About Island Press

Island Press is the only nonprofit organization in the United States whose principal purpose is the publication of books on environmental issues and natural resource management. We provide solutions-oriented information to professionals, public officials, business and community leaders, and concerned citizens who are shaping responses to environmental problems.

In 2000, Island Press celebrates its sixteenth anniversary as the leading provider of timely and practical books that take a multidisciplinary approach to critical environmental concerns. Our growing list of titles reflects our commitment to bringing the best of an expanding body of literature to the environmental community throughout North America and the world.

Support for Island Press is provided by The Jenifer Altman Foundation, The Bullitt Foundation, The Mary Flagler Cary Charitable Trust, The Nathan Cummings Foundation, The Geraldine R. Dodge Foundation, The Charles Engelhard Foundation, The Ford Foundation, The German Marshall Fund of the United States, The George Gund Foundation, The Vira I. Heinz Endowment, The William and Flora Hewlett Foundation, The W. Alton Jones Foundation, The John D. and Catherine T. MacArthur Foundation, The Andrew W. Mellon Foundation, The Charles Stewart Mott Foundation, The Curtis and Edith Munson Foundation, The National Fish and Wildlife Foundation, The New-Land Foundation, The Oak Foundation, The Overbrook Foundation, The David and Lucile Packard Foundation, The Pew Charitable Trusts, The Rockefeller Brothers Fund, Rockefeller Financial Services, The Winslow Foundation, and individual donors.

Society for Ecological Restoration

The Society for Ecological Restoration is an international, nonprofit organization. Its members are actively engaged in ecologically sensitive repair and management of damaged ecosystems through an unusually broad array of experience, knowledge sets, and cultural perspectives.

The mission of SER is to serve the growing field of ecological restoration by facilitating dialogue among restorationists, encouraging research, promoting awareness of and public support for restoration and restorative management, contributing to public policy discussions, and recognizing those who have made outstanding contributions to the field of restoration.

Society for Ecological Restoration, 1955 W. Grant Road #150, Tucson, AZ 85745. Tel. (520) 622-5485, Fax (520) 622-5491, E-mail: info@ser.org.

The Historical Ecology Handbook

The
Historical
Ecology
Handbook

A Restorationist's Guide to Reference Ecosystems

EDITED BY

DAVE EGAN
EVELYN A. HOWELL

SOCIETY FOR
ECOLOGICAL RESTORATION

ISLAND PRESS
Washington • Covelo • London

Copyright © 2001 Island Press

All rights reserved under International and Pan-American Copyright Conventions. No part of this book may be reproduced in any form or by any means without permission in writing from the publisher: Island Press, Suite 300, 1718 Connecticut Avenue NW, Washington, D.C. 20009.

Island Press is a trademark of The Center for Resource Economics.

No copyright claim is made in the work by M. Kat Anderson and Kenneth L. Cole, employees of the federal government.

The historical ecology handbook : a restorationist's guide to reference ecosystems / edited by Dave Egan and Evelyn A. Howell.
    p.   cm.
Includes bibliographical references.
    ISBN 1-55963-745-5 (cloth : alk. paper) — ISBN 1-55963-746-3 (paper : alk. paper)
    1. Human ecology—History.   2. Biotic communities—History.   3. Conservation of natural resources—History.   I. Egan, Dave.   II. Howell, Evenly A.   III. Title.
    GF13 .H58 2001
    577.27—dc21

                                                                00-011160

British Library Cataloging-in-Publication Data available.

Printed on recycled, acid-free paper ♻

Printed in Canada
10 9 8 7 6 5 4 3 2 1

Contents

III Synthesis: Case Studies Using Reference Conditions

Figures, Tables, and Boxes ·

Figures

Tables

Boxes

Acknowledgments

This book would not have been possible without the help and encouragement of many people. First, we would like to thank our colleagues at the University of Wisconsin–Madison Arboretum and the University of Wisconsin–Madison Landscape Architecture Department for their support and advice. In particular, we would like to recognize Pamela Nesbit of the Arboretum staff for her artistic work and Bill Jordan for his conversations about historical ecology and many other topics.

We are most grateful to Barbara Dean and Barbara Youngblood of Island Press for nurturing the idea for this book, helping us through the rough spots, and assisting us with the many stages of production. To you both, may your "garden of ideas" continue to flourish and bear fruit. Special thanks go to Cecilia González and Jennifer Alt and the rest of the staff at Island Press for doing a fine job with the copyediting and handling the artwork.

Thanks also go out to the Society for Ecological Restoration for its endorsement of this publication and for the forum it provided at the 1999 SER Annual Conference in San Francisco, where many of the contributors to this book presented papers in an all-day session. A special thanks goes to Don Falk for his continuing support of the project and to Eric Higgs for his interest in historical ecology and for sharing Jeanine Rhemtulla's thesis with us.

We also wish to recognize Kevin Ducey of Expresso Press in Madison, Wisconsin, for his conception and layout of the draft cover for this book.

Finally, we want to acknowledge all the contributors. This book would never have been completed if they had not taken time out of their busy schedules to write the chapters and answer all our various questions and comments. We hope they will be proud of what we have all accomplished.

Foreword

We change, the world we live in changes, and our appreciation of how change occurs is itself subject to constant change. For all those who care about the continually evolving relationship between people and the living earth, these basic facts of life have become increasingly and inescapably pertinent.

Conservation—never an easy endeavor—used to be so much easier: draw boundaries around a refuge or a reserve or a park and let it be; provide a market incentive or a government program and watch it work; protect a habitat or limit a harvest and see the populations recover. But we are dynamic creatures living in a dynamic world, and that realization has made conservation more difficult. We must now seek ways, in writer-naturalist Terry Tempest Williams's arresting phrase, to "find refuge in change." This volume helps all of us to find that refuge. It allows us to better understand how landscapes have changed, how we may investigate and interpret that change, and how our own conservation actions—and the ecosystems we inhabit—may benefit from that knowledge.

By chance, I am writing these words in a place where the fact of change is strongly in one's face. I sit on the extreme western edge of the North American Plate near Point Reyes, California. A mile away to the west, Douglas firs and Bishop pines adorn the granitic Inverness Ridge (gaunt silhouettes of pines, reminders of a 1995 fire, darken one stretch of the ridgeline). The ridge marks the eastern edge of the Pacific Plate. That side is grinding northward relative to this side. In the narrow basin between lies the San Andreas Fault. The fault zone here is buried beneath wetlands . . . or what once were wetlands, a coastal salt marsh. Between the mid-1800s and mid-1900s, settlers channelized the feeder streams, built dikes to control the tidal ebb and flow, and filled in the marsh to make pasture. The streams now run straighter toward their meeting with the sea. Two hundred Holsteins are meandering toward the main dike during their morning munch. But the dairy farmer and local conservationists have recently found some common ground here, and there are plans to restore the marsh's flux of brackish waters, and to bring back the saltgrass and pickleweed. The native Coast Miwok, who in 1579 greeted Francis Drake and the *Golden Hinde* here, are silent. They were uprooted from this place in the early 1800s, and by the end of that century their few survivors had scattered northward.

The scales of time—from geologic to ancient to historic to recent—and the types of change—from the purely natural to the human-induced—are displayed dramatically here along the California coast. But every place offers its past to those who seek it. Read it in the thick mud sediments of the Anacostia River basin in Washington, D.C.; in remnant stumps of white pine that still record the epic deforestation of the upper Great Lakes in the late 1800s; in the spread of cheat grass across the range-lands of the intermountain West. But you may also find the past in the excavated sites of the old ones; in stories still vivid in an elder's memory; in yellowed notes and records, filed away and forgotten. Every landscape provides materials by which we may calibrate its unique history of change. The contributors to this volume describe the tools and techniques we need to carry out this task.

It is worth pausing to consider just how profoundly the past few decades have altered our view of the earth's past. Geologists, climatologists, paleontologists, evolutionary biologists, and biogeographers have been hard at work. They have revealed how the changing configuration of the earth's tectonic plates, periodic asteroid impacts, differential rates of exchange of atmospheric gases, shifts in deep ocean currents, rising and falling sea levels, advancing and melting ice sheets, and the dispersal, extinction, and adaption of life-forms have conferred upon us our contemporary landscapes, seascapes, and biotas. Geneticists and paleo-anthropologists have sharpened our understanding of the origins, development, and diaspora of the human population over the millennia. Archaeologists, anthropologists, paleoecologists, cultural geographers, and environmental historians have shown how humans and ecosystems have influenced each other over varied scales of time and space. Ecologists and conservation biologists have challenged us to see the evidence of recent ecological change, and to understand how biological diversity is shaped by ecosystem disturbance, landscape-level processes, and, of course, people.

All of this has upset traditional approaches to "managing" a static and constant nature. It has rendered suspect our set formulae for conservation and compelled us to review our conservation philosophies. We no longer see the world as a piece of divine clockwork or as a superorganism whose behavior we can predict or control. But neither do we see change as simply random, chaotic, or inexplicable. The world is an integrated whole, and it has people in it. Its patterns of change are, to some extent, discernable. Landscapes have been shaped both by nonhuman forces and by human action, to varying degrees at varied times and places. All who work to reconstruct the past have brought us closer to that reality. In the process, they have disabused us (we may hope) of some of our naivete, our hubris, and our illusions.

In charting future directions in conservation, these recent scientific advances yield information that is absolutely essential, and yet insufficient. Science offers us knowledge, but it cannot tell us how to synthesize and use it, how to weave it into the stories that we confer on the land. It cannot motivate us to seek ways of living that replenish the systems that we depend on. It cannot protect the wild, or revive damaged systems, or reconnect people to their surroundings, or promote more just, durable, and resilient human communities. But the daily work of conservation, restoration, and environmental reform requires the reality check of science and history. Historical ecology, as the meeting ground of disciplines, is where we seek information and counsel. We need the diagnostic tools of historical ecology to help us get our bearings, to guide our restoration practices, and to inform our search for a viable conservation ethic.

It is fitting that our editors, Dave Egan and Evelyn Howell, have prepared this volume based on their many years of experience at the University of Wisconsin in Madison. There, in the spring of 1934, at the dedication of the university's arboretum, Aldo Leopold helped to inaugurate a new direction in conservation work. In his dedicatory remarks, Leopold laid out a vision for the site that emphasized the "reconstruction of original Wisconsin . . . to serve as a bench mark, a starting point, in the long and laborious job of building a permanent and mutually beneficial relationship between civilized men and a civilized landscape." In an era when the ecologies and economies of middle America were in crisis, the message rang sharply. "The time has come for science to busy itself with the earth itself," Leopold suggested. "The first step is to reconstruct a sample of what we had to start with."

Leopold may actually have missed a step. For even before reconstruction comes research. Others before Leopold had explored, from different angles, the place where the natural sciences and human history met: George Perkins Marsh in his classic *Man and Nature; or, Physical Geography as Modified by Human Action* (1864); Frederick Jackson Turner in his explication of the frontier thesis (1893); Alfred Russell Wallace, Charles Darwin, John Wesley Powell, Charles Van Hise, Carl O. Sauer, Walter Prescott Webb, Victor Shelford, Charles Elton (among other integrating minds in history, geography, and the biological sciences). The rivers of natural history and human history had joined, though their waters had not yet fully mingled.

With the emergence of ecology as a science, and ecological restoration as an applied art, history assumed a more prominent role in conservation. Understanding the history of the land, its biota, and its interactions (including the role of human beings) became the first task in restoration. Among other things, this placed new and greater importance on the continent's remnant wildlands. "The recreational value of wilderness has been often and ably presented," Leopold wrote in 1941, "but its scientific value is as yet but dimly understood." Increasingly, Leopold (and others as well) argued for the protection of wildlands as reference points, where the "science of land health" could find its "base datum of normality, a picture of how healthy land maintains itself. . . ." In the wild, it might be said, the past spoke with special clarity to the present.

Now historical ecology has emerged to help mingle the waters more purposefully. But beware: the awareness that historical ecology offers can be a burden. I have, for example, a friend whose family refuses to take a vacation with her anymore, because during a trip to Hawaii she would not stop complaining about all the beautiful but exotic plants engulfing the islands' native flora. "One of the penalties of an ecological education," Leopold wrote, "is that one lives alone in a world of wounds." If because of Leopold and other conservation visionaries we are no longer quite so alone, we must still find ways to reconcile ourselves to the temporal dimension of our work.

History complicates things. It undermines easy answers. It makes people, with all our confounded behavior, an unavoidable part of the puzzle. It messes with deeply rooted views of wildness and wilderness. To incorporate history in one's research and conservation plans takes time, money, persistence, imagination, concentration, self-criticism, attention to detail, a lot of reading, respect for the obscure, breadth of interest, and a capacity for respectful collaboration.

But history offers compensations. It bestows necessary knowledge. It makes the story of any landscape even more interesting. It can bring together people whose passions and philosophies may otherwise conflict. As well illustrated by the four case studies in this volume, it requires the tapping of diverse human talents, experiences, and perspectives. It helps us to appreciate wildness, not as a nostalgic illusion, but as an inherent attribute of all living things and all places. It records the steps in our fitful progress toward respect for that wildness. History does not confine us to the temporal dimension; rather it allows us to inhabit it with greater self-awareness, and perhaps even with grace.

In *Auguries of Innocence*, William Blake invited us

> To see the World in a Grain of Sand
> And Heaven in a Wild Flower
> Hold Infinity in the Palm of your hand
> And Eternity in an hour.

The contributors to this volume invite us to see the world in a pollen grain, a tree ring, a packrat midden, a soil layer. They ask us to mark time through the land record, the map, the oral tradition. Out of these frag- ments we reconstruct the earth's past. Even the case histories seem laden with the symbolic: Nantucket, where great ships under masts of white pine once went to sea, and where the cod ships and whalers came to harbor; the Indiana Dunes, where over a century ago the pioneer ecologist Henry C. Cowles first sought to understand changes in plant communities over time; the Grand Canyon, where all eyes may gaze into the sedimentary layers of deep time; and San Francisco Bay, near where the Coast Miwok met Drake at the west portal to North America.

We have changed since then, and so has our continent. Through the tools placed here in our hands, we may come to know this place better, to inhabit it more wisely, to restore some of what we have broken, and so begin to find our refuge in change.

Curt Meine
Point Reyes, California
May 15, 2000

Introduction

Dave Egan and Evelyn A. Howell

> *That which has been and that which is to come are not else-*
> *where—they are not autonomous dimensions independent of the*
> *encompassing present in which we dwell. They are, rather, the*
> *very depths of this living place—the hidden depth of its distances*
> *and the concealed depth on which we stand.*
>
> David Abram, *The Spell of the Sensuous:*
> *Perception and Language in a More-Than-Human World* (1996)

> *Restoration uses the past not as a goal but as a reference point for*
> *the future. If we seek to recreate the temperate forests, tallgrass*
> *savannas, or desert communities of centuries past, it is not to*
> *turn back the evolutionary clock but to set it ticking again.*
>
> Don Falk, "Discovering the Future, Creating the Past:
> Some Reflections on Restoration" (1990)

A fundamental aspect of ecosystem restoration is learning how to redis-
cover the past and bring it forward into the present—to determine what
needs to be restored, why it was lost, and how best to make it live again.
Unlike the protagonist in *Trout Fishing in America* (Brautigan 1967), who
goes to a wrecking yard and finds a complete, extant trout stream for sale,
restorationists must search out the missing, forgotten, and overlooked
aspects of the ecosystem they wish to restore and, once they find them,
begin to reassemble them into a viable system. This process requires ven-
turing through many doorways, talking with experts in a variety of disciplines, and sifting through countless documents, museum samples, and
pollen diagrams. It also means learning to live with uncertainty. Nevertheless, the answers are there—concealed, as David Abram (1996) puts
it, in "the very depths of this living place."

We hope this book will encourage ecosystem restorationists to look to the past and to those who study the past—historians, archaeologists, paleoecologists—as a means of discovering the reference conditions so important to their own work. To better describe how to make this connection between history and ecology—or, more specifically, between the emerging disciplines of historical ecology and ecosystem restoration—we set about here to answer the following questions: Why should history matter to restoration ecologists? What are historical ecosystems, and why are they needed in restoration ecology? How reliable are historic ecosystems as reference models, and what can we do to make them more reliable? First, however, we will discuss what we mean by historical ecology and ecosystem restoration.

Historical Ecology and Ecosystem Restoration

Historical ecology has been described variously as the interface between ecology and historical geography that undertakes studies of lost or degenerated historic ecosystems (Dirkx 1999), and as a discipline that "traces the ongoing dialectical relations between human acts and acts of nature, made manifest in the *landscape*" (Crumley 1994, emphasis in original). In general, historical ecologists agree on the following points:

1. Human influences, ranging from the subtle and benign to the overtly destructive, are pervasive throughout the earth's ecosystems. Historical ecologists recognize that the present geologic epoch—the Holocene (from ten thousand years ago to the present)—is the age of *Homo sapiens* living in both sustainable and surplus cultures, and always with some level of technological and ritualistic sophistication (Diamond 1997).

2. The interaction that takes place between the environment and human cultures is not deterministic, but rather a dynamic dialectic process that results in landscapes, which are, in effect, culturalized ecosystems. These landscapes are the common unit of analysis for historical ecologists because landscapes hold the record of human activity on the earth.

3. Humans, while pervasive and potentially destructive, especially when their population pressures become too high or when their technology goes unchecked, can produce and help to maintain sustainable, diverse ecosystems.

4. Despite its emphasis on the past, the work of historical ecologists is future seeking.

Finally, historical ecologists (Sheail 1980; Crumley 1998; Dirkx 1999) look at and interpret changes operating at different scales by using a variety of techniques—many of which will be covered in this book. This last point has recently received support in North America from ecologists (Christensen et al. 1996; Covington et al. 1997) and paleoecologists (Russell 1997; Delcourt and Delcourt 1998; Swetnam, Allen, and Betancourt 1999) who view the use of historical ecology techniques as beneficial to the management of ecosystems.

Historical ecologists and ecosystem restorationists share many ideas and values, although restorationists are interested not only in studying past ecosystems and landscapes, but also in returning them to a semblance of their former being.

A relatively young discipline, ecosystem restoration has many roots—landscape architecture, conservation, reclamation, the science of ecology, environmental mitigation—and a corresponding diversity of approaches and applications. Projects as different as planting former agricultural fields to native grasses to support pheasant populations in the Midwest, revegetating disturbed coastal areas with seagrasses, and planting buffer zones around remnant areas have been called restorations. One of the common themes that emerge from these efforts is the basic human instinct to care (Egan 1988; Oelschlaeger 1994). That is, ecological restoration efforts can be seen as a positive counterbalance to the disruptive effects of modern human activities. This implies a focus on efforts that promote biodiversity and complexity through the protection and restoration of native species and heterogeneous ecosystems.

The theory (restoration ecology [Jordan, Gilpin, and Abers 1987]) and practice (ecological restoration) of ecosystem restoration are, as is befitting a relatively young profession, still in a stage of self-discovery. Theorists and practitioners alike are striving to define the field and to identify a set of unifying principles or concepts—to decide what are the best, most authentic means of restoring what has been damaged or lost. This striving for authenticity brings restorationists face to face with the central role of time and requires that they understand past conditions in order to reestablish the historic processes and components needed to repair damaged ecosystems.

Why Should History Matter to Ecosystem Restorationists?

To examine why ecosystem restorationists should be concerned about history (the record of the passage of time), one needs to understand the procedural theory that grounds the practice of ecosystem restoration. The procedure can best be described as a series of linear steps (box I.1),

Box I.1. Outline of Ecological Restoration Project Procedures (Howell 1999)

A. Carry out preliminary research.
  1. Perform site inventory and analysis.
     a. The key to success in restoration is matching species and environment. Many restorations are dominated by broadly tolerant species perhaps because we have not been careful enough in the match.
     b. Initial conditions greatly influence the direction of vegetation change (colonization, inhibition, facilitation).
  2. Study prototypes (remnants and reports) to develop ecosystem models for the restoration to emulate.
  3. Review reports of previous restoration experiments and projects.
  4. Locate sources of materials.
B. Determine project purpose, site use policy, and research component.
C. Create the planting plan—describe the desired "end point" and *what* is to be planted *where* and *when* to achieve the end point.
  1. Determine ecosystem restoration goals and objectives based on ecosystem model.
     a. Specify species composition, abundance, distribution patterns
     b. Describe desired community structure
     c. Highlight desired ecological processes
  2. List numbers and proportions of species to be planted (if any).
  3. Choose materials: seed, seedlings, cuttings.
  4. Determine planting techniques.
     a. Specify method
     b. Specify timing
        i. Which season?
        ii. All at once or in phases?
  5. Specify (or not) locations of individual plants or seed mixes.
D. Prepare the site.
  1. Remove undesirable biota.
  2. Create a good planting medium.
  3. Enhance/ameliorate site conditions.
E. Implement project and research plan.
F. Monitor the site to see if objectives are being met.
  1. If so, continue as planned.
  2. If not, make mid-course correction.
G. Prepare restoration plan for animals, insects, etc.
H. Manage the site
  1. Discourage pests.
  2. Maintain natural processes.

although in practice the process is more dynamic and given to coordinated tasks. In essence, the restorationist first develops an accurate pre-modern model of the ecosystem or site and then prepares a prescription that will, within the context of modern restraints, move the system from its existing condition to one that more closely resembles the reference model. This procedure seems simple enough in concept—and is relatively easy to achieve if you are dealing with a mechanism like an old car that needs fixing. Ecosystem restorationists, however, are working with dynamic systems that are constantly changing over time and space, which makes the problem of developing and applying a reference model difficult and infuses it with a level of uncertainty. In order to do this type of work, the old paradigm of nature in balance must be forgotten (Botkin 1990), and the new metaphor of "flux of nature" (Pickett and Parker 1994) adopted.

Typically, there are two ways to develop such a reference model: (1) by studying the body of theory that concerns itself with the nature of ecosystems; and (2) by acquiring information about the composition, function, and structure of ecosystems in the past and present. Both ways are essential to make the model accurate because, as Pickett and Parker (1994) write, "Although sound ecological generalizations and predictions arise from regularities in species characteristics, environmental properties, and the interaction of species with one another and with physical environments, the specific dynamics of any one system will be contingent on its history, the accidents of arrival of species at the site, and the nature of the system's connections to the surrounding landscape."

Finally, and from a different perspective, developing a history of this type—one that emphasizes the human recording of both human and nonhuman events—may do more than help the restorationist model the systems that need repair. The involvement of the restorationist in this process of discovery will likely (1) help restorationists locate themselves within the "complementary opposition" (Whitehead 1998) of culture and nature; (2) provide them with a sense of personal, professional, and bioregional identity; and (3) serve as a guide or reference for present and future action. (Of course, as geographer David Lowenthal [1985] warns, the past can also be used as an escape from an unacceptable present, and its embrace may be viewed as a means "to inhibit change, embargo progress, dampen optimism, and stifle creativity.")

What Are Historic Ecosystems and Why Are They Important?

Historic ecosystems are those ecological systems that existed prior to this time. They may have existed several decades to many millennia ago.

Historic ecosystems include systems on a continuum from highly cultured landscapes to wilderness areas—systems that may have been influenced or modified by human activities to varying degrees over time. Historic ecosystems are important to restorationists because they can be useful as analogs or guides to current restoration actions.

To better understand why historic ecosystems are important, and to begin to establish a framework for working with the data derived from the techniques described in this book, we now focus our attention on several concepts that ground the use of historic ecosystems as reference systems. These include ideas about complex systems, initial conditions, range of variation, and reference conditions.

Complex Systems and Initial Conditions

Suffice it to say that ecologists have always been aware that the systems they studied were complex (McIntosh 1985, 272). However, contemporary ecological theorists (Botkin 1990; Pickett and Parker 1994; Wu and Loucks 1995; Brown 1995)—supported by advances in ecosystems ecology (Bormann and Likens 1979) and systems theory (Allen and Starr 1982; Kauffman 1993)—have begun to describe ecosystems in ways somewhat different from those used by their predecessors. Holling and Goldberg (1981) summarize this new perspective by pointing out that ecosystems possess four basic properties: (1) they have systemic qualities that indicate that the components are interacting in complex ways; (2) they are historical, meaning that their current conditions are shaped by past events; (3) they are open and spatial, meaning that their current conditions are shaped by the surrounding environment; and (4) they are nonlinear, meaning that successional pathways and other ecosystem processes are often multidirectional and may be characterized by lags and thresholds. Thus, a new paradigm is emerging in which ecologists view ecosystems as historically and spatially influenced systems that are complex, nonlinear, and open.

Perhaps most important, the development of these theories about complex, nonlinear systems has given ecologists a new language and framework to articulate what many have long believed: that initial conditions matter, and that current practice strongly influences future directions.

One of the trademarks of complex systems is a sensitivity to initial conditions (Lorenz 1963). Being sensitive to initial conditions means that complex systems respond to small perturbations or seemingly insignificant or inconsequential events. Prigogine and Stengers (1984, 169) note that the "mixture of necessity and chance constitutes the history of the system." Brown (1995, 182) puts it more clearly: "It means that historical events play a major role in ecology. Seemingly insignificant changes in abiotic conditions or species composition that happened long ago or far away can have large, irreversible effects on the structure and dynamics of local ecosystems." Knowing the initial conditions that made an ecosystem operate is, therefore, essential if restorationists seek an accurate starting point for their work. Indeed, if the idea is to set the clock ticking again, as Don Falk suggests, it will require that restorationists understand how the clock was initially set.

Historic Range of Variability

Accepting the idea that ecosystems are dynamic and complex does not deny ecologists or restorationists the opportunity to measure or observe ecosystems in an attempt to better learn how they operate. That idea merely indicates that what they measure or observe is likely to change over time and space, but within a range where the system remains basically recognizable.

This range of ecosystem operation is known by a variety of terms, *range of natural variation* (Caraher et al. 1992; Landres, Morgan, and Swanson 1999); *natural variability* (Swanson et al. 1994); *reference variation* (Manley et al. 1995); *ecosystem of reference* (Aronson, LeFloc'h, Floret, Ovalle, and Pontanier 1993); and *historic range of variation* (Morgan et al. 1994; Aplet and Keeton 1999). According to these authors, both *range of natural variation* and *natural variability* refer to the changes within ecosystems that are operating without human influence. *Reference variation* and *ecosystem of reference* are roughly similar; both identify standards for restoration activities that are derived from reference site studies.

While all of these terms acknowledge the need to recognize that ecosystems are dynamic, we are most comfortable with *historic range of variation*, or HRV. We prefer this term for two reasons: (1) it recognizes that Native Americans influenced ecosystems at various scales in many, although not all, areas where present-day restoration activities take place; and (2) it avoids the use of the word *natural*, which has been rightly attacked as being too ambiguous (MacCleery 1998; Jordan 1999).

In conceptual terms, HRV is a recognition that complex systems, including ecosystems, have a range within which they are self-sustaining and beyond which they move into a state of disequilibrium. Because many of today's ecosystems are in an unsustainable state due to modern interventions into their historic processes, finding ways to look back at the factors that made historic ecosystems sustainable is a logical step if those factors are to be restored (Aplet and Keeton 1999). Fortunately, there are several techniques that can be used to discover the HRV of the ecosystem being studied. These include the study of historic records (e.g., written and oral histories, photographs, maps, land office surveys, management and land-use records) and the analysis and interpretation of proxy records derived from biological sources such as pollen, spores, microfossils, packrat middens, tree rings, fire scars, woody debris, sediments and varves, ice cores, and other earth relics.

We are likewise fortunate that studies of these types have expanded since the growth in scientific disciplines such as ecology, and with the advent of improved technologies, including better microscopy and radiometric dating procedures (Libby 1952; Stuiver and Polach 1977). Indeed, since the emergence of the science of ecology in North America at the end of the ninteenth century, its practitioners—Frederic Clements (1924, 1949), John Curtis (1956, 1959), Henry Gleason (1953), Raymond Lindeman (1942), Paul Sears (1935a and b), and others—have utilized paleoecological and documentary data in their work (McIntosh 1985).

This type of study, which uses historical data in addition to contemporary information, allows restorationists to (1) illustrate the dynamics of the ecosystem they are studying (Morgan et al. 1994), (2) gauge how an ecosystem will react to a given initial condition, and (3) establish reference conditions for restoration and management activities.

There is no limit to the aspects of an ecosystem that could be measured to assess the historic range of variability—Manley et al. (1995) identified more than thirty-six such factors—and, in theory, all factors should be taken into consideration. Practically speaking, however, those working with historic range of variability in their restoration projects (Bay Institute 1998; Moore, Covington, and Fulé 1999; Stephenson 1999) tend to limit the number to several key variables that are specific to the project and can be measured by using available techniques. Typically, those variables attempt to measure some aspect of an ecosystem's composition, structure, and functional processes, in both qualitative and quantitative terms.

As with so many issues concerning ecosystems, selecting the appropriate temporal and spatial scale for a historic range of variability study is crucial. As V. Thomas Parker (1997, 302) points out, much depends on the goals of the project: "If we limit our goals to initiating a certain composition and leaving the system alone after that, then models that focus on biological interactions and organism adaptation to initial conditions are appropriate. If self-sustainability is also a goal, then larger spatial and temporal scale models are fundamental." Penelope Morgan and her colleagues (1994) suggest that "the objectives of the analysis" should determine the scale chosen for

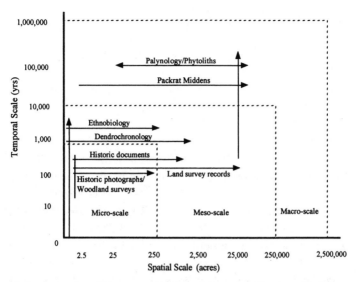

Figure I.1. Spatial and Temporal Scales of Historical Ecology Techniques (modified from Delcourt and Delcourt 1991; Swetnam, Allen, and Betancourt 1999)

most ecosystem patterns and processes. Furthermore, they recommend that appropriate ecological factors be chosen according to the scale of the study area—site, watershed, or landscape. They also suggest that the use of "multiple spatial and temporal scales is appropriate" (p. 94). Figure I.1 shows many of the techniques discussed in this book and the spatial and temporal scales they cover.

A key step, then, is to select a time period and geographical area that will provide enough heterogeneity to produce valuable information but will be relatively consistent in terms of climate and human use (Landres, Morgan, and Swanson 1999). Although the geographic area is determined largely by the scope of the project, restorationists should be aware that there is no fixed time period that must be used.

While HRV helps establish an understanding of the necessary kind, frequency, and magnitude of disturbances required to restore an ecosystem, it is not a "silver bullet." As Aplet and Keeton (1999) point out, there are some drawbacks: First, implementing such disturbances in the proper sequence and at the proper magnitude can be difficult and may not equal the effects of historic disturbance patterns. Second, the scale of observation must be accounted for, as noted above. Third, some systems may be so altered that using historic disturbances either may not work or may set the system off on an undesirable trajectory. Finally, restorationists need to be concerned about situations where their actions run up against other social concerns. For example, one might find that in the past a riverine system experienced periodic, large-scale flooding, which today would destroy homes and businesses now established along the river. Similarly, restoring areas with fire may prove problematic because of existing structures or land uses.

Reference Conditions

Reference conditions are determined by analyzing the data obtained for each of the variables chosen for the historic range of variation study. To use a simple example, a restorationist involved in a forest restoration may decide to use historic tree density as one of her variables. After compiling collaborative historic evidence from dendrochronology studies, photographs, and historic documents, she may determine that during the period 1650–1950 tree density in the forest ranged between 12 and 20 trees per acre. She can then set the reference condition somewhere in that historic range and undertake a plan to meet that goal within the context of present conditions. In reality such a plan would, of course, consider the results of the other variables studied as well as factors of scale, successional tendencies, and patch dynamics.

The selection of reference conditions is, as one restorationist has written, "the most important decision in ecological restoration. . . . Since future changes in an ecological community will always be dictated by its starting structure, the starting structure must accurately represent the reference ecosystem during the historical period" (Bonnickson 1994). Other restorationists echo this sentiment. For instance, Edith Allen, Wallace Covington, and Don Falk (1997) in their summary of the NSF-funded workshop "Developing a Conceptual Basis for Restoration Ecology," noted that the workshop participants found that "the need for reference conditions" was a problem intrinsic to restoration ecology.

Restorationists need reference conditions because they help (1) define what the original or preferred condition (composition, structure, processes, function) was compared to the present; (2) determine what factors caused the degradation; (3) define what needs to be done to restore the ecosystem; and (4) develop criteria for measuring the success of restoration treatments or experiments (Aronson et al. 1995; Swetnam, Allen, and Betancourt 1999; Noss 1985; Millar and Woolfenden 1999).

There are, as White and Walker (1997) point out, four types of reference models: (1) contemporary sites to be restored (same time, same place); (2) historic models of restoration sites (different time, same place); (3) contemporary remnants (same time, different place); and (4) historic remnants (different time, different place). While this book focuses on techniques that are useful in garnering information about historic ecosystems, we recommend that restorationists use the appropriate combination of site analysis (same time, same place), historic–same site information (different time, same place), and information from contemporary remnants (same time, different place) in their work. The combination of contemporary and historic information can help offset the deficiencies of each: contemporary information being only a "snapshot" in time, historic information being saddled with the incompleteness of the historic record. (We discourage the use of historic information from remnant sites because there is too much spatial and temporal uncertainty.)

How Reliable Are Historic Ecosystems as Reference Conditions?

No one should be fooled into thinking that reference conditions are precise. They can, however, be carefully determined guidelines that remain adaptable in the face of new information. As mentioned above, historic information suffers because we can never recover all the information of the historic record, and, thus, we must make interpretations and draw our conclusions on a relatively small sample. There is also a "decay" factor, in that the further away we are in time, the poorer our chances are of recovering the data we need. Other problems arise, not the least of which is the recurring problem with issues of scale. White and Walker (1997) provide an excellent discussion about how observations of variations within ecosystems are scale dependent, and Swetnam, Allen, and Betancourt (1999) also discuss the limitations of historical ecology techniques.

One thing that everyone agrees on is that no one technique can be used to etablish reference conditions. Moreover, as the contributors to this book point out again and again, each of the techniques they work with has limitations. In general, these limitations are recognized, and many disciplines have worked out methods to deal with inconsistencies and variations in the data obtained. However, no discipline has resolved all the problems its researchers encounter, nor is any likely to do so given the taphonomic nature of the data they are collecting. This is the case for both biological data and cultural data.

The answer to this problem of uncertainty—and to the problem of scale—is to recognize that all historical ecology techniques have their limitations (spatial and temporal) and inherent biases. Restorationists should be sure that standard correction factors for specific techniques have been used and then combine the appropriate techniques in a way

Table I.1. Generalized Climatic Trends and Ecosystem
Responses during the Holocene Epoch in North America

Date	Climatic Trends and Ecosystem Responses
10,000–9,500 B.P.	Pre-Boreal Period: warm and moist climate environments; more seasonal variation; rising sea levels; major ecotonal shifts of plants and animals.
9,500–8,500 B.P.	Boreal Period: warm and dry climate; sea-level rise continues; major ecotonal shifts of plants and animals; altithermal drying begins.
8,500–5,000 B.P.	Atlantic Period: warm and increasingly dry climate, especially in summer; maximum altithermal dryness about 6950 B.P.; maximum expansion of prairie in Midwest.
5,000–2,800 B.P.	Sub-Boreal Period: increasing moisture; local ecotone adjustments.
2,800–1,900 B.P.	Classic Roman Period: cool, increasing moisture; local ecotone adjustments.
1,900–1,550 B.P.	Late Roman Period: warming and increasingly dry.
1,550–950 B.P.	Post-Roman and Carolingian Period: warm temperatures in northern parts of North America, with temperatures about 1 degree C above present in central Canada.
950–700 B.P.	Medieval Warm Period: Little Climatic Optimum, worldwide warming.
700–450 B.P.	Early Medieval Cool Period: cooler temperatures; glacial advances in mountains.
450–100 B.P.	Medieval Little Ice Age: period of low solar activity with positive fluctuations from 410–360 B.P. and 180–100 B.P.; glacial advances in the Sierras and Alaska.
100 B.P. to present	Industrial Age: warming trend; anthropogenic changes abundant in North America.

that is multiscalar and cross-referential in order to build convincing, cor-roborative lines of evidence for their reference model. How certain fac-tors are chosen is of prime importance since some are natural pairs—fire history and forest structure, climate and fire history, repeat photography and forest structure, to name a few—while others—climate change and vegetation composition, for example—may not fit together, due to time lags or other discrepancies. More work is needed in determining which techniques work best together, although the case studies in this book pro-vide some good examples of how to select and use complementary research techniques.

Another, as yet unresolved but important, issue surrounds the use of historic ecosystems as reference models. This is the issue of the role climate plays in the historic model—*and* whether the contemporary climate is sim-ilar enough to make the historic data useful (table I.1). Millar and Woolfenden (1999), for example, argue that using presettlement condi-tions as the basis for restoration efforts accepts a model during which the climate was significantly cooler, that is, the Little Ice Age (A.D. 1400 to 1850). While over the long term, the climate of the Holocene has been rel-atively stable, the problem of climate variation is a real one and is further complicated by the lag time between climate change and vegetation response, which may be several centuries in the case of forests, for example.

There are other practical concerns about using historical ecology to study ecosystems. These include the costs involved in doing extensive research and the need to establish cooperative working relationships within an interdisciplinary team. In many cases, we suspect that site analysis and use of contemporary remnants will continue to serve the purposes of restorationists. However, agencies dealing with public lands and consultants working with large properties may have the incentive and the personnel to take on projects using historic references.

This appears to be the case in the United States Forest Service, where several historical ecology–related projects have been undertaken (e.g., Manley et al. 1995; Kaufmann et al. 1998; Marcot et al. 1998). In fact, larger-scale projects that have incorporated the concept of historical ecol-ogy have taken place or are underway throughout the United States and Canada. These include but are not limited to the historical ecology report of the Bay Institute (1998) and related work by hydrologists on the Sacra-mento and San Joaquin river systems (Greco 1999; Platenkamp, Brown, and Runlet 1999; Williams 1999); the EcoAtlas and Bay Area Historical Ecology Project from the San Francisco Estuary Institute (Grossinger 1999; see also chapter 17); the Culture, Ecology and Restoration Project in Canada's Jasper National Park (Higgs, Campbell, McLaren, J. Martin,

T. Martin, Murray, Palmer, and Rhemtulla 1999); the recommendations of a scientific advisory panel regarding the development of a comprehensive program for the restoration of the Kissimmee River in Florida (Karr et al. 1991); the work of Grace Brush, Stewart Pickett, and their colleagues and students in the Gwynns Falls watershed and other areas of Chesapeake Bay (Brush 1997); the Sierra Nevada Ecosystem Project (1996); various projects by Wallace Covington and his colleagues at Northern Arizona University restoring ponderosa pine and other ecosystems in the Greater Granyon Region (Covington et al. 1997; Moore, Covington, and Fulé 1999; McKnight 1999; see also chapter 16); various studies being undertaken as part of the USGS Land Use History of North America Program (Sisk 1998; Grahame 2000); the work of Ken Cole (Cole et al. 1998), including his work at Indiana Dunes National Shoreline (see chapter 15); the study of the Los Angeles coastal prairie by Rudi Mattoni and Travis Longcore (1997); the use of historic and other information in the restoration and management of prairies in Louisiana (Yerby, Stacey, and Mac-Roberts 1999); Elizabeth Lynch's (1998) study of vegetation mosaics at the Wind River Range in Wyoming; H.Y. Smith and Steve Arno's (1999) work with ponderosa pine forests in Montana and Idaho; and the work of Peter Dunwiddie and others in New England (see chapter 14; Motzkin et al. 1996). Also noteworthy are the ongoing efforts by various Native American tribes across North America, whose members are reviving the ancient ways of managing their cultural landscapes (Dublanica 1999; Holt-Padilla 1999; Kadlecik 1999; Martinez 1999).

The appearance and quality of these projects lead us to believe that cost and cooperation, while they may be limiting factors at some scale of operation, can be overcome, and that the benefits derived from such studies can provide very worthwhile information to restorationists, land managers, and decision makers alike.

Conclusion

Using historical information in ecosystem restoration projects is a new and exciting experience. While restorationists working in this way must learn to live with some level of uncertainty, the information they gather can serve as a responsible guide and coarse filter to more authentic restoration and management activities. Furthermore, we believe it can be used to inform restoration experiments, influence policy decisions, and engender public support and participation in restoration projects.

If there is a formula for success when using these techniques, it is this: Use a multiscale, multisource, cross-referential historical analysis that is compared to contemporary data to set your reference conditions. Finally, remain open and adaptive to the ongoing dialogue and findings that will surely come your way.

About This Book

This book is intended to provide the reader with a series of "primers" about the various techniques and source materials that can be used to identify historic reference conditions for restoration projects. While it will not make readers experts in any given discipline, we hope it will give them the necessary background knowledge and language to speak intelligently with experts, and to work intelligently with the data generated by experts or with other materials that exist in libraries and museums. Readers who wish to become more sophisticated in any of the techniques discussed in this book should look to primary sources or educational opportunities specific to their field of interest. This book, then, is a first step on a journey into the field of historical ecology and its application to ecosystem restoration.

Summary of Chapters

We have chosen to divide the first two sections of this book into categories that identify the type of historic evidence the authors are discussing. The first section contains techniques for discovering culturally derived evidence, such as documents, maps, photographs, oral history, and Native American land management practices. The second section consists of chapters devoted to techniques that identify biological (earth-relic) records, including standing woodlots, tree rings, pollen, packrat middens, opal phytoliths, animal remains, and records of changes in soil and hydrology. The third section, which we call "synthesis" because it brings together these otherwise disparate disciplines, highlights four case studies of restoration projects in which historical ecology data were used to establish reference conditions.

Why Historic Ecosystems?

The careful reader will note that we have tried to avoid the use of the terms *natural* and *prehistoric* when describing the past in North America. Both of these terms, we believe, cause problems because they fail to engage the past in a meaningful, authentic way. *Natural* is a term that describes a thing that exists in nature, a thing that is not artificial or derived from human activity. Of course, there are natural, universal processes (e.g., gravity, tectonics, evolution, meiosis) that hold sway, but we need to remember that the landscape forms and species these processes create are affected by historic incidents over time and space throughout the solar system and on Earth (e.g., asteroids, sunspots, volcanoes, ice ages), and by the practices of humans (e.g., horticulture, rituals, exploration, use of fire) and other species. Nature, as it is commonly interpreted, suggests that species, ecosystems, and environments exist in a static, often idealized, timeless state. Such thinking leads some to believe that natural areas or wilderness areas are pristine—never influenced by the ravages of history or humans. This has become a central issue in the debate over the extent to which Native Americans influenced the ecosystems of pre-Columbian North America (Denevan 1992; Anderson 1996; Vale 1998; McCann 1999) and remains a concern for restoration efforts in wilderness areas (Cole 2000).

Prehistoric, on the other hand, indicates a time prior to recorded history. While we understand the distinction, it seems that this is a European, academic division that fails to recognize that Native Americans have a history, which they preserve in their language, documents, customs, and land management techniques. "Prehuman" might be a better term to describe events in the Pleistocene or earlier in North America, but even that blinds us into thinking that the earth has no history of its own.

We would like to suggest that *historical* is a better way to describe the North American environment because it turns the restorationist away from searching for some ideal Eden and toward a more realistic, dynamic landscape where biodiversity can, through restorative and other efforts, exist in harmony with human needs (Jordan 1999). We couldn't agree more with Mr. Dan Huff of the United States National Park Service, who, in his opening talk of the Public Lands Symposium at the 1999 Society for Ecological Restoration Conference, said that the United States Park Service's definition of *natural* was no longer defensible and should be eradicated from its present-day use within the parlance of that organization. We suggest that restorationists and others consider that option on a larger scale, and we propose *historical* as an alternative.

Why the Holocene? Why North America?

The historic ecosystems we describe in this book are North American in space, and of the Holocene era in time. The Holocene, as described by geologists and others, comprises the past ten thousand years of the earth's history, or the period following the last glaciation (the Wisconsinan), during which the surface of North America (and, for that matter, the world) took its modern form, and after which time late Pleistocene vegetation and animals began to slowly and individually reassemble into Holocene-era guilds or communities. The Holocene climatic event marks the last synchronous global disturbance that affected every element of the environment from sea levels to soil-forming processes to the distribution of plants and animals, including humans. It was a true bifurcation point. The Holocene is, of course, the epoch during which several human cultures began to move away from foraging and harvester-based economies into horticulture and agriculturally based economies (Diamond 1997; Watson 1991).

We chose the Holocene for several reasons. First, while it may not be the earliest period of human entry or influence in the Americas (Bonnichsen and Turnmire 1999), the Holocene represents that historical period during which *Homo sapiens* significantly increased their own populations and their influence on North American ecosystems. Second, the composition of most contemporaneous North American plant and animal guilds or communities developed during this time. Third, it is the period in which all of humanity's recorded history (both oral and written) exists. Fourth, its history, both biological and cultural, can be known through standard chronological proxy dating methods as well as through the use of historic documents. Finally, it is the epoch we continue to live in, and in which restorationists must do their work to heal the enormous damage that has been done to the environment of North America (Noss, Laurie, and Scott 1995).

Readers should note that throughout the following chapters dates may be given in either calendar years (B.C. and A.D.) or in years "before the present" (B.P.). Those unfamiliar with the B.P. designation for time—a notation developed as part of the radiocarbon-dating process—should know that it indicates a calibrated point measured from 1950. Thus, 4950 B.P. is approximately the same as 3000 B.C., and 200 B.P. approximately the same as A.D. 1750. This approximation is necessary because there is typically a correction factor for B.P. dates, while there is none for calendar dates.

By North America, we mean that space occupied by the current nation-states of Canada, Mexico, and the United States. By selecting North America, we do not suggest that the use of historical information by restorationists should be limited to this continent. We hope that readers located elsewhere will use the basic concepts and other information in this book as a springboard for work in their own locales. In fact, much of the pioneering work in historical ecology is now underway in Central and South America, and Europe (Crumley 1994). Furthermore, European and other researchers have put considerable effort into studying the ecological history of their own countries (Roberts 1989; Smith and Cloutman 1988; Hooke and Kain 1982; Sheail 1980) and have often been at the forefront of using paleoecological and documentary data for ecological studies (Godwin 1934; Oldfield 1969; McArthur 1973; Hoskins 1975; Peterken 1979).

References

Abram, D. 1996. *The spell of the sensuous: Perception and language in a more-than-human world*. New York: Pantheon Books.

Allen, E.B., W.W. Covington, and D. Falk. 1997. Developing the conceptual basis for restoration ecology. *Restoration Ecology* 5(4):275–276.

Allen, T.F.H., and T.B. Starr. 1982. *Hierarchy: Perspectives for ecological complexity*. Chicago: University of Chicago Press.

Anderson, M.K. 1996. Tending the wilderness. *Restoration & Management Notes* 14(2):154–166.

Aplet, G.H., and W.S. Keeton. 1999. Application of historical range of variability concepts to biological conservation. Pages 71–86 in *Practical approaches to the conservation of biological diversity*, ed. R.K. Baydack, H. Campa III, and J.B. Haufler. Washington, D.C.: Island Press.

Aronson, J., E. LeFloc'h, C. Ovalle, and R. Pontanier. 1993. Restoration and rehabilitation of degraded ecosystems in arid and semiarid regions. 1. A view from the South. *Restoration Ecology* 1:8–17.

Aronson, J., S. Dhillon, and E. LeFloc'h. 1995. On the need to select an ecosystem of reference, however imperfect: A reply to Picket and Parker. *Restoration Ecology* 3(1):1–3.

Bay Institute. 1998. *From the Sierra to the sea: The ecological history of the San Francisco Bay–Delta Watershed*. San Rafael, Calif.: Bay Institute of San Francisco.

Bonnichsen, R., and K.L. Turnmire, eds. 1999. *Ice Age people of North America*. Corvallis: Oregon State University Press.

Bonnickson, T.M. 1994. Social and political issues in ecological restoration. Pages 108–114 in *Sustainable ecological systems: Implementing an ecological approach to land management*, tech. coords. W.W. Covington and L.F. DeBano., General Technical Report RM-247. Fort Collins, Colo.: USDA Forest Service, Rocky Mountain Forest and Range Experiment Station.

Bormann, F.H., and G.E. Likens. 1979. *Pattern and process in a forested ecosystem*. New York: Springer-Verlag.

Botkin, D.B. 1990. *Discordant harmonies: A new ecology for the twenty-first century*. New York: Oxford University Press.

Brautigan, R. 1967. *Trout fishing in America*. New York: Dell Publishing.

Brown, J.H. 1995. *Macroecology*. Chicago: University of Chicago Press.

Brush, G. 1997. History and impact of humans on Chesapeake Bay. Pages 125–145 in *Ecosystem function and human activities: Reconciling economics and ecology*, R.D. Simpson and N.L. Christensen. New York: Chapman and Hall.

Caraher, D.L., J. Henshaw, F. Hall, W.H. Knapp, B.P. MacCammon, J. Nesbitt, R.J. Pederson, I. Regenovitch, and C. Tietz. 1992. *Restoring ecosystems in the Blue Mountains: A report to the regional forester and the forest supervisors of the Blue Mountain forests*. Portland, Ore.: USDA Forest Service, Pacific Northwest Region.

Christensen, N.L., A.M. Bartuska, J.H. Brown, S. Carpenter, C. D'Antonio, R. Francis, J.F. Franklin, J.A. MacMahon, R.F. Noss, D.J. Parsons, C.H. Peterson, M.G. Turner, and R.G. Woodmansee. 1996. The report of the

Ecological Society of America committee on the scientific basis for ecosystem management. *Ecological Applications* 6:665–691.

Clements, F.E. 1924. *Methods and principles of paleo-ecology*. Yearbook 32. Washington, D.C.: Carnegie Institute of Washington.

———. 1949. The relict method in dynamic ecology. Pages 161–200 in *Dynamics of vegetation: Selections from the writings of Frederic E. Clements, Ph.D.*, ed. B.W. Allred and E.S. Clements. New York: H.W. Wilson.

Cole, D.N. 2000. Paradox of the primeval: Ecological restoration in wilderness. *Ecological Restoration* 18(2):77–86.

Cole, K.L., M.B. Davis, F. Stearns, G. Guntenspergen, and K. Walker. 1998. Historical landcover changes in the Great Lakes region. Pages 43–50 in *Perspectives on the land-use history of North America: A context for understanding our changing environment*, ed. T.D. Sisk. U.S. Geological Survey, Biological Resources Division, Biological Science Report USGS/BRD/BSR-1998-0003.

Covington, W.W., P.Z. Fulé, M.M. Moore, S.C. Hart, T.E. Kolb, J.N. Mast, S.S. Sackett, and M.R. Wagner. 1997. Restoration of ecosystem health in ponderosa pine forests of the Southwest. *Journal of Forestry* 95(1):23–29.

Crumley, C. 1994. *Historical ecology: Cultural knowledge and changing landscapes*. Sante Fe, N.M.: School of American Research Press.

———. 1998. Foreword. Pages ix–xiv in *Advances in historical ecology*, ed. William Balée. New York: Columbia University Press.

Curtis, J.T. 1956. The modification of mid-latitude grasslands and forests by man. Pages 721–736 in *Man's role in changing the face of the earth*, ed. W.L. Thomas in collaboration with C.O. Sauer, M. Bates, and L. Mumford. Chicago: University of Chicago Press.

———. 1959. *The vegetation of Wisconsin*. Madison: University of Wisconsin Press.

Delcourt, P.A., and H.R. Delcourt. 1991. *Quaternary ecology: A paleological perspective*. London and New York: Chapman and Hall.

———. Paleoecological insights on conservation of biodiversity: A focus on species, ecosystems, and landscapes. *Ecological Applications* 8:921–934.

Denevan, W.M. 1992. The pristine myth. *Annals of the Association of American Geographers* 82(3).

Diamond, J. 1997. *Guns, germs, and steel: The fates of human societies*. New York: W.W. Norton.

Dirkx, G.H.P. 1999. Workinggroup on Historical Ecology Web site: www.archweb.leidenuniv.nl/wlo/werkgr_ecol.html.

Dublanica, K. 1999. Ecological and cultural restoration of the Shokomish Tribe's estuary. In abstracts of the 1999 Society for Ecological Restoration Conference, San Francisco, Calif., September 22–25, 1999.

Egan, D. 1988. *Our heritage of landscaping with native plants: A hermeneutical study of texts from 1919–1929*. M.S. thesis. University of Wisconsin–Madison.

Falk, D. 1990. Discovering the future, creating the past: Some reflections on restoration. *Restoration & Management Notes* 8(2):71–72.

Gleason, H.A. 1953. Autobiographical letter. *Bulletin of the Ecological Society of America* 34:40–42.

Godwin, H. 1934. Pollen analysis: An outline of the problems and potentialities of the method. I. Technique and interpretations. *New Phytologist* 33:278–305. II. General applications of pollen analysis. *New Phytologist* 33:325–258.

Grahame, J. 2000. Land use history of the Colorado Plateau www.jan.ucc.nau. edu/~luhna/index.htm.

Greco, S. 1999. Floodplain history and dynamics of the Sacramento River: Implications for restoration and conservation. In abstracts of the 1999 Society for Ecological Restoration Conference, San Francisco, Calif., September 22–25, 1999.

Grossinger, R. 1999. Seeing time: A historical approach to restoration (California). *Ecological Restoration* 17(4):251-252.

Holling, C.S., and M.A. Goldbert. 1981. Ecology and planning. Pages 78–93 in *Contemporary anthropology: An anthology*, ed. D.G. Bates and S.H. Lees. New York: Alfred A. Knopf.

Holt-Padilla, H. 1999. Restoration using traditional cultural knowledge. In abstracts of the 1999 Society for Ecological Restoration Conference, San Francisco, Calif., September 22–25, 1999.

Hooke, J.M., and R.J.P. Kain. 1982. *Historical change in the physical environment.* London: Butterworth Scientific.

Hoskins, W.G. 1975, reprint. Historical sources for hedge dating. Pages 14–19 in *Hedges and local history.* London: NCSS/Bedford Square Press.

Howell, E.A. 1999. Course materials for Landscape Architecture 666: Restoration Ecology. University of Wisconsin–Madison.

Jordan III, W.R. 1999. Nature and culture. *Ecological Restoration* 17(4):187-188.

Jordan III, W.R., M.E. Gilpin, and J.D. Abers. 1987. *Restoration ecology: A synthetic approach to ecological research.* New York: Cambridge University Press.

Kadlecik, L. 1999. United Indian Health Service, Inc.—Restoring land, culture, and health. In abstracts of the 1999 Society for Ecological Restoration Conference, San Francisco, Calif. September 22–25, 1999.

Karr, J.R., S. Heinz, A.C. Benke, R.E. Sparks, M.W. Weller, J.V. McArthur, J.H. Zar. 1991. Design of restoration evaluation program. Report to the South Florida Water Management District from the Scientific Advisory Panel on evnironmental monitoring of Kissimmee River restoration. West Palm Beach, Fla.: South Florida Water Management District.

Kauffman, S.A. 1993. *The origins of order: Self-organization and selection in evolution.* New York: Oxford University Press.

Kaufmann, M.R., L.S. Huckaby, C.M. Regan, and J. Popp. 1998. *Forest reference conditions for ecosystem management in the Sacramento Mountains, New Mexico.* General Technical Report RMRS-GTR-19. Fort Collins, Colo.: USDA Forest Service, Rocky Mountain Research Station.

Landres, P.B., P. Morgan, and F.J. Swanson. 1999. Overview of the use of natural variability concepts in managing ecological systems. *Ecological Applications* 9(4):1179–1188.

Landres, P.B., P.S. White, G. Aplet, and A. Zimmerman. 1998. Naturalness and natural variability: Definitions, concepts and strategies for wilderness management. In *Proceedings of the Second Eastern Wilderness Conference*, ed. D.L. Kulhavy. Nacogdoches, Tx.: Center for Applied Studies, School of Forestry, Stephen F. Austin University.

Libby W.F. 1952. *Radio-carbon dating*. Chicago: Chicago University Press.

Linderman, R.L. 1942. The trophic-dynamic aspect of ecology. *Ecology* 23:399–418.

Lorenz, E. 1963. Deterministic nonperiodic flow. *Journal of Atmospheric Science* 20:163.

Lowenthal, D. 1985. *The past is a foreign country*. New York: Cambridge University Press.

Lynch, E.A. 1998. Origin of park-forest vegetation mosaic in the Wind River Range, Wyoming. *Ecology* 79(4):1320–1338.

MacCleery, D.W. 1998. When is a landscape natural? *Forest History Today* 4(1):39–41.

Manley, P., G.E. Brogan, C. Cook, M.E. Flores, D.G. Fullmer, S. Husari, T.M. Jimerson, L.M. Lux, M.E. McCain, J.A. Rose, G. Schmidtt, J.C. Schuyler, and M.J. Skinner. 1995. *Sustaining ecosystems: A conceptual framework*. R5-EM-TP-001. San Francisco: USDA Forest Service, Pacific Southwest Region.

Marcot, B.G., L.K. Croft, J.F. Lehmkuhl, R.H. Naney, C.G. Niwa, W.R. Owen, and R.E. Sandquist. 1998. *Macroecology, paleoecology, and ecological integrity of terrestrial species and communities of the interior Columbia Basin and northern portions of the Klamath and Great Basins*. General Technical Report PNW-GTR-410. Portland, Ore.: USDA Forest Service, Pacific Northwest Research Station. (T.M. Quigley, tech. ed., Interior Columbia River Basin Ecosytem Management Project: scientific assessment.)

Martinez, D. 1999. Takelma Intertribal Project: Restoration of oak/pine savanna as cultural landscape in southwest Oregon. In abstracts of the 1999 Society for Ecological Restoration Conference, San Francisco, Calif., September 22–25, 1999.

Mattoni, R., and T.R. Longcore. 1997. The Los Angeles coastal prairie: A vanished community. *Crossosoma* 23(2):71–102.

McArthur, A.G. 1973. Plotting ecological change. Pages 27–48 in *Recreating the past*, ed. D. Dufty et al. Sydney, Australia: Hicks Smith.

McCann, J.M. 1999. The making of the pre-Columbian landscape—Part II: The vegetation. *Ecological Restoration* 17(3):107–119.

McIntosh, R.P. 1985. *The background of ecology: Concept and theory*. London: Cambridge University Press.

McKnight, J. 1999. A project for the people: The Grand Canyon Forest Partnership Public Involvement Plan. In abstracts of the 1999 Society for Ecological Restoration Conference, San Francisco, Calif., September 22–25, 1999.

Millar, C.I., and W.B. Woolfenden. 1999. The role of climate change in interpreting historical variability. *Ecological Applications* 9(4):1207–1216.

Moore, M.M., W.W. Covington, and P.Z. Fulé. 1999. Reference conditions and ecological restoration: A southwestern ponderosa pine perspective. *Ecological Applications* 9(4):1266–1277.

Morgan, P., G.H. Aplet, J.B. Haufler, H.C. Humphries, M.M. Moore, and W.D. Wilson. 1994. Historic range of variability: A useful tool for evaluating ecosystem change. *Journal of Sustainable Forestry* 2(1&2):87–111.

Motzkin, G., D. Foster, A. Allen, J. Hared, and R. Boone. 1996. Controlling site to evaluate history: Vegetation patterns of a New England sand plain. *Ecological Monographs* 66(3):345–365.

Noss, R.F. 1985. On characterizing presettlement vegetation: How and why. *Natural Areas Journal* 5(1):5–19.

Noss, R.F., E.T. Laurie III, and J.M. Scott. 1995. *Endangered ecosystems of the United States: A preliminary assessment of loss and degradation.* Biological Report 28. Washington, D.C.: USDI, National Biological Service.

Oelschlaeger, M. 1994. *Caring for creation: An ecumenical approach to the environmental crisis.* New Haven, Conn.: Yale University Press.

Oldfield, F. 1969. Pollen analysis and the history of land use. *Advancement of Science* 25:298–320.

Parker, V.T. 1997. The scale of successional models and restoration objectives. *Restoration Ecology* 5(4):301–306.

Peterken, G.F. 1979. The use of records in woodland ecology. *Archives* 14:81–87.

Pickett, S.T.A., and V.T. Parker. 1994. Avoiding the old pitfalls: Opportunities in a new discipline. *Restoration Ecology* 2:75–79.

Platenkamp, G., C. Brown, and J. Runlet. 1999. Historical analysis of riparian habitat of the San Joaquin River, California. In abstracts of the 1999 Society for Ecological Restoration Conference, San Francisco, Calif., September 22–25, 1999.

Prigogine, I., and I. Stengers. 1984. *Order out of chaos.* New York: Random House.

Roberts, N. 1989. *The Holocene: An environmental history.* New York: Basil Blackwell.

Russell, E.W.B. 1997. *People and the land through time: Linking ecology and history.* New Haven, Conn.: Yale University Press.

Sears, P.B. 1935a. Types of North American pollen profiles. *Ecology* 16:488–499.
———. 1935b. Glacial and postglacial vegetation. *Botanical Review* 1:37–51.

Sheail, J. 1980. *Historical ecology: The documentary evidence.* Cambridge: Institute of Terrestrial Ecology.

Sierra Nevada Ecosystem Project. 1996. *Final report to Congress: Status of the Sierra Nevadas.* Volume 1: Assessment summaries and management strategies. Wildland Resources Center Report No. 36. University of California–Davis, Centers for Water and Wildland Resources.

Sisk, T.D., ed. 1998. *Perspectives on the land-use history of North America: A context for understanding our changing environment.* Biological Sciences Report USGS/BRD/BSR-1998-0003. USGS, Biological Resources Division.

Smith, A.G., and E.W. Cloutman. 1988. Reconstruction of Holocene vegetation history in three dimensions at Waun-Fignen-Felen, an upland site in South Wales. *Philosophical Transactions of the Royal Society of London* 322:159–219.

Smith, H.Y., and S.F. Arno, eds. *Eighty-eight years of change in a managed ponderosa pine forest.* General Technical Report RMRS-GTR-23. Ogden, Utah: USDA, Rocky Mountain Research Station.

Stephenson, N.L. 1999. Reference conditions for giant sequoia forest restoration: Structure, process, and precision. *Ecological Applications* 9(4):1253–1265.

Stuiver, M., and H.A. Polach. 1977. Discussion: Reporting ^{14}C data. *Radiocarbon* 19(3):355–363.

Swanson, F.J., J.A. Jones, D.O. Wallin, and J.H. Cissel. 1994. Natural variability—Implications for ecosystem management. Volume II: Ecosystem management principles and applications. Pages 80–94 in *Eastside forest ecosystem health assessment*, tech. eds. M.E. Jensen and P.S. Bourgeron, and assessment team leader R.L. Everett. General Technical Report PNW-GTR-318. Portland, Ore.: USDA Forest Service.

Swetnam, T.W., C.D. Allen, and J.L. Betancourt. 1999. Applied historical ecology: Using the past to manage the future. *Ecological Applications* 9(4):1189–1206.

Vale, T.R. 1998. The myth of the humanized landscape: An example from Yosemite National Park. *Natural Areas Journal* 18:231–236.

Watson, P.J. 1991. Origins of food production in western Asia and eastern North America. Pages 1–37 in *Quaternary landscapes*, ed. L.C.K. Shane and E.J. Cushing. Minneapolis: University of Minneapolis Press.

White, P.S., and J.L. Walker. 1997. Approximating nature's variation: Selecting and using reference information in restoration ecology. *Restoration Ecology* 5(4):338–349.

Whitehead, N.L. 1998. Ecological history and historical ecology: Diachronic modeling versus historical explanation. Pages 30–41 in *Advances in historical ecology*, ed. William Balée. New York: Columbia University Press.

Williams, P. 1999. Recreating forgotten landscapes. In abstracts of the 1999 Society for Ecological Restoration Conference, San Francisco, Calif., September 22–25, 1999.

Wu, J.G., and O.I. Loucks. 1995. From balance of nature to hierarchical patch dynamics: A paradigm shift in ecology. *Quarterly Review of Biology* 70:439–466.

Yerby, F., L. Stacey, and B. R. MacRoberts. 1999. Restoration and management of prairies on the Kisatchie National Forest, Louisiana. In abstracts of the 1999 Society for Ecological Restoration Conference, San Francisco, Calif., September 22–25, 1999.

Yesner, D.R. 1996. Environments and peoples at the Pleistocene-Holocene boundary in the Americas. Pages 243–252 in *Humans at the end of the Ice Age: The archaeology of the Pleistocene-Holocene transition*, eds. L.G. Straus, B.V. Eriksen, J.M. Erlandson, and D.R. Yesner. New York: Plenum Press.

I

Cultural Evidence

ARCHAEOLOGIST MICHAEL O'BRIEN begins this section, not with a chapter about a technique, but with an overview of how archaeologists have studied both changes in the physical environmental and the ways humans have adapted to those changes. He provides a summary of the techniques used by archaeologists and paleoecologists and stresses the effects of climate change on the activities of Native Americans in the Midwest. His case study of the Cannon Reservoir Human Ecology Project in northeastern Missouri is instructive because it identifies the complex interactions of climate, vegetation, animals, and human activities that must be considered when reconstructing the history of a site or watershed.

Kat Anderson is well known among restorationists as an advocate of historical ecology and for her work with Native Americans, whom she honors as "people with a sophisticated knowledge of how to harvest and manage plant and animal populations for sustained yields." In chapter 2, Kat discusses how she goes about doing her work as an ethnoecologist—conducting oral interviews with indigenous people, reviewing ethnographic literature, analyzing museum artifacts, and setting up field experiments. This work, which is rich in both a human and an other-than-human context, is essential to reconstruct the complex environment described in chapter 1.

For those who love a trip to the library, Michael Edmonds provides a spirited yet practical voyage through the archives as he discusses the "pleasures and pitfalls of written documents" in chapter 3. Written documents are pervasive in our culture and initially alluring to the first-time researcher. Edmonds puts things in perspective—sorting out biases and other problems—while exposing the reader to the wealth of primary and secondary documents that tell the tale of North America and its environmental past.

As Kat Anderson notes in her chapter, doing oral interviews is an essential part of a historical ecology project. In chapter 4, James Fogerty provides a no-nonsense guide to taking an oral history. He leads the reader through the basic steps of planning, interviewing, and transcribing—turning what were once words and ideas held in the mind of the narrator into information that can be used by everyone, including restorationists and land managers.

Seeing the past in the form of old maps and photographs is always fascinating, and Tina Reithmaier brings her experience in finding and accessing these documents to bear in chapter 5. She covers a wide spectrum of material, including maps by Native Americans, the federal government, and commercial interests; and photographs, both ground-based (including repeat photography) and aerial. When used effectively, as the case studies by Robin Grossinger, Ken Cole, and Peter Dunwiddie demonstrate in part III, these materials can provide a powerful tool for identifying change and for speaking to the general public.

The records (both written documents and maps) of the federal land surveys in North America are one of the resources historical ecologists and others use most often. In chapter 6, Gordon Whitney and Joseph DeCant recount the earliest land surveys on the continent and detail the emergence of the General Land Office surveys in the United States and the Canadian Crown and Dominion Land surveys in Canada. They provide practical information about where to find these documents and how to read them, pointing out their inherent biases and limitations. Using an example of work they undertook using survey records from northwestern Pennsylvania, they demonstrate how these surveys can be used to determine not only the species composition of presettlement woodlands, but also landscape-level disturbance processes, site-specific vegetation-environment relationships, and species associates and plant communities for mapping purposes.

I

Archaeology, Paleoecosystems, and Ecological Restoration

Michael J. O'Brien

Archaeologists have long been interested in the role the physical environment played in structuring the activities of prehistoric human groups. More recently, research has begun to shift toward the role of humans as active participants in paleoecosystems. This move toward paleoecology has not signaled an abandonment of traditional research questions having to do with humans and their environment—why groups lived in certain locales and not others; why they selected certain foods over others; and why they chose particular raw materials for their clothing, tools, and weapons. It has, however, signaled an end to the centuries-old belief in environmental determinism.

Despite this trend, paleoecological research is still an undercurrent in terms of actual archaeological practice. Although modern archaeologists are more familiar with paleoecology than their predecessors were, today's "ecologically oriented" archaeological applications are often based on methods more than on anything else. With a few exceptions—for example, the earlier work of Kent Flannery (1968) on systems theory and, later, the work of human evolutionary ecologists (Bettinger 1991; Kelly 1995)—theoretical work on such topics as grain response (MacArthur and Pianka 1966; Pianka 1974), patchiness (Wiens 1976), and central-place foraging (Orians and Pearson 1979) have not had the kind of impact in archaeology that one might have hoped.

One reason archaeologists fail to connect their studies of paleoenvironments to paleoecology is because of the difficulty inherent in reconstructing historic settings. Archaeologists are aware that attempts to understand both the paleoenvironment of a specific locality or region and how that environment influenced the actions of organisms living in it are difficult endeavors because environments change, and the rate and magnitude of change are never constant. They realize that, in the end, the best we can hope for are environmental snapshots taken at different times. If the data permit, we can stack those snapshots to create a moving picture, but we have to be honest about what it is that we have created—a jerky composite consisting of a set of still photographs taken at arbitrary points along a continuum. We might speak colloquially about having "reconstructed" paleoenvironments, but we need to keep in mind that we haven't reconstructed anything. What we have done is to model paleo-environments using available evidence, and, as we all know, models are merely educated guesses about how things might have been. On the positive side, the more lines of corroborating evidence there are, the more refined the model will be.

My goal in this chapter is threefold: (1) to present a brief overview of how archaeologists have adopted changing perspectives on human-environment interactions; (2) to discuss the sources of environmental information of which archaeologists routinely make use; and (3) to indicate some of the ways in which theoretical issues can be integrated into paleoecological research.

Human-Environment Interactions

Despite an early recognition of the importance of the environment and its effects on humans, archaeologists were for the most part slow to recognize the intricacies of human-environment interactions. Throughout the late nineteenth century and well into the twentieth century, most archaeologists were environmental determinists, viewing human actions simply as automatic responses to what the environment allowed (Wissler 1926). At an elementary level, the environment is deterministic—you can't, after all, grow corn at the North Pole—but to suggest that a particular environment triggers automatic, predictable responses on the part of any animal, particularly humans, is short-sighted. All organisms modify their environments—some in more dramatic fashion than others—and most enjoy a kind of phenotypic plasticity that allows them to escape sudden and automatic extinction in the face of environmental change.

By the 1950s, a significant portion of the discipline of archaeology had pushed aside the doctrine of environmental determinism of earlier decades. Archaeologists began leaning heavily on one of two sets of ideas: (1) environmental "possibilism"—a kind of indeterministic process in which the physical environment was seen not so much as determining cultural outcomes but as setting limits on cultural development; or (2) the cultural ecology of anthropologist Julian Steward (1949, 1955), which held that certain relational links between technology and environment, regardless of geographic locale, created similar cultural outcomes.

Included in the list of topics addressed in archaeological reports of the 1950s were the physiographic and geological setting of the locale, hydrologic resources, vegetation, climate, soils, and often the fauna native to the locality under investigation. However, those reports failed to consider both the changes that had taken place in the physical environment and any concomitant changes in human populations due to those changes. Lack of attention to those changes meant that the environment was really being viewed as a static backdrop against which human interactions were carried out. The lack of integration between archaeology and paleoecology was one of archaeologist Walter Taylor's major complaints in his 1948 summary of the state of the discipline. His (1957) report to the National Research Council's Committee on Archaeological Identification called for closer coordination of work between archaeologists and paleoenvironmentalists. The 1960s witnessed phenomenal growth in large-scale archaeological survey-and-excavation projects in the Near East, a significant number of which were directed by Robert J. Braidwood, Robert McCormick Adams, and their students (Adams 1962, 1965; Braidwood 1958, 1960; Flannery 1965; Hole 1966; Hole, Flannery, and Neely 1969; Kraelin and Adams 1960). These interdisciplinary archaeological studies, which focused on the physical environment and its role in the development of settled life, agriculture, and eventually urban areas, led to a series of conceptual changes in how archaeologists approached the topic of human-environment interactions. They spawned a whole new generation of similar studies in semiarid regions of the New World, such as Highland Mexico (Byers 1967; Flannery 1966, 1968; MacNeish 1964; MacNeish, Nelken-Terner, and Johnson 1967; MacNeish, Peterson, and Flannery 1970; MacNeish, Peterson, and Neely 1975). These studies became models both for later archaeological projects carried out in the United States (O'Brien, Warren, and Lewarch 1982) and for the currently emerging discipline of historical ecology (Crumley 1994; Balée 1998).

Sources of Environmental Information

One of the obvious problems facing archaeologists interested in understanding how aspects of the physical environment have changed through time is locating the data necessary to pinpoint the changes. The basic mechanics of landscape evolution became well known by the middle of the nineteenth century, at which time it became evident that the North American continent had undergone successive climatic changes, including periodic "ice ages." One of the burning issues of nineteenth-century prehistory was whether Ice Age humans had been present to hunt the megafauna, especially mastodons and mammoths, that amateur prehistorians had recovered from mid-continental bogs (O'Brien 1996). By the late nineteenth century the issue had been expanded as archaeologists attempted to determine whether there had been a North American Paleolithic period (Meltzer 1983, 1985) similar to that in Europe.

Answers to many of these questions came with the development of radiocarbon dating in the late 1940s (Marlowe 1999). We often think of radiocarbon dating as being solely the province of archaeologists, but its development was also a boon to paleoclimatologists, who could then date their pollen sequences and, like archaeologists, begin to focus on finer and finer units of time. It no longer was enough to place a terminal date on the last glacial episode and then to lump the last ten thousand or so years into a single unit. Through the use of radiocarbon dating, it became clear that the Holocene had witnessed considerable climatic variation and that if the proper data were available, the period could be subdivided into finer units of time.

Archaeologists quite naturally were interested in such research because the data would allow them to understand something of the past environments in which their subjects had lived. Some of the earliest work on paleoenvironments of the terminal Pleistocene and early Holocene (ca. 30,000–7,000 B.C.) was done in the western United States and the Mississippi River alluvial valley. Research done in various parts of the West, including the Rocky Mountains (Matthes 1951), the Great Basin (Antevs 1948; Heizer 1951), the Southwest (Bryan 1950; Sayles and Antevs 1941), and the Great Plains (Antevs 1950; Moss 1951; Schultz, Lueninghoener, and Frankforter 1951), incorporated a variety of data such as rates of varve buildup (Antevs 1950), cross-correlation of terrace sequences (Moss 1951), sediment analysis (Heizer 1951; Sayles and Antevs 1941; Schultz, Lueninghoener, and Frankforter 1951), the positioning of glacial moraines (Antevs 1950; Matthes 1951), and floral analysis (Schultz, Lueninghoener, and Frankforter 1951). Many of the paleoclimatic interpretations that grew out of this early research are now outdated, but what is important is that by 1950 archaeologists had begun to team up with geomorphologists and paleoclimatologists in an effort to document the myriad landscape and climatic changes that various localities had witnessed during the terminal Pleistocene and the Holocene.

Farther east, most of the work carried out in the Mississippi River alluvial valley—that portion of the valley from near Cairo, Illinois, to the Gulf of Mexico—was by Harold Fisk (1944) and those influenced by him (Saucier 1964, 1968). Fisk realized that the Mississippi Valley contained a chronicle of geomorphological responses to changing Tertiary and Quaternary climatic episodes that had affected the North American continent. His goal was to reconstruct the history of landscape development, especially during the terminal Pleistocene and Holocene epochs.

Archaeologists (Ford, Phillips, and Haag 1955; Phillips, Ford, and Griffin 1951) viewed Fisk's development of a relative chronology as a boon to their own work because it gave them another way to date their study sites. Although subsequent work, primarily by Roger Saucier (1974, 1968, 1981) and P. D. Royall and his colleagues, Paul and Hazel Delcourt (1991), has shown Fisk's chronology to be grossly inaccurate and flawed in terms of his postulations about the magnitude of certain processes, the importance of his work is unquestioned. He was the first researcher to tie the landscape evolution of the alluvial valley to climatic change and to the corresponding rates of water and sediment discharge in the upper reaches of the Mississippi system.

The region in which Fisk was working—an active floodplain setting in humid, mid-continental North America—was not comparable to western North America. In fact, many of the problems that Fisk encountered in his attempt to document the evolution of the Mississippi alluvial valley would have been foreign to researchers such as Ernst Antevs (1948, 1950), who was doing the same kind of work but in more stable environments. Thus it is quite understandable that the majority of paleoenvironmental research conducted in the 1940s and 1950s took place in the West (Bryan 1950; Heizer 1951; Matthes 1951; Moss 1951; Schultz, Lueninghoener, and Frankforter 1951).

Sustained interest in the Holocene climate and its relation to other aspects of the midwestern physical environment dates at least to the 1950s. Archaeologists viewed the upper Midwest, in particular, as an excellent laboratory for the study of environmental change because of its unique vegetational composition—a mixture of forest and prairie—with the specific makeup depending on location within the region. Stretching eastward from the Great Plains to central Indiana is a complex mosaic of tallgrass prairie and deciduous forest known as the Prairie Peninsula (Transeau 1935; Küchler 1964, 1972) (figure 1.1). The peninsula of interdigitating fingers of prairie upland and forested river valleys formed early in the Holocene and throughout its history has been vulnerable to climatic change. This vulnerability shows up in the pollen record and in such things as soil composition, valley-fill sequences, and archaeological site locations.

In 1955, W. H. Horr completed the first boreal pollen record in the midcontinent at Muscotah Marsh in northeastern Kansas (see also Wells [1970], who identified the pollen as being from spruce). The zone containing the boreal pollen was subsequently dated to 13,000 ± 1500 B.C. Here was evidence that during the close of the Pleistocene, spruce forests had grown where now there were tallgrass prairies. By the 1960s, pollen studies from other parts of the Midwest supported the long-held proposition that

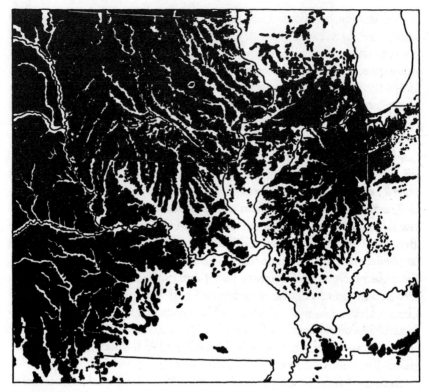

Figure 1.1. Map of the mid-continental Prairie Peninsula showing the interfingering of grasslands (black) and deciduous forests (white) (after Küchler 1964, 1972; Transeau 1935; from Warren 1982a).

boreal forests had been far south of their current latitudes during the terminal Pleistocene, and that, as these forests retreated northward with a rise in temperature, they were replaced in some areas by hardwood forests and in other areas by prairies. What happened next—that is, how climate changed throughout the Holocene—was open to question.

In 1960, James B. Griffin advanced the notion that climatic change contributed to the growth and decline of some northern prehistoric cultures through its effects on their crop cycles (Griffin 1960). The importance of that paper was not whether Griffin was correct (we now know that the situation was much more complex than he suspected) but that he tied the disappearance of a major Native American culture, termed Hopewellian by archaeologists and dating roughly A.D. 1–200, to climatic change.

This examination of the nature of the relation between climate change and human settlement and subsistence practices was the basis for a long-term study of late-ceramic-period cultures in the upper Midwest. It was titled "Climate, Ecology, and the Oneota Culture" and was done under the direction of archaeologist David Baerreis of the University of Wisconsin–Madison. That National Science Foundation–supported program involved intensive study of archaeological materials from Oneota and Mill Creek culture sites in Iowa, Missouri, Minnesota, extreme southeastern Nebraska, and western Wisconsin. It also involved studies of paleoclimatic indicators such as plant and animal remains, snails, and pollen. Baerreis's collaboration with climatologist Reid Bryson of the University of Wisconsin–Madison produced a series of reports and monographs (Baerreis and Bryson 1965, 1967; Bryson 1966; Bryson, Baerreis, and Wendland 1970; Henning 1970) that modeled Holocene climate in the upper Midwest and examined the archaeological record, especially the late portion, in terms of the documented changes in climate (see also Bryson [1966] and Bryson and Wendland [1967]). The site-specific analyses built on work that was more regionally extensive (Borchert 1950; Deevey and Flint 1957; Wright 1968) and produced a concise set of data that would repeatedly be incorporated into later work in the Midwest (Baerreis, Bryson, and Kutzbach 1976; Webb and Bryson 1972; Wendland 1978; Wendland and Bryson 1974).

As a result of numerous palynological and sedimentological analyses, paleoclimatologists (Bryson, Baerreis, and Wendland 1970; Bryson and Wendland 1967; Wendland 1978, 1995; Wendland and Bryson 1974) isolated ten postglacial climatic episodes, each of which affected portions of the Midwest, though the effects often differed substantially from area to area. Four episodes are of concern here: the pre-Boreal, dating between about 8050 B.C. and 7550 B.C., the Boreal (7550–6550 B.C.), the Atlantic (6550–3050 B.C.), and the sub-Boreal (3050–850 B.C.). These are shown in figure 1.2 along with generalized climatic conditions, vegetational changes, and cultural periods. Some of the general climatic trends that characterized these episodes can be extrapolated to regions outside the Midwest, but the magnitude of the trends is uncertain.

The boundary between the pre-Boreal and the Boreal is difficult to pinpoint because of the numerous continuities that carried over from one period to the other. By 8050 B.C. much of the Midwest contained essentially modern assemblages of plants and animals, which continued to extend their ranges throughout the Boreal. The slightly cooler and moister climate during the Boreal, which was extremely localized, may have allowed for the return of some more northerly plants and animals into portions of the upper Midwest, but on a regional basis the climate was becoming slightly warmer and drier. In Missouri, for example, grasses predominated in northern and western parts of the state; oaks (*Quercus*) and hickories (*Carya*) in the Ozark Highlands; oaks, hickories, ash

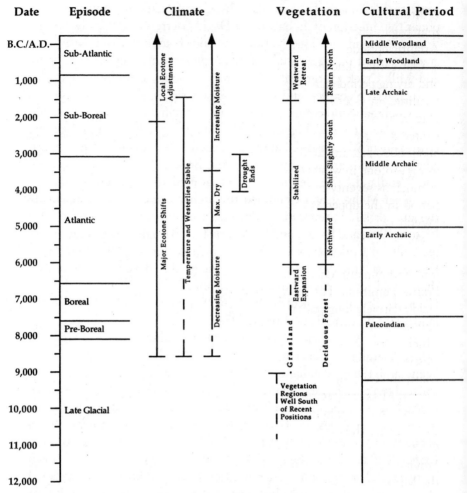

Figure 1.2. Chronological correlation between climatic episodes (left-hand column) and archaeological periods (right-hand column) between 12,000 B.C. and A.D. 250, along with generalized climatic conditions and vegetational changes (modified from Teter and Warren 1979).

(*Fraxinus*), elm (*Ulmus*), and maple (*Acer*) in the river valleys; and a host of water-tolerant species in the Mississippi alluvial valley.

An increased flow of dry, westerly winds in the Pacific air mass allowed prairie grasses to expand eastward from the Great Plains in a broad bisecting wedge that may have reached Missouri sometime around 7000–6550 B.C. Grasses took over the rapidly drying uplands, whereas forests retreated toward relatively moist positions along stream courses and sloping valley sides. This was the beginning of what has been referred to variously as the *Hypsithermal* (Deevey and Flint 1957), the *altithermal*

(Antevs 1948, 1950), and the *xerothermic* (Sears 1942)—a climatic event that began during the Boreal episode and reached its peak during the Atlantic episode.

Our earliest knowledge of the effects of this mid-Holocene warming and drying period came from pollen cores taken from upper-midwestern localities in South Dakota (Watts and Bright 1968) and Minnesota (McAndrews 1966; Winter 1962). These cores consistently demonstrated a decrease in tree pollen and an increase in herb pollen between about 6000 B.C. and 2000 B.C. Wright (1968) calculated that the prairie-forest ecotone in western Michigan might have moved northeastward by as much as seventy-five miles during that period. The height of the dry period in the upper Midwest appears to have occurred about 5000 B.C. (Webb and Bryson 1972; Wright 1971).

As James E. King and Walter Allen (1977) point out, there were as recently as two decades ago few pollen records for mid-Holocene vegetation and climatic change in areas south of the northern border of the Prairie Peninsula. Fortunately, spring bogs and swamps have begun to yield relatively long pollen sequences, and we now have a sample of data points from southeastern Missouri and northeastern Arkansas from which to examine the effects of the Hypsithermal on vegetation in the Mississippi alluvial valley. These include Powers Fort Swale (Royall, Delcourt, and Delcourt 1991) and Old Field (King and Allen 1977) in southeastern Missouri (see figure 1.3 for locations); and Big Lake (Guccione, Lafferty, and Cummings 1988) and Pemiscot Bayou (Scott and Aasen 1987) in northeastern Arkansas. They tell a tale of climatic variation similar to that of their northern counterparts. However, these cores do provide evidence that the xeric (dry) conditions evident over much of the Midwest during the Hypsithermal might not have been as drastic in the meander-belt portion of the Mississippi alluvial valley.

Another line of evidence for the effects of mid-Holocene climate on the Midwest is contained in sedimentological analyses. For example, it appears that there was a dramatic decrease in sediment size in Powers Fort Swale between 7550 B.C. and 2550 B.C., to the point where the percentage of clay fraction increased 31 percent from the early Holocene to the mid-Holocene. The changeover to clay particle dominance occurred at around 4650 B.C. (Royall, Delcourt, and Delcourt 1991), which is near the midpoint of the Atlantic episode. I interpret the decrease in grain size as reflecting the peak of the Hypsithermal, when little or no water was entering Powers Fort Swale and clay particles previously held in suspension began to be deposited as the water level in the swale fell. This phenomenon corresponds chronologically with the decrease in surface area of the Old Field swamp (King and Allen 1977) and was roughly contemporary with similar phenomena elsewhere in the Midwest. For example, a

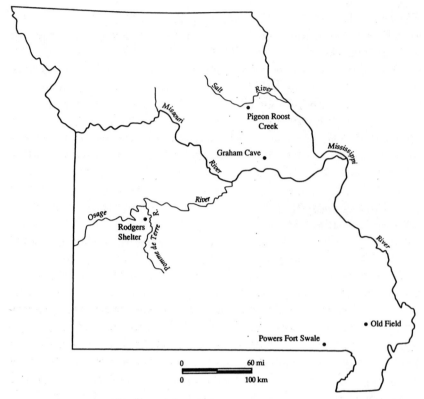

Figure 1.3. Map of Missouri showing locations of archaeological sites and pollen records.

decrease in stream discharge occurred in Illinois and Missouri (Hill 1975; Klippel, Celmer, and Purdue 1978), and a drop in lake levels occurred in Iowa and Minnesota (Brugman 1980; Van Zant 1979).

The death of mesic forests as a result of the onset of mid-Holocene drying could have led to increased wind erosion in certain areas. Stanley Ahler (1973, 1976) postulated that this occurred on the hillslopes around Rodgers Shelter, a stratified archaeological site in Benton County, Missouri (figure 1.3). Similarly, it is possible that some or all of the prairie mounds that dot the western lowlands along the Black and St. Francis Rivers (O'Brien, Lyman, and Holland 1989) were formed during the Hypsithermal as accumulations of windblown sediments derived from the Ozark Escarpment.

Some of the climatic trends mentioned above are mirrored in sources of data other than those from pollen and sediment profiles. For example, based on both the relative abundance of various grassland animal remains—bison, pronghorn, prairie chicken, jackrabbit, spotted skunk, badger, and plains pocket mouse—in the mid-Holocene levels of Rodgers Shelter, Bruce McMillan (1976) proposed that prairies had pushed as far eastward as the Pomme de Terre River valley by about 5000 B.C. A related study by McMillan and Walter Klippel (1981), which incorporated data from an earlier study (Klippel 1970, 1971) of fauna from Graham Cave (figure 1.3), demonstrated higher relative frequencies of edge species, such as deer and cottontails, in the mid-Holocene levels, suggesting that the prairie-forest ecotone had once been well east of its current position. Likewise, James R. Purdue (1980, 1982) found that body sizes of cottontails (*Sylvilagus floridanus*) and gray squirrels (*Sciurus carolinensis*) from archaeological deposits at Rodgers Shelter decreased significantly during the mid-Holocene to sizes that were comparable with those of modern cottontails and squirrels found farther west. Klippel (1970, 1971) noted the same body-size decrease in gray squirrels from Graham Cave.

Thus, despite spotty information, several lines of evidence suggest that the climate of the mid-continent changed dramatically during the early and mid-Holocene. Nevertheless, there still is some debate over the intensity of disruption. Although much of the Midwest was affected by the Hypsithermal, it is fairly clear that not all areas were affected equally (Wright 1976). Comparisons of climates and their effects on vegetation are risky, but there might be a modern analog to the mid-Holocene dry period. Although the drought that occurred in the central plains during the 1930s was much shorter than that which occurred during the Hypsithermal, results of that drought give us the opportunity to see what the short-term effects of a prolonged hot, dry spell are on vegetation communities.

In a series of papers written near the end of the 1930s drought and shortly thereafter, John Weaver and Frederick Albertson (1936; Albertson and Weaver 1945; Weaver 1943) documented wholesale changes in floral communities that occurred over a short period of time. They noted that the effects of the drought built up over a period of years, finally reaching a critical point where trees and grasses began to die. After four or five drought years, water in the uplands was so depleted that nowhere was it nearer to the surface than four feet—well beyond the ability of grasses and most trees to reach it. As conditions worsened, lower-elevation localities such as slopes and ravines began to be affected. Big bluestem (*Andropogon gerardi*), the dominant grass in lower-slope and streamside positions, decreased in relative frequency from about 75 percent of the grass community to about 50 percent at the peak of the drought. Weaver (1943) reported that as a result of the drought, an area of prairie 100–150 miles wide running north through Kansas, Nebraska, and South Dakota was transformed from a grassland in which little bluestem (*Schizachyrium scoparium*) was the dominant grass into a mixed-grass prairie of short grasses and western wheat grass (*Agropyron smithii*). Albertson and Weaver (1945) estimated 50–60 percent of the trees in the central plains died during or shortly after the drought. The losses were staggering: 28–70 percent loss (depending on area) of trees along bluffs and ravines; 59–75 percent loss along tributary streams; and 5–6 percent loss along the banks of continuously flowing streams.

These accounts lead one to suspect that during the Hypsithermal, the uplands would have been affected first and most severely. Tallgrass prairies would have been replaced by more drought-resistant grasses typical of the short-grass and mixed-grass prairies to the west. Upland forests would have been reduced in size as the drought persisted and the amount of available water declined. After a time, even the floodplains would have been affected by the prolonged effects of the Hypsithermal. Further reductions in composition, density, and extent of floodplain forests could be expected as drought conditions persisted.

Changes in vegetation would have caused simultaneous changes in the composition and distribution of fauna. Deer, squirrels, and other animals that feed on mast resources, such as acorns and hickory nuts, would have had to change their feeding behaviors in concordance with the shifting patterns of food distribution and abundance. Climatic change also would have affected the abundance and distribution of aquatic animals such as fish, reptiles, and mussels.

A Paleoecological Case Study: The Cannon Reservoir Human Ecology Project

I have yet to address the question of how climatic change affected humans residing in the Midwest during the Holocene. For that purpose, I will discuss the Cannon Reservoir Human Ecology Project (Warren 1976, 1979, 1982b; Warren and O'Brien 1981), an archaeological program that investigated changing adaptations on the part of indigenous peoples residing in the central Salt River valley of northeastern Missouri (figure 1.3). In this interdisciplinary study, fieldwork and analysis were designed to test the implications of specific propositions about the way indigenous hunters and gatherers structured their responses to changing physical and cultural environments.

Analysis of the physical environment of the project area (Warren 1982a, 1984) suggested that variation was expressed along two major dimensions. The first was an upland-lowland gradient of slope position that both reflected downslope increases in moisture, forest cover, and biotic diversity and correlated directly with proximity to major perennial streams. The second was an upstream (northwestward) gradient of decreasing relief, moisture, and density and width of forests. Despite the geographic independence of these two dimensions, common to both was variation in the abundance and diversity of forest and aquatic resources. Assuming that (1) subsistence economies of all indigenous groups in the region focused on forest and aquatic resources; (2) site locations were conditioned by access to important resources; and (3) environmental change during the Holocene was expressed along these same two geographic dimensions, sites were expected to be concentrated near waterways in the central and eastern parts of the project area, regardless of their ages.

Three hundred fifty-three sites—defined as any isolable aggregate of five or more surface artifacts—were discovered during the survey. Seventy-five of these sites were assigned to a temporal period by using temporally diagnostic projectile points. The locations of the Archaic components are shown in figure 1.4. With the exception of the Paleoindian–Early Archaic configuration (shown together), distinguished by three sites in level upland prairies that were at least three miles away from major perennial streams, all distributions appeared to fit expectations. Sites were more abundant along the Salt River and lower reaches of its major tributaries, and all sites more than a mile away from the major streams were located in the eastern half of the project area. Thus, sites tended to aggregate in those parts of the region where forest and aquatic resources were most abundant and diverse during the nineteenth and twentieth centuries. This association has an important implication: Differences in resource availability across the region were important enough to indigenous groups to influence relative values of different site locations, and upstream locations were generally less desirable than those downstream. Significantly, the causal direction of this relation was supported by the predominance, in excavated faunal and floral assemblages from the region, of the remains of forest and aquatic resources (Bozell and Warren 1982; King 1982).

A second perspective on site-context variation focused on characteristic positions of sites within regional environments, without regard to broad geographic distributions. Continuities and changes in physiographic contexts of dated sites were evaluated in light of hypothetical responses of regional floral communities to Holocene climatic change. Analysis of modern soils data and General Land Office records (see chapter 6) demonstrated that climatic change during the Neo-Boreal (Little Ice Age) climatic episode (ca. A.D. 1550–1850) caused extensive expansion of timber onto what previously were prairies. The magnitude of this episode and its effect on floral distributions were used as a baseline from

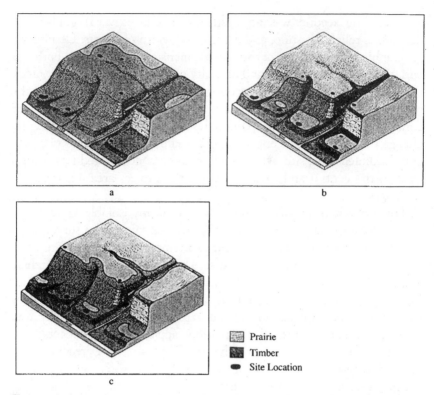

Figure 1.4. Models of site locations, showing hypothetical distributions of contemporary floral communities in the Cannon Reservoir sampling area, northeastern Missouri: (A) Paleoindian–Early Archaic period (eight out of eight sites plotted); (B) Middle Archaic period (9/18 plotted); (C) Late Archaic period (11/22 plotted) (from Warren 1982b).

which to predict the effects of other climatic episodes on the environment (Warren 1982b; Warren and O'Brien 1985). Assuming that the postulated magnitudes and directions of climatic trends during other periods were correct, Robert E. Warren (1982a) then projected hypothetical spatial configurations of floral communities for all major episodes of the Holocene.

To systematically evaluate site locations and to trace context changes through time, Warren (1982b) then compared the localities of all dated sites (including those postdating the Archaic period) in terms of their native physiographic, vegetational, and soil characteristics. A notably high incidence of sites—73 percent—were in bottomland contexts, whereas sites in upland contexts were relatively rare. This bias was significant in light of the fact that only 25 percent of the area surveyed was bottomland, but it was consistent with the proposition that access to resources generally favored bottomland settlement in the region. Proportions of components, calculated by cultural period and by context, illustrated several noteworthy trends. First, the bottomland bias began only during the Middle Archaic period (5000–3000 B.C.); no Paleoindian (9250–7500 B.C.) sites and only three of eight Early Archaic (7500–5000 B.C.) sites were located in bottomland contexts. Second, all periods had unique arrays of context occurrences. Proportional patterns between the Middle Archaic and Late Archaic (3000–600 B.C.) sites were similar but not identical. Third, there was a steady rise in the number of contexts in which sites occurred, from two in the Paleoindian period to six in the Late Archaic period. Warren (1982b) evaluated this trend of increasing site-context richness vis-à-vis two assumptions of the model that structured work in the Salt River valley: (1) hunter-gatherer population density in an environmentally diverse region increases as land use intensifies; and (2) population density increases with the varieties of environmental contexts that must be exploited to house and sustain the population. He found that the data supported both the notion of population density increase and the hypothesized change in land-use intensity throughout the Archaic period.

Specific contexts in which sites of various periods were located are noteworthy. Paleoindian sites occurred in two contexts—near small streams in locales that historically were prairie and on gently sloping margins of level upland forest (figure 1.4). Importantly, all four Paleoindian sites also contained Early Archaic components, signifying that later peoples used the same localities as earlier people. Early Archaic groups also exploited forested high and moderately high bottomland terraces near perennial streams, although no sites were found in those contexts during the probabilistic survey. However, excavations at the deep, stratified Pigeon Roost Creek site, located on a bottomland terrace near the main stem of the Salt River (figure 1.3), produced ample evidence that Paleoindian groups used bottomland contexts.

Despite several important continuities, site contexts from the Middle Archaic period represented a settlement pattern radically different from that of the Early Archaic period (figure 1.4). There was a sharp reduction in the proportion of upland sites to about 17 percent. Conversely, there was a sizable increase in the proportion of sites on very high bottomland terraces, and bluff-base sites occurred for the first time. The proportion of sites on margins of lower terraces changed very little. The new focus on lowland contexts probably represented either a major shift in resource orientation or significant shifts in the distribution of resources.

Prairies undoubtedly expanded beyond their nineteenth-century limits and probably also invaded many areas currently underlain by forest soils. Valley sides with relatively gentle slopes, which are common along the Salt River's major tributaries, may have been transformed into extensive hill prairies and open-canopy woodlands, or savannas. Many bottomland forests probably formed galleries along major streams and survived on steeper protected slopes. The resulting increase in resource accessibility could have obviated the value of many upland locations and could have encouraged recurrent occupation of stable bottomland contexts. Observed distributions were consistent, for the most part, with these propositions. Nevertheless, sites were common on upland rims, suggesting that the degree of settlement mobility was still quite high among Middle Archaic groups. Moreover, it also implies that the Middle Archaic settlement pattern may have been similar to the Early Archaic pattern. Although the distributions and physiographic contexts of sites changed a great deal, the biotic contexts and functions of sites may have remained the same.

Late Archaic period components in the central Salt River valley continued the trend of decreasing proportions of sites in upland contexts (roughly 9 percent). All but two components occurred in lowlands, and both exceptions were situated on the gently sloping edges of upland flats near major streams (figure 1.4). The proportion of bottomland sites was similar to that of the Middle Archaic period; most were located near major streams on the outer margins of high terraces. However, several other lowland contexts increased in relative frequency or were represented for the first time. Bluff-base sites in wide valley bottoms replaced upland rim components as the third most common context, and one site was located on the narrow terrace of a perennial tributary stream.

The increased proportion of lowland sites during the Late Archaic period represented a striking contrast to contemporary environmental changes. At the end of the Hypsithermal, effective moisture increased in the Prairie Peninsula, and timber reclaimed many contexts that previously had given way to prairie. Given these environmental changes, the relative decrease in numbers of upland sites during the Late Archaic period was anomalous from the perspective of changing resource distribution. If the Middle Archaic settlement-subsistence pattern had persisted, there should have been a proportional increase in upland sites, rather than a decline. Thus, observed trends indicated that there was a significant change after the Middle Archaic period, either in the kinds of resources exploited or in the settlement strategy used to house and sustain communities. Contrasts between site contexts of the Early Archaic and Late Archaic periods suggest that selection for patterns of settlement and subsistence after the Hypsithermal involved cultural factors rather than environmental ones. One important factor may have been population growth, whether that growth was simply the natural product of more births than deaths among native residential groups or was attributable in part to migration into the region.

In summary, settlement data from the central Salt River valley showed both an increase in the number of sites through time and an increase in the number of contexts that were used. These data, however, make little sense except when viewed in the context of changing Holocene environments. Even though our knowledge of Holocene environments and environmental change is incomplete, what we do know allows us to begin to understand why, for example, archaeological materials from certain periods are located in one topographic setting as opposed to another. Our knowledge of paleoclimatic regimes, especially the timing of the appearance and disappearance of those regimes, allows us to model vegetative and animal response, the former of which leaves its imprint in the soils it helps build and the latter in faunal assemblages in archaeological sites. As important as this information is, in and of itself it tells us little about what indigenous groups were doing at those sites and why they might have selected certain localities over others. This kind of information is derived in large part through excavation.

Archaeology and Restoration

Archaeology has come a long way in the past half century in terms of how it views human-environment interactions, but it has not reached the point where paleoecology is a decided research focus. Nonetheless, archaeologists have used a variety of methods and techniques to study previous environments, and there are signs of a growing interest in ecological theory among archaeologists—an interest and expertise that can contribute in significant ways to ecological restoration projects. I am in complete agreement with one of the central tenets of this volume—that the success of restoration ecology rests in large part on its incorporation of the historical dimension.

In this chapter, I have discussed the effect of climate on vegetation and on human and animal populations. Climatic change may, in fact, be the ultimate cause of future changes in the environment, but restoration ecologists have to wrestle with myriad other aspects of the historical dimension. From my perspective, one of the more important ones is human agency. Humans, as I've noted, are not simply passive recipients of whatever nature happens to throw their way—that is, they are not environmentally determined. Rather, they can and do modify their environment, sometimes with devastating effects. We need not restrict our focus to the twentieth century or even to the last few hundred years to see how humans can radically alter an ecosystem. As Raymond Wood and I have pointed out (O'Brien and Wood 1998), among the greatest such transformations are those that have come about by the human release of fire, which was an important environmental component long before humans tried to control it. Fire in most landscape settings is not only natural, it is historic, desirable, and inevitable (Pyne 1982; Wright and Bailey 1982).

In the popular mind, and until recently in much of the academic literature (Cronon 1983; Denevan 1992; McCann 1999), the pre-Columbian eastern United States is perceived as having been a vast and essentially uninterrupted tract of dense forest—a collection of pristine ecosystems that were massively disrupted by Euroamerican settlers. Today many restorationists and land managers are devoted to returning regional vegetation to a pre-Euroamerican standard—without realizing that what the first Europeans saw was a landscape that had been molded by fires and other management practices of Native Americans. For example, early historical narratives, whether by explorers, settlers, or scientists, "display a compelling uniformity in their depiction of Missouri woodlands as far more open than today" (Ladd 1991, 70–71). Henry Rowe Schoolcraft's travels through the Ozarks in the early nineteenth century led him through the countryside near the Meramec River, where he noted that "a tall, thick, and rank growth of wild grass covers the whole country, in which the oaks are standing interspersed, like fruit trees in some well cultivated orchard" (Schoolcraft 1821, 54). Accounts of regions as far east as the forests of Virginia echo this language and reinforce the importance of fire in Native American land management practices (Hammett 1992). Similarly, as Kat Anderson points out in this volume (chapter 2), ethnologies and ethnobotanical studies of indigenous peoples throughout North America also demonstrate their use of various techniques, including fire, to acquire food, medicine, and materials for clothing, shelter, transportation, defense, and ritual.

In conclusion, those interested in restoration ecology cannot ignore the temporal dimension, nor can they ignore perhaps the most important players in the ecosystems that evolved along that dimension: humans. Ecologists can learn from archaeologists as they explore the ways in which human groups have helped shape past ecosystems, and I would maintain that archaeologists have a lot to learn from restoration ecologists, especially as members of their project teams.

References

Adams, R. M. 1962. Agriculture and urban life in early southwestern Iran. *Science* 136:109–122.

———. 1965. *Land behind Baghdad: A history of settlement on the Diyala Plains.* Chicago: University of Chicago Press.

Ahler, S. A. 1973. Post-Pleistocene depositional change at Rodgers Shelter. *Plains Anthropologist* 18:1–26.

————. 1976. Sedimentary processes at Rodgers Shelter. Pages 123–139 in *Prehistoric man and his environments: A case study in the Ozark Highland*, ed. W. R. Wood and R. B. McMillan. New York: Academic Press.

Albertson, F. W., and J. E. Weaver. 1945. Injury and death or recovery of trees in prairie climate. *Ecological Monographs* 15:394–433.

Antevs, E. 1948. *The Great Basin, with emphasis on glacial and postglacial times*. III. Climatic changes and pre-white man. Bulletin 38, pages 168–191. Salt Lake City: University of Utah.

————. 1950. Postglacial climatic history of the Great Plains and dating the records of man. Pages 46–50 in *Proceedings of the Sixth Plains Archaeological Conference, 1948*. Anthropological Papers 11. Salt Lake City: University of Utah.

Baerreis, D. A., and R. A. Bryson. 1965. Climatic episodes and the dating of the Mississippian cultures. *The Wisconsin Archeologist* 46:203–220.

Baerreis, D. A., and R. A. Bryson, eds. 1967. *Climatic change and the Mill Creek culture of Iowa*. Archives of Archaeology No. 29. Madison: University of Wisconsin,

Baerreis, D. A., R. A. Bryson, and J. E. Kutzbach. 1976. Climate and culture in the western Great Lakes region. *Midcontinental Journal of Archaeology* 1:39–57.

Balée, W. 1998. *Advances in historical ecology*. New York: Columbia University Press.

Bettinger, R. L. 1991. *Hunter-gatherers: Archaeological and evolutionary theory*. New York: Plenum.

Borchert, J. R. 1950. The climate of the central North American grassland. *Annals of the Association of American Geographers* 40:1–39.

Bozell, J. R., and R. E. Warren. 1982. Analysis of vertebrate remains. Pages 171–195 in *The Cannon Reservoir Human Ecology Project: An archaeological study of cultural adaptations in the southern Prairie Peninsula*, ed. M. J. O'Brien, R. E. Warren, and D. E. Lewarch. New York: Academic Press.

Braidwood, R. J. 1958. Near Eastern prehistory. *Science* 127:1419–1430.

————. 1960. *Excavations in the Plains of Antioch: An archaeological survey*. Publication No. 61. Chicago: University of Chicago, Oriental Institute.

Brugman, R. B. 1980. Postglacial diatom stratigraphy of Kirchner Marsh, Minnesota. *Quaternary Research* 13:133–146.

Bryan, K. 1950. The geology of Ventana Cave. Pages 75–126 in *The stratigraphy and archaeology of Ventana Cave, Arizona*, ed. E. W. Haury. Tucson: University of Arizona Press.

Bryson, R. A. 1966. Airmasses, streamlines, and the boreal forest. *Geographical Bulletin* 8:228–269.

Bryson, R. A., D. A. Baerreis, and W. M. Wendland. 1970. The character of late-glacial and post-glacial climatic changes. Pages 53–74 in *Pleistocene and recent environments of the central Great Plains*, eds. W. Dort Jr. and J. K. Jones Jr. Lawrence: University Press of Kansas.

Bryson, R. A., and W. M. Wendland. 1967. Tentative climatic patterns for some late glacial and post-glacial episodes in central North America. Pages

271–298 in *Life, land and water*, ed. W. J. Mayer-Oakes. Winnipeg: University of Manitoba Press.

Byers, D. S., ed. 1967. *The prehistory of the Tehuacán Valley. Vol. 1: Environment and subsistence*. Austin: University of Texas Press.

Cronon, W. 1983. *Changes in the land: Indians, colonists, and the ecology of New England*. New York: Hill and Wang.

Crumley, C. L. 1994. *Historical ecology: Cultural knowledge and changing landscapes*. Sante Fe, N.M.: School of American Research Press.

Cutter, B. E., and R. P. Guyette. 1994. Fire frequency on an oak-hickory ridgetop in the Missouri Ozarks. *American Midland Naturalist* 132:393–398.

Deevey, E. S., and R. F. Flint. 1957. Postglacial hypsithermal interval. *Science* 125:182–184.

Denevan, W. M. 1992. The pristine myth: The landscape of the Americas in 1492. *Association of American Geographers, Annals* 82:369–385.

Fisk, H. N. 1944. *Geological investigation of the alluvial valley of the lower Mississippi Valley*. Vicksburg, Miss.: U.S. Army Corps of Engineers.

Flannery, K. V. 1965. The ecology of early food production in Mesopotamia. *Science* 147:1247–1255.

———. 1966. The postglacial "readaptation" as viewed from Mesoamerica. *American Antiquity* 31:800–805.

———. 1968. Archaeological systems theory and early Mesoamerica. Pages 132–177 in *Anthropological archeology in the Americas*, ed. B. J. Meggers. Washington, D.C.: Anthropological Society of Washington.

Ford, J. A., P. Phillips, and W. G. Haag. 1955. The Jaketown site in west-central Mississippi. *Anthropological Papers* (American Museum of Natural History) 46(1).

Griffin, J. B. 1960. Climatic change: A contributory cause of the growth and decline of northern Hopewellian culture. *The Wisconsin Archeologist* 4(2): 21–33.

Guccione, M. J., R. H. Lafferty III, and L. S. Cummings. 1988. Environmental constraints on human settlement in an evolving Holocene alluvial system, the lower Mississippi Valley. *Geoarchaeology* 3:65–84.

Hammett, J. E. 1992. Ethnohistory of aboriginal landscapes in the southeastern United States. *Southern Indian Studies* 41:1–50.

Heizer, R. F. 1951. A preliminary report on the Leonard Rockshelter site, Pershing County, Nevada. *American Antiquity* 17:89–98.

Henning, D. R. 1970. Development and interrelationships of Oneota culture in the lower Missouri River valley. *The Missouri Archaeologist* 32.

Hill, F. C. 1975. *Effects of the environment on animal exploitation by Archaic inhabitants of the Koster site*. Ph.D. dissertation, Department of Biology, University of Louisville.

Hole, F. 1966. Investigating the origins of Mesopotamian civilization. *Science* 153:605–611.

Hole, F., K. V. Flannery, and J. A. Neely. 1969. *Prehistory and human ecology of the Deh Luran Plain: An early village sequence from Khuzistan, Iran*. Memoir No. 1. Ann Arbor: University of Michigan, Museum of Anthropology.

Horr, W. H. 1955. A pollen profile study of the Muscotah Marsh. *Science Bulletin* (University of Kansas) 37:143–149.

Kelly, R. L. 1995. *The foraging spectrum: Diversity in hunter-gatherer lifeways.* Washington, D.C.: Smithsonian Institution Press.

King, F. B. 1982. Analysis of archaeobotanical remains. Pages 197–213 in *The Cannon Reservoir Human Ecology Project: An archaeological study of cultural adaptations in the southern Prairie Peninsula,* ed. M. J. O'Brien, R. E. Warren, and D. E. Lewarch. New York: Academic Press.

King, J. E., and W. H. Allen Jr. 1977. A Holocene vegetation record from the Mississippi River valley, southeastern Missouri. *Quaternary Research* 8:307–323.

Klippel, W. E. 1970. *Prehistory and environmental change along the southern border of the Prairie Peninsula during the Archaic period.* Ph.D. dissertation, Department of Anthropology, University of Missouri–Columbia.

———. 1971. *Graham Cave revisited: A reevaluation of its cultural position during the Archaic period.* Memoir No. 9. Columbia: Missouri Archaeological Society.

Klippel, W. E., G. Celmer, and J. R. Purdue. 1978. The Holocene naiad record at Rodgers Shelter in the western Ozark Highland of Missouri. *Plains Anthropologist* 23:257–271.

Kraelin, C. H., and R. M. Adams, eds. 1960. *City invincible: A symposium on urbanization and cultural development in the ancient Near East.* Oriental Institute of the University of Chicago, December 4–7, 1958. Chicago: University of Chicago Press.

Küchler, A. W. 1964. *Potential natural vegetation of the coterminous United States.* Special Publication No. 36. New York: American Geographical Society.

———. 1972. The oscillations of the mixed prairie in Kansas. *Erdkunde* 26:120–129.

Ladd, D. 1991. Reexamination of the role of fire in Missouri oak woodlands. Pages 67–80 in *Proceedings of the Oak Woods Management Workshop.* Charleston: Eastern Illinois University.

MacArthur, E., and E. R. Pianka. 1966. On optimal use of a patchy environment. *American Naturalist* 100:603–609.

MacNeish, R. S. 1964. Ancient Mesoamerican civilization. *Science* 143: 531–537.

MacNeish, R. S., A. Nelken-Terner, and F. W. Johnson. 1967. *The prehistory of the Tehuacán Valley. Vol. 2: Nonceramic artifacts.* Austin: University of Texas Press.

MacNeish, R. S., F. A. Peterson, and K. V. Flannery. 1970. *The prehistory of the Tehuacán Valley. Vol. 3: Ceramics.* Austin: University of Texas Press.

MacNeish, R. S., F. Peterson, and J. A. Neely. 1975. *The prehistory of the Tehuacán Valley. Vol. 5: Excavations and reconnaissance.* Austin: University of Texas Press.

Marlowe, G. 1999. Year one: Radiocarbon dating and American archaeology, 1947–1948. *American Antiquity* 64:9–32.

Matthes, F. E. 1951. Rebirth of the glaciers of the Sierra Nevada during late post-Pleistocene time. *Geological Society of America Bulletin* 52:2030.

McAndrews, J. H. 1966. Postglacial history of prairie, savanna and forest in northwestern Minnesota. *Torrey Botanical Club Memoirs* 22:1–72.

McCann, J. M. 1999. The making of the pre-Columbian landscape. Part II: The vegetation, and implications for restoration for 2000 and beyond. *Ecological Restoration* 17(3):3–15.

McMillan, R. B. 1976. The dynamics of cultural and environmental change at Rodgers Shelter, Missouri. Pages 211–232 in *Prehistoric man and his environments: A case study in the Ozark Highland*, ed. W. R. Wood and R. B. McMillan. New York: Academic Press.

McMillan, R. B., and W. E. Klippel. 1981. Environmental changes and hunter-gatherer adaptation in the southern Prairie Peninsula. *Journal of Archaeological Science* 8:215–245.

Meltzer, D. J. 1983. The antiquity of man and the development of American archaeology. *Advances in Archaeological Method and Theory* 6:1–51.

———. 1985. North American archaeology and archaeologists 1879–1934. *American Antiquity* 50:249–260.

Moss, J. H. 1951. *Early man in the Eden Valley*. Philadelphia: University of Pennsylvania, University Museum, Museum Monographs.

O'Brien, M. J. 1996. *Paradigms of the past: The story of Missouri archaeology*. Columbia: University of Missouri Press.

O'Brien, M. J., R. L. Lyman, and T. D. Holland. 1989. Geoarchaeological evidence for prairie-mound formation in the Mississippi alluvial valley, southeastern Missouri. *Quaternary Research* 31:83–93.

O'Brien, M. J., R. E. Warren, and D. E. Lewarch, eds. 1982. *The Cannon Reservoir Human Ecology Project: An archaeological study of cultural adaptations in the southern Prairie Peninsula*. New York: Academic Press.

O'Brien, M. J., and W. R. Wood. 1998. *The prehistory of Missouri*. Columbia: University of Missouri Press.

Orians, G. H., and N. E. Pearson. 1979. On the theory of central place foraging. Pages 155–177 in *Analysis of ecological systems*, ed. D. J. Horn, G. R. Stairs, and R. D. Mitchell. Columbus: Ohio State University Press.

Phillips, P., J. A. Ford, and J. B. Griffin. 1951 *Archaeological survey in the lower Mississippi alluvial valley, 1940–1947*. Papers 25. Cambridge, Mass.: Harvard University, Peabody Museum of American Archaeology and Ethnology.

Pianka, E. R. 1974. *Evolutionary ecology*. New York: Harper and Row.

Purdue, J. R. 1980. Clinal variation in some mammals during the Holocene in Missouri. *Quaternary Research* 13:242–258.

———. 1982. The environmental implications of the fauna recovered from Rodgers Shelter. Pages 199–261 in *Holocene adaptations within the lower Pomme de Terre River Valley, Missouri*, ed. M. Kay. Report submitted to the U.S. Army Corps of Engineers, Kansas City District.

Pyne, S. J. 1982. *Fire in America*. Princeton, N.J.: Princeton University Press.

Royall, P. D., P. A. Delcourt, and H. R. Delcourt. 1991. Late Quaternary paleoecology and paleoenvironments of the central Mississippi alluvial valley. *Geological Society of America Bulletin* 103:157–170.

Saucier, R. T. 1964. *Geological investigation of the St. Francis Basin, lower Mississippi Valley*. Technical Report No. 3-659. Vicksburg, Miss.: U.S. Army Engineer Waterways Experiment Station.

———. 1968. A new chronology for braided stream surface formation in the lower Mississippi Valley. *Southeastern Geology* 9:65–76.

———. 1974. *Quaternary geology of the lower Mississippi Valley*. Research Series No. 6. Fayetteville: Arkansas Archeological Survey.

———. 1981. Current thinking on riverine processes and geologic history as related to human settlement in the Southeast. *Geoscience and Man* 22:7–18.

Sayles, E. B., and E. Antevs. 1941. *The Cochise culture*. Medallion Papers No. 29. Globe, Ariz.: Gila Pueblo.

Schmits, L. J. 1978. The Coffey site: Environment and cultural adaptation at a prairie Plains Archaic site. *Midcontinental Journal of Archaeology* 3:69–185.

Schoolcraft, H. R. 1821. *Journal of a tour into the interior of Missouri and Arkansaw . . . performed in the years 1818 and 1819*. London: Phillips.

Schultz, C. B., G. C. Lueninghoener, and W. D. Frankforter. 1951. A graphic resume of the Pleistocene of Nebraska (with notes on the fossil mammalian remains). Lincoln: *Bulletin of the University of Nebraska State Museum*, Contribution of the Division of Vertebrate Paleontology.

Scott, L. J., and D. K. Aasen. 1987. Interpretation of Holocene vegetation in northeastern Arkansas. Pages 100–132 in *A cultural resources survey, testing, and geomorphic examination of ditches 10, 12, and 29, Mississippi County, Arkansas*, by R. H. Lafferty III, M. J. Guccione, L. J. Scott, D. K. Aasen, B. J. Watkins, M. C. Sierzchula, and P. F. Bauman. Report submitted to the U.S. Army Corps of Engineers, Memphis District.

Sears, P. B. 1942. Xerothermic theory. *Botanical Review* 8:708–736.

Steward, J. H. 1949. Cultural causality and law; a trial formulation of early civilization. *American Anthropologist* 51:1–27.

———. 1955. *Theory of culture change*. Urbana: University of Illinois Press.

Taylor, W. W., Jr. 1948. *A study of archeology*. Memoir No. 69. Arlington, Va.: American Anthropological Association.

Taylor, W. W., Jr., ed. 1957. *The identification of non-artifactual archaeological remains; report of a conference held in Chicago, March 11–13, 1956, by the Committee of Archaeological Identification, Division of Anthropology and Psychology, National Academy of Sciences, National Research Council*. Publication No. 565. Washington, D.C.: National Research Council.

Teter, D. C., and R. E. Warren. A dated projectile point sequence from the Pigeon Roost Creek site. Pages 227–251 in *The Cannon Reservoir Human Ecology Project: A regional approach to cultural continuity and change*, eds. M. J. O'Brien and R. W. Warren. Technical Report No. 79–14. Lincoln: University of Nebraska, Department of Anthropology.

Transeau, E. N. 1935. The Prairie Peninsula. *Ecology* 16:423–437.

Van Zant, K. 1979. Late glacial and postglacial pollen and plant macrofossils from Lake West Okoboji, northwestern Iowa. *Quaternary Research* 12: 358–380.

Warren, R. E. 1976. Site survey and survey design. Pages 1–333 in *Cannon Reservoir Archaeological Project report* (appendix II), ed. D. R. Henning. Technical Report No. 79-03. Lincoln: University of Nebraska, Department of Anthropology.

———. 1979. Archaeological site survey. Pages 71–100 in *Cannon Reservoir Human Ecology Project: A regional approach to cultural continuity and change*, eds. M. J. O'Brien and R. E. Warren. Technical Report No. 79–14. Lincoln: University of Nebraska, Department of Anthropology.

———. 1982a. The historical setting. Pages 29–70 in *The Cannon Reservoir Human Ecology Project: An archaeological study of cultural adaptations in the southern Prairie Peninsula*, eds. M. J. O'Brien, R. E. Warren, and D. E. Lewarch. New York: Academic Press.

———. 1982b. Prehistoric settlement patterns. Pages 337–368 in *The Cannon Reservoir Human Ecology Project: An archaeological study of cultural adaptations in the southern Prairie Peninsula*, eds. M. J. O'Brien, R. E. Warren, and D. E. Lewarch. New York: Academic Press.

———. 1984. The physical environment: A context for frontier settlement. Pages 95–134 in *Grassland, forest, and historical settlement: An analysis of dynamics in northeast Missouri*, by M. J. O'Brien. Lincoln: University of Nebraska Press.

Warren, R. E., and M. J. O'Brien. 1981. Regional sample stratification: The drainage class technique. *Plains Anthropologist* 26:213–227.

———. 1985. Archaeological sites and their contexts. In Archaeology of the central Salt River valley: An overview of the prehistoric occupation by M. J. O'Brien. *The Missouri Archaeologist* 46:11–36.

Watts, W. A., and R. C. Bright. 1968. Pollen, seed and mollusk analysis of a sediment core from Pickerel Lake, northeastern South Dakota. *Geological Society of America Bulletin* 79:855–876.

Weaver, J. E. 1943. Replacement of true prairie by mixed prairie in eastern Kansas and Nebraska. *Ecology* 24:421–434.

Weaver, J. E., and F. W. Albertson. 1936. Effects of the great drought on the prairies of Iowa, Nebraska and Kansas. *Ecology* 17:567–639.

Webb III, T., and R. A. Bryson. 1972. Late- and postglacial climatic change in the northern Midwest, USA: Quantitative estimates derived from fossil pollen spectra by multivariate statistical analysis. *Quaternary Research* 2:70–115.

Wells, P. V. 1970. Postglacial vegetational history of the Great Plains. *Science* 167:1574–1582.

Wendland, W. M. 1978. Holocene man in North America: The ecological setting and climatic background. *Plains Anthropologist* 23:273–287.

Wendland, W. M., Environmental history at Lubbock Lake and the episodic nature of Holocene climates. In *Ancient peoples and landscapes*, ed. E. Johnson. Lubbock: Museum of Texas Tech University.

Wendland, W. M., and R. A. Bryson. 1974. Dating climatic episodes of the Holocene. *Quaternary Research* 4:9–24.

Wiens, J. A. 1976. Population response to patchy environments. *Annual Review of Ecology and Systematics* 7:81–120.

Winter, T. C. 1962. Pollen sequences at Kirchner Marsh, Minnesota. *Science* 138:526–528.

Wissler, C. 1926. *The relation of nature to man in aboriginal America.* New York: Oxford University Press.

Wright, H. A., and A. W. Bailey. 1982. *Fire ecology.* New York: Wiley.

Wright, H. E., Jr. 1968. History of the Prairie Peninsula. Pages 78–88 in *The Quaternary of Illinois*, ed. R. E. Bergstrom. Special Publication No. 14. Urbana: University of Illinois, College of Agriculture.

———. 1971. Late Quaternary vegetational history of North America. Pages 425–464 in *Late Cenozoic glacial ages*, ed. K. K. Turekian. New Haven, Conn.: Yale University Press.

———. 1976. The dynamic nature of Holocene vegetation: A problem in paleoclimatology, biogeography, and stratigraphic nomenclature. *Quaternary Research* 6:581–596.

2

The Contribution of Ethnobiology to the Reconstruction and Restoration of Historic Ecosystems

M. Kat Anderson

The notion of pristine wilderness areas where passive Indians wandered and collected resources is being dismantled as more people begin to recognize that many ecosystems were profoundly influenced at each level of biological organization by Native American land uses and management techniques (Anderson 1996; McCann 1999a, 1999b). This recognition of Native Americans as gardeners, horticulturalists, and plant dispersers—as people with a sophisticated knowledge of how to harvest and manage plant and animal populations for sustained yields (Fowler 1986; Turner and Kuhnlein 1983; Anderson 1990)—means that the restoration of an historic ecosystem, in order to be authentic, must take into account the rich knowledge of regional native cultures. This involves studying and understanding a native group's material culture, ecological knowledge, and management practices and knowing the plants, animals, and fungi that were important to that particular group (Turner 1995; Balick and Cox 1996).

One relatively new discipline that can help restorationists retrieve this knowledge is ethnobiology, which is the study of how different human societies interact with the natural environment (Soulé and Kohm 1989; 65). Ethnobiological studies are multidisciplinary in nature and use methods from anthropology and biology to elucidate the historic and current interrelationships between human cultures and the natural environment (Cox 1989; Posey 1992). Major topics within the field include the study of how different cultures perceive, classify, evaluate, and use other species; how they manage ecosystems for their own needs; and the limitations and consequences of their actions (Bye 1979; Ford 1981; Prance 1995). Ethnobiologists acquire this information by studying, tallying, and cataloguing the vast anthropological collections of useful plants and animals that are housed in museums throughout North America. They also record the detailed information that lives in the memories of elderly Native Americans, and they meticulously read the diaries, field notes, and published treatises of early anthropologists who studied Native American uses and management of the natural world.

In addition, ethnobiologists are beginning to use the concepts and methods of historical ecology as a framework for their research (Ford 1978; 43). According to ethnobiologist William Balée, historical ecology provides a powerful paradigm for comprehending the interactions between natural environments and associated indigenous societies—a paradigm in which the relation between nature and culture is seen as a dialogue rather than a dichotomy (Balée 1994, 1). Historical ecologists and ethnobiologists are concerned with looking at a world in which humans are active members of the land community.

Up to this point, the relationship between ethnobiologists, historical ecologists, and ecological restorationists has yet to be fully appreciated or explored. However, through their studies, ethnobiologists can provide evidence of both the former biological richness of historic ecosystems and the management techniques used by indigenous peoples to support the structure and richness of those systems—such studies should support the work of restorationists as they seek to restore historic ecosystems (Jordan 1994; Jordan, Peters, and Allen 1998).

Unraveling the Past: Methods Used by Ethnobiologists

Ethnobiologists use five principal means to retrieve information about past environments and land-use histories. These include (1) oral interviews and participant observations with indigenous peoples; (2) reviews of ethnographic literature; (3) analysis of museum artifacts; (4) ecological field experiments; and (5) analysis of plant and animal remains in archaeological contexts. (The last method is discussed in chapters 1 and 11.) Ethnobiologists critically analyze this information using multiple lines of evidence to support their reconstructions (Anderson 1996; Pearsall 1989, 1994) and allow for independent cross-checking of their conclusions (Merchant 1993; Crumley 1994). In doing that, they attempt to disclose the dynamic interactions between people and plants, people and animals, and people and ecosystems.

Oral Interviews and Participant Observation

The majority of traditional ecological knowledge about the use of plant and animal species and former management practices and disturbance regimes resides in the memories of elderly Native Americans and the oral traditions and knowledge they pass down. Fortunately, there are still Native Americans living in remote communities who were raised in traditional ways, and who still speak their native language, harvest wild plants and animals, practice traditional horticulture adjacent to their homes or on wildlands, or have memories of how such practices were conducted. To build a rapport with these individuals requires persistent, long-term contact, a sensitivity to their cultural values, and an ability to explain how sharing their knowledge will further the well-being of their communities. As Davis (1995, 45) points out, "The depth of one's knowledge of any aspect of a people's ethnobotany is directly proportional to one's overall knowledge of the culture." Moreover, anyone seeking knowledge of Native American ways should be aware that ecologists have typically dismissed the traditional knowledge of Native Americans as folklore because Native Americans do not speak the language of science and their knowledge is derived from trial and error and keen observation rather than through well-designed quantitative experiments (La Barre 1943, 200).

Ethnobiologists use two principle ways to retrieve knowledge about traditional practices: oral interviews and participant observations. In both cases, the ethnobiologist pays the participants for their time and knowledge. In addition, both unpublished and published reports that the ethnobiologist might generate from interviews or other means are copied and given back to the native participants and the respective tribal councils. When herbarium collections are made, an extra set, which is laminated or preserved under glass, is presented to the tribe (figure 2.1).

Ethnobiologists use two interview methods developed by social scientists. The first method uses qualitative, open-ended interviews in which respondents give extensive responses to a series of general questions on specific subjects (see chapter 4). The second interview method involves conducting highly structured interviews that are designed to be quantitative in scope (Alexiades 1996a; Martin 1995) and that utilize clusters of specific questions focused on particular topics (Briggs 1986). The questions for these interviews are meticulously designed to avoid "leading" the respondent to a particular answer, but rather to reveal the truth. Questions are designed to be nontechnical and easily understandable to the respondent yet to disclose information that is detailed, pertinent, and repeatable by scientists in disciplines such as restoration ecology, conservation biology, and fire ecology. If the respondent grants permission, both types of interviews should be recorded with a tape recorder and the tapes transcribed.

Ethnobiologists can conduct highly structured interviews with a group of randomly selected respondents for the purpose of statistically analyzing

Figure 2.1. A sample of a plant voucher for tribal use.

the responses. In most cases, however, the results of interviews with Native Americans in North America come from small sample sizes and the selection of respondents cannot be done randomly. This means that the normal quantitative methods of the social science do not apply. Still, responses can be tallied and displayed in tabular form as numbers and percentages and recorded as actual responses to questions.

A reference collection of slides, photographs, and specimens of plants and fungi should be assembled to help the respondent identify species and recall the harvesting methods, management techniques, and uses of a species. This is extremely helpful in substantiating and enriching information gained from oral interviews. Ethnobiologists can also ask respondents to press plant specimens for future identification by the ethnobiologist.

In addition to interviews, the ethnobiologist should, whenever possible, accompany native people into the field (Agar 1980, 70, 75). Called participant observations, these visits are made to different sites where interactions between native people and plants, animals, and fungi can be witnessed firsthand (Jorgensen 1989). The ethnobiologist should ask Native Americans to identify plants, fungi, and animals and to talk about their particular uses, harvesting (times and methods), and management practices (see figure 2.2). High-quality plant specimens should be gathered and pressed on the spot, directly tying each specimen to its locale, altitude, uses, harvesting patterns, and management through handwritten notes entered in a notebook. Photographs and detailed ethnobotanical and management information, such as a map of the harvest area, should also be included. Each specimen should be identified by several Native American informants, by the ethnobiologist, and later by a taxonomist. Once properly identified, the specimens should be preserved as vouchers at one or several major herbaria. These vouchers are important for later review and assessment of the ethnobiologist's work and can be correlated with field notes (Alexiades 1996b). They also provide an important historical record and environmental education tool for the tribes. Finally, a careful record of the etymology of the plant names, and of the cultural terminology surrounding them, should be made.

The types of information gathered by the ethnobiologist include (1) native plant species, their uses by indigenous people, and the relevant harvesting variables (season, frequency, tools, scale, quantity, pattern) associated with those species; (2) former and contemporary specific vegetation management practices employed by indigenous groups for each useful native plant species and community, as well as the cultural purposes for specific horticultural practices (e.g., to improve the quality of the plant material, to decrease insect infestations and pathogens, to recycle

Figure 2.2. Melba Beecher, a very knowledgeable Western Mono elder, holding an edible mushroom, *Neolentinus ponderosus*, that had not previously been recorded by anthropologists.

nutrients); (3) comparisons of the parameters necessary for useful plant material (e.g., young age for palatability, anthocyanins for decoration, cell density and uniformity to prevent warping) with the characteristics of plant materials gathered from unmanaged, "natural" areas to elucidate former management practices; (4) investigation of why the tribal elders perceive that the native plants are disappearing along with the tribe's memories of the abundance and distribution of these species; and (5) estimates of the quantities of managed native plants or plant parts needed for the making of various cultural items.

Ethnobiologists and others can establish nonarbitrary criteria for judging the validity of the findings from oral interviews. First, the accuracy of the account can be verified by cross-referencing the information with testimony from other Native American families within, and when appropriate between, tribes of the region, checking for inconsistencies in the information. Second, ethnographic research can be judged by cross-checking its conclusions independently through varied sources of data such as archaeobotanical remains, ecological field experiments, pollen studies, fire scars present in tree rings, analysis of museum artifacts, and written accounts (Crumley 1994). Third, ethnographic research can be evaluated by the extent to which it contributes to the development of a generic conceptual framework—that is, one that identifies patterns that apply to a wide variety of social phenomena (Lofland 1974). Fourth, the research can be judged according to the extent to which it generates formal theories (Athens 1984).

Ethnographic Literature

There are numerous photographs, maps, land surveys, books, field notes, diaries, journals, and reports that contain information concerning indigenous cultures and their use of land in North America (see chapters 3 and 5). These materials are typically found in university libraries, government archives, museums, and historical societies across the continent and overseas. In addition to books, diaries, and reports, back issues of social science journals such as *American Antiquity*, *American Anthropologist*, *Economic Botany*, *Human Ecology*, *International Journal of American Linguistics*, *Journal of American Folk-Lore*, *Journal of Ethnopharmacology*, and *Journal of Ethnobiology* contain articles on the cultural traditions of indigenous peoples. Literature reviewed by ethnobiologists can be divided into three sections: general history, ethnohistory, and ethnographic information. In this chapter, I discuss only the third category.

Ethnography can be defined as the detailed scientific description of specific human cultures. Many university libraries have access to the "Human Relations Area Files" (HRAF)—a database of thousands of articles and books that pertain to the ethnography of more than three-hundred cultural groups throughout the world (Alexiades 1996a). West-erman (1994) provides an aid for finding bibliographic sources in the field of anthropology, the discipline that produced many ethnographies during the late nineteenth and early twentieth centuries. The federal government and many museums sponsored ethnographic studies, the results of which can be found in publications such as *The Smithsonian Annual Report* and *The Bureau of American Ethnology Bulletin* (Ford 1978).

Specific ethnographic studies can be found about certain aspects of native cultures such as language, kinship, ethnobotany, and mythology. For example, thorough ethnobotanies exist for such tribes as the Hocak (Winnebago), Menomini, Meskwaki, and Ojibwe in the Great Lakes region (Kindscher and Hurlburt 1998; Smith 1923, 1928a, 1928b); the Southern Paiute and Western Shoshone in the Great Basin (Bye 1972; Chamberlin 1911); the Hopi, Navajo, Pima, and Tewa in the Southwest (Mayes and Lacy 1989; Wyman and Harris 1951; Curtin 1984; Robbins, Harrington, and Freire-Marreco 1916); and the Cahuilla, Kawaiisu, and Sierra Miwok in California (Bean and Saubel 1972; Zigmond 1981; Bar-rett and Gifford 1933). (See figure 2.3.) There are also summaries of indigenous food and medicinal plants (Havard 1895, 1896; Henkel 1906; Moerman 1986; Vogel 1970; Kindscher 1987, 1992). In addition, many ethnobotanical studies that exist as unpublished master's theses or doc-toral dissertations provide a wealth of information (Banks 1953). Dock-stader (1973) has catalogued some of these early works in a helpful two-volume set. Other unpublished studies contain significant amounts of plant data, such as those of ten tribes listed for the southwestern United States in Ford (1985; 411).

Field notes that were taken during the course of various ethnographic studies also contain important information. Particularly valuable are the field notes of collectors that can be correlated with museum artifacts. Botanists also identified pressed plant specimens for anthropologists, and their correspondence and unpublished writings often contain important information. These field notes can be found in city, county, state, and national museums as well as in the library collections of botanic gardens, universities, and state academies of science.

Classic, multivolume works for referencing North American tribes include W. C. Sturtevant's *Handbook of North American Indians* (1978–ongoing) and E. S. Curtis's *The North American Indian* (1907–1930).

Ethnobiologists peruse all these materials looking for at least three types of information: (1) early landscape descriptions of a region;

Figure 2.3. A sampling of the large corpus of published ethnobotanies from California that describe the many kinds of plants used by Native American tribes.

(2) descriptions of the tribe and its material culture; and (3) descriptions of burning, hunting, and gathering practices of indigenous people.

Museum Artifact Analysis

Artifacts and plant parts in museums have become disenfranchised from their biological and cultural contexts—they lie hidden away in drawers and on shelves in museum archives. They are, however, important vestiges of the historic landscape and remain vital links to piecing together the wealth and diversity of the land.

Museum collections include the artifacts of diverse indigenous cultures, including the fungi and plant parts that were used for foods, medicine, basketry, and cordage. Many of these artifacts—shredded bark medicines, basketry coils, bags of seeds—are nearly a century old, and some, especially the fleshy bulbs and tubers, are disintegrating rapidly. Interestingly, collections for a specific geographic region are often housed in museums in other parts of the continent. For example, collections of the Pomo in California exist not only in California museums, but also in the Smithsonian Institution in Washington, D. C., the Museum of the American Indian in New York City, the Field Museum of Natural History in Chicago, and the Public Museum of Milwaukee. (See figure 2.4.)

Figure 2.4. Jars of seeds that were utilized in great quantities by the Pomo tribe of central California in the collection of the Public Museum of Milwaukee (Samuel Barrett, collector).

Museum artifact analysis is an emerging technique that is designed to enrich the ethnobiologist's knowledge about the relation between indigenous peoples and nature. This method involves detailed studies of artifacts and partially processed plant and animal parts to answer questions about such topics as indigenous diets and pharmacopoeias, the utility of specific woods, indigenous harvesting strategies and disturbance regimes, plant densities and abundance, and species assemblage patterns (Anderson 1993, 1997). Researchers analyze the collections and the accompanying card catalogue entries in addition to unpublished and published field notes and oral interviews. Their work tends to cover five general areas: (1) museum collection inventories, (2) taxonomic identification of unidentified plant parts, (3) comparisons of mature and young shrub growth, (4) taxonomic identification of unidentified woody materials and artifacts, and (5) counting the number of plant parts needed for specific cultural items.

Museum Collection Inventories

All artifacts and loose plant, fungi, and animal materials are inventoried and tallied for tribes in the specific area being studied. This involves verifying the taxonomic identity of each collection item and determining which plant or animal part was used, in which way, and by which tribe. The researcher then lists the species according to the plant community type in which they occur based on information gained from floras and faunas, plant community classification systems, and the advice of leading experts in plant demography and floristics. In some cases, the ethnobiologist further distinguishes and evaluates the plant species according to light requirements, nitrogen-fixing capability, modes of reproduction, and relationship to disturbance.

Taxonomic Identification of Previously Unidentified Plant Parts

In cases where plant parts have been collected but not identified taxonomically, ethnobiologists typically borrow small samples of the parts and make detailed efforts to identify them as to their genus and, when possible, to the species level. This involves working with museum staff, staff at seed bank facilities, horticultural experts, staff at botanical gardens, overseers of private reference collections, and native elders, as well as reviewing unpublished field notes.

Comparisons of Mature and Young Shrub Growth

To determine how woody plants were manipulated by indigenous groups, the ethnobiologist analyzes and compares the morphology and anatomy of shrub and tree shoots from several types of collections, including

historical collections from herbariums, new collections made by the ethnobiologist, and museum collections of indigenous artifacts such as
cordage rods and coils, game sticks, and weapons. The ethnobiologist
examines the shoot tissues to determine the time since the last disturbance and to formulate a list of diagnostic characteristics (usually found
in leaf scars, lenticels, and anthocyanins) that will help identify each
shrub and tree species used and the typical age of the part being used. For
example, if the shoot growth is young, the shrub or tree may have been
managed by fire or pruning. These characteristics are then compared to
the availability of similar plant parts from the same species of shrub or
tree in an unmanaged, "natural" forest, woodland, grassland, or riparian
community. These comparisons between materials found in collections
and "naturally growing" plants give the ethnobiologist a good idea of the
extent of indigenous management. For example, an analysis of the morphology of bundles of branches of willow (*Salix* spp.), redbud (*Cercis occidentalis*), sumac (*Rhus trilobata*), oak (*Quercus* spp.), and other species in
museum collections of California Indian basketry revealed branches that
were young, long, and straight with no diseases, insects, or lateral branch-
ing. These young shoots do not occur readily in "natural" plants in the
absence of disturbance.

Taxonomic Identification of Previously Unidentified Woody Materials and Artifacts

Working in collaboration with scientists at forest products laboratories,
ethnobiologists use nondestructive techniques (if possible) to taxonomically identify those collected woody materials and artifacts that have no
scientific identifications. They analyze samples of loose, woody materials
and artifacts under high-powered microscopes, using cell shape, size, and
anatomy along with diagnostic characteristics such as leaf scars, lenticels,
and anthocyanins to make their identifications.

Counting the Number of Plant Parts Needed to Make a Cultural Item

The ethnobiologist works closely with museum experts and native elders
to understand the intricacies of making cultural artifacts because the
elders have made, or may still make these items. There are two facets to
this work—one at the scale of a single item, the other at the level of a collection of items at the village scale. At the level of the single artifact, the
ethnobiologist selects a subset of cultural items that require large amounts
of plant material and then tallies the number of plant parts and individual plants needed to complete each of the items selected. The ethnobiologist then compares the availability of that plant or plant part in both
managed and unmanaged plant communities. For example, Blackburn

and I (1993) determined that a California Indian feather skirt or cape contained about one hundred feet of cordage, made from approximately five hundred plant stalks of milkweed (*Asclepias* spp.), while a forty-foot-long deer net contained some seven thousand feet of cordage, which would have required a staggering thirty-five thousand milkweed stalks.

At a different level, the ethnobiologist tries to determine the amount of plant material needed by an average-sized indigenous village. This process involves discussions with native elders and non-Indian craftspeople to obtain estimates of the number of plants or plant parts needed to make a particular item from both wild and managed plant communities. With this estimate, the ethnobiologist can compute the number of managed plants and plant parts needed. This calculation provides restorationists with a good grasp of the quantities of plant materials needed from wildlands, the management practices necessary to achieve sustained yields, and the strict cultural parameters required before plants were deemed suitable for use (Blackburn and Anderson 1993).

Ecological Field Experiments

Only recently have ethnobiologists begun to move beyond the descriptive stage of analysis and into the area of quantifying the ecological effects of indigenous harvesting regimes and horticultural practices on vegetation dynamics. This involves enlisting the expertise of disturbance ecologists and statisticians in the design of ecological field experiments. These experiments are designed to mimic or simulate indigenous manipulations, such as the experimental removal of plant parts or whole plants in order to measure the productivity and growth response of the plant populations being harvested. One such example was an experiment that simulated indigenous digging practices with blue dicks (*Dichelostemma capitatum*), one of the most widely eaten corms in California. Native elders assert that without digging, the plants become sparse. Indeed, some cultural groups harvest blue dicks and replant cormlets and spare plants and harvest them after seeding to ensure replenishment of seed. To more thoroughly understand this Indian-plant interaction, Rowney and I designed a field experiment to determine the degree to which differences in the intensity and timing of harvest, both with and without the replanting of cormlets, affect corm and cormlet production of blue dicks (Anderson and Rowney 1999).

This experimental approach has the advantage of focusing on specific questions and/or hypotheses that relate to the effects of indigenous practices on specified features or characteristics of individual species, populations, or plant communities. Moreover, results from these experiments could serve as guidelines for harvesting populations of native plants in a sustainable manner and help return management regimes that would create patch sizes, edge-area ratios, connectivity, and contiguity similar to that experienced in earlier times by Native American tribes.

Ethnobiology and Ecological Restoration

Indigenous knowledge that resides in both the historic literature and within living indigenous cultures is essential for the identification and cataloguing of historic ecosystems in different regions. By reconnecting artifacts, the testimonies of elders, and literature about the past with living landscapes, ethnobiologists like myself hope to open the eyes of restorationists to the animals, plants, and fungi that no longer exist in these landscapes. For example, ethnobiologist Catherine Fowler's (1996) field studies among the Timbisha Shoshone of Death Valley National Monument in southern California revealed several of their management practices. These include pruning lower limbs and clearing brush from under mesquite and pinyon trees, coppicing willows to promote long switches for basketry, and pruning panamint prince's plume (*Stanleya elata*) and desert prince's plume (*S. pinnata*), two important edible greens. This valuable information could be used to design experiments that measure the growth response of these plants to simulated management regimes with the long-term dual goals of managing various areas for seed, greens, and basketry production, and enhancing biodiversity. Likewise, ethnobiologist Jan Timbrook and her colleagues (1982) did a thorough literature review that disclosed vegetation burning by the Chumash in Southern California. That study could be used to reconstruct indigenous burning regimes that specify season, frequency, extent, severity, and pattern of burns for different cultural purposes. Future studies might then measure the reproductive success of herbaceous plants with edible seeds under indigenous burning regimes. Similarly, Helen McCarthy (1993) and other ethnobiologists have discovered that Indian tribes burned areas under native oaks (*Quercus* spp.) to reduce insect pests (*Curculio* and *Melissopus* spp.). Studies could be designed to measure pest incidence in acorns in existing stands with known fire histories, and then field experiments could be conducted to determine the effect of different fire treatments on incidence of these insects.

In addition to generating knowledge for both experiments and practice, ethnobiologists can also assist restorationists by establishing regional libraries or regional databases that contain the ethnographic and ethnohistoric information discussed in this chapter. Such systems would allow the restorationist (or other interested parties) to cross-reference the information, allowing the user to trace the number and variety of historical references that refer to specific plant uses or other facts, thereby increasing the validity of the data.

In all these ways, ethnobiologists, historical ecologists, and restorationists should continue to work with indigenous peoples to show the extent to which their interactions with plant communities shaped and maintained the diversity, abundance, and health of those communities— and can show us a way to a sustainable future.

References

Agar, M.H. 1980. *The professional stranger: An informal introduction to ethnography*. New York: Academic Press.

Alexiades, M.N. 1996a. Anthropology-related resources for ethnobotanists. Pages 285–288 in *Selected guidelines for ethnobotanical research: A field manual*, ed. M.N. Alexiades. New York: New York Botanical Garden.

———. 1996b. Standard techniques for collecting and preparing herbarium specimens. Pages 99–126 in *Selected guidelines for ethnobotanical research: A field manual*, ed. M.N. Alexiades. New York: New York Botanical Garden.

Anderson, M.K. 1990. California Indian Horticulture. *Fremontia* 18(2):7–14.

———. 1993. Native Californians as ancient and contemporary cultivators. Pages 151–174 in *Before the wilderness: Environmental management by native Californians*, eds. T.C. Blackburn and M.K. Anderson. Menlo Park, Calif.: Ballena Press.

———. 1996. Tending the wilderness. *Restoration & Management Notes* 14(2):154–166.

———. 1997. From tillage to table: The indigenous cultivation of geophytes for food in California. *Journal of Ethnobiology* 17(2):149–169.

———. 1999. The fire, pruning, and coppice management of temperate ecosystems for basketry material by California Indian tribes. *Human Ecology* 27(1):79–113.

Anderson, M.K., and D.L. Rowney. 1999. The edible plant *Dichelostemma capitatum*: Its vegetative reproduction response to different indigenous harvesting regimes in California. *Restoration Ecology* 7(3):231–240.

Athens, L. 1984. Scientific criteria for evaluating qualitative studies. In *Studies in symbolic interaction*, vol. 5, ed. N.K. Denzin. Greenwich, Conn.: JAI Press.

Balée, W. 1994. *Footprints of the forest*. New York: Columbia University Press.

Balick, M.J., and P.A. Cox. 1996. *Plants, people, and culture: The science of ethnobotany*. New York: Scientific American Library.

Banks, W.A. 1953. *Ethnobotany of the Cherokee Indians*. Master's thesis, University of Tennessee.

Barrett, S.A., and E.W. Gifford. 1933. Miwok Material Culture. *Bulletin of the Public Museum of the City of Milwaukee* 2(4):117–376.

Bean, L.J., and K.S. Saubel. 1972. *Temalpakh: Cahuilla Indian knowledge and usage of plants*. Morongo Indian Reservation, Banning, Calif.: Malki Museum Press.

Blackburn, T.C., and M.K. Anderson, eds. 1993. Introduction: Managing the domesticated environment. Pages 15–25 in *Before the wilderness: Native Californians as environmental managers*, ed. T.C. Blackburn and M.K. Anderson. Menlo Park, Calif.: Ballena Press.

Briggs, C. 1986. *Learning to ask: A sociolinguistic appraisal of the role of the interview in social science research*. New York: Cambridge University Press.

Bye, R.A. 1972. Ethnobotany of the Southern Paiute Indians in the 1870s. Pages 87–104 in *Great Basin cultural ecology: A symposium*, ed. D.D. Fowler. Publications in the Social Sciences 8. Reno: University of Nevada, Desert Research Institute.

———. 1979. Incipient domestication of mustards in Northwest Mexico. *Kiva* 44:237–256.

Chamberlin, R.V. 1911. Ethno-botany of the Gosiute Indians of Utah. *Memoirs of the American Anthropological Association* 2(5):329–405.

Crumley, C.L. 1994. Historical ecology: A multidimensional ecological orientation. Pages 1–16 in *Historical ecology: Cultural knowledge and changing landscapes*, ed. C.L. Crumley. Santa Fe, N.M.: School of American Research Press.

Curtin, L.S.M. 1984. *By the prophet of the earth: Ethnobotany of the Pima*. Tucson: University of Arizona Press.

Curtis, E.S. 1907–30. *The North American Indian*. 20 volumes. F.W. Hodge, ed. Norwood, Mass.: Plimpton Press (Reprinted New York: Johnson Reprint, 1970).

Davis, E.W. 1995. Ethnobotany: An old practice, a new discipline. Pages 40–51 in *Ethnobotany Evolution of a discipline*, ed. R.E. Schultes and S.V. Reis. Portland, Ore.: Dioscorides Press.

Dockstader, F.J. 1973. *The American Indian in graduate studies: A bibliography of theses and dissertations*, vols. 1 and 2. New York: Heye Foundation and New York Museum of the American Indian.

Duke, J.A. 1986. *Handbook of northeastern Indian medicinal plants*. Lincoln, Mass.: Quarterman Press.

Ford, R.I., ed. 1978. *The nature and status of ethnobotany*. Anthropological Paper No. 67. Ann Arbor: University of Michigan, Museum of Anthropology.

———. 1981. Ethnobotany in North America: An historical phytogeographic perspective. *Canadian Journal of Botany* 59(11):2178–2189.

———. 1985. Anthropological perspectives of ethnobotany in the greater Southwest. *Economic Botany* 39(4):400–415.

Foster, S., and J.A. Duke. 1990. *A field guide to medicinal plants: Eastern and central North America*. Boston: Houghton Mifflin.

Fowler, Catherine S. 1986. Subsistence. Pages 64–97 in *Handbook of North American Indians*. Volume 11: Great Basin, ed. W.L. D'Azevedo. Washington, D.C.: Smithsonian Institution.

———. 1996. Historical perspectives on Timbisha Shoshone land management practices, Death Valley, California. In *Case studies in environmental archaeology*, ed. E.J. Reitz, L.A. Newsom, and S.J. Scudder. New York: Plenum Press.

Havard, V. 1895. Food plants of the North American Indians. *Bulletin of the Torrey Botanical Club* 22(3):98–123.

————. 1896. Drink plants of the North American Indians. *Bulletin of the Torrey Botanical Club* 23(2):33–46.

Henkel, A. 1906. *Wild medicinal plants of the United States.* Bulletin 89. Washington, D.C.: U.S. Department of Agriculture, Bureau of Plant Industry, 1–76.

Jordan III, W.R., 1994. "Sunflower forest": Ecological restoration as the basis for a new environmental paradigm. Pages 17–34 in *Beyond preservation: Restoring and inventing landscapes*, eds. A.D. Baldwin Jr., J. De Luce, and C. Pletsch. Minneapolis: University of Minnesota Press.

Jordan III, W.R., R.L. Peters II, and E.B. Allen. 1988. Ecological restoration as a strategy for conserving biological diversity. *Environmental Management* 12:55–72.

Jorgensen, D.L. 1989. *Participant observation: A methodology for human studies.* Applied Social Research Methods Series 15. Newbury Park, Calif.: Sage Publications.

Kindscher, K. 1987. *Edible wild plants of the prairie: An ethnobotanical guide.* Lawrence: University of Kansas Press.

————. 1992. *Medicinal wild plants of the prairie: An ethnobotanical guide.* Lawrence: University of Kansas Press.

Kindscher, K., and D.P. Hurlburt. 1998. Huron Smith's ethnobotany of the Hocak (Winnebago). *Economic Botany* 52(2):352–372.

La Barre, W. 1942. Folk medicine and folk science. *Journal of American Folklore* 55(218):197–203.

Lofland, J. 1974. Styles of reporting qualitative field research. *American Sociologist* 9:101–111.

Martin, G. J. 1995. *Ethnobotany: A methods manual.* London: Chapman and Hall.

Mayes, V.O., and B.B. Lacy. 1989. *Nanise' a Navajo herbal: One hundred plants from the Navajo reservation.* Tasiale, Ariz.: Navajo Community College Press.

McCann, J. 1999a. Before 1492: The making of the pre-Columbian landscape. Part I: The environment. *Ecological Restoration* 17(1&2):15–30.

————. 1999b. Before 1492: The making of the pre-Columbian landscape. Part II: The vegetation, and implications for restoration for 2000 and beyond. *Ecological Restoration* 17(3):105–127.

McCarthy, H. 1993. Managing oaks and the acorn crop. Pages 213–228 in *Before the wilderness: Native Californians as environmental managers*, ed. T.C. Blackburn and M.K. Anderson. Menlo Park, Calif.: Ballena Press.

Merchant, C. 1993. *What is environmental history? Major problems in American environmental history.* Lexington, Mass.: D.C. Heath.

Moerman, D.E. 1986. *Medicinal plants of native America.* Research Reports in vols. 1 and 2. Ann Arbor: University of Michigan, Museum of Anthropology.

Pearsall, D.M. 1989. *Paleoethnobotany: A handbook of procedures.* San Diego: Academic Press.

————. 1994. Editor's view. *Journal of Ethnobiology* 14(2):iii–iv.

Posey, D.A. 1992. Interpreting and applying the "reality" of indigenous concepts: What is necessary to learn from the natives? Pages 21–34 in *Conservation of* neotropical forests: Working from traditional resource use, ed. K.H. Redford and C. Padoch. New York: Columbia University Press.

Prance, G.T. 1995. Ethnobotany today and in the future. Pages 60–68 in Ethnobotany: Evolution of a discipline, ed. R.E. Schultes and S.V. Reis. Portland, Ore.: Dioscorides Press.

Robbins, W.W., J.P. Harrington, and B. Freire-Marreco. 1916. Ethnobotany of the Tewa Indians. Bureau of American Ethnology Bulletin 55. Washington, D.C.: Smithsonian Institution.

Smith, H.H. 1923. Ethnobotany of the Menomini Indians. Bulletin of the Public Museum of the City of Milwaukee 4(1):1–174.

———. 1928a. Ethnobotany of the Meskwaki Indians. Bulletin of the Public Museum of the City of Milwaukee 4(2):175–326.

———. 1928b. Ethnobotany of the Ojibwe Indians. Bulletin of the Public Museum of the City of Milwaukee 4(3):327–525.

Soulé, M.E., and K.A. Kohm. 1989. Research priorities for conservation biology. Washington, D.C.: Island Press.

Stimson, A.K. 1946. Contributions towards a bibliography of the medicinal use of plants by the Indians of the USA. Master's thesis, University of Pennsylvania.

Sturtevant, W.C. 1978–present. Handbook of North American Indians, 20 volumes. Washington, D.C.: Smithsonian Institution.

Timbrook, J., J.R. Johnson, and D.D. Earle. 1982. Vegetation burning by the Chumash. Journal of California and Great Basin Anthropology 4(2):163–186.

Turner, N.J. 1995. Ethnobotany today in northwestern North America. Pages 264–283 in Ethnobotany evolution of a discipline, ed. R.E. Schultes and S. von Reis. Portland: Dioscorides Press.

Turner, N.J., and H.V. Kuhnlein. 1983. Camas (Camassia spp.) and riceroot (Fritillaria spp.): Two liliaceous "root" foods of the Northwest Coast Indians. Ecology of Food and Nutrition 13:199–219.

Vogel, V.J. 1970. American Indian medicine. Norman: University of Oklahoma Press.

Westerman, R.C. 1994. Field work in the library: A guide to anthropology and related area studies. Chicago: American Library Association.

Wyman, L.C., and S.K. Harris. 1951. The ethnobotany of the Kayenta Navaho. University of New Mexico Publications in Biology. 5:1–59.

Zigmond, M.L. 1981. Kawaiisu ethnobotany. Salt Lake City: University of Utah Press.

3

The Pleasures and Pitfalls
of Written Records

Michael Edmonds

About A.D. 1020, Thorfin Karlsefni discovered on a beach in Newfound-land or Labrador "so many eider-duck . . . that a man could hardly take a step for the eggs" and "no shortage of provisions, for there was hunting of animals on the mainland, eggs in the island breeding-grounds, and fish from the sea." This remained the only European eyewitness description of a North American environment for five hundred years. But shortly after Columbus blundered into the Caribbean in the autumn of 1492, the European captains who quickly followed in his wake began to catalogue the natural resources of the "new" world.

By the mid-sixteenth century, descriptions of North American envi-ronments were spilling off European printing presses in substantial num-bers. Before Copernicus revealed that the earth revolved around the sun, several Spanish writers had described American habitats from Florida to New Mexico. Before Galileo faced the Inquisition, French explorers had described the St. Lawrence River and the Great Lakes region as far west as the head of Lake Superior. Before Shakespeare's celebrated "First Folio" reached even one London reader, dozens of works had already reported on English travels in American landscapes. And those were just the beginning. By the early eighteenth century, hundreds of descriptions of the new continent had been published; and over the next two cen-turies, every expedition seemed to be immediately chronicled by a partic-ipant or an enterprising journalist.

The astonishing number of textual sources that can be used to research the natural history of North America is a mixed blessing. On the one hand, testimony of past witnesses about the state of the landscape does exist for many parts of the continent. On the other, their sheer number can make it quite difficult to discover exactly what may have been said about any given place at any given time. Further adding to this confusion is the fact that what a text *says* may seem straightforward, while what it *means* is obscured by the cultural assumptions and discursive practices of an earlier age. This chapter lays out strategies for coping with those difficulties, while also quoting eyewitness accounts that show some of the pleasures of working with textual evidence.

Identifying and Locating Textual Sources

General Strategies

All textual records have been created, disseminated, and preserved according to certain established conventions of authorship, publishing, and librarianship. Research is always easier if you follow these main currents, and nearly impossible if you ignore them.

First rule: Think geographically, whenever possible. That is, structure your research around a specific locality or finite region rather than around a particular zoological species or a type of habitat. Because all history happened in some *place*, writers often shaped their narratives around particular locations. Similarly, publishers usually indexed their texts with specific place names but are likely to have omitted references to biological terms. Librarians and bibliographers always provided geographic access points, if possible. Before beginning your search for textual sources, compile a controlled vocabulary of relevant geographic names, starting with the most specific and proceeding to broader ones.

Second, check regional bibliographies such as those listed below for works that cover your area. Use Beers (1982) to see if a specialized bibliography exists that will lead to primary sources. Examine Arksey (1983) and Kaplan (1962) to find diaries, journals, memoirs, and autobiographies of people who traveled through or settled in your area. Use Kaminkow (1975) to identify local histories of the region and check the indices to Evans (1901–55) for works printed before 1801.

Third, consult the American Association for State and Local History (1990) to identify local historical organizations that may possess unpublished texts or unique in-house finding aids. For example, every small town in New York has an officially designated historian who knows the local resources. Contact institutions in your area, such as county historical societies or village public libraries, for advice and suggestions.

Fourth, search two important databases—OCLC *WorldCat* and *America: History & Life*—for texts that may not appear in the tools mentioned in the previous points. OCLC *WorldCat* contains descriptions of forty million books and journals owned by tens of thousands of libraries. It is available at nearly every academic library and most large public libraries but is *not* available to the public over the Internet. To find texts that appeared only as articles, search the database *America: History & Life*. It gives access to articles published since 1982 in more than two thousand periodicals devoted to North American history. Like OCLC, it is not available to the general public over the Internet. Because all bibliographic databases such as OCLC and AHL are formed from a controlled vocabulary, try searches that combine your place name with the qualifier "description and travel"—a standard phrase used by librarians to provide access to any account of a geographic area.

Types of Textual Sources

For purposes of this chapter, I have divided textual source material into eight general categories: (1) classic early explorations, (2) the Jesuit Relations, (3) travelers' accounts, (4) Native American sources, (5) official United States government expeditions, (6) local histories, (7) census schedules, and (8) early scientific investigations.

Classic Early Explorations

Seventy-five years before the English stepped ashore at Jamestown, the Spanish explorer Hernando de Soto encamped across the Mississippi from present-day Memphis, Tennessee. One of his officers noted, "This land is higher, drier, and more level than any other along the river that had been seen until then. In the fields were many walnut trees, bearing tender-shelled nuts in the shape of acorns, many being found stored in the houses. . . . There were many mulberry trees, and trees of plums (persimmons), having fruit of vermillion hue, like one of Spain, while others were grey, differing, but far better. All the trees, the year round, were as green as if they stood in orchards, and the woods were open" (Spanish explorers 1907, 206).

As this demonstrates, eyewitness accounts from the major Renaissance exploring expeditions can be fruitful sources of firsthand data on North American landscapes. Although they are particularly prone to the problems of nomenclature and interpretation discussed later in this chapter, such difficulties are usually solved by consulting dependable critical editions. For a summary of what happened on the expeditions themselves, consult Brebner (1933) or a similar secondary work. The liveliest anecdotes and most interesting passages from these documents are brought together in the five large volumes edited by Quinn (1979). Meinig (1986) puts the classic accounts in proper geographical perspective, and the works of Sauer (1966, 1968, 1971, 1980) provide a superb synthesis of their environmental data. You may also find it helpful to keep an atlas, such as Roberts (1973), close at hand.

Although there's nothing quite like the pleasure of handling a six-teenth-century, vellum-bound first edition of a Renaissance voyage, you will probably find a modern scholarly version more convenient. The Hakluyt Society has published more than two hundred well-edited reprints of early explorations over the last century and a half, and reliable texts of most European voyages to the Caribbean, the Gulf Coast, and the Atlantic Coast can be found in their series. While a few of their earliest publications fall somewhat short of modern editorial standards, many of the more recent ones—such as Quinn's volumes on the English voyages to Virginia and New England—are impeccable. Other scholarly organizations that have published similar editions of basic primary sources include the Champlain Society (more than sixty explorations of Canada through the nineteenth century), the Book Club of California (more than one hundred accounts of the Pacific Coast), and the Quivira Society (Spanish exploration in the Southwest, 1590s through 1890s). Search OCLC or the catalogue of any large research library under the names of these organizations for complete lists of their publications.

The amount and quality of ecological description in early explorations varies considerably, though you can usually find helpful descriptions, such as this 1609 description of New York Harbor: "[A crew sent toward shore by Henry Hudson] caught ten great mullets, of a foote and a halfe long a peece, and a ray as great as foure men could hale into the ship. . . . They went into the woods, and saw great store of very goodly oakes and some currants. . . . The lands, they told us, were as pleasant with grasse and flowers and goodly trees as ever they had seene, and very sweet smells came from them" (Juet 1625, 79–80). In the West, Pedro de Castenada, who traveled with the Coronado expedition from Mexico to Kansas in 1540–42, catalogued the landscape in equal detail: "The ravine which the army had now reached was a league wide from one side to the other, with a little bit of a river at the bottom, and there were many groves of mulberry trees near it, and rose bushes with the same sort of fruit that they have in France. They made verjuice from the unripe grapes at this ravine, although there were ripe ones. There were walnuts and the same kind of fowls as at New Spain, and large quantities of prunes like those of Castile" (Spanish explorers 1907, 333–34).

The Jesuit Relations and Allied Documents

Starting in 1610, Jesuit priests traveled an arc stretching from Maine and Nova Scotia in the east, through Quebec, Ontario, and the Great Lakes, down the Mississippi Valley to Louisiana. While the spiritual effect of their missionary work is debatable, the historical value of the extremely detailed annual reports they sent back to France is unquestioned. Long before the habitats in those regions were disrupted by modern civilization, the missionaries submitted very personal, meticulously detailed, and highly anecdotal accounts of their activities.

These texts are known collectively as the Jesuit Relations because their original titles usually begin *Relation de ce qui se passe dans la nouvelle France* . . . ("Report of what happened in New France . . ." during the preceding year). They were complemented by a similar series, *Lettres edifiantes et curieuses*, letters written from missions all around the world and published in Paris, 1703–76, which also contains much on natural history. The standard edition encompassing both series (French and English on facing pages) is Thwaites (1901), in seventy-three volumes.

The Jesuit Relations often shed unique light on the historical ecology of a specific area. For example, a priest traveling through Green Bay, Wisconsin, in 1673 reported that the Indians:

> perceiving that Ducks, Teal, and other birds of that kind dive into the water in quest of grains of wild rice to be found there toward the Autumn season, . . . stretch nets for them with such skill that, without counting the fish, they sometimes catch in one night as many as a hundred wild fowl. This fishing is equally pleasant and profitable; for it is a pleasure to see in a net, when it is drawn out of the water, a Duck caught side by side with a pike, and Carp entangled in the same meshes with Teal. The Savages subsist on this manna nearly three months. (Dablon 1673, 121)

Such careful descriptions abound in the Jesuit Relations, and careful editing and fastidious indexing by Thwaites and his staff almost always make it possible to identify their location. Unfortunately, the English equivalents of French botanical and zoological terms are occasionally inaccurate.

Travelers' Accounts

The Jesuit missionaries were only one type of traveler to follow in the footsteps of the first explorers. People in all walks of life, from European noblemen to semiliterate fur traders, left written records of various parts of North America. The number of these published accounts, tourists' letters, travelers' diaries, emigrant pamphlets, and early settlers' reminiscences is staggering. For example, my research on birds in early America turned up more than twelve hundred primary sources written before 1828 that describe American birds or their habitats. Obviously, finding only the texts you need in this wealth of sources can be a challenge.

Start by consulting regional bibliographies. Use Parks (1989) for the northeastern United States, Vail (1933) for the East Coast, Hubach

(1961) for the Midwest, Clark (1956) for the Southeast, Mintz (1987) and Mattes (1988) for the Great Plains and Rocky Mountains, Wagner and Camp (1982) for the Western United States, Rittenhouse (1971) for the Southwest, Cowan (1964) for California, Smith (1950) and Bjoring et al. (1982) for the Pacific Northwest, and Staton (1934–85) and Waterston (1989) for Canada. The scope and contents of all of these works are described in the bibliography at the end of this chapter, and they should be obtainable at large research libraries or through interlibrary loan.

The most frequently cited travel accounts of North America are those reproduced in three large reprint series. Excerpts from the earliest travels and voyages (before 1612) were printed in the five massive volumes of Quinn (1979). While Quinn was more sensitive to environmental information than many earlier editors, his selections can do no more than scratch the surface, and you will want to use his bibliography to work back to the full texts of the primary sources. For the colonial era, C. Scribner's Sons' issued selections from hundreds of early texts in its Original Narratives of Early American History series. These twenty-eight books, each covering a different geographic region and published independently, provide lengthy selections from primary sources. The third series, and the only project to issue the full text of many later, overland narratives, is Thwaites (1907), whose thirty titles are thoroughly edited and usefully indexed.

Many other publishers have produced the complete texts of less well-known travel narratives through specific regions. Dozens of descriptions of the western and southwestern United States in the nineteenth century have been carefully reprinted over the last several decades by the Lakeside Press of Chicago in its Lakeside Classics series. The Book Club of California has issued a similar number of early travels through that state, and the University of Alaska Press and the Limestone Press of Fairbanks, Alaska, have brought out English translations of early Russian works about that state and the Pacific Northwest. For Canada, the Hudson's Bay Record Society and the Champlain Society have between them issued dozens of primary accounts. All these works can be found in major library catalogues with a keyword search under the publishers' names. The full texts of three thousand works on Canada printed before 1900 are currently available from "Early Canadiana Online" http://www.canadiana.org/cgibin/ECO/mtq, a Web site jointly maintained by the National Library of Canada, the Bibliothèque Nationale du Quebec, the University of Toronto, and other partners.

The reliability, accuracy, and level of detail provided by travelers vary enormously, of course. Most were far more interested in human society than in natural history, and you may need to spend hours carefully searching for descriptions of plants, animals, birds, or climatological events. Nonetheless, educated writers with a penchant for natural history tended to describe the landscapes they passed through in great detail. For example, Captain Aleksei Chirikov, second in command on Bering's expedition, noted that on the Alaska coast at the end of July 1741: "We saw whales, sea lions, walruses, porpoise, white feathered ducks and a multitude of others, some with curved red bills, and many kinds of seagulls. There are high mountains everywhere on that coast" (Dmytryshyn, Crownhart-Vaughan, and Vaughan 1988, 148). Paradoxically, many less sophisticated writers were equally thorough. Seventeenth-century merchant Nicolas Denys (1908) recorded detailed ecological data for the Canadian maritimes, for example, and a century later fur trader Samuel Hearne (1958) amassed substantial collections of scientific observations in the far north.

Merchants and Indian agents sometimes collected important information from Native American trading partners. For example, Pierre Gaultier de Varennes de la Verendrye left this account of the region northeast of Lake Winnipeg, as described by the Cree in 1737: "The country is very open—no mountains. They found a shrub the wood and leaves of which are odoriferous, and which might be the laurel; another which bore seeds like the pepper I showed them; also a tree which produced a kind of cocoa from which exude drops like blood when it is in flower. There are also mines, all kind of wild beasts in abundance, and snakes of a prodigious size" (La Verendrye 1927, 247–48). Fifty years later, the intrepid Scotish trader Alexander Mackenzie—who crossed from the Atlantic to the Pacific two decades before Lewis and Clark—noted of today's Wood Buffalo National Park, in northern Alberta, "The Indians informed me, that, at a very small distance from either bank of the [Slave] river, are very extensive plains, frequented by large herds of buffaloes; while the moose and reindeer keep in the woods that border on it. The beavers, which are in great numbers, build their habitations in the small lakes and rivers, as, in the larger streams, the ice carries everything along with it, during the spring. The mud-banks in the river are covered with wild fowl; and we this morning killed two swans, ten geese, and one beaver, without suffering the delay of an hour . . ." (Mackenzie 1927, 141).

The quite different experiences and intentions of these authors make travelers' accounts especially liable to the problems of nomenclature, geography, and interpretation discussed below. The editors who published their manuscripts also had specific goals in mind, goals that led, for example, to indices listing every human being mentioned but none of the other species of animals or plants. A researcher must consequently be prepared to comb every traveler's account page by page and paragraph by paragraph in order to extract environmental data that seemed inconsequential to the people who wrote or issued the text. Despite these difficulties, however, the reminiscences, diaries, letters, and narratives of travelers can provide a very rich, unfiltered, source of information on American landscapes.

Native American Sources

Long before the *National Enquirer*, Americans' appetite for the bizarre and horrific was partly met by a literary genre known today as "captivity narratives." These first-person narratives of hardship and torture fed the demand for titillation among curious white readers, and despite their ephemeral nature, more than two hundred of those texts survive today. They generally provide colorful and intimate descriptions—albeit culturally biased—of eighteenth- and nineteenth-century frontier environments and the ways that native peoples inhabited them. Their plots usually follow a predictable course: Indians capture the frontier narrator; he or she undergoes a traumatic journey to a native community in the depths of the wilderness; after surviving a period of life among the Indians, he or she eventually escapes or is repatriated. Contemporary readers consumed these texts out of fascination with the "other"—Indians and their sometimes (to white readers) horrifying ways. We read them today for glimpses into how Native Americans interacted with each other and the landscapes that surrounded them.

To find captivity narratives that may shed light on your area, start with Vaughan (1983). This bibliography was the basis for The Garland Library of Narratives of North American Indian Captivities, a 225-volume series issued in the 1970s. For pre-1800 texts that may include descriptions of Indians and their ecological relationships to the land, also search the indices to Evans (1901–55). For early Canada and the northeastern United States, a magnificent compendium was published in 1724 by Joseph-François Lafitau (Lafitau 1974–77), and a wealth of data is scattered through the Jesuit Relations (Thwaites 1901).

Fortunately, we need not rely exclusively on the dominant culture for information about the natural environments inhabited by Native Americans prior to white settlement. Indian autobiographies and memoirs began to appear in English at the turn of the nineteenth century, and many of these describe landscapes before European immigrants arrived in significant numbers. The helpful annotations and index in Brumble (1981) will guide you to first-person accounts by Indian writers and help you predict whether a given memoir is likely to include descriptions of the land and how it was used.

Many native authors described nature in great detail because it was one of the most important characters in their story. Here, for instance, a

Papago woman describes her childhood home in southern Arizona in the mid-nineteenth century:

> We lived at Mesquite Root and my father was chief there. That was a good place, high up among the hills, but flat, with a little wash where you could plant corn. Prickly pear grew there so thick that in summer, when you picked the fruit, it was only four steps from one bush to the next. . . . There were birds flying around, doves and woodpeckers, and a big rabbit sometimes in the early morning, and quails running across the flat land. Right above us was Quijotoa Mountain, the one where the cloud stands up high and white when we sing for rain." (Chona 1936)

Such careful evocation of childhood landscapes are quite common in Native American memoirs. Most Indian autobiographers saw themselves as an inseparable part of the divine natural creation: "Our breath is the wind and it is also our soul," wrote a nineteenth-century Crow warrior; "our words are our breath and they are sacred" (Two Leggings 1967, 25). For this reason they often provided thorough, precise, and detailed accounts of the animals, plants, climate, and topography of the landscape.

Other sources of Native American information about the environment are the serial publications of the Smithsonian Institution and its Bureau of American Ethnology. Starting in the late nineteenth century, academic anthropologists visited and lived among a wide variety of native peoples in the western United States. Their published research often includes the full texts of Indian descriptions of their lands before European contact, as well as a great deal of information on the ways indigenous peoples related to the plants and animals with whom they shared their environment (see chapter 2). The unpublished field notes of professional ethnologists, many of which are available on microfilm in major libraries, provide further details, often including verbatim testimony from Indian informants.

The annual reports of the Smithsonian Institution began in 1846 and contain increasing amounts of environmental and scientific information as the decades pass. The Bureau of American Ethnology's annual reports (fifteen volumes, 1879–94) and *Bulletin* series (two hundred volumes, 1887–1971) published monographs of varying length on a wide variety of Native American research topics. The easiest and most direct access to this massive collection of primary data is the CD-ROM version of Murdock and O'Leary (1975).

Official United States Government Expeditions

Almost as fast as the federal government came into possession of the landscape, it sent soldiers and surveyors to explore and report upon it. The best-known United States government explorations that crossed the interior during the nineteenth century—those of Lewis and Clark, Pike, Long, and Frémont—were intended in large part to gather scientific data. Their personnel were ordered to maintain detailed journals, and because scientists were deliberately recruited to record zoological, botanical, and meteorological data, these reports can be extremely useful to anyone doing environmental history on the Great Plains or western United States.

Not as well known, but typical of this genre, are the Pacific Railroad Surveys of 1853–55. The federal government financed six separate expeditions to locate the best route for constructing a railroad from St. Louis to the Pacific Ocean. Those six surveys produced twelve massive volumes of scientific reports, including three volumes of separately published zoological monographs. For example, Lieutenants Joseph Ives and A. W. Weeks led an expedition west along the thirty-fifth parallel, and their report includes more than two hundred pages on the botany and eighty pages on the zoology they encountered.

Meisel (1924–29) provides an overview of the scientific data collected on all those surveys undertaken before 1865. In all, more than seventeen hundred reports of official, federally financed explorations are listed in Hasse (1899), with full citations back to the appropriate government publications. These include two important later surveys conducted by the U.S. Army Corps of Engineers and the U.S. Geological Survey, respectively, each of which collected substantial amounts of ecological information about the western United States.

The first of these, the so-called Hayden Survey (technically, the "Geological and Geographical Survey of the Territories") covered most of the area from New Mexico north to the Yellowstone Valley in 1867–79. It produced twelve annual reports and thirteen large monographs on natural history and anthropology, including accounts of geology, topography, drainage, vegetation, ethnology, and zoology. The other major project of these years is the Powell Survey ("Geographical and Geological Survey of the Rocky Mountain Region"), 1874–79. Despite its title, this survey covered not just the Rockies but also the Black Hills of South Dakota and the desert and high plateau regions of Utah. Its report occupied twelve massive volumes, with another nine devoted to the ethnology of Native Americans. Other Army surveys after 1865 that have substantial natural history components are Jones (1875), King (1870–80), and Ludlow (1875a and 1875b).

Because accumulation of scientific evidence was a stated purpose of these expeditions, the reports issued at the time give detailed environmental data. For example, botanist Sereno Watson's report on the Great Basin in northern Nevada and Utah, which was based on collecting done in 1867–69, provides a detailed topographical and climatological overview of the region, followed by a 500-page illustrated catalogue of all plants encountered, including the locations where most were found (Watson 1871). Farther north, junior officers Elliott Coues and J. T. Rothrock produced similarly meticulous volumes on the birds, fur-bearing animals, and plants of the West. Coues, in particular, is especially useful. His 750-page, species-by-species account of all the birds encountered during explorations of the Missouri River includes quotes from and citations to dozens of previously published texts as well as many charming first-person anecdotes from the field (Coues 1877, 1878; Rothrock 1878).

Although these nineteenth-century government publications can be found in dozens of libraries in their original formats or on microfilm, they often lack useful indices. In some cases this difficulty is solved by modern critical editions such as the University of Nebraska Press multivolume edition of Lewis and Clark (1983) or by earlier scholarly editions. For example, Coues's late-nineteenth-century editions of Pike and of Lewis and Clark are heavily annotated with footnotes that attempt to clarify every botanical and zoological reference.

In addition to the official reports issued by government exploring expeditions, private journals, field notes, and reminiscences by participants have been published. William Clark's journal, for example, describes the party's encampment near Sioux City, Iowa, in August 1804: "I walked on Shore with one man Collins, . . . The Misqutors [mosquitoes] were So troublesom and thick Musqutors in the Plains that I could not Keep them out of my eyes, with a bush. In my absens Capt Lewis Killed a Pelican on Pelicans Island, at which place maney Hundreds had collected . . ." (Clark 1964, 102). Similar private records kept by professional scientists who accompanied other major expeditions, such as Titian Peale on Stephen Long's 1819–20 expedition to the Rockies or physician John Richardson on Sir John Franklin's first attempt to discover a northwest passage in 1821–23 have also been published (Peale 1947; Richardson 1984).

To discover which scientists accompanied each expedition, consult volumes two and three of Meisel (1924–29). Remember, however, that in the decades since Meisel compiled his pioneering work, many journals and diaries of naturalists have been printed for the first time. Use Meisel to identify a scientist who may have kept notes on a locality in which you are interested, and then search OCLC and America: History & Life to find their field notes, memoirs, or other texts.

Local Histories

Only twenty years after the Pilgrims arrived at Plymouth Rock, their leader, William Bradford, sat down to write a history of the town. Ever since then every community—every village, town, county, and state—seems to have nurtured its sense of identity by researching and publishing at least one monograph on its own history. Although many exist from the seventeenth and eighteenth centuries, only in the nineteenth did the local history genre truly come into its own. Sparked by centennial celebrations of the American Revolution in 1876, communities all across the continent began to display civic pride in having grown from puny hamlets to substantial settlements. Between 1880 and 1920, hundreds of stout, sometimes multivolume works—their ponderous, self-important outsides belying the mundane historical approach and the pedestrian prose snoring within—appeared from commercial or vanity presses.

Local histories tend to follow a predictable arrangement that begins with a survey of the county or region, followed by chapters on individual townships or communities. Each of these sections is likely to start with an account of geography and natural features, and here you will often find some description of the environmental conditions at the time of European settlement. For example, the standard history of Ashley County, Arkansas, includes this description by an early surveyor: "I cannot but observe the wild and desolate looking appearance by the overflow [of Coffee Creek]. Long grape vines and ratan vines hang in disorder on all sides. Huge trunks of trees lie on the ground blackened by the fire and broken into fragments by their fall. Nothing indicates the presence of man. We have seen no sign of life save that exhibited by the black mosquito, the rattlesnake, and the bear" (Etheridge 1959).

Since these works incline toward self-promotion, their descriptions must be taken with caution. The land that became "our town" is likely to be portrayed as an idyllic Eden whose natural situation and fertility possessed few, if any, equals. Almost as often, though, these texts depicted the land as a hostile wilderness that had to be conquered and "improved" by pioneer settlers.

Between the lines, however, readers can usually gather a reliable account of the environment as seen by the locals, with precise references to very specific features of the landscape. Sometimes it's not necessary to read between the lines at all, as in this typical paragraph from the opening pages of a Colorado county history, concerning the impression the shortgrass prairie made on its first settlers: "The absence of trees and vegetation was noted by these soldiers. They realized the truth of the remark of one of their number, that one could not find a riding switch between Julesburg and a point 70 miles west on the way to Denver. Other observations were that the alkali was dangerous for cattle and that the water was alkaline to such an extent that it could not be used for drinking or cooking" (Conklin 1928). Use Kaminkow (1975) to discover local histories available for the community you are researching.

In addition to standard histories, most communities also produced at least one local newspaper. Gregory (1937) remains the best bibliography of these, although many can also be found on OCLC. Local newspapers contain a great deal of information about the settlement of any area but are rarely, if ever, indexed. One usually has no choice but to turn every page of every issue (or crank through reel after reel of microfilm) hunting for relevant data. Occasionally an unpublished finding aid will have been created at the newspaper office or in the local public library. Many towns, for example, used W.P.A. funds in the 1930s to create card-file indices to their own newspapers. Consult the American Association for State and Local History (1990) to identify local institutions that may possess newspaper indices.

The magazines and serial publications of local historical societies are another source that can be extraordinarily helpful. These range from venerable scholarly titles such as the *Collections of the Massachusetts Historical Society* to special interest publications such as *Preliminary Studies of the Texas Catholic Historical Society* (both of which have published early travel accounts with unique ecological information). Even more ephemeral publications may have been produced at the grassroots level: one hundred years ago many communities had an Old Settlers Society or Pioneer Settlers Association that published the recollections of people who arrived in the area before it was transformed by industry and agriculture. Check with the local historical society or public library for advice on sources of this type.

Census Schedules

Every ten years since 1790, the federal government has knocked on the door of every dwelling in the country and asked a set of questions about the people within and the activities at which they work. Similar information was collected by the Canadian government. The data collected in these surveys was divided into "schedules"—a population schedule detailing demographic data about households; an agriculture schedule showing tremendous detail about crops grown and land use; and a manufacturing schedule depicting the raw materials, labor, and production of factories and other industrial facilities. The types and the amount of data collected varies over time. In general, the censuses from 1790 to 1840 are not sufficiently detailed to be of much use in environmental history, but those from 1850 to 1920 can be employed in a wide variety of ways to reconstruct human communities and show how they affected their environments.

Because federal census data have been collected systematically at the most fundamental geographical levels—door to door, block to block (or farm to farm, lumber camp to lumber camp)—it provides high-resolution snapshots of every area in the United States at ten-year intervals. The original handwritten ledger volumes are at the National Archives, but microfilm copies of them are widely distributed. Many large research institutions possess microfilm of the population schedule for the entire country from 1790 to 1920 (the last year currently available). Census schedules are normally held at the state archives or the state library, though many academic and large public libraries also have them. Search OCLC or your institution's on-line catalogue with a general keyword search such as "Louisiana and census and 1870." Many states conducted additional census surveys of their own in other years, and these usually parallel or logically complement the federal schedules in content.

If assembled and then analyzed over decades, census data can provide an intricate and reliable framework showing settlement and land-use patterns. This framework can serve as a quantitative grid against which the narrative and anecdotal evidence gathered from the prose sources described above can be understood. The population schedules, for example, show the occupation of every adult in the community, allowing one to make certain generalizations about the ways that natural resources were exploited at different points in the community's history. The agriculture schedules may permit construction of detailed land-use plans for most localities in the country, although researchers must be alert to the changing vocabulary employed by census workers. The manufacturing schedules can enable one to assess the historical development and the environmental impact of nineteenth-century factories, mills, and extractive industries across the decades.

Census records are far from the only government documents that can be used to reconstruct alterations in the environment by human settlement. Clawson and Stewart (1965) provide access to a wide variety of statistical data about land use, collected by various government agencies.

Early Scientific Investigations

Modern science is often said to date from the founding of the Royal Society in London in 1660, and only a few decades later English-speaking Americans embraced the methods of their protoscientific colleagues across the Atlantic. By the early eighteenth century, for example, Carolina physician John Lawson and Massachusetts clergyman Cotton Mather were systematically collecting information on the passenger pigeon (Lawson 1709; Schorger 1955 [1938]). Other eighteenth-century investigators who provided excellent detail on the natural history of the eastern United States were Mark Catesby and William Bartram, whose reports on the plants, birds, and animals of the Southeast have become classics (Catesby 1754; Bartram 1958). Meanwhile, in California, Father Miguel Venegas attempted "an accurate description of that country, its soil, mountains, harbours, lakes, rivers and seas; its animals, vegetables, minerals . . ." (Venegas 1759). Descriptions by American intellectuals and visiting naturalists began to appear in large numbers following the ascendancy of the Linnean system and the founding of the first American scientific institutions late in the century. Harkanyi (1990) lists texts written by more than 500 "scientists" active in America between 1760 and 1790.

Many reports by eighteenth- and early nineteenth-century botanists and zoologists were issued in the serial publications of fledgling scientific institutions, such as the American Philosophical Society (founded in Philadelphia in 1769) or in now obscure technical journals including *The Western Quarterly Reporter of Medical, Surgical and Natural Science* (issued in Cincinnati in 1822–23). Many of the investigations conducted by the first generations of American professional scientists are found only in their pages, revealing much about the ecology of areas that have since been completely transformed by industrialization, immigration, and modern agriculture.

To find early scientific works, start with Bridson (1994), whose 7,500 citations to secondary sources will provide helpful context. For citations to American works, consult Tucher (1985) for the earliest periods and Harkanyi (1990) and Meisel (1924–29) for the late eighteenth and nineteenth centuries. Meisel is especially helpful for its itemized accounts of the contents of scientific journals. To complement those and leave no stone unturned, consult the library catalogue of the Academy of Natural Sciences of Philadelphia (ANSP 1972). The academy has aggressively collected natural history works since its beginnings in 1812. Its sixteen-volume alphabetical catalogue lists 150,000 separate works by both author and subject.

The work of early ecologists often provides a gateway to primary evidence on specific regions (Shelford 1926). By the mid-nineteenth century, a handful of naturalists in the eastern and midwestern United States were sensitive to the ecological effects of the human migration and development occurring around them. Brewer (1960) will lead researchers back to their pioneering texts. By the end of the century, scientific approaches to agriculture and forestry had led scholars to cast a retrospective look toward the state of nature prior to modern management. The bibliographies by Bidwell and Falconer (1941), Bowers (1969), Fahl (1977), and Harvey (1979) yield many useful citations to early scientific work in these two areas.

Problems with Textual Evidence

Identifying and locating works that describe vanished environments is only the first step in using textual sources. Understanding what they say is the second. Despite their seeming transparency, historical texts are not a clear lens that zooms in on the past to tell us faithfully how the world was. Chipped, cracked, and fogged, laced with errors, omissions, prejudices, silent assumptions, and preconceptions, they don't reflect the past so much as refract it. Contemporary accounts are more like a kaleidoscope than a microscope: they fragment and rearrange the past rather than truthfully reveal it. The principal problems in using textual evidence arise from nomenclature, geography, and biases.

The Problem of Nomenclature

The first European explorers carried across the Atlantic preconceptions about nature that affected both their perceptions and the texts they left to posterity. The things they noticed and the things they overlooked, what they understood and what baffled them, were all shaped by the languages and concepts they brought from home. As they tried to comprehend a new world where flying fish leaped out of the sea and wingless birds swam under water, they were inevitably constrained by ideas and thought processes carried from Europe.

The most crucial part of this intellectual baggage was a centuries-old biological vocabulary, names originally coined by Greek and Latin observers in the Mediterranean hundreds of years before. Seeing an osprey dive for fish in Chesapeake Bay or paddling beneath pendulous clouds of hanging moss in a Louisiana bayou, European travelers could describe their experience only in ancient terms preserved in medieval herbals and bestiaries. Although common enough in their own day, their colloquial Renaissance names for plants and animals were quite different from those used today.

Consider the following brief mention of New England plants by John Josselyn, who lived in Maine from 1663 to 1671: "'Tis true, the Countrie hath no *Bonnerets*, or *Tartarlambs*, no glittering coloured *Tuleps*; but here you have the *American Mary-gold*, the *Earth-nut* bearing a princely Flower, the beautiful leaved *Pirola*, the honied *Colibry*, etc." (Josselyn 1674, 43). Terms equally unfamiliar to us were widely used for other species, as well: about half the bird names used by the earliest French travelers in Canada and the Mississippi Valley came from a sixteenth-century French ornithology, and early English explorers took 90 percent of their avian vocabulary from Elizabethan ornithological books. Reading their texts, even veteran birders might be hard put to identify a hernshawe, puit, ninmurder, stannel, gripe, or sea-pie (heron, plover, shrike, kestrel, eagle, and oystercatcher, respectively)—terms that needed no definition to the original readers of early accounts of America.

Many New World plants and animals escaped the confines of traditional European nomenclature altogether, leaving observers baffled about *what* to call them. Cruising the Atlantic Coast early in the seventeenth century, Captain John Smith found among the familiar waterfowl "some other strange kinds to us unknowne by name." A generation later, one of the first Dutch settlers in New York noted "falcons, sparrow-hawks, sailing-hawks, castrills, church-hawks, fish-hawks, and several other kinds, for which I have no name" (Smith 1607, 18:434; Donck 1968, 48).

This lack of widely accepted names led to vagueness that can make it difficult to identify many species. Faced with ninmurders, Mary-Golds (sunflowers), puits, carcajous (wolverines), and ortolans (any edible small bird, rather than the particular Old World species of that name), what can a researcher do? Unfortunately, there is no comprehensive historical dictionary of biological nomenclature. For texts in English, the classic *Oxford English Dictionary* is still the best starting place, and it can be usefully supplemented by the recent multivolume *Dictionary of American Regional English*. For French texts, Ganong (1909), McDermott (1941), and Imbs (1971–94) will solve the most commonly encountered problems.

The editors of any given text may have spent a great deal of effort trying to identify specific ecological terms used in the texts they were issuing. When puzzled, consult footnotes in the modern reprints of an early text, including those editions produced as long ago as the mid-nineteenth century. It may also be necessary to consult academic colleagues in history, area studies, or linguistics in order to unravel the most baffling terms. One must be prepared to accept that, in the end, some terms may altogether defy accurate definition because they are obsolete slang terms, transliterations of forgotten Native American names, or simply printers' errors.

The Problem of Location

The environmental information preserved in early textual sources is obscured by similar problems in geographical nomenclature. Observers who traveled through landscapes not yet surveyed or settled had only the most rudimentary geographical knowledge and so could describe locations only in approximate terms. To make matters worse, until the invention of the chronometer about the time of the American Revolution, explorers simply couldn't tell how far west they had traveled.

For example, in March and April 1543, the Spanish explorer Garcilaso de la Vega (a member of the De Soto expedition) kept notes on a dramatic flood somewhere in the lower Mississippi River valley: "Its water began to move swiftly out over some immense strands that lay between the main channel and its cliffs. Afterward the water rose gradually to the tops of these cliffs and overflowed to the fields with the greatest speed and volume . . . the river entered the gates of the little village of Aminoya in the wildness and fury of its flood, and two days later one could not pass through the streets of this town except in canoes. The flood was forty days in reaching its crest, which came on the twentieth of April" (Vega 1951, 553–54). This is the first description of the seasonal flooding of the Mississippi River, but where, exactly, did it happen? We cannot easily say.

In most cases, such vagueness is compounded by the fact that the travelers themselves had no clear idea of where they were. "We had now penetrated a great distance into the interior of a wild and uninhabited country," wrote Charles Johnston, who was taken captive by Shawnee Indians in 1790 and marched "I knew not how many miles" into the barren wilderness of central Ohio. "During the whole march, we subsisted on bear's meat, venison, turkeys, and raccoons, with which we were abundantly supplied, as the ground over which we passed afforded every species of game in profusion, diminishing, however, as we approached their villages" (Johnston 1827, 46). Nice ecological data about mammals and the impact of human communities; but for what locale?

Solving difficulties such as these usually turns out to be either simple and straightforward or nearly impossible, with few cases falling between those extremes. To unravel such mysteries, first search OCLC and *America: History & Life* for critical editions, biographies of the writer, and modern secondary sources on the specific expedition in question. Chances are good that their editors and authors will have investigated this problem before you. For example, recent conference proceedings about the De Soto expedition include a careful reconstruction of its route by Dr. Charles Hudson of the University of Georgia, based on archaeological as well as textual evidence, that fixes the flooded village of Aminoya outside the current town of Clarksdale, Mississippi (Hudson 1993).

If there is a shortage of secondary scholarship, or if it failed to solve the geographical problem in sufficient detail, take note of any place names mentioned in the text, estimate their approximate locations, and use Kaminkow (1975) to identify local historical sources for the area. Standard county histories frequently begin with quotations from, or discussions of, the first travelers to enter any area, and these may identify conspicuous natural features. In addition, most states have an official historical society that produced a series such as *Wisconsin Historical Collections*, a nineteenth-century publication that later grew into a scholarly quarterly. These periodicals generally provided the best outlet for local history research, and in them you may find detailed accounts of localities that refer to early textual sources.

Finally, use any names of physical features that may be mentioned in the text, no matter how small or specific, and search them in the *USGS Geographic Names Information System*. This massive database contains information about almost two million physical and cultural geographic features in the United States, including all the names used on USGS topographic maps. You can search it for free on the World Wide Web at http://mapping.usgs.gov/www/gnis/ or check a printed version almost as large in book format (Abate 1991).

Unfortunately, many landscapes described in textual sources published before the mid-nineteenth century simply cannot be identified with any acceptable level of precision. To precisely locate an early description of a habitat on a modern map and find it on the ground can therefore be impossible. Charles Johnston, for example, traveled from the southeastern corner of Ohio to Detroit, yet we have no way to accurately pinpoint the habitats that he described en route.

Problems of Interpretation

The first European witnesses of native American flora and fauna saw through eyes spectacularly different from our own. They surveyed the rugged landscape of the new world through a lens composed of different beliefs, desires, and values than our own. Even the best educated did not know that the earth moved around the sun and could not comprehend an eclipse or explain what caused thunder and lightning. Our scientific worldview was not shared by seventeenth-century New Englanders, for example, some of whom knew—with as much certainty as we know our own commonsense facts—that they could be possessed by the devil, and consequently, with eyes wide open and in good conscience, tortured to death their neighbors who appeared to be possessed. Such problems of cultural bias permeate nearly every text written about North American environments before the mid-nineteenth century, and many later ones as well.

A more familiar problem of interpretation arises from authors' biases. For example, many early accounts of the eastern seaboard were written by merchant adventurers seeking exploitable commodities. Their frequent references to sassafras, grapes, and various herbs and berries are not so much a report on botany as "a commentary on the agricultural and medicinal commodities in vogue in England in the 1600s . . ." (Whitney 1994, 11). Similarly, the pamphlets and texts written by promoters and colonizers, whether in Virginia in 1630 or Indiana in 1830, usually exaggerate the benefits and omit the difficulties of settling in their particular vicinity.

Still other problems arise from what one may think of as "structural" limitations in the observer. For example, texts extolling the vast number of wild fowl in any locality may have been written by witnesses who visited it only during spring or fall migration (these were sometimes followed by other works, written in the depths of winter or a midsummer drought, complaining of the author's deceit). Similarly, early descriptions of North American flora and fauna are usually confined to species that were visible from major transportation routes such as rivers, turnpikes, and heavily traveled roads. See chapter two of Whitney (1994), "Reconstructing the Past," for further examples.

To surmount these difficulties, researchers should first be aware of their own biases. To dismiss a seventeenth-century text or a Native American autobiography because their authors did not display our scientific worldview reveals more about ourselves than about the text in hand. Although every text should be treated with a certain amount of skepticism, it must first be approached with faith, empathy, and imagination.

Second, consider the writer's purpose and background, either as expressed in the text's prefatory matter or surmised from what can be learned about him or her from secondary sources. Every author was equipped with a skill set and wrote with some purpose and audience in mind. Ask yourself, is the account that of an educated military officer or a common foot soldier? Was it written to gather backers, persuade adherents, sell a product, or communicate scientific data? Is it based on eyewitness testimony or hearsay provided by informants whose reliability is unknown to us? Anticipating such biases will throw light on the subjects the writer covered or omitted, what he or she could see and what went unobserved.

Third, whenever possible compare texts with one another to discover inconsistencies and contradictions. Assembling multiple accounts of the same ecological phenomenon can produce a sort of intellectual triangulation, each author's viewpoint communicating slightly different facts that intersect at a few common points.

Finally, use the other chapters of this book to balance documentary evidence with that gained from pollen samples, sedimentation studies, archaeological investigation, and other work in the field.

Annotated References

Abate, Frank. 1991. *The Omni gazetteer of the United States of America.* Detroit: Omnigraphics.

American Association for State and Local History. 1990. *Directory of historical organizations in the United States and Canada.* Nashville, Tenn.: AASLH Press.

ANSP. 1972. *Catalog, Academy of Natural Sciences of Philadelphia Library,* 16 vols. Boston: G.K. Hall. Cites 150,000 separate works, including virtually all the important scientific literature on America from the seventeenth century to 1970.

Arksey, L. 1983. *American diaries: An annotated bibliography of published American diaries and journals to 1980,* 2 vols., ed. Laura Arksey, Nancy Pries, and Marcia Reed. Detroit: Gale Research. Describes more than 5,000 published diaries kept between 1492 and 1980 and provides geographical access through a detailed index that includes occupations such as "naturalist" and general topics such as "explorations" and "loggers and logging."

Bartram, W. 1958. *Travels*. Edited with commentary and an annotated index by Francis Harper. New Haven: Yale University Press.

Beers, H. P. 1982. *Bibliographies in American history, 1942–1978*, 2 vols. Woodbridge, Conn.: Research Publications. Lists nearly 12,000 bibliographies, with excellent subject and geographic indexing.

Bidwell, P. W., and J. I. Falconer. 1941. *History of agriculture in the northern United States, 1620–1860*. Carnegie Institute Publication No. 358. New York: Peter Smith.

Bjoring, B., et al. 1982. *Explorers' and travellers' journals documenting early contacts with Native Americans in the Pacific Northwest, 1741–1900*. Compiled by Bob Bjoring and Susan Cunningham. Bibliography Series No. 3. Seattle: University of Washington Libraries. Arranged geographically, this handy list of 682 items provides good citations to overland trips, Russian coastal expeditions, and government reports that detail not only native peoples, but also the environments they inhabited.

Bowers, D. 1969. *A list of references for the history of agriculture in the United States: 1790–1840*. Davis: University of California, Agricultural History Center.

Brebner, John B. 1933. *The explorers of North America, 1492–1806*. New York: Macmillan.

Brewer, R. 1960. *A brief history of ecology. Part I: Pre-nineteenth century to 1919*. Occasional papers of the C.C. Adams Center for Ecological Studies, no. 1. Kalamazoo: Western Michigan University.

Bridson, G. 1994. *The history of natural history: An annotated bibliography*. New York: Garland Publications. Although international in scope, these 7,500 citations provide access to the most authoritative secondary sources on American scientists.

Brumble, H. D. 1981. *An annotated bibliography of American Indian and Eskimo autobiographies*. Lincoln: University of Nebraska Press.

Catesby, M. 1754. *The natural history of Carolina, Florida, and the Bahama Islands*. London: C. Marsh.

Chona, M. 1936. The autobiography of a Papago woman. In *Memoirs of the American Anthropological Association* 46 (1936). Also reprinted in Ruth Underhill, *Papago Woman*, Prospect Heights, Ill.: Waveland Press, 1985.

Clark, Thomas D. 1956–59. *Travels in the old South: A bibliography*, 3 vols. Norman: University of Oklahoma Press. Lists and comments upon more than 1,000 books published before 1860; additional volumes cover later periods. Index entries in each volume on specific place names and "flora and fauna" lead to first-person descriptions of natural environments.

Clark, William. 1964. *The field notes of Captain William Clark, 1803–1805*. New Haven, Conn.: Yale University Press.

Clawson, M., and C. L. Stewart. 1965. *Land use information: A critical survey of U.S. statistics including possibilities for greater uniformity*. Washington, D.C.: Resources for the Future.

Conklin, E. B. 1928. *A brief history of Logan County, Colorado: With reminiscences by pioneers*. Sterling, Colo.: Daughters of the American Revolution, Elbridge Gerry Chapter.

Conzen, M., T. A. Rumney, and G. Wynn. 1993. *A scholar's guide to geographical writing on the American and Canadian past*. Chicago: University of Chicago Press. Geographically arranged, this volume surveys more than 10,000 sources that provide data on historical environments across the continent.

Coues, E. 1877. *U.S. Geological Survey of the Territories (Hayden Survey). Fur-bearing animals: A monograph of North American Mustelidae . . .* Miscellaneous Publications 8. Washington, D.C.: Government Printing Office.

———. 1878. *U.S. Geological Survey of the Territories (Hayden Survey). Birds of the northwest: A hand-book of the ornithology of the region drained by the Missouri river and its tributaries*. Miscellaneous Publications no. 3. Washington, D.C.: Government Printing Office.

———. 1903. *Key to North American birds*. 4th edition. 2 vols. Boston: D. Estes and Co.

Cowan, R. E., and R. G. Cowan. 1933. *A bibliography of the history of California, 1510–1930*, 4 vols. Los Angeles: No publisher. More than 7,500 citations with title, subject, and chronological indexes.

Dablon, C. 1673. Relation of what occured most remarkable in the missions of the fathers of the Society of Jesus, in the years 1671 and 1672. Page 121 in *Jesuit relations and allied documents*, vol. 56, ed. Reuben Gold Thwaites. Cleveland: Burrows Bros. 1896–1901.

Denys, N. 1908. *The description and natural history of the coasts of North America (Acadia)*. Toronto: Champlain Society.

Dmytryshyn, B., E. A. P. Crownhart-Vaughan, and T. Vaughan. 1988. *Russian penetration of the North Pacific Ocean, 1700–1797*. Volume 2: A documentary record. Portland: Oregon Historical Society Press.

Donck, A. van der. 1968. *A Description of the New Netherlands*. Syracuse, N.Y.: Syracuse University Press.

Etheridge, Y. W. 1959. *History of Ashley County, Arkansas*. Van Buren, Ark.: Press-Argus.

Evans, C. 1901–55. *The American bibliography: A chronological dictionary of all books, pamphlets, and periodical publications printed in the United States of America from the genesis of printing in 1639 down to and including the year 1800*, 13 vols. Worcester, Mass.: American Antiquarian Society. Lists all 39,000 publications printed in America before 1801. Each volume contains a "classified subject index" that includes sections on history, geography, and travel.

Fahl, R. J. 1977. *North American forest and conservation history, a bibliography*. Santa Barbara, Calif.: Clio Press.

Ganong, W. F. 1909. The identity of the animals and plants mentioned in the early voyagers to eastern Canada and Newfoundland. *Proceedings and trans-*

actions of the Royal Society of Canada. 3rd ser., vol. 3, sec. 2. Ottawa: Royal Society of Canada.

Gregory, W. 1937. *American newspapers, 1821–1936: A union list.* New York: 1937; reprinted New York: Kraus, 1967. Contains about 45,000 geographically arranged entries listing local newspapers around the country.

Harkanyi, K. 1990. *The natural sciences and American scientists in the revolutionary era: A bibliography.* Westport, Conn.: Greenwood Press. Provides good access to more than 5,000 primary and secondary sources on late-eighteenth-century American natural history. A helpful companion to Meisel (1924–29) and Tucher (1985).

Harvey, C. L. 1979. *Agriculture of the American Indian: A select bibliography.* Washington, D.C.: USDA.

Hasse, A. 1899. *Reports of explorations printed in the documents of the United States government: A contribution toward a bibliography.* Washington, D.C.: Government Printing Office; reprinted New York: B. Franklin, 1969. Gives clear citations to about 1,700 scientific reports buried in hundreds of official documents issued by the United States government. Arranged geographically, it permits easy access to all the scientific data collected in the classic nineteenth-century exploring expeditions.

Hearne, S. 1958. *A journey from Prince of Wales's fort in Hudson's Bay to the Northern Ocean, 1769, 1770, 1771, 1772,* ed. Richard Glover. Toronto: Macmillan.

Hubach, R. 1961. *Early midwestern travel narratives: An annotated bibliography, 1634–1850.* Detroit: Wayne State University Press; reprinted 1998. Describes and annotates more than 1,000 primary sources covering the region from Pennsylvania west to the Great Plains and north to the Canadian border. Very detailed annotations describe each work's content, and a comprehensive index pinpoints geographical names.

Hudson, C. 1993. Reconstructing the de Soto expedition route west of the Mississippi River: Summary and contents. Pages 143–154 in *The Expedition of Hernando de Soto west of the Mississippi, 1541–1543.* Proceedings of the de Soto symposia, 1988 and 1990. Fayetteville: University of Arkansas Press.

Imbs, P. 1971–94. *Trésor de la langue française; dictionnaire de la langue du XIXe et du Xxe siècle (1789–1960),* publié sous la direction de Paul Imbs. Paris: Editions du Centre national de la recherche scientifique. Despite the subtitle, also useful for earlier periods.

Johnston, C. 1827. *A narrative of the incidents attending the capture, detention, and ransom of Charles Johnston.* New York: Harper; reprinted New York: Garland, 1975.

Jones, W. 1875. *Reconnaissance of northwestern Wyoming, including Yellowstone National park, made in summer of 1873.* Washington, D.C.: Government Printing Office.

Josselyn, J. 1674. *An account of two voyages to New-England.* London; edition quoted: Hanover, N.H.: University Press of New England, 1988.

Juet, R. 1625. The third voyage of Master Henry Hudson, toward Nova Zembla. First published in 1625. Reprinted in *Henry Hudson the Navigator: The original documents in which his career is recorded*, ed. G. M. Asher, London: Haklyut Society, 1860.

Kaminkow, M. J. 1975. *United States local histories in the Library of Congress: A bibliography*, 5 vols. Baltimore: Magna Carta. Contains citations to more than 87,000 histories of villages, towns, cities, and counties. Most were published in the late nineteenth or early twentieth century and usually begin with a chapter that surveys the topography and environmental conditions at the time of European contact.

Kaplan, L. 1962. *A bibliography of American autobiographies*. Madison: University of Wisconsin Press. More than 6,300 autobiographies and memoirs, all of which are available in full text on microfiche, with a useful geographical index.

King, C. 1870–80. *Report of geological exploration of the fortieth parallel, 1866–1877*. Washington, D.C.: Government Printing Office.

Lafitau, J.-F. 1974–77. *Customs of the American Indians compared with the customs of primitive times*. Edited and translated by William N. Fenton and Elizabeth L. Moore. Toronto: Champlain Society.

La Verendrye, P. G. de V., sieur de. 1927. *Journals and letters of Pierre Gaultier de Varennes de la Verendrye and his sons*. Edited by Lawrence J. Burpee. Toronto: Champlain Society.

Lawson, J. 1709. *A new voyage to Carolina*. First published London; reprinted Chapel Hill: University of North Carolina Press, 1967.

Lewis and Clark. 1983–. *The journals of the Lewis and Clark expedition*. Ed. Gary E. Moulton. 11 volumes to date. Lincoln: University of Nebraska Press.

Ludlow, W. 1875a. *Report of reconnaissance of Black Hills of Dakota made in summer of 1874*. Washington, D.C.: Government Printing Office.

———. 1875b. *Report of reconnaissance from Carroll, Montana Territory, on upper Missouri, to Yellowstone National Park and return, made in summer of 1875*. Washington, D.C.: Government Printing Office.

Mackenzie, A. 1927. *Voyages from Montreal on the River St. Lawrence through the continent of North America to the Frozen and Pacific Oceans in the years 1789 and 1793*. First published London, 1801; edition quoted Toronto: Radisson Society of Canada.

Mattes, M. J. 1988. *Platte River road narratives: A descriptive bibliography of travel over the great central overland route to Oregon, California, Utah, Colorado, Montana, and other western states and territories, 1812–1866*. Urbana: University of Illinois Press. Describes more than 2,000 first-person accounts of travels across the Great Plains and Rocky Mountains between 1812 and 1866. Although each is thoroughly annotated, geographical indexing is superficial.

McDermott, J. F. 1941. A glossary of Mississippi French, 1673–1850. *Washington University Studies*. New series, Language and literature: no. 12. St. Louis: Washington Univ.

Meinig, D. W. 1986. *The shaping of America, a geographical perspective on 500 years of history*, 2 vols. New Haven, Conn.: Yale University Press. A historical geographer presents his history of the continent, continually bearing environmental issues in mind.

Meisel, M. 1924–29. *A bibliography of American natural history; the pioneer century, 1769–1865; the role played by the scientific societies; scientific journals; natural history museums and botanic gardens; state geological and natural history surveys; federal exploring expeditions in the rise and progress of American botany, geology, mineralogy, paleontology and zoology*, 3 vols. New York: Premier Publishing; reprinted New York: Hafner, 1967. Provides comprehensive access to all early American scientific literature, especially to the many articles and papers in nineteenth-century scholarly journals.

Mintz, L. W. 1987. *The trail: A bibliography of the travelers on the overland trail to California, Oregon, Salt Lake City, and Montana during the years 1841–1864.* Albuquerque: University of New Mexico Press.

Monaghan, F. 1933. *French travellers in the United States, 1765–1932.* New York: New York Public Library; reprinted New York: Antiquarian Press, 1961, with a supplement by Samuel J. Marino. Lists more than 1,800 sources, with some annotations and an excellent index including place names of localities observed.

Murdock, G. P., and T. J. O'Leary. 1975. *Ethnographic bibliography of North America*, 4th edition. New Haven, Conn.: Human Relations Area Files Press. A supplement by Marlene M. Martin was issued in 1990, and the two works were issued together in 1992 on CD-ROM as *Bibliography of native North Americans on disc* by ABC-CLIO.

Palmer, J. 1818. *Journal of travels in the United States of North America, and in lower Canada, performed in the year 1817.* London: Sherwood, Neely, and Jones.

Parks, R. 1989. *New England, a bibliography of its history, prepared by the Committee for a New England bibliography.* Hanover, N.H.: University Press of New England. With its six companion volumes dedicated to individual states, this set provides access to thousands of primary and secondary sources.

Peale, T. 1947. The journal of Titian Ramsay Peale, pioneer naturalist. *Missouri Historical Review* 41:147–163, 266–284.

Prucha, F. P. 1987. *Handbook for research in American history: A guide to bibliographies and other reference works.* Lincoln: University of Nebraska Press.

Quinn, D. B. 1979. *New American world: A documentary history of North America to 1612*, 5 vols. New York: Arno Press.

Richardson, J. 1984. *Arctic ordeal: The journal of John Richardson, surgeon-naturalist with Franklin, 1820–1822.* Edited by C. Stuart Houston. Kingston: McGill–Queen's University Press.

Rittenhouse, J. D. 1971. *The Santa Fe Trail: A historical bibliography.* Albuquerque: University of New Mexico Press. Lists and annotates more than 700 eyewitness accounts, including Spanish and American government reports.

Roberts, G. 1973. *Atlas of discovery.* New York: Crown. Lays out the routes and dates of all major expeditions, with short prose commentary.

Rothrock, J. T. 1878. *U.S. Geographical Surveys west of the one hundredth meridian.* Vol. 6: Reports upon the botanical collections made in portions of Nevada,

Utah, California, Colorado, New Mexico, and Arizona during the years 1871, 1872, 1873, 1874, and 1875. Washington, D.C.: Government Printing Office.

Sauer, C. O. 1966. *The early Spanish main*. Berkeley: University of California Press.

———. 1968. *Northern mists*. Berkeley: University of California Press.

———. 1971. *Sixteenth-century North America: The land and people as seen by Europeans*. Berkeley: University of California Press.

———. 1980. *Seventeenth-century North America*. Berkeley: Turtle Island Press.

Schorger, A. W. 1955. Unpublished manuscripts by Cotton Mather on the passenger pigeon (1938). *The Auk* 55.

Shelford, V., ed. 1926. *Naturalist's guide to the Americas*. Baltimore: Williams and Wilkins.

Smith, C. W. 1950. *Pacific Northwest Americana: A checklist of books and pamphlets relating to the history of the Pacific Northwest*, 3rd edition, revised and extended by Isabel Mayhew. Portland: Oregon Historical Society. Despite the word "checklist," this volume contains citations to more than 11,000 sources arranged, unfortunately, only by author. Subject access is available only in a typescript index prepared by Mayhew. This index has been microfilmed and is available at a handful of libraries in the region.

Smith, J. 1607. Description of Virginia, 1607. In *Hakluytys Posthumus, or Purchas His Pilgrimes Purchas, Samuel, 1625*. London; edition quoted Glasgow: J. MacLehose and Sons, 1905–07.

Spanish explorers. 1907. *Spanish explorers in the southern United States, 1528–1543*. New York: Scribners.

Staton, F. M. 1934–85. *A bibliography of Canadiana: Being items in the public library of Toronto relating to the early history and development of Canada*, 4 vols. Edited by Frances M. Staton, Marie Tremaine, et al. Toronto: Public Library. Describes more than 8,000 primary sources with full publication data and brief annotations about content; a thorough index in each volume gives access by locality.

Thwaites, Reuben Gold, ed. 1901. *The Jesuit relations and allied documents: Travels and explorations of the Jesuit missionaries in New France, 1610–1791*, 73 vols. Cleveland: Burrows Bros., 1896–1901. The standard edition, with French and English on facing pages. A more complete and scholarly edition of only the French texts is currently under way.

———. 1907. *Early western travels, 1748–1846; a series of annotated reprints of some of the best and rarest contemporary volumes of travel, descriptive of the aborigines and social and economic conditions in the middle and far West, during the period of early American settlement, ed. with notes, introductions, index, etc.* 32 vols. Cleveland: A. H. Clark, 1904–07.

Tucher, Andrea. 1985. *Natural history in America, 1609–1860: Printed works in the collections of the American Philosophical Society, the Historical Society of Pennsylvania, the Library Company of Philadelphia*. New York: Garland, 1985.

Two Leggings. 1967. *Two Leggings: The making of a Crow warrior*. Edited by Peter Nabokov. New York: Crowell.

Vail, R. W. G. 1933. *The voice of the old frontier.* Philadelphia: University of Philadelphia Press. Cites about 1,000 accounts published before 1800 by settlers, Indian captives, and promoters of areas within the United States. Detailed bibliographic description of the volumes as artifacts and of the different editions of each work, but no annotations on content and no subject indexing by place.

Vaughn, A. T. 1983. *Narratives of North American Indian captivity: A selective bibliography.* New York: Garland.

Vega, G. de la. 1951. *The Florida of the Inca.* Austin: University of Texas Press.

Venegas, M. 1759. *A civil and natural history of California, containing an accurate description of that country, its soil, mountains, harbours, lakes, rivers and seas; its animals, vegetables, minerals.* London: J. Rivington and J. Fletcher.

Wagner, H. R., and Charles L. Camp. 1982. *The Plains & the Rockies: A critical bibliography of exploration, adventure and travel in the American West, 1800–1865,* 4th edition, revised, enlarged, and edited by Robert H. Becker. San Francisco: John Howell–Books.

Waterston, E. 1989. *The Travellers. Canada to 1900: An annotated bibliography of works published in English from 1577.* Guelph, Ont.: University of Guelph. Provides citations and full annotations on 700 English-language publications about Canada.

Watson, S. 1871. *U.S. Geological Exploration of the Fortieth Parallel (King Survey).* Vol. 5: Botany. Washington, D.C.: Government Printing Office.

Whitney, G. G. 1994. *From coastal wilderness to fruited plain: A history of environmental change in temperate North America 1500 to the present.* New York: Cambridge University Press.

4

Oral History: A Guide to Its Creation and Use

James E. Fogerty

Oral history is a flexible tool that is particularly well suited for use in projects that involve understanding and reconstructing historic ecosystems. Many farmers, landowners, wildlife preservationists, American Indians, and others have given considerable thought and attention to issues surrounding land and its uses and are living repositories of information on earth and water resources. They have knowledge of changing patterns of land use and are the holders of information on past land uses and on cultural and related values attached to land. Unfortunately, they will seldom have written down that information in any form—much less a form that is organized for research needs. However, given a carefully organized construct, like the one provided by an oral historian, such people are able to provide that information.

As a research tool, oral history has gained considerable currency over the past twenty-five years. In gaining this acceptance, oral historians have overcome the prejudice of those who believe that unless information comes from a written record, or is scientifically validated, it cannot possibly be relevant. To be sure, the designation "oral history" is sometimes bestowed rather casually upon products that hardly meet the requirements of research use—a fact that continues to trouble oral historians as they attempt to ensure the credibility of their work. The use of oral history techniques in popular works by authors such as Studs Terkel and in the widely acclaimed Foxfire series of school projects has helped popularize the term but has sometimes confused its meaning. That all recorded or videotaped conversation is not oral history seems obvious to the oral historian, but that distinction is not so well defined in the minds of the public or those of oral history's skeptics. Nevertheless, oral history is here to stay and, thus, understanding what it is and how to use it creditably and credibly is a topic of some importance (Ritchie 1995).

Definition and History

Oral history is generally defined as a structured conversation between two people—an interviewer pursuing a carefully defined line of inquiry, and a narrator with information that the interviewer seeks to acquire. While an oral history interview may involve more than one interviewer and/or more than one narrator, the usual configuration is one on one.

As a structured discipline that uses sound and, more recently, visual recording equipment, oral history may be said to date to the post–World War II era. While recording devices were certainly available before that time, the development of relatively inexpensive magnetic recording tape and tape recorders in the late 1940s and early 1950s fueled the boom in oral history. This trend continued with the advent of cassette tapes and smaller, more portable recording devices.

Credible Oral History

Any credible oral history has the following qualities: (1) it is designed to collect substantive information and is conducted as a multiple-interview project; (2) it has a defined direction and is not a series of random conversations; and (3) it results in a series of products that will be of use beyond the immediate needs of the interviewer.

Very few topics, including the retelling of the history of a place, lend themselves to an interview with one person. The best approach to a credible oral history lies in the careful selection of a group of narrators whose complementary interviews will provide a more complete understanding of the issues at hand. It is better, then, to think of a project rather than a single interview or a series of discrete interviews. A project offers a basic structure within which an oral history inquiry can be guided toward a defined goal. It allows the interviewer to use research information from a number of related interviews. The multiple-narrator approach also helps corroborate and cross-reference information obtained from the narrators and offers a greater variety of perspectives on a subject. This alone makes the project approach of particular value.

Any oral history project needs a sense of direction and a set of defined and realistic goals. Focus and scope are critical issues in the construction of any such project. However, it is important to recognize that no series of interviews, no matter how well conceived and carried out, can answer every question on a broad subject. Therefore, interviewers need to limit conversations to those areas that are most likely to generate substantive information. To determine a workable focus and scope for a project, it is helpful to work with a small committee of people who are interested in the project and have complementary knowledge of the field.

Audience and *product* are two words that should receive consideration from anyone carrying out an oral history project. Since oral histories are created to be used, the interviewer should have at least one potential audience in mind when framing the topics to be covered during an interview. If the interviewer fails to do that, the interview will likely contain little useful or interesting information. As to product, interviewers must not forget that in completing a project, they are creating a series of products, from audio- or videotapes to the edited transcript. These products should be planned as carefully as the interview topics because they will be listened to, read, or viewed. Therefore, their quality—like the quality of any product—should be evident and durable.

Finally, anyone involved in an oral history project should always remember that oral history is not collected. Oral history is the joint creation of the narrator and the interviewer. The narrator is, of course, the principal creator, for it is the narrator who has the information, insight, perspective, and experience the interviewer seeks to capture. Thus, the success of any interview is dependent on the interviewer's ability to establish rapport with the narrator and to create an atmosphere of comfort and partnership.

Key Considerations in an Oral History Project

There are six key points that an oral historian must consider and act on when creating a high-quality oral history: planning, resources, research, scheduling, selecting narrators, and ethics.

Planning

Any oral history interview must be defined by the reasons for which it will be conducted, including its intended audience and the gaps in available information that it is intended to fill. As stated above, planning is best done with a small committee of interested colleagues.

One of the most important items produced by the committee is the project statement, which should be a brief statement outlining the purpose of the project. I suggest that it be no longer than three paragraphs. The project statement is used to explain the project to potential narrators and give them some reason to participate. It is also useful when seeking funding and in dealing with other requests for information about the project. Oral historians should remember that projects that cannot be defined in concise, plain language are unlikely to impress either narrators or potential funders.

The next task for the committee involves developing a basic interview format. In laying out an interview, write down the major subjects you feel are important and then expand them by adding related and secondary information that you gain as part of the conversation within the committee. Keep a relatively narrow focus and construct an interview framework that will produce a good depth of information within that focus area. Resist the urge to fill the interview with technical terms and jargon—language that will either puzzle the narrator or result in an unusable conversation between two insiders. Also resist the urge to add more topics. Keep in mind that there is nothing worse than an interview that skates lightly over the surface of a number of subjects and explores none of them in depth.

Every interview should have a framework that will emerge from the process of research and analysis. The framework should be carefully structured to produce a relatively orderly progression of discussion, thus aiding the narrator and future researchers. In laying out the framework, one should think in terms of topics rather than discrete questions. Listing topics and several layers of subtopics helps focus the interview on the information, rather than on the questions themselves. Moreover, a written list of questions can narrow the interviewer's focus to the wording of the question rather than to information being explored. It also allows the interviewer to be as spontaneous in asking questions as one hopes the narrator will be in answering them. When questions are developed or asked, they should be brief and to the point—"Establish what you want to know and give the narrator a clear field to reply" is a good rule of thumb (Morrissey 1987).

Although the framework provides the interview's basic structure, it should not be used during the interview to discourage the narrator's initiative in introducing related information. If carefully constructed, the framework will provide the interviewer with a written outline of objectives and aid in ensuring that they are met. The framework will also provide a modicum of form and structure to the interview, which will help most interviewers move through the interview process.

Resources

Few projects happen without adequate funding. However, the question of how much funding is necessary must be predicated on real needs. Among the most important elements of an oral history project that require funding are the costs associated with scheduling, conducting, transcribing, editing, printing, and binding the interviews. Other costs include those required to maintain control of the various interview products and processes and to prepare an electronic (or other) finding aid, so that the interviews can be found and used. There is also the cost of the tape that is needed for both the master and duplicate copies and the one-time cost of recording equipment.

Research

Research is a key ingredient in interview preparation and, to some extent, in determining the success of the interviewer in gathering information. Obviously, most interviewers in the field of ecological restoration will have some interest in that subject and/or in the history of a place to be restored and the land-use practices that occurred on it. Knowledge, however, can be computed in various ways, and simple interest in a subject or residence in an area will not an expert interviewer make. Research is always necessary to provide adequate understanding and to enable an interviewer to ask intelligent questions, especially the all important follow-up questions. Even when an interviewer possesses considerable knowledge of a subject or region, he or she will need to prepare for interviews by carefully framing the topics for discussion and learning as much as possible about the narrators and their relationships to the topics.

If, for example, one is to interview a farmer about the history of a prairie, it will be important to have some idea of his or her relationship to that land. Is the farmer a third-generation landowner—the grandchild of an immigrant who homesteaded the land and passed it down through the generations? Was the farmer raised on the land, or is the prairie on a piece of land that was purchased later and added to the existing acreage? Or is the landowner an ex-urbanite who acquired the land recently for aesthetic and preservation purposes, and for whom the prairie may represent a personal and, perhaps, political statement? Understanding and incorporating knowledge of such distinctions is critical to any oral history project. It establishes the interview's validity and keeps the interviewer from asking questions that are inappropriate and betray an ignorance of either the subject or the narrator.

The knowledge the interviewer gains by doing research must, however, be used properly. An interviewer's role is to elicit information, not to provide it or use it to manipulate the narrator. The interviewer's knowledge may aid in the acquisition of information from the narrator, but it should never be used to display either that information or the interviewer's opinions. Nothing is more apparent to a researcher than a leading question or the attempts of an interviewer who is determined to use a narrator to support his own conclusions. The resulting product will only diminish the interviewer and his or her reputation and leave the narrator's potential contribution unrealized.

Scheduling, Travel, and Interview Time

Since the interviewer generally cannot stride into the narrator's home or office, plunk down a tape recorder, slip in a tape, and command the narrator to talk, one must plan time for a preliminary conversation, a possible mid-interview break, and the post-interview pleasantries that accompany most productive human relations. It also takes time to schedule interviews and interview segments and time to travel to and from the interview location.

Selecting the Narrators

Another important task for the committee is the selection of narrators. In preparing for the interviews, and while discussing the scope of the project, the committee should also make a list of possible people to interview. Do not edit the list in its initial stage. List everyone who might contribute to the project and include basic information about how their contribution might enhance the project. Then narrow the list to a realistic number of potential narrators. The narrators should be chosen according to whether their views will both complement and add to the body of information being gathered, and according to the resources available to the project.

Carefully evaluate the list of potential narrators to ensure that, while providing an opportunity to corroborate information by discussing the same subjects with several narrators, you do not duplicate information and perspectives to no useful purpose. Build in the chance to document a diversity of opinions. One of the beauties of oral history is its ability to document similarities and differences in opinion, leaving the eventual users to draw their own conclusions. This diversity of perspectives is important to ecological restorationists not only as a means of discovering how various people perceive the history of a place, but also as a guide to managing the cultural aspects of future restoration projects in the area.

Ethical Considerations

Critical to the whole field of oral history is the belief that the opinions of the narrators are important, and that their reasons for believing and acting as they have or do are central to the information gathering process. Interviewers must treat each narrator with respect, regardless of whether they agree with the views or opinions expressed by that narrator. Interviewers must remember that they are gathering information, not passing judgment—something that is reserved for the eventual users of the interview. The interviewer must remember to stay on task and carry out the objectives of the interview.

The Oral History Association provides the following guidelines concerning the ethics of oral history as it pertains to the relationship between the interviewer and the narrator:

> While these principles and standards provide a general framework for guiding professional conduct, their application may vary according to the nature of specific oral history projects. Regardless of the purpose of the interviews, oral history should be conducted in the spirit of critical inquiry and social responsibility, and with a recognition of the interactive and subjective nature of the enterprise . . .

1. Narrators should be informed of the purposes and procedures of oral history in general and of the aims and anticipated uses of the particular projects to which they are making their contribution.

2. Narrators should be informed of the mutual rights in the oral history process, such as editing, access restrictions, copyrights, prior use, royalties, and the expected disposition and dissemination of all forms of the record.

3. Narrators should be informed that they will be asked to sign a legal release. Interviews should remain confidential until interviewees have given permission for their use.

4. Interviewers should guard against making promises to interviewees that they may not be able to fulfill, such as guarantees of publication and control over future uses of interviews after they have been made public.

5. Interviews should be conducted in accord with any prior agreements made with the interviewee, and such preferences and agreements should be documented for the record.

6. Interviewers should work to achieve a balance between the objectives of the project and the perspectives of the interviewees. They should be sensitive to the diversity of social and cultural experiences, and to the implications of race, gender, class, ethnicity, age, religion, and sexual orientation. They should encourage narrators to respond in their own style and language, and to address issues that reflect their concerns. Interviewers should fully explore all appropriate areas of inquiry with the narrator and not be satisfied with superficial responses.

7. Interviewers should guard against possible exploitation of narrators and be sensitive to the ways in which their interviews might be used. Interviewers must respect the right of the narrator to refuse to discuss certain subjects, to restrict access to the interview, or under extreme circumstances even to choose anonymity. Interviewers should clearly explain these options to all narrators. (Oral History Association, 1991)

I would also like to suggest that the Archivist's Code of Ethics merits consideration. It makes clear that archivists must realize that in selecting records for retention or disposal they act as agents of the future in determining its heritage from the past. Therefore, insofar as their intellectual attainments, experience, and judgment permit, they must be ever conscious of the future's needs, making decisions impartially and without taint of ideological, political, or personal bias.

This dictum is equally true for oral historians, who must frame each interview to include a collection of facts and opinions that will be of maximum research value.

Preparing for the Interview

Once the oral history project is defined, the project statement written and approved, the research done, and the narrators chosen, it is time to prepare for the interview itself. Each narrator must be contacted in advance and arrangements made for the interview session. Contact should normally be made by the person who will conduct the interview, since introduction of a variety of people will serve only to confuse the prospective narrator.

The first contact should be made in a letter written on the letterhead of the organization sponsoring the project. The letter should briefly explain the project and the reasons the person was chosen as a narrator. A copy of the project statement should also be enclosed. The letter should state that the interviewer will contact the narrator shortly by telephone to arrange a meeting to discuss the interview. After waiting a week or two to ensure that the letter has been received and read, the interviewer should telephone the narrator and arrange a meeting, preferably at the location where the interview will take place. This pre-interview meeting will give interviewer and narrator an opportunity to become acquainted. The interviewer will be able to assess the ease with which the narrator speaks and gauge the need for additional research or other enhancements that might be necessary. During the pre-interview (and indeed during the interview itself), the interviewer should be alert to the narrator's body language. If the person seems tense or ill at ease, it is the interviewer's job to deal with that situation, establishing whatever rapport is possible and cultivating the role of friendly and interested student.

The interviewer may take a tape recorder to the pre-interview (to let the narrator see the machine) but should never arrive with tape! This precaution is easily explained by noting that occasionally a narrator may launch into a full-fledged reminiscence during the pre-interview. The interviewer should not hesitate to intervene if this happens, halting the flow of memories by saying that the narrator's information is exactly what is needed and should be saved until the day of the actual interview. A mention that the interviewer has no tape to record will definitely seal the issue.

In the real world, of course, pre-interviews are not always possible. If narrators live in another state or are otherwise unavailable, the interviewer will have to make do with mail, telephone, and (increasingly) e-mail. Some telephone contact is critical in such a situation, however, since neither mail nor e-mail will give narrator and interviewer the sense of each other gained by conversation.

During the initial contact the interviewer must be prepared to explain the project and to outline areas the narrator should be prepared to discuss. The interviewer might provide the narrator with a list of topics to be discussed but never a list of actual questions. A list of questions may lead the narrator to expect that only those questions will be asked, with the result that the interviewer may have difficulty introducing the inevitable follow-up questions and discussing other subjects. Narrators may sometimes express concern about their memory or whether they should do some research of their own before an interview. While a well-prepared narrator is indeed welcome, in the real world few people are willing or able to devote time to research before being interviewed. Interviewers should make it clear that the important elements in oral history interviews are the narrators' memories of people, events, interactions, contexts, and the myriad of informal details that other research would not bring. Exact dates, over which many narrators express initial concern, are hardly ever of prime importance. Dates can almost always be found through other sources. Memories of what happened, and how, and with whom are a narrator's important contributions.

Interview Location

Whenever possible, arrange for the interview to take place in a location of the narrator's choosing, most often his or her home or office. Most interviews are held in such places for practical as well as contextual considerations. This arrangement ensures that narrators are not faced with driving, directions to another location, parking, and a host of other concerns that can easily create stress and difficulty and add time that the narrator may not have. It also ensures that narrators will be on their "home turf," in familiar surroundings that provide a relaxed atmosphere for the session and give more comfort to the interview process.

In selecting a location, every effort should be made to remove the narrator from areas that others must use and in which background noise is likely to prove a problem for both concentration and the audio quality of the tape. Interruptions should be avoided; it is the interviewer's job to make certain that the narrator understands that interruptions disrupt the interview and decrease the value of the narrator's contribution.

The interviewer should avoid sitting in the narrator's usual chair when deciding where to sit while conducting the interview. Interviewer and narrator should sit as closely as people normally do while conducting a personal conversation. They should be able to hear one another easily and to feel in contact with each other throughout the session.

Interview Style: Conversation, not Interrogation

Control and direction of the interview are major concerns for the interviewer. Too often oral history interviews tend to fall into one of two kinds—the rambling, nondirected interview that starts nowhere and ends in much the same place, or the overdirected, interviewer-dominated session that has an almost staccato rhythm to it. Neither is good; both are the products of interviewers who have overemphasized a single aspect of the process. The rambler has either not done his homework and has few questions to ask, or is afraid to interject an occasional comment that will keep the narrator within the bounds of the interview. The dominating interviewer, on the other hand, is either afraid of losing control of the situation by allowing the narrator to discuss anything beyond strictly defined limits of the topic, or is fond of the sound of his own voice. Both need to rethink their objectives and methods of approach.

Conversation, not interrogation ought to be the motto of every interviewer. The successful interviewer is one who is at home as a listener and conducts interviews because he or she genuinely wants to know what a narrator thinks or remembers about a topic. Only in a relaxed atmosphere will the narrator feel at ease to relate personal views and experiences. Few narrators are likely to respond positively to an adversarial relationship with an interviewer. Nothing is more inhibiting than to be interviewed by someone with a long list of "must ask" questions, who waits for each answer with barely concealed impatience to get on to the next. The interviewer may nod comprehension as necessary but should avoid interjecting "uh-huh" repeatedly, which can become an annoying distraction during listening and transcribing.

It is up to the interviewer to establish the tone of the interview session. The interviewer should be pleasant and encouraging, and above all nonjudgmental. Understanding, acceptance, and respect are critical elements that the interviewer must project: understanding of the narrators' comments, acceptance of their statements, and respect for their right to have their own opinions about the people and events they discuss. There is no need for interviewers to ratify opinions they find problematic or to dispute or argue with a narrator's commentary. Each narrator has presumably been selected because his or her views are important to a project. Creating a climate conducive to a free and comfortable discourse is an important duty of any interviewer. However, it is also important not to allow the interview to become so informal and unstructured that the product resembles a television talk show. Just as there is a decided difference between conversation and interrogation, there is one also between directed conversation and small talk.

Interview discipline is a critical ingredient in any oral history. The interviewer must maintain a working control of the interview. If an interviewer believes that something related by a narrator is incorrect or misleading, he or she should use care in contradicting the narrator. It may be possible to note other opinions and invite reaction to them, but that should be left to the discretion of an experienced interviewer. Most narrators are unlikely to appreciate the intimation that either their memory or their veracity is in question. In accounts of a specific event such as a flood, fire, labor strike, or election, for instance, the fact that a number of narrators may tell the story differently demonstrates one of the strengths of oral history—its ability to document the breadth of human perception.

Taping the Interview

All equipment should be assembled well before departing for an interview. Include your list of topics, a notepad and pencil, the recorder and microphone, a supply of twice as many tapes as needed, an extension cord or extra batteries, and two copies of the donor agreement.

Before leaving for the interview, record an introduction on the first tape. Some interviewers prefer to record this information after the interview, leaving sufficient tape at the beginning for that purpose. One is probably better prepared, however, by recording the information prior to the interview session. This allows the interviewer to check the sound levels, ensure that all is in working order, and depart for the interview with the confidence that the mechanical components are ready for the interview session. Never record the introduction in the presence of the narrator—nothing will more surely inhibit subsequent conversation.

The introduction should resemble the following example (the information should be standard regardless of the form used):

Today is August 15, 2000. I am John Doe of the Spruce County Historical Society, and the following interview is with Clementine Hall Roberts, who operates a farm near the town of Spruce Meadows. The farm includes an important tract of remnant prairie. The interview is being held in Mrs. Roberts's home.

Note that this introduction includes the following items of information:

- date of the interview
- name of the interviewer
- name of the narrator
- brief description of the narrator's relationship to the subject of the interview
- location of the interview

Each element of information is important, and including each on the first tape ensures that all are recorded and can be included as an opening to the interview transcript.

On Site: Setting Up

Once in the narrator's home or office, set up the equipment as smoothly and quickly as possible. Place the recorder in a position from which it can be monitored to make certain that it is operating, and from which the tape can be changed without disturbing the flow of conversation. Place the microphone between you and the narrator for maximum recording effect. Never place the recorder on a table where the clatter of coffee cups or the rustle of paper or other sounds will disrupt the recording. When using the microphone without a stand, place a magazine or cushion beneath the recorder and beneath the microphone to deaden vibrations that might mar the quality of the recording.

Let the narrator know that you will be either turning the cassette or inserting a new one every thirty minutes. You will be using standard sixty-minute cassettes, and the abrupt clicking sound and engagement of the interviewer in turning or changing the tape can be disconcerting to a narrator who is not prepared.

Try not to place the recorder within the direct sight line of the narrator. The inescapable presence of a tape recorder is unlikely to promote spontaneity. The narrator is certainly aware that the interview is being recorded. It is unnecessary to drive home the point by displaying the recorder prominently.

During the interview, take a few notes, mainly of names and references you will wish to check after the interview, or as the basis for questions you may wish to interject at a later time. Do not disrupt the flow of conversation or break the narrator's train of thought by asking for spellings or similar information that can be obtained following the taping session.

As the interview progresses, do not be disturbed by moments of silence. Leave the recorder running at all times, even when the narrator pauses to search for a word or for an elusive thought or memory. No one can talk continuously without pausing for breath or to collect one's thoughts. Occasional silence is not a waste of tape and may in fact contribute to an understanding of the narrator's feelings in providing a particular comment or description.

When the narrator appears to tire, or when the flow of information ebbs noticeably, bring the interview smoothly to an end. Exhausting a narrator by prolonging the session beyond sensible limits will not help either the present or future interviews. It is much better to return for a second session than to tire a narrator in the first.

Before leaving the interview site, have the narrator sign two copies of the oral history agreement form (discussed in the following section). It is best to do this at the conclusion of the interview, while everything is clear in the minds of both narrator and interviewer.

The Interview Contract

Each oral history interview must be covered by a contract between the narrator and the interviewer's institution (or, less frequently, the interviewer personally). The contract should establish the date of the interview (or interviews) and the terms under which the interview is given (see box 4.1). Most interviews will be given without restriction on public use and should clearly state the narrator's understanding of that provision. Occasionally an interview will need to be restricted for a period of time due to the narrator's concern with access to sensitive information. The period of restriction should be stated clearly, and the interviewer should ensure that it is reasonable (see box 4.2). The stipulation "closed until death" of the narrator is never acceptable, since it creates a substantial burden on the repository to determine an event that may occur

---

Box 4.1. Sample Oral History Agreement Form

I, **[name of narrator]**, a participant in an interview recorded on **[date]**, hereby give and deliver to **[name of institution]** all the incidents of ownership in that interview, including copyright, from this time forward.

Signed (donor): _____

Address: _____

Date: _____

Signed (interviewer):_____

Box 4.2. Sample Restricted Oral History Agreement Form

I, **[name of narrator]**, a participant in an interview recorded on **[date]**, hereby give and deliver to **[name of institution]** all the incidents of ownership in that interview, including copyright, from this time forward, with the single exception that access should be given until **[date]** only to those persons having the written permission of **[name of narrator]**, his or her heir(s), or his or her designee(s), as specified below.

Signed (donor): _____

Address: _____

Date: _____

Signed (interviewer):_____

Specified heir(s) or designee(s): _____

far in the future and be largely unreported. Very few interviews will merit restriction for more than twenty years.

Restrictions should be imposed only when interview content and narrator concerns make them necessary. An additional consideration should also be made clear when a restricted contract is signed: restriction does not mean that an interview cannot be used. It simply ensures that requests to use an interview during the period of restriction will be referred to the narrator, who thus retains control of access for the duration of the restriction.

Narrators are rarely paid for their interviews. Most people are genuinely interested in providing information and contributing to the historical record. An offer of payment would be inappropriate in most instances and could easily skew the resulting interview and researchers' views of its validity. In some cases, however, a form of payment may conform to cultural practice. The custom of offering food, tobacco, and other such items to American Indian narrators is often followed as a traditional sign of respect for the narrator and his knowledge.

Transcribing and Editing

As soon as possible following the interview session, the interviewer should ensure that a complete copy is made of the interview tapes. The master and copies should be clearly labeled as such, together with the name of the narrator and the date of the interview. The copy tapes should be transcribed within a reasonable time and the transcript edited for clarity. Transcription is a time-consuming and expensive process, though the expense has been greatly reduced by the use of word-processing programs that permit easy correction and rapid changes in font and structure. Transcribing machines, such as the Sony BM-815 micro-transcriber, are available, and they work well. There is also an increasing number of professional transcription services that provide excellent products that benefit from the familiarity that comes from transcribing hundreds of interviews. In contracting for transcription, one may specify the word-processing program one prefers, as well as the basic format that provides the least amount of editing work for the interviewer or program editor. One may also specify the formats in which the completed interview should be returned. For example, the transcription service used by the Minnesota Historical Society provides a computer disk with the completed transcript, as well as a paper copy for editing. Editing is done by the interviewer or by a member of the Society's Oral History Office, and edits are then entered in the electronic version in the Office. The final version is then ready for printing and binding. Each interview in an oral history project is bound with a title page, copyright statement, introduction describing the project of which the interview is part, and a photograph of the narrator. Transcripts may include other photographs as well if they are judged to add illustrative value to the interview.

Transcript editing is a diverse practice among oral historians. Some prefer a minimalist approach, leaving the transcript a largely accurate record of the conversation between narrator and interviewer. Others allow narrators to rewrite much of the text, or largely rewrite it themselves to create a document that may be vastly different than the taped interview on which it is based. The latter practice is unfortunate, leaving the eventual user to wonder why oral history was employed at all.

However, some editing is usually necessary—especially that aimed at eliminating false starts, consolidating run-on sentences, and reducing the number of conversational idiosyncrasies (such as the ubiquitous "you know") that appear in the text. Much of this editing is done to increase the readability of the printed text, since some things (such as false starts) that are quite understandable on tape may be confusing and even misleading when transcribed.

Another key element in editing is the correction of spelling errors and the checking of facts. Names should always be spelled correctly, and footnotes or bracketed insertions provided to explain references that are not otherwise identified. Depending on the skill of the transcriber, some basic editorial work such as paragraphing and revising sentence structure may be necessary as well. The question of whether to have narrators edit their transcripts often can be answered in terms of time and reality. Many narrators are busy people with little time to provide more than a casual read-through of a transcript. Narrators should be discouraged from making extensive alterations, and difficulty in completing narrator review should be handled by establishing a clearly understood deadline. A number of oral history programs use a thirty- or sixty-day limit, with the understanding that if a transcript is not returned within that limit, it will be considered to have received the narrator's approval.

Above all, the narrator should be coached before and after the interview to understand that the transcript is meant to reflect a conversation. It is not, and should not appear to be, a highly polished piece of prose from which all spontaneity and most facts have been drained.

Final Production

Print and bind the completed transcript as well as you can afford. Remember that the transcript is something in which a narrator should take pleasure and pride, and that the volume should be attractive and easy to use. Printing and binding may be done as expensively or inexpensively as resources permit; the current availability of a wide variety of reasonably priced, high-quality commercial printing and binding services makes production of an attractive product much easier. The Minnesota Historical Society produces a minimum of three bound copies of each interview—one is catalogued in the library, one is held in reserve for interlibrary loans or other requests, and one is presented to the narrator. Additional copies are often produced for narrators or for use in other libraries.

Record Keeping

Establishing provenance and control for oral history interviews is an important part of the process. Provenance refers to the record of when, how, where, why, and by whom an interview was created. Each interview should be backed by a file containing correspondence with the narrator, the master copy of the interview agreement, photographs, research notes, and other items that document the interview's history and creation. Each interview should have a data sheet in both electronic and printed form that provides basic information on its creation and content. (See box 4.3.)

Equipment

High-quality audiotape recorders are relatively easy to use, and the general use of cassette tape has eliminated the need to worry over management of the machine. The quality of both the recorder and the external microphone is important. Recorders in the range of $300 to $500 each

Box 4.3. Interview Data Sheet

Narrator:

Address:

Biographical Information:

Date of Interview:

Interviewer:

Location of Interview:

Number of Cassettes:

Length of Cassettes (i.e., 60 minutes):

Length of Interview:

Subjects Discussed:

are preferable to ensure quality and trustworthy operation. An omnidirectional external microphone in the $100 range is important to ensure the necessary sound quality. If you use lavelier microphones, you will need two microphones—one for the narrator and one for the interviewer—and the recorder will need to have two microphone jacks.

Always use sixty-minute cassette tapes, with thirty minutes of taping time on each side. Pencil in the name of the narrator on each side of the tape, with the number of the side being used. This will guard against inadvertent tapeovers.

Videotaping Oral History

The use of videotape in oral history production has increased dramatically in recent years. While used in a minority of all interviews, its growth has been spurred by the increased flexibility and portability of equipment and by the undoubted uses to which the video components of oral history can be put.

Videotape is variously employed in oral history, sometimes to tape entire interviews as an adjunct to audiotaping, sometimes to incorporate illustration of a narrator's descriptions. Video provides significant opportunities and also has several drawbacks.

Video offers the viewer the opportunity to see the places or processes a narrator is describing. For example, the use of video in the Minnesota Environmental Issues Oral History Project allows users to virtually walk through the Black Dog Prairie, and, thereby, to better understand its beauty, importance, and vulnerability to surrounding development pressures. When the head of the Minnesota chapter of The Nature Conservancy kneels down to describe a prairie forb, you can see the flower and begin to comprehend its fragility in the prairie landscape. Video also offers increased opportunities for post-interview use of the visual images, which may be used alone or in concert with other images.

On the other hand, video is expensive, in terms of both equipment and personnel. Moreover, videotape itself makes poor archival material because it is not permanent and it cannot be easily transcribed (although when expensive, high-quality master tape is used, it copies extremely well and provides excellent images on dubbed tape).

Taking everything into account, video should be used only when it brings something unique to the project. The most thoughtful and appropriate process for creating videohistory is one I have dubbed the Perlis Plan after Vivian Perlis of Yale University. A pioneer in defining the use of video in oral history, Perlis discarded the idea of simply turning the camera on a seated narrator and letting the tape run. Instead, she correctly noted that what users wanted was to see the things the narrator described, or better still, to see the narrator doing something rather than talking about it. Video footage of a farmer using his land and showing the accommodations he has made to wetland preservation, for example, offers a great deal of visual information to supplement the interview text.

Digital Future

There is every reason to believe that oral historians will become increasingly involved in the use of digital images to create oral history presentations. At present, film, photographs, diaries, minute books, and correspondence are all being digitized with the grand aim of making the information accessible to more people.

Will Schneider of the Polar Regions Oral History Office at the University of Alaska at Fairbanks was among the first to understand the promise offered by linking images of photographs and interview text with the narrator's voice. His work pointed the way for many subsequent projects, and if its promise has not yet been fully realized, it is because of concerns that have little to do with Schneider's pioneering efforts. As is true for similar uses of music and books, questions of control and copyright cannot be ignored, and, at least at this time, oral history transcripts are best left to more easily controlled situations, rather than putting them on the Internet.

Summary

Oral history can serve those interested in learning about the history of a place and the people who have lived there. With an understanding of its realities and care in its production, oral history can contribute to research into historic ecosystems in many important ways. It requires time and resources, to be sure, but so do most other valuable endeavors.

Oral history is special because of the interaction it demands of the interviewer and the narrator. It brings together two people in an unusual partnership, aimed at creating documents of value from the knowledge possessed by the narrator. In doing so it provides marvelous opportunities for the development of personal relationships between its co-creators, enriching both of them as it creates information for wider use.

It offers a priceless chance to gain something truly unique—the perspective and knowledge that each narrator brings to an interview. It can capture information that would otherwise be lost and bring fresh insight to the problems and the prospects we face in this complex, fast-changing, interdependent world in which we live.

References

Baum, Willa K. 1977. *Transcribing and editing oral history*. Nashville, Tenn.: American Association for State and Local History.

Dunaway, David K., and Willa K. Baum. 1984. *Oral history: An interdisciplinary anthology*. Nashville, Tenn.: American Association for State and Local History.

Morrissey, Charles T. 1987. Public historians and oral history: Problems of concept and methods. *Public Historian* 2:22–29.

Oral History Evaluation Guidelines. 1991. 2nd ed. Waco, Tex.: Oral History Association.

Perks, Robert, and Alistair Thomson. 1998. *The oral history reader*. London: Routledge.

Ritchie, Donald A. 1995. *Doing oral history*. New York: Twayne Publishers.

5

Maps and Photographs

Tina Reithmaier

> *Maps break down our inhibitions, stimulate our glands, stir our imagination, loose our tongues. The map speaks across the barrier of language; it is sometimes claimed as the language of geography.*
>
> Carl O. Sauer, *The Education of a Geographer*

> *Locating human actions in space remains the greatest intellectual achievement of the map as a form of knowledge.*
>
> Brian Harley, *From Sea Charts to Satellite Images*

Throughout history, humans have made images to convey the geographic locations of their lives. Early peoples drew maps in the dirt, carved them out of wood, or painted them on animal skins. Today's maps and photographs, while technically sophisticated and supported by recent innovations in satellites, computers, and various sensing technologies, convey the same basic message: here is a place where I live or where I have been, and these are the things I know about that place.

While introductory in its scope, this chapter will explore how restoration ecologists can locate maps and photographs to discover what they can tell us about historic ecosystems in North America. In doing so, it will cover maps made by the following groups: Native Americans, early European explorers, early American explorers and naturalists, various agencies of the federal and state governments, and commercial publishers. It will also discuss where to find and how to use ground and aerial photographs as well as repeat photography.

It is important to note that modern maps and vertical aerial photographs come in a variety of scales. In this case, scale defines the relationship between the linear distance on a map or photograph and the corresponding actual distance on the ground. This relationship is expressed as a ratio, such as 1:24,000, where 1 is the unit of distance on the map or photograph, and 24,000 is the unit of distance on the ground. The scale makes a dramatic difference in terms of resolution. The general rule of thumb is the larger the scale (the closer the ratio is to 1:1), the finer the resolution. Thus, larger-scale maps and photographs cover less area but provide greater detail or information about that area. For example, a 7.5-minute orthophotoquad at a scale of 1:24,000, or 1 inch equals 2,000 feet, provides slightly more than 2.5 times the resolution of a 15-minute topographic map (scale 1:62,500, or 1 inch equals 5,208 feet).

Maps

General Works

There are a number of standard titles that describe and analyze the history of mapping in North America. *From Sea Charts to Satellite Images*, edited by David Buisseret (1990), is a collection of essays by noted contemporary historians of cartography. These scholars provide a series of essays that explore the use of maps to study history in a broader context. The book's subjects range from European antecedents of New World maps and eighteenth-century large-scale maps to twentieth-century highway maps and aerial imagery. Each essay gives a brief description of a type of map, provides a bibliography for further reading, and shows a series of maps with commentary. This work is useful in becoming familiar with the types of maps available to the researcher. It also explores how to read maps and their usefulness as sources for historical study.

North America: The Historical Geography of a Changing Continent, edited by Robert D. Mitchell and Paul A. Groves (1990), is divided into five parts that cover the chronological study of the geography of the United States and Canada. In eighteen essays, the authors explore historical geography, colonization, expansion prior to the 1860s, consolidation from the 1860s to 1920, and the reorganization of the continent since the 1920s. These essays, complemented by maps, provide a useful text for understanding North America's changing continent.

Various maps and atlases that were produced from the colonial period through the establishment of the United States Geological Survey are examined in Walter W. Ristow's *American Maps and Mapmakers* (1985). In addition to the discussion of the maps themselves, Ristow identifies the mapmakers and the technology that was used to produce these historic sources. The book provides an excellent overview for understanding the evolution of mapmaking in North America and complements an earlier work by John Noble Wilford, *The Mapmakers* (1981), which focuses on earlier mapmakers in Europe and the United States.

David Greenhood's *Mapping* (1951) is a good book for the beginner who needs some help understanding the principles and terms used by cartographers and map librarians. Numerous books have also been written or compiled about where maps are located in research libraries, historical societies, government agencies, and private institutions throughout North America. David K. Carrington and Richard W. Stephenson have, for example, compiled *Map Collections in the United States and Canada: A Directory* (1985), which lists the numerous map collections throughout the continent. *A Guide to U.S. Map Resources* by David Cobb (1990) also lists map libraries and resource centers in the United States.

Another invaluable source is the National Archives of the United States, whose *Guide to Cartographic Records in the National Archives* is available both in paper (1971) and on the Internet at www.nara.gov. The guide is a finding tool to more than two million maps produced by the federal government since 1774. The National Archives has more than six hundred map collections and more than three million aerial photographs. Other plans and maps can be found within the country's ten regional archive branches. In addition to the National Archives, another government source is the Library of Congress. *A List of Maps in the Library of Congress* was produced in 1901 and was updated by the Library of Congress under the title *A List of Biographical Atlases in the Library of Congress, 1909–1992*. The most recent work in updating its finding aids is *Library of Congress Geography of Maps: An Illustrated Guide* (1966) by Ralph E. Ehrenberg and staff. The Library of Congress Web site lcweb.loc.gov/rr/geogmap/gmpage.html is also an invaluable tool in identifying the numerous historic maps it houses. The Web site has a search mode and explains how you can order copies of the maps you are interested in studying. For example, searching for topographical maps brought up twenty-eight items, including the *Virginia Atlas and Gazetteer* and the *Topographic Mapping Index*. Another useful finding aid is *Archives in the Library of Congress* by John C. L. Andreassen.

Checklist of Printed Maps of the Middle West to 1900, edited by Robert W. Karrow Jr. (1981), is a fourteen-volume compendium that lists printed maps at research libraries, university libraries, and some local historical societies and libraries. The maps are identified by geographical location and described by year, cartographer, scale, and size. Researchers should be aware, however, that many of these institutions have updated their records and have acquired finding aids for new materials since this book was published.

Maps can be found in a number of collections including books and periodicals. *The Index to Maps in Books and Periodicals* (American Geographical Society of New York Map Department 1968, 1974, 1978) is a good source for seeking out these hard-to-discover maps.

In addition to these general works, many research libraries have published catalogues of their map collections. These works, in addition to state and local inventories, will assist the researcher in finding maps pertinent to a particular site but not locally archived.

Finally, the World Wide Web also contains some excellent searching tools. For example, the Web site www.dir.yahoo.com/Science/Geography/Cartography/maplibraries lists research and university map library Web sites, many of which have on-line catalogues.

Native American Maps

Maps drawn by Native Americans show that they had a working knowledge of the landscape in which they lived. Fortunately, copies of many of these maps have been compiled and annotated by geographers, cartographers, and historians.

Atlas of Great Lakes Indian History by Helen Hornbeck Tanner (1987) is a narrative of Native American life in the Great Lakes region. In numerous chapters Tanner covers the natural vegetation ca. 1600, the Iroquois Wars, the French era, Native American villages and tribal distribution, the frontier transition, Native American villages ca. 1820, the Black Hawk War, land cessions, and reservations and Native American villages ca. 1870. A sequence of thirty-three maps, by Miklos Pinther, accompany Tanner's text and visually describe the movement of Native American tribes from 1600 to 1870 in the Great Lakes region.

Barbara Mundy's *The Mapping of New Spain: Indigenous Cartography and the Maps of the Relaciones Geográficas* (1996) includes 101 illustrations that complement the descriptive stories of Spain and its imperial ideology of mapping and describing the New World, colonial Spanish officials and the response to the *Relaciones Geográficas* questionnaire, and the Native American mapping tradition in this colonial period. Mundy argues that Amerindians were mapping the world at the same time the Spanish and Creole colonists were. Their maps were different from those of the Europeans, however, because they had a different cultural perception of space. Mundy contends that the Native American maps changed as their relationship to the land changed following European colonization.

Mark Warhus in *Another America* (1997) comments on some eighty Native American maps from the colonial period to the present with an emphasis on maps from the Great Plains. By using maps as his driving force of study, he has created a useful history of the Native American.

Cartographic Encounters: Perspectives on Native American Mapmaking and Map Use includes a number of essays derived from the Kenneth Nebenzhal Jr. Lectures in the History of Cartography, which were held at the Newberry Library in 1993. G. Malcolm Lewis (1998) has edited the book into three sections: Part 1, The 400-Year First Encounter; Part 2,

The Ongoing Second Encounter; and Part 3, Future Encounters in New Contexts. These essays include some maps but are mostly narrative.

Another source for information about Native Americans is the U.S. Bureau of Indian Affairs (BIA), whose files contain more than 16,000 maps, covering the period 1800–1939. These maps pertain to treaties, removal policy, reservations, and land use but also contain substantial information about the historical geography of Native American lands. Laura E. Kelsey has compiled the *List of Cartographic Records of the Bureau of Indian Affairs* (1954), which is a key finding aid to maps housed at the BIA.

Mapping by Early European Explorers

The maps of Europeans—from Columbus to the first settlers of the Virginia and Massachusetts colonies—may also be of interest to restoration ecologists. Many of these maps, such as John White's "A Map of Virginia with a Description of the Countrey, The Commodities, People, Government and Religion," can be found in the map libraries of various universities, institutes, and government agencies. The Library of Congress, for example, holds Samuel de Champlain's 1606 chart showing his three-year exploration of the northeast coast of North America. It and other LOC holdings are described in *Nautical Charts on Vellum in the Library of Congress* by Walter W. Ristow and Raleigh A. Skelton (1977).

The map collection of the Newberry Library in Chicago www.newberry.org includes 100,000 maps and 4,000 atlases. More than 900 maps of the Trans-Mississippi West are catalogued in the library's Graff Collection. The collections of the John Carter Brown Library at Brown University www.brown.edu/Facilities/University_library/general/libraries/jcb.htm include more than 54,000 books, maps, and prints reflecting the history of discovery, exploration, and settlement of North America. The materials date from the late fifteenth century to 1825, and include European travel accounts. The natural history records group includes maps and prints of various North American plants and their usefulness for food and medicine.

The Bancroft Library www.lib.berkeley.edu/EART/MapCollections .html at the University of California–Berkeley has one of the largest map collections of any university in the United States. Its 360,000 maps cover not only this early period in North America, but up to the present. The 420,000 maps and 20,000 books and atlases held in the Map Division and Rare Book Division of the New York Public Library www.nypl.org/research/chss/map/map.html date from the sixteenth century.

Copies of maps by early Europeans can also be found in various books. For example, "Colonial Settlement from Europe" is an essay in *The Cadastral Map in the Service of the State* by Robert J. P. Kain and Elizabeth Baignet

(1992) that discusses the production of cadastral maps (landownership maps) and the surveying of the new colonies. The authors explain the metes and bound system that was employed in the colonies to divide the newly acquired land (see chapter 6). There is also a section explaining the land division of long lots, which was used in areas settled by the French.

The Mapping of America by R. V. Tooley (1980) offers the reader a variety of maps including descriptions of Virginia, maps of French-controlled areas, marine surveys by James Cook (1758–68), and the Jansson Visscher map of New England.

In The Cartography of North America, 1500–1800, Pierluigi Portinaro and Franco Knirsch (1987) reproduce more than three hundred color and black-and-white images, many of which are maps. The authors include maps by John Smith (1612), Willem Blaeu (1645), Jean Nicolas Bellin (1757), and Antonio Zatta (1778) to illustrate the mapping of North America.

The Mapping of America by Seymour I. Schwartz and Ralph E. Ehrenberg (1980) discusses the mapping of the United States from 1500 through 1800, looking at the nation's history, colonization, seaboard expansion, and emergence as a new nation. Though it is a highly informative work, it stops short of discussing settlement of the West and the production of commercial maps in the nineteenth century.

Historical Maps of the United States by Michael Swift (1998) contains more than one hundred maps from the Public Records Office of London. The content ranges from Virginia in 1612 to Montreal in 1907. Though the title refers to the United States, Swift has included maps from Jamaica, Antigua, Quebec, St. Croix, Guadeloupe, Newfoundland, Montreal, and Panama. The images are cited in chronological order, which gives the reader a sense of not only the history of cartography but also the development of the United States.

The description and reproduction of maps produced by the Jesuits, the U.S. Coastal Survey, the U.S. Navy, and the U.S. Topographical Engineers, can be found in Maps and Plans in the Public Records Office (Volume 2. America and West Indies). At first glance, this work, edited by P. A. Penford (1974), might seem an unlikely source because it was published by Her Majesty's Stationery Office in London. Nevertheless, it provides a wealth of historic maps dating to the eighteenth and nineteenth centuries.

An excellent guide to mapping in Canada during this period is Richard Ruggles's A Country So Interesting: The Hudson Bay Company and Two Centuries of Mapping, 1670–1870 (1991). Ruggles searched company archives in Manitoba and London and was able to locate 838 maps and 557 sketches made by company employees and Native Americans. He includes 66 of those maps in this book.

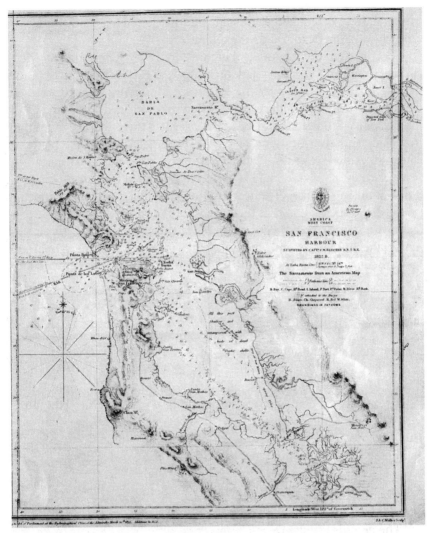

Figure 5.1. An 1872 map of San Francisco Harbor, San Pablo Bay, and the lower Sacramento River (Great Britain Hydrographic Department Nautical Chart, scale 1:81,000. UC–Berkeley Earth Sciences and Map Library).

Mapping by the United States Government

Early Western Surveys

Beginning in the early nineteenth century, under the leadership of President Thomas Jefferson, the United States government set about the task of mapping large portions of the continent. These maps were intended to serve as baseline information for both commercial and military purposes. However, the explorers employed by the federal government to make these maps also acquired significant information about plants, animals, and Native Americans on their explorations.

Shortly after the Louisiana Purchase in 1803, Jefferson sent Meriwether Lewis and William Clark on a two-year expedition from St. Louis up the Missouri River, over the Bitterroot Mountains to the Columbia River, and on to the Pacific Ocean. When they returned, Lewis and Clark had maps that showed the vast country they had traversed, the rivers they traveled, and the locations of Native American tribes. As historian Stephen Ambrose writes, "Jefferson's first purpose was good maps—he wanted to know what he had bought. He explained his purpose to naturalist William Dunbar: 'The work we are now doing is, I trust, done for posterity, in such a way that they need not repeat it. . . . We shall delineate with correctness the great arteries of this great country: those who come after us will extend the ramifications as they become acquainted with them, and fill up the canvas we begin" (Ambrose 1996; inner quote, Jackson 1978, 245).

Other expeditions into the interior of the continent followed. Zebulon Pike explored the Rocky Mountains from 1805 to 1807. Stephen Long returned in 1819 to the area Pike had explored earlier and continued to survey the Rocky Mountains until 1820. George W. Featherstonhaugh was sent in 1834 to explore the Ozark Mountains, and in 1839 David Dale Owen surveyed the mineral lands of the Upper Mississippi Valley.

After the Civil War, four separate expedition teams surveyed the West: the Clarence King Expedition (the area between the Rocky Mountains and the Sierra Nevadas); the F. V. Hayden Expedition (New Mexico, Colorado, Wyoming, Montana, Idaho); the John Wesley Powell Expedition (Colorado River, Arizona, Nevada, Utah, Wyoming); and the George Wheeler Expedition (Nebraska, Texas, Kansas, the Dakotas, California, and the Rocky Mountain states). Each of these teams recorded extensive observations of the land, flora, and fauna in surveys, annual reports, and maps (see chapter 3).

Various materials, including correspondence of the King, Hayden, Powell, and Wheeler surveys, have been catalogued with the unpublished government documents in the National Archives. In addition to these documents, maps, sketches, and a photographic collection of the surveys can be reviewed at the National Archives within the Still Pictures section and the Cartographic and Architectural branch. The documents of these great western surveys can be examined in the annual reports (1867–79) of the Smithsonian Institution, the Department of the Interior, the Secretary of War, the Chief of Engineers, and the Hayden Survey at the National Archives. The United States Geological Survey has published Bulletin 222, *Catalogue and Index of the Hayden, King, Powell, and*

Wheeler Surveys by Lawrence F. Schmeckebier (1904). The reports and accompanying maps of the surveys can be found in the holdings of the Library of Congress, Geography and Map Division. Additional information can also be obtained in the records of the United States Congress.

Richard A. Barlett provides one of the better narratives for further study of these surveys in *Great Surveys of the American West* (1962). An exhaustive bibliography has been compiled in Bonnie Skell Hardwick's dissertation, *Science and Arts: The Travel Writings of the Great Surveys of the American West after the Civil War* (1977). A number of individual biographies also have been written including *Clarence King: A Biography* by Thurman Wilkins (1988) and *Powell of the Colorado* by William Culp Darrah (1951).

U.S. Geological Survey

Following this period of exploration, and as the United States began to expand westward following the Civil War, it became increasingly clear that a national mapping program was needed. In 1879, President Rutherford Hayes signed a bill establishing the United States Geological Survey, and the agency quickly set to the task of creating a series of quadrangular land maps at scales of 1:250,000 for one-degree maps and 1:125,000 for thirty-minute maps. (Today the standard scale is 1:24,000.) Henry Nash Smith examines the beginnings of the United States Geological Survey in his 1947 article "Clarence King, John Wesley Powell, and the Establishment of the United States Geological Survey."

Topographic maps are, perhaps, the maps for which the USGS is best known. These maps show the natural and humanmade features of geographical areas throughout the United States. They show the contour of the land, rivers, mountains, and areas of wooded vegetation, as well as street grids and cultural features. These topographical maps are a valuable source for the researcher who is looking for changes in topography, geology, hydrology, land use, or vegetation.

P. D. A. Harvey's *The History of Topographical Maps* (1980) serves as a general introduction to topographic maps. There are also a variety of finding aids for the voluminous amount of mapping created by the USGS and the U.S. Army Corps of Engineers, which was established in 1838. They include *Descriptive Catalog of Maps Published by Congress, 1817–1843* by Clausen and Friis (1941), *Maps Index to Topographic Quadrangles of the United States, 1882–1940* by Moffat (1985), and *National Lands Index: An Index to Nationally Designated Lands on National Topographic Maps* by Markham (1980).

The USGS has also preserved thousands of historic maps, many of which can be obtained from its library Web site www.mapping.usgs.gov/

index/2library.html. The library includes maps dating back to the 1880s. They are indexed chronologically and alphabetically by state and quadrangle name. Some data indexing, however, has not been completed.

In addition to topographic maps, the USGS has mapped floodplains, geologic formations (especially in mountainous areas), land use (including national parks), land cover, and hydrology (including river basin and watershed studies) throughout the United States.

Morris Thompson's *Maps for America* is a concise and inclusive book about the different types of maps produced by the USGS. Thompson uses many illustrative examples of the maps the USGS has produced since 1879. *The National Atlas of the United States*, edited by Arch C. Gerlach (1970), complements Thompson's work and provides a variety of maps on which to base further research. For an overview of the maps produced by the USGS, consult its map resource Web site at www.mapping.usgs.gov/mac/isb/pubs/booklets/usgsmaps/usgsmaps.html.

Most of these government-initiated surveys and maps can also be found at the Library of Congress Geography and Map Reading Room, Map Collections 1597–1988. However, these maps, which were normally bound in House and Senate documents and can be found in the LOC Geography and Map Division's Congressional Serial Set Collection, are often difficult to use because of their large format and fragile nature. They are described and reproduced in Carl Wheat's five-volume, *Mapping the Transmississippi West* (1963). Another source is the USGS Historical Map Archives, which is located in Reston, Virginia. This archive holds maps from 1880 to the present. This reference collection complements the USGS historical library with scientific and technical reports.

Coastal Surveys

In 1807, President Jefferson signed a bill establishing the Survey of the Coast of the Federal Government, the purpose of which was to provide ships' captains with navigation charts to use as they plied the coastlines of the new country. This effort became the United States Coast Survey in 1836 and, in 1878, the United States Coast and Geodetic Survey. Today, these surveys are conducted by the National Oceanic and Atmospheric Administration. The Library of Congress, Geography and Map Division, holds an estimated twenty-five thousand sheets of coast surveys. Another source for coastal surveys is the USGS Historical Maps Archives, which are located in Reston, Virginia, and hold maps from 1880 to the present.

The Survey of the Coast was divided into three divisions to study geodesy, topography, and hydrography. Ferdinand R. Hassler, the appointed director, required rigid directives, though some of the techniques for surveying were crude. The coast survey of 1843 includes nine thousand miles of shoreline from Rhode Island to the Chesapeake Bay. The Coast Survey included hydrographic surveys of New York Bay, Long Island Sound, Delaware Bay, and the Delaware River, all giving a sound base for further studies. Techniques were improved and surveys were completed of all coastal areas of the United States, including Alaska after 1867. The Coast Survey's Historical Collection can be viewed at its Web site www.chartmaker.ncd.noaa.gov/ocs/text/MAP-COLL.htm. The collection includes nautical charts, Civil War maps, and early exploration maps of the Pacific Northwest.

General Land Office Surveys

From 1785 through 1787, parts of Ohio became the first tracts of land surveyed under the township-range land survey system. This national method of land surveying became law following the passage of the Land Ordinance of 1787 and the establishment of the General Land Office in 1812 (see chapter 6). In effect, this legislation put a one-mile-by-one-mile grid across the country from the Ohio River Valley to the Pacific Ocean. Laura Kelsey has compiled a *List of Cartographic Records of the General Land Office* (1964), which is useful for locating GLO survey maps.

Thematic Maps

The United States government also produces thematic maps—maps devoted to a single phenomenon such as temperature, precipitation, population, and vegetation. However, as Ralph Ehrenberg (1977) notes, the federal government produced very few thematic maps prior to the Civil War. Such maps became more common as the United States expanded westward and there arose a need to inventory and display the country's natural and human resources. Of particular interest to restoration ecologists are thematic maps dealing with vegetation. A good resource for locating such maps is *The Checklist of On-line Vegetation and Plant Distribution Maps* compiled by Claire Englander and Philip Hoehn (2000) of Stanford University's Branner Library. The Web site is www.sul.stanford.edu/depts/branner/vegmaps.htm. Other finding aids include *Index to Plan Distribution Maps in North American Periodicals through 1972* (Phillips and Stuckey 1976) and the *International Bibliography of Vegetation Maps* (Küchler 1980).

Other thematic maps of interest include weather maps, United States Postal Service maps, and census maps. The weather maps that were originally produced by the United States Navy in the 1840s charted wind and currents. By the 1850s, Joseph Henry of the Smithsonian Institution was charting national weather land surface data. The Western Union Telegraph Company produced weather maps charting storms, weather patterns, and cloud conditions until 1871 as well. Originally maps were posted publically, and, by 1911, became common in newspapers around the country (Ehrenberg 1977).

In the late 1830s, the United States Post Office Department starting mapping transportation routes under the direction of H. A. Burr. Between 1839 and 1866, Burr prepared numerous maps of postal routes. Among other information, these maps indicate postal routes and any "natural or artificial objects." The Postal Office Department continued to publish a series of route maps between 1866 and 1894 that included drainage features and waterways. These maps were updated until 1930. Narratives by local postmasters describing the landscape around their post office and along the routes accompany many of these maps. These maps and reports are held in the National Archives (Ehrenberg 1977; Record Group 28, Records of the Post Office Department Division of Topography), and a list of them can be found on the archive's Web site www.nara.gov/guide/rg028.html.

The 1850 census is the first to contain any maps. During the Civil War, the Census Office created annotated maps from the 1860 Agricultural Census under the supervision of Joseph Kennedy. Shortly after the Civil War, Francis A. Walker introduced the *Statistical Atlas of the United States*, which included numerous thematic maps that portrayed census data collected from the Ninth Census of 1870. The census data was transformed into maps and graphs showing agriculture, physical geography, and other vital statistics (Ehrenberg 1977). Similar atlases were produced for subsequent census schedules (see chapter 3). Many of these atlases can be found at your local or state historical society, research or university library, if not at your local public library. Other finding aids can be found at www.census.gov/cgi-bin/gazetteer.

Commercial Map Publishers

Not all maps were published by or for government purposes, however. Private mapmakers and publishers also made and sold a wide variety of maps. A good source for finding sixteenth- and seventeenth-century, privately made, hand-drawn maps of the thirteen colonies is *Maps and Charts Published in America before 1800: A Bibliography* by James Wheat and Christian Brown (1969).

Among the most widely distributed commercial maps were the cadastral, or landownership, maps, which were produced from the 1830s until the 1930s. Today, these are known as plat maps. Purchased on a subscription basis, these maps show the ownership of rural property within a county. All landownership maps made before 1861 were of the large, wall-sized, single-sheet format. Following the Civil War, the atlas format was most prominent. In this format a township of the county was assigned to each page, and then additional pages contained illustrations, especially lithographs of buildings and farms, along with information about family and town histories, ethnic composition, and agricultural statistics. (See figure 5.2.) For more information on the commercial process of nineteenth-century mapping, see Michael Conzen's (1984) essay "The County Landownership Map in America: Its Commercial Development and Social Transformation 1814–1939." There are also a few chapters in *From Sea Charts to Satellite Images* (Buisseret 1990) that discuss commercial publishing of maps and town plans in more detail.

Map historians estimate that five thousand cadastral maps and atlases of North American counties were published. These maps tend to follow the periods of agrarian settlement across the continent, leaving the non-agrarian parts of North America unmapped. Michael Conzen (1990) writes, "Early coverage from the 1830s to the 1860s is good for the Middle Atlantic states, New England, and Ohio. Counties in the Middle West, the Great Plains, Ontario, and Maritimes were quite widely and frequently covered between 1850 and 1875, and those in the Middle West and Great Plains again, along with the Pacific Northwest and Canadian Prairies, between 1890 and 1925." These nineteenth-century maps are useful to the restorationists because they show topography, land cover, land use, and ownership—all of which can be compared with similar maps within a series or with other archival information, including General Land Office surveys, to determine changes in the cultural and natural features of the agrarian landscape.

The Library of Congress Geography and Map Division has the largest single collection of county maps and atlases in the United States. It has also microfiched numerous landownership maps and made that microfiche set available to research, university, and some local libraries. There are several sources for searching the Library of Congress for cadastral maps, including: *Landownership Maps: A Checklist of Nineteenth Century United States Maps in the Library of Congress* by David A. Carrington and Richard W. Stephenson (1967); *A List of Geographical Atlases in the Library of Congress* by Clara E. LeGear (1963); *State Atlases: An Annotated Bibliography* by David A. Cobb and Peter B. Ives (1983); *American maps, 1795–1895: A Guide to Values: wall maps, folding maps, atlases and maps from atlases* by K. A. Sheets (1985); *Index to Nineteenth Century City Plans appearing in Guide Books* (1980), and an *Index to Early Twentieth Century City Plans appearing in Guide Books* (1978), both by Harold M. Otness.

The National Map Collection of the Public Archives of Canada holds the best collection of Canadian county maps and atlases. There are two research sources for that collection: *County Maps: Land Ownership Maps of*

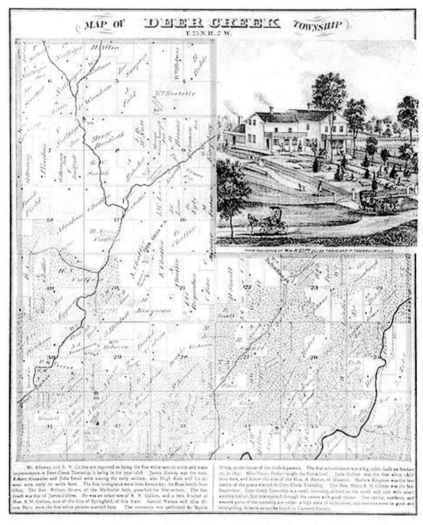

Figure 5.2. A cadastral map of Deer Creek Township.

Canada in the Nineteenth Century compiled by Heather Maddick (1976), and *County Atlases of Canada* compiled by Betty May (1970). The Golda Meir Library at the University of Wisconsin–Milwaukee has a large number of county maps and atlases from both the United States and Canada.

Interpreting Maps

The map, when interpreted correctly, complements the study of historical change because it provides visual cues and supporting evidence to other sources of historic and contemporary information. Maurice Beresford (1957, 1971) argues in *History on the Ground* that the map is the second part of a research triangle. According to Beresford, one must begin historical questioning in the field; followed by research in the archives, which includes studying maps; and then return to the site in order to tell a complete story of a locality.

Several problems are inherent in interpreting information from a map. First, one needs to determine if the map is to scale. This is not the case with most maps by Native Americans and early explorers; it becomes less of a concern with modern maps. If the distance between two points on a map is out of proportion to the actual distance on the ground, the map is essentially useless in terms of matching it to any other existing maps or photographs. This isn't to say that such maps are completely without merit, just that they have no spatial integrity. Information on such maps—village sites, battle sites, rivers, vegetation, geologic formations—might still be useful, but it would have to be corroborated with other sources before being put into a study.

Second, as Robin Grossinger and Joshua Collins (unpublished) discovered when using historical topographic sheets from the U.S. Coastal Survey to study the coastal areas of San Francisco Bay, maps need to be checked for geomorphic accuracy. To do this, Grossinger and Collins suggest using (1) multiple, contemporaneous source materials to corroborate map accuracy, and (2) carefully studied remnant habitats as analogs to judge the accuracy of the maps against. Like Beresford, they recommend going back to the field to "resolve questions about the accuracy of the best maps."

Third, researchers should remember that a map is merely a snapshot in time. Knowing this, the researcher should attempt to find series of maps that show changes over time, or other maps or photographs in which changes could be seen by comparison. Again, the presence of a map scale and the compatibility of scale are important.

Fourth, as Brian Harley (1989) points out, the researcher needs to place the map in context of time, place, and society. By this he means that the researcher needs to understand or look for the motivation of the cartographer when interpreting a map. It becomes necessary to ask questions such as: Was the map made for speculative reasons? as part of an exploration? for military purposes? as part of a town planning effort? Each of these motivations will produce a map with different information. The researcher needs to be aware that some items may be overemphasized and others omitted. In the ideal world, maps should show little or no bias, but in reality some bias always creeps in, so the map researcher must always be vigilant. Using other source material to verify the accuracy of the map is one way to overcome this problem.

In reading a map, the researcher should study its orientation (north, south, east, west), check to see if it's drawn to a scale, learn the date of production and the identity of the cartographer and the publisher. The researcher can then begin to look at the map in terms of terrain and place names to provide a sense of space. Again, a series of maps should be studied, if possible, to help determine the cultural context and identify the silences or embellishments of the map. Census materials, aerial photographs, diaries, and newspaper articles are all sources that should be considered to help identify the accuracy of a map. Finally, as Beresford (1971) so strongly suggests, one should visit the site in question where the researcher can piece together all the sources and then fully interpret the site.

For further reading on the interpretation of maps see *The Making of the English Landscape* by W. G. Hoskins (1963), *How to Lie with Maps* by Mark Monmonier (1996), and *Artifacts and the American Past* by Thomas Schlereth (1980).

Photography

Photography, which first started in Europe, had become part of American culture by the 1840s. Large American cities had photo studios, while villages and towns were visited by traveling photographers. For example, the first history of San Francisco, which was published in 1855, is replete with photographs documenting the rapid growth of that city following the Gold Rush of 1849.

A general book for understanding the processes of photography is *Looking at Photographs: A Guide to Technical Terms* by Gordon Baldwin (1991). Alan Trachenberg's (1989) book *Reading American Photographs: Images as History* is a wonderful survey of the history of American photographers such as Mathew Brady. A variety of images produced as tintypes, daguerreotypes, stereoscopes, postcards, and most recent developing techniques can be found at the National Archives, the Library of Congress Prints and Photographs Division, and in private collections, in university research libraries, in archives, and at state and local historical societies.

Restorationists working outside urban areas may be interested in photographs taken after the Civil War by photographers such as Andrew J. Russell, Carlton Watkins, Timothy O'Sullivan, and William Henry Jackson. Both Russell and Watkins worked for railroad companies. Russell is best known for his photograph of the completion of the first transcontinental railroad; Watkins for his landscape portraits of Yosemite, the Columbia River, and Alaska. O'Sullivan and Jackson, on the other hand, went west as members of government-sponsored survey teams. O'Sullivan participated in both the King and the Wheeler surveys and accompanied the Hayden survey team. His works have been published in *Timothy O'Sullivan, America's Forgotten Photographer* by James D. Horan (1966) and *The Photographic Artifacts of Timothy O'Sullivan* by Rick Dingus (1982). Jackson is known for his photographs of the Yellowstone area and Mesa Verde. The biography *William Henry Jackson and the Transformation of the American Landscape* by Peter B. Hales (1988) is a good introduction to his work. Jackson's photographs can be found at the Library of Congress (Detroit Publishing Company Collection www.rs6.loc.gov/detroit/dethome.html), the National Archives, and the Colorado Historical Society. There is also a Web site on Jackson entitled "Time Exposures" at www.fit.edu/IntoTechSys/resources/cogei/hhjte.html.

The National Archives has an impressive number of still photographs. *Guide to the Holdings of the Still Picture Branch of the National Archives* by Barbara Lewis Burger is an excellent work for researching those holdings. The Library of Congress also has an illustrated guide of prints and photographs on its Web site www.lcweb.loc.gov/rr/print/guide/port-6.html. State historical societies, museums, and photographic archives of government agencies such as the U.S. Forest Service, U.S. National Park Service, U.S. Geological Survey, and U.S. Bureau of Land Management and their counterparts in Canada are also important sources for historic ground-base photographs.

While photographs can be powerful tools, they have to be used wisely. As G. F. Roders and his colleagues (1984) point out, photographs can be (1) altered ("skies printed in, tonal changes introduced by pencil work"), (2) made misleading by various artistic techniques, and (3) unrepresentative of the entire landscape. This last point is especially important to be aware of because early photographers were most likely interested in "attractive" or "unusual" aspects of the environment they saw, while the contemporary researcher may be looking for something different. Finally, because it is a relatively new technology, photography is limited in its temporal scale to the past 150 years. Scale, in a spatial sense, also becomes an issue if a quantitative analysis is being undertaken.

Aerial Photography

In 1861, the Union army used a tethered hot-air balloon equipped with a camera to take the first aerial photograph in the United States: a bird's-eye picture of the Virginia countryside between Richmond and the Chickahominy River (Thompson 1981). With the invention of the airplane and improvements in cameras and film, aerial photography became an extremely accurate means of determining landscape features and changes over time. There are three types of aerial photographs: low-oblique photos that show the ground from an angle but with no horizon, high-oblique photos that show the ground from an angle and include the horizon and the sky, and vertical photos that show the ground directly below the camera. Oblique air photos provide images that are closest to our own perspective when looking out an airplane window—a panorama—but because of this they are distorted in terms of scale. Vertical photos, on the other hand, have relatively little distortion and are, therefore, used exclusively for accurate mapping and interpretation of the land. Like very old maps, oblique air photos cannot be used for quantitative analysis but can provide supplementary information to that obtained from vertical air photos.

A good introductory work to the subject is *Aerial Photography: The Story of Aerial Mapping and Reconnaissance* by Grover Heiman (1972). Mary Rose Collins's *The Aerial Photo Sourcebook* (1998) provides basic information about aerial photos and good information about how to acquire them from federal and state sources in the United States. *Fundamentals of Remote Sensing and Airphoto Interpretation* by Thomas Avery and Graydon Berlin (1992) is an excellent book for learning how to interpret air photos.

There are many sources for air photos within the United States (Collins 1998). The Library of Congress Prints and Documents Division contains the oldest air photos, dating from ca. 1900 to the 1940s. Most vertical air photos of the United States taken for federal agencies, mainly the Department of Agriculture, between 1935 and 1945 are housed in the Cartographic Archives and Architectural Division of the National Archives. They cover approximately 80 percent of the land area of the conterminous states and are organized by county. These photos range in scale from 1:15,000 to 1:56,000. Air photo collections are also maintained by the USGS, the Forest Service, the Natural Resources Conservation Service, the National Park Service, the Tennessee Valley Authority, and the National Ocean Service. Additional air photo sources can be found in state agencies, especially departments of transportation and natural resources, and at universities, historical societies, and commercial sources.

Vertical air photos can be used in a variety of ways to study vegetation, archaeological sites, riverine systems, and soils. Avery and Berlin (1992) provide excellent information for the beginner regarding air photo interpretation of these various factors. Air photos also can be successfully compared to maps if the two scales are compatible. This can be a powerful tool, as Robin Grossinger has demonstrated in the EcoAtlas project (see chapter 17).

In some cases, the researcher may locate vertical aerial photographs (those taken with the camera directly over the scene and perpendicular to the horizon) but not know their scale. The scale can be determined by calculating the relationship between a measurement on the photo and the same measurement on a map with a known scale (Avery and Berlin 1992). This relationship can be expressed as PS = 1/(MD)(MS) ÷ PD, where PS = photo scale, MD = map distance between two points, MS = map scale, and PD = photo distance between two points. The points should be at the same elevation.

Repeat Photography

One important use of old photographs is to compare them with newer photographs taken at the same location, or to compare a time series of photographs taken at the same location. This process, which is known as repeat photography, has interested ecologists for some time as a means of comparing changes in vegetation (Clements 1905; Farrow 1915; Cooper 1928; Tansley 1946; Daubenmire 1968). Both ground-based photos and air photos can be used in this manner. For example, Ken Cole (chapter 15) uses both ground-based photo monitoring stations and vertical air photos taken in different years to document vegetation change at Indiana Dunes National Lakeshore. Tom Swetnam and his colleagues (1999, 1196) write that "repeat photography is a simple, inexpensive, and elegant tool for reconstructing past environmental changes and for monitoring future ones." Robert H. Webb, author of *Grand Canyon: A Century of Change* (1996), noted, "There is no more basic scientific technique than interpreting old photographs. We discovered changes in the Grand Canyon that could not have been determined any other way" (p. 214).

Work of this sort using ground-based photographs involves the following steps: (1) locating an existing series of historic photographs of the area being studied; (2) locating and reoccupying the original camera station; (3) matching the direction and angle of sunlight to the original in order to reproduce the proper shadows; (4) taking the photograph; (5) making field notes of weather, time of day, and condition of subject being photographed; and (6) making records of the new camera station (Rogers, Malde, and Turner 1984; Veblen and Lorenz 1991; Rhemtulla 1999).

A classic example of repeat photography can be seen in *The Changing Mile* (1966) by J. R. Hastings and R. M. Turner. Between 1960 and 1966, Hastings and Turner took repeat photos of images taken by various photographers in Arizona. Turner and Dominic Oldershaw took another set of matches between 1987 and 1996 for the second edition of the book. Other works using repeat photography include *Then and Now: A Photographic*

History of Vegetation Change in the Central Great Basin Desert (1982) by G. F. Grant; *Changes in Vegetation and Land Use in Eastern Colorado: A Photographic Study, 1904 to 1986* (1991) by W. J. McGinnies, H. L. Shantz, and W. G. McGinnies; *Arizona Then and Now: A Comprehensive Rephotographic Project* (1981) by A. A. Dutton and D. T. Bunting; and *The Colorado Front Range: A Century of Ecological Change* (1991) by T. T. Veblen and D. C. Lorenz.

Agencies such as the Forest Service have made use of repeat photography. The Santa Rita Experimental Range, originally administered by the Forest Service, has used and continues to use repeat photography to monitor the land it oversees. Evidence of its work can be found on its Web site www.ag.arizona.edu/SRER/srer.html. Forester George Gruell has been using repeat photography since the early 1970s to document changes in the land. His collaborative 1982 publication, *Seventy Years of Vegetative Change in a Managed Ponderosa Pine Forest in Western Montana*, is an excellent example of how to document changes in a plant community. It has recently been updated (Smith and Arno 1999).

While most studies using repeat photography have been qualitative, Jeanine Rhemtulla (1999), a recent graduate student at the University of Alberta, has developed a procedure using overlays, standard air photo interpretation, and Geographic Information Systems to quantify land cover types from ground-based photos taken eighty years apart at Jasper National Park.

While elegant, repeat photography suffers from the same limitations as other photographs (see above). Readers interested in repeat photography, especially in the western states, should consult the Bibiliography of *Repeat Photography for Evaluating Landscape Change* (Rogers, Malde, and Turner 1984).

Conclusion

In studying the history of the ecosystem, one can leave no map unread, no photograph unobserved. The researcher must keep in mind, however, that such documents are not all revealing and must be used in conjunction with other sources such as field notes, diaries, travel accounts, guidebooks, and census data. When consulting with a reference librarian or collections manager, researchers should know the state, county, township or town, and geographic coordinates of the site in question. The geographic coordinates can easily be located in an atlas or on a state map. When citing a map, the researcher should include the name of the map; the cartographer, surveyor, or compiler if known; the publisher of the map; the year and date of publication; the location of publication; and the edition or volume of the publication.

References

Ambrose, S. 1996. *Undaunted courage: Meriwether Lewis, Thomas Jefferson, and the opening of the American West*. New York: Simon and Schuster.

American Geographical Society of New York Map Department. 1968, 1974, 1978. *Index to maps in books and periodicals*. Boston: G.K. Hall.

Andreassen, J.C.L. 1949. *Archives in the Library of Congress*. Menasha, Wisc.

Ashby, C.M., et al. 1971. *Guide to cartographic records in the National Archives*. Washington, D.C.: National Archives and Records Service.

Avery, T.E., and G.L. Berlin. 1992. *Fundamentals of remote sensing and airphoto interpretation*. New York: Maxwell Macmillan International.

Baldwin, G. 1991. *Looking at photographs*. Malibu, Calif.: J. Paul Getty Museum.

Bancroft Library. 1975. *Catalog of manuscript and printed maps in the Bancroft Library*. Boston: G.K. Hall.

Barlett, R. 1962. *Great surveys of the American West*. Norman: University of Oklahoma Press.

Beers, H.P. 1942. A history of the U.S. topographical engineers, 1813–1863. *Military Engineer* 34:290–291.

Beresford, M. 1957, 1971. *History on the ground: Six studies in maps and landscapes*. London: Methuen.

Buisseret, D., ed. 1990. *From sea charts to satellite images*. Chicago: University of Chicago Press.

Burger, B.L. 1990. *Guide to the holdings of the Still Picture Branch of the National Archives*. Washington, D.C.: National Archives and Records Administration.

Carrington, D.K., and R.W. Stephenson, eds. 1967. *Landownership maps: A checklist of nineteenth century United States maps in the Library of Congress*. Washington, D.C.: Library of Congress.

———. 1985. *Map collections in the United States and Canada: A directory*. New York: Special Libraries Association.

Clausen, M., and H.R. Friis. 1941. *Descriptive catalog of maps published by Congress 1817–1843*. Privately published.

Clements, F.E. 1905. *Research methods in ecology*. Lincoln, Nebr.: University Publishing.

Cobb, D.A., compiler. 1990. *Guide to U.S. map resources*. Chicago: American Library Association.

Cobb, D.A., and P.B. Ives. 1983. *State atlases: An annotated bibliography*. Chicago: CPL Bibliographies.

Collins, M.R. 1998. *The aerial photo sourcebook*. Lanham, Md.: Scarecrow Press.

Conzen, M. 1984. The county landownership map in America: Its commercial development and social transformation 1814–1939. *Imago Mundi* 36:9–31.

———. 1990. North American county maps and atlases. Pages 186–211 in *From sea charts to satellite images*, ed. D. Buisseret. Chicago: University of Chicago Press.

Cooper, W.S. 1928. Seventeen years of successional change upon Isle Royale, Lake Superior. *Ecology* 9(1):1–5.

Darrah, W.C. 1976. *Powell of the Colorado*. Princeton, N.J.: Princeton University Press.

Daubenmire, R. 1968. *Plant communities: A textbook of plant synecology*. New York: Harper and Row.

Deák, G.-G. 1976. *American views: Prospects and vistas*. New York: Viking Press.

Dickinson, G.C. 1969. *Maps and air photographs*. London: Edward Arnold.

Dingus, R. 1982. *The photographic artifacts of Timothy O'Sullivan*. Albuquerque: University of New Mexico.

Dutton, A.A., and D.T. Bunting. 1981. *Arizona then and now: A comprehensive rephotographic project*. Phoenix: Ag2 Press.

Ehrenberg, R.E., compiler. 1973. *Cartographic records in the National Archives of the United States useful for urban studies*. Washington, D.C.: National Archives and Records Service.

———. 1977. Taking the Measure of the Land. *Prologue* (Fall):129–150.

———. 1987. *Scholar's guide to Washington, D.C., for cartography and remote sensory imagery*. Washington, D.C.: Smithsonian Institution Press.

Ehrenberg, R.E., et al. 1996. *Library of Congress geography and maps: An illustrated guide*. Washington, D.C.: Library of Congress.

Englander, C., and P. Hoehn, comps. N.d. Checklist of online vegetation and plant distribution maps. Palo Alto, Calif.: Stanford University Branner Library Web site: www.sul.stanford.edu/depts/branner/vegmaps.htm

Farrow, E.P. 1915. On a photographic method of recording developmental phases of vegetation. *Journal of Ecology* 3(2):121–124.

Gerlach, A.C. 1970. *The National Atlas of the United States of America*. Washington, D.C.: Department of the Interior.

Grant, G.F. 1982. *Then and now: A photographic history of vegetation change in the central Great Basin Desert*. Salt Lake City: University of Utah Press.

Greenwood, D. 1951. *Mapping*. Chicago: University of Chicago Press.

Grossinger, R., and J. Collins. N.d. *Geomorphic accuracy of the first coast survey of San Francisco Bay, 1850–1860*. Unpublished manuscript.

Hales, P.B. 1988. *William Henry Jackson and the transformation of the American landscape*. Philadelphia: Temple University Press.

Hardwick, B.S. 1977. *Science and art: The travel writings of the great surveys of the American West after the Civil War*. Ph.D. dissertation, University of Pennsylvania, Philadelphia.

Harley, J.B. 1968. The evolution of early maps: Towards a methodology. *Imago Mundi* 22:62–74.

———. 1989. Deconstructing the Map. *Cartographica* 26(2):1–20.

Harvey, P.D.A. 1980. *The history of topographical maps*. London: Thames and Hudson.

Hastings, J.R., and R.M. Turner. 1966. *The changing mile: An ecological study of vegetation change with time in the lower mile of an arid and semiarid region*. Tucson: University of Arizona Press.

Hebert, J.R., and P.E. Dempsey, compilers. 1984. *Panoramic maps of cities in the United States and Canada: A checklist of maps in the collections of the Library of Congress.* Washington, D.C.: Library of Congress.

Heiman, G. 1972. *Aerial photography: The story of aerial mapping and reconnaissance.* New York: Macmillan.

Horan, James David. 1966. *Timothy O'Sullivan, America's forgotten photographer.* Garden City, N.Y.: Doubleday.

Hoskins, W.G. 1963. *The making of the English landscape.* London: Hodder and Stoughton.

Jackson, D., ed. 1978. *Letters of the Lewis and Clark Expedition, with related documents:1783–1854.* Urbana: University of Illinois Press.

Johnson, H. 1976. *Order of the land.* New York: Oxford University Press.

Jones, E.L. 1924. The evolution of the nautical chart. *Military Engineer* 16:224–226.

Kain, R.J.P., and E. Baignet. 1992. *The cadastral map in the service of the state.* Chicago: University of Chicago Press.

Karrow Jr., R.W., ed. 1981. *Checklist of printed maps of the Middle West to 1900.* 14 volumes. Boston: G.K. Hall.

Kelsey, L.E., compiler. 1954. *List of cartographic records of the Bureau of Indian Affairs.* Washington, D.C.: National Archives and Records Service.

———. 1964. *List of cartographic records of the General Land Office.* Washington, D.C.: National Archives and Records Service.

Küchler, A.W. 1980. *International bibliography of vegetation maps.* Lawrence: University of Kansas, Publication Library Series, no. 45.

LeGear, C.E. 1950. *U.S. atlases: A list of national, state, county, city, and regional atlases in the Library of Congress.* Washington, D.C.: Library of Congress.

———. 1963. *A list of geographical atlases in the Library of Congress.* Washington, D.C.: Government Printing Office.

Lewis, M., ed. 1998. *Cartographic encounters: Perspectives on Native American mapmaking and map use.* Chicago: University of Chicago Press.

Library of Congress. 1992. *A list of geographical atlases in the Library of Congress, with bibliographical notes.* Washington, D.C.: Government Printing Office.

———. 1993. *A descriptive list of treasure maps and charts in the Library of Congress.* Indianapolis: Universal Scandinavian.

———. 1995. *Prints and photographs: An illustrated guide.* Washington, D.C.: Library of Congress.

Maddick, H., compiler. 1976. *County maps: Land ownership maps of Canada in the 19th century.* Ottawa, Canada: National Map Collection, Public Archives of Canada.

Manning, T.G. 1947. *The influence of Clarence King and John Wesley Powell on the early history of the United States Geological Survey.* Reprint, Washington, D.C.: Proceedings of the Geological Society of America.

Markham, R.P. 1980. *National lands index: An index to nationally designated lands on national topographic maps.* Greeley: University of Northern Colorado Press.

May, B., compiler. 1970. *County atlases of Canada*. Ottawa, Canada: National Map Collection, Public Archives of Canada.

McDonald, D., ed. 1990. *Directory of historical societies in the United States*. Nashville, Tenn.: American Association for State and Local History.

McGinnies, W.J., H.L. Shantz, and W.G. McGinnies. 1991. *Changes in vegetation and land use in eastern Colorado: A photographic study, 1904 to 1986*. Fort Collins, Colo.: USDA, Agricultural Research Service.

Mitchell, R.D., and P.A. Groves. 1990. *North America: The historical geography of a changing continent*. Savage, Md.: Rowman and Littlefield.

Moffat, R.M. 1985. *Map index to topographic quadrangles of the U.S., 1882–1940*. Occasional Paper No.10. Santa Cruz, Calif.: Western Association of Map Libraries.

Monmonier, M. 1996. *How to lie with maps*. Chicago: University of Chicago Press.

Mundy, B. 1996. *The mapping of New Spain: Indigenous cartography and the maps of the Relaciones Geográficas*. Chicago: University of Chicago Press.

New York Public Library. 1971. *Directory catalog of the Map Division*. Boston: G.K. Hall.

Otness, H.M. 1978. *Index to early twentieth century city plans appearing in guidebooks*. Santa Cruz, Calif.: Western Association of Map Libraries.

———. 1980. *Index to nineteenth century city plans appearing in guidebooks*. Santa Cruz, Calif.: Western Association of Map Libraries.

Pattison, W. 1976. Use of the US Public Land Survey plats and notes as descriptive Sources. *Professional Geographer* 8(January):1014.

Penford, P.A. 1974. *Maps and plans in the Public Records Office*. Volume 2: America and West Indies. London: Her Majesty's Stationery Office.

Philips, P.L. 1901. *A list of maps of America in the Library of Congress*. Washington, D.C.: Government Printing Office.

Philips, W.L., and R.L. Stuckey. 1976. *Index to plan distribution maps in North American periodicals through 1972*. Boston: G.K. Hall.

Portinaro, P., and F. Knirsch. 1987. *The cartogaphy of North America, 1500–1800*. New York: Facts on File.

Rhemtulla, J.M. 1999. *Eighty years of change: The montane vegetation of Jasper National Park*. Master's of science thesis, Department of Renewable Resources, University of Alberta.

Ristow, W.W. 1977. *Maps for an emerging nation: Commercial cartography in nineteenth century America*. Washington, D.C.: Library of Congress.

———. 1985. *American maps and mapmakers: Commercial cartography in the nineteenth century*. Detroit, Mich.: Wayne State University Press.

Ristow, W.W., and R.A. Skelton, compilers. 1977. *Nautical charts on vellum in the Library of Congress*. Washington, D.C.: Library of Congress.

Rogers, G.F., H.E. Malde, and R.M. Turner. 1984. *Bibliography of repeat photography for evaluating landscape change*. Salt Lake City: University of Utah Press.

Ruggles, R.I. 1991. *A country so interesting: The Hudson Bay Company and two centuries of mapping, 1670–1870.* Montreal: McGill-Queens University Press.

Schlereth, T. 1980. *Artifacts and the American past.* Nashville, Tenn.: Association for State and Local History.

Schmeckebier, L.F. 1904. *Catalogue and index of the Hayden, King, Powell and Wheeler Surveys,* Bulletin 222. Washington, D.C.: United States Geological Survey.

Schwartz, S.I., and R.E. Ehrenberg. 1980. *The mapping of America.* New York: Harry N. Abrams.

Shalowitz, A. 1957. 150 years of nautical charting progress. *Surveying and Mapping* 17:250.

Sheets, K.A. 1985. *American maps, 1795–1895. A guide to values: wall maps, folding maps, atlases and maps from atlases.* Ann Arbor, Mich.: K.A. Sheets.

Smith, D.L., and C.G. Crampton, eds. 1987. *The Colorado River survey.* Salt Lake City: Howe Bros.

Smith, H.N. 1947. Clarence King, John Wesley Powell, and the establishment of the United States Geological Survey. *Mississippi Valley Historical Review* 34:37–58.

Smith, H.Y., and S.F. Arno, eds. 1999. *Eighty-eight years of change in a managed ponderosa pine forest.* General Technical Report RMRS-GTR-23. Ogden, Utah: USDA, Rocky Mountain Research Station.

Swetnam, T., C. Allen, and J.L. Betancourt. 1999. Applied historical ecology: Using the past to manage the future. *Ecological Applications* 9(4):1189–1206.

Swift, M. 1998. *Historical maps of the United States.* London: PRC Publishing.

Tanner, H. 1987. *Atlas of Great Lakes Indian history.* Norman: University of Oklahoma Press.

Tansley, A.G. 1946. *Introduction to plant ecology: A guide for beginners in the study of plant communities.* London: George Allen and Unwin.

Thompson, M.M. 1981. *Maps for America,* 2nd edition. Reston, Va.: U.S. Department of the Interior.

Thrower, N.J.W. 1961. The county atlas of the United States. *Surveying and Mapping* 21:365–373.

———. 1972. *Maps and civilization: Cartography in culture and society.* Chicago: University of Chicago Press.

Tooley, R.V. 1980. *The mapping of America.* London: Holland Press Cartographica 2.

Trachenberg, A. 1989. *Reading American photographs.* Toronto: Hill and Wang.

U.S. Coast and Geodetic Survey. 1916. *Centennial celebration of the United States Coast and Geodetic Survey.* Washington, D.C.: U.S. Coast and Geodetic Survey.

U.S. Geological Survey. 1904. *The US Geological Survey: Its origin, development, organization and operation.* Washington, D.C.: U.S. Geological Survey.

Veblen, T.T., and D.C. Lorenz. 1991. *The Colorado front range: A century of ecological change.* Salt Lake City: University of Utah Press.

Warhus, M. 1997. *Another America—Native American maps and the history of our land.* New York: St. Martin Press.

Webb, R.H. 1996. *Grand Canyon, a century of change: Rephotography of the 1889–1890 Stanton expedition*. Tucson: University of Arizona Press.

Wheat, C.I. 1963. *1540–1861: Mapping the transmississippi West*, 5 volumes. San Francisco: Institute of Historical Cartography.

Wheat, J.C., and C.F. Brown. 1969. *Maps and charts published in America before 1800: A bibliography*. New Haven, Conn.: Yale University Press.

Wilford, J.N. 1981. *The mapmaker*. New York: Vintage Books.

Wilkins, T. 1988. *Clarence King: A biography*. Albuquerque: University of New Mexico Press.

William Clements Library. 1972. *Research catalog of maps of America to 1860 in the William L. Clements Library, University of Michigan*. Boston: G.K. Hall.

6

Government Land Office Surveys and Other Early Land Surveys

Gordon G. Whitney and Joseph P. DeCant

North Americans are fortunate because they can access a spatially comprehensive database—the land surveys—that provides a representation of its vegetation prior to significant European settlement. The federal government of the United States alone has over 6,500 volumes of General Land Office (GLO) survey notes and 100,000 plat maps of township surveys (Pattison 1956). Although naturalists, such as Increase Lapham, used the federal land surveys to construct maps of the vegetation of the Midwest as early as 1855 (Dorney 1983), ecologists waited until the early nineteenth century to make them part of their work (Sears 1925). Today, archaeologists, ecologists, foresters, geographers, and range managers all employ land survey records to construct a picture of the presettlement landscape. In recent years the number of theses, maps, and published papers that have used land surveys to describe the presettlement vegetation of various townships, counties, states, provinces, and geographic regions in the United States and Canada has grown dramatically, until it now totals more than several hundred references.

Threading one's way through the data and interpreting the notes contained in those surveys can, however, be a relatively daunting task. In this chapter, we provide a guide to the interpretation, the limitations, and the uses of the early colonial, crown, state, dominion, and federal (GLO) survey records.

Colonial Surveys

Although the early land surveys were not designed specifically to record vegetation, they contain a wealth of information about North America's historic plant communities and ecosystems. The earliest recorded land grants in the 1600s simply listed the acreage, the type of land (meadow, upland, woodland, etc.), and the abutting parcels of land. Typical is a 1653 grant of land in the south quarter of Concord, Massachusetts: "22 acres on pine plaine by brooke meadow: bounded on the n. with sp[ruce] swamp: with the highway on the se: on the south with Th stow: on the w. with Luke Potter." Their emphasis on the more unique forms of vegetation, such as pine plains and spruce swamps in the otherwise oak-dominated landscape of southern New England, provides clues to the nature of the early vegetation (Whitney and Davis 1986).

The need for a more accurate or precise measurement of lots, coupled with improvements in the magnetic compass, led to the metes and bounds surveys of the late seventeenth century (Stilgoe 1976). This survey technique forms the basis of many of the colonial surveys and a number of the early state land surveys. In the metes and bounds surveys, the corners of the lots are tied to natural landmarks, such as trees and geological features, or to stakes and stones. George Washington's 1750 survey notes of Frederick County, Maryland, demonstrates a typical metes and bounds survey: "beg[inning]: at a white Oak a white Hickory & white Wood Tree just on ye Mouth of Wiggan's Run & opposite to a nob of ye Mountains in Maryland & run thence S^o 25 W^t Two hund^d & twenty Eight Poles to a white hickory an Elm & Mulberry about 30 Pole from Cacapehon thence N° 75 W^t One hund^d & forty Poles to a Chesnut Oak & white Oak thence N° 25 E^t Two hund^d & Sixty Poles to a white Oak red Oak & Iron Wood on ye Riverside thence down ye several Meanders thereof S^o 67$\frac{1}{2}$ E^t 37 Po S^o 58$\frac{1}{2}$ E^t 74 Po S^o 55 E^t to ye big Con^g 210 Acres-" (Spurr 1951). (A pole or rod is equal to 16.5 feet. Four poles make up a chain of 66 feet.)

Although counts of the corner tree species provide a quantitative estimate of the composition of the early forests, this type of survey suffers from its "irregular pattern and inconsistent use of trees" (Winer 1955). Surveyors frequently attempted to make sure that the better lands were joined or included in the plot. The resulting asymmetric shapes of the lots often make it difficult to tie the corner trees to specific sites on the landscape or locations on modern maps. In addition, lot size and the use of stakes and stones versus trees as corner markers often varied from the lowlands to the uplands (Winer 1955). Larger lot sizes or the increased use of stakes and stones in the more rugged terrain of the higher elevations occasionally meant that the tree species of those areas were underrepresented in the tree counts (Whitney 1994).

General Land Office Survey

Pressures to expedite the sale of the land and to form a contiguous block of settlements that could easily be defended eventually led to the rectangular system of survey employed sporadically by several northeastern states (Clewley 1976 [1910]). The Land Ordinance of 1785 made the rectangular system of survey the norm of the federal government. Most of the federal surveys were carried out under the auspices of the General Land Office (GLO), which was established within the Treasury Department in 1812. Jamison (1958), Love (1971), and Schroeder (1981) provide good reviews of the field techniques employed by the colonial and GLO surveyors. A brief summary of the basic format of the GLO surveys and their interpretation follows.

The six-miles-square township, divided into thirty-six square-mile (640-acre) sections, formed the heart of the GLO's rectangular land survey system (figure 6.1). Townships in turn were related to two "standard" north-south and east-west coordinates or lines to which the township could be referred. Sherman (1925) drew a map showing the major east-west *baselines* and the major north-south *meridians* established across the United States. The townships were numbered Twp 1, or 2 or 3, etc., north or south of a specific baseline and Range 1, or 2 or 3, etc., east or west of a specific meridian.

Distances along the north-south and east-west township section lines were measured with a 66-foot chain composed of one hundred 7.92-inch links. Eighty chains equaled a mile, or the side of a section. Stakes were set at every mile (section corner) and half-mile (quarter-section corner) interval on the surveyed section lines (note representative description of section line, taken from surveyor's field notes, in box 6.1).

Surveyors in the first Seven Ranges in eastern Ohio set a precedent by marking the section number or the mark "$\frac{1}{4}$ S." on two or more "witness" trees adjacent to the posts (Pattison 1970 [1957]). Witness trees to which the bearing and distance from the post were noted were known as "bearing" trees (Surveyor General E. Tiffin's 1815 "Instructions for Deputy Surveyors" reprinted in White [1983]). Besides recording the names, diameters, bearings, and distances of all bearing trees (box 6.1), surveyors were required to record trees that fell on the survey line—the "line" trees. They also recorded the kinds of timber and undergrowth and the quality of the soil along each section line (Tiffin 1815 in White [1983]). Subsequent instructions required that the kind of timber be noted "in the order of which it is most prominent" (White 1983).

Information about the occurrence of prairies, swamps, groves, windfalls, and other natural phenomena were frequently mandatory in the section line descriptions (White 1983). Section line descriptions are particularly useful for the information they provide on the physiognomy of the vegetation (prairie, timber, barrens, etc.) and the occasional comments on interesting herbaceous species, such as "rosin weeds" in the prairies (Hutchison 1988). Terms and phrases such as *open plains or prairies, thinly timbered lands, barrens,* and *oak openings* were also commonly employed in the line

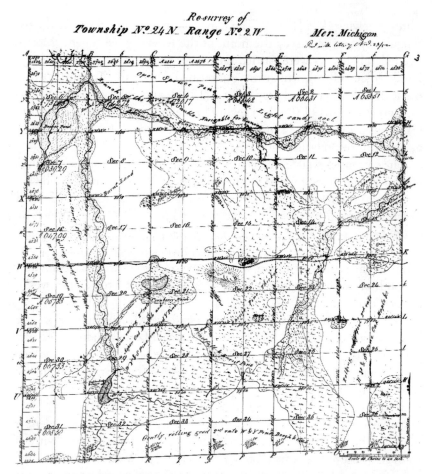

Figure 6.1. 1852 General Land Office plat map of Township 24N, Range 2W, part of present-day Roscommon County, Michigan. Sections are numbered consecutively, starting in the upper left-hand corner with section 1, moving left to right, right to left, etc., until section 36 is encountered in the lower right-hand corner. Note references to vegetation, burnt areas, and beaver ponds. Stippled areas are predominately wetlands. Courtesy of U.S. Bureau of Land Management, public information.

descriptions (Schroeder 1981; Whitney and Steiger 1985). What they meant, however, and the degree to which they reflected the surveyor's cultural perspective or geographic background remain to be determined (Schroeder 1983; Anderson 1996). Indeed, it was often difficult to separate the different communities when they merged imperceptibly into one another. As E. F. Lucas, a deputy surveyor in Iowa in 1837, noted: "In places the timber is standing thick, then is scattering, that it is hard to distinguish between timber and prairie" (Anderson 1996). John White's

Box 6.1. Sample of deputy surveyor William Burt's 1852 field notes for Township 24N, Range 2W, Michigan. Left-hand column represents distances in chains along survey line. (Copied from notes in Lands Division of Michigan's Department of Natural Resources. Items in brackets are chapter authors' explanation of notes.)

West	Random between sections 7 & 18
40.00	Set temporary post
80.54	Intersect west boundary of Township 79 links North of Post [Random survey line was run west from southeast corner of section 7. Temporary post was set at 40.00 chains or 1/2 mile (1 chain = 100 links or 66'). Line went for 80.54 chains until it hit western boundary of township, 79 links (52.1') north of previously established post on southwestern corner of section. To insure correct closure of section, a true or corrected line (see below) was established from the southwestern corner post to the southeastern corner post. The temporary posts were moved to the true line.]
N89°27'E	Corrected between section 7 & 18
	Maple 8 N33°E 27 links
	W Oak 6 S6°E 12 links

[Two bearing trees were noted at the corner post on the township's western boundary: an 8″-diameter red maple bearing N33°E 27 links (17.8') from the post and a 6″-diameter white oak bearing S6°E 12 links (7.9') from the post.]

2.00	Descend hill 40 feet S.S.E.
11.30	Y Pine 18 in diam [an 18″-diameter yellow (red) pine line tree].
30.44	DO 6 in diam. [ditto, another red pine on the line].
40.54	Set quarter section post
	S Pine 10 N25°W 43 links
	Y Pine 8 S50°E 64 links

[Two bearing trees noted at corrected quarter section post, a 10″-diameter spruce (jack) pine and an 8″-diameter yellow (red) pine.]

43.02	S Pine 8 in diam.
77.00	Enter alder bottom N.W.
78.70	Stream 25 N.W. [stream 25 links (16.5') wide, course NW].
80.50	Section Corner

Land west half gently rolling soil sandy 2^d rate [rating refers to agricultural potential of soil, i.e., 1st = good, 2^d = mediocre, 3^d = poor], East half level, Timber burnt & gone & sandy as a desert. On west half, Timber small. W [white], Y [yellow (red)], & S [spruce (jack)] Pine, Oak Aspen Maple etc.

(1994) exhaustive historical review of the use of the terms *savanna, barrens,* and *oak openings* is a good starting point for understanding the nineteenth-century terminology.

The surveyors usually concluded their field notes with a brief, one- to two-paragraph, general description of the township (box 6.2), focusing on the topography, the timber, and the soil of the region (White 1983).

Line notes formed the basis of the surveyor's township plat map. Produced at a scale of two inches per mile, plat maps are extremely useful because they frequently provide a picture of the presettlement landscape replete with occurrence of prairies, timber, wetlands, beaver ponds, windfalls, and burnt areas as well as notes on the vegetation and soils of the township (see figure 6.1 and Hutchinson [1988] for examples).

Box 6.2. Transcribed copy of deputy surveyor William Burt's general description of Township 24N, Range 2W, part of present-day Roscommon County, Michigan. (From Burt's 1852 field notes in the Lands Division of Michigan's Department of Natural Resources.)

The surface of this township is generally quite level, soil light sand. Timber W Y & S Pine Aspen Oak Beech birch etc. In the swamps Cedar Tamerack Spruce W Birch & Pine. In sections 32, 33, 34 & 35 is some good land Soil good second rate Sandy loam, Timber W & Y [Red] Pine Oak Beech & Birch. A portion of sections 23, 24, 25, & 26 is second rate land and nearly as good as the above mentioned. Sections 1, 2, 3, 4 & 5 are Spruce [Jack] Pine Plains. Very open and nearly barren. Soil light sand a few black Oak were seen. The remainder of the township, except swamps Marshes and bottoms on streams, is light sandy soil, Timber generally small and stunted Spruce Pines. A portion of sections 7, 17, & 18 is nearly barren, the timber has been burnt and left the bare sand which drifts with the wind. Following the course of the large stream in the north part of the township is Alder bottom interspersed with "patches" of blue joint grass [*Calamagrostis canadensis*], good for mowing. The above stream is navigable for canoes. In the South west part of the large marsh in sections 20 & 21 Cranberrys were seen in abundance. The Beaver pond in sections 29 & 32 is deep and looks much like a Lake. The Indians have canoes and a lodge on the NW side of the pond. The large Beaver pond in sections 6 & 7 is shallow and covers much land all the timber is dead in & near the pond. The hills in sections 21, & 22 appear to have a good soil and support a heavy growth of Pine, Oak, Beech, Aspen, etc. When on the North west side of the hills, the country to the NW can be seen for many miles. In the small pond or lake in section 22 are fish of the "Bass tribe."

Because the instructions issued by the GLO varied slightly from one region or time period to the next, it's important to consult the instructions governing your region. Most states have books or references on surveying procedures in the state, such as Sherman's (1925) *Original Ohio Land Subdivisions*. C. Albert White (1983) has complied a number of the instructions in his book A *History of the Rectangular Survey System*.

Canadian Crown Surveys and Dominion Land Surveys

Canada also experimented with various rectangular systems of survey, although much of the data pertaining to the vegetation are limited to lists of the major kinds of trees encountered along the surveyed lines. Nonetheless, the eighteenth- and nineteenth-century crown surveys of Ontario are very similar to the section line descriptions of the GLO surveys and have been used to map the vegetation and analyze species associations (Gentilcore and Donkin 1973). The later Dominion Land surveys of western Canada have township plat maps that are very similar to those of the GLO (Archibold and Wilson 1980).

Availability of Land Survey Records

Because land survey records are often difficult to locate or poorly indexed, knowing where to look for the appropriate records can be as important as knowing how to correctly interpret them. Records are generally more sporadic and difficult to locate in the case of the older colonial surveys and the surveys of the states that lack land laws. For instance, only roughly 25 percent of the original records for Tennessee and Kentucky can be located (Hutchinson 1988), and connected drafts or survey maps have been completed for only 25 to 35 percent of Pennsylvania's townships.

Start your search at the local level. In New England, this means the town records and the proprietors' records at the town clerk's office. The survey records and deeds or deed registries stored at the county courthouse are a good starting point in Kentucky, Massachusetts, New York (county clerk's office), Pennsylvania, Virginia, and West Virginia. At the state level, one should consult the appropriate State Archives (Georgia, Illinois, Maine, Michigan, New York); State Library (Connecticut, Indiana, Tennessee); Secretary of State's Office (Alabama, Iowa, Missouri, New Hampshire, Vermont); Department of Natural Resources (Michigan, Missouri, Wisconsin); State Historical Society (Iowa, Kentucky, Minnesota); State Auditor's Office (Ohio); State Land Office (Louisiana); or General Land Office (Texas). Finally, don't overlook the local historical society and university libraries as repositories for surveyors' field notes. Whitney (1994, table 2.2) provides a table showing the location of land survey records in the Northeast and the Midwest.

Since the GLO maintained parallel sets of records at its local district office and at its headquarters in Washington, D.C., multiple copies of its field notes and plats usually exist. The National Archives in Washington, D.C., has headquarter plats and field notes for Ohio, Indiana, Illinois, Missouri, Kansas, and Iowa (Bouman 1976), most of which are available on microfilm. The remaining public land records of most of the Great Plains, the Midwest, and the South were turned over to the individual states or state archives (Bouman 1976). Plats and field notes of the remaining western states are housed in the eleven western state offices of the Bureau of Land Management (Galatowitsch 1990). Where duplicate copies of the field notes exist, it is probably best to utilize the "original" field office records to avoid errors that may have occurred in the hand copying procedure in the Washington office (Almendinger 1997) or the occasional Works Progress Administration typescript copies (Anderson 1996).

Biases and Limitations

There are a number of thorough reviews as to the reliability and utility of the early land survey records (Bourdo 1956; Galatowitsch 1990; Whitney 1994; Almendinger 1997). The records have been critiqued on a number of grounds, described in the following sections.

Error and Ambiguity in Tree Identification

Surveyors typically employed common names in their identification of woody and herbaceous plant species. The wide variety of tree species noted in many of the surveys indicates that surveyors were familiar with at least the tree flora. Comparisons of the trees reported in the surveys with bearing trees still existing in the Midwest suggest a high degree of accuracy (Kilburn 1958; Whitney 1994).

The use of colloquial or common names, which varied from region to region or are no longer used, is another problem. Many investigators have prepared tables showing the equivalency of the common name and the scientific name (Shanks 1953; Anderson and Anderson 1975; Galatowitsch 1990; Almendinger 1997). Early editions of Gray's (1848, 1867) *Manual of Botany*, Darlington's (1859) *American Weeds and Useful Plants*, and other early taxonomic guides are often useful in deciphering the common names. Some species can be eliminated on the basis of their known geographic distribution today. The Spanish oak noted in the early land surveys of northwestern Pennsylvania, for instance, was not the *Quercus falcata* of the southern United States but the scarlet oak (*Q. coccinea*) of the uplands or the swamp Spanish oak (*Q. palustris*) of the lowlands. Both species resembled the Spanish oak of the South and were frequently confused with it (Darlington 1859).

Survey Contract Fraud

Surveyors occasionally submitted fictitious survey records to the GLO. Government field examiners caught most of these fakes, however, and the townships were subsequently resurveyed (Almendinger 1997). Significant differences between the descriptions of landscape features on the survey section lines and those crossed by section lines on USGS topographic maps can indicate a fraudulent survey.

Surveyor Bias in Selection of Bearing Trees

Some GLO instructions stated that the trees chosen should be those nearest the corner post; other instructions simply required that the bearing trees be adjacent to the corner post (White 1983). Although there undoubtedly was some bias with respect to the size and the species of the tree selected (Bourdo 1955, 1956), it is unlikely that they obscured real differences in the relative abundances of the species. Distance tests to assess the significance of the bias are unreliable, as they violate many statistical assumptions (Grimm 1981). The consistency of tree references by surveyors working in the same general area (Whitney 1994), the similarity of species counts in references to bearing trees and references to line trees in the same survey (Almendinger 1997), and the fact that the choice of species next to the corner post was probably limited (Bourdo 1956)—all argue for the reliability of the surveys.

Inappropriate Use of Survey Records

A number of investigators have applied Cottam's (1949) random pairs method or Cottam and Curtis's (1956) point-centered quarter method to the distance and diameter measurements of the bearing trees to develop density and basal area estimates of the presettlement woodlands. These techniques assume that the trees were randomly distributed and that the bearing trees were nearest neighbors (random pairs) or trees nearest the corner post (quarter method). However, neither assumption is justified (Bourdo 1955; Grimm 1984) since single species in mixed-species stands are likely to have a clumped distribution (Mueller-Dombois and Ellenberg 1974). Thus, most determinations using these methods result in *underestimates* of the true tree density and basal area (Bourdo 1955; Almendinger 1997; Nelson 1997).

Although they do not provide absolute measures of tree density, bearing tree distances can tell us much about the relative structure of the woods. Nelson (1997), for instance, used bearing tree distances to show that the oak forests of the Ozarks were much more open than the oak forests of the northern till plains of Missouri. Early work at the University of Wisconsin (Cottam 1949; Curtis 1959) and subsequent studies (Moran

1978; Packard 1988; Henderson and Epstein 1995; Leach and Ross 1995) have highlighted the importance of low-density oak savannas in the historic landscapes of the Midwest. Ken Cole (chapter 15) and Robert Taylor used GLO surveys to show how prairies and oak savannas in the Indiana Dunes National Lakeshore have filled in due to the suppression of fires.

Temporally Precise Nature of the Survey

Because they were completed over a limited span of time, the land surveys represent a snapshot of a dynamic, ever changing ecosystem and force us to consider just how representative they are as a true picture of the "presettlement" vegetation (Noss 1985). Changes in the climate or changes in the density of Native American populations could alter the frequency of fires, which, in turn, could affect the vegetation. Moreover, the GLO surveys of the Midwest in the nineteenth century coincided with the "Little Ice Age" and the expansion of the forests onto the prairie (Wood 1976). Only paleoecological studies, such as Grimm's (1983) study of the recent development of the Big Woods in Minnesota, can provide answers to how fixed and stable the vegetation was over the long term.

Underestimation of Smaller Features of the Landscape on Township Plat Maps

Surveyors likely missed or underestimated the areas of small features within a section, such as beaver floodings, small wetland areas, and relict stands of pines, because they only recorded what they saw along the surveyed section lines and interpolated the boundaries between the lines (Comer et al. 1995). Iversen and Risser (1987), for instance, noted that the percentage of area designated as wetlands was higher inside as opposed to outside a two-hundred-meter buffer zone running along the section lines of several Illinois counties. They applied an empirically determined calibration factor to correct for the underestimate.

Applications

Despite their limitations, land survey records have contributed significantly to our understanding of the structure of North America's presettlement ecosystems and the processes that maintained them. They have figured prominently in the restoration of a number of historic ecosystems. Schroeder (1981), for instance, studied GLO surveys from Missouri and found that they described savanna-like landscapes in that state—a bit of research that serves as a foundation for the Missouri Department of Natural Resources efforts to restore savanna ecosystems in that state's parks (McCarty 1998).

By way of summary, land surveys can be used to determine (1) species compositions of presettlement woodlands, (2) landscape-level disturbance processes, (3) site-specific determinants, (4) species associations and community classification, and (5) vegetation types for mapping purposes. We will review their use by highlighting some of our own work with the early land survey records of northwestern Pennsylvania, which were done in the late eighteenth and early nineteenth centuries, frequently in the form of rectangular lots of two hundred to four hundred acres. Although they are not as well known as the GLO studies, a number of excellent studies have used similar surveys to determine the presettlement vegetation of the states that lack public land laws in the eastern United States (Siccama 1971; Lorimer 1977; Marks, Gardescu, and Seischab 1992).

Source of Information on the Species Composition of Presettlement Ecosystems

The land surveys are unexcelled as a source of baseline information. Counts of the witness or corner trees in the land survey records have been compared with counts of trees in old-growth forest remnants to determine the degree to which the remnants approximated or were representative of the presettlement forest (Stearns 1949; Bryant 1987). Witness or corner tree counts have also been used to determine the nature of the presettlement vegetation—grassland or forested—in several riparian habitat restoration projects in the West (Galatowitsch 1990) and the East (Nelson et al. 1998). They have frequently been combined with more recent surveys to assess (1) regional changes in the composition of the forest (Whitney 1994; Habeck 1994), and (2) range trends (Christensen and Johnson 1964; Buffington and Herbal 1965; Bahre 1991) over the last one hundred to two hundred years.

Comparisons of presettlement and old-growth forest remnants in the Midwest, for example, have shown that today's remnants are an artifact of near total protection from fire. Moreover, many old-growth oak forests are undergoing a conversion to the more fire-sensitive but shade-tolerant sugar maple (Wuenscher and Valiunas 1967; Fralish et al. 1991)—a change that has suppressed the recruitment of oaks and is currently a serious management problem (Ebinger 1986).

In our study, counts of the corner trees provided an estimate of the forest composition in the three major physiographic regions of northwestern Pennsylvania (figure 6.2 and table 6.1). The spatially precise nature of the database—the corner trees—encouraged us to use a geographic information system (GIS) to analyze the data. We found that beech and sugar maple dominated the northern half of the region with outliers to the

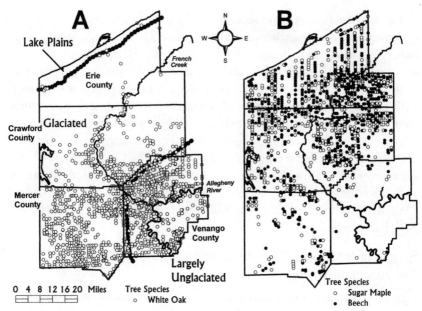

Figure 6.2. Distribution of major tree species in early land survey records of northwestern Pennsylvania. Dotted lines indicate limits of major physiographic regions of four-county study area.

south, while white oak blanketed the south with an extension up French Creek (figure 6.2). Red maple and black cherry appear to have been the major beneficiaries of human activities in northwestern Pennsylvania during the last two hundred years (table 6.1). Red maple's increase throughout much of the Northeast is probably due to fire suppression, its opportunistic response to cutting, and widespread farm abandonment (Abrams 1998).

Source of Information on Landscape-Level Disturbance Processes

Landscape-level disturbances in the form of fires and windthrows can have a profound impact on the vegetation of a forest. Surveyors' notes on the occurrence of windthrows and burnt areas on section lines have been used to determine the frequency of natural disturbances in the presettlement forest (Lorimer 1977; Canham and Loucks 1984; Whitney 1994).

In lieu of developing a spatial model of disturbance, there is a simple mathematical formula for using the GLO data to determine the areal extent and cyclical nature of disturbance events. This can be accomplished by dividing the percentage of the total length of the surveyed section lines affected by fire or windfall by the estimated number of years the disturbance is visible. Dividing 100 by the resulting percent affected

Table 6.1. Presettlement forest composition based on corner tree percentages of early surveys and current percentage composition of all trees with a 5+" diameter based on 1989 U.S. Forest Service Continuous Forest Inventory estimates for northwestern Pennsylvania.[1]

	Presettlement — 1785–1840				Current–1989
	Lake Plains	Glaciated Appalachian Plateaus	Unglaciated Appalachian Plateaus	Total	
Hemlock	7.7	3.3	3.4	3.4	6.6
White Pine[2]	2.1	1.8	2.0	1.8	0.7
Maple[3]	9.1	8.9	7.4	8.5	22.3
Sugar Maple	9.1	11.6	0.8	8.9	6.3
Birch[4]	0.7	2.6	1.8	2.4	3.3
Hickory	9.8	4.0	5.6	4.6	2.3
Chestnut	0.7	4.3	10.4	5.7	—
Dogwood	0.7	2.0	0.3	1.6	—
Beech	16.8	16.9	1.3	13.2	3.7
Ash[5]	9.1	5.0	0.5	3.9	4.9
Walnut[6]	0.7	1.0	0.7	0.9	0.2
Poplar[7]	3.5	1.1	0.1	0.9	1.9
Cucumber tree[8]	4.9	1.1	0.4	1.0	0.6
Ironwood	5.6	3.5	1.1	3.0	0.3
Aspen[9]	—	0.4	1.2	0.6	6.9
Black Cherry	—	1.8	1.8	1.7	14.2
White Oak	2.8	16.3	35.5	20.6	3.1
Scarlet Oak	—	0.2	3.9	1.0	1.3
Red Oak	0.7	0.9	5.4	2.0	4.0
Black Oak[10]	2.1	4.7	9.9	5.9	1.8
Basswood	7.7	2.1	0.6	1.8	1.5
Elm	4.9	2.1	0.1	1.7	1.5
Miscellaneous	1.4	4.3	5.7	4.6	12.6
# Trees	143	4438	1455	6036	

[1]Based on 189 USDA Forest Service Inventory and Analysis 1-acre plots sampled by means of several fixed radius and variable radius points.
[2]Includes a few *Pinus rigida* in early surveys.
[3]*Acer rubrum*, probably includes a few *A. saccharinum* in early surveys.
[4]Predominately *Betula lutea*, some *B. lenta*.
[5]*Fraxinus americana*, with a few *F. nigra* in early surveys.
[6]*Juglans cinerea* and *J. nigra*.
[7]*Liriodendron tulipifera*.
[8]*Magnolia acuminata*.
[9]*Populus tremuloides* and *P. grandidentata*.
[10]Probably includes a limited number of red oak in early surveys.

annually gives the return time or disturbance rotation period, the number of years it takes to disturb an area equal to the area in question.

Soils, topography, and the scarcity of natural firebreaks have frequently been shown to be major determinants of the more fire-prone presettlement oak- and pine-dominated forests and savannas of the East (Cowell 1995) and the Midwest (Will-Wolf and Montague 1994; Brugam and Patterson 1996; Batek et al. 1999). There is increasing interest in restoring these ecosystems. Mendelson, Aultz, and Mendelson (1992), however, have criticized what they believe is the rush to recreate savannas on sites that never supported savannas. A better understanding of vegetation–site–fire frequency relationships as exemplified by studies of the land surveys (Bowles, Hutchison, and McBride 1994) can improve the effectiveness of our restoration efforts.

Unfortunately, we could not locate any good survey field notebooks for our four-county study area in northwest Pennsylvania. Frequent references to "timber destroyed by fire" in A. Comley's (1814) field notes (Huidekoper Collection Papers, Holland Land Company, Crawford County Historical Society) of the oak forests of Clarion County, directly to the southeast of Venango County, suggest that fires were common in the southern part of our study area. We suspect that the flat, exposed ridge tops of Venango County—with their dry, coarse-textured, sandstone-derived soils—were conducive to the spread of fires and the maintenance of the fire-tolerant forests of oak and chestnut.

Source of Information on Site-Specific Determinants of Presettlement Ecosystems

Successful restoration often depends on matching species with their appropriate site requirements such as soils, surface geology, and topographic position. Land survey records are an important source of information on such vegetation-environment relationships (Tans 1976; Whitney 1982; Lange 1990; Leitner et al. 1991; Barrett et al. 1995; Nelson et al. 1998; Batek et al. 1999).

In our study, we transcribed the location and species of each corner tree (approximately six thousand) in our study area onto USGS 7.5-minute topographic maps, coded the trees, and stored the resulting data as point features within the GIS. We overlaid the corner tree map on various layers containing information on the surficial geology, topography, and soil drainage of the region. By constructing a 2 x C contingency table based on counts of the presence and absence of each species across the various categories (C) of each site factor, we were able to determine the degree to which each species was positively or negatively associated with each category. Cell frequencies of tables with a significant χ^2 or G statistic were then converted to standardized residuals (d-values of Haberman [1973] or post-hoc cell contribution values of SAS [1998]) to show whether the species occurred on that feature more or less frequently than expected by chance (Strahler 1978; Whitney 1982).

The results, which are shown in table 6.2, are distinctive. The location of the beech and sugar maple forests on the fine-textured, more calcareous, less well-drained soils of the rolling plains and plateaus of the northern half of the study area is immediately apparent, as is the location of the oak and chestnut forests on the better-drained, but nutrient-poor leached till and sandstone-derived soils of the ridge tops and upper slopes of Mercer and Venango Counties. Black cherry, elm, hemlock, and white pine were preferentially associated with the alluvial and moister outwash soils

Table 6.2. Relationship of species to specific site factors. A plus (+) indicates a significant association; i.e., species is more frequent than expected. A minus (–) indicates a significant negative association; i.e., species is less frequent than expected.

	ash	basswood	beech	birch	black cherry	black oak	chestnut	elm	hemlock	maple (red)	red oak	scarlet oak	sugar maple	walnut	white oak	white pine
Soil Drainage																
Very poorly	++	+	++			=	=	++	++						=	++
Poorly			++			−	=	++		++	−	=	++	++	=	
Somewhat poorly			++			=	−				−	=	++	=	−	=
Moderately well	=	−	=		++	++	=	=				++	=		++	
Well to excessively			=			+			++		++	++	=	+		++
Surficial Geology																
Alluvial or muck					++	=	=	++	++					++	=	++
Outwash	++	++			++	=	=	++	++		−				=	++
Calcareous till		++	++		−	=	=	++	++	=	=	=	++	−	=	−
Low-lime till			=	+	=	+	+	=	=	++	=	=			+	=
Leached, acidic till	=	=	=	=		++	++	=	−		++	++	=		−	++
Residual shale	=		=	−					++			++	=		++	
Residual sandstone	=		=			++	++	=	++	=	++	++	=	−	++	++
Topographic Position																
Floodplains	+				+	=	=	+	++					++	=	
Coves	−		=	++					++		+		=			
Lower hill slopes			−			+			++	=						
Rolling plains	+		++			−	=		−		=	=	++		=	=
Terminal moraine			−		−					+						
High plateau		+	++	++	=						=	−	++		=	
Ridge top	=	=	=	=		++	++	=	=	−	++	++	=		−	++
Upper hill slopes	−		=			++	++	−	−		++	++	=			++

Single plus (+) or minus (–) indicates p (of no association) <0.05. Double plus (++) or minus (=), p<0.01 under hypothesis of independence (SAS 1998).

of the broad floodplains and valley terraces. The more northern hemlock and birch (predominantly yellow birch) showed a preference for the cooler, moister lower slopes, coves, and ravines and the higher (1,500+ feet elevation) plateaus.

Source of Information on Species Associations and Community Classification

A better understanding of the affinities or the association of the various species is essential to community classification and the mapping of the presettlement vegetation. Typically one analyzes the co-occurrence of (1) witness trees at corner or section posts or (2) trees cited in section or boundary line descriptions, utilizing a coefficient of association like Cole's Coefficient and an appropriate clustering program (Whitney 1990; Marks, Gardescu, and Seischab 1992; Almendinger 1997). The result is a dendrogram showing the degree of association of the various species. Species near each other in the dendrogram are most likely to occur together, forming a distinctive community.

Since we lacked data on the co-occurrence of species, we analyzed the tree species' habitat similarities and dissimilarities. The habitat dissimilarities of the species were calculated for soil drainage class, topographic position, and surficial geology, utilizing Schoener's (1970) proportional dissimilarity. Values ranged from 0.0 in the case of no habitat overlap to 1.0 in the case of complete habitat overlap. We then averaged the three dissimilarity values and subjected the resulting dissimilarity matrix to McQuitty's linkage, a weighted agglomerative method of clustering (Minitab 1997). The resulting dendrogram (figure 6.3) again shows the dichotomy between the oak and chestnut forests at one end of the spectrum and the beech and sugar maple forests with their elm-ash phase at the other end of the spectrum. The dendrogram represents an objective determination of the major community types of the presettlement period, an important consideration given that some communities lack modern analogs and that some of our modern communities are artifacts of human disturbance.

Mapping Vegetation Types

Mapping the presettlement vegetation has been a major goal of a number of early land survey studies. Developed at the scale of the township, county, or state, accurate maps provide valuable baseline information on the occurrence and extent of North America's presettlement ecosystems.

Notable examples of published vegetation maps at the state level include Gordon's (1966) map of Ohio, Marschner's (1974) map of Minnesota, Finley's (1976) map of Wisconsin, and Gross and Dick-Peddie's (1979) map of New Mexico. Many of the earliest maps employed a more

Similarity

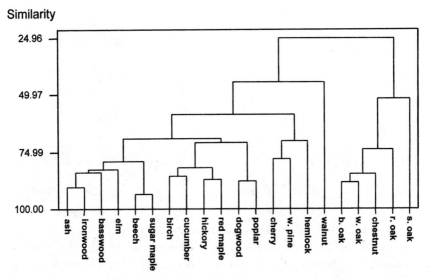

Figure 6.3. Dendrogram showing habitat similarity of major tree species in early land surveys of northwestern Pennsylvania. Note shift from species more characteristic of beech and sugar maple community on left to species more characteristic of oak and chestnut community on right.

subjective and broad-based interpretation of the major community or ecosystem types. Recent maps such as Comer and Albert's (1998) map of the "vegetation of Michigan circa 1800" represent a refinement of the earlier mapping techniques. Comer and Albert relied on an intelligent geographic information system to map the communities based on dominants and a simplified version of the Michigan Natural Feature's Inventory community classification system (Comer et al. 1995). Iowa's State Reserves Board and Department of Natural Resources funded a study that digitized vegetation data from GLO township plat maps to produce a statewide GIS map of Iowa's presettlement vegetation broken down into a few broad categories: prairie, timber, barrens, openings, etc. (Anderson 1996).

Occasionally the maps derived from land survey records disagree with the more idealized maps of the potential "natural" vegetation. For instance, as part of our study we produced a map of the presettlement vegetation of northwestern Pennsylvania based on the occurrence of the dominant and the more characteristic species of the beech–sugar maple and the oak-chestnut forest types (figure 6.4B). There are a number of differences between our map and the vegetation of the same area as shown in Küchler's (1964) map of the potential natural vegetation of the conterminous United States (Figure 6.4A). Küchler's map for Pennsylvania was apparently developed from Pennsylvania Bureau of Forestry data, which in turn was largely based on Illick and Frontz's (1928) map of

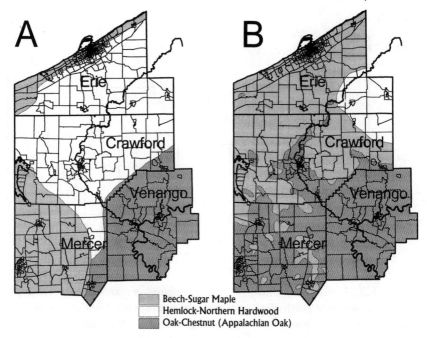

Figure 6.4. Maps of the presettlement vegetation of northwestern Pennsylvania. (A) Küchler's (1964) map of the potential natural vegetation. (B) Map based on the location of dominant and indicator species of the beech–sugar maple community (beech, sugar maple, ash, ironwood, basswood, elm), the oak–chestnut community (most oaks and chestnut), and the hemlock–northern hardwoods community (hemlock and yellow birch).

second- and third-growth northern hardwood forests in the state. We mapped most of the northern half of the region as beech–sugar maple as opposed to the hemlock–northern hardwood type shown in Küchler's map. Yellow birch and hemlock are dominants of the hemlock–northern hardwood community. With the exception of northeastern Crawford County and southeastern Erie County, however, they represented less than 15 percent of the corner trees (table 6.1). The oak-chestnut community or forest type covered a larger area in our map, penetrating the northern half of the study area along French Creek valley, an area frequented by Native Americans and their incendiary practices (Burkett and Cunningham 1997).

Maps such as these are useful in understanding historic vegetation patterns and vegetation change. The U.S. Forest Service and various state agencies in the Midwest have used GLO survey notes and plat maps to relocate various savanna and barren sites for ecosystem restoration (Stritch 1990; Cornett 1994).

Maps also provide a visual and quantitative record of change over time. John T. Curtis's (1956) classic paper showing the increasing fragmentation of the forests of Cadiz Township, Wisconsin, is probably the best-known example. MacRoberts, MacRoberts, and Stacey (1997) and Iverson et al. (1989) utilized data from the land survey records and remotely sensed data gathered today to show a 90 percent decrease in northern Louisiana's prairies and a 99.9 percent decrease in Illinois's prairies since settlement. Hansen, Kurmis, and Ness (1974), Whitney (1987), and White and Mladenoff (1994) produced township scale maps showing forest cover changes in the pine and hardwood forests of the Upper Great Lakes region over the last 150 to 200 years. Cole et al. (1998) and Silbernagel et al. (1997) recently extended the cover change studies to the multicounty and multistate level. Many of these studies have suggested that it may be difficult to recreate the original white pine– and hemlock-dominated forest ecosystems of the Great Lakes due to historic factors and human-mediated changes in the disturbance regime.

Conclusion

Researchers have expressed varying opinions about the utility of the early land survey records (Grimm 1981; Almendinger 1997). Good records are not available for all sections of North America, particular the East Coast. The records vary in terms of their accuracy and their detail. On the positive side, however, they provide a relatively unbiased picture of North America's plant communities at the time of earliest European settlement (Curtis 1959). They have given us insight into the restoration and maintenance of a number of historic ecosystems at both the local (Cottam 1949; Wilhelm 1991) and the regional levels.

Acknowledgments

We thank the respective county recorders' offices for access to the warrantee township tract survey maps of the Pennsylvania Historical and Museum Commission (Erie, Mercer, and Venango Counties) and the surveyor's docket book (Crawford County); the Erie Historical Museum for access to the Pennsylvania Population Company surveys in Crawford County; and Robert Ilisevich of the Crawford County Historical Society for letting us review the records of the Holland Land Company and the Donation Land Surveys. Terry Bensel kindly allowed us the use of Allegheny College's GIS lab facilities. Kevin Kelly and Claudine Tobalske assisted in the GIS analysis. Brenda Metheny typed the manuscript.

References

Abrams, M. 1998. The red maple paradox. *BioScience* 48: 355–364.

Almendinger, J. L. 1997. *Minnesota's bearing tree database.* Biological Report No. 56. St. Paul: Minnesota Department of Natural Resources.

Anderson, P. F. 1996. *GIS research to digitize maps of Iowa 1832–1859 vegetation from General Land Office township plat maps.* Des Moines: Iowa Department of Natural Resources.

Anderson, R. L., and M. R. Anderson. 1975. The presettlement vegetation of Williamson County, Illinois. *Castanea* 40: 345–363.

Archibold, O. W., and M. R. Wilson. 1980. The natural vegetation of Saskatchewan prior to agricultural settlement. *Canadian Journal of Botany* 58: 2031–2042.

Bahre, C. J. 1991. *A legacy of change: Historic human impact on vegetation of the Arizona borderlands.* Tucson: University of Arizona Press.

Barrett, L. R., J. Liebens, D. G. Brown, R. J. Schaetzl, P. Zuwerink, T. W. Cate, and D. S. Nolan. 1995. Relationships between soils and presettlement forests in Baraga County, Michigan. *American Midland Naturalist* 135: 264–285.

Batek, M. J., A. J. Rebertus, W. A. Schroeder, T. L. Haithcoat, E. Compas, and R. P. Guyette. 1999. Reconstruction of early nineteenth-century vegetation and fire regimes in the Missouri Ozarks. *Journal of Biogeography* 26: 397–412.

Bouman, L. J. 1976. The survey records of the General Land Office and where they can be found today. Pages 263–272 in *Proceedings of the American Congress on Surveying and Mapping,* 36th Annual Meeting, February 22–28.

Bourdo Jr., E. A. 1955. *A validation of methods used in analyzing original forest cover.* Ph.D. thesis, University of Michigan, Ann Arbor.

———. 1956. A review of the General Land Office survey and of its use in quantitative studies of former forests. *Ecology* 37: 754–768.

Bowles, M. L., M. D. Hutchison, and J. L. McBride. 1994. Landscape pattern and structure of oak savanna, woodland, and barrens in northeastern Illinois at the time of European settlement. Pages 65–73 in *Proceedings of the North American Conference on Savannas and Barrens,* eds. J. S. Fralish, R. C. Anderson, J. E. Ebinger, and R. Szafoni. Chicago, Ill.: U.S. Environmental Protection Agency, Great Lakes National Program Office.

Brugam, R. B., and M. J. Patterson. 1996. Application of geographic information system to mapping presettlement vegetation in southwestern Illinois. *Transactions of the Illinois State Academy of Science* 89: 125–141.

Bryant, W. S. 1987. Structure and composition of the old-growth forests of Hamilton County, Ohio, and environs. Pages 317–324 in *Proceedings of the Central Hardwood Forest Conference VI,* eds. R. L. Hay, F. W. Woods, and H. DeSelm. Knoxville: University of Tennessee.

Buffington, L. C., and C. H. Herbal. 1965. Vegetational changes at a semidesert grassland range from 1858 to 1963. *Ecological Monographs* 35: 139–164.

Burkett Jr., C. K., and R. K. Cunningham. 1997. The McFate site and late woodland settlement and subsistence in French Creek valley, northwestern Pennsylvania. *Bulletin of the Society for Pennsylvania Archaeology* 67: 5–20.

Canham, C. D., and O. L. Loucks. 1984. Catastrophic windthrow in the preset-tlement forests of Wisconsin. *Ecology* 65: 803–809.

Christensen, E. M., and H. B. Johnson. 1964. Presettlement vegetation and veg-etational change in three valleys in central Utah. *Brigham Young University Science Bulletin, Biological Series* 4(4): 1–16.

Clewley, F. A. 1976 (1910). *Colonial precedents of our national land system as it existed in 1800.* Reprint. Philadelphia: Porcupine Press.

Cole, K. L., M. B. Davis, F. Stearns, G. Guntenspergen, and K. Walker. 1998. Historical landcover changes in the Great Lakes region. Pages 43–50 in *Per-spectives on the land-use history of North America: A context for understanding our changing environment,* ed. T. D. Sisk. Biological Science Report USGS BRD/BSR-1998-0003. USGS, Biological Resources Division.

Comer, P. J., and D. A. Albert. 1998. *Vegetation of Michigan circa 1800: An inter-pretation of the General Land Office surveys (map).* Lansing: Michigan Depart-ment of Natural Resources, Michigan Natural Features Inventory and Wildlife Division.

Comer, P. J., D. A. Albert, H. A. Wells, B. L. Hart, J. B. Raab, D. L. Price, D. M. Kashian, R. A. Corner, and D. W. Schuen. 1995. *Michigan's native landscape, as interpreted from the General Land Office surveys 1816–1856.* Report to the U.S.E.P.A. Water Division and the Wildlife Division, Michigan Depart-ment of Natural Resources. Lansing: Michigan Natural Features Inventory.

Comley, A. 1814. Field notes of surveys for Holland Land Company. In Huidekoper Collection Papers, Holland Land Company. Meadville, Pa.: Crawford County Historical Society.

Cornett, D. R. 1994. Using General Land Office survey notes in ecosystem map-ping. *Wild Earth* 4: 58–60.

Cottam, G. 1949. The phytosociology of an oak woods in southwestern Wiscon-sin. *Ecology* 30: 271–287.

Cottam, G., and J. T. Curtis. 1956. The use of distance measures in phytosocio-logical sampling. *Ecology* 37: 451–460.

Cowell, C. M. 1995. Presettlement piedmont forests: Patterns of composition and disturbance in central Georgia. *Annals of the Association of American Geographers* 85: 65–83.

Curtis, J. T. 1956. The modification of mid-latitude grasslands and forests by man. Pages 721–736 in *Man's role in changing the face of the earth,* ed. W. L. Thomas Jr. Chicago: University of Chicago Press.

———. 1959. *Vegetation of Wisconsin: An ordination of plant communities.* Madi-son: University of Wisconsin Press.

Darlington, W. 1859. *American weeds and useful plants: Being a second and illus-trated edition of agricultural botany.* New York: Orange Judd & Company.

Dorney, C. H., and J. R. Dorney. 1989. An unusual oak savanna in northeastern Wisconsin: The effect of Indian-caused fire. *American Midland Naturalist* 122: 103–113.

Dorney, J. R. 1983. Increase A. Lapham's pioneer observations and maps of land forms and natural disturbances. *Transactions of the Wisconsin Academy of Sciences, Arts, and Letters* 71: 25–30.

Ebinger, J. 1986. Sugar maple, a management problem in Illinois forests? *Transactions of the Illinois Academy of Science* 79: 25–30.

Finley, R. W. 1976. *Original vegetation cover of Wisconsin (map)*. St. Paul, Minn.: USDA Forest Service, North Central Forest Experiment Station.

Fralish, J. S., F. B. Crooks, J. L. Chambers, and F. M. Harty. 1991. Comparison of presettlement, second-growth and old-growth forest on six site types in the Illinois Shawnee Hills. *American Midland Naturalist* 125: 294–309.

Galatowitsch, S. M. 1990. Using the original land survey notes to reconstruct presettlement landscapes in the American West. *Great Basin Naturalist* 50: 181–191.

Gentilcore, L., and K. Donkin. 1973. Land surveys of southern Ontario: An introduction and index to the field notebooks of the Ontario land surveyors 1784–1859. Cartographica monograph no. 8. Supplement no. 2 to *Canadian Cartographer*, vol. 10.

Gordon, R. B. 1966. *The natural vegetation of Ohio at the time of the earliest land surveys (map)*. Columbus: Ohio State University, Ohio Biological Survey.

Gray, A. 1848. *A manual of the botany of the northern United States, from New England to Wisconsin and south to Ohio and Pennsylvania inclusive*. Boston: James Munroe.

————.1867. *Manual of the botany of the northern United States, including the district east of the Mississippi and north of North Carolina and Tennessee*. 5th ed. New York: Ivison, Blakeman, and Taylor.

Grimm, E. C. 1981. *An ecological and paleoecological study of the vegetation in the Big Woods region of Minnesota*. Ph.D. dissertation, University of Minnesota.

————. 1983. Chronology and dynamics of vegetation change in the prairie-woodland region of southern Minnesota. *New Phytologist* 93: 311–350.

————. 1984. Fire and other factors controlling the Big Woods vegetation of Minnesota in the mid-nineteenth century. *Ecological Monographs* 54: 291–311.

Gross, F. A., and W. A. Dick-Peddie. 1979. A map of primeval vegetation in New Mexico. *Southwestern Naturalist* 24(1): 115–122.

Habeck, J. R. 1994. Using General Land Office records to assess forest succession in ponderosa pine/Douglas-fir forests in western Montana. *Northwest Science* 68: 69–78.

Haberman, S. J. 1973. The analysis of residuals in cross-classified tables. *Biometrics* 29: 205–220.

Hansen, H. L., V. Kurmis, and D. D. Ness. 1974. *The ecology of upland forest communities and implications for management in Itasca State Park, Minnesota*. Technical Bulletin No. 298, Forestry Series 16. St. Paul: University of Minnesota, Agriculturist Experiment Station.

Harrison, R. W. 1954. Public land records of the federal government. *Mississippi Valley Historical Review* 41: 277–288.

Henderson, R. A., and E. J. Epstein. 1995. Oak savannas in Wisconsin. Pages

230–232 in *Our living resources: A report to the nation on the distribution, abundance, and health of U.S. plants, animals, and ecosystems*, ed. E. T. LaRoe. Washington, D.C.: USDI, National Biological Service.

Hutchison, M. 1988. A guide to understanding, interpreting, and using the public land survey field notes in Illinois. *Natural Areas Journal* 8: 245–255.

Illick, J. S., and L. Frontz. 1928. The beech-birch-maple forest type in Pennsylvania. Bulletin No. 46. Harrisburg: Pennsylvania Department of Forests and Waters.

Iverson, L. R., R. L. Oliver, D. P. Tucker, P. G. Risser, C. D. Burnett, and R. G. Rayburn. 1989. *Forest resources of Illinois: An atlas and analysis of spatial and temporal trends.* Special Publication No. 11. Urbana-Champaign: Illinois Natural History Survey.

Iverson, L. R., and P. G. Risser. 1987. Analyzing long-term changes in vegetation with geographic information system and remotely sensed data. *Advances in Space Research* 7: 183–194.

Jamison, K. 1958. The survey of the public lands in Michigan. *Michigan History* 42: 197–214.

Kilburn, P. D. 1958. Historical development and structure of the aspen, jack pine, and oak vegetation types on sandy soils in northern lower Michigan. Ph.D. dissertation, University of Michigan, Ann Arbor.

Küchler, A. W. 1964. *The potential natural vegetation of the conterminous United States. Map and Manual.* Special Publication No. 36. New York: American Geographical Society.

Lange, K. I. 1990. *A postglacial vegetational history of Sauk County and Caledonia Township, Columbia County, south central Wisconsin.* Technical Bulletin No. 168. Madison: Wisconsin Department of Natural Resources.

Leach, M., and L. Ross, eds. 1995. *Midwest oak ecosystems recovery plan: A call to action.* Chicago: U.S. Environmental Protection Agency, Great Lakes National Program Office.

Leitner, L. A., C. P. Dunn, G. R. Guntenspergen, F. Stearns, and D. M. Sharpe. 1991. Effects of site, landscape features, and fire regime on vegetation patterns in presettlement southern Wisconsin. *Landscape Ecology* 5: 203–217.

Lorimer, C. G. 1977. The presettlement forest and natural disturbance cycle of northeastern Maine. *Ecology* 58: 139–148.

Love, J. B. 1971. *The colonial surveyor in Pennsylvania.* Ph.D. dissertation, University of Pennsylvania, Philadelphia.

MacRoberts, M. H., B. R. MacRoberts, and L. M. Stacey. 1997. Historical notes on Louisiana prairies: Size changes in a century and a half. *Phytologia* 83: 102–108.

Marks, P. L., S. Gardescu, and F. K. Seischab. 1992. *Late eighteenth century vegetation of central and western New York State on the basis of original land survey records.* Bulletin No. 484. Albany: New York State Museum, University of the State of New York.

Marschner, F. J. 1974. *The original vegetation of Minnesota* (map). St. Paul, Minn.: USDA Forest Service, North Central Forest Experiment Station.

McCarty, K. 1998. Landscape-scale restoration in Missouri savannas and wood-lands. *Restoration & Management Notes* 16(1): 22–32.

Mendelson, J., S. P. Aultz, and J. D. Mendelson. 1992. Carving up the woods: Savanna restoration in northeastern Illinois. *Restoration & Management Notes* 10(2): 127–131.

Minitab, Inc. 1997. *Minitab user's guide 2: Data analysis and quality tools*. Release 12 for Windows. State College, Penn.: Minitab.

Moran, R. C. 1978. Presettlement vegetation of Lake County, Illinois. Pages 12–18 in *Proceedings of the Fifth Midwest Prairie Conference*, eds. D. C. Glen-Lewin and R. Q. Landers. Ames: Iowa State University.

Mueller-Dombois, D., and H. Ellenberg. 1974. *Aims and methods of vegetation ecology*. New York: John Wiley.

Nelson, J. C. 1997. Presettlement vegetation patterns along the 5th principal meridian, Missouri Territory, 1815. *American Midland Naturalist* 137: 79–94.

Nelson, J. C., R. E. Sparks, L. DeHaan, and L. Robinson. 1998. Presettlement and contemporary vegetation patterns along two navigation reaches of the upper Mississippi River. Pages 51–60 in *Perspectives on the land-use history of North America: A context for understanding our changing environment*, ed. T. D. Sisk. Biological Science Report USGS BRD/BSR-1998-0003. USGS, Biological Resources Division.

Noss, R. F. 1985. On characterizing presettlement vegetation: How and why. *Natural Areas Journal* 5(1): 5–19.

Packard, S. 1988. Just a few oddball species: Restoration and the rediscovery of the tallgrass savanna. *Restoration & Management Notes* 6(1): 13–20.

Pattison, W. D. 1956. Use of the U.S. public land survey plats and notes as descriptive models. *Professional Geographer* 8(1): 10–14.

———. 1970 (1957). *Beginnings of the American rectangular land survey system, 1784–1800*. Columbus: Ohio Historical Society.

SAS. 1998. *StatView Reference*, 2nd edition. Cary, N.C.: SAS Institute.

Schoener, T. W. 1970. Non-synchronous spatial overlap of lizards in patchy habitats. *Ecology* 51: 408–418.

Schroeder, W. A. 1981. *Presettlement prairie of Missouri*. Natural History Series, Publication No. 2. Jefferson City: Missouri Department of Conservation.

Sears, P. B. 1925. The natural vegetation of Ohio. I. A map of the virgin forest. *Ohio Journal of Science* 25: 139–149.

Shanks, R. E. 1953. Forest composition and species association in the beech-maple forest region of western Ohio. *Ecology* 34: 455–466.

Sherman, C. E. 1925. *Original Ohio land subdivisions*. Columbus: Ohio Cooperative Topographic Survey.

Siccama, T. G. 1971. Presettlement and present forest vegetation in northern Vermont with special reference to Chittenden County. *American Midland Naturalist* 85: 153–172.

Silbernagel, J., J. Chen, M. R. Gale, K. S. Pregitzer, and J. Probst. 1997. *An interpretation of landscape structure from historic and present land cover data in the eastem *Upper Peninsula of Michigan*. General Technical Report NC-192. St. Paul, Minn.: USDA Forest Service, North Central Forest Experiment Station.

Spurr, S. H. 1951. George Washington, surveyor and ecological observer. *Ecology* 32: 545–549.

Stearns, F. W. 1949. Ninety years change in a northern hardwood forest in Wisconsin. *Ecology* 30: 350–358.

Stilgoe, J. 1976. Documents in landscape history. *Journal of Architectural History* 30(1): 15–18.

Strahler, A. H. 1978. Binary discriminant analysis: A new method for investigating species-environment relationships. *Ecology* 59: 108–116.

Stritch, L. R. 1990. Barrens restoration in the Cretaceous hills of Pope and Massac Counties, Illinois. Pages 31–37 in *Environmental restoration: Science and strategies for restoring the earth*, ed. J. J. Berger. Washington, D.C.: Island Press.

Tans, W. 1976. *The presettlement vegetation of Columbia County, Wisconsin, in the 1830s*. Technical Bulletin No. 90. Madison: Wisconsin Department of Natural Resources.

White, C. A. 1983. *A history of the rectangular survey system*. Washington, D.C.: U.S. Department of the Interior, Bureau of Land Management.

White, J. 1994. How the terms savanna, barrens, and oak openings were used in early Illinois. Pages 25–63 in *Proceedings of the North American Conference on Barrens and Savannas*, eds. J. S. Fralish, R. C. Anderson, J. B. Ebinger, and R. Szafoni. Chicago: U.S. Environmental Protection Agency, Great Lakes National Program Office.

White, M. A., and D. J. Mladenoff. 1994. Old-growth forest landscape transitions from pre-European settlement to present. *Landscape Ecology* 9: 191–205.

Whitney, G. G. 1982. Vegetation-site relationships in the presettlement forests of northeastern Ohio. *Botanical Gazette* 143: 225–237.

———. 1987. An ecological history of the Great Lakes forest of Michigan. *Journal of Ecology* 75: 667–684.

———. 1990. The history and status of the hemlock-hardwood forests of the Allegheny Plateau. *Journal of Ecology* 78: 443–458.

———. 1994. *From coastal wilderness to fruited plain: A history of environmental change in temperate North America from 1500 to the present*. Cambridge, England: Cambridge University Press.

Whitney, G. G., and W. C. Davis. 1986. From primitive woods to cultivated woodlots: Thoreau and the forest history of Concord, Massachusetts. *Journal of Forest History* 30: 70–81.

Whitney, G. G., and J. R. Steiger. 1985. Site-factor determinants of the presettlement prairie-forest border areas of north-central Ohio. *Botanical Gazette* 146: 421–430.

Wilhelm, G. 1991. Implications of changes in floristic composition of the Morton Arboretum's East Woods. Pages 31–54 in *Proceedings of the oak woods management workshop*, eds. G. V. Burger, J. E. Ebinger, and G. S. Wilhelm. Charleston: Eastern Illinois University.

Will-Wolf, S., and T. C. Montague. 1994. Landscape and environmental con-
straints on the distribution of presettlement savannas and prairies in south-
ern Wisconsin. Pages 97–101 in *Proceedings of the North American
Conference on Barrens and Savannas*, eds. J. S. Fralish, R. C. Anderson, J. E.
Ebinger, and R. Szafoni. Chicago, Ill.: U.S. Environmental Protection
Agency, Great Lakes National Program Office.

Winer, H. 1955. *History of the Great Mountain forest, Litchfield County, Connecticut*. Ph.D. dissertation, Yale University, New Haven, Connecticut.

Wood, W. R. 1976. Vegetation reconstruction and climatic episodes. *American
Antiquity* 41: 206–208.

Wuenscher, J. E., and A. Valiunas. 1967. Presettlement forest composition of the
River Hills region of Missouri. *American Midland Naturalist* 78: 487–495.

II

Biological Evidence

OBSERVATION is one of the cornerstones of any scientific endeavor, so it seems appropriate that the biological evidence section begins with a chapter about how to infer the history of a wooded site through careful inspection and attention to detail. P. L. Marks and Sana Gardescu are plant ecologists who see history in the way a tree has formed, in dead trees and logs, and in the presence or absence of understory vegetation. They "read the landscape." The method of inferring the history of a forest from observational field evidence that they describe in chapter 7, while qualitative, is, nevertheless, a vital first step in many restoration projects. The information from such work can also be used effectively to initiate and support more detailed, quantitative studies.

Dendrochronology or tree-ring dating is arguably one of the most widely recognized and versatile techniques for studying past environmental conditions. Working in the lineage of A. E. Douglas, the founder of modern dendrochronology, Kurt Kipfmueller and Thomas Swetnam (chapter 8) discuss the principles, practice, applications, and limitations of their science. As they explain, there is more to this work than simply counting tree rings.

Owen Davis describes another versatile technique—the analysis of pollen and related microfossils—in chapter 9. Like dendrochronology, palynology is a powerful means of studying past ecosystems, providing evidence over long periods of time and at a variety of scales. In addition to describing the basics of palynological investigation, Davis provides several examples of how palynology has been used to reconstruct historic vegetation.

The study of packrat middens is a relatively new way of learning about past environments in arid regions and one that complements other studies, such as palynology and dendrochronology. In chapter 10, David Rhode provides an overview of the work being done in that field, the strengths and weaknesses of the technique, and an outline of midden collection and analysis methods.

Historic animal assemblages is the subject of chapter 11, in which Michael Morrison wrestles with the problem of how to find good historical data about beings that are much more mobile than plants. His approach is multifaceted and includes discussions of the work done by zooarchaeologists and paleontologists in addition to advice about how to use museum collections and databases, literature, and relict fauna to determine historic animal assemblages. He also provides the reader with valuable guidelines for working with incomplete data sets.

In chapter 12, Stanley Trimble provides a myriad of documentary and database sources for the restorationist who needs historic information about factors such as soils, geomorphology, and hydrology.

Finally, in chapter 13, Glen Fredlund discusses another kind of micro-fossil—opal phytoliths, the "jewels of the plant world"—and its use in reconstructing historic ecosystems, especially those associated with grass-lands. Like several other contributors, he is quick to point out the limitations of the approach under discussion, which is, nevertheless quite powerful when properly applied.

7

Inferring Forest Stand History from Observational Field Evidence

P. L. Marks and Sana Gardescu

There are many reasons for wanting to know the history of a forest. For a restoration ecologist, learning how a current forest stand—its vegetation, structure, and species composition—came into being is a fundamental issue. With that knowledge and a familiarity with the local flora, a restorationist can begin to plan how to use environmental conditions, successional pathways, disturbance, or plantings to return a forest to a historic or other desired state. Awareness of a site's history is also important for anyone interested in understanding the relationship between vegetation and environment, since variations in stand history can lead to spurious correlations and misinterpretations of the effects of current conditions. Information on species-site relationships is fundamental both for basic ecology and for restoration efforts (Aber 1987), while retrospective studies can often provide important insights into ecological processes (Foster, Orwig, and McLachlan 1996).

This chapter focuses on ways that site history can be inferred from evidence that can be directly observed from a careful search through a piece of forest. In the following section of this chapter, we describe the kinds of field evidence that an experienced naturalist might use. In the subsequent section, we provide examples that demonstrate how the various types of field observations can be used to differentiate forest stands with different histories, such as old-growth forest vs. second-growth logged stands, or secondary post-agricultural forests vs. primary forest. We use the term *secondary forest* for stands that developed on land that was once cleared for farming, in contrast to *primary forests*, which were never cleared for agriculture but are not necessarily undisturbed *old growth*. Little old-growth forest is left in the United States because most forest stands have been logged or cleared for farming or urbanization. Since logged stands are also commonly referred to as "secondary" forest, to avoid confusion we will use *post-agricultural* for forest stands that developed on former farm fields.

Observations of Field Evidence

There are a variety of field clues that, if properly interpreted, reveal significant aspects of a forest's history (table 7.1). These include features of the trees and understory plants in the stand, microtopography, and the stand edges. Because of their longevity, trees preserve a record of previous growing conditions, both while they are living and, in many cases, long after they die. How far back in time one can extrapolate depends on the type of evidence as well as the species and climate, but most field observations reflect primarily the most recent hundred years—or in the case of a young post-agricultural stand, a few to several decades. Often the signs are indistinct, or have more than one possible interpretation, so it is important to observe more than one kind of feature and, where possible, combine field evidence with other types of historical information.

Stand Edges

Where a forest stand of interest is surrounded by, or adjacent to, other forest, the shape and edges of the stand can often be revealing. An abrupt shift in stand structure or species composition that does not correspond to changes in environment, such as differences in drainage or slope, suggests that the history of the stand differs from that of the surrounding forest. Straight boundaries or rectilinear stands found within continuous forest

Table 7.1. Types of observations that can be used to infer forest history

Features	Examples	Interpretations
Stand edges	• straight (rectilinear) discontinuities	farmed or logged on one side or both
	• line of low-branched trees in forest	former hedgerow between fields
Stand composition	• old hawthorns and apple trees	former pasture
	• maples (fire-sensitive) absent	burned
Tree form	• branchy, spreading, or "wolf" trees	former field or savanna
Dead or damaged trees	• abundant cut stumps	logged
	• tip-ups	windthrow
	• fire scars	burned
Understory plants	• weedy species present	former old field or pasture
	• sparse understory vegetation	possible grazing or browsing
Microtopography	• windthrow pits and mounds	never plowed

usually indicate human activity rather than natural disturbance—one side or the other, or both, may have been farmed or logged (Russell 1997). Former agricultural field edges are sometimes visible as wire fencing or stone walls within what is now forest. Evidence that a former edge, now embedded in forest, was once adjacent to an open field can be seen in the asymmetric form of the trees along the old edge (figure 7.1).

Property boundaries (frequently indicated by posted signs) within continuous forest are also important to note because the stands on either side are likely to have different management histories. Current or former landowners may have helpful information about a stand's history and past management (see chapter 4). Former fields and hedgerows, clear-cuts, and large natural-disturbance openings are often evident in old aerial photographs (see chapter 5). Such visual information can be useful for determining the boundaries of the current stand.

Stand Structure and Composition

The forest trees within a stand—their forms, sizes, and species composition—reveal much about its history. Trees develop specific shapes depending on whether they grow in the interior of a forest, along an edge,

Figure 7.1. A well-defined woodland edge (above the arrow) between two stands of different ages. The younger, post-agricultural forest is to the left, evident in the profusion of spreading branches on the left-hand side of the trees along the former open edge.

or in the open (Egler 1977; Oliver and Larson 1996). Low, spreading branches on trees that are now surrounded by forest are diagnostic of stands that originated on abandoned farm fields, large forest clearings, or former savannas. However, branchy, open-grown trees can also be found in primary forest, on soils where a dense canopy does not develop, such as oak woodlands on dry ridges, so it is important to be familiar with the local natural variation in forest types. Open-grown forms are not seen if the regenerating saplings or residual stems were at high density, which is normally the case in stands that developed after windthrow or logging.

Stand size and age structure can be a useful diagnostic tool. Large-diameter trees are characteristic of old-growth stands, although not all old forests have large trees, depending on site conditions (Oliver and Larson 1996). Uniformity in diameter of the canopy trees often indicates that the stand initiated after a large disturbance, such as logging or a windstorm. Alternatively, the absence of one or more size classes from a full range of tree diameters suggests a failure in tree establishment for a period of time, possibly due to fires or grazing.

There are several caveats to using stand structure to infer history. One needs to know what the normal structure is for that forest type in order to recognize departures, which can be subtle (Veblen 1992). In some cases it may be necessary to sample the stand to determine the size distribution and composition (Bonham 1989). Since it is the age structure that shows the pattern of stand development, and because stem diameters and tree heights are frequently not reliable indicators of relative ages (Cooper 1960; Veblen 1992; Oliver and Larson 1996), it is better to age the trees using annual tree rings whenever possible (see chapter 8). Even so, age structure can sometimes give a false impression. For instance, an empty age class can be due to high sapling mortality rather than a period of no seedling establishment (Johnson, Miyanishi, and Kleb 1994).

Tree species composition is often a good indicator of important aspects of a stand's past. Knowledge of the natural variations in forest type within the local landscape is key, because departures from expectation are a clue that something has altered the pattern. For instance, a stand of red maple (Acer rubrum) and white ash (Fraxinus americana) in a region where nearby forests on similar upland soils are mixtures of American beech (Fagus grandifolia) and sugar maple (Acer saccharum) is likely to have had a different history. In central New York, dominance by red maple and white ash is indicative of post-agricultural forest (Nyland, Zipperer, and Hill 1986; Mohler 1991). Certain species are associated with particular site histories, for example, jack pine (Pinus banksiana) with fire, or apple and hawthorn (Malus and Crataegus spp.) with pastures. Others, such as aspen and birch (Populus and Betula spp.), can be found in a variety of clearings, including old fields, clear-cuts, and stands opened up by fire or wind. The absence of a species can also be informative. For example, fire-sensitive species such as eastern hemlock (*Tsuga canadensis*) are missing in forests that have burned, and beech trees are not found in the canopy of young post-agricultural stands. The associations between particular indicator species, habitat, and site history vary across regions, so it is important to know the local vegetation. For example, tulip poplar (*Liriodendron tulipifera*), a mesophytic forest species, is not an old-field invader toward the northern end of its range in New York but is common in many post-agricultural old-field stands in some regions farther south.

Dead and Damaged Trees

Another stand feature that can reflect forest history is the presence and abundance of dead timber—standing dead trunks, stumps, and downed logs. Dead trees can provide useful information, especially if they are large, numerous, or of a different species or growth form than the current live canopy trees. For example, large, branchy, dead white pines (*Pinus strobus*) standing in a forest now overgrown by hardwoods are often diagnostic of a former old field (figure 7.2). Cut or charred stumps indicate previous logging or fire, while snaps and tip-ups indicate windthrow. The evidence at times is confusing, as fires may occur following large blow-downs or in logging slash, and salvage logging may have been done in stands that were damaged by fire, wind, or disease.

Disturbances can be dated by the condition of the dead timber, the ages of stems that established after the disturbance, and the growth responses of older trees. Often a combination of methods is best for determining such dates (Dynesius and Jonsson 1991). Inferring the previous stand species and size composition from stumps and downed logs is not straightforward, since species vary in decay rates and many stems may no longer be evident. Determining ages of the live trees requires more than basic field observation because, except for some pines that have annual branch whorls, most stems must be either cored or cut, to count the annual growth rings. The ages of saplings and trees that established on rotting logs and stumps, or on windthrow pits and mounds, provide a minimum age estimate of the disturbance (Dynesius and Jonsson 1991). A more exact determination can be made by examining the annual rings of any older, residual saplings or trees. The date of disturbance will be seen as a sharp increase in growth in response to the canopy opening.

The disturbance date can also be determined from cross-dating any damage scars, such as fire-charred bark or windthrow fell scars, on older trees in the patch that survived the event. Using tree-ring dating, fire scars on live and dead trees have been used to determine the fire history

Figure 7.2. A standing dead white pine in a forest that developed on an abandoned agricultural field. The branchiness of the pine reveals its open-grown origin.

of a stand and map the areas affected by each burn (Heinselman 1973; Agee 1993; see chapter 8). It is important to verify that the scars were caused by fire, since similar scars can be produced by disease, sunscald, insects, bears or other animals, or logging damage (Agee 1993; Oliver and Larson 1996; Wessels 1997). Historical records and aerial photographs, or analysis of charcoal in lake sediments, can be important sources of corroboration of the times and locations of fires, in combination with fire-scar dating of the trees (Heinselman 1973; Clark 1990).

Dead trees, logs, and stumps can sometimes provide evidence of the presence of a species long after it has been lost from a stand due to succession, logging, or disease, especially trees with decay-resistant wood. Examples include red cedar (*Juniperus virginiana*) in old-field forests, and stumps of white or longleaf pine (*Pinus strobus* or *P. palustris*) in logged stands. American chestnut (*Castanea dentata*) is an interesting special case. Once an important species in the oak-chestnut forests and some of the more mesophytic forests of the eastern United States (Braun 1950), chestnut was practically eliminated by a fungal blight in the early 1900s. Because the wood is very rot-resistant, one can still determine the distribution of chestnut in different kinds of forests and in some cases reconstruct its original abundance and size distribution in a stand. Even where chestnut was salvage-logged, the stumps remain as evidence.

Understory Vegetation

The herbs, shrubs, and tree seedlings in a stand may also offer clues to site history. Stands that developed on abandoned plowed fields typically have patches of remnant, open-field herbs and shrubs that are able to linger on in the developing forest stand; other species are good indicators of former pasture (Stover and Marks 1998). In the same way, patches of cultivated plants, such as vinca, lilac, and daylily, leave lasting local legacies that mark abandoned home sites and schoolhouses. Other species, such as deerbrush (*Ceanothus integerrimus*), are evidence that the site was burned. In some cases a depauperate ground layer may be the result of past disturbances, such as fire or cattle grazing, but it can also be due to current environmental factors such as poor soils, excessive shade, or ongoing deer browsing.

The Forest Floor

Several clues to stand history can be found by examining the ground surface and soil. Variations in microtopography provide evidence of windthrow, as the uprooting of trees produces pits and mounds several feet or more across that remain for many centuries, long after the logs have rotted away (Schaetzl et al. 1990). Blowdowns of large, deeply rooted trees produce especially noticeable pits and mounds. Uprooting is generally more common in stands on slopes or where trees are shallowly rooted, such as on wet sites or soils with a fragipan (Schaetzl et al. 1989). Since plowing smoothes the ground, the presence of pit and mound microtopography is evidence that the area was not plowed. The converse is not true, however, as not all stands that were never plowed have pits and mounds. This is especially true on sites with sandy soils. Examination of the pits and mounds, especially if the downed logs remain, can indicate the direction of windthrow. Also, the state of deterioration of the pits and mounds, and sizes of trees growing on them, can indicate whether they were formed at one time in a major disturbance or have accumulated over centuries.

Within the soil, a history of plowing can be inferred from a uniform plow layer (Ap horizon), while charred wood indicates former fire. Examination of soils requires some expertise; for example, to differentiate plow zones from other natural soil horizons or to interpret and date charcoal fragments (which can be confused with wood decayed by black fungi (Wessels 1997; see chapter 9). In addition, seeds in the soil can be sieved out to identify species in the seedbank. The presence of numerous seeds of field weeds or early successional woody plants would indicate a former large natural-disturbance opening, clear-cut, or agricultural field (Livingston and Allessio 1968; Marks 1974). A number of fire-adapted species also produce a dormant seedbank (Agee 1993). However, the process of collecting, sorting, and germinating seed samples to identify species is labor intensive.

Interpretations and Applications

In this section we expand on the features introduced in the previous section—stand edges, tree species composition and stand structure, dead timber, understory plants, and the forest floor—to discuss how these can be used to determine the disturbance or land-use history of a stand. Four areas are covered: disturbance openings in primary forest, logged stands, post-agricultural secondary forest, and stands that developed on former pastures.

Reconstructing Stand Disturbance History in Primary Forest

A well-established tenet of forest ecology holds that canopy-opening disturbances are important for tree recruitment and forest composition, even in old-growth stands (Pickett and White 1985; Lorimer and Frelich 1994; Oliver and Larson 1996). Canopy openings can be caused by many agents of natural disturbance, including wind, fire, ice storms, flooding, disease, and insect defoliation (Stearns 1949; Spurr and Barnes 1980; Pickett and White 1985). A restorationist interested in determining the extent to which a stand is the product of natural disturbance events or an artifact of human impacts needs to recognize that there is a spectrum of possible stand age structures and species compositions, depending on the disturbance regime. At one extreme are forests of shade-intolerant species with cohort age structures, created by large-scale windstorms or stand-renewing fires. At the other end of the spectrum would be the classic old-growth stands of trees of multiple sizes and ages resulting from centuries of recruitment in small gaps. While each stand can have a particular disturbance history, the kind of disturbance regime that is likely varies regionally. Lightning fires are common across parts of the southern and northern United States, hurricanes are more important near the coast, and small windthrows are the primary natural disturbance in the central regions of the eastern forest (Runkle 1990; Oliver and Larson 1996).

The edges of large-scale natural disturbances vary from sharp to diffuse (Foster, Knight, and Franklin 1998), but except where they run into roads or firebreaks, they seldom produce straight stand edges. In cases where the boundary is relatively sharp, the trees surrounding a former disturbance opening show asymmetric growth. Within the opening, because of the dense thickets that develop, the trees generally do not have an open-grown form.

A number of shade-intolerant species can provide evidence of former large openings in a forest caused by natural disturbance or people. Which trees invade varies regionally. A few examples of species that indicate large canopy openings are yellow and paper birch (*Betula alleghaniensis* and *B. papyrifera*) and tulip poplar (*Liriodendron tulipifera*) in eastern North America; Douglas-fir (*Pseudotsuga menziesii*) and lodgepole pine (*Pinus contorta*) in the West; and loblolly pine (*Pinus taeda*) in the South. Understory species that establish following large disturbances include bracken fern (*Pteridium aquilinum*), fireweed (*Epilobium angustifolium*), and various brambles (*Rubus* spp.). How long the early successional species persist as evidence of the opening varies. Many of the fast-growing trees are short-lived and are replaced by other species within a few decades. Others survive for centuries.

Size structure of trees in a stand can sometimes reflect the disturbance history, but aging stems is a better way to locate and date cohort patches that established in large openings. Tree-ring analysis has been used to document pulsed recruitment histories in a number of forest types, including southwestern ponderosa pine (*Pinus ponderosa*) forest where fire was the primary disturbance (Cooper 1960), and a northeastern stand of beech and hemlock with patches of tulip poplar that established after windstorms (Marks, Gardescu, and Hitzhusen 1999). Even in all-aged stands of shade-tolerant species, peaks in the age distributions suggest occasional episodes of enhanced recruitment, as in Appalachian mixed-mesophytic old growth (Lorimer 1980). Tree-ring growth-rate differences between trees in the open and trees under a canopy have been used to deduce stand history. The stem growth (tree-ring width of the first ten years) and basal branches (diameter) of open-grown vs. partially shaded white pines, when compared to the early growth history of trees in two old-growth stands, showed that the pines at one site had originated in small forest gaps, whereas the pines at the other had established in open conditions (Lutz and McComb 1935).

Dead trees provide evidence of stand disturbances, from single-tree windthrows to large-scale lightning fires or hurricanes. Old-growth stands with a long history of small gaps accumulate large amounts of dead and decaying wood, both on the ground and standing dead (Spurr and Barnes 1980; Martin 1992). In contrast, stands burned by crown fires have less coarse woody debris on the ground due to consumption in hot fires, and can have conspicuous charred snags. Major windstorms leave large numbers of broken and downed trees but with less variation in stages of decay than in small-gap old growth. For thunderstorm down-bursts or hurricanes, the orientation of trunks in a blowdown can indicate the wind direction; in contrast, tornadoes scatter trunks spirally (Foster, Orwig, and McLachlan 1996; Oliver and Larson 1996; Wessels 1997).

In places where a former regime of frequent or intense disturbances has been suppressed or altered, it is sometimes possible to discern evidence of a shift in species composition. The changes can include both invasion by species that were not able to establish previously, such as fire-sensitive or flood-intolerant trees following fire suppression or flood control, and losses of species that required the disturbance to maintain their populations. Whether the invading species are seen as a sapling layer or sub-canopy trees will depend on the time since the disturbance regime was altered. Release from flooding may allow seedling establishment in many more years, producing a noticeable increase in understory lushness. Wetland drainage frequently leads to changes in stand dominants and losses of such species as black ash (*Fraxinus nigra*) and silver maple (*Acer saccharinum*) (Whitney 1994). Stream channelization also affects species composition (Hupp 1992). In forests with a former history of periodic surface fires, stands with a diverse, grassy understory can decrease in herb cover as the pine litter builds up and the canopy shade increases (Cooper 1960, 1961; Sackett, Haase, Harrington 1994). Some herbaceous species that require open patches may disappear from unburned areas, such as *Eryngium cuneifolium* in Florida scrub (Menges and Kimmich 1996). Where enough time has elapsed for fire-intolerant trees to become dominant, the flammability characteristics of the stand can change such that subsequent fires become unlikely (Streng and Harcombe 1982). The particular responses to fire or flood suppression vary widely, depending on the previous disturbance regime, such as surface vs. crown fire, as well as species, region, and environmental factors. Correctly interpreting the field signs requires detailed knowledge of the local species and disturbance patterns, and in most cases where fire or flooding frequency has been altered, sources such as management records would be important for corroboration.

Interpreting Logged Forests

The vast majority of forests in North America have a history of at least some cutting. Signs of recent or intensive logging are easily observed, but a single moderate harvest a century ago can be difficult to detect. Stumps with level tops clearly indicate tree cutting. Stumps can provide evidence of the species that were present, their diameters, abundance, and spatial distribution. Sometimes a common, economically valuable tree species can be eliminated from a stand by cutting, but the legacy of the species persists for a time as stumps. Wood and bark structure can be used to iden-tify stumps to genus and often to species (Panshin and de Zeeuw 1970), and some trees (such as white pine and chestnut) have distinctive stumps even after many decades of decay (Wessels 1997).

In cases where stands that regrew after logging are surrounded by other forest, evidence of the logging may be clearest at the edges, indicated by a change in size or species composition. Logging operations that track property boundaries often have straight edges. A clear-cut will have a much more noticeable edge and stronger differences in stand structure across that boundary than a thinning cut. The size of the clear-cut affects tree species composition and stand structure (Dale, Smith, and Pearcy 1995). Fast-growing shade-intolerant trees, with a single cohort age structure, are abundant in former clear-cuts, but that is not diagnostic, as the same occurs following large natural disturbances. Stands with a his-tory of repeated cutting can even approach the species composition and range of stem sizes of natural old growth (Oliver and Larson 1996).

If it is important to know the date of the harvest (if not available from timber records or conversation with landowners), then determining the sizes, ages, and release dates of trees in and around the logged area can provide a good estimate. Variations in stump decay rates among species can be used to estimate the time of logging; for instance, maple and birch rot quickly, while large white pine stumps last a hundred years or more. The tops of the trees, which are normally left behind by loggers, can also provide a clue because fine twigs rot away within a few years.

Determining that a stand was cut, and how much timber was removed, can be difficult for stands logged some time in the past. The absence of large trees (greater than three feet in diameter) can indicate cutting, but stands on poor soils also lack large trees, and natural disturbances such as blowdowns and crown fires can eliminate large stems. Logged stands do not necessarily have less dead timber than uncut forests, because of vari-ations in decay rate and other factors (Oliver and Larson 1996), although in general there tends to be much more of both standing dead and downed logs in old growth.

Some tree species will stump sprout when cut, producing a distinctive, persistent stand structure with clusters of multiple stems (Wendel 1975; Whitney 1994; Russell 1997). Red oak (Quercus rubra) and red maple often sprout after cutting. As stems damaged by wind, fire, or browsing can also form sprout clumps, it is important to look for other clues to verify that the stand was logged. It should be noted that some species, such as bass-wood (Tilia americana), routinely form clumps without being damaged.

Ground-layer plants are not often helpful in distinguishing forests that were logged. Clear-cutting in some forests may reduce the species richness of forest-interior herb species (Duffy and Meier 1992; Duffy 1993; Bratton 1994), but evidence for such a decline is controversial (Johnson, Ford, and Hale 1993; Elliott and Loftis 1993) and some forest understory species respond positively to canopy removal (Hughes and Fahey 1991). There are several fast-growing open-habitat herbs, such as pokeweed (*Phytolacca americana*) and fireweed, that typically become common after major timber harvests, but they can decline or disappear within decades, making their diagnostic value limited.

Forests on Land That Was Once Plowed

In many parts of the eastern United States, post-agricultural forests are abundant today, often more so than stands that were never cleared and plowed (Hart 1968; Turner and Ruscher 1988; Foster 1992; Smith, Marks, and Gardescu 1993). This is especially true in regions with less productive soils where agriculture once thrived but has now declined. A restorationist or forest ecologist needs to be able to distinguish post-agricultural stands because they differ markedly from primary forest in species composition of the trees, the understory plants, and potentially the animals. The effects of an agricultural history are extremely persistent, both for plants (Nyland, Zipperer, and Hill 1986; Whitney and Foster 1988) and for other species, such as worms (Kalisz and Dotson 1989).

Where a post-agricultural stand is now adjacent to or surrounded by older forest, the old edges provide evidence of the former field. Farm fields are normally rectilinear in outline, and these straight edges, with distinct changes in tree structure, species composition, and understory at the boundary, are typical of post-agricultural stands. (Exceptions occur where the original forest was cleared up to the rim of a gorge or the base of a steep slope, leaving curved edges.) Where the fields were adjacent to forest, the old trees along the former edge are typically asymmetrical in shape, with low, often large-diameter, spreading branches on the side that once faced the open field. Conversely, the shaded, forest sides of the trunks have few branches except in the overstory crown (see figure 7.1). Sometimes the low, spreading branches may be dead or remain only as huge, protruding branch stubs, but the asymmetrical growth form is still clear. Some tree trunks in former edges lean noticeably in the direction of what was once open field. A row of old trees that are more upright and symmetrical, with large, low branches on both sides, is evidence of a former hedgerow between open fields, which are now post-agricultural forest stands (figure 7.3). Old hedgerows can also be recognized by the frequent bird-dispersed trees and shrubs, such as cherries (*Prunus* spp.).

Figure 7.3. A former hedgerow that marks the edge between two post-agricultural stands. Note the spreading branches on both sides of the old hedgerow, which runs from the left foreground to the center rear of the photograph.

Other indicators of former field edges, in stands that now appear to be continuous forest, are old wire fences, stone walls, and rock piles. Stones were moved to the edge of a field in the early years of farming to facilitate plowing, and, given the difficulty in moving heavy rocks, they generally indicate that the site was plowed and not just pastured.

The overstory trees in a post-agricultural stand generally show a structural uniformity because they invaded the abandoned field over a limited period, often less than ten to twenty years. The older trees frequently have a branchy and spreading growth form. The degree of branchiness of the canopy trees is an excellent diagnostic characteristic because normally it is so unambiguous, especially for white pine. However, the absence of low branches on old trees in a stand does not rule out the possibility of post-agricultural forest. A branchy growth form may be missing if dense thickets of saplings developed in the abandoned field, or simply because some old-field trees, such as loblolly pine, do not retain the lower branches.

In some post-agricultural forests there are scattered, distinctively large and branchy trees that contrast with the many smaller, younger stems. This occurs where some trees were already present within the field when it was abandoned. When such a site reverts to forest, the huge,

Figure 7.4. A large, open-grown tree in a post-agricultural stand.

open-grown "wolf" trees stand out from the matrix of smaller stems (figure 7.4). It is important not to base stand age estimates on these older wolf trees.

Characteristic tree species of young post-agricultural forests include a number of less shade-tolerant species with good seed dispersal. The common colonizers of abandoned fields vary from region to region, such as eastern red cedar and gray birch (*Betula populifolia*) in southern New England (Raup 1940), and loblolly pine in the Southeast (Oosting 1942). Eastern red cedar and gray birch are generally diagnostic of former agricultural fields, but loblolly pine can also occur in natural-disturbance openings and logged stands. In central New York the primary old-field trees are white pine, white ash, and red maple. Although these three are also found in primary forest, they are dominants only in post-agricultural stands (Mohler 1991). Several late-successional species are characteristically absent from post-agricultural forests, but over time the distinction in species composition is reduced as the initial invaders die and more shade-tolerant trees take over.

Even dead trees can provide evidence that a stand was once open field, if they have an open-grown form or are identifiable as old-field species. A diagnostic feature in some regions of the eastern United States is the dead, branchy, old-field conifers that have been overtopped by hardwoods but can remain standing for many decades.

Compared to primary forests, post-agricultural forests typically contain more open-field species of herbs and shrubs and fewer forest-interior understory species (Whitney and Foster 1988; Matlack 1994; Singleton 1998; Stover and Marks 1998). These patterns attenuate with time, but colonization by forest herbs is slow (Matlack 1994; Brunet and von Oheimb 1998), and the richness and cover of forest-interior herbs in even century-old stands can be lower than in primary forest (Bossuyt, Hermy, and Deckers 1999). Relict field plants in post-agricultural forests include gray dogwood (*Cornus racemosa*), strawberry (*Fragaria virginiana*), golden-rod (*Solidago rugosa*), dandelion (*Taraxacum officinale*), and speedwell (*Veronica officinalis*). While some common primary forest species, such as false Solomon's seal (*Smilacina racemosa*) and woodferns (*Dryopteris* spp.), can be found in post-agricultural stands, other forest herbs and shrubs, including maple-leaved viburnum (*Viburnum acerifolium*) and tall white lettuce (*Prenanthes altissima*), remain sparse or absent. Thus, what is distinctive about the understory species composition of post-agricultural forests is the combination of the absence of a number of typical forest herbs and the presence of some otherwise open-habitat, field plants.

Additional evidence that a site was plowed is that the ground surface characteristically lacks conspicuous irregularities in microtopography because the treefall pits and mounds were smoothed by repeated plowing. For most post-agricultural stands in North America, there has not yet been time for tree growth and windthrow to accumulate new pits and mounds. A plow layer may be visible in the soil profile. It should be noted that not all farm fields were plowed, especially some land used as pasture. The soil seedbank, at least for a few decades after abandonment, can also be used to differentiate post-agricultural stands from primary forest, since a number of agricultural weeds have long-lived seeds.

Forests on Former Pastures

Post-agricultural stands have also developed on sites that were once in pasture, and these can often be distinguished from forests on former plowed fields. Pasture use ranged in intensity, and thus legacy, from land that was plowed and planted with pasture grasses, to open meadows that were not plowed, to grazed woods that were never cleared. Pastured sites can often be identified by old fencing, especially barbed wire. The direction the wire turns at a corner can indicate which side the animals were on.

The presence of fencing does not always imply that the site was open field because in many regions of the United States a high percentage of the farm woodlots in the early 1900s were used for cattle (Whitney 1994). Grazing and trampling have major impacts on both understory plants and canopy trees (Lutz 1930; Day and DenUyl 1932), and stands with a history of heavy grazing can retain evidence in the abundance of species that were less palatable or resprouted readily (Whitney 1994).

The most useful diagnostic feature of stands that developed on former open pastures is the abundance of thorny species of shrubs and small trees (Wessels 1997; Stover and Marks 1998). Typical species are multiflora rose (*Rosa multiflora*), hawthorn (*Crataegus* spp.), buckthorn (*Rhamnus cathartica*), apple, and eastern red cedar. These species invade active pastures, and if not removed by the farmer, persist for many decades after abandonment. An extremely densely branched, stunted, conical or hour-glass form of woody pasture plants, particularly apples and hawthorns, often reflects a long period of browsing by cattle (Scott 1915). In time, abandoned pastures are colonized by the same types of trees that colonize abandoned plowed fields, but the thorny species can be seen in the understory as living and dead stems. Any of the "pasture" species can occasionally be found in unpastured or nonagricultural sites—it is their abundance that is diagnostic of pastures.

Other features are less reliable for differentiating former pastures from abandoned plowed crop fields. The old forest-edge or hedgerow trees will be the same in both cases, and structural characteristics within the stands will be similar, although multiple wolf trees (former shade trees) are more characteristic of old pastures. Herbaceous plants are not especially helpful in distinguishing stands on former pastures, because the vegetation soon after abandonment converges to typical old-field vegetation and then largely disappears as the tree canopy develops. In rare instances where a pasture was never plowed, patches of forest herbs that could be relicts from the original forest may be found (Stover and Marks 1998). Post-agricultural stands on former unplowed pastures can combine residual forest traits (forest species, pits and mounds) with features acquired from the history of farming (open-field species and open-grown trees).

Conclusion

One can walk into a forest stand and look for salient features of the edge, the trees, the dead timber, the understory, and the ground (table 7.1) that indicate whether it was old growth, logged, a former field, or pasture. Other, complementary, approaches may reveal more definitive information about stand history. For example, a more quantitative approach could include sampling tree rings to determine the age structure of the trees, and analyzing ring width to date the times of canopy opening (e.g., Eggler 1938; Abrams, Orwig, and Demeo 1995).

At the Harvard Forest in New England, researchers used a more elaborate field method to infer stand disturbance histories (Henry and Swan 1974; Oliver and Stephens 1977). In each study, a small plot of forest was carefully taken apart, including each live and dead tree, to determine their species, size, age, release dates, and locations, and for dead trees whether they broke or uprooted, the direction of fall, and the relative vertical positions of downed trees. When combined with information such as logging management records and known hurricane dates, a detailed picture of the history of human and natural disturbances emerged. Clearly, this is an extremely intensive effort, whose strength is the synthesis and corroboration that result. It is a limited approach, however, because it can realistically be applied only to very small areas, which may not be representative of the whole stand.

In contrast to the intensive methods just described, basic field observation is the most straightforward and cheapest approach to inferring stand history over the past decades or century and is worthwhile in any stand of interest even when other documentation or methodology is available. The method is nonquantitative for the most part, although careful field notes about the features that are present and absent, and maps or sketches of feature locations and patch dimensions, are useful. Judgments should be based on multiple signs, which will sometimes be conflicting. It is important both to avoid overinterpretation or jumping to conclusions from one sign, and to be able to accept exceptions and see the overall pattern. There are no indicator species that are both diagnostic of a particular history and characteristic of every such stand, and the current forest composition and structure frequently give only an incomplete indication of past history (Foster, Orwig, and McLachlan 1996). The best interpretations of field observation are those that can be supported by other sources of information, such as management records and information from landowners, historical documents, old aerial photographs, and tree-ring dating.

The use of field observations does require some familiarity with the local vegetation, history, and environments. Regional vegetation descriptions are helpful (such as Curtis 1959; Wells 1967; Franklin and Dyrness 1973; Barbour and Major 1977; Barbour and Billings 1988; Collins and Anderson 1994), as are local or state floras (e.g., Yatskievych 1999).

The time over which evidence remains visible in a forest is limited. This is especially true for post-agricultural stands, as the vegetation that was there before clearing can only be guessed at by assuming it was similar to nearby undisturbed stands on the same soil type, if any remain. In older stands, the timescale of field evidence is restricted by the ages of surviving or decay-resistant trees (Foster, Orwig, and McLachlan 1996), though some signs, such as stone walls or pits and mounds, can last for centuries. Both recent minor disturbances, such as grazing or selective thinning, and major clear-cutting or agricultural clearing a century ago, can be nearly imperceptible today (Foster, Orwig, and McLachlan 1996).

An important point is that most sites have multiple kinds of field evidence that point toward their histories. The more evidence one can recognize and use for a site, the more likely one is to infer the correct history. And the more one can deduce of its history, the better one understands the current forest.

References

Aber, J. D. 1987. Restored forests and the identification of critical factors in species-site interactions. Pages 241–250 in Restoration ecology: A synthetic approach to ecological research, ed. W. R. Jordan III, M. E. Gilpin, and J. D. Aber. Cambridge, England: Cambridge University Press.

Abrams, M. D., D. A. Orwig, and T. E. Demeo. 1995. Dendroecological analysis of successional dynamics for a presettlement-origin white-pine–mixed-oak forest in the southern Appalachians, USA. Journal of Ecology 83: 123–133.

Agee, J. K. 1993. Fire ecology of Pacific Northwest forests. Washington, D.C.: Island Press.

Barbour, M. G., and W. D. Billings, eds. 1988. North American terrestrial vegetation. New York: Cambridge University Press.

Barbour, M. G., and J. Major, eds. 1977. Terrestrial vegetation of California. New York: John Wiley.

Bonham, C. D. 1989. Measurements for terrestrial vegetation. New York: John Wiley.

Bossuyt, B., M. Hermy, and J. Deckers. 1999. Migration of herbaceous plant species across ancient-recent forest ecotones in central Belgium. Journal of Ecology 87: 628–638.

Bratton, S. P. 1994. Logging and fragmentation of broadleaved deciduous forests: Are we asking the right ecological questions? Conservation Biology 8: 295–297.

Braun, E. L. 1950. Deciduous forests of eastern North America. New York: Hafner.

Brunet, J., and G. von Oheimb. 1998. Migration of vascular plants to secondary woodlands in southern Sweden. Journal of Ecology 86: 429–438.

Clark, J. S. 1990. Fire and climate change during the last 750 yr in northwestern Minnesota. Ecological Monographs 60: 135–159.

Collins, B. R., and K. H. Anderson. 1994. Plant communities of New Jersey: A study in landscape diversity. New Brunswick, N.J.: Rutgers University Press.

Cooper, C. F. 1960. Changes in vegetation, structure, and growth of southwest pine forests since white settlement. Ecological Monographs 30: 129–164.

———. 1961. The ecology of fire. Scientific American 204: 150–160.

Curtis, J. T. 1959. The vegetation of Wisconsin. Madison: University of Wisconsin Press.

Dale, M. E., H. C. Smith, and J. N. Pearcy. 1995. *Size of clearcut opening affects species composition, growth rate, and stand characteristics.* Research Paper NE-698. USDA Forest Service, Northeastern Forest Experiment Station.

Day, R. K., and D. DenUyl. 1932. *Studies in Indiana farmwoods.* I. The natural regeneration of farm woods following the exclusion of livestock. Bulletin No. 368. Lafayette, Ind.: Purdue University Agricultural Experiment Station.

Duffy, D. C. 1993. Seeing the forest for the trees: Response to Johnson et al. *Conservation Biology* 7: 436–439.

Duffy, D. C., and A. J. Meier. 1992. Do Appalachian herbaceous understories ever recover from clearcutting? *Conservation Biology* 6: 196–201.

Dynesius, M., and B. G. Jonsson. 1991. Dating uprooted trees: Comparison and application of eight methods in a boreal forest. *Canadian Journal of Forest Research* 21: 655-665.

Eggler, W. A. 1938. The maple-basswood type in Washburn County, Wisconsin. *Ecology* 19: 243–263.

Egler, F. E. 1977. *The nature of vegetation: Its management and mismanagement: An introduction to vegetation science.* Norfolk, Conn.: Aton Forest, and Connecticut Conservation Association.

Elliott, K. J., and D. L. Loftis. 1993. Vegetation diversity after logging in the southern Appalachians. *Conservation Biology* 7: 220–221.

Foster, D. R. 1992. Land-use history (1730–1990) and vegetation dynamics in central New England, USA. *Journal of Ecology* 80: 753–772.

Foster, D. R., D. H. Knight, and J. F. Franklin. 1998. Landscape patterns and legacies resulting from large, infrequent forest disturbances. *Ecosystems* 1: 497–510.

Foster, D. R., D. A. Orwig, and J. S. McLachlan. 1996. Ecological and conservation insights from reconstructive studies of temperate old-growth forests. *Trends in Ecology and Evolution* 11: 419–424.

Franklin, J. F., and C. T. Dyrness. 1973. *Natural vegetation of Oregon and Washington.* General Technical Report PNW-8. USDA Forest Service, Pacific Northwest Forest and Range Experiment Station.

Greeley, W. B. 1925. The relation of geography to timber supply. *Economic Geography* 1: 1–14.

Hart, J. F. 1968. Loss and abandonment of cleared farm land in the eastern United States. *Annals of the Association of American Geographers* 58: 417–440.

Heinselman, M. L. 1973. Fire in the virgin forests of the Boundary Waters Canoe Area, Minnesota. *Quaternary Research* 3: 329–382.

Henry, J. D., and J. M. A. Swan. 1974. Reconstructing forest history from live and dead plant material—An approach to the study of forest succession in southwest New Hampshire. *Ecology* 55: 772–783.

Hughes, J. W., and T. J. Fahey. 1991. Colonization dynamics of herbs and shrubs in a disturbed northern hardwood forest. *Journal of Ecology* 79: 605–616.

Hupp, C. R. 1992. Riparian vegetation recovery patterns following stream channelization: A geomorphic perspective. *Ecology* 73: 1209–1226.

Johnson, A. S., W. M. Ford, and P. E. Hale. 1993. The effects of clearcutting on herbaceous understories are still not fully known. *Conservation Biology* 7: 433–435.

Johnson, E. A., K. Miyanishi, and H. Kleb. 1994. The hazards of interpretation of static age structures as shown by stand reconstructions in a *Pinus contorta–Picea engelmannii* forest. *Journal of Ecology* 82: 923–931.

Kalisz, P. J., and D. B. Dotson. 1989. Land-use history and the occurrence of exotic earthworms in the mountains of eastern Kentucky USA. *American Midland Naturalist* 122: 288–297.

Livingston, R. B., and M. L. Allessio. 1968. Buried viable seed in successional field and forest stands, Harvard Forest, Massachusetts. *Bulletin of the Torrey Botanical Club* 95: 58–69.

Lorimer, C. G. 1980. Age structure and disturbance history of a southern Appalachian virgin forest. *Ecology* 61: 1169–1184.

Lorimer, C. G., and L. E. Frelich. 1994. Natural disturbance regimes in old-growth northern hardwoods. *Journal of Forestry* 60: 33–38.

Lutz, H. J. 1930. Effect of cattle grazing on vegetation of a virgin forest in north-western Pennsylvania. *Journal of Agricultural Research* 41: 561–570.

Lutz, H. J., and A. L. McComb. 1935. Origin of white pine in virgin forest stands of northwestern Pennsylvania as indicated by stem and basal branch features. *Ecology* 16: 252–256.

Marks, P. L. 1974. The role of pin cherry (*Prunus pennsylvanica* L.) in the maintenance of stability in northern hardwood ecosystems. *Ecological Monographs* 44: 73–88.

Marks, P. L., S. Gardescu, and G. E. Hitzhusen. 1999. Windstorm damage and age structure in an old growth forest in central New York. *Northeastern Naturalist* 6: 165–176.

Martin, W. H. 1992. Characteristics of old-growth mixed mesophytic forests. *Natural Areas Journal* 12(3): 127–135.

Matlack, G. R. 1994. Plant species migration in a mixed-history forest landscape in eastern North America. *Ecology* 75: 1491–1502.

Menges, E. S., and J. Kimmich. 1996. Microhabitat and time-since-fire: Effects on the demography of *Eryngium cuneifolium* (Apiaceae), a Florida scrub endemic plant. *American Journal of Botany* 83: 185–191.

Mohler, C. L. 1991. Plant community types of the central Finger Lakes region of New York: A synopsis and key. *Proceedings of the Rochester Academy of Science* 17: 55–107.

Nyland, R. D., W. C. Zipperer, and D. B. Hill. 1986. The development of forest islands in exurban central New York State. *Landscape and Urban Planning* 13: 111–123.

Oliver, C. D., and B. C. Larson. 1996. *Forest stand dynamics.* New York: John Wiley.

Oliver, C. D., and E. P. Stephens. 1977. Reconstruction of a mixed species forest in central New England. *Ecology* 58: 562–572.

Oosting, H. J. 1942. An ecological analysis of the plant communities of Piedmont, North Carolina. *American Midland Naturalist* 28: 1–126.

Panshin, A. J., and C. de Zeeuw. 1970. *Textbook of wood technology*, vol. 1, 3rd edition. New York: McGraw-Hill.

Pickett, S. T. A., and P. S. White, eds. 1985. *The ecology of natural disturbance and patch dynamics*. New York: Academic Press.

Raup, H. M. 1940. Old field forests of southeastern New England. *Journal of the Arnold Arboretum* 21: 266–273.

Runkle, J. R. 1990. Gap dynamics in an Ohio *Acer-Fagus* forest and speculations on the geography of disturbance. *Canadian Journal of Forest Research* 20: 632–641.

Russell, E. W. B. 1997. *People and the land through time*. New Haven, Conn.: Yale University Press.

Sackett, S., S. Haase, and M. G. Harrington. 1994. Restoration of southwestern ponderosa pine ecosystems with fire. Pages 115–120 in *Sustainable ecological systems: Implementing an ecological approach to land management*, Tech. coord. W. W. Covington and L. F. DeBano. General Technical Report RM-247. USDA Forest Service, Rocky Mountain Forest and Range Experiment Station.

Schaetzl, R. J., S. F. Burns, T. W. Small, and D. L. Johnson. 1990. Tree uprooting: Review of types and patterns of soil disturbance. *Physical Geography* 11: 277–291.

Schaetzl, R. J., D. J. Johnson, S. F. Burns, and T. W. Small. 1989. Tree uprooting: Review of terminology, process, and environmental implications. *Canadian Journal of Forest Research* 19: 1–11.

Scott, E. L. 1915. A study of pasture trees and shrubbery. *Bulletin of the Torrey Botanical Club* 42: 451–461.

Singleton, T. A. 1998. *Recovery of the forest herb community in post-agricultural forests in central New York: Pattern and process.* Ph.D. dissertation, Cornell University, Ithaca, New York.

Smith, B. E., P. L. Marks, and S. Gardescu. 1993. Two hundred years of forest cover changes in Tompkins County, New York. *Bulletin of the Torrey Botanical Club* 120: 229–247.

Spurr, S. H., and B. V. Barnes. 1980. *Forest ecology*, 3rd edition. New York: John Wiley.

Stearns, F. W. 1949. Ninety years change in a northern hardwood forest in Wisconsin. *Ecology* 30: 350–358.

Stover, M. E., and P. L. Marks. 1998. Successional vegetation on abandoned cultivated and pastured land in Tompkins County, New York. *Journal of the Torrey Botanical Society* 125: 150–164.

Streng, D. R., and P. A. Harcombe. 1982. Why don't East Texas savannas grow up to forest? *American Midland Naturalist* 108: 278–294.

Turner, M. G., and C. L. Ruscher. 1988. Changes in landscape patterns in Georgia, USA. *Landscape Ecology* 1: 241–251.

Veblen, T. T. 1992. Regeneration dynamics. Pages 152–187 *in Plant succession: Theory and prediction*, ed. D. C. Glenn-Lewin, R. K. Peet, and T. T. Veblen. New York: Chapman and Hall.

Wells, B. W. 1967. *The natural gardens of North Carolina*. Chapel Hill: University of North Carolina Press.

Wendel, G. W. 1975. *Stump sprout growth and quality of several Appalachian hard-wood species after clearcutting.* Research Paper NE-329. USDA Forest Service, Northeastern Forest Experiment Station.

Wessels, T. 1997. *Reading the forested landscape: A natural history of New England.* Woodstock, Vt.: Countryman Press.

Whitney, G. G. 1994. *From coastal wilderness to fruited plain: A history of environmental change in temperate North America 1500 to the present.* Cambridge, England: Cambridge University Press.

Whitney, G. G., and D. R. Foster. 1988. Overstory composition and age as determinants of the understory flora of woods of central New England. *Journal of Ecology* 76: 867–876.

Yatskievych, G. 1999. *Steyermark's flora of Missouri*, vol. 1, revised edition. St. Louis: Missouri Botanical Garden Press.

8

Using Dendrochronology to Reconstruct the History of Forest and Woodland Ecosystems

Kurt F. Kipfmueller and Thomas W. Swetnam

Tree rings are an important source of long-term proxy information that can be used in reconstructing and understanding the history of past cultures, landscapes, and environments. Dendrochronology—or tree-ring dating—relies on the practice of cross-dating, which is the assignment of exact calendar dates to each annual ring through the matching of patterns of growth and other tree-ring characteristics. The best-known applications of dendrochronology have been in the fields of archaeology and paleoclimatology (e.g., Stokes and Smiley 1968; Fritts 1976; Baillie 1995; Schweingruber 1996). The tree-ring dating of ancient cliff dwellings and pueblos of the southwestern United States, for example, is widely known and celebrated in both scientific and popular literature (Douglass 1929; Baillie 1995). Likewise, the unique insights derived from tree-ring reconstructions of past climatic variations are commonly referenced in assessments of climatic change and its implications at global scales (Oldfield 1998; USGCRP 1999).

A somewhat less well-known application of dendrochronology is in the field of historical ecology (or paleoecology). Although the potential of tree rings for ecological research was recognized by the founder of modern dendrochronology, A. E. Douglass (1920), it is only recently that the subdiscipline of dendroecology has received much attention by dendrochronologists or ecologists (e.g., Fritts and Swetnam 1989; Schweingruber 1996). In 1986, for example, an international conference on the ecological aspects of tree-ring research resulted in seventy-nine conference papers (Jacoby and Hornbeck 1987), and a recent tree-ring conference with the broad theme of "Environment and Humanity" (Dean, Meko, and Swetnam 1996) contained about thirty papers (out of a total of eighty-two) that directly addressed ecological topics. Moreover, the utility of tree rings in addressing important ecological questions is gaining recognition among the larger community of ecologists. This trend is exemplified by recent W. S. Cooper Awards (for "outstanding contributions in geobotany, physiographic ecology, or plant succession") presented by the Ecological Society of America to the authors of four papers that made extensive use of dendrochronological techniques (Hupp 1992; Fastie 1995; Arseneault and Payette 1997; Lloyd and Graumlich 1997).

A primary reason for this expanded interest in dendroecology is that both ecologists and natural resource managers have become increasingly aware of the fundamental importance of historical perspectives. This appreciation stems, in part, from recognition of the ubiquity of nonequilibrium dynamics arising from historical processes, such as climatic change and aperiodic disturbances (Sprugel 1991). To understand how ecosystems arrived at their current configurations, we must know about past events and trajectories of change (Brown 1995; Christensen et al. 1996). This interest in history is reflected in an increasing demand for reconstructions of past ecosystem processes and structures that would be useful in defining the "historical or natural range of variability" (Morgan et al. 1994; Kaufmann et al. 1994; Landres, Morgan, and Swanson 1999; Stephenson 1999; Swetnam, Allen, and Betancourt 1999).

Dendrochronology is particularly well suited to historical-ecological research because trees tend to be long-lived and the variations in characteristics of their annual rings can be used to reconstruct long and detailed histories of the surrounding environment. Another reason is that *cross-dating*—the most important principle and practice of dendrochronology —facilitates a multidisciplinary and multiple-lines-of-evidence approach that is very effective in historical reconstruction (Swetnam, Allen, and Betancourt 1999). Cross-dating is the matching of tree-ring characteristics within and among trees across a range of temporal and spatial scales for the purpose of exactly dating individual rings and the structures and elements contained within the rings. Cross-dating is most commonly due to regional climatic variations (e.g., drought and wet years) that cause synchronous changes in tree growth processes (Douglass 1941; Stokes and Smiley 1968; Fritts 1976). Hence, by carrying out tree-ring cross-dating, most dendrochronologists are at least indirectly involved in the study of climatic variability, even though their primary focus may be on the study of ecological and cultural events and processes (e.g., births and deaths of trees, wildfires, insect outbreaks, and construction of ancient dwellings and human demography).

The use of dendrochronological principles and techniques affords several important advantages over other dating techniques. The primary advantage of dendrochronology is accuracy of dating. The use of dendrochronological principles ensures that the assignment of annual dates to a series of tree rings is exact. This accuracy in turn facilitates the establishment of connections between the temporal occurrence of events and the timing of other changes to the physical system. Without this level of accuracy, dendrochronologists cannot establish important relationships between tree growth and events in the surrounding environment.

Second, tree-ring data represent an extraordinary natural archive of ecological variation over long periods of time. Depending upon the physical environment and the rate of decay, tree rings can be used to reconstruct past events or changes in ecological systems spanning centuries and, in some cases, millennia. This is especially true when a large number of samples are cross-dated, as opposed to simple ring counting of a few samples. Simple ring counting is limited temporally by the longevity of the tree species being sampled. Though this may be very long in some species that attain great age, such as bristlecone pine (*Pinus longaeva*), the cross-dating of remnant material (i.e., samples from logs, stumps, and standing dead trees) can extend the record of change considerably. The bristlecone pine chronology developed by cross-dating currently exceeds nine thousand years, almost twice as long as the oldest currently living individual (the oldest living bristlecone pine that we know of is about forty-eight hundred years old). Remnant material has also been an integral part of development of fire histories in the Southwest (e.g., Baisan and Swetnam 1990) and of documentation of changes in forest communities (LaMarche 1973; Lloyd and Graumlich 1997; Donnegan and Rebertus 1999).

Another benefit of dendrochronology is that it can assist in identifying potential mechanisms of variability. For instance, tree-ring–based fire history reconstructions indicate that fires occurred in many mountain ranges of the southwestern United States during 1748 (Swetnam and Baisan 1996; Swetnam and Betancourt 1998) (figure 8.1). Study of historical documents and climate reconstructions from tree rings and corals indicate that the El Niño–Southern Oscillation was probably a climatic mechanism for those events (Swetnam and Betancourt 1990). An unusually strong El Niño event occurred in 1747 and may have led to an increase in fine-fuel abundance, leading to those widespread fires during the dry year of 1748. The regional climate signal is clearly evident in the growth characteristics of precipitation-sensitive conifers collected throughout the region, with a wide ring forming in 1747 followed by an extremely narrow ring during the dry year of 1748 (figure 8.1). Similar relationships between climate and natural disturbance exist in the case of insect-caused epidemics, as we will describe later.

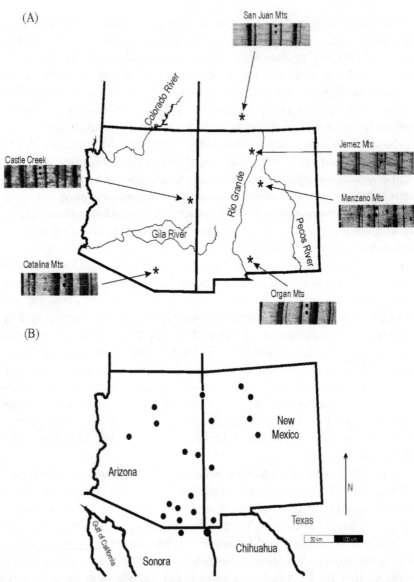

Figure 8.1. (A) The characteristic ring sequence that occurred across a broad region of the Southwest around 1750. Growth is from left to right. Double black dots indicate the 1750 ring. The rings of 1748 and 1752 are noticeably narrow; that of 1747 is wide in some series, likely due to higher amounts of winter-spring precipitation associated with a strong El Niño year. (B) The network of fire history sites that contain evidence of the 1748 fire year throughout the Southwest, indicating the regional nature of that event.

Cross-dated and measured tree-ring width chronologies are commonly incorporated into networks of chronologies for broad-scale climatic reconstruction (e.g., Fritts 1991; Cook et al. 1999). As spatial networks of climate and disturbance are built up for landscapes and regions, it becomes possible to directly compare independently derived time series of the key events and processes over long temporal and broad spatial scales. Examples include comparisons of climatic reconstructions with chronologies of fire events (Swetnam 1993; Veblen et al. 1999); tree births and deaths (Betancourt et al. 1993; Allen and Breshears 1998; Villalba and Veblen 1998); and human population changes (Dean et al. 1985). These multiple, independent lines of evidence can be particularly effective in disentangling natural from cultural causes of ecosystem variations (Allen, Betancourt, and Swetnam 1998; Swetnam and Betancourt 1998; Veblen et al. 1999).

Historical knowledge and understanding are often of central importance in the field of restoration ecology because "restoration" directly implies the return of degraded ecosystems to some desired condition or state that existed in the past. The identification of specific reference or desired conditions, however, is problematic in that a given condition at a particular time and place represents a "snapshot" of a system's structure and composition (Stephenson 1999). However, natural systems are dynamic, i.e., they fluctuate at a variety of spatial and temporal scales due to complex interactions among periodic natural disturbances, humans, atmospheric variability, and changes in species composition through successional processes (White and Walker 1997). Recognition of the dynamic, nonequilibrial nature of most ecosystems has led to the conceptualization of a "historical range of variability" as a framework for evaluating current ecosystem conditions relative to the range and variation of past conditions (Cissel 1994; Morgan et al. 1994). Deciding on specific goals or targets for restoration, however, is dependent on other considerations as well, such as costs and practicality. Even if historical conditions are not useful for identifying restoration goals, the knowledge of past conditions and changes is often important for understanding how current conditions developed.

In this chapter we review the guiding principles of dendrochronology as they relate to reconstruction of the ecological history of forests and woodlands. We also discuss some basic techniques and practices used to cross-date and ensure accurate dating of tree rings. Using "classic" and recent examples, we focus on the use of dendrochronology to understand the mechanisms of ecological change and variability across time and space, and on applications toward the restoration of ecosystems. Finally, we discuss some important limitations of dendrochronology as a tool for historical ecology.

The Principles of Dendrochronology

Refined over the last century, the principles that have served as the foundation of dendrochronological practice are still central to the science of dendrochronology. The following principles lead directly to cross-dating and are essential as guiding concepts and approaches to the analysis and interpretation of tree rings. The principles outlined here are discussed in greater detail elsewhere (e.g., Fritts 1976; Fritts and Swetnam 1989).

The Principle of Uniformity. Simply put, this principle states, "The present is the key to the past." This means that those processes operating at present are assumed to be reasonably similar to processes that operated in the past. Although processes may be similar, their rates or other aspects of the processes may vary through time. The principle of uniformity as applied to dendrochronology implies that the factors currently controlling tree growth are similar to those that affected tree growth in the past. This principle is the logical basis for quantitatively estimating (reconstructing) variations of past processes from tree rings.

The Principle of Limiting Factors. The rate and timing of tree growth can be affected by many different factors, such as moisture, temperature, animals, and others. Although different factors can affect tree-growth processes, growth is usually limited by the factor that is most critically in demand; that is the most limiting factor (Fritts 1976; Barbour, Burk, and Pitts 1987; Kozlowski, Kramer, and Pallardy 1991). For example, in arid climates, moisture is typically the factor most limiting to tree growth. During exceptionally dry periods, trees throughout a region will grow very slowly and produce a narrow annual ring. The factors limiting to growth in a particular setting in a particular sequence of years establishes the pattern of wide and narrow rings that is useful in cross-dating.

The Principle of Site Selection. Site selection is an important aspect of most dendrochronological investigations. Dendroclimatological investigations typically focus on sites that maximize tree-growth responses to the climate variable of interest. For example, if a climate reconstruction focuses on summer temperature, then sites are selected near the upper elevation or latitudinal limits of a species range where temperature is most limiting to growth. Site selection for investigations focusing on the reconstruction of ecological parameters, such as natural disturbance or successional processes, however, may be more often based on a need to obtain spatially representative information for particular landscapes or ecosystems. In the case of restoration, for example, the site to be restored is often predetermined, and therefore the selection of a particular site to maximize an environmental signal may not be warranted, but is driven by the objectives of the investigation.

The Principle of Ecological Range. The principle of ecological range refers to the range of habitats and abiotic conditions in which a given species can survive and reproduce (Fritts 1976). A given species can usually be found growing across a gradient or a range of habitats with differing physical characteristics. The differing physical characteristics of trees along such gradients have an important influence on the growth characteristics of annual rings and the data that are recorded (Fritts 1976). Generally, species most suitable for dendroclimatic investigations are found growing near the margins of their ecological range. Trees growing near these range limits often have greater responsiveness to limiting factors such as precipitation or low temperatures than species growing near the center of their ecological range (Fritts 1976).

The Principle of Replication. The reduction of "noise" in a tree-ring data set is typically achieved by increasing the number of samples collected both from an individual tree and from a site as a whole (Fritts 1976; Wigley, Jones, and Briffa 1987; Cook and Kairiukstis 1990). The climatic "signal" in tree-ring records refers to the information contained within a tree-ring record that can be directly attributed to environmental variability, as opposed to the "noise," or random or residual variation in tree growth, that cannot be related to environmental variations (Fritts 1976). The principle of replication, then, is the maximization of the climate signal through an increase in sample size and temporal depth. The collection of additional samples for any given year may amplify the signal of interest (up to a point) while helping to identify characteristics that may be restricted to one or a few trees.

The Principle of Cross-Dating. The most important principle (and technique) in dendrochronology is cross-dating (Fritts 1976). Cross-dating is a technique used to ensure the assignment of accurate calendar dates to individual growth rings. The technique of cross-dating involves the systematic comparison of annual ring-width patterns between radii from the same tree, from several trees from the same area, and from trees over regions (Douglass 1941, 1946; Ferguson 1970; Fritts 1976). The most common mechanism creating cross-dating is interannual climatic variability at a scale broader than a forest stand. This extrinsic environmental variability results in synchroneity of growth relationships in trees growing within a given area, thus yielding characteristic sequences of ring growth identifiable between trees (Stokes and Smiley 1968).

The annual ring of a tree is composed of both early wood and late

Late Wood

Early Wood

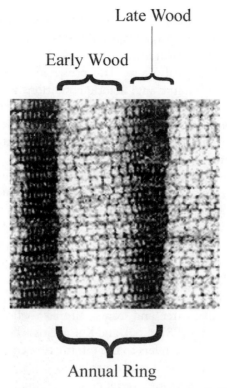

Annual Ring

Figure 8.2. The annual ring structure of subalpine larch (*Larix lyallii* Parl.) from Montana. The lighter portion of the ring is the early wood, when tree growth is relatively rapid. Those cells are lighter because their walls are thinner than the cell walls of late wood, which is noticeably darker.

wood (figure 8.2). The early-wood portion of the annual growth ring is composed of cells with thinner cell walls than the cells forming the late wood. The thicker cell walls in the late wood result in that portion of the ring appearing darker. Cross-dating ensures that all rings in a given series are dated to annual precision by aiding the identification of locally absent and false rings (figures 8.3, 8.4d, and 8.4e) (Douglass 1946; Ferguson 1970; Fritts 1976; Swetnam, Thompson, and Sutherland 1985). In some tree-ring series, an annual ring may be missing from part or all of a tree stem due to extreme climatic conditions or an injury that limits growth in a given year.

False rings, or intra-annual growth bands, result from changes in cell structure within an annual ring, resulting in a band of cells that resembles true late wood. The occurrence of false rings, like the occurrence of locally absent rings, can often be attributed to changes in water availability or an injury during the growing season (Telewski and Lynch 1991).

**False Ring within
the 1893
Ring**

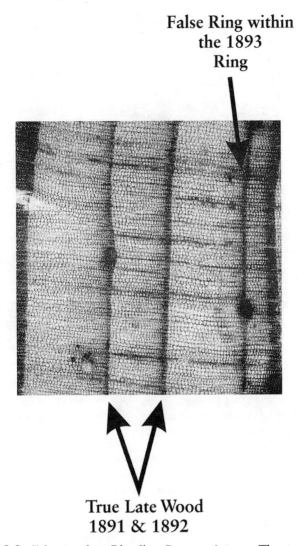

**True Late Wood
1891 & 1892**

Figure 8.3. False ring from Rhyollite Canyon, Arizona. The rings 1891 and 1892 have noticeably thinner late wood. A false ring, interrupted by a resin duct, is evident in 1893. Historical evidence suggests that the summers of 1891 and 1892 were extremely dry, resulting in the death of numerous cattle in the southwestern United States. This is generally attributed to the failure of the summer monsoon (photo courtesy of C. H. Baisan).

False rings can be distinguished from true annual rings by their morphological appearance and by comparisons with other samples. False rings usually show a gradual transition from late-wood cells to early-wood cells, whereas true late-wood boundaries are very abrupt. Resin ducts are often useful in the identification of false rings because they interrupt the false

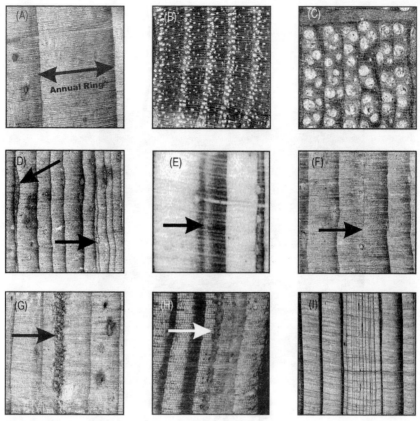

Figure 8.4. Tree-ring diagnostic features: (A) annual ring in an eastern white pine (*Pinus strobus*); (B) annual ring from ash (*Fraxinus* spp.), a ring-porous species showing clustered vessels in the early wood of the annual ring; (C) annual ring from an oak (*Quercus* spp.) collected in Arizona, showing diffuse porous-ring structure in which vessels are distributed throughout the annual ring; (D) locally absent rings of 1610 and 1616 found in a whitebark pine (*Pinus albicaulis*) collected in Idaho; (E) intra-annual growth band (false ring, in a conifer collected in the Southwest; common in areas experiencing an arid fore-summer followed by monsoonal rains) in a conifer collected in the Southwest; (F) thin late wood characteristic of the 1801 annual ring in whitebark pine growing at upper elevations of Idaho and Montana, is a useful cross-dating marker year; (G) frost ring showing disrupted cells in the late wood of the 1866 ring in whitebark pine; (H) catastrophic resin ducts in the 1993 ring of sub-alpine larch (*Larix lyallii*); (I) growth suppression in Douglas fir (*Pseudotsuga menziesii*) beginning in 1851 due to defoliation by western spruce budworm.

ring while the true late wood forms around resin ducts (figure 8.3). The occurrence of false rings or locally absent rings can be determined for certain only by using cross-dating techniques.

Dendrochronology in Practice

Tree-ring specimens require careful preparation to ensure that accurate measurements can be taken and the information contained within annual ring structures processed accordingly. A brief description of some of the techniques used to prepare suitable wood surfaces to carry out cross-dating is presented here, but more thorough treatments can be found in Stokes and Smiley (1968) and Swetnam, Thompson, and Sutherland (1985).

Upon selection of a study site, dendrochronologists usually collect tree-ring specimens using a drill-like tool called a Swedish increment borer. Increment borers are used to remove a very small, cylindrical sample of wood (commonly referred to as a tree core or increment core). Two or more increment cores are traditionally sampled from each tree to reduce the effects of intra-tree growth differences and aid in the identification of false or missing rings (Stokes and Smiley 1968). Increment core sampling of fire scars or other kinds of injuries is difficult, but it is possible when only a single injury needs to be dated along the sampled axis (Sheppard, Means, and Lassoie 1988; Barrett and Arno 1988). Dating of multiple scars on the same tree, or of scars in highly resinous or decayed trees, can be infeasible or impractical.

In the case of sampling fire scars or other types of cambial scars, full or partial cross sections are usually collected (Arno and Sneck 1977). The sampling of partial cross sections involves the removal of a small portion of wood, eliminating the need to fell trees completely. Partial cross sections can be taken with a chainsaw from the boles of trees, and if carefully done, the tree may not be significantly weakened. Although detailed follow-up studies have not yet been done, it appears that most fire-scarred trees will survive when relatively small partial sections (less than about one-third of the basal area) are taken from their boles (personal observation of the authors).

To protect partial and full cross sections for transportation to a laboratory, filament tape or plastic shrink wrap is often used to prevent damage and keep broken pieces with their respective samples. Increment cores can be stored and transported using paper or plastic drinking straws or core holders. If plastic drinking straws are used, increment cores should be removed from them as soon as possible, or slits should be cut in the straws to allow cores to dry and prevent molding.

In preparation for surfacing, increment cores are removed from the straws or carriers and secured into grooved wooden core mounts in such a way that the tracheid cells (the tube-like cells that form most of the wood tissue) are aligned in a vertical position. The vertical alignment of tracheid cells produces the cross-sectional surface that is required to identify ring boundaries. Preparation of full or partial cross sections involves gluing broken samples back together and, in some cases, mounting cross sections on pieces of plywood to prevent further damage during the surfacing process.

The development of highly polished surfaces on tree-ring samples is of the utmost importance in order to identify false, micro, or locally absent rings. Very fine surfaces are also needed for proper dating of scars. Surfaces should be of sufficient quality to distinguish individual tracheid cells under 20x to 30x magnification. This can be accomplished by sanding samples with successively finer grades of sandpaper. Sanding should progress through grades of 100, 220, 320, and 400 to ensure a high-quality surface. In the case of tree-ring samples with very narrow rings, sandpaper of 15 μm can be used to provide a very high polish that more clearly distinguishes annual rings.

Once the samples are prepared, the dendrochronologist can begin to analyze and record the data—a skill that comes only through practice and experience. This includes recognizing the pattern of wide and narrow rings and other features, such as light-colored or thin late wood or frost damage (figures 8.4f and 8.4g). One of the most common dating tools used by dendrochronologists is known as "skeleton plotting." It involves graphically representing the wide and narrow features of a tree-ring series on a strip of graph paper (figure 8.5). Beginning traditionally with trees that were living when sampled, plotting begins at the innermost ring and progresses outward. By convention, one dot is placed on every tenth ring, two on every fiftieth, and three on every hundredth ring. As additional samples are plotted and the dates verified by comparing plots with one another and making adjustments for false and missing rings, the common features between samples begin to emerge. They are summarized as a master skeleton plot or master dating chronology. Samples collected from dead material can also be plotted and the patterns compared to the master chronology, thereby extending the chronology further back in time as additional remnant wood is dated. This process is commonly referred to as chronology building (figure 8.6). With practice, and as familiarity with the ring-width patterns increases, these patterns are gradually committed to memory and cross-dating can sometimes be done directly on the wood without the use of skeleton plot aids.

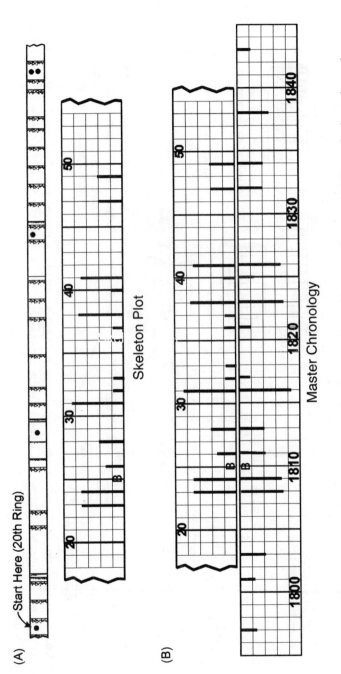

Figure 8.5. Skeleton plotting is a commonly used graphical cross-dating technique. (A) From the hypothetical increment core, longer lines are drawn for rings that are narrower than those around them. Single black dots denote decades, double black dots are used to mark fifty-year intervals. It is also sometimes useful to denote larger rings, or other anatomical features such as frost rings or resin ducts, with a "B." (B) The skeleton plot patterns can be matched to a master chronology to assign exact dates to each annual ring.

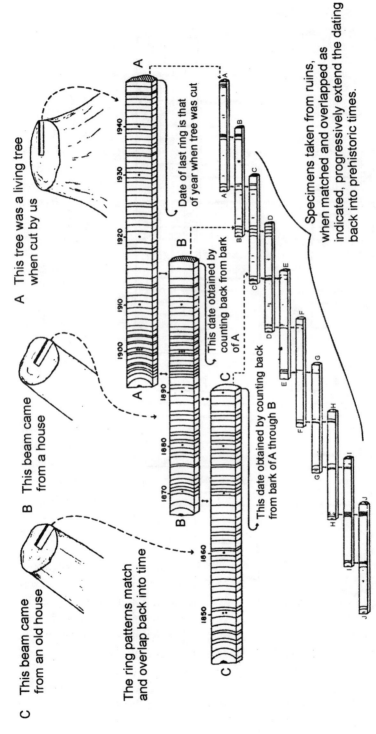

Figure 8.6. The overlapping of successive series (chronology building) is used to extend tree-ring chronologies back in time. Remnant materials (logs, stumps, and standing dead trees) or archaeological materials are especially useful for chronology extension (from Stokes and Smiley 1968).

A This tree was a living tree when cut by us

B This beam came from a house

C This beam came from an old house

The ring patterns match and overlap back into time

Date of last ring is that of year when tree was cut

This date obtained by counting back from bark of A

This date obtained by counting back from bark of A through B

Specimens taken from ruins, when matched and overlapped as indicated, progressively extend the dating back into prehistoric times.

Dendrochronologists also use other methods of cross-dating. These methods are sometimes used in combination with skeleton or visual dating. Computer software programs, for example, can be used to statistically compare the dating among measured tree-ring series (Baillie and Pilcher 1973; Holmes 1983). If computer techniques are used to cross-date measured series, it is imperative that the dating also be verified by reexamining the actual specimens (and graphical plots of ring series) for common patterns and to ensure that the dating is correct. For example, if the computer output from a cross correlation of ring-width series suggests that an absent or false ring problem exists at a certain point in the measured time series, one should visually examine the wood specimen in question before inserting a zero value (for an absent ring) or deleting a ring value (for a suspected false ring). If a full or partial cross section (or multiple cores from the same tree) is available, a search around the circumference of the specimen (or of the paired core) often results in discovery of the locally absent ring as a "partial" ring, or verification that a ring is indeed false by its morphological characteristics at another position on the stem. In material with many false or missing rings, the best use of computerized programs is to verify the dating on tree-ring series after careful visual and graphical cross-dating techniques have been used.

The Application of Dendrochronology in Forest Ecosystem Restoration

Dendrochronology is a broad, interdisciplinary field of investigation, and new approaches and applications are constantly being developed. Although there are many applications of dendrochronology, they are linked by the use of cross-dating and are often pursued in a combined and comparative manner. For instance, it is common for dendroecological investigations to be conducted simultaneously with dendroclimatic reconstructions, such as in fire climatology investigations, insect outbreak studies, and climate studies.

Changes in forest ecosystems can be examined using dendrochronological techniques by determining the natality and mortality rates of forest species, the growth patterns preserved within annual rings, or the occurrence of cambial scars resulting from discrete events. Forest demography may be reconstructed from tree-ring dating the births and deaths of trees. Birth or "recruitment" processes may be estimated by obtaining and dating the tree rings near the pith at ground level (Villalba and Veblen 1998). Death processes can be evaluated by cross-dating the outermost rings, or the last formed ring beneath the bark of dead trees (Allen and Breshears 1998; Swetnam and Betancourt 1998; Mast et al. 1999).

Annual accuracy is not always possible in determining germination dates or the timing of events that caused changes in growth rates. Several years may be necessary for a tree to reach the height at which a sample is collected, which makes determination of the precise year of germination difficult. The loss of annual rings due to decay processes may also make determination of accurate death dates difficult (Lloyd and Graumlich 1997). In addition, dramatic reduction in the rate of growth or an increase in a tree's rate of growth lags somewhat following the event that caused the growth change (Lorimer 1985; Veblen et al. 1991). The use of cambial scarring (e.g., fire scarring) does not have this limitation, however, because the actual year or season in which the scarring event occurs is preserved with the annual ring (Dieterich and Swetnam 1984).

Historic Forest Structure and Change

The reconstruction of past forest structures is being used to assess changes during the twentieth century in forest conditions due to human land use, and to better understand the composition of old-growth forests in the past (Abrams, Orwig, and Demeo 1995; Foster, Orwig, and McLachlan 1996; Fulé, Covington, and Moore 1997). Researchers at Northern Arizona University, for example, have made extensive use of dendrochronological techniques and principles to evaluate changes in forested ecosystems since the time of EuroAmerican settlement, and have used this information in support of restoration plans (Covington and Moore 1994; Fulé, Covington, and Moore 1997; Mast et al. 1999; Moore, Covington, and Fulé 1999). They have collected information on the current structure and composition of forests and on fire history in northern Arizona and determined changes through time. They have also made use of remnant materials, such as logs and snags, to obtain a more complete reconstruction of presettlement forest structure. Their research indicates that relative to past forest structure and composition, the modern landscape has higher tree density and basal area. Their research also indicates that the mean diameter of ponderosa pine has diminished significantly compared with periods prior to settlement, suggesting an increase in the abundance of small-diameter ponderosa pines and a possible decline in the number of large trees that were likely present prior to EuroAmerican settlement.

The power of dendroecological approaches in historical ecology over the well-known "chronosequence" method of inference was elegantly demonstrated by Fastie (1995) in a reexamination of the classic successional studies in Glacier Bay, Alaska (Cooper 1923). Fastie examined ring-width releases and growth rates, and used remnant materials to reconstruct the chronological order of succession. He found that succession at

Glacier Bay had multiple trajectories, and that successional patterns previously inferred at Glacier Bay were not as orderly as had previously been thought. Citing the lack of ring-width characteristics of suppression-and-release patterns as evidence, Fastie showed that spruce (*Picea* spp.) and hemlock (*Tsuga* spp.) became established on oldest sites in the absence of an initial shrub layer. In contrast, spruce and hemlock collected from more recently deglaciated sites had reduced initial growth followed by a dramatic release. Fastie used experimental canopy gaps to show that more recently deglaciated sites were composed of a shrub layer, and that spruce and hemlock germinating on those sites had reduced growth until they were able to attain heights great enough to extend above the shrub layer.

Disturbance

Perhaps the most important application of dendroecology is the reconstruction of the history of disturbances in forests and woodlands. Dendrochronologists can reconstruct and investigate some of the most important characteristics of disturbance regimes—disturbance size, duration, intensity, seasonality, and frequency (Pickett and White 1985). Numerous disturbances can be examined using dendrochronology, including windthrow (Veblen et al. 1989), hydrological changes (Hupp 1992; Tardif and Bergeron 1997), volcanic eruptions (Lamarche and Hirschboeck 1984; D'Arrigo and Jacoby 1999), earthquakes (Van Arsdale et al. 1998), and snow avalanches (Veblen et al. 1994). We focus here on the application of dendrochronology to reconstruct the history of fire and insect epidemics.

Fire

Fire is a nearly ubiquitous disturbance of North American forests (Pyne 1982; Williams 1989; Agee 1993). Fire regimes range from frequent, low-intensity surface fires to relatively infrequent, catastrophic events that initiate new growth. Human land uses and activities, such as grazing, have reduced fire frequencies in some southwestern forests (Savage and Swetnam 1990; Swetnam, Allen, and Betancourt 1999), and the suppression of fires across much of North America has also reduced the frequency and extent of fires and resulted in current forest conditions, unlike those of past forest conditions (Covington and Moore 1994). Fire history investigations suggest that the effects of reduced fire activity have led to increased and possibly unnatural fuel accumulations that could lead to large catastrophic fires in areas historically dominated by smaller, patchy, nonlethal, surface fires. The restoration of landscapes through the reintroduction of fire, using prescribed burning or management policies that allow some natural fires to burn under certain conditions, is becoming more common across most federal land management agencies (Arno and Brown 1991; Agee 1993; Stephenson 1999). However, the proper prescriptions for restoration of landscapes with altered fire regimes require information concerning the natural occurrence of fire at long timescales. In addition, information concerning the factors that influence fire activity, such as climate or subsequent disturbance, is also necessary to ensure ecosystem sustainability for the long term (Christensen et al. 1996). Cross-dated fire histories are often essential for understanding how and why fire regimes have changed, relative to the modern record of fire.

The development of fire histories to better understand fire frequency at different timescales is generally approached using fire-scar analysis, stand-origin dating, or a combination of those two techniques (Johnson and Gutsell 1994). The dating of fire scars is the most commonly used technique, especially in areas where frequent, low-intensity fires occur.

A fire scar is a lesion formed when a fire is sufficiently intense to partially kill the cambium of a tree (figure 8.7; Gutsell and Johnson 1996). As a tree heals, new wood forms around the lesion and preserves the date of the fire event. Subsequent fires burning around the tree can result in the formation of an additional fire scar. In some instances, the seasonal

(A)

(B)

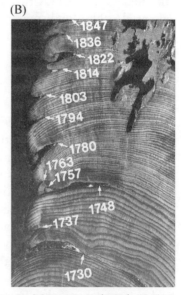

Figure 8.7. (A) A fire-scarred snag in the Rincon Mountains of southern Arizona; this tree recorded multiple fire events prior to its death. (B) A fire-scarred cross section showing the dates of the fire scars within the annual rings (photos courtesy of C. H. Baisan).

occurrence of fire can be determined based on the positioning of a fire-scar lesion within an annual ring (Baisan and Swetnam 1990). The dating of fire scars is the most precise method of assigning dates to the occurrence of fire, providing annual resolution. However, missing or false rings within a fire-scarred sample can lead to errors in the assignment of calendar dates to individual fires, so cross-dating should always be used to ensure annual precision (Madany, Swetnam, and West 1982; Johnson and Gutsell 1994). This may require additional time when compared to simple ring-counting procedures. In our experience, most time involved in accurately dating fire scars is spent securing good specimens and preparing them for visual assessment. This time is well spent, whether in ring-counting approaches or in cross-dating, as we have found poorly prepared surfaces are the most common source of error.

The dates of fires determined from fire-scar analysis can then be compiled into a single figure, and inferences concerning the spatial characteristics of fire events can be explored. For example, fire history studies conducted in twenty-seven mountain ranges of the southwestern United States indicate that some fires were widespread (figure 8.8). Other fire years were more localized. In addition, around 1900 there is a nearly synchronous reduction in fire occurrence throughout the Southwest due to the effects of fire suppression. Examination of fire events at multiple spatial scales can help elucidate some of the spatial characteristics of fire and determine potential factors that influence the occurrence and spread of fire.

In areas where relatively infrequent catastrophic crown fires destroy most or all living trees, the dating of fires is often done using stand-origin dating techniques (Arno, Reinhardt, and Scott 1993; Johnson and Gutsell 1994; Larsen 1997). Stand-origin dating involves the collection and dating of age data from trees that regenerate following a catastrophic fire event. Patches created by catastrophic fire events are first identified using aerial photography or remote-sensing methods. The patches are then visited, and the date of stand-origin is determined by collecting increment cores or cross sections from species likely to colonize a site shortly after a fire. However, stand-origin dating does not always provide precise dates of fire occurrence. The unknown time required for vegetation to become established following a catastrophic fire, or a difficulty in determining the number of years required for trees to reach the height at which age samples are collected can be potential sources of error. Moreover, the accuracy of a fire date is dependent in part upon the number of trees sampled to determine its occurrence (Kipfmueller and Baker 1998). To overcome these problems, fire-scar-dating techniques can be used in conjunction with stand-origin dating to improve the accuracy of fire date estimates. Fire scars can often be found along the boundaries of patches. Trees

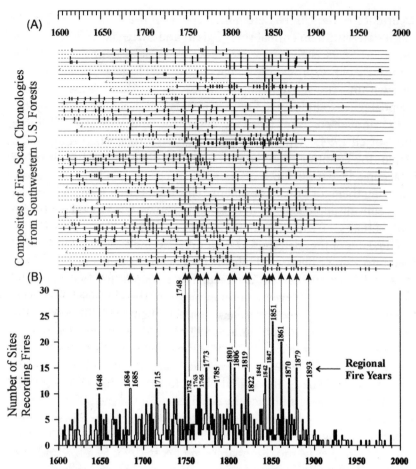

Figure 8.8. Composite fire-scar chronologies from fifty-five fire history sites located in Arizona, New Mexico, and northern Mexico. (A) In the upper chart, each horizontal line represents one fire history site, and the vertical tick marks represent the recording of a fire event using fire-scar dating. When fires are synchronous between adjacent sites, the tick marks form a continuous vertical line. (B) The bottom graph tracks the total number of sites recording a fire event each year. Years that have fire events recorded in at least ten sites across the network are labeled indicating regional fire years (reprinted from Allen, Betancourt, and Swetnam 1998).

within a patch may also survive a fire and record its occurrence as a fire scar (Kipfmueller and Baker 1998).

Several measurements can be used to identify the history of fire within an area and identify changes through time. The most commonly used measurements include fire frequency (the number of fires occurring within a given area through time) and mean fire interval (a measure of the average number of years between successive fires, measured either at a point on the landscape or for an area of known dimensions) (Arno and Petersen 1983; Agee 1993). Fire rotation (a measure of the number of years required to burn an area equal in size to the area under investigation) (Heinselman 1973; Agee 1993) is sometimes estimated. Fire rotation requires either mapped fire perimeters (e.g., fire atlases compiled by management agencies (McKelvey and Busse 1996) or the reconstruction of fire boundaries using other sources of information (Agee 1993). Statistical approaches have been developed for the description of fire regimes using stand-origin and time-since-fire data and are treated in detail by Johnson and Gutsell (1994).

The analysis of climate variability in conjunction with fire history investigations is a particularly important aspect of determining potential courses of action for the restoration of forests affected by fire suppression. Although twentieth-century changes in fire regimes are most often attributed to human activities and forest management practices, climate has undoubtedly been a major determinant of fire regime changes at long timescales. Increasingly, fire history studies are being conducted concurrently with reconstructions of climate. This enables comparisons of fire and climate variability to assess the relative roles of climate and human land uses on fire regimes. Short-term, interannual controls on fire frequency, for example, have been attributed to year-to-year changes in precipitation (Swetnam 1993; Veblen et al. 1999), which are often related to large-scale atmospheric anomalies, such as El Niño. Longer-term, multidecadal fluctuations in fire occurrence, for example, have been shown to be related to long-term temperature changes in giant sequoia forests in California (Swetnam 1993) and precipitation patterns in the Southwest (Grissino-Mayer and Swetnam 2000).

The restoration of fire in forested landscapes is not without difficulty. Because fire frequency can vary considerably through time, even in the absence of significant human impacts, it is difficult to determine which fire frequency characteristics should be used as baseline conditions (Stephenson, Parsons, and Swetnam 1991). In addition, spatial heterogeneity within past fire regimes can be difficult to reconstruct or restore. Fires are often patchy in nature, with some areas experiencing low-intensity fires and others more destructive fires. It is imperative that the design and implementation of fire restoration plans examine not only the frequency by which fire has occurred, but also the spatial variation inherent in fire occurrence.

Insects

The temporal occurrence of insect-caused epidemics has been examined using the dates of tree death (Perkins and Swetnam 1996) as well as changes in the growth patterns of both host and nonhost tree species (e.g., Swetnam, Thompson, and Sutherland 1985, Veblen et al. 1991; Hadley and Veblen 1993; Swetnam and Lynch 1993). The effects of climate can be removed, and suppressions due to insect defoliation enhanced, by comparing the growth between host and nonhost tree species (Swetnam, Thompson, and Sutherland 1985). A similar approach uses the growth patterns of trees that survive insect-caused epidemics, but rather than examining suppressions in the host species, the researcher identifies ring-width releases in surviving nonhost trees (Veblen et al. 1991; Fastie, Berg, and Swetnam, in review). Other approaches have also been used that rely simply on visual identification of suppressions and releases to assign dates to the outbreaks (Weber and Schweingruber 1995; Weber 1997).

Like fire, the patterns of insect outbreaks can be related to variability in climate and the impacts of human land use. Swetnam and Lynch (1989, 1993), for example, identified important relationships between western spruce budworm outbreaks in northern New Mexico and wetter than average conditions. In addition, they identified outbreak changes during the twentieth century that may have been due to fire suppression and past timber harvesting practices. Their results indicate that relative to earlier time periods, the twentieth century has experienced the longest intervals of reduced budworm activity, and that recent outbreaks have been among the most severe. Extensive logging of pine trees and severe fires reduced the density of trees in these forests. This was followed by a period of favorable climate and fire suppression that enabled host species (Douglas fir and true firs) to establish in these forests. In the decades following the logging and severe fires, these forests were less susceptible to disturbance by budworms, but as they reached maturity, host species became more homogenous across the landscape, leading to an abundance of susceptible host species over a large area. This resulted in more widespread and severe defoliation events in the late twentieth century than had occurred in previous centuries (Swetnam and Lynch 1989, 1993; Hadley and Veblen 1993; Weber and Schweingruber 1995).

The Limitations of Dendrochronology

Although there are important advantages to the use of dendrochronologic data, it is important to note its limitations. First, dendrochronology is limited to areas where trees form annual rings, so that variability can be used for cross-dating. Generally, these are areas where trees are sufficiently sensitive to climate (Fritts and Swetnam 1989). For example, tropical areas lack well-defined growing seasons, and, as a result, most tropical tree species lack clearly defined, annual growth rings. However, exploratory advances in tropical dendrochronology are being made using a variety of techniques to explore potential relationships with seasonal changes in environmental variability (Jacoby 1989). In contrast, some locations contain trees that may be too sensitive to variations in environmental conditions. For example, in some extremely arid regions, trees may be so sensitive to climate that a large number of annual rings are missing, making them difficult to date and utilize in dendrochronological investigations (Fritts and Swetnam 1989).

Tree rings, and other sources of paleoecological data, are subject to loss with increasing time before present. As tree-ring materials decay and are lost, the record and resolution of changes within the ecosystem diminishes. The resolution of the record may also be limited with respect to the sample depth during early portions of the record. This can be especially problematic in examinations of fire events but is a factor in all types of dendrochronological investigations.

Like most proxy records, tree rings record events through complicated physical and biological processes. Tree growth, therefore, acts as a filter through which environmental variability is recorded imperfectly. Our ability to accurately reconstruct the processes recorded by tree rings is directly related to our ability to understand and model this complicated filtering process, and therefore understand the signal recorded by tree rings (Swetnam, Allen, and Betancourt 1999).

Related to the problem of filtering complex environmental signals through biological processes is the concept of "no analogue." The "no-analogue" problem arises from processes or events that occur either during the modern period or in the past for which there is no related reference condition. This can lead to problems relating past or current growth characteristics with those for which there is no record. This may lead to complications in interpreting environmental variability from tree-ring data and may violate some aspects of the principle of uniformity.

Although tree rings can be applied to many aspects of historical ecology, it may not always be an appropriate approach to some questions of particular management concern or restoration. Care must be taken to determine if tree rings are appropriate recorders of a particular environmental variable, either through the matching of historical records with tree-ring data or through experiments that manipulate specific environmental conditions and monitor tree response.

Tree-ring analysis does have limits in its applicability to restoration ecology. Nevertheless, tree rings represent a useful, dynamic tool that can help capture the history of landscape change. Tree rings are a valuable source of long-term information that can be used to discover the range of environmental variability within forests and woodlands. The power of dendrochronology lies not only in the determination of events in time, but also in its ability to make inferences concerning the processes of environmental change. Information on the long-term fluctuations within the environment is crucial to the design and implementation of plans that seek to restore and maintain forests and woodlands within a range of their natural variation. New dendrochronological techniques and approaches aimed at understanding ecosystem variability will continue to evolve as resource managers and restorationists are faced with new problems and questions concerning our ever changing environment.

Resources for Dendrochronologists

There are a number of good references that can help those with little experience in dendrochronology. Guidelines for collecting, preparing, and cross-dating tree-ring samples can be found in M. A. Stokes and T. L. Smiley's book *An Introduction to Tree Ring Dating* (1968). Several texts focusing on the theoretical and practical aspects of dendrochronology have also been produced, including *Methods of Dendrochronology: Applications in the Environmental Sciences* (Cook and Kairiukstis 1990). A mainstay of the dendrochronology community is *Tree Rings and Climate* by H. C. Fritts, published in 1976. Unfortunately, it is out of print, but it can be found in most university libraries. A good resource for those interested in using tree rings to reconstruct insect-caused epidemics can be found in Swetnam, Thompson, and Sutherland, 1985.

In addition, the World Wide Web has become an important source of information on tree-ring research. The NOAA Paleoclimatology Program www.ngdc.noaa.gov/paleo/ archives includes more than one thousand tree-ring chronologies representing five continents. Those chronologies can be downloaded free of charge for a variety of uses. An additional online resource for those interested in pursuing dendrochronology is Henri Grissino-Mayer's Tree-Ring Web Pages web.utk.edu/~grissino. They include information on where to find commonly used dendrochronology supplies and useful links to tree-ring resources, as well as a searchable database of books and articles related to tree-ring research. An additional tool found on the World Wide Web is an interactive cross-dating tutorial developed by Dr. Paul Sheppard at the Laboratory of Tree-Ring Research tree.ltrr.arizona.edu/skeletonplot/introcross-date. htm. This tool allows users to apply skeleton-plotting techniques to date hypothetical tree-ring series.

References

Abrams, M.D., D.A. Orwig, and T.E. Demeo. 1995. Dendroecological analysis of successional dynamics for a presettlement-origin white-pine–mixed-oak forest in the southern Appalachians, USA. *Journal of Ecology* 83: 123–133.

Agee, J.K. 1993. *Fire ecology of Pacific Northwest forests.* Washington, D.C.: Island Press.

Allen, C.D., J.L. Betancourt, and T.W. Swetnam. 1998. Landscape changes in the southwestern United States: Techniques, long-term data sets, and trends. Pages 71–84 in *Perspectives on the land use history of North America: A context for understanding our changing environment,* ed. T. Sisk. Biological Science Report USGS/BRD/BSR-1998-0003. U.S. Geological Survey.

Allen, C.D., and D.D. Breshears. 1998. Drought-induced shift of a forest-woodland ecotone: Rapid landscape response to climate variation. *Proceedings of the National Academy of Science USA 95:* 14839–14842.

Arno, S.F., and J.K. Brown. 1991. Overcoming the paradox in managing wildland fire. *Western Wildlands 17:* 40–46.

Arno, S.F., and T.D. Petersen. 1983. *Variation in estimates of fire intervals: A closer look at fire history on the Bitterroot National Forest.* General Technical Report INT-301, USDA Forest Service, Intermountain Forest and Range Experiment Station, Ogden, Utah.

Arno, S.F., E.D. Reinhardt, and J.H. Scott. 1993. *Forest structure and landscape patterns in the subalpine lodgepole pine type: A procedure for quantifying past and present conditions.* General Technical Report INT-294, USDA Forest Service, Intermountain Research Station, Ogden, Utah.

Arno, S.F., and K.M. Sneck. 1977. *A method for determining fire history in coniferous forests in the mountain West.* General Technical Report INT-12, USDA Forest Service, Intermountain Forest and Range Experiment Station, Ogden, Utah.

Arseneault, D., and S. Payette. 1997. Landscape change following deforestation at the Arctic treeline in Québec, Canada. *Ecology 78:* 693–706.

Baillie, M.G.L. 1995. *A slice through time: Dendrochronology and precision dating.* London: B.T. Batsford.

Baillie, M.G.L., and J.R. Pilcher. 1973. A simple cross-dating program for tree-ring research. *Tree-Ring Bulletin 33:* 7–14.

Baisan, C.H., and T.W. Swetnam. 1990. Fire history on a desert mountain range: Rincon Mountain Wilderness, Arizona, U.S.A. *Canadian Journal of Forest Research 20:* 1559–1569.

Barbour, M.G., J.H. Burk, and W.D. Pitts. 1987. *Terrestrial Plant Ecology,* 2nd edition. Menlo Park, Calif.: Benjamin/Cummings.

Barrett, S.W., and S.F. Arno. 1988. Increment-borer methods for determining fire history in coniferous forests. General Technical Report INT-244, USDA Forest Service, Intermountain Research Station, Ogden, Utah.

Betancourt, J.L., E.A. Pierson, K. Aasen-Rylander, J.A. Fairchild-Parks, and J.S. Dean. 1993. Influence of history and climate on New Mexico pinyon-juniper woodlands. In *Managing pinyon-juniper ecosystems for sustainability and social needs,* ed. E.F. Aldon and D.W. Shaw. USDA Forest Service General Technical Report RM-236:42–62. Proceedings of the symposium April 26–30, Santa Fe, New Mexico.

Brown, J.H. 1995. *Macroecology.* Chicago: University of Chicago Press.

Christensen, N.L., A.M. Bartuska, J.H. Brown, S. Carpenter, C. D'Antonio, R. Francis, J.F. Franklin, J.A. MacMahon, R.F. Noss, D.J. Parsons, C.H. Peterson, M.G. Turner, and R.G. Woodmansee. 1996. The report of the Ecological Society of America committee on the scientific basis for ecosystem management. *Ecological Applications* 6: 665–691.

Cissel, J.H., F.J. Swanson, W.A. McKee, and A.L. Burditt. 1994. Using the past to plan the future in the Pacific Northwest. *Journal of Forestry* 92: 30–31, 46.

Cook, E.R., and L.A. Kairiukstis, eds. 1990. *Methods of dendrochronology: Applications in the environmental sciences.* Boston: Kluwer Academic.

Cook, E.R., D.M. Meko, D.W. Stahle, and M.K. Cleaveland. 1999. Drought reconstructions for the continental United States. *Journal of Climate* 12: 1145–1162.

Cooper, W.S. 1923. The recent ecological history of Glacier Bay, Alaska: II. The present vegetation cycle. *Ecology* 4: 223–246.

Covington, W.W., and M.M. Moore. 1994. Southwestern ponderosa forest structure and resource conditions: Changes since Euro-American settlement. *Journal of Forestry* 92: 39–47.

D'Arrigo, R.D., and G.C. Jacoby. 1999. Northern North American tree-ring evidence for regional temperature changes after major volcanic events. *Climatic Change* 41: 1–15.

Dean, J.S., R.C. Euler, G.J. Gumerman, F. Plog, R.H. Hevly, and T.N.V. Karlstrom. 1985. Human behavior, demography, and paleoenvironment on the Colorado plateaus. *American Antiquity* 50: 537–554.

Dean, J.S., D.M. Meko, and T.W. Swetnam, eds. 1996. *Tree rings, environment, and humanity.* Tucson, Ariz.: Radiocarbon.

Dieterich, J.H., and T.W. Swetnam. 1984. The dendrochronology of a fire scarred ponderosa pine. *Forest Science* 30: 238–247.

Donnegan, J.A., and A.J. Rebertus. 1999. Rates and mechanisms of subalpine forest succession along an environmental gradient. *Ecology* 80: 1370–1384.

Douglass, A.E. 1920. Evidence of climatic effects in the annual rings of trees. *Ecology* 1: 24–32.

———. 1929. Secrets of the Southwest solved by talkative tree rings. Vol. 56. *National Geographic Magazine.*

———. 1941. Cross-dating in dendrochronology. *Journal of Forestry* 39: 825–831.

———. 1946. *Precision of ring dating in tree-ring chronologies.* Laboratory of Tree-Ring Research Bulletin 17. Tucson: University of Arizona.

Fastie, C.L. 1995. Causes and ecosystem consequences of multiple pathways of primary succession at Glacier Bay, Alaska. *Ecology* 76: 1899–1916.

Fastie, C.L., E.E. Berg, and T.W. Swetnam. In review. The response of boreal forests to lethal outbreaks of spruce beetles on the Kenai Peninsula, Alaska. *Ecological Applications.*

Ferguson, C.W. 1970. Concepts and techniques of dendrochronology. Reprinted from chapter 7 in *Scientific methods in medieval archaeology,* ed. R. Berger. Berkeley: University of California Press.

Foster, D.R., D.A. Orwig, and J.S. McLachlan. 1996. Ecological and conservation insights from reconstructive studies of temperate old-growth forests. *Trends in Ecology and Evolution* 11: 419–424.

Fritts, H.C. 1976. *Tree rings and climate*. New York: Academic Press.

———. 1991. *Reconstructing large-scale climatic patterns from tree-ring data: A diagnostic analysis*. Tucson: University of Arizona Press.

Fritts, H.C., and T.W. Swetnam. 1989. Dendroecology: A tool for evaluating variations in past and present forest environments. *Advances in Ecological Research* 19: 111–188.

Fulé, P.Z., W.W. Covington, and M.M. Moore. 1997. Determining reference conditions for ecosystem management of southwestern ponderosa pine forests. *Ecological Applications* 7: 895–908.

Grissino-Mayer, H.D., and T.W. Swetnam. 2000. Century-scale climate forcing of fire regimes in the American Southwest. *Holocene* 10: 207–214.

Gutsell, S.L., and E.A. Johnson. 1996. How fire scars are formed: Coupling a disturbance process to its ecological effect. *Canadian Journal of Forest Research* 26: 166–174.

Hadley, K.S., and T.T. Veblen. 1993. Stand response to western spruce budworm and Douglas-fir bark beetle outbreaks, Colorado Front Range. *Canadian Journal of Forest Research* 23: 479–491.

Heinselman, M.L. 1973. Fire in the virgin forests of the Boundary Waters Canoe Area, Minnesota. *Quaternary Research* 3: 329–382.

Holmes, R.L. 1983. Computer assisted quality control in tree-ring dating and measurement. *Tree-Ring Bulletin* 43: 69–78.

Hupp, C.R. 1992. Riparian vegetation recovery patterns following stream channelization: A geomorphic perspective. *Ecology* 73: 1209–1226.

Jacoby, G.C. 1989. Overview of the use of tree-ring analysis in tropical regions. *International Association of Wood Anatomists Bulletin* 10: 99–108.

Jacoby, G.C., and J.W. Hornbeck, eds. 1987. *Proceedings of the International Symposium on Ecological Aspects of Tree-Ring Analysis*. Publication CONF-8608144. Washington, D.C.: U.S. Department of Energy.

Johnson, E.A., and S.L. Gutsell. 1994. Fire frequency models, methods and interpretations. *Advances in Ecological Research* 25: 239–287

Kaufmann, M.R., R.T. Graham, D.A. Boyce Jr., W.H. Moir, L. Perry, R.T. Reynolds, R.L. Bassett, P. Mehlhop, C.B. Edminster, W.M. Block, and P.S. Corn. 1994. *An ecological basis for ecosystem management*. General Technical Report RM-GTR-246. Fort Collins, Colo.: USDA Forest Service.

Kipfmueller, K.F., and W.L. Baker. 1998. A comparison of three approaches to date stand-replacing fires in lodgepole pine forests. *Forest Ecology and Management* 104: 171–177.

Kozlowski, T.T., P.J. Kramer, and S.G. Pallardy. 1991. *The physiological ecology of woody plants*. New York: Academic Press.

LaMarche, V.C. 1973. Holocene climate variations inferred from treeline variations in the White Mountains, California. *Quaternary Research* 3: 632–660.

LaMarche, V.C., and K.K. Hirschboeck. 1984. Frost rings in trees as records of major volcanic eruptions. *Nature* 307: 121–126.

Landres, P., P. Morgan, and F. Swanson. 1999. Evaluating the usefulness of natural variability in managing ecological systems. *Ecological Applications* 9: 1179–1188.

Larsen, C.P.S. 1997. Spatial variations in boreal forest fire frequency in northern Alberta. *Journal of Biogeography* 24: 663–673.

Lloyd, A.H., and L.J. Graumlich. 1997. Holocene dynamics of treeline forests in the Sierra Nevada. *Ecology* 78: 1199–1210.

Lorimer, C.G. 1985. Methodological considerations in the analysis of forest disturbance history. *Canadian Journal of Forest Research* 15: 200–213.

Madany, M.H., T.W. Swetnam, and N.E. West. 1982. Comparison of two approaches for determining fire dates from tree scars. *Forest Science* 28: 856–861.

Mast, J.N., P.Z. Fulé, M.M. Moore, W.W. Covington, and A.E. Waltz. 1999. Restoration of presettlement age structure of an Arizona ponderosa pine forest. *Ecological Applications* 9: 228–239.

McKelvey, K.S., and K.K. Busse. 1996. Twentieth-century fire patterns on Forest Service lands. Pages 1119–1138 in *Sierra Nevada Ecosystem Management Project: Final report to congress*. Volume 2: Assessments and scientific basis for management options. Davis: University of California, Centers for Water and Wildland Resources.

Moore, M.M., W.W. Covington, and P.Z. Fulé. 1999. Reference conditions and ecological restoration: A southwestern ponderosa pine perspective. *Ecological Applications* 9: 1266–1277.

Morgan, P., G.H. Aplet, J.B. Haufler, H.C. Humphries, M.M. Moore, and W.D. Wilson. 1994. Historical range of variability: A useful tool for evaluating ecosystem change. *Journal of Sustainable Forestry* 2: 87–111.

Oldfield, F., ed. 1998. *Past Global Changes (PAGES): Status report and implementation plan*. Stockholm: International Geosphere-Biosphere Program.

Perkins, D.L., and T.W. Swetnam. 1996. A dendroecological assessment of whitebark pine in the Sawtooth-Salmon River region, Idaho. *Canadian Journal of Forest Research* 26: 2123–2133.

Pickett, S.T.A., and White, P.S. 1985. *The ecology of natural disturbance and patch dynamics*. New York: Academic Press.

Pyne, S. 1982. *Fire in America: A cultural history of wild land and rural fire*. Princeton, N. J.: Princeton University Press.

Savage, M., and T.W. Swetnam. 1990. Early 19th-century fire decline following sheep pasturing in a Navajo ponderosa pine forest. *Ecology* 71: 2374–2378.

Schweingruber, F.H. 1996. *Tree rings and environment: Dendroecology*. Berne, Switzerland: Paul Haupt Publishers.

Sheppard, P.R., J.E. Means, and J.P. Lassoie. 1988. Cross-dating cores as a nondestructive method for dating living, scarred trees. *Forest Science* 34: 781–789.

Sprugel, D.G. 1991. Disturbance, equilibrium, and environmental variability: What is "natural" vegetation in a changing environment? *Biological Conservation* 58: 1–18.

Stephenson, N.L. 1999. Reference conditions for giant sequoia forest restoration: Structure, process, and precision. *Ecological Applications* 9: 1253–1265.

Stephenson, N.L., D.J. Parsons, and T.W. Swetnam. 1991. Restoring natural fire to the sequoia–mixed conifer forest: Should intense fire play a role? Pages 321–337 in *Proceedings 17th Tall Timbers Ecology Conference*, Tallahassee, Fla., May 18–21, 1989. Tall Timbers Research Station.

Stokes, M.A., and T.L. Smiley. 1968. *An introduction to tree ring dating.* Chicago: University of Chicago Press.

Swetnam, T.W. 1993. Fire history and climate change in giant sequoia groves. *Science* 262: 885–889.

Swetnam, T. W., C.D. Allen, and J.L. Betancourt. 1999. Applied historical ecology: Using the past to manage for the future. *Ecological Applications* 9: 1189–1206.

Swetnam, T.W., and C.H. Baisan. 1996. Historical fire regime patterns in the southwestern United States. Pages 11–32 in *Fire effects in southwestern forests: Proceedings of the second La Mesa Fire Symposium*, tech. ed. C.D. Allen. RM-GTR-286. USDA Forest Service, Fort Collins, Colorado.

Swetnam, T.W., and J.L. Betancourt. 1990. Fire–Southern Oscillation relations in the southwestern United States. *Science* 249: 1017–1020.

———. 1998. Mesoscale disturbance and ecological response to decadal climate variability in the American Southwest. *Journal of Climate* 11: 3128–3147.

Swetnam, T.W., and A.M. Lynch. 1989. Tree-ring reconstructions of western spruce budworm history in the southern Rocky Mountains. *Forest Science* 35: 962–986.

———. 1993. Multicentury, regional-scale patterns of western spruce budworm outbreaks. *Ecological Monographs* 63: 399–424.

Swetnam, T.W., M.A.Thompson, and E.K. Sutherland. 1985. *Using dendrochronology to measure growth of defoliated trees: Spruce budworms handbook.* USDA Agricultural Handbook No. 639. Washington, D.C.: USDA.

Tardif, J., and Y. Bergeron. 1997. Ice-flood history reconstructed with tree rings from the southern boreal forest limit, western Quebec. *Holocene* 7: 291–300.

Telewski, F.W., and A.M. Lynch. 1991. Measuring growth and development of stems. In *Techniques and approaches in forest tree ecophysiology*, eds. J.P. Lassoie and T.M. Hinckley. Boston: CRC Press.

USGCRP. 1999. *Our changing planet. U.S. Global Change Research Program, The nation's research investments to understand the complexity of global environmental change.* A report by the Subcommittee on Global Change Research, Committee on Environment and Natural Resources of the National Science and Technology Council, Washington, D.C.

Van Arsdale, R.B., D.W. Stahle, M.K. Cleaveland, and M.J. Guccione. 1998. Earthquake signals in tree-ring data from the New Madrid seismic zone and implications for paleoseismicity. *Geology* 26: 515–518.

Veblen, T.T., K.S. Hadley, E.M. Nel, T. Kitzberger, M.S. Reid, and R. Villalba. 1994. Disturbance interactions in a Rocky Mountain subalpine forest. *Journal of Ecology* 82: 125–135.

Veblen, T.T., K.S. Hadley, M.S. Reid, and A.J. Rebertus. 1989. Blowdown and stand development of a Colorado subalpine forest. *Canadian Journal of Forest Research* 19: 1218–1225.

———. 1991. The response of subalpine forests to spruce beetle outbreak in Colorado. *Ecology* 72: 213–231.

Veblen, T.T., T. Kitzberger, R. Villalba, and J. Donnegan. 1999. Fire history in northern Patagonia: The roles of humans and climatic variation. *Ecological Monographs* 69: 47–67.

Villalba, R., and T.T. Veblen. 1998. Influences of large-scale climatic variability on episodic tree mortality in northern Patagonia. *Ecology* 79: 2624–2640.

Weber, U.M. 1997. Dendroecological reconstruction and interpretation of larch budmoth (*Zeiraphera diniana*) outbreaks in two central alpine valleys of Switzerland from 1470–1990. *Trees* 11: 277–290.

Weber, U.M., and F.H. Schweingruber. 1995. A dendroecological reconstruction of western spruce budworm outbreaks (*Choristoneura occidentalis*) in the Front Range, Colorado, from 1720 to 1986. *Trees* 9: 204–213.

White, P.S., and J.L. Walker. 1997. Approximating nature's variation: Selecting and using reference information in restoration ecology. *Restoration Ecology* 5: 338–349.

Wigley, T.M.L., P.D. Jones, and K.R. Briffa. 1987. Cross-dating methods in dendrochronology. *Journal of Archaeological Science* 14: 51–64.

Williams, M. 1989. *Americans and their forests: A historical geography*. New York: Cambridge University Press.

9

Palynology: An Important Tool for Discovering Historic Ecosystems

Owen K. Davis

Palynology is among the most powerful tools for studying past ecosystems because pollen and related microfossils are very abundant and well preserved in a variety of sediment types, from ocean mud to the dung of extinct animals. Palynology provides evidence of past ecosystems over long and short time periods on both regional and local geographic scales. It can record both historic and prehistoric (archaeological) records of human interactions with the landscape.

Certain general rules apply to the suitability of sediments for pollen analysis, but there are exceptions to almost every palynology rule. As palynologists often say, "Pollen is where you find it." The type of sediment determines the time-resolution of the reconstruction. Rapidly deposited, annually layered sediments (varves) permit the analysis of seasonal and annual change. The geographic scale depends on the kind of "palynomorph" used. Some types are distributed short distances (a few meters), while others may travel hundreds of kilometers.

Palynology is more than the identification of pollen grains. In fact, the word *palynology* was originally coined to make this distinction. In 1944 Ernst Antevs objected to using the phrase *pollen analysis* for this science, because it also included the study of spores, algae, charcoal, and other microscopic plant and animal remains in the pollen preparation (now called *palynomorphs*; see below). And, just as important, the science encompassed more than just the identification of such remains. Those who came to be known as palynologists related changes in the abundances of the various microfossils to changes in the abundances of plants in the region. The distinction is as important as that between flora and vegetation. The first is a list of the plants, the second treats the importance or abundance of plants—the trees vs. the forest.

Antevs's (1944) observation received wide interest, and Hyde and Williams (1944) responded by proposing the word *palynology* from Greek and Latin roots. As such, the word is a collective noun, like *flour* and is not properly used in the plural. Palynologists study plant pollen, not plant "pollens." The term is also useful for understanding the origin of the science. The "things" studied by palynologists share two traits: they are microscopic, and they are highly resistant to most acids. So palynology can be traced to Paulus F. Reinsch, who in 1884 was the first scientist to dissolve the rock containing pollen and spores with a mixture of acids and other chemicals. He shares the distinction of originating the science with Lenart von Post, who in 1916 applied quantitative techniques to understand the postglacial vegetation history of northern Europe (Jansonius and McGregor 1996).

The chemical resistance of pollen and the other palynomorphs is what sets them apart from all other fossils. Palynologists study what survives the chemical extraction process. Pollen grains, plant and fungus spores, and certain algae are all palynomorphs, but diatoms and coccoliths (algae) are not, because they are dissolved by the hydrofluoric acid and hydrochloric acid used in routine pollen processing. This processing concentrates the pollen many thousandfold, so a single microscope slide can contain hundreds of fossil pollen grains—enough to provide a very reliable estimate of the nature of the past populations of plants and other organisms.

Note that "fossil" pollen is the same organic material that was deposited in sediments hundreds, thousands, or millions of years ago. It is not a "replacement fossil" like the silicates that make up petrified wood or trilobite fossils. The resistant pollen (or spore) wall is made of a biopolymer called sporopollenin (Brooks 1971), whose function is to protect the genetic material within the pollen or spore grain. One can think of pollen and spores as miniature plastic milk cartons of the plant world, designed to be light yet strong and transport precious genetic material safely through the air.

The Theory of Palynology

The historical applications of palynology include archaeology, biogeography, climate studies, environmental restoration, fire history, and paleoecology. In addition, palynology has contemporary applications in aeroallergy, plant breeding, and honey production.

The power of palynology to portray ancient environments is based on the ubiquity and durability of pollen and other palynomorphs. It is not unusual for a cubic centimeter of sediment to contain tens of thousands of pollen grains, and in aquatic sediment far more algal remains. And, in favorable environments, the palynomorphs are preserved indefinitely. The pollen grains of the earliest flowering plants contain the original carbon atoms deposited three hundred million years ago. Furthermore, the fossil pollen grains bear a quantifiable relationship to the plants that produced them (M. B. Davis 1963)—a relationship that can produce numerical estimates of temperature, precipitation, and other environmental parameters.

Although quantifiable, the relationship of pollen to vegetation is not simply proportional. Many factors influence the relationship between a fossil pollen assemblage and the vegetation that produces it, and between other palynomorphs and their original populations. The palynology assemblage is a function of **P**roduction, **D**ispersal, p**R**eservation, and **I**dentification:

$$P = f(P, D, R, I)$$

Identification is discussed below; the other three factors are treated in the later sections on interpretation (production and dispersal) and preservation.

Identification

The key to all forms of palynology is identification. Each organism produces a characteristic and relatively invariant kind of pollen, spore, or other palynomorph. Furthermore, pollen and spores of closely related species are self-similar; for example, the fir and pine genera of the pine family are similar but distinctive. This permits the reliable identification of ancient plants from their pollen. Routinely, each plant genus can be identified; for example, pine vs. fir, vs. spruce. For certain plants, routine identification is to the species taxonomic level (e.g., *Typha latifolia* pollen), but for others, the entire family may produce just one pollen type (e.g., grass pollen). Detailed study of well-preserved pollen or spores can result in identification to the species taxonomic level when necessary. However, the additional time needed for species-level identification is often not warranted for routine pollen analysis.

Complementary analyses using other paleoecological techniques are frequently undertaken for the same sediment sample. This approach can overcome the genus-level taxonomic resolution of pollen. For example, grasses can be routinely identified to the species taxonomic level by their fruits (caryopses).

Identification is the most time-consuming aspect of palynology, in terms of both data collection and the never-ending process of learning new pollen types. Beginning palynologists typically can recognize a few tens of pollen types without consulting identification keys; experienced palynologists may recognize hundreds. Many pictured keys have been produced (see chapter appendix for a list of sources), but they are idealized two-dimensional representations of an idealized "type" to which a fossil (often poorly preserved) can be assigned. The picture keys illustrate the "important" taxa of a region, but they can cover only a small fraction of the total plant diversity. Microscope slide collections of the regional flora are the ultimate authority for palynological research. Because pollen identification has not been automated, high-quality research relies on years of experience and research collections containing thousands of pollen reference slides. Experience is even more critical to the identification of other palynomorphs such as fungal spores or dinoflagellates, for which collections of reference specimens are rare.

Careful identification of palynomorphs other than pollen is important, but few keys exist. Changes of the abundance of charcoal in pollen preparations can be used to estimate changes in fire frequency, for example. Charcoal is resistant to the pollen extraction procedure because it is primarily inert carbon—having been burned. Charcoal particles can be counted at the same time pollen and spores are tallied on the microscope slide. However, other opaque particles also occur in the pollen preparation (figure 9.1), so identification is important. Much of the original cell pattern is retained in the microscopic charcoal fragment, so rudimentary identification (e.g., whether tissue was woody or herbaceous) is possible (figure 9.2).

Due to the lack of keys and comparative collections, the identification of fungal spores is more difficult than the identification of pollen so fungal spores are less often reported in palynological studies. Other difficulties include the facts that the number of fungal species is greater than

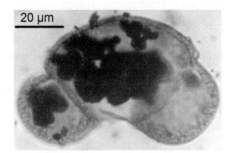

Figure 9.1. Pine pollen grain containing crystals of opaque iron pyrite (FeS), an example of opaque particles other than charcoal. John Wayne Marsh, California, 190 cm.

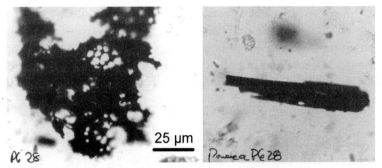

Figure 9.2. Charcoal particles from the Panaca Formation, Nevada (Late Miocene), demonstrating the antiquity and morphological distinctness of these microfossils. Left, herbaceous; right, woody.

that of plant species, that many fungi produce more than one spore type, and that the taxonomy of fungi is not as well known as that of flowering plants. Moreover, many fungal spores are not preserved as fossils, or do not survive the pollen extraction process. Therefore, it is not surprising that fungal spores are often ignored in palynological studies. Most of the spores present are probably from the *fungi imperfecti*, which have no known sexual stage. These spores are comparatively large and dark and can be classified by the *Sacardian system* of fungal spore morphology (figure 9.3).

Palynology samples of aquatic sediment often contain the remains of aquatic algae. These include the spores of species such as *Spirogyra*, a filamentous green algae, but the most common algal palynomorphs are the colonies of the planktonic and benthic green algae *Pediastrum* and *Botryococcus* (figure 9.4). These can reach great abundance in lake sediment (many times that of pollen). Their ecology is not very well known, but they indicate year-round standing water of moderate temperature and nutrient status.

Pollen and spore identification is based on the physical characteristics of size, structure, and sculpture. The terminology for the physical characteristics is large and complicated, and several variations exist. Recently Punt et al. (1994) have attempted to simplify and standardize the extensive pollen morphology terminology.

Size is the most obvious and least diagnostic of the identification criteria. Most pollen grains are 20–40 micrometers (μm) in diameter—about one-half to one-third the diameter of a human hair. Size is more variable than the other two characteristics. Pollen grains of a single species may vary by 50 percent in diameter depending on geographical conditions that include various genetic and environmental differences. The sedimentary environment affects pollen size, as does the chemical processing of the sediment sample. However, the relative sizes of pollen grains are important keys for identification when counting fossil samples.

The major categories of pollen and spores are called classes. A pollen grain may consist of one cell (a monad) or many cells (a tetrad or polyad).

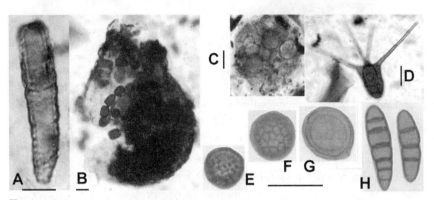

Figure 9.3. Algal and fungal spores.
(A) *Gleotrichia* (cyanobacteria, Playa Vista 1472 cm)
(B) *Sporormiella* (dung fungus, ascomycete John Wayne, 30 cm) spores in ascomycete spore body)
(C) *Thecaphora* (plant pathogen, basidiomycete John Wayne, 30 cm)
(D) *Tetraploa* (decay fungus, *fungi imperfecti* John Wayne, 30 cm)
(E) *Ustilago bromivora*
(F) *Tilletia caries*
(G) *Puccinia tanaceti*
(H) *Leptosphaeria artemisiae*
E–H basidiomycete plant pathogens, reference collection, Washington State University. Bars near letters are 10 μm.

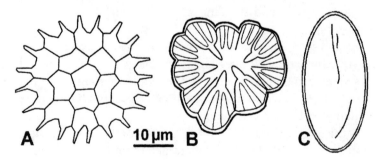

Figure 9.4. Drawings of algal palynomorphs.
(A) *Pediastrum* (green alage colony)
(B) *Botryococcus* (green algae colony)
(C) *Spirogyra* (spore, filamentous green algae)

Most pollen classes are characterized by a pattern of apertures (shown in fenestrate through periporate in figure 9.5). Special classes such as ferns and similar plants without seeds have trilet or monolet spore (not pollen) classes. The illustrated keys for pollen identification listed in the chapter appendix typically begin with the pollen classes, then branch out using pollen sculpture (see figure 9.7), and reach genus-level identifications using diagnostic features.

Structure refers to the general form of the pollen grain and its wall. The pollen wall (figure 9.6) usually is made up of a layer of radial elements

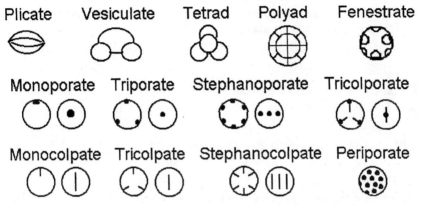

Figure 9.5. Pollen classes. These general shapes are the basic categories for pollen identification. Black circles represent pores; lines represent furrows; open circles within circles represent large apertures.

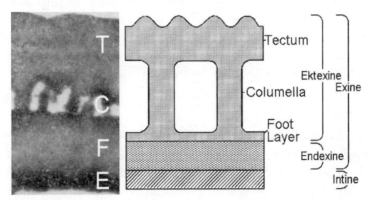

Figure 9.6. Pollen wall morphology and terminology. Transmission electron micrograph at left is *Nyssapollenites* (Eocene) intine (innermost layer of wall) not present (Kedevs 1990).
T = tectum, C = columella, F = foot layer, E = endexine.

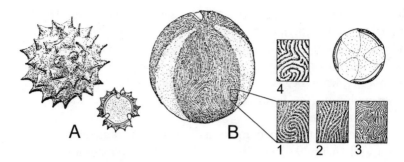

Figure 9.7. Pollen sculpture
(A) echinate sunflower pollen
(B) striate to rugulate maple pollen B2 striate B 1, 2, 3, 4 rugulate.
Drawings by Allen Solomon.

called columella, bounded by an inner foot layer and outer tectum. The wall is only a few µm thick, so it must be viewed at high power (1,000x) for diagnostic treatment, but the characteristics of the wall can be important for identifying pollen and spores. The wall of the spores of ferns and similar plants is generally made up of two layers, and the wall of fungi is usually simple.

Pollen and spore *sculpture* refers to the surface ornamentation of the pollen grain. Sculpture is often useful to distinguish the genera within pollen classes. In addition to the basic categories, the size of the pattern and its distinctness are useful for pollen identification. Each sculpture type is an "ideal" encompassing considerable variability. The sculpturing elements are of two general types. They may be elongated perpendicular to the pollen grain surface and round in plan view (e.g., gemmate, verrucate, echinate), or they may be elongated parallel to the surface (reticulate, rugulate, striate). Some major sculpture categories are shown in figure 9.7. Many other categories are used in the texts listed in the chapter appendix.

Methods

Palynology technique begins with sediment collection. The primary consideration is that the sample not be contaminated by pollen from older or younger sediment or from the atmosphere. Sediment cores from lakes and bogs are a primary source for pollen analysis. An extensive literature exists on site selection and coring devices (Moore, Webb, and Collinson 1991; Faegri, Kaland, and Krzywinski 1989). The goal is to obtain an uncontaminated sequence without gaps or duplications. Piston corers, which prevent sediment compaction and allow recovery from deep water, are typically used. The cores (columns of lake sediment) are opened in a pollen-free environment, the mixed "surface smear" of the core is removed, and volumetric samples are taken.

In addition to lake cores, many other kinds of sediment are sampled for palynological analysis. These include natural exposures of sediments as well as archaeological excavations. In each case, the goal is to obtain an uncontaminated sample. A fresh exposure is made immediately before sampling, collecting tools are cleaned between samples, and the sediment is stored in clean containers. The nature of the sediments from which the samples are obtained provides valuable information about the origin, transport, and age of the pollen samples. Therefore, detailed sediment descriptions are routinely taken during pollen sample collection. Chronological studies, such as radiocarbon dating, are particularly useful, so samples for dating are collected along with the palynology samples.

Sample preparation must be performed in a setting that avoids contamination. The palynology laboratory is ordinarily equipped with air filtration to remove airborne pollen, and laboratory procedures minimize cross-contamination among samples and exposure to modern pollen. The goal of processing the pollen sample is to remove as much of the non-pollen matrix as possible in order to reduce the time required to identify and count the pollen and spores under a microscope. Three general processes are used that rely on the physical properties of pollen and spores. First, pollen can be separated from larger (and smaller) particles by screening. Metal and plastic screens can be used to remove particles that are both coarser and finer than pollen and other palynomorphs.

Second, sporopollenin (Brooks 1971)—the biopolymer that makes the pollen wall—is extremely resistant to strong acids. Therefore, sediments can be treated with hydrofluoric acid (HCl) and hydrochloric acid (HF) to dissolve the silicates, carbonates, and other minerals that constitute the inorganic portion of the sediments. The sporopollenin is also resistant to the chemical procedure of *acetolysis*, which breaks down the cellulose that constitutes much of the organic mater in sediments. Weak bases do not destroy pollen or spores (although they cause them to swell), so pollen extraction may include treatment with 10 percent potassium hydroxide (KOH) or sodium hydroxide (NaOH) to remove humates—organic compounds found in most sediments. Box 9.1 lists a typical chemical extraction sequence.

Finally, the density or specific gravity of pollen (1.9–1.8 g/l) is sufficiently different from the minerals and organic particles of sediments that the technique of "density separation" can be used to concentrate pollen preserved in inorganic sediments. Various dense chemicals and solutions can be used, but all of the chemical techniques (acid digestion, density

Box 9.1. Routine Pollen Extraction Procedure

1. Add 1 cm^3 sample to ca. 50 ml water with detergent; agitate 10 minutes.

2. Swirl solution and screen (180 μm mesh, stainless steel) into second beaker.

3. Add 10 ml 10% HCl or concentrated HCl until effervescence stops.

4. Add 1 Lycopodium tablet (or other tracers).

5. Transfer screened solution to 50 ml Nalgene test tubes. Centrifuge, decant, and water rinse.

6. Add 40 ml HF and let stand overnight. Centrifuge, decant, and water rinse; then transfer to 15 ml glass tubes.

7. Perform acetolysis:

    a. add 5 ml glacial acetic acid centrifuge and decant;

    b. stir sample, add 5 ml acetic anhydride (use volumetric pipet);

    c. add 0.55 ml H_2SO_4 to acetic anhydride solution (use volumetric pipet), mix, centrifuge, and decant into glacial acetic acid;

    d. add 5 ml glacial acetic acid centrifuge and decant.

8. Add 10 ml 10% KOH 2 min. and place tube in boiling water bath. Centrifuge, decant, and rinse with hot water until super natent is clear.

9. Stain with safranin "O."

10. Transfer to labeled 1-dram shell vials.

11. Add a few drops of glycerin.

12. Desiccate to remove water.

separation) are hazardous and must be conducted by trained personnel in a contamination-free laboratory.

Pollen data are usually displayed on stratigraphic profiles as percentages. The percentages are calculated based on various "pollen sum" divisors. For example, the divisor may include only the pollen of trees—an "arboreal sum," or it may include the pollen of all non-wetground plants—a "terrestrial sum." It may or may not include fern spores. Although an individual type (for example, cattail pollen) may not be included in the pollen sum, its percentage calculation is nonetheless based on the "pollen sum." The sums are designed to reflect specific properties of the vegetation, such as aquatic vs. upland or regional vs. local.

Percentages are the most widely used data type. They require the fewest assumptions, and are the easiest to calculate. However, percentage data suffer from a serious problem of *constraint*. The percentage of an individual pollen type is influenced by abundances of all other types in the pollen sum. Any type may increase either because that pollen type has become more abundant, or because one or more of the other types in the sum have decreased.

The problem of constraint in *relative* percentage data is avoided in *absolute* palynology techniques (Maher 1972). Absolute techniques require volumetric pollen processing, and typically the addition of a *tracer* or *spike* that is used to calculate the amount of pollen in the volumetric sample. The absolute data may be either concentrations—expressed as the number of grains per volume (grains/cm^3) or mass (grains/gm)—or accumulation rates (grains/cm^2/yr). The advantage of the accumulation rate data is that concentrations may increase or decrease due to changes in the sedimentation rate of the nonpollen matrix. Accumulation rate (or "influx") data correct these changes in sedimentation rate.

All three types of data (percentage, concentration, accumulation rate) are usually displayed on stratigraphic "pollen diagrams." These consist of a vertical axis of time (figure 9.8) or depth (figure 9.9) (with the youngest or uppermost sample at the top of the diagram) and horizontal axes of percentage, concentration, or accumulation rate for each palynomorph (figure 9.8 and 9.9). The sequence of types in the diagram is selected to emphasize taxonomic, physiognomic, or ecological relationships—for example, trees-shrubs-herbs. Because the diversity of palynomorphs is high, often exceeding one hundred types, only the most abundant types are shown.

Less abundant types may be shown with 5x or 10x exaggeration curves. For example, in figure 9.8, fir (*Abies*), juniper (*Juniperus*), and spruce (*Picea*) do not exceed 10 percent, so the percentages are multiplied by 10 to produce the gray curve, which shows a single spruce pollen grain near the surface that would not otherwise be apparent. Summaries are used to portray general trends. In figure 9.8, this consists of curves labeled "woody, shrubs, herbs, and deteriorated." The "woody" curve combines fir, juniper, spruce, and pine (*Pinus*) and several rare taxa. The many types comprising the "herb" curve are too rare to show individually, but together they steadily increase in abundance toward the top of the diagram.

Interpretation

Data collection and display are the most time-consuming steps in paly-nology, but interpretation is the most critical. Because there is no simple relationship between the pollen abundance in a sample and the

LAKE CLEVELAND, CASSIA CO., IDAHO
Pollen Percent

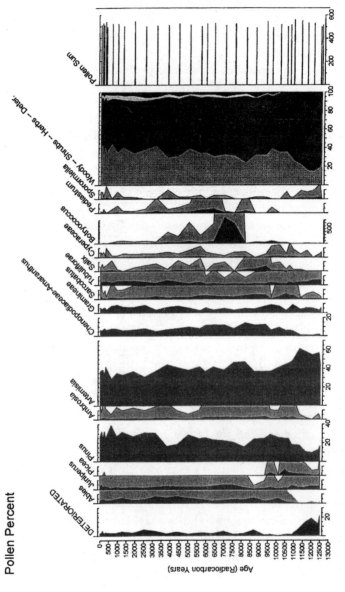

Figure 9.8. Percentages pollen diagram, gray-shaded areas tenfold exaggerations of black areas for selected pollen types. The curves *Salix* through *Sporormiella* are not included in the pollen sum. Note the abbreviated horizontal (percentage) scale for very abundant *Botryococcus* algae.

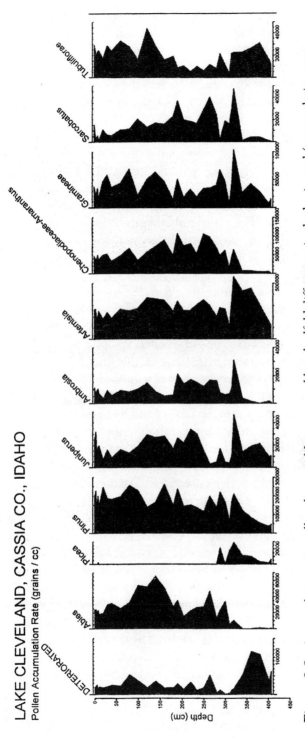

Figure 9.9. Accumulation rate pollen diagram. Note ten- and hundredfold differences in the horizontal (accumulation rate, grains/cm³/year) scales.

abundance of plants on the landscape, interpretation must take into account the variables of production, dispersal, and preservation to interpret past populations, then use the changing abundance of organisms to infer environmental change. As is often said, "First the pollen, then the vegetation, finally the climate." Pollen is the best-studied palynomorph, so the discussion will focus on it, but the approach can be applied to algae, fungi, and other palynomorphs.

Some features of pollen diagrams are relatively easy to interpret. The pollen diagram in figure 9.8 shows curves for abundant pollen types, but four-fifths of the pollen types are too rare to plot. Pine and sagebrush (*Artemisia*), the most abundant types, reflect the steppe-forest vegetation matrix characteristic of the mountains of the northern Great Basin (O. K. Davis 1984). The greater abundance of sagebrush pollen before 11,000 B.P. represents the relatively greater importance of sagebrush steppe, because the concentration of sagebrush pollen was greater then (figure 9.9).

However, the other features of figure 9.8 are more subtle. The relatively low percentages of Chenopodiaceae-*Amaranthus* pollen represents long-distance transport from low-elevation vegetation zones. The increase of Chenopodiaceae-*Amaranthus* pollen from 9500 B.P. to 5500 B.P. indicates upward migration of the low-elevation vegetation. This trend coincides with peak values of willow (*Salix*) pollen and aquatic algae *Pediastrum* and *Botryococcus* because the lake from which the sediments were collected became shallower and more productive in response to the increased heat and lower precipitation that drove vegetation zones upslope. Such conclusions are based on the comparison of the percentage and concentration values (figures 9.8 and 9.9), and on the plant macrofossils preserved in the pollen core (O. K. Davis et al. 1986).

Note that in figure 9.8, the percentages of local fir are generally lower than those of distant Chenopodiaceae-*Amaranthus* because the latter has greater production and better dispersal. In general, differences in pollen production and dispersal correspond to two pollenation "strategies" followed by flowering plants. Although many intermediates and exceptions exist, plants are generally either "wind pollinated" or "animal pollinated." The reproductive success of a plant depends on a pollen grain reaching the female part of the flower in viable condition. Wind pollination relies on a "sweepstakes" strategy characterized by the production of vast quantities of buoyant pollen that travels great distances. In contrast, animal-pollinated species produce much less pollen and instead rely on showy petals, perfume, and nectar to attract animals that transport pollen.

The wind-pollination and animal-pollination strategies follow taxonomic lines in some cases and cut across them in others. The only reliable way to establish the relationship between vegetation and the pollen rain (or between other palynomorphs and the organisms that produce them) is to compare the contemporary vegetation to palynology samples taken from that vegetation. This relationship varies regionally, so major palynological studies are usually accompanied by contemporary analysis of "surface samples."

Despite the many regional differences, some general patterns can be recognized. Plants are said to be underrepresented in the pollen rain if their pollen abundance is low relative to the importance of the correlative plant in the vegetation, and overrepresented if their pollen is too abundant. In general, elm and creosote bush are underrepresented types, and pine and ragweed are overrepresented. Over- and underrepresentation are particularly evident in percentage pollen studies, but the fundamental differences in production and dispersal influence concentration and influx data, too.

Figure 9.10 shows examples of over- and underrepresented pollen types. In these surface samples from southern Idaho (O. K. Davis 1984), sagebrush (*Artemisia*) is an overrepresented pollen type that is present at 30 percent in samples where the plant is locally absent. In contrast, Douglas-fir (*Pseudotsuga menziesii*) pollen is not found in forests where that tree is locally present until it reaches a vegetative coverage of 40 percent. Its pollen is underrepresented in the pollen rain. Greasewood (*Sarcobatus*) is neither under- nor overrepresented.

These relationships are dependent on the geographical scale over which the vegetation data are collected and the type of sediment sample from which the pollen is taken. For figure 9.10, the vegetation scale is small. That is, on a scale of 100s of meters, greasewood produces about as much pollen as the regional pollen rain, sagebrush produces more, Douglas fir less. This relationship scale is appropriate for mountainous regions, where vegetation patterns are relatively fine scaled.

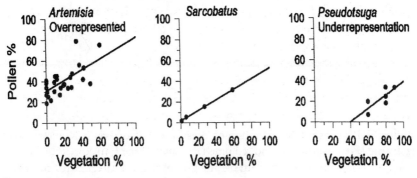

Figure 9.10. Pollen over- and underrepresentation.

On larger geographical scales, different factors govern plant abundances, and the relationship of vegetation to pollen generally is better for pollen types with good long-distance dispersal. However, on both small and large scales, the relationship shows considerable variability among regions (Delcourt and Delcourt 1987) with only a few types (e.g., spruce and greasewood) showing consistent relationships.

Once the patterns of production and dispersal have been investigated by surface sample study, the stratigraphic sequence of fossil samples can be applied to either floristic or vegetational problems—that is, floristic issues of ecologically or biogeographically important species, or vegetational issues such as the kind of environment. For example, Margaret Davis (1976) has used palynology to trace the northward migration of individual plant species following the last glaciation (figure 9.11). This floristic approach shows that plants migrate at different rates from different Ice Age population centers. In contrast, Delcourt and Delcourt (1980) used similar data to trace the movement of major vegetation boundaries during the Holocene. During the middle-Holocene, boreal forest was farther north, and the northern boundary of deciduous forest was farther south. The prairie-savanna border was farther east, and the savanna between prairie and deciduous forest was less extensive than two hundred years ago (figure 9.12).

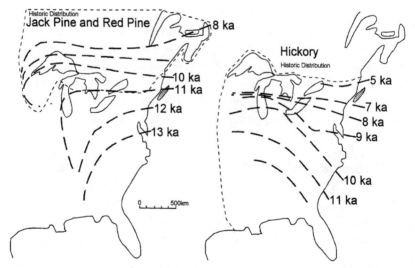

Figure 9.11. Postglacial migration of forest species, based on palynology. Left, jack pine (*Pinus banksiana*) and red pine (*P. resinosa*); right, hickory (*Carya ovata*). Dashed line shows modern distribution of the species (after M. B. Davis 1976).

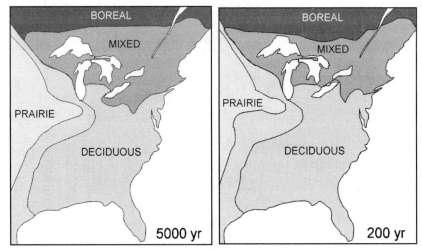

Figure 9.12. Migration of major vegetation types based on palynology (simplified from Delcourt and Delcourt 1980).

Surface sample studies allow pollen data to be calibrated against environmental data to provide numerical estimates of past environments. For example, the fossil pollen spectrum may be directly transformed into temperature, precipitation, plant abundance, or vegetation type using a variety of numerical techniques. Fossil palynological samples may be compared directly to modern samples, to climate patterns that exist in the modern samples, or to statistical relationships between the modern samples and environmental data such as precipitation or temperature.

Figure 9.13 compares two palynology-based temperature records. Each fossil sample from the two sites was compared to a database of 1,367 modern surface samples (O. K. Davis 1995) using the squared-chord distance measure of dissimilarity, in which

$$d_{ij} = \sum_k (p_{ik}^{1/2} - p_{jk}^{1/2})^2$$

where d_{ij} = squared-chord distance

and p_{ik} = the proportion of pollen type k in sample i

The temperature value for each fossil sample is computed as the average temperature for the modern surface samples that have squared-chord distances of less than 0.15 to the fossil sample. The standard deviation for these "close analogs" is also shown; the accuracy is ± 1–2 °C.

Preservation

Although pollen is nearly inert in the proper sedimentary environment, it is readily destroyed by household bleaches (5.25 percent sodium hypochlorite or 3 percent hydrogen peroxide). These are oxidizing agents

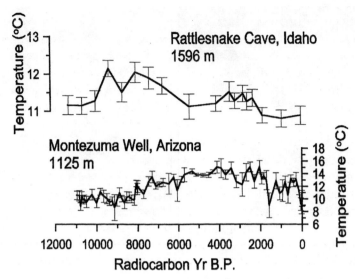

Figure 9.13. Annual temperature reconstructed from the numerical comparison of pollen percentages in fossil samples with those in modern samples.

that readily destroy sporopollen and similar biopolymers. Pollen preservation is best in anoxic environments and is variable in other environments. As palynologists often say, pollen is where you find it. European literature sometimes states that high pH destroys pollen, but palynomorph preservation is excellent in alkaline (pH 9) Mono Lake, which has anoxic sediments.

Aerial oxidation of pollen produces shrunken grains with "melted" or "blurred" sculpture and wall structure. High temperatures darken the pollen wall. Biological oxidation produces a different pattern. Certain fungi and bacteria possess enzymes that can break down the pollen wall. They produce characteristic "etching" or "erosion" patterns on the pollen wall (Cushing 1967; Delcourt and Delcourt 1980). The shrinking and swelling that accompany the wetting and drying of sediment also destroys pollen (Campbell and Campbell 1994).

Because pollen grains vary in their resistence to deterioration (Sangster and Dale 1964; Havinga 1967), pollen deterioration alters the preserved assemblage in favor of the more resistant pollen types. The thickness of the pollen wall and amount of sporopollenin are important factors for pollen preservation, but the recognizability of the grain may be an equally important factor in producing a biased assemblage. Less distinctive grains may be misidentified, or not recognized as pollen, thereby producing a biased pollen assemblage. For example, Chenopodiaceae-*Amaranthus* and Tubuliflorae pollen are thick walled and are easily recognized by the regular placement of pores or spines, even in poorly preserved samples, whereas juniper pollen is thin walled and indistinctive.

Deterioration leaves some grains unidentifiable but still recognizable as pollen. The abundance of deteriorated pollen serves as an index of the reliability of the pollen count and routinely is presented as a separate curve on pollen diagrams (figures 9.8 and 9.9). If deteriorated pollen is not included in the pollen sum, the bias toward well-preserved types is worsened, because the percentages of resistant and easily recognized pollen types are inflated even more.

Figures 9.8 and 9.9 show high abundances of deteriorated pollen in basal sediment. Is the basal assemblage biased by poor preservation? Chenopodiaceae-*Amaranthus* and Tubuliflorae are elevated, but so are the percentages of juniper and the tiny, thin-walled *Sporormiella* spores. Because fragile and indistinct grains are abundant, it is unlikely that deterioration has altered the pollen assemblage.

Applications

Climate reconstructions are based on the environmental tolerances of plants and vegetation. Shifts in abundances and distributions occur when limiting and optimum conditions change, and these shifts can be traced palynologically. Many different numerical approaches have been applied to directly transform palynological data to temperature, precipitation, and other environmental data (Overpeck, Webb, and Prentice 1985).

Figure 9.13 compares palynological reconstructions of climate for two sites in the United States—one in the Northwest, the other in the Southwest. The technique compares each fossil sample with modern surface samples, each of which has been assigned precipitation and temperature values based on local climate records. The annual average of monthly temperature is shown. The temperatures and precipitation shown in figure 9.13 are the averages for the modern samples that are close analogs to each fossil sample.

Archaeological applications of palynology can be divided among studies of human economy and human behavior. Economic applications of archaeological palynology include tracing the domestication of plants and the study of human diet. Examples of behavioral applications include determining the source and function of a given artifact or feature, funerary practices, and human environmental impact.

An example of the impact of indigenous people on local vegetation is shown in figure 9.14. Their population density is estimated from the number of rooms in dwellings in the Hay Hollow region of central Arizona. The juniper pollen percentages (Hevly 1988) are for radiocarbon-dated samples from several archaeological sites, dated to the same time period.

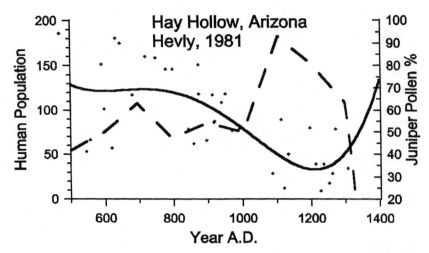

Figure 9.14. Effect of human population on juniper (a fuel) in central Arizona. Dashed line is human population, solid line is smoothed juniper pollen percentage, dots are juniper pollen data points (after Hevly 1988).

Biogeographical applications of palynology include the plant migration studies of Mary Davis and Paul and Hazel Delcourt discussed earlier (figures 9.11 and 9.12). In general, the distributions of plants were closer to the equator during the last glaciation than they are today. Comparison of the long pollen records from Owens Lake, California (Woolfenden 1996; Litwin et al. 1997) and the Great Salt Lake (O. K. Davis 1998) demonstrate that these north-south migrations have been repeated with each successive glacial and interglacial period. During interglacials, such as the present Holocene, juniper woodland surrounds the valleys of the northern Great Basin, but that vegetation type is not particularly well developed in the southern Great Basin. During glaciations, the opposite is true. The lower mountain slopes host cold, treeless vegetation in the northern Great Basin, but woodland dominates the lower slopes of the southern Great Basin.

North-south migrations are not the dominant response of vegetation to climate change in mountainous regions. Throughout the world, the response to climate change in mountainous regions has been altitudinal migration, with full glacial vegetation zones up to 1,000 m lower than today. Figure 9.15 shows the elevational pattern of plant migrations in southern Idaho over the last twenty thousand years (Davis, Sheppard, and Robertson 1986).

Palynological examples of biogeographic shifts in California include the presence of giant sequoia (*Sequoiadendron*) east of the Sierra

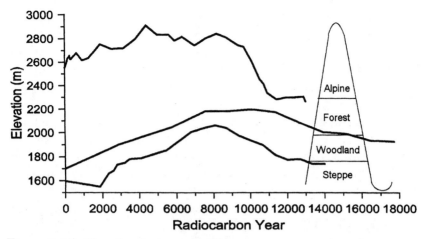

Figure 9.15. Elevational migration of three vegetation-zone boundaries in southern Idaho based on pollen analysis of three sites. Timing and amount of migration vary among the three boundaries, but modern analogs exist for all fossil samples shown (after Davis, Sheppard, and Robertson 1986).

Nevada Crest during the end of the last glaciation, eleven thousand years ago (O. K. Davis 1999); the presence of spruce in the Sierra Nevada up to the end of the last glaciation, eighteen thousand years ago (Litwin et al. 1997); and the presence of greasewood (*Sarcobatus*) east of the Sierra Nevada Crest until seven thousand radiocarbon years ago (O. K. Davis 1999).

Rate-of-change studies are palynological analyses of both biogeographical and paleoecological interest. The goal of these analyses is to determine when vegetation change was most rapid in the past. This is done by calculating the dissimilarity between adjacent pollen samples over the time elapsed between samples. Several measures of dissimilarity can be used (Overpeck, Webb, and Prentice 1985); the most commonly used is the squared-chord distance.

Local and regional compilations of rates of change exist for eastern North America (Jacobsen, Webb, and Grimm 1987) and Europe (Huntley 1990). A comparison of two local rates of change is shown in figure 9.16. In general, these investigations show the greatest change at the glacial-interglacial transition about ten thousand years ago and during the last one thousand years. The middle Holocene is frequently shown to be a time of relative quiet. The curve for Lake Cleveland (figure 9.16) matches this general trend. However, the curve for Montezuma Well shows maximum changes 8,000 ^{14}C (radiocarbon) years ago, coincident with the collapse of juniper woodland, and about 1,300 years ago, coincident with the expansion of the Hohokam culture. Both curves show reduced change during the middle Holocene, consistent with other studies. The differences between the two curves can be explained by the different environmental histories of the Pacific Northwest and the American Southwest (figure 9.13), and by the greater population density of humans in the Southwest.

Environmental restoration typically proceeds with the goal of returning an area to its "undisturbed state." Determining this state can be accomplished by palynological study. In most cases humans are the agents of recent disturbance, including their accidental and intentional introduction of non-native animals and plants. Since humans have been present in nearly every environment of the earth for thousands of years, it is ordinarily assumed that the amplitude or kind of human depredation has recently increased, and the goal is to determine the nature of the environment prior to this raise. See, however, the peak in rates of change 1,300 ^{14}C years ago at Montezuma Well (figure 9.16).

In the southwestern United States, wetlands are rare and are particularly valuable to humans. Wetlands have long been the focus of human habitation and a source of food and materials (Adams 1988). Historic photographs (O. K. Davis and Turner 1987) have documented the trans-

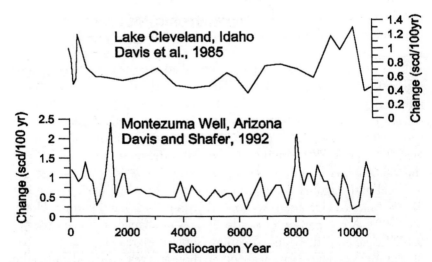

Figure 9.16. Rates of vegetation change based on palynology of two sites in the northwestern (Lake Cleveland [Davis, Sheppard, and Robertson 1985]) and southwestern (Montezuma Well [Davis and Shafer 1992]) United States. Very high (>2 squared chord distance/100 yr) peaks in the Montezuma Well diagram date to the demise of juniper woodland ca. 8,000 ^{14}C (radiocarbon) yr B.P. and to the spread of Hohokam agriculture 1,300 ^{14}C yr B.P.

formation of wetland vegetation during the historic period. Cienegas (marshes) that were previously open and herb dominated now are covered with dense canopies of willow, ash, walnut, and other woody plants.

This transformation is also recorded in palynological studies of the wetland sediment (O. K. Davis 1994). In all six sites investigated, this transformation followed a substantial decrease of charcoal percentages (figure 9.17) and the first occurrence of the pollen exotic taxa. The presence of charred seeds and fruits of wetland plants establishes the burning of the cienega itself. Accompanying the marked expansion of wetland taxa—primarily woody plants—is the conversion of the cienega sediment from silt to peat, and increased percentages of fungal spores including the decay fungus (*Tetraploa*) and the dung fungus (*Sporormiella*). *Tetraploa* apparently colonized the senescent plant material that accumulated after the cessation of burning. The increase of *Sporormiella* (figure 9.3) has been shown to follow the introduction of grazing animals in several sites from western North America (O. K. Davis 1987).

During the late prehistoric period, burning was sufficiently frequent to exclude most woody plants (*Celtis, Cephalanthus, Populus, Fraxinus, Salix*) from the southwestern wetlands. The cienegas appear to have been burned seasonally as a management tool to harvest cienega animals and foster agriculture. Prehistoric human utilization of the southwestern

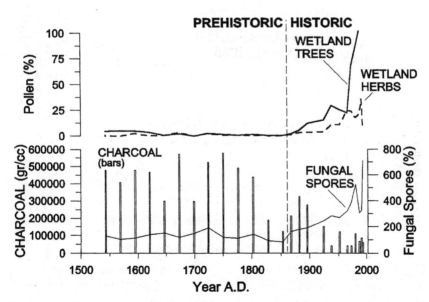

Figure 9.17. Summary of the historic transformation of southwestern wetlands (cienegas). Average curves for six pollen diagrams near the San Pedro River, Arizona. Reduced burning led to increases in woody plants.

cienegas is demonstrated by the presence of corn (*Zea mays*) and pre-Columbian weeds such as purslane (*Portulaca oleraceane*).

Appendix: Pollen Morphology Texts and Databases

Adams, R. J., and J. K. Morton. 1972–79. *An atlas of pollen of the trees and shrubs of eastern Canada and the adjacent United States*, parts 1–4. University of Waterloo Biology Series 8–11.

American Association of Stratigraphic Palynogists. 2000. Palydisks. www.opal. geology.toronto.ca:80/AASP/aasppalydisk.html.

Bambara, S. B., and N. A. Leidy. 1991. *An atlas of selected pollen important to honey bees in the eastern United States*. Raleigh: North Carolina State Bee-keepers Association. 38 pp.

Bassett, I. J., C. W. Crompton, and J. A. Parmalee. 1978. *Airborne pollen grains and common fungus spores of Canada*. Monograph No. 18. Canada Department of Agriculture, Research Branch. 321 pp.

Crompton, C. W., and W. A. Wojtas. 1993. *Pollen grains of Canadian honey plants*. Publication 1892/E. Center for Land and Biological Resources Research, Ottawa, Ontario: Research Branch Agriculture Canada. 228 pp.

Dalmau, J. M. P. 1961. *Polen, estractura y características de los granos de polen*. Gerona, Spain: J. M. P. Dalmau.

Erdtman, G. 1952. *Pollen morphology and plant taxonomy, Angiosperms*. Waltham, Mass: Chronica Botanica.

Gonzalez Quintero, Lauro. 1967. *Flora polinica y tipos de vegetacion del Valle del Mezquital*. Thesis, National School of Biological Sciences, Mexico City, Mexico.

Hevly, R. H. 1981. Pollen production, transport and preservation: Potentials and limitations in archaeological paylnology. *Journal of Ethnobiology* 1: 39–54.

Jones, G. D., V. M. Bryant Jr., M. H. Lieux, S. D. Jones, and P. D. Lingren. 1995. *Pollen of the southeastern United States: With emphasis on melissopalynology and entomopalynology*. Contribution Serial 30. Dallas, Tex.: American Association of Stratigraphic Palynologists Foundation. 76 pp. 104 plates.

Kapp, R. O. 1969. *How to know pollen and spores*. Dubuque, Iowa: W. C. Brown. 249 pp.

McAndrews, J. H., A. A. Berti, and G. Norris. 1973. *Key to the pollen and spores of the Great Lakes region*. Life Science Miscellaneous Publication. Toronto: Royal Ontario Museum. 61 pp.

Moore, P. D., J. A. Webb, and M. E. Collinson. 1991. *Pollen analysis*. London: Blackwell Scientific. 216 pp.

National Oceanic and Atmospheric Administration. 2000a. Latin American Pollen Database. www.ngdc.noaa.gov/paleo/lapd.html.

———. 2000b. North American Pollen Database. www.ngdc.noaa.gov.paleo/napd.html.

Roubik, D. W., and P. Moreno. 1991. *Pollen and spores of Barro Colorado Island*. Monographs in Systematic Botany 36. St. Louis: Missouri Botanical Garden. 268 pp.

Salgado Labouriau, Maria Lea. 1971. *Contribuicao a palinològia dos cerrados*. Editado pela Academica Brasileria de Ciencias.

Ting, W. S. 1966. Determination of *Pinus* species by pollen statistics. *University of California Publications in Geological Science* 58: 1–183.

Wodehouse, R. P. 1959. *Pollen grains, their structure, identification and significance in science and medicine*. New York: Hafner Publishing.

References

Adams, K. R. 1988. *The ethnobotany and phenology of plants in and adjacent to two riparian habitats in southeastern Arizona*. Ph.D. dissertation, University of Arizona, Tucson.

Antevs, E. V. 1944. The right word? *Pollen Analysis Circular* 6: 2.

Behre, K.-E. 1986. *Anthropogenic indicators in pollen diagrams*. Boston: A. A. Balkema.

Brooks, J., ed. 1971. *Sporopollenin*. Proceedings of a symposium held at the Geology Department, Imperial College, London. New York: Academic Press.

Campbell, I. D., and C. Campbell. 1994. Pollen preservation: Experimental wet-dry cycles in saline and desalinated sediments. *Palynology* 18: 5–10.

Cushing, E. J. 1967. Evidence for differential pollen preservation in late Quaternary sediments in Minnesota. *Review of Palaeobotany and Palynology* 4: 87–101.

Davis, M. B. 1963. On the theory of pollen analysis. *American Journal of Science* 261: 897–912.

———. 1976. Pleistocene biogeography of temperate deciduous forests. *Geoscience and Man* 8: 13–26.

Davis, O. K. 1984. Pollen frequencies reflect vegetation patterns in a Great Basin (USA) mountain range. *Review of Palaeobotany and Palynology* 40: 295–315.

———. 1987. Spores of the dung fungus *Sporormiella*: Increased abundance in historic sediments and before Pleistocene megafaunal extinction. *Quaternary Research* 28: 290–294.

———. 1994. *Pollen analysis of borderland cienegas*. Contract Number HQ/AZ-920815 1. Report submitted to Richard P. Young, The Nature Conservancy, Arizona Field Office, 300 E. University Blvd., Suite 230, Tucson, Arizona 85704.

———. 1995. Climate and vegetation patterns in surface samples from arid western U.S.A.: Application to Holocene climatic reconstructions. *Palynology* 19: 97–120.

———. 1998. Palynological evidence for vegetation cycles in a 1.5-million-year pollen record from the Great Salt Lake, Utah, USA. *Palaeogeography, Palaeoclimatology and Palaeoecology* 138: 175–185.

———. 1999. Pollen analysis of Tulare Lake, California: Great Basin–like vegetation in Central California during the Full-glacial and early Holocene. *Review of Palaeobotany and Palynology* 107: 249–257.

Davis, O. K., and D. S. Shafer. 1992. A Holocene climatic record for the Sonoran Desert from pollen analysis of Montezuma Well, Arizona, USA. *Palaeogeography, Palaeoclimatology and Palaeoecology* 92: 107–119.

Davis, O. K., J. C. Sheppard, and S. Robertson. 1986. Contrasting climatic histories for the Snake River Plain result from multiple thermal maxima. *Quaternary Research* 26: 321–339.

Davis, O. K., and R. M. Turner. 1987. Palynological evidence for the historic expansion of juniper and desert shrubs resulting from human disturbance in Arizona, U.S.A. *Review of Palaeobotany and Palynology* 49: 177–193.

Delcourt, P. A., and Delcourt, H. R. 1980. Pollen preservation and Quaternary environmental history in the southeastern United States. *Palynology* 4: 215–231.

———. 1987. *Long-term forest dynamics of the temperate zone.* New York: Springer Verlag.

Faegri, K., P. A. Kaland, and K. Krzywinski. 1989. *Textbook of pollen analysis,* 4th edition. New York: John Wiley.

Havinga, A. J. 1967. Palynology and pollen preservation. *Review of Palaeobotany and Palynology* 2: 81–98.

Hevly, R. H. 1988. Prehistoric vegetation and paleoclimates on the Colorado Plateaus. Pages 92–118 in *The Anasazi in a changing environment,* ed. G. J. Gumerman. New York: Cambridge University Press.

Huntley, B. 1990. Dissimilarity mapping between fossil and contemporary pollen spectra in Europe for the past 13,000 years. *Quaternary Research* 33: 360–367.

Hyde, H. A., and D. A. Williams. 1944. The right word. *Pollen Analysis Circular* 8: 2.

Jacobsen Jr., G. L., T. Webb III, and E. C. Grimm. 1987. Patterns and rates of vegetation change during the deglaciation of eastern North America. In *Geology of North America.* Vol. K: North America and adjacent oceans during the last deglaciation, eds. W. F. Ruddiman and H. E. Wright Jr. Boulder, Colo.: Geological Society of America.

Jansonius, J., and D. C. McGregor. 1996. Chapter 1, Introduction. In *Palynology: Principles and Applications,* 3 vols., eds. J. Jansonius and D. C. McGregor. Dallas, Tex.: American Association of Stratigraphic Palynologists Foundation.

Kedevs, M. 1990. *Transmission electron microscopy of the fossil angiosperm exines.* Hungary. Foundation for Szeged, Hungary and the OTKA, Poland.

Litwin, R. J., D. P. Adam, N. O. Frederiksen, and W. B. Woolfenden. 1997. An 800,000 year pollen record from Owens Lake, California: Preliminary analyses. Pages 127–142 in *Geological Society of America Special Paper 317.* Washington, D. C.: Geological Society of America.

Maher, L. J. 1972. Absolute pollen diagram of Redrock Lake, Boulder County, Colorado. *Quaternary Research* 2: 531–533.

Moore, P. D., J. A. Webb, and M. E. Collinson. 1991. *Pollen analysis.* London: Blackwell Scientific.

Overpeck, J. T., T. Webb III, and I. C. Prentice. 1985. Quantitative interpretation of fossil pollen spectra: Dissimilarity coefficients and the method of modern analogs. *Quaternary Research* 23: 87–108.

Punt, W., S. Blackmore, S. Nilsson, and A. Le Thomas. 1994. *Glossary of pollen and spore terminology.* Laboratory for Paleobotany and Palynology Contributions Series 1.

Reinsch, P. 1884. Micro-paleo phytologia formationis carbonifera. *Erlangen*. 1: I–vii, 1–80; 2: I–xi, 1–56.

Sangster, A. G., and H. M. Dale. 1964. Pollen grain preservation of underrepresented species in fossil spectra. *Canadian Journal of Botany* 42: 437–449.

Von Post, L. 1916. Om skogstrSdpollen I sydsvenska torfmosselagerfsljder. *Geologiska Fsreningens I Stockholm Fsrhandlingar* 38: 384–390.

Woolfenden, W. B. 1996. *Late-Quaternary vegetation history of the southern Owens Valley region, Inyo County, California*. Ph.D. dissertation, University of Arizona, Tucson.

10

Packrat Middens as a Tool for Reconstructing Historic Ecosystems

David Rhode

Several species of mammals and birds accumulate large quantities of biological remains in nests or waste heaps. Under favorable conditions these "midden" deposits may be preserved for thousands of years, providing a detailed fossil record of past environmental conditions. Packrat middens are among the best known of these fossil accumulations, so-called because rodents of the genus *Neotoma*, the woodrats or packrats, create them. Packrat middens contain abundant, exquisitely preserved remains of plants and animals that (1) can be well dated by the radiocarbon method, (2) yield detailed information about the past spatial distribution of particular taxa and ecosystems, and (3) provide valuable insights into the changing ecophysiology of particular taxa in response to climate change, atmospheric composition, and other factors.

The paleoenvironmental value of packrat middens was first recognized in the early 1960s (Wells and Jorgensen 1964; Wells and Berger 1967), and since then they have revolutionized our knowledge of the history of dryland ecosystems in western North America. Packrat middens exhibit certain strengths, shortcomings, and biases that must be considered when using them to make inferences about past ecosystems. Nevertheless, they provide a uniquely localized, detailed, and diversified archive of past environmental conditions from dryland regions where other records are sometimes quite scarce. The information derived from middens complements regional data available from other paleoenvironmental sources (e.g., pollen profiles, dendrochronology, alluvial or lake chronologies), so that reconstructions of past ecosystems can be independently tested, refined, and expanded.

This chapter explores the utility of packrat midden analysis for learning about past ecosystems. Characteristics of middens are discussed first, followed by a brief outline of midden collection and analysis techniques. Strengths, weaknesses, and biases of the method are then considered. Some examples of the significant findings of midden analysis are then presented to illustrate how midden research has shed light on various paleoecological issues. Finally, the applicability of midden research for restoration ecology is considered.

Packrats and Their Middens

The genus *Neotoma* consists of twenty-one species of cricetid rodents (figure 10.1), ranging in size from 100 g to 400 g adult weight, with large eyes, prominent rounded ears, long tails, soft fur that ranges from pale buff to nearly black, and strongly built feet adapted to climbing (Vaughn 1990). The genus inhabits a wide variety of habitats and is widely distributed in North America from Nicaragua northward to the Northwest Territories of Canada and from California east to Florida (Vaughn 1990). Packrats

Figure 10.1. Bushy-tailed woodrat (*Neotoma cinerea*), living in a nest atop a large indurated midden deposit.

are typically solitary-dwelling, territorial rodents that den in shelters such as rocks and rock overhangs, trees and hollow tree stumps, under bushes, and occasionally in burrows (Finley 1990). Although habits, dietary specialization, and habitats are quite variable among different species, packrats generally have two main habitat requirements: adequate shelter and succulent plants, which make up most of their diet. They are noted for their propensity to build large dens from materials they collect within a 30–50-meter radius. Packrats typically bring back a wide variety of items: sticks, grasses, animal bones, carnivore or herbivore dung, cactus pads and spines, and other nearby items that attract their curiosity. They heap these around their den as protection from predators and the elements (figure 10.2). Some species of packrats make "houses" that are quite substantial in size, while other species make only small, rudimentary houses. Within the house are separate areas for nesting, food storage, and elimination of waste (Finley 1990).

The loose debris of a packrat den may be protected for long periods of time under properly sheltered conditions, but these debris piles usually decompose with time. More commonly, however, the collected materials

Figure 10.2. Modern packrat house. Loose sticks, rocks, and other debris collected by the rat surround the partially indurated midden. The midden, if soaked with amberat and indurated, may be preserved for long periods of time, but the loose debris usually does not last for very long.

are preserved in the packrat's viscous urine. Packrats tend to urinate copiously, even in arid environments, and their urine coats and saturates the collected plant materials. When dry, the urine becomes a dark brown to black, glossy, rock-hard mass called *amberat* (Orr 1957; Wells and Berger 1967). A midden cemented with amberat is said to be *indurated* (Spaulding et al. 1990). Amberat is hygroscopic, soft and sticky when wet, and hard and rocklike when dry. When the air is humid, amberat rehydrates and flows through capillary action to the outside of the midden, where it dries to form a hard, lustrous rind. This rind adds extra protection to the enclosed plant and animal remains. Through time, the rind incorporates dust, pollen, and other airborne debris, creating rinds that are often dull, grayish, and cracked in very old middens. The amberat prevents microbial growth and decay, and it keeps termites and other insects from consuming the saturated plant material (Spaulding et al. 1990).

Ancient packrat middens are typically found in caves, rockshelters, or overhanging cliffs, where they are protected from the elements. The midden looks like a layered lump of dirty asphalt adhering a rock wall, containing a jumbled assortment of plant materials, fecal pellets, other organic debris, and rocks, all encased in amberat (figure 10.3). Amberat is strongly adhesive and will stick to the sides of dry caves or protected rockshelters for millennia, as long as the shelter remains dry. Middens do not last very long in rock overhangs if subject to repeated wetting, or if the rock surface exfoliates quickly. If a midden is repeatedly wetted, the amberat eventually flows or dissolves out, and the midden will fall apart and decompose. For this reason, middens are well preserved in arid areas, but they do not tend to last in very humid or mesic climates.

Generations of rats may inhabit the same crevice in a cave or shelter periodically over thousands of years, each rat living on and around the midden accumulated by its predecessors. As a result, a midden can develop complex internal stratigraphy and layering, indicating multiple episodes of deposition. These different layers may be of very different ages, so care is taken not to mix them when collecting and processing the midden for analysis (Wells 1976).

Middens made by packrats are the most commonly studied, but other mammals (including humans) create middens that can be valuable archives of paleobiological information. For example, porcupines (*Erethizon*) create middens composed primarily of vegetal materials (Betancourt, Van Devender, and Rose 1986), and certain genera of birds, notably raptors, also create middens that may be immensely valuable archives for studying regional faunal history (Andrews 1990). Owls and other raptors regurgitate pellets containing indigestible parts of their diet: bones, hair, feathers, insect parts, and even plant remains (Rhode and

Figure 10.3. Ancient packrat midden. This large midden, from the Eleana Range in southern Nevada, was sampled and studied by W. G. Spaulding (Spaulding 1985, 1990). Note the fine stratification in the midden (right), indicating separate depositional events. These strata have been radiocarbon-dated to a range of ages from ten thousand years to seventeen thousand years.

Madsen 1998). The pellets are often examined to determine the birds' diet (Bent 1937; Gleason and Craig 1979; Marti 1974). Over time, deep midden deposits composed largely of regurgitated pellets may develop beneath frequently used roosts in caves or on overhangs, providing a rich fossil record. One such deposit is located in Homestead Cave, located in the Lakeside Range near Great Salt Lake, Utah (figure 10.4). This deep (>11 ft), well-stratified midden deposit contains literally millions of identifiable bones, providing an exceedingly detailed record of small mammal and bird abundance dating through the last eleven thousand years (Grayson 1998; Madsen 2000).

Humans also produce middens. Human settlement or campsites typically have dark, organically rich soils that contain fragments of charcoal, bones, and shells. So-called shell middens are found by archaeologists throughout coastal areas and along major rivers worldwide (Stein 1992). These ancient garbage heaps are densely packed with layers of shellfish, which can also serve as detailed paleobiological archives. For example,

Figure 10.4. The well-stratified deposits in Homestead Cave represent eleven thousand years' worth of owl pellets, resulting in an extremely rich fossil record of small mammal occupation of the region (Grayson 1998; Madsen 2000).

shell middens in coastal Southern California have provided information about the changing abundance of shellfish populations in estuaries and coasts in response to changing environmental conditions as well as human predation habits (Glassow and Wilcoxon 1988; Jones 1996). Isotopic dating of shells can also provide proxy data for changing ocean conditions through time (Arnold and Tissot 1993; Jones and Kennett 1999).

Packrat Midden Collection and Analysis

Collection and basic preparation of packrat middens are fairly straightforward and do not require elaborate equipment. However, most analyses require specialized expertise and training. Identification of plant and animal macrofossils requires a strong knowledge of the regional flora and fauna, a good reference collection or herbarium for identification, and a talent for recognizing taxa from a few isolated seeds, leaves, twigs, bones, or teeth. Other kinds of analyses, related to ecophysiological function, anatomy, genetics, or chemical composition, usually require the collaboration of specialists.

Once a suitable packrat midden is found in the field, a portion of it is usually removed with a hammer and chisel, for subsequent analysis

Figure 10.5a. Removing chunks of an indurated packrat midden, using a rock hammer.

Figure 10.5b. A piece of indurated midden ca. 13,000 ^{14}C years old, showing abundant pine needles.

(figures 10.5a and b). Notes are taken on slope, aspect, elevation, rock type, and vegetation growing in the vicinity of the sampling locality. These data allow the investigator to identify how similar the contents of the packrat midden are to modern conditions, and to assess whether plant or animal remains are present in the midden that do not occur in the vicinity at the time of collection. If a packrat currently inhabits the same locale, a sample of its modern midden is often taken to compare against the ancient sample.

Once in the lab, the midden sample is prepared. The midden is first closely examined to identify obvious stratification. This step often requires splitting the midden and removing the exterior rind with a hammer and chisel. Different strata within the midden sample are separated and their exterior rinds are cleaned off, again using a hammer and chisel. Some investigators may simply examine plant remains exposed on the surfaces of these "split" samples, without further preparation (e.g., Wells 1976). More frequently, however, these splits are immersed in water to dissolve the amberat and disaggregate the samples (Van Devender 1973). Soaking can take several days, and heavily indurated middens may require more than one soaking to dissolve out all the amberat. The result of soaking is a slurry of disaggregated macrofossils, fine silty matrix, and dissolved amberat (urine). Most of this slurry is poured through a fine mesh sediment sieve and washed. The macrofossils retrieved on the sieve are then dried under low heat. A sample of the slurry is often retained for pollen analysis as well. A urine sample may also be retained for other purposes, such as chemical or immunospecific analyses (Lowenstein, Rainey, and Betancourt 1991) or cosmogenic dating (Plummer et al. 1997).

The dried macrofossil sample is weighed, then sorted to retrieve and identify plant remains, animal bones and hair, insect parts, rodent fecal pellets, and other materials. The identification of fossil parts is conducted by comparing them with reference specimens and published descriptions, often with the assistance of taxonomists who specialize in particular taxa. Counting fossil remains is done using a variety of scales (Spaulding et al. 1990): nominal (presence/absence), ordinal ranks (e.g., Van Devender 1973; Thompson 1984); interval (counts or weights), ratio (proportion) measures (Spaulding 1985); or some measure of macrofossil concentration (e.g., logged number of elements per unit weight of midden; Cole and Webb 1985). Samples can contain thousands of individual plant fossils, so it is sometimes preferable, from the standpoint of cost and efficiency and without the loss of critical information, to quantify the presence of different types of fossils on some ordinal scale (e.g., present, rare, common, abundant), rather than a more labor-intensive interval scale (Van Devender 1973). In some cases, counting abundant small remains may require identification under a binocular microscope, and some form of sampling such as a point-count frame similar to those used in fecal pellet or rumen analysis (Chamrad and Box 1964). Once segregated, various fossil materials can be analyzed for a wide range of applications (see below).

Age determination is typically accomplished through radiocarbon dating, either through bulk dating of midden constituents (e.g., fecal pellets or unidentified plant matter), or dating of a specific fossil type (e.g., juniper twigs or pine needles). Bulk dating provides a general date of the sample as a whole and is often necessary when using conventional radio-carbon-dating methods that require fairly large sample sizes. However, the bulk date may not apply to specific fossil types of interest, which may be intrusive into the sample from an older or younger deposition event. If the age of a specific plant or animal fossil is the objective, it is better to date it directly, rather than rely on a possibly tenuous association with bulk dates. Accelerator-based radiocarbon-dating methods require very small samples, so even small or rare fossils usually provide a sample large enough to date (Van Devender et al. 1985).

Midden results are represented diagrammatically in a variety of ways, some of them similar to the diagrams of pollen analysis (Betancourt, Van Devender, and Martin 1990a; cf. Faegri and Iversen 1975). Constituents of middens from a single area are often depicted as *time series*, using a set of histograms (or sometimes pie diagrams) to show changing abundance of major plant taxa through time (figure 10.6). Midden records may also be represented in a *time-elevation curve* (figure 10.7), showing changing elevations of various plant taxa through time. Occasionally, researchers will compute a similarity measure between midden constituents and modern vegetation (Spaulding 1985; Cole 1990), and then show how similarity between a midden sample and modern vegetation has tended to decrease with the age of the midden (figure 10.8). This graphical tech-nique can be useful for illustrating variable rates of vegetation change during the past several millennia, but it tends to lose utility when assess-ing rates of change in earlier periods. This limitation occurs because glacial-age vegetation often differed so much from modern conditions that any changes in glacial-age vegetation would not necessarily result in change in the similarity index relative to modern vegetation.

Strengths, Weaknesses, and Biases of the Midden Method

One of the major strengths of packrat middens as a paleoecological tool is the spatio-temporal specificity of individual midden samples. The macro-fossils preserved in a midden usually are derived from a very localized area, on the order of 2.5 acres (1 hectare) centered on the midden, and usually represent a relatively brief amount of time, on the order of several years to a few decades. This spatio-temporal specificity of middens creates a record of past biotic conditions that is quite different in character from that typically derived from pollen records. Many pollen records from lakes or bogs can be treated as regional in coverage and continuous through time, analogous to a broad panoramic movie sequence. The record from a packrat midden does not have this regional, continuous

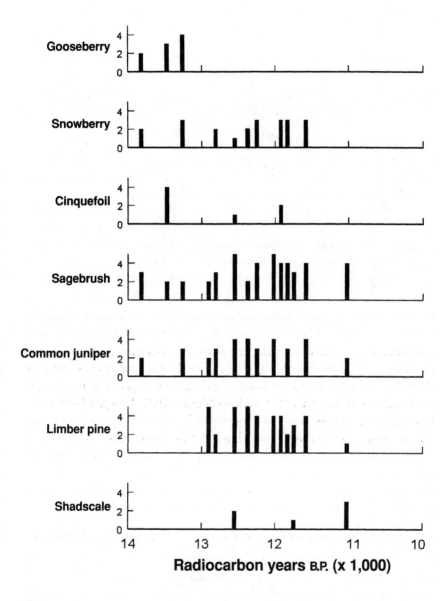

Figure 10.6. Example of a time series diagram, showing changing abundance of various plant taxa in midden samples dating 14,000–10,000 ^{14}C yr B.P. in the western Bonneville Basin, Nevada-Utah. Abundance is scaled ordinally: 0 = absent, 1 = rare, 2 = occasional, 3 = common, 4 = abundant. (Data from Rhode and Madsen 1995.)

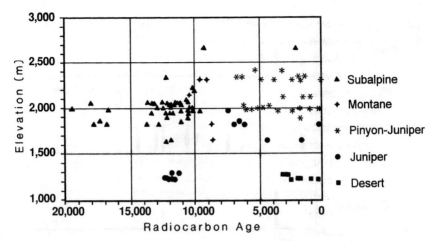

Figure 10.7. Example of a time-elevation diagram, showing changing elevations of vegetational assemblages represented in middens in the central Great Basin (38–40° N) for the last twenty thousand years (Thompson 1990).

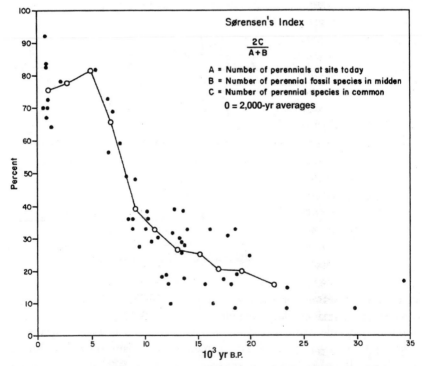

Figure 10.8. Example of a similarity diagram for the Grand Canyon, Arizona (Cole 1985), showing that the similarity between the plant taxa represented in middens and the modern vegetation at the midden sites decreases through time. Dots are midden localities, open circles are averages from two-thousand-year segments. (Reprinted by permission of the University of Chicago Press.)

character—it is analogous to a detailed, close-up snapshot. Individually, the snapshot can give an excellent picture of conditions within its localized frame of reference, but it does not provide a continuous record of biotic change, nor can the regional conditions outside of the snapshot's narrow frame be identified with any certainty. But the two different kinds of records are additive and complementary. If a large number of midden "snapshots" representing different times and places are put together, and if these midden records are combined with the continuous regional record available from pollen profiles, then a very detailed regional record of terrestrial vegetation change emerges (Mehringer and Wigand 1990).

Another strength of packrat middens as an archive of paleoenvironmental information is the diversity of remains that are typically preserved for analysis. Plant macrofossils are often found in such exquisite condition that they are suitable for a wide range of analyses. Plant parts can be examined for anatomical features, such as stomatal density on leaves that may provide clues to changing ecophysiological function of certain plant taxa through time (Van de Water, Leavitt, and Betancourt 1994). Stable isotopes of a variety of elements (carbon, hydrogen, oxygen, sulfur), found in cellulose or other tissue, may also provide important data, such as growing season temperature, seasonal precipitation, plant water-use efficiency, and plant stress (Long et al. 1990; Van de Water, Leavitt, and Betancourt 1994; Wigand, Hemphill, and Patra 1994). Pollen is also very common in packrat middens, derived from a mixture of local plants as well as the regional pollen rain (Anderson and Van Devender 1992; O. K. Davis and Anderson 1987; Thompson 1985; Van Devender 1988). Pollen in the midden can complement and extend the localized picture of plant macrofossils by showing that some plants not represented by macrofossils were present or even common in the region around the midden. (However, the varied sources of both local and regional pollen deposition in a midden can complicate and confound easy interpretation.)

Animal remains, including bones, hair, desiccated muscle or other tissue, feathers, scales, fecal pellets, and insect or arthropod parts, are also frequently found in middens. Many of these materials are derived from the locality around the midden, providing an indication of faunal associates of the local plant community, such as local pollinators. Invertebrate remains may also be derived from insects and arthropods that inhabit the midden commensally with the rats, or from parasites of the packrats. Because insect species often have narrow climatic and habitat requirements, insect remains can be very useful for making inferences about past climatic conditions or the existence of certain plant or animal taxa in the region (Elias 1994, 1996).

Faunal remains (bones, feathers, skin, fecal pellets, etc.) can provide physiological and genetic information about past animal populations as well. For example, fecal pellets can provide evidence of the packrat's diet (Finley 1990; Nelson, Webb, and Long 1990), internal parasite load, and changing body size in response to climate variation (Smith, Betancourt, and Brown 1995; Smith and Betancourt 1998). Isotopic composition of bones or preserved tissue may yield evidence of changing diet through time (Kohn 1999; Sillen and Lee-Thorp 1994). Recent advances in retrieval of genetic information from well-preserved fossil materials (Poinar et al. 1998) open the door to many different investigations relating evolutionary and biogeographic dynamics to climatic, ecophysiological, and ecosystem changes through time.

A third major strength of the packrat midden method is that middens are often ubiquitous in rocky areas of drylands—locations where other fossil records are scarce. For example, more than three thousand dated packrat middens have been analyzed in the dry interior region of North America, making its late Pleistocene and Holocene vegetation history among the best known in the world (Betancourt, Van Devender, and Martin 1990b). This is a region where well-dated pollen sequences are scarce compared to more mesic parts of the world.

The midden record also contains a number of weaknesses and biases that need to be considered when making inferences about past biotic conditions at both local and regional scales. One weakness is that the information contained in middens is largely nominal or ordinal in scale, consisting largely of a roster of biotic remains, a local floral or faunal list. Comparison between plant remains found in modern middens and the modern vegetation around the middens often shows a fairly strong correspondence with the *kinds* of plants growing in the vicinity, but little correspondence with the *relative abundance* of plants in the area (Dial and Czaplewski 1990; Frase and Sera 1993; Spaulding et al. 1990). This difference between what is most abundant in the nest and what is most abundant in the local area reflects biases in a packrat's collection behavior. That is, even though a packrat often has fairly catholic collecting habits, it still favors certain plants in its diet or to build its nest or house. Furthermore, different species of packrats may have different collecting preferences, so that a midden site sequentially inhabited by different packrat species may show significantly different plant records, even in the absence of significant vegetation change. Hence, the abundance of plant remains found in an ancient midden probably does not correspond directly with the abundance of plants that grew near the midden when it was created.

The midden record also provides little direct evidence of biotic community structure or function. For example, pine needles in a midden may demonstrate that a certain species of pine grew at a locality but not whether the needles came from a single tree, a stand of trees, or a shrubby krummholz form. If the midden record does not also contain seeds, cones, or pollen, a researcher may not be certain whether the pines were healthy and capable of reproducing, or were beyond their reproductive tolerances. Other key ecological parameters and processes such as biomass, age structure, nutrient cycling, and dynamic interpopulation and interspecific relationships, such as predation and competition, are often difficult or impossible to identify in the fossil remains left in packrat middens.

An additional weakness of the midden record relates to sampling biases. The vast majority of fossil middens are preserved in protected rocky localities, so that the vegetation record is strongly biased toward plant communities inhabiting rocky outcrops, mountains, and canyons. Vegetation communities located away from rock outcrops tend to be underrepresented. A few exceptions to this generalization apply. For instance, middens more than one thousand years old have been found in protected crevices in the walls of arroyos cut through consolidated alluvial fill in southern Nevada and elsewhere, providing evidence for vegetation change in valley or wash settings (Cole and Webb 1985; Hunter and McAuliffe 1994; Spaulding 1990).

A second possible source of sampling bias is that, in general, younger middens may be more common than older middens, simply as a function of the increasing probability of degradation through time (Webb and Betancourt 1990). However, in many parts of the American Southwest, the number of middens known from the late Wisconsin glacial period (14,000–10,000 B.P.) is greater than the number dating to the subsequent early Holocene (9000–6000 B.P.). This pattern runs counter to expectations based on increasing degradation through time. Webb and Betancourt (1990) suggest that this bias may be the result of the collection habits of researchers, who tend to favor the analysis and dating of middens containing plant remains that are significantly different from modern vegetation. However, others suggest that packrats may also have been more plentiful during the late Wisconsin than during the early Holocene in many areas (Brown 1971; Grayson 1998).

A final, and important, weakness has to do with the radiocarbon method of dating. Radiocarbon dating can provide reliable, and often quite precise, ages for organic materials that are as much as forty thousand years old. This range is sufficient to date most packrat middens encountered (though the ages of a few known middens exceed that limit), and it is usually entirely sufficient for the purposes of reconstructing historic landscapes. However, radiocarbon dating lacks precision with samples from the last four hundred years or so (figure 10.9). There are two reasons for this imprecision. First, every radiocarbon age determination contains

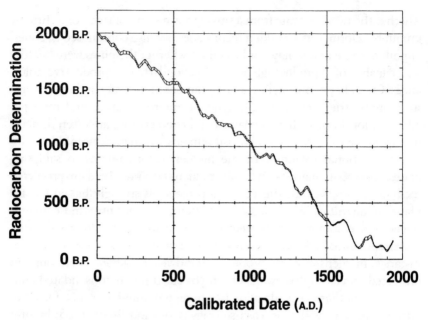

Figure 10.9. A calibration curve showing the measured relationship between radiocarbon dates and calendar dates for the last two thousand calendar years. Data are from Stuiver et al. 1998, and the curve is taken from the OxCal calibration program, version 3.0 (Bronk Ramsey 1995). Note that the curve flattens out from A.D. 1550 to 1950, so that a single radiocarbon date may reflect several distinct calendar dates.

a degree of measurement uncertainty. This means that every radiocarbon date is really a normal probability distribution with a standard deviation typically on the order of several decades. Thus, the range of radiocarbon dating is quite good for tracking environmental change on the scale of centuries to millennia but not so good for finer-scale temporal changes. Second, radiocarbon ages do not necessarily correspond uniquely or closely to calendar ages. A one-to-one correspondence between radiocarbon dates and calendar dates assumes a constant decay rate of the carbon isotope ^{14}C *and* a constant initial amount of ^{14}C in the dated object. However, the atmospheric abundance of ^{14}C varies through time and, as a result, plants and animals may contain different initial amounts of ^{14}C at the time of death. This difference adversely affects the relationship between radiocarbon dates and calendar dates (Stuiver and Reimer 1993; Stuiver, Reimer, and Braziunas 1998). If the initial amount varies, then a radiocarbon age does not necessarily correspond closely to a given calendar date and indeed may correspond to several different possible calendar dates. Moreover, variation in solar radiation has caused significant fluctuations in the atmospheric ^{14}C content during the last few hundred years, and any single radiocarbon age within that time period may correspond probabilistically to a wide range of possible calendar dates. Modern (i.e., post-Hiroshima) samples can be readily distinguished from pre-nuclear testing samples, but samples dating between about A.D. 1500 and A.D. 1945 cannot be readily assigned a single calendar age within that interval.

When the imprecision of radiocarbon dating is coupled with the amount of time represented by individual midden samples (probably several decades), it becomes clear that packrat middens are a rather coarse-grained data source for tracking vegetation changes during the last few hundred years. Middens dating older than about fifty years can be compared with modern vegetation, and middens older than a few hundred years can be usefully compared with middens that are younger than three hundred years. Such comparisons yield evidence of dramatic changes in rangeland vegetation composition during the past four hundred years (e.g., Cole, Henderson, and Shafer 1997; Cole and Webb 1985; Hunter and McAuliffe 1994), but that is close to the limit of discrimination presently available. It is much harder to document changes in vegetation using middens having radiocarbon ages of 250 ± 50 yr B.P. and 100 ± 50 yr B.P., simply because of the dating problems associated with the radiocarbon method (figure 10.10). These dating difficulties introduce serious limitations in using packrat middens to examine in close detail the empirical record of vegetation change in western North America during the past few hundred years. During that period, rangelands in western North America underwent extensive vegetation changes as a result of Euro-American settlement. At the same time, vegetation also responded to climatic warming after the end of the Little Ice Age—a cold period that affected many western North American plant communities from ca. A.D. 1550 to 1850. Sorting out the effects of climatic variation from human-induced effects to vegetation patterns during the last few hundred years is an important and rather difficult scientific task, requiring an integrated, multidisciplinary, fine-grained, regional approach toward detecting change and its causes (e.g., Allen, Betancourt, and Swetnam 1998)—one with policy implications for ecological restoration and management of rangelands. Unfortunately, fine-grained documentation of vegetation change during this period can be quite difficult if it employs radiocarbon dating as the main chronological tool.

If one is not concerned with the nature of vegetation change or ecosystem dynamics during the last few hundred years, but instead wishes to obtain general information about pre-disturbance vegetation as a historical reference point for restoration efforts, then this dating imprecision

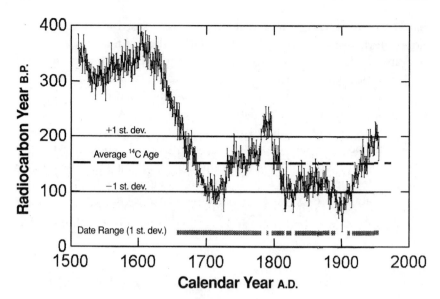

Figure 10.10. Close-up of radiocarbon age–calendar date calibration curve for last 450 years (data from Stuiver et al. 1998). Horizontal dashed line represents a hypothetical average radiocarbon date of 150 years, and horizontal thin lines represent one standard deviation of 50 years (i.e., 150 – 50 ^{14}C yr B.P.). This radiocarbon date would correspond, at one standard deviation (~ 67 percent likelihood of being the correct radiocarbon age), with the calendar ages spanned by the thick horizontal bands at the bottom of the graph labeled "Date Range." Note that this single date spans nearly all of the last 300 years. At two standard deviations (~ 95 percent likelihood of being the correct radiocarbon age), the entire 300-year interval is spanned.

may not be an important problem. However, it should always be kept in mind that plant communities experience considerable and continuous change in response to variations in climate, geomorphic processes, fire frequency, and human action, on spatial scales ranging from the localized to the broadly regional and on timescales of decades to millennia (Chambers et al. 1998; Tausch 1999a; Wigand 1997; Wigand et al. 1995; Wigand and Rhode, in press). Treating "presettlement" environments as having been uniform or "average" during the past millennium neglects a great deal of the spatio-temporal variation that occurred and that is an essential historical legacy of modern ecosystems (see below). Understanding that essential variability and its causes in a historical perspective requires control of the time element, and that is why the imprecision of radiocarbon dating can be troublesome.

Middens as Ecological and Paleoecological Tools: Some Examples

Despite these various shortcomings, packrat middens have proven extremely valuable for addressing a wide range of ecological and paleoecological issues in dryland regions. A selection of recent analyses is described here to give the reader a sense of the range of ecological and paleoecological applications that midden analysis provides. These include (1) reconstructing the vegetation history of southwestern North America; (2) tracing the migration histories of particular taxa; (3) determining the effects of climate on the anatomy and physiology of plant and animal species; (4) using plant and animal distributions as proxy estimators of past climatic conditions; and (5) gauging the effects of human disturbance on plant communities.

Reconstructing the Vegetation History of the American Southwest

The current reconstruction of past vegetation in arid North America (Betancourt, Van Devender, and Martin 1990b, 437) differs substantially from previous reconstructions that were based on regional pollen records (e.g., Martin and Mehringer 1965; see Betancourt, Van Devender, and Martin 1990c, 4–5), largely because of the wider coverage of numerous packrat middens and the finer taxonomic resolution to which the macrofossils could be identified. General surveys of vegetation history in arid North America that are based largely on packrat midden records include Van Devender and Spaulding (1979); Spaulding, Leopold, and Van Devender (1983); Van Devender, Thompson, and Betancourt (1987); Wells (1983); Wigand and Rhode (in press); and several chapters in *Packrat Middens: The Last 40,000 Years of Biotic Change* (Betancourt, Van Devender, and Martin 1990a), a landmark reference book often considered the packrat midden bible.

Among the important lessons that have arisen from this large body of work, several key findings stand out. First, *biotic associations developed and changed during the past 200,000 years largely in response to climatic change* (see also Barnosky 1987; Whitlock and Bartlein 1997). The abrupt shifts from glacial-type climates (e.g., the late Wisconsin) to interglacial-type climates (e.g., the Holocene) resulted in especially dramatic biotic response. The distribution and abundance of biota probably also changed significantly in response to the so-called Dansgaard-Oeschgar (D-O) events, millennial-scale climate cycles that punctuated the glacial periods (Behl and Kennett 1996; Bond and Lotti 1995; Clark and Bartlein 1995; Dansgaard et al. 1993; Oviatt 1997). The resolution of the paleovegetation record is often insufficient to mark these millennial-scale changes, however. Biotic communities have also responded to the lesser-magnitude climatic variation during the last ten thousand years, including smaller, D-O-like climatic events that apparently persisted through the Holocene (Bond et al. 1997; Madsen 2000).

Second, *biotic changes involved numerous taxa experiencing large range shifts, both elevationally and latitudinally.* At times during the late Wisconsin glacial period, the lower treeline of some conifers in the Great Basin and American Southwest was as much as 1,000 m lower than at present (Cole 1985; Thompson 1990; Wells and Berger 1967; Van Devender and Spaulding 1979). Some plant taxa, including ponderosa pine (*Pinus ponderosa*), singleleaf pinyon (*P. monophylla*), and creosotebush (*Larrea tridentate*), migrated hundreds of kilometers northward as the cold glacial climates waned. In some cases, these migrations may have been initiated by the dramatic glacial-to-interglacial climate shift, but local effects were not exhibited until centuries or millennia later, a lag that has sometimes been called vegetational inertia (Cole 1985, 1990; M. B. Davis 1986; cf. Markgraf 1986).

Third, *the biotic communities that prevailed during the late Wisconsin and the first half of the Holocene often were not like those found today.* They contained mixtures of taxa that do not presently co-occur, mixtures we would now consider "anomalous" or nonanalog (Spaulding, Leopold, and Van Devender 1983; Graham 1986, 1992). (On the other hand, some plant communities (e.g., sagebrush steppe) seem to have been fairly stable over the long term). As Graham (1992, 79) notes, "Climatic warming during the late glacial (14,000 to 10,000 years ago) caused individual species distributions to change along environmental gradients in different directions, at different rates, and during different times. The individualistic response of the biota caused the emergence of new community patterns. Changes in the distribution of individual taxa continued during the Holocene (the last 10,000 years), but the magnitude of these changes was not the same as those of the late glacial." This is perhaps the most important lesson: that long-term biotic change in North America during the late Quaternary epoch has generally been an individualistic response of particular taxa to shifting climate conditions, in a sort of dynamic equilibrium. Some taxa evolved under the highly variable conditions characteristic of the Quaternary period by developing relatively wide climatic tolerances or phenotypic flexibility, while other populations adapted through gene pool fragmentation, effective dispersal mechanisms, and the ability to migrate rapidly from isolated refugia (Barnosky 1987; Huntley and Webb 1989; Nowak et al. 1994; Prentice 1992; Thompson 1988;

Whitlock and Bartlein 1993). Individualistic responses of biota to environmental variability appear to be a lasting evolutionary legacy of the dynamic Quaternary period (Bartlein and Prentice 1989; M. B. Davis 1986; FAUNMAP Working Group 1997; Foster, Schoonmaker, and Pickett 1990; Huntley 1991; Schoonmaker and Foster 1991; Tausch, Wigand, and Burkhardt 1993; Thompson 1988), with expectable repercussions for future biotic change (Graham 1992).

Finally, *remains from packrat middens have been used to document significant changes at the plant community level as well as the level of individual taxa.* For example, Chambers et al. (1998) used a series of middens from mountains in central Nevada dating from the last eight thousand years to show how the number of shrub and forb taxa in the local community changed in response to changing climates, generally as a function of available moisture. They found that increased moisture resulted in greater numbers of taxa (especially forbs), while decreased moisture tended to reduce the number of taxa (see also Wigand et al. 1995). As another example, data from middens near the Bonneville Basin of eastern Nevada concern the distribution of woodland communities dominated by limber pine (*Pinus flexilis*), which is restricted to scattered subalpine occurrences in the Great Basin today. During the last glacial period, however, limber pine woodlands tended to become widespread recurrently during periods marked by cold, dry climates (Rhode and Madsen 1995; Rhode 2000a, 2000b; see figure 10.6). The shrub associates of these limber pine communities varied during different episodes, however, probably in response to variable moisture levels, the abundance of atmospheric CO_2, and historical antecedents, among other factors. The prevailing paradigm of the individualistic nature of biotic response to environmental change is indicated once again. This individualistic response does not, however, preclude the likelihood of species interacting in similar ways to recurring environmental stimuli, nor the possibility of recurrent community-level patterns resulting from those stimuli, nor the development of positive and persistent correlations and interactions among different species.

Tracing the Migration Histories of Individual Plant Taxa

Packrat midden studies have been especially valuable for documenting regional migration dynamics of several important range plants in arid North America. For example, packrat midden studies have shown that several conifer species expanded rapidly over long distances, including ponderosa pine (Anderson 1989); singleleaf pinyon pine (Thompson 1990; Madsen and Rhode 1990; Rhode and Madsen 1998); Colorado pinyon (*Pinus edulis*) (Betancourt et al. 1991; Lanner and Van Devender

1998); and Utah juniper (*Juniperus osteosperma*) (Miller and Wigand 1994; Nowak et al. 1994; Wigand and Rhode, in press). Likewise, other studies show that characteristic desert shrub taxa, such as the creosotebush and bursage (*Ambrosia dumosa*) that now dominate vast areas of the warm southwestern deserts, expanded to their present range during the early to middle Holocene (Spaulding 1990; Van Devender 1990). Meanwhile, other taxa, such as ponderosa pine, singleleaf pinyon, and Utah juniper, reached their present distribution only recently—within the past few thousand years.

The migration histories of these western taxa should be very useful for testing theoretical models of long-distance plant dispersal (Clark 1998) and the supposed genetic consequences of migration dynamics and founder events (Betancourt et al. 1991; Hamrick, Schnabel, and Wells 1994). For example, current models of the northward spread of single-needled pinyon pine into the eastern Great Basin about seven thousand years ago (Madsen and Rhode 1990; Rhode and Madsen 1998; Thompson 1990) apparently exceed estimates of possible range expansion based on modern avian dispersal agents (Lanner 1983; Vander Wall and Balda 1977). This rapid migration may have involved a different dispersal mechanism, such as movement of viable seeds by nomadic Native American groups (Mehringer 1986; Rhode and Madsen 1998; see also Betancourt et al. 1991 for a related case with Colorado pinyon).

Determining the Climatic Effects on Individual Plant and Animal Taxa

Fossils from packrat middens have shown that various species of plants and animals significantly altered their anatomy and physiological functions during the past twenty thousand years in response to changing temperature, precipitation, and atmospheric CO_2 concentration. As noted previously, fecal pellets of the bushy-tailed woodrat, found in ancient middens at several localities on the Colorado Plateau, have been used to estimate adult body size through the last twenty-five thousand years (Smith, Betancourt, and Brown 1995; Smith and Betancourt 1998). Estimated body size was found to track closely with estimates of late Quaternary temperature in the region, suggesting that the bushy-tailed woodrat followed Bergmann's Rule relating larger body sizes to colder temperatures. Smith and Betancourt (1998, 1) suggest that "woodrat size is a precise paleothermometer, yielding information about temperature variation over relatively short-term temporal and regional scales."

A second example involves limber pine, a conifer that occupies scattered subalpine habitats in the intermountain West today and that, during the last glacial period, was much more widespread and grew at much lower elevations. Fossils from packrat middens show that glacial-age limber pine populations also had a different anatomy and physiological capacity for water stress than do modern populations. Van de Water, Leavitt, and Betancourt (1994) examined needles from forty-two middens spanning the last thirty thousand years in the Great Basin. They found that stomatal density of the needles decreased 17 percent and $\delta^{13}C$ values decreased ca. 1.5 parts per mil concentration in needle tissue during the deglacial period from fifteen thousand to twelve thousand years ago, indicating increased water-use efficiency during that period. At the same time, atmospheric CO_2 rose approximately 30 percent, from ~190–200 parts per mil to ~270–280 parts per mil. The investigators estimated that water-use efficiency of limber pine increased ca. 15 percent during deglaciation, a significant change in adaptive tolerances.

Estimates of Past Climates

A number of studies have used fossils from packrat middens to estimate past climatic conditions in various regions. Spaulding and Graumlich (1986), for example, interpreted relatively abundant remains of juniper, grass, and succulents (e.g., cacti) in early Holocene middens from the Sonoran and Mojave deserts to indicate a substantially stronger summer precipitation regime than occurs today in that region. Van Devender (1990) disagreed with that interpretation, suggesting instead that those remains could indicate somewhat greater precipitation generally, but not necessarily an increase in summer "monsoons." The question of the strength of early Holocene summer monsoon systems in the intermountain West is an important, and as yet unresolved, test of certain general circulation models of global climate based on Earth's orbital dynamics (Bartlein et al. 1998; Kutzbach et al. 1993; Thompson et al. 1993).

In another study, David Madsen and I (1995) used fossil evidence of limber pine growing near the margins of the Bonneville Basin, in Utah and eastern Nevada, to suggest that the growing-season temperature thirteen thousand to eleven thousand years ago was at least 6 °C cooler than it is today. As noted above, during this period limber pine was in the process of increasing its water-use efficiency in response to rising atmospheric CO_2 and was able to rapidly expand into the Bonneville Basin lowlands. However, the climate still had to be significantly cooler (though not necessarily wetter) than what prevails in the area today. This result contrasts with estimates of climate based on the magnitude and timing of the decline of Pleistocene Lake Bonneville, adduced from geomorphological evidence (Oviatt, Currey, and Sack 1992), which indicates that Lake Bonneville rapidly declined to a level below that of the present-day Great Salt Lake by thirteen thousand years ago, implying temperatures as warm as or somewhat warmer than those of today.

Human Impacts on Vegetation Communities

Two brief examples illustrate the use of packrat middens to understand human impacts to environments. The first case involves Chaco Canyon, located in the arid center of the San Juan Basin, northwestern New Mexico. During the tenth through the thirteenth centuries A.D., Chaco Canyon was the center of the Anasazi culture in the Southwest (Vivian 1990), which included a core of pueblo-style villages now represented by spectacular archaeological ruins such as Pueblo Bonito, Chetro Ketl, and other "great houses." Betancourt and Van Devender (1981) used packrat midden data to show that the Anasazi occupying Chaco Canyon had effectively deforested their local area by about eight hundred years ago. This local environmental degradation may ultimately have played a role in the abandonment of Chaco Canyon by the Anasazi.

Another example of more recent human impacts comes from Capitol Reef National Park, in Utah, where Ken Cole and his colleagues (1997) examined the effects of grazing on native vegetation. They used macrofossils and pollen from a series of packrat middens spanning the last five thousand years to show that presettlement vegetation contained abundant remains of species palatable to large herbivores, as well as a variety of trees and shrubs. By contrast, remains of those species were rare to absent in modern middens, which were dominated by taxa characteristic of overgrazed rangelands. Cole and his colleagues (1997, 323) found that "the magnitude of change in vegetation during the last 200 [years] was far greater than during the previous 5000 [years]." Using tree-ring, meteorological, and historical grazing records, they suggested that intensive nineteenth-century sheep grazing, particularly during periods of drought, was the main cause of the great historic vegetation change.

Middens as a Tool for Restoration Ecology

This brief survey illustrates the value of packrat middens to various paleoecological concerns. Now, how can the study of ancient middens contribute to the modern concerns of restoration ecology? How does information derived from middens fit into the goals of successful restoration projects? There are a number of potential ways.

First, packrat middens can prove highly useful as historical reference data in dryland areas, for the purposes of ecological restoration at specific sites (White and Walker 1997; Wigand 1998). Remains found in middens provide a detailed list of the plants and animals that grew in or near a specific locality before it was disturbed. Through genetic or chemical studies, these remains can be matched to the closest living subspecies or population, allowing for a more ecologically appropriate selection of seed or plant stocks for reintroduction (Linhart 1995). Associated pre-disturbance faunas may also be identified in certain cases, providing useful information for the restocking of pollinators or seed dispersers to help restore a fully functioning habitat (Montalvo et al. 1997; Neal 1998).

Second, remains from middens can provide background data on pre-disturbance levels of certain chemicals or elements in the soils of an area. For example, levels of mercury found in certain species of plants represented by fossils in packrat middens, compared with mercury levels measured in modern plants of the same species, may show to what extent historic mining activities increased the amount of mercury in the soils above pre-disturbance "background" levels.

Third, apart from site-specific "background" reference data for particular restoration projects, the study of middens can provide a wealth of information about long-term population dynamics and response of biota to various environmental constraints—information that is crucial to successful restoration ecology (Allen 1995; Montalvo et al. 1997; Palmer, Ambrose, and Pobb 1997; Tausch 1999b; White and Walker 1997). Packrat middens provide a long-term perspective on spatio-temporal fluctuation and stability of plant communities in dryland environments on a scale of decades to centuries. This can enlighten restorationists about ecological processes, especially when the midden studies are coupled with long-term climate reconstructions, showing the strong correlation between distribution and composition of major vegetation formations and climate. In turn, data from packrat middens can be coupled with geomorphic information about watershed and landscape dynamics in the context of changing climate and human land use to provide a powerful tool for understanding the functioning of modern ecosystems and their recovery potential (Chambers et al. 1998; Tausch 1999a). Equally important, the midden record demonstrates the individualistic response of plant taxa to environmental change. The midden paleorecord can also provide an excellent gauge of the resistance potential of certain plant communities (Rejmánek 1999) to migrants, such as pinyon pine, Utah juniper, and exotic rangeland weeds. Packrat middens also have relatively fine-grained spatio-temporal resolution compared to records, such as pollen sequences, which makes contemporaneous middens useful for indicating the heterogeneity of vegetation associations within a single area at a certain time.

Fourth, middens may provide information regarding the potential causes of past environmental degradation, loss of habitat, and extirpation of a particular species. As noted in the examples above, fossils from pack-rat middens can provide information about plant stress under certain climatic conditions, or the decline of native taxa as a result of factors such as the introduction of exotics, overgrazing, and changes in fire regime.

Fifth, but perhaps most important, midden analysis helps to solidify our understanding of the historical legacy of modern landscapes and biological communities (Brown 1995; Schoonmaker and Foster 1991). Today's dryland biotic communities are palimpsests, accumulated results of past environmental conditions: decades of drought or cold or overgrazing, during which certain taxa could outcompete others (Bahre and Shelton 1993; Betancourt 1996); years when "pulses" of certain plants were able to germinate and survive to reproductive age (Betancourt et al. 1993; Neilson 1986; Romney, Wallace, and Hunter 1987; Savage, Brown, and Feddema 1996); seasons when certain kinds of animals could migrate across intervening hostile terrain and colonize distant habitats (Grayson et al. 1996); or days when wildfire cleared a landscape and started the process anew (Ffolliott et al. 1996; Krammes 1990; Swetnam and Baisan 1996). Restoration ecologists need to internalize this perspective on the influence of past environmental processes because in many instances the area requiring restoration has been stripped of its biological and environmental heritage, robbed of its legacy from the past. *The restoration ecologist begins the process of rebuilding that environmental history.* Doing so successfully requires an appreciation of the long-term perspectives: of historical process, of spatio-temporal scale, of the variability inherent in ecosystem operation, and of historical contingency. The study of packrat middens helps to provide these viewpoints.

Against these positive aspects, several features of midden analysis need to be kept in mind when considering their use in a restoration context. Middens fit far better at the interface between macroecology and biogeography than they do in traditional ecosystem ecology. Middens are not short-term records, at least in the sense of most modern ecological studies. Ecological measures of community function, biomass, age structure, nutrient cycling, competition, and so on are largely not available from middens. Midden records are not continuous in space or time, nor are they distributed evenly or randomly through a landscape. Also, the midden record is strongly biased by the predilections of rats and by the vagaries of preservation, biases that can present interpretive problems. Finally, experience shows that, in many areas, a good midden can be very hard to find.

Despite these caveats, packrat middens and other preserved animal nests or garbage heaps have proven to be extremely valuable fossil records of past ecological change, with many potential uses in investigating and restoring modern ecosystems. It should be remembered that packrat midden analysis is a relatively new field, little more than three decades old. Its potential has only begun to be tapped, and new innovative applications of midden studies are reported yearly (e.g., Chambers et al. 1998; Hunter et al., in review; Plummer et al. 1997; Smith and Betancourt 1998). Midden analysis is by no means a mature science. It is not really a science at all, but rather an approach to a diverse and fruitful archive for the study of historical ecology, with many useful lessons and applications for the present.

References

Allen, C.D., J.L. Betancourt, and T.W. Swetnam. 1998. Landscape changes in the Southwestern United States: Techniques, long-term data sets, and trends. In *Perspectives on the land use history of North America: A context to understanding our changing environment*, ed. T. Sisk. U.S. geological survey. Biological resources division, biological science report USGS/BRD/BSR-1998-0003.

Allen, E.B. 1995. Restoration ecology: Limits and possibilities in arid and semi-arid lands. Pages 7–15 in *Proceedings: Wildland Shrub and Arid Land Restoration Symposium, October 19–21, 1993, Las Vegas, NV*, comp. B.A. Roundy, E.D. McArthur, J.S. Haley, and D.K. Mann. General Technical Report INT-GTR-315. Ogden, Utah: USDA Forest Service.

Anderson, R.S. 1989. *Development of the southwestern ponderosa pine forests: What do we really know?* Paper presented at Multiresource Management of Ponderosa Pine Forest Symposium, Northern Arizona University, Flagstaff.

Anderson, R.S., and T.R. Van Devender. 1992. Comparison of pollen and macrofossils in packrat (*Neotoma*) middens: A chronological sequence from the Waterman Mountains of southern Arizona, U.S.A. *Review of Palaeobotany and Palynology 69*.

Andrews, P. 1990. *Owls, caves, and fossils*. Chicago: University of Chicago Press.

Arnold, J.E., and B.N. Tissot. 1993. Measurement of significant marine paleotemperature variation using black abalone shells from prehistoric middens. *Quaternary Research 39*:390–394.

Bahre, C., and M.L. Shelton. 1993. Historic vegetation change, mesquite increases, and climate in southeastern Arizona. *Journal of Biogeography 20*:489–504.

Barnosky, C.W. 1987. Response of vegetation to climate changes of different duration in the late Neogene. *Trends in Ecology and Evolution 2*:247–250.

Bartlein, P.J., K.H. Anderson, P.M. Anderson, M.E. Edwards, C.J. Mock, R.S. Thompson, T. Webb III, and C. Whitlock. 1998. Paleoclimate simulations for North America over the past 21,000 years: Features of the simulated climate and comparisons with paleoenvironmental data. *Quaternary Science Reviews 17*:549–585.

Bartlein, P.J., and I.C. Prentice. 1989. Orbital variations, climate, and paleoecology. *Trends in Ecology and Evolution 4*:195–197.

Behl, R.J., and J.P. Kennett. 1996. Brief interstadial events in Santa Barbara basin, northeastern Pacific, during the past 60 kyr. *Nature* 379:243–246.

Bent, A.C. 1937. *Life histories of North American birds of prey.* U.S. National Museum Bulletin 167. Washington, D.C.: Smithsonian Institution.

Betancourt, J.L. 1996. Long- and short-term climatic influences on southwestern shrublands. Pages 5–9 in *Proceedings: Symposium on Shrubland Ecosystem Dynamics in a Changing Climate;* 1995 May 23–25, Las Cruces, NM, comp. J.R. Barrow, E.D. MacArthur, R.E. Sosebee, and R.J. Tausch. General Technical Report INT-GTR-338. Ogden, Utah: USDA Forest Service.

Betancourt, J.L., E.A. Pierson, K. Aasen-Rylander, J.A. Fairchild-Parks, and J.S. Dean. 1993. Influence of history and climate on New Mexico pinyon-juniper woodlands. Pages 42–62 in *Managing pinyon-juniper ecosystems for sustainability and social needs: Proceedings of the Symposium, April 26–30, Santa Fe, New Mexico,* eds. E.F. Aldon and D.W. Shaw. General Technical Report RM-236. Fort Collins, Colo.: USDA Forest Service.

Betancourt, J.L., W.S. Schuster, J.B. Mitton, and R.S. Anderson. 1991. Fossil and genetic history of a pinyon pine (*Pinus edulis*) isolate. *Ecology* 72:1685–1697.

Betancourt, J.L., and T.R. Van Devender. 1981. Holocene vegetation in Chaco Canyon, New Mexico. *Science* 214:656–658.

Betancourt, J.L., T.R. Van Devender, and P.S. Martin, eds. 1990a. *Packrat middens: The last 40,000 years of biotic change.* Tucson: University of Arizona Press.

———. 1990b. Synthesis and prospectus. Pages 435–447 in *Packrat middens: The last 40,000 years of biotic change,* eds. J.L. Betancourt, T.R. Van Devender, and P.S. Martin. Tucson: University of Arizona Press.

———. 1990c. Introduction. Pages 2–11 in *Packrat middens: The last 40,000 years of biotic change,* eds. J.L. Betancourt, T.R. Van Devender, and P.S. Martin. Tucson: University of Arizona Press.

Betancourt, J.L., T.R. Van Devender, and M. Rose. 1986. Comparison of plant macrofossils in woodrat (*Neotoma* sp.) and porcupine (*Erethizon dorsatum*) middens from the western United States. *Journal of Mammalogy* 67:266–273.

Bond, G., and R. Lotti. 1995. Iceberg discharges into the North Atlantic on millennial time scales during the last glaciation. *Science* 267:1005–1010.

Bond, G., W. Showers, M. Cheseby, R. Lotti, P. Almasi, P. deMenocal, P. Priore, H. Cullen, I. Hajdas, and G. Bonani. 1997. A pervasive millennial-scale cycle in North Atlantic Holocene and glacial climates. *Science* 278:1257–1266.

Bronk Ramsey, C. 1995. Radiocarbon calibration and analysis of stratigraphy: The OxCal program. *Radiocarbon* 37(2):425–478.

Brown, J.H. 1971. Mammals on mountaintops: Nonequilibrium insular biogeography. *American Naturalist* 105:467–478.

———. 1995. *Macroecology.* Chicago: University of Chicago Press.

Chambers, J.C., K. Farleigh, R.J. Tausch, J.R. Miller, D. Germanoski, K. Martin, and C. Nowak. 1998. Understanding long- and short-term changes in vegetation and geomorphic processes: The key to riparian restoration. Pages

101–110 in *Rangeland management and water resources*, ed. D.F. Potts. Proceedings of AWRA Specialty Conference, Technical Publication Series TPS 98-1. Herndon, Va.: American Water Resources Association.

Chamrad, A.D., and T.W. Box. 1964. A point frame for sampling rumen contents. *Journal of Wildlife Management* 28:473–477.

Clark, J.S. 1998. Why trees migrate so fast: Confronting theory with dispersal biology and the paleorecord. *American Naturalist* 152(2):204–224.

Clark, P.U., and P. Bartlein. 1995. Correlation of late Pleistocene glaciation in the western United States with North Atlantic Heinrich events. *Geology* 23:483–486.

Cole, K.L. 1985. Past rates of change, species richness, and a model of vegetational inertia in the Grand Canyon, Arizona. *American Naturalist* 125:289–303.

———. 1990. Late Quaternary vegetation gradients through the Grand Canyon. Pages 240–258 in *Packrat middens: The last 40,000 years of biotic change*, eds. J.L. Betancourt, T.R. Van Devender, and P.S. Martin. Tucson: University of Arizona Press.

Cole, K.L., N. Henderson, and D.S. Shafer. 1997. Holocene vegetation and historic grazing impacts at Capitol Reef National Park reconstructed using packrat middens. *Great Basin Naturalist* 57(4):315–326.

Cole, K.L., and R.H. Webb. 1985. Late Holocene vegetation changes in Greenwater Valley, Mojave Desert, California. *Quaternary Research* 23:227–235.

Dansgaard, W., S.J. Johnsen, H.B. Clausen, D. Dahljensen, N.S. Gundestrup, C.U. Hammer, C.S. Hvidberg, and J.P. Steffensen. 1993. Evidence for general instability of past climate from a 250 kyr ice-core record. *Nature* 364:218–220.

Davis, M.B. 1986. Climatic instability, time lags, and community disequilibrium. Pages 269–284 in *Community ecology*, eds. J. Diamond and T.J. Case. New York: Harper and Row.

Davis, O.K., and R.S. Anderson. 1987. Pollen in packrat (*Neotoma*) middens: Pollen transport and the relationship of pollen to vegetation. *Palynology* 11:185–198.

Dial, K.P., and N.J. Czaplewski. 1990. Do woodrat middens accurately represent the animals' environments and diets? The Woodhouse Mesa study. Pages 43–58 in *Packrat middens: The last 40,000 years of biotic change*, eds. J.L. Betancourt, T.R. Van Devender, and P.S. Martin. Tucson: University of Arizona Press.

Elias, S.A. 1994. *Quaternary insects and their environments*. Washington, D.C.: Smithsonian Institution Press.

———. 1996. Late Pleistocene and Holocene seasonal temperatures reconstructed from fossil beetle assemblages in the Rocky Mountains. *Quaternary Research* 46:311–318.

Faegri, K., and J. Iversen. 1975. *Textbook of pollen analysis*. New York: Hafner Press.

Fall, P.L., C.A. Lindquist, and S.E. Falconer. 1990. Fossil hyrax middens from the Middle East: A record of paleovegetation and human disturbance. Pages

408–427 in *Packrat middens: The last 40,000 years of biotic change*, eds. J.L. Betancourt, T.R. Van Devender, and P.S. Martin. Tucson: University of Arizona Press.

FAUNMAP Working Group. 1997. Spatial response of mammals to late Quaternary environmental fluctuations. *Science* 272:1601–1606.

Ffolliott, P.F., L.F. DeBano, M.B. Baker Jr., G.J. Gottfried, G. Soliz-Garza, C.B. Edminster, D.G. Neary, L.S. Allen, and R.H. Hamre, tech. coords. 1996. *Effects of fire on Madrean Province ecosystems: Symposium proceedings*. General Technical Report RM-GTR-289. Fort Collins, Colo.: USDA Forest Service,

Finley, Jr., R.B., 1990. Woodrat ecology and behavior and the interpretation of paleomiddens. Pages 28–42 in *Packrat middens: The last 40,000 years of biotic change*, eds. J.L. Betancourt, T.R. Van Devender, and P.S. Martin. Tucson: University of Arizona Press.

Foster, D.R., P.K. Schoonmaker, and S.T.A. Pickett. 1990. Insights from paleoecology to community ecology. *Trends in Ecology and Evolution* 5:119–122.

Frase, B.A., and W.E. Sera. 1993. Comparison between plant species in bushy-tailed woodrat middens and the habitat. *Great Basin Naturalist* 53(4):373–378.

Glassow, M., and L. Wilcoxon. 1988. Coastal adaptations near Point Conception, California, with particular regard to shellfish exploitation. *American Antiquity* 53:36–51.

Gleason, R.L., and T.H. Craig. 1979. Food habits of burrowing owls in southeastern Idaho. *Great Basin Naturalist* 39:274–276.

Graham, R.W. 1986. Response of mammalian communities to environmental changes during the late Quaternary. Pages 300–313 in *Community ecology*, eds. J. Diamond and T.J. Case. New York: Harper and Row.

Graham, R.W. 1992. Late Pleistocene faunal change as a guide to understanding effects of greenhouse warming on the mammalian fauna of North America. Pages 76–87 in *Global warming and biological diversity*, eds. R.L. Peters and T.E. Lovejoy. New Haven, Conn.: Yale University Press.

Grayson, D.K. 1998. Moisture history and small mammal community richness during the latest Pleistocene and Holocene, northern Bonneville Basin, Utah. *Quaternary Research* 49:330–334.

Grayson, D.K., S.D. Livingston, E. Rickart, and M.W. Shaver. 1996. The biogeographic significance of low elevation records for *Neotoma cinerea* from the northern Bonneville Basin, Utah. *Great Basin Naturalist* 56:191–196.

Hamrick, J.L., A.F. Schnabel, and P.V. Wells. 1994. Distribution of genetic diversity within and among populations of Great Basin conifers. Pages 147–162 in *Natural history of the Colorado Plateau and Great Basin*, eds. K.T. Harper, L.L. St. Clair, K.H. Thorne, and W.M. Hess. Niwot: University Press of Colorado.

Hunter, K.L., and J.R. McAuliffe. 1994. Elevational shifts of *Coleogyne ramossissima* in the Mojave Desert during the Little Ice Age. *Quaternary Research* 42:216–221.

Hunter, K.L., B.R. Riddle, J.L. Betancourt, K.L. Cole, T.R. Van Devender, and W.G. Spaulding. N.d. Polyploidy changes during the past 18,000 ^{14}C years in the North American desert shrub *Larrea tridentata*. Submitted to *Nature*.

Huntley, B. 1991. How plants respond to climate change: Migration rates, individualism and the consequences for plant communities. *Annals of Botany* 67:15–22.

Huntley, B., and T. Webb III. 1989. Migration: Species' response to climatic variations caused by changes in the earth's orbit. *Journal of Biogeography* 16:5–19.

Jones, T.L. 1996. Mortars, pestles, and division of labor in prehistoric California: A view from Big Sur. *American Antiquity* 61:243–264.

Jones, T.L., and D.J. Kennett. 1999. Late Holocene sea temperatures along the central California coast. *Quaternary Research* 51:74–82.

Kohn, M.J. 1999. You are what you eat. *Science* 283:335–336.

Krammes, J.S., tech. coord. 1990. *Effects of fire management of southwestern natural resources: Proceedings of the symposium*. General Technical Report RM-191. Fort Collins, Colo.: USDA Forest Service.

Kutzbach, J.E., P.J. Guetter, P.J. Behling, and R. Selin. 1993. Simulated climatic changes: Results of the COHMAP climate-model experiments. Pages 24–93 in *Global climates since the Last Glacial Maximum*, eds. H.E. Wright Jr., J.E. Kutzbach, T. Webb III, W.F. Ruddiman, F.A. Street-Perrott, and P.J. Bartlein. Minneapolis: University of Minnesota Press.

Lanner, R.M. 1983. The expansion of singleleaf piñon in the Great Basin. Pages 169–171 in "The Archaeology of Monitor Valley 2. Gatecliff Shelter", by D.H. Thomas. *American Museum of Natural History Anthropological Papers* 59(1).

Lanner, R.M., and T.R. Van Devender. 1998. The recent history of pinyon pines in the American Southwest. Pages 171-182 in *Ecology and biogeography of Pinus*, ed. D. Richardson. London: Cambridge University Press.

Linhart, Y.B. 1995. Restoration, revegetation, and the importance of genetic and evolutionary perspectives. Pages 271–287 in *Proceedings: Wildland Shrub and Arid Land Restoration Symposium, October 19–21, 1993, Las Vegas, NV*, comps. B.A. Roundy, E.D. McArthur, J.S. Haley, and D.K. Mann. General Technical Report INT-GTR-315. Ogden, Utah: USDA Forest Service.

Long, A., L.A. Warneke, J.L. Betancourt, and R.S. Thompson. 1990. Deuterium variations in plant cellulose from fossil packrat middens. Pages 380–396 in *Packrat middens: The last 40,000 years of biotic change*, eds. J.L. Betancourt, T.R. Van Devender, and P.S. Martin. Tucson: University of Arizona Press.

Lowenstein, J.M., W.N. Rainey, and J.L. Betancourt. 1991. Immunospecific albumin in fossil packrat, porcupine and hyrax urine. *Naturwissenschaften* 78:26–27.

Madsen, D.B. 2000 *Late Quaternary paleoecology in the Bonneville Basin*. Salt Lake City: Utah Geological Survey.

Madsen, D.B., and D. Rhode. 1990. Holocene pinyon (*Pinus monophylla*) in the northeastern Great Basin. *Quaternary Research* 33:94–101.

Markgraf, V. 1986. Plant inertia reassessed. *American Naturalist* 127:725–726.

Marti, C.D. 1974. Feeding ecology of four sympatric owls. *Condor* 76:45–61.

Martin, P.S., and P.J. Mehringer Jr. 1965. Pleistocene pollen analysis and bio-geography of the Southwest. Pages 433–451 in *The Quaternary of the United States*, ed. H.E. Wright Jr. New Haven, Conn.: Yale University Press.

Mehringer, Jr., P.J. 1986. Prehistoric Environments. Pages 31–50 in *Handbook of North American Indians*, Volume 11: Great Basin, ed. W.L. d'Azevedo. Washington, D.C.: Smithsonian Institution.

Mehringer, Jr., P.J., and P.E. Wigand. 1990. Comparison of Late Holocene envi-ronments from woodrat middens and pollen: Diamond Craters, Oregon. Pages 294–325 in *Packrat middens: The last 40,000 years of biotic change*, eds. J.L. Betancourt, T.R. Van Devender, and P.S. Martin. Tucson: University of Arizona Press.

Miller, R.F., and P.E. Wigand. 1994. Holocene changes in semiarid piñon-juniper woodlands: Response to climate, fire, and human activities in the US Great Basin. *BioScience* 44(7):465–474.

Montalvo, A.M., S.L. Williams, K.J. Rice, S.L. Buchmann, C. Cory, S.N. Han-del, G.P. Nabhan, R. Primack, and R.H. Robichaux. 1997. Restoration biol-ogy: A population biology perspective. *Restoration Ecology* 5(4):277–290.

Neal, P.R. 1998. Pollinator restoration. *Trends in Ecology and Evolution* 13(4):132–133.

Neilson, R.P. 1986. High-resolution climatic analysis and southwest biogeogra-phy. *Science* 232:27–34.

Nelson, D.J., R.H. Webb, and A. Long. 1990. Analysis of stick-nest rat (*Leporil-lus: muridae*) middens from Central Australia. Pages 428–434 in *Packrat mid-dens: The last 40,000 years of biotic change*, ed. J.L. Betancourt, T.R. Van Devender, and P.S. Martin. Tucson: University of Arizona Press.

Nowak, C.L., R.S. Nowak, R.J. Tausch, and P.E. Wigand. 1994. Tree and shrub dynamics in northwestern Great Basin woodland and shrub steppe during the Late-Pleistocene and Holocene. *American Journal of Botany* 81(3):265–277.

Orr, P.C. 1957. On the occurrence and nature of "amberat." *Western Speleological Institute, Observations* 2:1–3.

Oviatt, C.G. 1997. Lake Bonneville fluctuations and global climate change. *Geology* 25:155–158.

Oviatt, C.G., D.R. Currey, and D. Sack. 1992. Radiocarbon chronology of Lake Bonneville, eastern Great Basin, USA. *Palaeogeography, Palaeoclimatology, Palaeoecology* 99:225–241.

Palmer, M.A., R.F. Ambrose, and N.L. Poff. 1997. Ecological theory and com-munity restoration ecology. *Restoration Ecology* 5(4):291–300.

Plummer, M.A., F.M. Phillips, J. Fabryka-Martin, H.J. Turin, P.E. Wigand, and P. Sharma. 1997. Chlorine-36 in fossil rat urine: An archive of cosmogenic nuclide deposition during the past 40,000 years. *Science* 277:538–541.

Poinar, H.N., M. Hofreiter, W.G. Spaulding, P.S. Martin, B.A. Stankiewicz, H. Bland, R.P. Evershed, G. Possnert, and S. Pääbo. 1998. Molecular coproscopy: Dung and diet of the extinct ground sloth *Nothrotheriops shas-tensis*. *Science* 281(5375):402–406.

Prentice, I.C. 1992. Climate change and long-term vegetation dynamics. Pages 293–339 in *Plant succession: Theory and prediction*, eds. D.C. Glenn-Lewin, R.A. Peet, and T. Veblen. London: Chapman and Hall.

Rejmánek, M. 1999. Holocene invasions: Finally the resolution ecologists were waiting for! *Trends in Ecology and Evolution* 14(1):8–10.

Rhode, D. 2000a. Middle and late Wisconsin vegetation in the Bonneville Basin. In *Late Quaternary paleoecology in the Bonneville Basin*, by D.B. Madsen. Salt Lake City: Utah Geological Survey. 137–147.

———. 2000b. Holocene vegetation history in the Bonneville Basin. Pages 149–163 in *Late Quarternary paleoecology in the Bonneville Basin*, by D.B. Madsen. Salt Lake City: Utah Geological Survey.

Rhode, D., and D.B. Madsen. 1995. Late Wisconsin vegetation in the northern Bonneville Basin. *Quaternary Research* 44(2):246–256.

———. 1998. Pine nut use in the early Holocene and beyond: The Danger Cave archaeobotanical record. *Journal of Archaeological Science* 25:1199–1210.

Romney, E.M., A.Wallace, and R.B. Hunter. 1987. Pulse establishment of woody shrubs on denuded Mojave Desert land. Pages 54–57 in *Proceedings—Symposium on Shrub Ecophysiology and Biotechnology*, eds. E.D. McArthur, A. Wallace, and M.R. Haferkamp. General Technical Report INT-256. Ogden, Utah: USDA Forest Service.

Savage, M., P.M. Brown, and J. Feddema. 1996. The role of climate in a pine forest regeneration pulse in the southwestern United States. *Ecoscience* 3:310–318.

Schoonmaker, P.K., and D.R. Foster. 1991. Some implications of paleoecology for contemporary ecology. *Botanical Review* 57(3):204–245.

Sillen, A., and J.A. Lee-Thorp. 1994. Trace element and isotopic aspects of predator-prey relationships in terrestrial foodwebs. *Palaeogeography, Palaeoclimatology, Palaeoecology* 107:243–255.

Smith, F.A., and J.L. Betancourt. 1998. Response of bushy-tailed woodrats (*Neotoma cinerea*) to Late Quaternary climatic change in the Colorado Plateau. *Quaternary Research* 50(1):1–11.

Smith, F.A., J.L. Betancourt, and J.H. Brown. 1995. Effects of global warming on woodrat (*Neotoma cinerea*) body size during the last deglaciation. *Science* 270:2012–2014.

Spaulding, W.G. 1985. *Vegetation and climates of the last 45,000 years in the vicinity of the Nevada Test Site, southcentral Nevada*. U.S. Geological Survey Professional Paper 1329.

———. 1990. Vegetational and climatic development of the Mojave Desert: The last glacial maximum to present. Pages 166–199 in *Packrat middens: The last 40,000 years of biotic change*, eds. J.L. Betancourt, T.R. Van Devender, and P.S. Martin. Tucson: University of Arizona Press.

Spaulding, W.G., Betancourt, J.L., Croft, L.K., and K.L. Cole. 1990. *Packrat middens: Their composition and methods of analysis*. Pages 59–84 in *Packrat middens: The last 40,000 years of biotic change*, eds. J.L. Betancourt, T.R. Van Devender, and P.S. Martin. Tucson: University of Arizona Press.

Spaulding, W.G., and L. Graumlich 1986. The last pluvial climatic episodes in the deserts of southwestern North America. *Nature* 320:441–444.

Spaulding, W.G., E.B. Leopold, and T.R. Van Devender. 1983. Late Wisconsin paleoecology of the American Southwest. Pages 259–293 in *Late-Quaternary environments of the United States*; Volume 1: The Late Pleistocene, ed. S.C. Porter. Minneapolis: University of Minnesota Press.

Stein, J.K., ed. 1992. *Deciphering a shell midden.* San Diego: Academic Press.

Stuiver, M., and P.J. Reimer. 1993. Extended ^{14}C database and revised CALIB radiocarbon calibration program. *Radiocarbon* 35:215–230.

Stuiver, M., P.J. Reimer, E. Bard, J.W. Beck, G.S. Burr, K.A. Hughen, B. Kromer, F.G. McCormac, J. van der Plicht, and M. Spurk. 1998. INTCAL98 radiocarbon age calibration 24,000–0 cal B.P. *Radiocarbon* 40:1041–1083.

Stuiver, M., P.J. Reimer, and T.F. Braziunas. 1998. High-precision radiocarbon age calibration for terrestrial and marine samples. *Radiocarbon* 40:1127–1152.

Swetnam, T.W., and C.H. Baisan. 1996. Historical fire regime patterns in the southwestern United States since A.D. 1700. Pages 11–32 in *Fire effects in southwestern forests: Proceedings of the second La Mesa Fire Symposium*, ed. C. Allen. General Technical Report RM-GTR-286. Fort Collins, Colo.: USDA Forest Service.

Tausch, R.J. 1999a. Historic pinyon and juniper woodland development. Pages 12–19 in *Proceedings: Ecology and Management of Pinyon-Juniper Communities within the Interior West*, comp. S.B. Monsen and R. Stevens. USDA Forest Service Rocky Mountain Research Station Proceedings RMRS-P-9. Fort Collins, Colo.

————. 1999b. Transitions and thresholds: Influences and implications for management in pinyon and juniper woodlands. Pages 361–365 in *Proceedings: Ecology and Management of Pinyon-Juniper Communities within the Interior West*, comp. S.B. Monsen and R. Stevens. USDA Forest Service Rocky Mountain Research Station Proceedings RMRS-P-9. Fort Collins, Colo.

Tausch, R.J., P.E. Wigand, and J.W. Burkhardt. 1993. Viewpoint: Plant community thresholds, multiple steady states, and multiple successional pathways: Legacy of the Quaternary? *Journal of Range Management* 46:439–447.

Thompson, R.S. 1984. Late Pleistocene and Holocene environments in the Great Basin. Ph.D. dissertation, Department of Geosciences, University of Arizona, Tucson.

————. 1985. Palynology and *Neotoma* middens. Pages 89–112 in *Late Quaternary vegetation and climates of the American Southwest*, eds. B.L. Fine-Jacobs, P.L. Fall, and O.K. Davis. American Association of Stratigraphic Palynologists Contributions Series 16. Dallas, Tex.: American Association of Stratigrophic Palynologists Foundation.

————. 1988. Western North America. Pages 415–459 in *Vegetation history*, eds. B. Huntley and T. Webb III. *Handbook of Vegetation Science*, Volume 7. Dordrecht: Kluwer Academic Publishers.

————. 1990. Late Quaternary vegetation and climate in the Great Basin. Pages 200–239 in *Packrat middens: The last 40,000 years of biotic change*, eds. J.L. Betancourt, T.R. Van Devender, and P.S. Martin. Tucson: University of Arizona Press.

Thompson, R.S., C. Whitlock, P.J. Bartlein, S.P. Harrison, and W.G. Spaulding. 1993. Climate changes in the western United States since 18,000 yr B.P. Pages 468–513 in *Global climates since the Last Glacial Maximum*, eds. H.E. Wright Jr., J.E. Kutzbach, T. Webb III, W.F. Ruddiman, F.A. Street-Perrott, and P.J. Bartlein. Minneapolis: University of Minnesota Press.

Vander Wall, S.B., and R.P. Balda. 1977. Coadaptations of the Clark's nutcracker and the piñon pine for efficient seed harvest and dispersal. *Ecological Monographs* 47:89–111.

Van Devender, T.R. 1973. Late Pleistocene plants and animals of the Sonoran Desert: A survey of ancient packrat middens in southwestern Arizona. Ph.D. dissertation, University of Arizona, Tucson.

————. 1988. Pollen in packrat (*Neotoma*) middens: Pollen transport and the relationship of pollen to vegetation. *Palynology* 12:226–229.

————. 1990. Late Quaternary vegetation and climate of the Sonoran Desert, United States and Mexico. Pages 134–165 in *Packrat middens: The last 40,000 years of biotic change*, eds. J.L. Betancourt, T.R. Van Devender, and P.S. Martin. Tucson: University of Arizona Press.

Van Devender, T.R., P.S. Martin, R.S. Thompson, K.L. Cole, A.J.T. Jull, A. Long, L.J. Toolin, and D.J. Donahue. 1985. Fossil packrat middens and the tandem accelerator mass spectrometer. *Nature* 317:610–613.

Van Devender, T.R., and W.G. Spaulding. 1979. Development of vegetation and climate in the southwestern United States. *Science* 204:701–710.

Van Devender, T.R., R.S. Thompson, and J.L. Betancourt. 1987. Vegetation history of the desert of southwestern North America: The nature and timing of the Late Wisconsin-Holocene transition. In *North America and adjacent oceans during the last deglaciation*, eds. W.F. Ruddiman and H.E. Wright Jr. *The geology of North America K-3*. Boulder, Colo.: Geological Society of America.

Van de Water, P.K., S.W. Leavitt, and J.L. Betancourt. 1994. Trends in stomatal density and $^{13}C/^{12}C$ ratios of *Pinus flexilis* needles during the last Glacial-Interglacial cycle. *Science* 264:239–243.

Vaughn, T.A. 1990. Ecology of living packrats. Pages 14–27 in *Packrat middens: The last 40,000 years of biotic change*, eds. J.L. Betancourt, T.R. Van Devender, and P.S. Martin. Tucson: University of Arizona Press.

Vivian, R.G. 1990. *The Chacoan Prehistory of the San Juan Basin*. New York: Academic Press.

Webb, R.H., and J.L. Betancourt. 1990. The spatial and temporal distribution of radiocarbon ages from packrat middens. Pages 85–102 in *Packrat middens: The last 40,000 years of biotic change*, eds. J.L. Betancourt, T.R. Van Devender, and P.S. Martin. Tucson: University of Arizona Press.

Webb, III, T., 1992. Past changes in vegetation and climate: Lessons for the future. Pages 59–75 in *Global warming and biological diversity*, eds. R.L. Peters and T.E. Lovejoy. New Haven, Conn.: Yale University Press.

Wells, P.V. 1976. Macrofossil analysis of wood rat (*Neotoma*) middens as a key to the Quaternary vegetational history of arid America. *Quaternary Research* 6:223–248.

————. 1983. Paleobiogeography of montane islands in the Great Basin since the last Glaciopluvial. *Ecological Monographs* 53:341–382.

Wells, P.V., and R. Berger. 1967. Late Pleistocene history of coniferous woodlands in the Mohave Desert. *Science* 155:341–382.

Wells, P.V., and C.D. Jorgensen. 1964. Pleistocene wood rat middens and climatic change in the Mohave Desert: A record of juniper woodland. *Science* 143(3611):1171–1174.

White, P.S., and J.L. Walker, 1997. Approximating nature's variation: Selecting and using reference information in restoration ecology. *Restoration Ecology* 5(4):338–349.

Whitlock, C., and P.J. Bartlein. 1993. Spatial variations of Holocene climatic change in the Yellowstone region. *Quaternary Research* 39:231–238.

————. 1997. Vegetation and climate change in northwest America during the past 125 kyr. *Nature* 388(6637):57–61.

Wigand, P.E. 1997. A late-Holocene pollen record from Lower Pahranagat Lake, southern Nevada, USA: High resolution paleoclimatic records and analysis of environmental response to climate change. Pages 63–77 in *Proceedings of the Thirteenth Annual Pacific Climate (PACLIM) Workshop, April 15–18, 1996*, eds. C.M. Isaacs and V.L. Tharp. Interagency Ecological Program Technical Report 53. Sacramento: California Department of Water Resources.

————. 1998. *Selection of plant species to be used in effective re-vegetation of mining affected areas through examination of the reconstructed vegetation communities of the last 700 years and their climatic settings: A proposal for exploratory work in the Osgood Mountains in close proximity to the Getchell gold mine of north-central Nevada.* Proposal submitted by Wigand to Getchell Gold Corporation, Battle Mountain, NV.

Wigand, P.E., M.L. Hemphill, and S.M. Patra. 1994. Late Holocene climate derived from vegetation history and plant cellulose stable isotope records from the Great Basin of western North America. Pages 2574–2583 in *High level radioactive waste management: Proceedings of the fifth annual international conference, Las Vegas, Nevada, May 22–26, 1994.* La Grange Park, Ill.: American Nuclear Society; New York: American Society of Civil Engineers.

Wigand, P.E., M.L. Hemphill, S. Sharpe, and S. Patra. 1995. Great Basin semi-arid woodland dynamics during the late Quaternary. Pages 51–70 in *Proceedings: Climate change in the Four Corners and adjacent regions: Implications for environmental restoration and land-use planning,* ed. W.J. Waugh. Grand Junction, Colo.: U.S. Department of Energy.

Wigand, P.E., and D. Rhode. In press. Great Basin vegetation history and aquatic systems: The last 150,000 years. In *Great Basin aquatic systems history,* eds. R. Hershler, D. Currey, and D.B. Madsen. Contributions to Earth Science Series, Washington, D.C.: Smithsonian Institution.

11

Techniques for Discovering Historic Animal Assemblages

Michael L. Morrison

All restoration changes conditions for wildlife. A stated or unstated goal of most restoration is improving conditions for native species of wildlife. To be ultimately successful, restoration plans must be guided in large part by the needs of current or desired wildlife species in the project area. Such information includes data on species abundance and distribution, both current and historic; details on habitat requirements, including proper plant species composition and structure; problems associated with exotic species of plants and animals; and many additional factors. Thus, proper consideration of wildlife—their habitat needs and numbers—is a complicated process that requires careful consideration during all stages of restoration. Additionally, the success of a restoration project should be judged, in part, by how wildlife species respond to the project.

The initial step in a restoration project is determining specific goals and desired endpoints. These goals often include establishing a time period for replicating all or part of a preexisting plant community. To date, however, few studies have explicitly included historic animal communities as part of the planning process. Each animal species requires specific combinations of environmental conditions and resources for occupancy and survival that must be accounted for in the restoration plan. Simply providing a general vegetation type or plant association may not provide the necessary components to allow occupancy by many animal species. Such factors include the seasonal availability of water and resting sites (e.g., dens, hybernacula), microhabitat features (e.g., down logs, rocks), and the presence of specific food sources.

Thus, any project seeking to restore the ecology of an area needs to determine the animal species likely to be present. Restoring a degraded area to match currently existing conditions in relatively nondegraded sites is possible through new studies. Such work is often part of required mitigation as a requirement for development, or as part of a legal settlement following accidental environmental impacts (e.g., toxic spills). However, restoring an area to match some preexisting condition is difficult unless data on historic conditions are available. Thus, attempting to reconstruct historic conditions is a worthwhile endeavor that will enhance a restoration project.

The goal of this chapter is to describe techniques useful in reconstructing the historic assemblage of animals in an area. This will be accomplished by (1) discussing the conceptual foundation for exploring historic animal assemblages, (2) describing direct and indirect techniques for gathering historic data, (3) providing examples of using such techniques in designing restoration, and (4) determining the uncertainty associated with historic data.

Concepts and Definitions

There is little standardization in the use of many ecological terms. Failure to use terms in a standard manner, or provide an explicit definition of each, causes confusion among scientists and those trying to apply results of research studies (Hall, Krausman, and Morrison 1997). Thus, I will first define several key ecological terms. I define *habitat* as the resources and conditions present in an area that produce occupancy by an organism. Habitat is *organism specific*; it relates the presence of a species, population, or individual (animal or plant) to an area's physical and biological characteristics. Habitat involves more than vegetation or vegetation structure; it is the sum of the specific resources that are needed by organisms. Wildlife habitat is therefore *not* equivalent to "habitat type," which was coined by Rexford Daubenmire (1968, 27–32), and refers only to the type of vegetation association in an area, or the potential of vegetation to reach a specified climax stage. The term *habitat type* should not be used when discussing wildlife-habitat relationships. When people want to refer only to the vegetation that an animal uses, they should use *vegetation association* or *vegetation type* instead. The definition of habitat as organism specific is a critical concept. It means that restoring vegetation alone, regardless of how well it matches some desired condition, can easily fail to restore the desired assemblage of wildlife.

In contrast to habitat, the *niche* of an animal is defined as the strength and frequency of interactions between the individual and entities (e.g., resources, other animals) in its habitat. Whereas the habitat defines a physical space occupied by an animal, the niche defines how the animal interacts with entities within that area. Thus, determining the niche (i.e., niche parameters) of an animal includes quantifying factors such as the size distribution of food and the strength of interactions with predators and competitors. Providing adequate "habitat" is not sufficient to allow for successful occupancy of a restoration site if niche parameters are not recognized and also restored. Such restoration could involve removal of predators or competitors of a target (e.g., endangered) species.

The terms *community* and *ecosystem* are used in multiple ways throughout the ecological literature (King 1997). A goal of restoration often revolves around reconstruction of a plant or animal "community." Strictly, an animal community is a group of interacting species in a defined location. Because we seldom have data on interspecific interactions, we seldom know the true community. John Wiens (1989, 257–258) chose to "accept the operational utility of talking about bird communities as assemblages of individuals of several species that occur together." He added that regardless of how one defines *community*, the group of birds being investigated and the criteria used to categorize the group should be described explicitly. It is exceedingly difficult to reconstruct a historic animal community. Thus, we should probably restrict our efforts to simply listing the species of interest that appeared to occur in the study region. The term *assemblage* has been used to describe the group of species under study without assigning any level of biological organization. That is how it will be used in this chapter. Finally, in most cases, researchers will have little knowledge of an ecosystem, including its interactions and boundaries. It is probably safer and less confusing to simply refer to the spatial boundaries of the study area and restrict discussion to the functions and relationships observed in that area.

Setting the Stage

The Pleistocene epoch, which began about 2–3 million years ago, is thought to have ended about ten thousand years before the present. The Pleistocene was characterized by a series of advances and retreats of continental ice sheets and glaciers. Our recent epoch is, in fact, probably another interglacial period of the Pleistocene (Cox and Moore 1993). This advance and retreat of ice obviously had a dramatic impact on vegetation and the general environmental conditions. Many animals, however, had time to seek and occupy different areas.

Most animal species currently occupying the earth are survivors of the abiotic and biotic influences of the Pleistocene, especially the last several advance-retreat cycles. Thus, the distribution and abundance of animal species existing currently can be linked to the geological events of the Pleistocene. The retreat of the ice sheet opened the way for occupation of vast areas either by species pre-adapted to the newly developing vegetation or by those able to adjust to the new environmental conditions. The identity of the pool of potential colonists is unknown but was probably related to the types of species and their abundance in refugia and in the more southern, ice-free areas (Morrison, Marcot, and Mannan 1998, 16–19; figure 11.1). Many taxa probably reached their present ranges in the early Holocene, although some survived in refugia until the late Holocene (Elias 1992). The influence of glacial-interglacial cycles

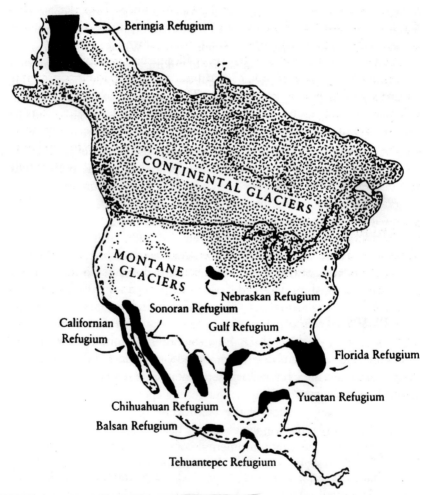

Figure 11.1. Postulated glacial-age refugia of the arid lands and certain other regions of North America. The northern portion indicated as the Sonoran Refugium probably was occupied by the biota of the Great Basin, and the southern part, by that of the Sinaloan shrublands. (Figure used by permission of John P. Hubbard and Cornell Laboratory of Ornithology; from an article in *The Living Bird* 12:155–196, 1973.)

on species' geographic range has been substantial (e.g., review by Gutier-rez 1997).

Biogeographic patterns of animal distribution have been explained by vicariance (the distribution that results from the replacement of one member of a species pair by the other, geographically) and dispersal. For example, in some regions of the Southwest, Russell Davis and his col-leagues (1988) concluded that both post-Pleistocene dispersal and subse-quent colonization, as well as vicariant events and subsequent extinction, have influenced the current assemblages of mammals. They stressed that the degree to which each process influences animal distribution should be considered in explaining current faunal composition.

The restorationist can use these post-Pleistocene phenomena to both understand the pattern of animal distribution and help identify potential animal assemblages in a project region. The current disjunct (patchy) dis-tribution of many animal species resulted from post-Pleistocene coloniza-tion and not negative human-induced impacts. In the desert Southwest, for example, many species of small mammals were unable to survive in the woodlands of mountain ranges that were isolated by intervening desert scrub (Brown 1978).

Techniques

Techniques available to assemble understanding of the historic wildlife of a project area can generally be divided between direct and indirect meth-ods. Direct methods provide proof of species occupancy through personal observation or other evidence (e.g., remains). Indirect methods require assembling a picture of what species likely occurred based on indirect data. In most cases, the restorationist will require information from both direct and indirect techniques to reassemble the historic wildlife assem-blage of a project site. Below I outline examples of data sources available for both techniques.

Direct Studies and Resources

Zooarchaeology

Zooarchaeology is an interdisciplinary field of research in which scien-tists study animal remains (subfossils, fossils, and bones) from archaeo-logical sites to determine the distribution, species morphology, and level of interactions with humans of historic animal assemblages. Zooarchaeol-ogists typically look for faunal remains in three types of sites: (1) village refuse areas; (2) butchering or kill sites; and (3) intentional burial sites. In general, the best finds are in areas that are environmentally stable with low levels of bacteria—that is, areas under still water, in dry desert caves, or where specimens were buried quickly (Reitz and Wing 1999).

To grasp the work of zooarchaeologists and understand some of the limits to their findings, one must understand the process by which a living animal or animal assemblage is transformed into a typically small sample assemblage. This latter assemblage is the result of various factors in the process, including: (1) the ephemeral nature of a species' anatomy; (2) the displacement and deep burial of bones by fluvial, sedimentary, or volcanic processes; (3) decisions by indigenous groups as to which animals to use; and (4) decisions by zooarchaeologists about where to take the sample. Since very little of this can be controlled by the zooarchaeologists, it means that some animals are not sampled, and their presence can, at best, be inferred but never known for certain. (See figure 11.2.)

Determining the distribution of animal parts can also be a problem because animals were killed and butchered away from a village or butchering site, animals and animal parts were traded among indigenous peoples, and domesticated animals were used by indigenous peoples outside the animal's original range. In terms of proximal and distant assemblages, it is fair to say, however, that one finds fewer animal remains outside the "catchment" area than within it. However, as zooarchaeologists Elizabeth Reitz and Elizabeth Wing (1999) point out, "These difficulties form challenges that should be met rather than boundaries that cannot be crossed. When prudently and cautiously studied in well-reasoned steps, animal remains, incomplete as they are, do provide insights into the past." They go on to suggest that (1) methods should match research objectives; (2) interpretations of results should be verified by further observation, experiments, and replication; and (3) an interdisciplinary approach should be used.

Zooarchaeologists have used bones as small as vertebraes and leg bones of mice to help reconstruct the fauna of an area (Olsen 1964). These zooarchaeological reconstructions can then be compared to contemporary distributions of species to determine the species that have apparently occupied an area from the date of the archaeological material. Using this method, Kay (1998) reconstructed the pre-Columbian ungulate and predator (including human) composition of North America. He used evidence from (1) firsthand personal accounts, (2) photos from the 1870s, (3) data on berry use (as an indicator of environmental conditions), (4) data on beaver abundance (also an indicator of environmental conditions), and (5) archaeological data (percent composition of different species in bone remains). Work such as Kay's could have significant implications for deciding how restoration projects are directed because it

Figure 11.2. Diagrammatic drawing of the taphonomic deposition process. (Courtesy of Pamela Nesbit.)

establishes goals for the composition of animal assemblages, and thus vegetation types, and successional patterns.

Along with the classic book *The Archaeology of Animals* by Simon J. M. Davis (reprinted in 1995) and the recent book *Zooarchaeology* by Elizabeth Reitz and Elizabeth Wing (1999), there are several resources for information about zooarchaeology. Many of these can be found at the zooarchaeology home page borealis.lib.uconn.edu/zhp, where the reader will find access to zooarchaeology labs, collections, bibliographies, research, zooarchaeologists, and related topics.

Paleontology

The work of paleontologists is similar in nature to, and often overlaps with, that of zooarchaeologists, but paleontologists study sites that had little or no direct human contact. Paleontology is divided into four subdisciplines: invertebrate paleontology, vertebrate paleontology, micropaleontology, and paleobotany. Paleontologists study the same hard bones, teeth, and other animal parts that zooarchaeologists study. However, they also study fossilized animal and plant remains and tend to take their studies much further back in time than the Holocene epoch, often doing research into the Paleozoic. Nevertheless, paleontologists such as Harris (1993) used paleontological methods and data to reconstruct the succession of microtene rodents from the mid- to late-Wisconsin period in New Mexico, and Goodwin (1995) used similar techniques to reconstruct the Pleistocene distribution of prairie dogs (*Cynomys* spp.).

Micropaleontology, or the study of subfossils, has also been used to give clues to historic animal assemblages. As David Rhode explains in chapter 10 on packrat middens, such middens often contain the remains of animals, including local plant pollinators, from a small, well-defined area and over a relatively short period of time. These subfossils can, nevertheless, be used to provide information about the climate and the physiological and genetic makeup of the animal assemblage. N. Philip Ashmole and Myrtle Ashmole (1997) used bird subfossils to help them reconstruct the ecosystem of Ascension Island in the equatorial Atlantic (see also Olson 1977).

Identifying fossil or subfossil remains requires the availability of reference specimens for comparison with the unknown items. Because we are restricting our analyses to the Holocene and forward in time, it is likely that any major natural history museum will contain adequate specimens for comparison. Knowledge of vertebrate morphology is necessary to speed the identification process, although people with good undergraduate training in wildlife science or zoology can usually perform the analyses.

Collections of Animal Remains

Much of the work of zooarchaeologists and paleontologists resides in collections that are housed at a variety of private and public universities, museums, and research organizations. Such collections represent fairly good attempts at cataloguing the fauna of a region. Many larger museums have gathered specimens from throughout North America and the rest of the world. (For a list of museum and lab sites, see www.borealis.uconn.edu/zhp/labs.htm or www.service.uga.edu/natmus/WWWSTS. html#US.)

Natural history collections are housed at a variety of private and public universities, museums, and research organizations. These collections were usually accumulated to characterize the fauna of a region, just as herbariums have been developed to characterize the flora of an area. The specimens usually consist of amphibians and reptiles preserved in alcohol; birds preserved as skins; and mammals preserved as skins, skulls, and sometimes other bones. An original tag accompanying each specimen lists the date and location of collection, the collector, the species identity, and perhaps a few natural history notes.

Although museums naturally concentrate on species within their geographic region, many of the larger museums have gathered specimens from throughout North America and the rest of the world. Large research museums sponsored collecting trips to locations that had previously received little natural history work. Such collecting trips were common throughout the world as nations began to explore their boundaries; they are relatively rare in developed countries today. Thus, some museums contain specimens from outside their immediate area.

Bird eggs are housed in some ornithological collections. Eggs have been collected by scientists, amateur birders, and egg traders. The science of studying eggs is called oology and was extremely popular in the early 1900s—several oological journals were published. Egg collections have been valuable in the analysis of natural history parameters (e.g., clutch size, breeding phenology), breeding distributions, and pesticide-caused eggshell thinning. The data slip accompanying the egg sets usually includes clutch size, nest location (height, plant substrate), and related data.

Richard Banks and his colleagues (1973) and Mary Clench and her colleagues (1976) summarize the holdings of major ornithological collections in North America and identify museums by state and province, contact information, and the size of their holdings. Overall, the museums they contacted housed more than 4 million study skins, 150,000 skeletal specimens, 50,000 fluid-preserved specimens, and 650,000 egg sets. Lloyd Kiff and Dan Hough (1985) provide a detailed summary of information on the location, specimen holdings, geographic coverage, and related information of egg collections in North America.

A conservative estimate of the total number of specimens in major herpetological collections in the United States was 3.5 million in the mid-1980s (L. Trueb, California Academy of Sciences, pers. comm.). Fortunately, most of those specimens have been catalogued, which means that summary information, date of collection, and location of collection are available to researchers. Hafner and his colleagues (1997) have compiled a thorough review of the mammalian collections of North and South America.

With so much data to catalogue, an increasing number of museums, such as the Museum of Paleontology at the University of California–Berkeley (www.ucmp.berkeley.edu/collections/catalogs.html), the National Museum of Natural History at the Smithsonian (www.nmnh.si.edu/collections.html), and the Florida Museum of Natural History (www.flmnh.ufl.edu/databases/zooarch/intro.html), have developed collection databases. This is a favorable trend because it assists curators in managing collections and helps researchers determine what is in specific collections. There are, however, a number of issues that researchers should consider when using a museum collection database.

First, researchers should be aware that mistakes in the transcription of original data can and do happen, and that few museums transcribe all the original information—especially field notes—into the database. With these problems in mind, the researcher should (1) request a computer printout of specimen holdings sorted by date and location, and (2) request photocopies of the original data slips for the specimens of interest.

Second, in some cases, the museum staff may not have verified the identification of the species (this can be determined by asking the curator). If this is the case, it is often necessary to visit the collection and identify the specimen, or request the curatorial staff to confirm the identification. In some rare cases, it may be necessary to request a loan of critical specimens for identification purposes, but such requests should be kept to a minimum because handling and shipping specimens often harms them and reduces their usefulness.

Third, researchers should remember that museum specimens were often collected as part of short-term surveys or archaeological excavations. Moreover, sampling was usually conducted in concentrated areas that promised relatively high species diversity. Thus, researchers should not consider the available specimens a complete representation of the species present in either the specific sampling locale or the surrounding area. The presence of a specimen indicates only that the species was present at the time of collection.

Fourth, it is important to determine the authenticity of museum records. For example, curators of egg collections are aware that some egg collectors may have misrepresented where the eggs were collected because location, rather than authenticity, dictated price during the early

1900s boom in egg trading. Novice users of museum data should consult with people experienced with such matters rather than accepting all information at face value.

Finally, researchers should act professionally and be willing to pay for the photocopy work they request and even the labor involved in accessing and printing computer databases. Potential users of museum information should also be aware that some curators may be reluctant to cooperate with them unless the purpose of the research is clearly elucidated. It is critical that researchers understand and discuss the limitations and biases in any records they hope to use since this will indicate to the reluctant curator that they are experienced.

Nonmuseum Databases

In addition to museum databases, there are several other data sources that researchers and restorationists should be aware of. Two important data sources for birds are the National Audubon Christmas Bird Count (CBC) and the North American Breeding Bird Surveys (BBS). Begun in 1900, the annual CBC has grown into a valuable database for long-term monitoring of bird populations. Counting areas were initially concentrated in the eastern United States but have become more common throughout the country since the 1950s. The density of counting areas has also increased over time. The CBC data have been summarized by the U.S. Fish & Wildlife Service and by various researchers (Wing 1947). The *Canadian Field Naturalist* recorded similar count data from 1924 through 1939. The *National Audubon Society Field Notes* (formerly *American Birds* and *Audubon Field-Notes*) publishes the annual results of the counts, and there is a Web site with a database that can be consulted: birdsource.tc.cornell.edu/cbcdata. At this point, however, the CBC data alone do not provide significant historical information for many locations. Moreover, users of the Web database are warned that the data contains errors and should not be used in scientific studies until it is reviewed and corrected by CBC compilers.

In 1965, the U.S. Fish & Wildlife Service's Bureau of Biological Survey (now the Biological Resource Division of the U.S. Geological Survey) developed the Breeding Bird Survey in order to monitor changes in bird distribution and population trends. The BBS consists of more than two thousand randomly located, permanent survey routes established along secondary roads throughout the continental United States and southern Canada. These routes are surveyed annually during the height of the breeding season. The data from these surveys and their interpretations, which can be found at www.mp1-pwrc.usgs.gov/ bbs/bbs.html, are most useful in determining the likely assemblage of birds in a locality.

Other databases worth consulting are the Man & the Biosphere Program (MAB) Fauna Database (www.ice.ucdavis.edu/mab/fauna.html). This site includes absence-presence information about fauna on MAB sites throughout North America. Similarly, the National Parks Fauna Database (www.ice.ucdavis.edu/nps) provides basic information about animals found in national parks and on lakeshores. The Cornell University Fauna Databases (gopher://biodiversity.bio.uno.edu:70/77/.indices/ bird/cubird) and that of the Slater Museum of Natural History in Tacoma, Washington (gopher://biodiversity.bio.uno.edu:70/77/.indices/slater/bird) are also worth reviewing.

Literature

Libraries and museums house the field notes, journals, and other written records of scientists and other observers of wildlife. These written records and recollections often contain species-specific information on animal distribution, abundance, breeding status, and other aspects of natural history. They can aid in reconstructing the animal assemblage for a region and the region's environmental conditions at the time.

Take, for example, this account of a roadrunner, which was made near San Diego, California, in April 1827 by Paolo Emilio Botta, a naturalist collecting for the Museum of Natural History in Paris:

> One finds about the anchorage, that running bird which I have already mentioned by the name of Churay, to which is attributed the ability to kill snakes for food. The Churay is slightly larger than a magpie; as to form it is very similar to the native of our country. Like it, it has a long tail which it raises at times to an almost perpendicular position. Its color is tawny with green feathers and iridescences. It seldom flies and only for short distances; but it runs as fast as a horse. It is said that, when it finds a sleeping snake, it erects a rampart made of the spiny branches of a cactus about it and, when this accomplished, wakes the snake suddenly, by crying; the snake, expecting to flee, impales itself on the long barbs which decorate its prison, and the bird finishes it off with blows of its beak. (Botta 1835)

Dennis Power (1994) published a good example of assembling historic avifauna records. He used historic survey reports through the early 1900s to reconstruct the distribution and abundance of birds on the coastal islands of California.

Similarly, Ned Johnson (1994) used *The Checklist of North American Birds*, fifth edition (American Ornithologists' Union 1950) to help him reconstruct changes in avifauna in the western United States. He calculated these changes by comparing this midcentury baseline with subsequently published regional bird compilations, including more recent editions of *The Checklist*. He also tallied nesting season records cited in *Audubon Field Notes* to gain information about pioneers (a singing male or a pair in an appropriate breeding habitat) and extralimital nesting during the last three decades. From this work, he was able to reconstruct the expanding range of the Scott's oriole (*Icterus parisorum*) in the southwestern United States (figure 11.3) and of other species elsewhere. He concluded that these range expansions were due to climatic changes (increased summer moisture and higher mean summer temperatures) and were not due to human causes. Such analysis can help restorationists to understand the history of species and establish priorities regarding the restoration of suitable plant associations.

See chapter 3 for more detailed information about the use of historical documents.

Indirect Techniques

Reconstruction of the biogeographic history of indicator species provides another means, albeit indirect, of knowing the historic habitats and their associated faunal assemblages. This procedure works best when the indicator species are specialists with a restricted range of vegetation types. For example, Hafner (1993) used the Nearctic pikas (*Ochotona princeps* and *O. collaris*) as biogeographic indicators (i.e., species that are thought to be diagnostic of specific environmental conditions) of cool, mesic, rocky areas. He then hypothesized that species known to co-occur with these pika species would use similar habitat.

Relict faunas still exist within continental North America in areas where they have found suitable habitat that has sustained them through numerous generations, and they can be a good indicator of historic faunal assemblages. For example, Hartwell Welsh (1990) reported that the Del Norte salamander (*Plethodon elongates*), Olympic torrent salamander (*Rhyocotriton olympicus*), and tailed frog (*Ascaphus trueii*) are paleoecological relicts that have long been associated with the ancient conifer forests of the Pacific Northwest. Bruce Marcot and his colleagues (unpublished data) compared the existing fauna of the interior of the western United

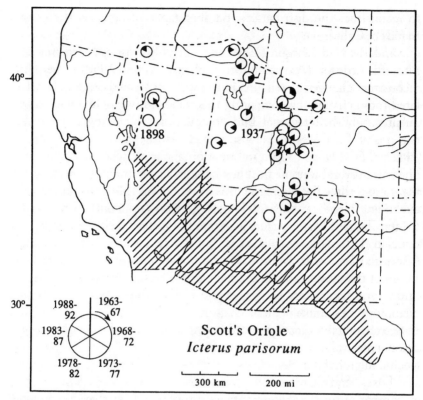

Figure 11.3. The pattern of diagonal lines shows the approximate nesting range of the Scott's oriole in the Southwest as of the middle of the 1900s. Records of the past three decades document pioneering and extralimital nesting to the extent of the dashed line. All symbols represent specific localities of summer presence. Blackened pie slices denote occurrence in the half-decade period indicated by the diagram in the lower left. A line protruding from the pie slice represents positive evidence of breeding. (Reprinted with permission, Cooper Ornithological Society.)

States to Tertiary fossil fauna and found seven relict fauna genera (represented by thirty-two species) and twenty relict fauna families (represented by fifty-five genera). These genera and families occupy a wide range of vegetation, including grasslands, shrublands, and forests.

Although it may be tempting to use relict faunas as ecological indicators, there are some caveats that should be considered. First, relicts tend to occur in odd and disjunct locations and, therefore, do not necessarily represent zonal or climatic climax conditions. Second, insofar as relicts are holdovers from earlier environments, their distributions do not necessarily reflect the suitability of current conditions. Thus, restorationists should be wary of defining habitat and landscape requirements from the current habitat use patterns of relics without knowing the paleoecological history of the population and the site. Nonetheless, plant and animal relics are often of scientific interest and deserve special conservation consideration (Millar and Libby 1991).

Applications

There are several ways to work with the historic evidence to help solve restoration-related problems. In this section, I cite examples from a relatively "wild" landscape, an urban landscape, and a genetic study.

Jerry Franklin and his colleagues (1995) reconstructed the floral and faunal conditions existing at Mt. St. Helens prior to its 1980 eruption. Although their research task was relatively simple given the recent nature of the event and the quantity of biological information they had to draw on, the process they followed, nevertheless, remains a good example of reestablishing habitat in order to rehabilitate wildlife species. Their work included relatively large-scale plantings of preexisting vegetation types, plantings of forage species, and provisioning of species-specific microhabitat elements such as standing dead trees, water holes, nest boxes, and raptor roosts and perches. They increased the rate of recolonization of the area by certain animals by providing key habitat elements that would otherwise take years or decades to develop naturally. Nest boxes, for example, substitute for natural cavities because trees take many decades or even over a century to grow to a diameter of sufficient size to provide adequate nesting locations.

Along with several colleagues, I prepared a wildlife habitat restoration plan for Sweetwater Regional Park in San Diego County, California (Morrison, Tennant, and Scott 1994). We surveyed the park to obtain the current distribution and abundance of vegetation and wildlife, and then compared those results with historical data (pre-1975) about amphibians, reptiles, mammals, and birds from specimens housed at the San Diego Natural History Museum. We also used literature sources to supplement the museum records. What we discovered was a substantial loss of native amphibians and reptiles, including four amphibians, three lizards, and eleven snake species. The small mammal assemblage was depauperate and dominated by the exotic house mouse (*Mus musculus*) and the native western harvest mouse (*Reithrodontomys megalotis*). There was also an apparent net loss of thirteen other mammal species. We found six new species of birds, but a loss of eighteen other bird species. The park managers used these data, in part, to develop a restoration plan of the local plant and animal communities (Morrison, Scott, and Tennant 1994). The data we collected on likely historic assemblages of animals provides direction for potential reintroduction of selected native species to the site. For example, we recommended that the abundance of exotic mice and rats should probably be reduced to promote recolonization of the site by native rodents.

In 1997, Juan Bouzat and his colleagues used museum specimens of the greater prairie chicken (*Tympanuchus cupido*) from the Illinois Natural History Survey ornithological collection to test the hypothesis that an existing Illinois population of greater prairie chicken has less genetic variability than historic populations (Bouzat, Lewin, and Paige 1998). Their method of testing involved taking DNA samples from the feather roots of the museum specimens and comparing them with DNA from the population in Illinois, and with other current populations in Kansas, Minnesota, and Nebraska. Their findings confirmed the existence of a "genetic bottleneck" in the Illinois population—a population that is missing alleles found in the historic specimens and in DNA from greater prairie chickens in nearby states. This study should suggest to restorationists not only the merits of genetic sampling, but the need to consider crossbreeding animals (much like restorationists and horticulturalists have done with endangered plants) to help them recover their historic genetic vigor.

Uncertainty: How to Work with an Incomplete and Altered Record

Despite all the information we have, the historic records for species, faunal assemblages, and habitats are far from complete. This lack of information was not lost on those involved in the Sierra Nevada Ecosystem Project (1996), who, in their attempt to use historic reference conditions to determine the ecological sustainability of the area, found that "historic wildlife distributions were the most difficult to infer, being based on historic forest habitats and estimates of historic use of habitat." Likewise, Brina Kessel and Daniel Gibson (1994) explain that today it is almost impossible to determine whether some perceived change in an animal population is a real directional change or just a fluctuation. They define this situation as one where apparent changes fall into the following categories: (1) those we believe are real changes; (2) those that reflect our increased knowledge of an animal assemblage; (3) those that may be natural fluctuations; and (4) those attributable to confused species identifications.

Without direct observations of a species or specimens, we can only guess at the likely effectiveness of a reconstructed animal assemblage. Recall that habitat is a species-specific concept that includes more than vegetation. The more thoroughly we can describe the historic vegetation and environmental conditions—for example, the presence of water and the soil conditions—the more complete will be our list of potential animal species.

I would further suggest that we should assess the quality of our historic reconstruction by assigning probabilities of certainty to each data source that is used. These probabilities of certainty could be qualitative. Factors to include in assigning certainty include:

1. *Age of the data source.* Older data per se are not of lower quality. Rather, the techniques used to collect specimens, the intensity of field observations, and related aspects of data gathering have changed with time. Therefore, all workers should carefully consider the strengths and weaknesses of the techniques used to gather the data being evaluated.

2. *Physical distance from the data source to the study site.* Intuitively, the more distant a source of data on the occurrence of a species is from the project area, the greater the extrapolation that is necessary to assume that the animal once occurred at the area. Factors to use in evaluation include likely habitat continuity and the dispersal ability of the animal.

3. *Quantity and quality of data sources:*
   - *One record or numerous records.* Intuitively, the greater the number of records, the greater the likelihood that the species occurred in the area of interest.

   - *Records from a brief time span or a long time span.* Specimens that appear in records over a period of time lessen the probability of misidentification.

   - *Actual specimens or visual observations.* People make mistakes, rendering voucher specimens an invaluable source of confirmation of the occurrence of a species.

   - *Completeness of data record.* Information on date, location, vegetation association, and related natural history parameters strengthen the quality of a historic record.

   - *Reputation of data source.* It is helpful, when using historic records, to determine the qualifications of the data collector, especially when visual records are involved.

If such an assignment is attempted, each conclusion and assumption needs to be discussed, and those accepted should be stated as part of the report.

Finally, restorationists should not confuse what should be present in an area with what people would like to be there. Predicting past occurrences of currently protected species will meet with criticism from certain stakeholders. It is best, therefore, to discuss any uncertainties and keep any conclusions and recommendations within the data.

Conclusion

Reconstructing the likely animal assemblages of a proposed restoration site is a valuable goal for any restoration project. Unfortunately, it is not easily accomplished and always is undertaken with some level of uncertainty. There is no guarantee that if restorationists build the "correct" habitat, a species that historically occupied such a habitat will come. Small sites or sites that are surrounded by inhospitable boundary influences may always remain unsuitable for recolonization by animals, no matter how well constructed the habitat. Thus, restoration goals for wildlife should be developed in light of both historic possibilities and current conditions.

References

American Ornithologists' Union. 1950. *The Checklist of North American Birds*. 5th ed. New York: American Ornithologists' Union.

Ashmole, N.P., and M.J. Ashmole. 1997. The land fauna of Ascension Island: New data from caves and lava flows, and a reconstruction of the prehistoric ecosystem. *Journal of Biogeography* 24:549–589.

Banks, R.C., M.H. Clench, and J.C. Barlow. 1973. Bird collections in the United States and Canada. *Auk* 90:136–170.

Botta, P.E. 1835. Description du Saurothera Californiana (Coucou Churea). *Nouvelles Annales de Museum History* 4.

Bouzat, J.L., H.A. Lewin, and K.N. Paige. 1998. The ghost of genetic diversity past: Historical DNA analysis of the greater prairie chicken. *American Naturalist* 152(1):1–6.

Brown, J.H. 1978. The theory of insular biogeography and the distribution of boreal birds and mammals. *Great Basin Naturalist Memoirs* 2:209–227.

Clench, M.H., R.C. Banks, and J.C. Barlow. 1976. Bird collections in the United States and Canada: Addenda and corrigenda. *Auk* 93:126–129.

Cox, C.B., and P.D. Moore. 1993. *Biogeography: An ecological and evolutionary approach*. 5th edition. Boston: Blackwell Scientific Publications.

Daubenmire, R. 1968. *Plant communities: A textbook of plant synecology*. New York: Harper and Row.

Davis, R., C. Dunford, and M.V. Lomolino. 1988. Montane mammals of the American Southwest: The possible influence of post-Pleistocene colonization. *Journal of Biogeography* 15:841–848.

Davis, S.J.M. 1995 reprint. *The archaeology of animals*. New Haven, Conn.: Yale University Press.

Elias, S.A. 1992. Late Quaternary zoogeography of the Chihuahuan Desert insect fauna, based on fossil records from packrat middens. *Journal of Biogeography* 19:285–197.

Franklin, J.F., P.M. Frenzen, and F.J. Swanson. 1995. Re-creation of ecosystems at Mount St. Helens: Contrasts in artificial and natural approaches. Pages 287–333 in *Rehabilitating damaged ecosystems*, 2nd edition, ed. J. Cairns Jr. Boca Raton, Fla.: Lewis Publishers.

Goodwin, H.T. 1995. Pliocene-Pleistocene biogeographic history of prairie dogs, genus *Cynomys* (Sciuridae). *Journal of Mammalogy* 76:100–122.

Gutierrez, D. 1997. Importance of historical factors on species richness and composition of butterfly assemblages (Lepidoptera: Rhopalocera) in a northern Iberian mountain range. *Journal of Biogeography* 24:77–88.

Hafner, D.J. 1993. North American pika (*Ochotona princeps*) as a late Quaternary biogeographic indicator species. *Quaternary Research* 39:373–380.

Hafner, M.S., W.L. Gannon, J. Salazar-Bravo, and S.T. Alvarez-Castaneda. 1997. *Mammal collections in the Western Hemisphere. A survey and directory of existing collections*. Lawrence, Kansas: American Society of Mammalogists.

Hall, L.S., P.R. Krausman, and M.L. Morrison. 1997. The habitat concept and a plea for standard terminology. *Wildlife Society Bulletin* 25:173–182.

Harris, A.H. 1993. Wisconsinan pre-plenighacial biotic change in southeastern New Mexico. *Quaternary Research* 40:127–133.

Heermann, A.L. 1859. Report upon the birds collected on the survey. *U.S. Pacific Railroad Survey Reports* 10:29–80.

Hubbard, J.P. 1973. Avian evolution in the aridlands of North America. *Living Bird* 12:155–196.

Johnson, N.K. 1994. Pioneering and natural expansion of breeding distributions in western North America. Pages 27–44 in *A century of avifaunal change in western North America*, eds. J.J. Jehl Jr. and N.K. Johnson. Studies in Avian Biology Series 15. San Diego, Calif.: Cooper Ornithological Society.

Kay, C.E. 1998. Are ecosystems structured from the top-down or bottom-up: A new look at an old debate. *Wildlife Society Bulletin* 26:484–498.

Kessel, B., and D.D. Gibson. 1994. A century of avifaunal change in Alaska. Pages 4–13 in *A century of avifaunal change in western North America*, eds. J.J. Jehl Jr. and N.K. Johnson. Studies in Avian Biology Series 15. San Diego, Calif.: Cooper Ornithological Society.

Kiff, L.F., and D.J. Hough. 1985. *Inventory of bird egg collections of North America*. American Ornithologists' Union and Oklahoma Biological Survey, Norman, Okla.

King, A.W. 1997. Hierarchy theory: A guide to system structure for wildlife biologists. Pages 185–212 in *Wildlife and landscape ecology: Effects of pattern and scale*, ed. J.A. Bissonette. New York: Springer-Verlag.

McIntosh, R.P. 1986. *The background of ecology: Concept and theory*. New York: Cambridge University Press.

Millar, C.I., and W.J. Libby. 1991. Strategies for conserving clinal, ecotypic, and disjunct population diversity in widespread species. Pages 149–170 in *Genetics and conservation of rare plants*, eds. D.A. Falk and K.E. Holsinger. Oxford, England: Oxford University Press.

Morrison, M.L., B.G. Marcot, and R.W. Mannan. 1998. *Wildlife-habitat relationships: Concepts and applications*. 2nd edition. Madison: University of Wisconsin Press.

Morrison, M.L., T.A. Scott, and T. Tennant. 1994. Wildlife-habitat restoration in an urban park in Southern California. *Restoration Ecology* 2:17–30.

Morrison, M.L., T. Tennant, and T.A. Scott. 1994. Laying the foundation for a comprehensive program of restoration for wildlife habitat in a riparian floodplain. *Environmental Management* 18:939–955.

Olsen, S.J. 1964. Mammal remains from archaeological sites. Part 1. Southeastern and southwestern United States. *Papers of the Peabody Museum of Archaeology and Ethnology* 56(1):1–162.

Olson, S.L. 1977. Additional notes on subfossil bird remains from Ascension Island. *Ibis* 119:37–43.

Power, D.M. 1994. Avifaunal change on California's coastal islands. Pages 75–90 in *A century of avifaunal change in western North America*, eds. J.J. Jehl Jr. and N.K. Johnson. Studies in Avian Biology 15.

Reitz, E.J., and E.S. Wing. 1999. *Zooarchaeology*. New York: Cambridge University Press.

Robbins, C.S., D. Bystrak, and P.H. Geissler. 1986. The breeding bird survey: Its first fifteen years, 1965–1979. U.S. Fish and Wildlife Service Research Publication 157. Washington, D.C.

Sierra Nevada Ecosystem Project. 1996. *Final report to Congress: Status of the Sierra Nevada*. Volume 1: Assessment summaries and management strategies. Wildland Resources Center Report No. 36. Centers for Water and Wildland Resources. University of California, Davis.

Welsh, H.H. 1990. Relictual amphibians and old-growth forest. *Conservation Biology* 4:309–319.

Wiens, J.A. 1989. *The ecology of bird communities*. Volume 2: Processes and variations. Cambridge, England: Cambridge University Press.

Wing, L. 1947. *Christmas census summary, 1900–1939*. Pullman: State College of Washington. Mimeograph.

Web and Gopher Sites

National Museum of Natural History/Smithsonian
    www.mnh.si.edu/rc/db/databases.html
Florida Museum of Natural History/Comparative Collection Database
    www.flmnh.ufl.edu/databases/zooarch/intro.htm
North American Breeding Bird Survey
    www.mp1-pwrc.usgs.gov/bbs/bbs.html
Man & Biosphere Fauna Database
    www.ice.ucdavis.edu/mab/fauna.html

National Parks Fauna Database
 www.ice.ucdavis.edu/nps
University of California at Berkeley Museum of Paleontology
 www.ucmp.berkeley.edu/collections/catalogs.html
Cornell University Fauna Databases
 gopher://biodiversity.bio.uno.edu:70/77/.indices/bird/cubird
Slater Museum of Natural History (Tacoma, Washington)
 gopher://biodiversity.bio.uno.edu:70/77/.indices/slater/bird
Cornell University CBC Count Report
 birdsource.tc.cornell.edu/cbcdata
Biodiversity and Biological collections Gopher
 www.biodiversity.bio.uno.edu/:70/11/collections_info/institution

12

Geomorphology, Hydrology, and Soils

Stanley W. Trimble

For more than a century, the historical reconstruction of past landscapes has been an important tool in the study of geomorphology and hydrology (Marsh 1864; Goudie 1999). This importance has increased, and several surveys and compendia published in the past two decades indicate the scope and utility of this approach (Thornes and Brunsden 1977; Hooke and Kain 1982; Gregory 1979, 1987; Grove 1988; Cooke and Doornkamp 1990; Trimble and Cooke 1991; Goudie 1999; Whitney 1994; Trimble 1998; Trimble, in press). The recent interest in the restoration of aquatic ecosystems and the need to know reference conditions make historical reconstruction even more important (National Research Council 1992, 1999; White and Walker 1997). This chapter will briefly cover geological surveys; soil surveys; soil erosion surveys; stream and sediment discharge records; stream, valley, estuary, and coastal surveys; use of stream structures such as bridges and mills; reservoir surveys; wetland drainage records; and irrigation records. It will also provide examples of studies that use these records so that the user may read further. The reader should be cautioned that every technique or approach has so many variations that anyone deciding on a given record or technique would be well served to examine different permutations presented by the problems at hand and by the availability of data.

Geological Surveys

Historical geological surveys are rarely valuable for their information about bedrock geology—modern surveys are usually better—but the older surveys were written in a period when geologists were earth scientists in the broad sense. As a result, their reports often contain a wealth of information about landforms, rocks, minerals, soils, vegetation, animals, agriculture, and drainage. An example is E. W. Hilgard (1860), who wrote a long treatise concerning the effects of agriculture on soils and soil erosion and the consequent stream sedimentation in antebellum Mississippi. Such surveys were usually produced by states rather than the federal government, and investigators would do well to read these often obscure state publications (e.g., Hall and Hall 1908; McCallie 1911; Barrows and Phillips 1917). In addition, states often produced significant studies that were never published and may be in some available repository such as the office of the state geologist. Although somewhat less comprehensive in scope, early reports of the U.S. Geological Survey can be useful. An outstanding example is the work of G. K. Gilbert (1917), who showed that hydraulic mining in California had caused mountain valleys to be buried and San Francisco Bay to be partially filled with sediment. However, these reports require a great deal of patience and determination on the part of the researcher because they tend to be rare, obscure, or hidden away in little-used archives or collections.

Soil Surveys

In 1899, the U.S. Department of Agriculture began systematic soil surveys, generally at the county level. Often, even more than geologists, soil scientists were in fact early ecologists or natural historians who had a good understanding of the relationships among soils, landforms, drainage, climate, vegetation, animals, agriculture, and even demography, and they frequently and insightfully addressed environmental relationships and problems they observed. Frequent themes in these early soil surveys are poor agricultural and forestry practices, soil erosion, and changes of landscape drainage, such as the filling of stream bottoms from accelerated sedimentation (Trimble 1970a and b; Trimble 1974; Wilson 1989).

Most soil surveys give keen observations on plant communities existing at the time of survey. Mattoni and Longcore (1997) found such insights useful when reconstructing the characteristics and extent of coastal prairie in Southern California.

Most early (1899–1955) soil surveys contained detailed maps, often superimposed over USGS topographic sheets at a scale of 1:62,500 (one inch = one mile), but the soils maps usually contain more information than the USGS sheets. After about 1955, soils information was mapped directly over vertical aerial photography at a scale of 1:20,000, and more recently it has been mapped over orthophotos (congruent with USGS topographic maps) at 1:24,000. More modern soil surveys contain much more technical soils information but are less broad and integrative. On the other hand, one may now follow more closely edaphic or pedologic change such as podzolization or gleization and changes of bulk density, nutrient levels, organic content, structure, and degree of erosion. Moreover, modern soil surveys relate more closely to urbanization so that related environmental changes may be better understood. Many counties have had several soil surveys since 1899, and restorationists and others may use these like a time series to follow soil and landscape changes over time.

Soil Erosion Surveys

Most modern soil surveys report the degree of previous erosion or profile truncation for each mapping unit, but these data are not detailed. Earlier USDA surveys were more detailed, the most comprehensive being the Reconnaissance Erosion Survey of 1934 (U.S. Department of Agriculture 1935). While the state maps were published at 1:500,000, the original field maps were more detailed, mostly being done at 1:62,500 (Trimble 1975c). These field maps are available in the National Archives (Record Group 114).

Far more detailed studies (1:15,840) were done for scattered parts of the United States between 1935 and 1942 by the USDA Soil Conservation Service. The first twenty-two of these were called Erosion Surveys, but the last twenty-one were called Physical Land Inventories (Bennett 1944). Additional studies were not published, although mimeographed copies may be in the National Archives (Record Group 114; see Heynen 1981) or in state or county Natural Resources Conservation Service offices. These studies not only contain important baseline information concerning soils, agriculture, forests, streams, reservoirs, and related land-use practices, they also offer penetrating analyses of contemporary problems such as the relation of tenancy to soil erosion. Using these sources, I (Trimble 1974, 1975c, 1977) was able to quantify the total soil erosion during the historical agricultural period for the Southern Piedmont.

Stream Discharge and Water Quality

Stream discharge measurements began to be taken in the nineteenth century but were not taken on a widespread basis until the early 1900s. Earlier reports gave only daily or monthly discharge rates, while more recent data are recorded hourly. Even so, stream gauging is so expensive that only a very small proportion of streams have been gauged, and as a result the data are often chronologically discontinuous. Furthermore, many agencies have collected the data, causing the data to be scattered and often inaccessible. Since 1980, stream discharge data have been collected and electronically stored. They are now online at "Geological Survey Real Time and Historical Stream Flow, Water Quality, Water Use Data" www.h2o.usgs.gov. Despite some problems finding good data sets, stream discharge records have been used in many studies of streamflow changes as related to environmental controls such as urbanization, afforestation, and agriculture (Knox et al. 1975; Trimble, Weirich, and Hoag 1987; Sutcliffe 1987; Potter 1991; Price 1998; Van Steeter and Pitlick 1998).

Water quality data are more problematic. Sediment discharge data exist from early in the twentieth century, but it was midcentury before the data were widespread and dependable. Such data are normally given in mass per day, but are sometimes given in concentrations. Occasionally, one finds turbidity data. Even more than water discharge, sediment transport data are scattered and discontinuous. Thus, the probability of having historical stream and sediment discharge data for any particular stream is small, and one must often make regional transfers and use surrogates— techniques that Costa and Baker (1981) do a good job of presenting. Trimble and Cooke (1990) offer a detailed listing of sediment discharge data, but many of the data are now online at water.usgs.gov/nawqa/data. The Geological Survey National Stream Quality Accounting Network www.water.usgs.gov/publicnasgan provides water quality information from the Mississippi, Columbia, Rio Grande, and Colorado river systems.

Studies relating historic sediment discharge and environmental changes are Hadley (1974), Trimble (1975a, 1977), Meade (1982), Meade and Trimble (1974), Meade and Parker (1985). Other water quality data (BOD, pH, nitrogen, heavy metals, etc.) are generally available from scattered and discontinuous sampling. More on water quality, including Web sites and GIS applications, may be found in National Research Council or NRC (1999).

Reservoir Surveys

Stream sediment discharge is much better measured in reservoirs such as the Tennessee Valley Authority system than in streams (NRC 1999; Trimble and Bube 1990). This is because reservoirs intercept all streamflow and trap the coarser sediment load, or bedload, not measured by suspended sediment sampling. Moreover, reservoir data can sometimes provide more than a hundred years' worth of information. Trap efficiency can be estimated so that measured rates of reservoir accumulation can be adjusted to give reasonable approximations of actual stream sediment discharge (Brune 1953; Trimble and Bube 1990; NRC 1999). Trimble and Carey (1984, 1992) showed how reservoir sedimentation rates could be combined with runoff rates to retrodict historical sediment concentrations. Very little work has been done on the quality (chemical, biological) of reservoir sediment.

During the past century or so, most reservoirs have been periodically surveyed to measure the rates of sediment accumulation (figure 12.1), and these rates have been periodically collated and published (Dendy and Champion 1978; U.S. Geological Survey 1983). Unfortunately,

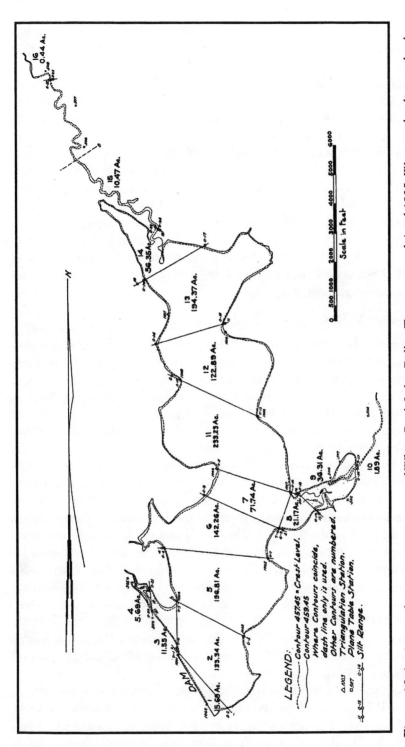

Figure 12.1. A typical reservoir survey map, of White Rock Lake, Dallas, Texas, surveyed April 1935. Water and sediment depths are measured along each "silt range" (from Eakin 1936).

fewer agencies now appear to be doing the surveys and no agency has taken responsibility for collating and publishing the results for the period since 1980. Of course, scientists can survey reservoirs themselves (Eakin 1936; Trimble and Lund 1982; Trimble 1983; Trimble and Carey 1992). For example, investigators in the United Kingdom have greatly extended the time and utility of reservoir surveys by using isotopic dating methods such as ^{210}Pb and ^{137}Cs (Oldfield 1977; Burt, Donohoe, and Vann 1984; Petts 1984; McManus and Duck 1985, 1993; Petts and Foster 1985; Foster et al. 1985; Foster, Dearing, and Appleby 1986; Foster et al. 1990; Duck and McManus 1987, 1990; Stott 1987; Stott, Butcher, and Pemberton 1988; Labadz, Burt, and Potter 1991; Dearing and Foster 1993). Some of these studies have established nineteenth-century stream basin sediment yields, and D. P. Butcher and his colleagues have done a study that extends back to 1840. Small reservoirs in continuous use in the United States date back to 1677 (Graf 1999), and older records should have considerable utility.

Stream, Valley, and Coastal Surveys

By far the best baseline data for determining long-term landform and hydrographic changes are provided by instrumented ground surveys. There are considerable amounts of data of this type.

Stream and valley surveys are often done together, usually in the form of cross-sectional profiles, but longitudinal profiles (water level or stream bottom) are often included. In exceptional cases, floodplains and other areas adjacent to the stream are mapped using contour lines (figure 12.2). The most common source of such stream and valley surveys is the U.S. Army Corps of Engineers (COE), and most are found in the Congressional Serials (e.g., U.S. Congress 1943). Surveys tend to be on larger rivers and estuaries (harbors or potential harbors) and have been indexed by Jones and Holland (1948). Their study and similar studies have been indispensable for research of stream and valley aggradation and degradation and lateral channel migration (Adler 1980; Kondolf and Curry 1986; James 1989; and Kesel, Yoder, and McCraw 1992). Using similar data, Costa (1978) was able to reconstruct bankfull discharge capacity in 1858 for a stream in Denver, Colorado. Other such studies were done by Emmett and Hadley (1968); Leopold and Emmett (1965); Osterkamp, Emmett, and Leopold (1990); Thoms and Walker (1992); and Brizga and Finlayson (1994).

An extremely detailed series of stream and valley surveys was done in 1935–41 by the Soil Conservation Service to measure historic sediment in about sixty drainage basins (Happ, Rittenhouse, and Dobson 1940; Happ 1975). Only a few of these have ever been restudied (Trimble

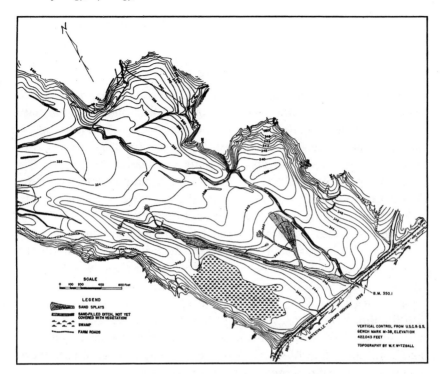

Figure 12.2. A precisely mapped stream valley, East Goose Valley near Oxford, Mississippi, ca. 1938. The valley was being rapidly filled with sand at the time (from Happ, Rittenhouse, and Dobson 1940).

1975b; Trimble 1983; Trimble 1999; Trimble and Lund 1982; Magilligan 1985). Many of the extant data were collected by Happ and placed in the National Archives (Record Group 114).

Another source of stream profiles is the stage-discharge relationship at older gauging stations. Some of these were established in the nineteenth century, and each successive revision, done every few years, required one or more surveyed cross section. Cooke and Reeves (1976), Williams and Wolman (1984), and Van Steeter and Pitlick (1998) used such profiles to show historic stream channel changes.

Detailed coastal surveys have been done by the U.S. Coast and Geodetic Survey starting before 1850, and many locations have been resurveyed several times (see Reingold 1958; Johnson and Heynen 1971; Guthorn 1984). These excellent surveys, which can be found in most major libraries, have been used to measure estuarine sedimentation (Gottschalk 1945), coastal erosion (Dolan and Bosserman 1972), and shoreline evolution (El-Ashry and Wanless 1968). Carr (1980),

Robinson (1955, 1966), Ren (1985), and Bird (1987) provide other important coastal studies.

Bridges, Mills, and Other Riparian Features

In the absence of stream and valley surveys, good inferences may be made by examining stream features. Bridges, for example, often give immediate clues as to stream changes with small openings suggesting channel aggradation (Happ, Rittenhouse, and Dobson 1940; Trimble 1970b; Costa 1978) and large openings and old waterlines suggesting degradation (Williams and Wolman 1984). Bridges can also be an index to lateral shifts (Williams 1978). Schumm and Lichty (1963), Lewin (1979), and Brooks and Brierley (1997) provide other important papers related to this topic.

When available, bridge plans offer far more information. They may include one or more stream profiles, and some may include local contour maps. Road bridge plans may go back to the early twentieth century and are usually available from state agencies, such as the state highway department (figure 12.3). Railroad bridge plans often extend back well into the nineteenth century and are available from the railroad or from state agencies, such as the public service commission (Happ, Rittenhouse, and Dobson 1940; Cooke and Reeves 1976). In many places, there has been a succession of bridges and surveys so that channel changes can be ascertained. Survey datum normally remains the same. Bridges are sometimes inspected periodically—usually by state agencies—and photographs may be on file (Hoag 1983).

Cultural riparian features may be used to document stream changes. Small dams, weirs, and diversions, fish traps, fords, and buildings are especially susceptible to stream change (Gilbert 1917; Thornthwaite, Sharpe, and Dosch 1942; Cooke and Reeves 1976). For example, Vita-Finzi (1969) used Roman dams and irrigation works to trace two millennia of stream changes. Similar work could be done in the United States, where continuously operated milldams date back to 1677 (Graf 1999). Both state and federal agencies have done extensive surveys (U.S. Bureau of the Census 1887; Hall and Hall 1908) that often give detailed data about existing and potential sites for water power. I (Trimble 1970a and b) used milldams, fish traps, and fords to trace stream aggradation and degradation in Georgia. This work was taken a step further by Ferguson (1997a and b), who used subsurface radar and magnetometer surveys to find datable subsurface features.

A technical knowledge of historical mills as well as other riverine landscape features is very useful. Some states performed surveys, much like those for bridges, that include photographs of mills and associated phenomena (Trimble 1998). The 1880 U.S. Census included detailed

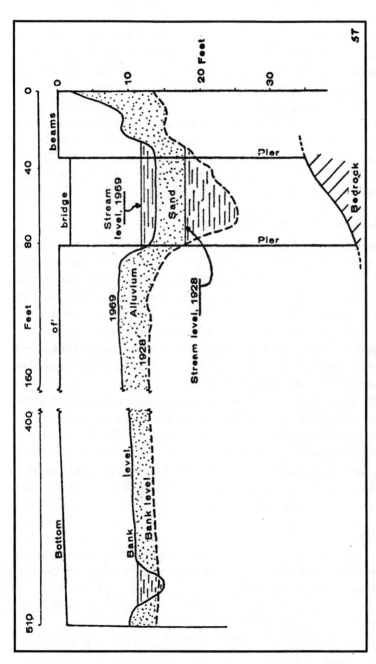

Figure 12.3. Stream and valley aggradation demonstrated from a bridge plan. Federal Highway 11 bridge over Middle Oconee River, Jackson County, Georgia (from Trimble 1970b).

data on mills of that date (U.S. Bureau of the Census 1887), although the census manuscripts, when available in archives, contain the best and most complete information. Other studies using cultural stream features are those of Cooke and Reeves (1976); Eschner, Hadley, and Crowley (1981); Limbrey (1983); and Thoms and Walker (1992, 1993).

Archaeologists have long used buildings to date landform changes (Butzer 1964, 1971; Butzer and Hansen 1968; Vita-Finzi 1969, 1973; Limbrey 1983) and geomorphologists have followed suit (Bryan 1925; Womack and Schumm 1977; Cooke and Reeves 1976). Examinations of buildings, even if they have to be excavated, will often reveal important information about previous stream configuration and regime (Trimble 1998). Previous flood levels are sometimes marked on extant buildings, especially in Europe, and these may be used to extend flood series.

Irrigation and Wetland Records

I consider these two categories together because the U.S. Census did so, beginning with their first decadal report in 1920 (U.S. Bureau of the Census 1922). Irrigation records are important because of the impacts of irrigation on soil and water and, thus, on ecosystems. Additionally, landscapes may have been severely reshaped to accommodate flood or furrow irrigation. In some cases, county records can be very helpful.

Wetland drainage records are plentiful. As stated, the Census started recording drainage projects in 1920, but local and county records are more complete and detailed, often going back to the earliest drainage. States often did detailed surveys and reports (McCallie 1911; Barrows and Phillips 1917). These sometimes include detailed topographic maps of the wetland drainage projects as well as photographs and informative narratives about processes occurring at the time (Trimble 1970a, 1974). Some of these are included in the National Archives (Record Groups 8, 114, and 221; see also Reingold 1953). Gordon Whitney (1994) cites several examples of historical wetland studies.

References

Adler, L.L. 1980. *Adjustment of the Yuba River, California, to the influx of hydraulic mining debris, 1849–1979.* M.A. thesis, Department of Geography, University of California, Los Angeles.

Barrows, H.H., and J.V. Phillips. 1917. Agricultural Drainage in Georgia. *Geological Survey of Georgia Bulletin* No. 32. Atlanta, Ga.

Bennett, J. 1944. *Physical land conditions in Clarke County, Georgia.* USDA Soil Conservation Service, Physical Land Survey 35. Washington, D.C.

Bird, E.C.F. 1987. Coastal processes. Pages 87–116 in *Human activity and environmental processes*, ed. K.J. Gregory and D.E. Walling. Chichester, England: Wiley.

Brizga, S.O., and B.L. Finlayson. 1994. Interactions between upland catchment and lowland rivers: An applied Australian case study. *Geomorphology* 9: 189–201.

Brooks, A.P., and G.J. Brierley. 1997. Geomorphic responses of lower Bega River to catchment disturbance, 1851–1926. *Geomorphology* 18: 291–304.

Brune, G.M. 1953. Trap efficiency of reservoirs. *Transactions, American Geophysical Union* 34: 407–418.

Bryan, K. 1925. Date of channel trenching (arroyo cutting) in the arid Southwest. *Science* 62: 474–478.

Burt, T.P., M.A. Donohoe, and A.R. Vann, 1984. Changes in the yield of sediment from a small upland catchment following open ditching for forestry drainage. *Catena Supplement* 5: 63–74.

Butcher, D.P., J.C. Labadz, A. Potter, and P. White, 1993. Reservoir sedimentation rates in the southern Pennine Region, UK. Pages 73–92 in *Geomorphology and Sedimentology of Reservoirs*, eds. J. McManus and R.W. Duck. Chichester, England: Wiley.

Butzer, K.W. 1964. *Environment and archeology: An Introduction to Pleistocene Geomorphology*. Chicago: Aldine.

———. 1971. *Recent history of an Ethiopian delta*, Research Paper 136. Chicago: University of Chicago. Department of Geography.

Butzer, K.W., and C.L. Hansen. 1968. *Desert and river in Nubia*. Madison: University of Wisconsin Press.

Carr, A.P. 1980. The significance of cartographic sources in determining coastal change. Pages 69–78 in *Timescales in geomorphology*, ed. R.A. Cullingford, D.A. Davidson, and J. Lewin. Chichester, England: Wiley.

Cooke, R.U., and J.C. Doornkamp. 1990. *Geomorphology in environmental management*. Oxford, England: Clarendon Press.

Cooke, R.U., and R. Reeves. 1976. *Arroyos and environmental change in the American Southwest*. Oxford, England: Oxford University Press.

Costa, J.E. 1978. *Hydrologic and hydraulic investigations of Cherry Creek, Denver, Colorado*. Technical Paper no. 78-1. Denver: University of Denver, Department of Geography.

Costa, J.E., and V.R. Baker. 1981. *Surficial Geology*. New York: John Wiley.

Dearing, J.A., and I.D.L. Foster. 1993. Lake sediments and geomorphological processes: Some thoughts. Pages 5–14 in *Geomorphology and sedimentology of lakes and reservoirs*, ed. J. McManus and R.W. Duck. Chichester, England: Wiley.

Dendy, F.E., and W.A. Champion. 1978. *Sediment deposition in U.S. reservoirs: Summary of data reported through 1975*. U.S. Department of Agriculture Miscellaneous Publication 1362.

Dolan, R., and K. Bosserman. 1972. Shoreline erosion and the lost colony. *Annals of the Association of American Geographers* 62: 424–426.

Duck, R.W., and J. McManus. 1987. Sediment yields in lowland Scotland derived from reservoir surveys. *Transactions of the Royal Society of Edinburgh: Earth Sciences* 78: 369–377.

————. 1990. Relationships between catchment characteristics, land use and sediment yield in the Midland Valley of Scotland. Pages 285–299 in *Soil erosion on agricultural land*, ed. J. Boardman, I.D.L. Foster, and J.A. Dearing. Chichester, England: Wiley.

Eakin, H.M. 1936. *Silting of reservoirs*. U.S. Department of Agriculture Technical Bulletin 524.

El-Ashry, M.T., and H.R. Wanless. 1968. Photo interpretation of shoreline changes between Capes Hatteras and Fear (North Carolina). *Marine Geology* 6: 347–379.

Emmett, W.W., and R.F. Hadley. 1968. *The Vigil Network: Preservation and access of data*. U.S. Geological Survey Circular 460-c.

Eschner, T.R., R.F. Hadley, and K.D. Crowley. 1981. *Hydrologic and morphologic changes in channels of the Platte River basin: A historical perspective*. U.S. Geological Survey Open-File Report 81-1125.

Ferguson, B.K. 1997a. The alluvial progress of Piedmont streams. Pages 132–141 in *Effects of watershed development and management on aquatic ecosystems*, ed. L. Roesner. New York: American Society of Civil Engineers.

————. 1997b. Flood and sediment interpretation at the historic Scull Shoals Mill. In *Proceedings of the 1997 Georgia Water Resources Conference, Athens, GA, 20–22 March*.

Foster, I.D.L., J.A. Dearing, and P.G. Appleby. 1986. Historical trends in catchment sediment yields: A case study in reconstruction from lake sediment records in Warwickshire, UK. *Hydrological Sciences Journal* 31: 427–443.

Foster, I.D.L., J.A. Dearing, R. Grew, and K. Orend. 1990. The late sedimentary database: An appraisal of lake and reservoir-based studies of sediment yield. *IASH Publication* 189: 14–43.

Foster, I.D.L., J.A. Dearing, A. Simpson, A.D. Carter, and P.G. Appleby. 1985. Lake catchment based studies of erosion and denudation in the Mereuck catchment, Warwickshire, UK. *Earth Surface Processes and Landforms* 10: 45–68.

Gilbert, G.K. 1917. *Hydraulic mining debris in the Sierra Nevada*. U.S. Geological Survey Professional Paper 105.

Gottschalk, L.C. 1945. Effects of soil erosion on navigation in Upper Chesapeake Bay. *Geographical Review* 35: 219–38.

Goudie, A. 1999. *The human impact on the natural environment*. Cambridge, Mass. MIT Press.

Graf, W.L. 1999. Damnation: A geographic census of American dams and their large-scale hydrologic impacts. *Water Resources Research* 35: 1305–1311.

Gregory, K.J. 1979. River channels. In *Man and environmental processes*, eds. K.J. Gregory and D.E. Walling. Folkestone, England: Dawson.

————. 1987. River channels. Pages 207–235 in *Human activity and environmental processes*, eds. K.J. Gregory and D.E. Walling. London: John Wiley.

Grove, J.M. 1988. *The Little Ice Age*. London: Methuen.

Guthorn, P.J. 1984. *United States Coast Charts, 1783–1861*. Exton, Penn.: Schiffer.

Hadley, R.F. 1974. Sediment yield and land use in the southwest United States. *International Association of Hydrological Science Publicaton* 113: 96–98.

Hall, B.M., and M.R. Hall. 1908. Water-powers of Georgia. *Geological Survey of Georgia Bulletin* No. 16.

Happ, S.C. 1944. Effects of sedimentation on floods in the Kickapoo Valley, Wisconsin. *Journal of Geology* 52: 53–68.

———. 1975. Valley sedimentation as a factor in sediment yield determinants. Pages 57–65 in *Present and prospective technology for predicting sediment yields and sources*. USDA, Agricultural Research Service, Publication S-40.

Happ, S.C., G. Rittenhouse, and G.C. Dobson. 1940. *Some principles of accelerated stream and valley sedimentation*. U.S. Department of Agriculture Technical Bulletin 695.

Heynen, W.J. 1981. *Preliminary inventory of the cartographic records of the Soil Conservation Service*, Record Group 114. Washington, D.C.: National Archives and Records Service.

Hilgard, E.W. 1860. *Report on the geology and agriculture of the State of Mississippi*. Jackson: Mississippi Geological Survey.

Hoag, B.L. 1983. *Channel erosion as a source of sedimentation in Newport Bay, California*. M.A. thesis, Department of Geography, University of California, Los Angeles.

Hooke, J.M., and R.J.P. Kain. 1982. *Historical change in the physical environment*. London: Butterworth Scientific.

James, L.A. 1989. Sustained storage and transport of hydraulic gold mining sediment in the Bear River, CA. *Annals of the Association of American Geographers* 79: 570–592.

Johnson, M., and W.J. Heynen. 1971. *Inventory of the records of the Hydrographic Office*, Record Group 37. Washington, D.C.: National Archives and Records Service.

Jones, B.E., and R.O. Holland. 1948. *Index to river surveys made by the United States Geological Survey and other agencies*. U.S. Geological Survey Water Supply Paper 995.

Kesel, R.H., E.G. Yoder, and D.J. McCraw. 1992. An approximation of the sediment budget of the lower Mississippi River prior to major human modification. *Earth Surface Processes and Landforms* 17: 711–722.

Knox, J.C., P.J. Bartlein, K.K. Hirschbeck, and R.J. Muckenhirn. 1975. *The response of floods and sediment yields to climate variation and land use in the Upper Mississippi Valley*. Madison: University of Wisconsin, Institute for Environmental Studies.

Kondolf, G.M., and R.R. Curry. 1986. Channel erosion along the Carmel River, Monterey County, California. *Earth Surface Processes and Landforms* 11: 307–319.

Labadz, J.C., T.P. Burt, and A. Potter. 1991. Sediment yields and delivery in the blanket peat moorlands of the southern Pennines. *Earth Surface Processes and Landforms* 16: 255–271.

Leopold, L.B., and W.W. Emmett. 1965. Vigil Network sites: A sample of data for permanent filing. *Bulletin, International Association of Scientific Hydrology* 10: 12–21.

Lewin, J. 1979. Historical river changes. Pages 161–175 in *Paleohydrology in practice*, eds. K.J. Gregory, J. Lewin, and J.B. Thornes. Chichester, England: Wiley.

Limbrey, S. 1983. Archaeology and paleohydrology. Pages 189–212 in *Background to palaeohydrology*, ed. K.J. Gregory. Chichester, England: Wiley.

Magilligan, F.S. 1985. Historical floodplain sedimentation in the Galena River basin, Wisconsin and Illinois. *Annals of the Association of American Geographers*, 75: 583–594.

Marsh, G.P. 1864. *Man and Nature*. New York: Scribner.

Mattoni, R., and T.R. Longcore. 1997. The Los Angeles Coastal Prairie, a vanished community. *Crossosoma* 23: 71–102.

McCallie, S.W. 1911. *A preliminary report on drainage reclamation in Georgia*. Geological Survey of Georgia Bulletin No. 25.

McManus, J., and R.W. Duck. 1985. Sediment yield estimated from reservoir siltation in the Ochil Hills, Scotland. *Earth Surface Processes and Landforms* 10: 193–200.

McManus, J., and R.W. Duck, eds. 1993. *Geomorphology and sedimentology of lakes and reservoirs*. Chichester, England: Wiley.

Meade, R.H. 1982. Sources, sinks, and storage of river sediment in the Atlantic drainage of the United States. *Journal of Geology* 90: 235–252.

Meade, R.H., and R.S. Parker. 1985. *Sediment in rivers of the United States, National Water Summary, 1984*. U.S. Geological Survey Water Supply Paper 2275, pp. 49–60.

Meade, R.H., and S.W. Trimble. 1974. Changes in sediment loads in rivers of the Atlantic drainage of the United States since 1900. *International Association of Hydrological Science Publication* 113: 99–104.

National Research Council. 1992. *Restoration of aquatic ecosystems*. Washington, D.C.: National Academy Press.

———. 1999. *New strategies for America's watersheds*. Washington, D.C.: National Academy Press.

Oldfield, F. 1977. Lakes and their drainage basins as units of sediment-based ecological study. *Progress in Physical Geography* 1: 460–504.

Osterkamp, W.R., W.W. Emmett, and L.B. Leopold. 1990. The Vigil Network: A reviving of interest. *Transactions, American Geophysical Union* 71: 338.

Petts, G. *Impounded Rivers*. Chichester, England: Wiley.

Petts, G., and I. Foster. 1985. *Rivers and landscapes*. London: Edward Arnold.

Petts, G., A. Large, M. Greenwood, and M. Bickerton. 1992. Floodplain assessment for restoration and conservation: Linking hydrogeomorphology and ecology. Pages 217–234 in *Lowland floodplain rivers: Geomorphological perspectives*, eds. P. Carling and G. Petts. Chichester: Wiley.

Potter, K.W. 1991. Hydrological impacts of changing land management practices in a moderate-size agricultural catchment. *Water Resources Research* 27: 845–355.

Price, A.P. 1998. *The effect of climate and landuse on the hydrology of the Upper*

Oconee River Basin, Georgia. Ph.D. dissertation, Department of Geography, University of California, Los Angeles.

Reingold, N. 1953. *Records of the Bureau of Agricultural Engineering,* Preliminary Inventory No. 53. Washington, D.C.: National Archives and Records Service.

———. 1958. *Records of the Coast and Geodetic Survey,* Record Group 23. Washington, D.C.: National Archives and Records Service.

Ren, M., ed. 1985. *Modern sedimentation in coastal and nearshore zone of China.* Beijing: China Ocean Press.

Robinson, A.H. 1955. The harbour entrances of Poole, Christchurch and Pagham. *Geographical Journal* 121: 33–50.

———. 1966. Residual currents in relation to shoreline evolution of the East Anglian coast. *Marine Geology* 4: 57–84.

Schumm, S.A., and R.W. Lichty. 1963. *Channel widening and floodplain construction along Cimmarron River in southwestern Kansas.* U.S. Geological Survey Professional Paper 352D.

Stott, A.P. 1987. Medium-term effects of afforestation on sediment dynamics in a water supply catchment: A mineral magnetic interpretation of reservoir deposits in the Macclesfield Forest, NW England. *Earth Surface Processes and Landforms* 12: 619–630.

Stott, A.P., D.P. Butcher, and T.J.L. Pemberton. 1988. Problems in the use of reservoir sedimentation data to estimate erosion rates. *Zeitschrift für Geomorphologie* 30: 205–226.

Sutcliffe, J.V. 1987. The use of historical records in flood frequency analysis. *Journal of Hydrology* 96: 159–171.

Thoms, M.C., and K.F. Walker. 1992. Channel changes related to low-level weirs on the River Murray, South Australia. Pages 233–249 in *Lowland floodplain rivers: Geomorphological perspectives,* eds. P.A. Carling and G.E. Petts. Chichester, England: Wiley.

———. 1993. Channel changes associated with two adjacent weirs on a regulated lowland alluvial river. *Regulated Rivers: Research and Management* 8: 271–284.

Thornes, J.B., and D. Brunsden. 1977. *Geomorphology and time.* London: Methuen.

Thornthwaite, C.W., C.F.S. Sharpe, and E.F. Dosch. 1942. Climate and accelerated erosion in the arid and semi-arid Southwest with special reference to the Polacca Wash drainage basin, Arizona. U.S. Department of Agriculture Technical Bulletin 808. Washington, D.C.

Trimble, S.W. 1970a. The Alcovy River swamps: The result of culturally accelerated sedimentation. *Bulletin of the Georgia Academy of Sciences* 28: 131–141.

———. 1970b. *Culturally accelerated sedimentation on the Middle Georgia Piedmont.* Ft. Worth, Tex.: U.S. Department of Agriculture, Soil Conservation Service.

———. 1974. *Man-induced soil erosion on the Southern Piedmont, 1700–1970.* Ankeny, Iowa: Soil Conservation Society of America.

———. 1975a. Denudation studies: Can we assume stream steady state? *Science* 188: 1207–1208.

————. 1975b. Response of Coon Creek watershed to soil conservation measures. Pages 24–29 in *Landscapes of Wisconsin*, ed. B. Zakrzewska-Borowiecki. Washington, D.C.: Association of American Geographers.

————. 1975c. A volumetric estimate of man-induced soil erosion on the Southern Piedmont Plateau. Pages 142–154 in *Present and prospective technology for predicting sediment yields and sources*, USDA-ARS Publication S-40.

————. 1977. The fallacy of stream equilibrium in contemporary denudation studies. *American Journal of Science* 277: 876–887.

————. 1983. A sediment budget for Coon Creek basin in the Driftless Area, Wisconsin, 1853–1977. *American Journal of Science* 283: 454–474.

————. 1998. Dating fluvial processes from historical data and artifacts. *Catena.* 31: 283–304.

————. 1999. Decreased rates of alluvial sediment storage in the Coon Creek Basin, Wisconsin. *Science* 285: 1444–1446.

————. In press. The use of historical data in geomorphology. In *Geomorphological Techniques*, ed. T. Burt. Oxford: Blackwell.

Trimble, S.W., and K.P. Bube. 1990. Improved reservoir trap efficiency prediction. *Environmental Professional* 12: 255–272.

Trimble, S.W., and W.P. Carey. 1984. *Sediment characteristics of Tennessee streams and reservoirs.* U.S. Geological Survey Open-File Report 84–279.

————. 1992. *A comparison of the Brune and Churchill methods for computing sediment yields applied to a reservoir system.* U.S. Geological Survey Water Supply Paper 2340, pp. 195–202.

Trimble, S.W., and R.U. Cooke. 1991. Historical sources for geomorphological research in the United States. *Professional Geographer* 43: 212–228.

Trimble, S.W., and S.W. Lund. 1982. *Soil conservation and the reduction of erosion and sedimentation in the Coon Creek Basin, Wisconsin.* U.S. Geological Survey Professional Paper 1234.

Trimble, S.W., F.H. Weirich, and B.L. Hoag. 1987. Reforestation and the reduction of water yield on the Southern Piedmont since circa 1940. *Water Resources Research* 23: 425–437.

U.S. Bureau of the Census. 1887. *Reports on the water powers of the United States.* 10th Census, Washington, D.C.: Government Printing Office.

————. 1922. *Irrigation and Drainage*, 14th Census. Washington, D.C.: Government Printing Office.

U.S. Congress. 1943. *Survey of the Coosa River watershed in Georgia and Tennessee.* House Document 236, 78th Congress, 1st session.

U.S. Department of Agriculture. 1935. Reconnaissance erosion survey. Washington D.C.: U.S. Department of Agriculture.

U.S. Geological Survey. 1983. *Sediment deposition in U.S. reservoirs—Summary of data reported 1976–1980.* Reston, Va.: Office of Water Data Coordination.

Van Steeter, M.M., and J. Pitlick. 1998. Geomorphology and endangered fish habitats of the upper Colorado River. 1. Historic changes in streamflow, sediment load, and channel morphology. *Water Resources Research* 34: 287–304.

Vita-Finzi, C. 1969. *The Mediterranean valleys: Geological changes in historical times*. Cambridge: Cambridge University Press.

———. 1973. *Recent earth history*. London: Macmillan.

White, P.S., and J.L. Walker. 1997. Approximating nature's variation: Selecting and using reference information in restoration ecology. *Restoration Ecology* 5(4): 338–349.

Whitney, G.G. 1994. *From coastal wilderness to fruited plain: A history of environmental change in temperate North America from 1500 to the present*. Cambridge, England: Cambridge University Press.

Williams, G.P. 1978. *The case of shrinking channels—the North Platte and Platte Rivers in Nebraska*. U.S. Geological Survey Circular 781.

Williams, G.P., and M.G. Wolman. 1984. *Downstream effects of dams on alluvial rivers*. U.S. Geological Survey Professional Paper 1286.

Wilson, J.P. 1989. Soil erosion from agricultural land in the lake Simcoe-Couchiching basin, 1800–1981. *Canadian Journal of Soil Science* 69: 137–151.

Womack, W.R., and S.A. Schumm. 1977. Terraces of Douglas Creek, northwestern Colorado: An example of episodic erosion. *Geology* 5: 72–76.

13

Inferring Vegetation History from Phytoliths

Glen G. Fredlund

Phytoliths are the jewels of the plant world. These translucent, microscopic bodies are composed of hydrated silica deposited within and between the living cells of plants. Phytoliths are released into the environment upon the death and decay of the plant tissues and are subsequently deposited in soils and sediments. If not subjected to dissolution, fossil phytoliths can persist in sedimentary rocks for millions of years (Thomasson 1986). Phytoliths have attracted the attention of many allied fields of study including soil science, archaeology, geology, plant systematics, and ecology. Although the research done by these allied disciplines is relevant, this chapter is intended as an introduction to phytolith analysis as a means of reconstructing past vegetation, especially in conjunction with restoration ecology.

Paleoecological phytolith analysis shares much theory with other techniques for vegetation reconstruction, especially palynology (see chapter 9). In spite of these similarities, phytolith analysis has both advantages and some unique limitations that distinguish it from other proxy data. My goal is to make the interested novice reader aware of both the limitations and the advantages of phytolith analysis in vegetation reconstruction. The review here addresses issues as they occur throughout the life history of a phytolith and its analysis. After a brief history of phytolith research, I present topics related to phytolith production, classification, taphonomy, depositional context, and preservation. In my view, it is critical for researchers planning to use phytoliths as a guide to historical vegetation restoration to have a realistic understanding of these issues. They determine the potential chronological and spatial resolution of the fossil record. Next, I introduce techniques for obtaining phytoliths

from soils and sediments. Last, I discuss approaches to vegetation reconstruction and current trends in the discipline.

History of Method

Phytolith research has its roots in the European Age of Discovery
(Piperno 1988; Powers 1992) when Christian Ehrenberg, the renowned
German microbiologist and father of phytolith analysis, first began to
explore the microscopic characteristics of soils, sediments, and other
materials. Among the *infusoria* (microscopic plant and animal life)
Ehrenberg described was a preponderance of *phytolitharia*—a term he
adapted from the Greek words *phyto* and *litho*, which together mean
"plant stones." Ehrenberg correctly traced the source of phytoliths to
extant plants and constructed the first key for their classification (Ehrenberg 1846). He also identified phytoliths as a major component of the
dust samples Charles Darwin collected on board the *Beagle* off the coast
of Africa in 1833 (Darwin 1846). Today fossil phytolith analysis of atmospheric dust and deep ocean sediments is being resurrected as a tool in
global climate change research.

Following Ehrenberg's pioneering work, the efforts of phytolith
researchers shifted away from paleoecology toward several related botanical concerns—plant anatomy, physiology, and plant systematics. Until
World War II, a number of German researchers continued the work of
identifying and classifying phytoliths begun by Ehrenberg (Piperno 1988,
4–5). Beginning in the 1950s, botanical phytolith studies become more
international. The contributions of this period are too numerous and too
varied to review in this chapter, but a few do deserve recognition. Metcalfe's *Anatomy of Monocotyledons: I. Gramineae*, published in 1960, is of
particular interest to restoration ecologists working with grasslands. Other
important works in grass phytolith taxonomy include works by Parry and
Smithson (1964, 1966) and Ellis (1979). Descriptions of phytolith production and phytolith forms also occur throughout the taxonomic literature but are most common for plant families in which phytoliths are most
abundant (e.g., the grasses; Watson 1987). Detailed descriptions and
three-dimensional illustrations of phytolith forms are not generally provided in taxonomic literature because other anatomical structures are considered more taxonomically significant, and because taxonomists typically
do not describe individual, disarticulated phytoliths. Nevertheless, the
taxonomic literature does provide contemporary researchers with a starting point for understanding phytolith production and classification.

A second cluster of post-Ehrenberg research focused on phytoliths in
soils and ecological functions. Soil scientists and their collaborators in
ecology were primarily interested in the role of phytoliths in soil develop-

ment, mineral and nutrient cycling, and plant ecology. During the 1950s, collaborative efforts between soil scientists, ecologists, and botanists at the University College of North Wales in Bangor resulted in significant advances in phytolith analysis (Powers 1992). Smithson, the leading British soils phytolith researcher of this school, credits Russian soil scientists with pioneering the topic (Smithson 1958), but early examples of phytolith-related soils research can be found elsewhere. Throughout the 1950s and 1960s, phytolith research by soil scientists continued on an international scale—Kanno and Arimura (1958) in Japan, Baker (1959b) in Australia, and Beavers and Stephen (1958) in the United States.

Naturally, some of these phytolith researchers recognized the potential for using phytolith analysis to reconstruct past vegetation. Referring to the phytolith assemblages in soils, Smithson (1956, 128) stated, "They [phytoliths] might, with careful study, provide information about former vegetation and soil conditions of the sites where they occur." In the early 1960s, soil scientists in Australia (Baker 1959a) and the United States (Jones and Beavers 1963) began to recover phytoliths from Quaternary and other geologic deposits and analyze them as plant fossils representative of past vegetation disconnected from modern soil development. In 1967 Larry Wilding, a soils researcher interested in the persistence of phytoliths in the soils system, published the first radiocarbon dates obtained from organic matter occluded within phytoliths. With proof of the antiquity of soil phytoliths, Wilding and Drees (1968) were among the first Americans to use fossil phytoliths as evidence of vegetation history.

Phytolith research in archaeology has a history intertwined with the soils and ecological research (Piperno 1988). Identification of economically important plants, especially cultigens, from archaeological sediments is the most common application of phytolith analysis in archaeology (Grob 1897; Bozarth 1987; Kaplan, Smith, and Sneddon 1992; Fujiwara 1993). These efforts center on finding phytolith forms that are reasonably specific to the plant in question. Some archaeological researchers have adopted a morphometric analysis (measurement of phytolith size and shape) to discriminate the use of cereal crops, including Indian corn (*Zea mays*) and wheat (*Triticum* spp.), from the nondomesticated relatives (Pearsall 1978; Piperno 1984; Ball, Gardner, and Brotherson 1996; Piperno and Pearsall 1998a, 1998b). These morphometric approaches use inferential statistics to test for the presence of domesticated crops in archaeological samples. Both approaches can be reasonable and effective for documenting domestication for most archaeological contexts. These archaeological efforts at improving the taxonomic resolution of phytolith analysis may provide a test track for refining all phytolith classification.

In 1969, Page Twiss and two other geoscientists published a pivotal paper entitled "*Morphology Classification of Grass Phytoliths.*" Although this paper did not pioneer the classification of grass phytoliths, it is important for three reasons. First, it stated explicitly the systematic and ecological relevance of grass phytolith classification in the Great Plains. Second, it demonstrated how this classification system could be used quantitatively to evaluate Quaternary changes in vegetation and climate. Finally, because the basis for this research was eolian dust traps, it implicitly suggested the analogy between phytolith analysis and the far more advanced development of fossil pollen analysis. This paper stimulated a new wave of researchers in Quaternary studies and archaeology (Rovner 1971; Palmer 1976; Lewis 1981; and Fredlund, Johnson, and Dart 1985). In the last decade there has been an international explosion continuing the application of phytoliths as a tool for vegetation reconstruction. Paleoecological research is currently being conducted in nearly ever major biome, from Brazil (Alexandre et al. 1999) to Thailand (Kealhofer and Penny 1998) to east Africa (Runge and Runge 1995), to cite but a few examples.

Phytolith Production

Silica is present to some degree in practically all plants. In many plants phytoliths are the product of passive silica uptake from the rooting solution and its progressive concentration in leaves and other tissues as waters are lost through transpiration. Phytoliths may serve a variety of functions within plants, including being a defense against herbivory and as structural reinforcement.

The amount of silica varies greatly among species and, indeed, between families of plants even within the same environment. A study of twenty-seven plants from the coastal wetlands of Mississippi by Lanning and Eleuterius (1985) illustrates this extreme. They found that the silica content of leaves ranged from less than 0.1 to more than 44 percent by dry weight, depending on the taxon. Although the silica content of most plants has yet to be investigated, synthesis of the botanical literature shows clear taxonomic patterns (Piperno 1988; Pearsall 1998). The plants of some families, including Equisetaceae (horsetail), Cyperaceae (sedges), Poaceae (grasses), Marantaceae (arrowroot), Palmae (palm), and Zingiberaceae (ginger), are far more likely to have high silica content (greater by 5 percent by weight of dry leaves) than are plants from other families. Families with relatively low silica content (less than 2 percent of the dry weight of leaves) include the Pinaceae (pines), Aceraceae (maples), Fagaceae (beech and oak), and Salicaceae (willows) (Geis 1973; Klein and Geis 1978). Taxonomic patterns of silica contents may also be extremely variable even within families. For example, the leaves of *Celtis* (hackberry) and *Ulmus* (elms) have relatively high silica content, while other genera in the same plant family have almost no silica. These significant taxonomic patterns of silica content reflect what anatomical botanists have long known: silica uptake and deposition within the tissues of many plants is an adaptive, active process.

The vast disparities in phytolith content alone suggest that some plants may be overrepresented in the phytolith record, while others are all but absent. However, to obtain the complete picture of phytolith production needed for vegetation reconstruction, researchers need to consider two additional factors. The first is the rate of phytolith cycling into the environment. For example, the ray cells of wood often include spherical or nodular silica bodies (Carlquist 1988). These woody-tissue phytoliths are not cycled into the environment until the death and decay of the wood, which for many trees could take centuries. Meanwhile, other phytoliths, typically those produced in leaves and flowers, are released into the environment on an annual cycle. It is these rapidly cycled forms that tend to dominate phytolith records. This difference in the cycle of production results in phytolith assemblages that are out of proportion to the biomass of the plants within a plant community.

The second consideration is the chemical stability and morphological regularity of the silica bodies being produced. Much of plant silica occurs as thin, weakly deposited intercellular sheets. Even roots and other subsurface organs can include such intercellular silica deposits (Sangster and Hodson 1992). These sheets do not preserve well in many depositional environments. Fragments of these intercellular sheets that do survive are not typically taxonomically diagnostic and are, therefore, of little use in vegetation reconstruction. In contrast, even a single blade of grass may yield tens of thousands of taxonomically diagnostic phytoliths.

The implications of these productivity variables for vegetation reconstruction are critical. Together they result in vastly different annual yields of morphologically distinctive phytoliths. This makes correlation between phytolith forms and vegetation complex. At its simplest level, this difference in productivity should make it relatively easy to distinguish grasslands from forest because grasslands annually yield tremendous numbers of distinctive phytoliths, while closed forests do not. In fact, these broad differences in production have been used in landscape ecology studies to argue for vegetation dynamics (Fisher, Jenkins, and Fisher 1987). However, as I will discuss later, vegetation reconstruction derived solely from bulk soil phytolith recovery can be problematic.

Classification and Identification

Taxonomically significant phytoliths are typically created as silica precipitates along the inside of cell walls, where it produces a cast fossil. These cast phytoliths may include a very detailed impression of the inside of a cell that can be used for taxonomic identification (e.g., Bozarth 1992).

The identification and classification of phytoliths, however, remain complicated and somewhat in disarray. This complexity is the product of two factors. First, similar or identical phytolith forms can be produced in homologous structures in unrelated plants (Rovner 1999). This results in phytoliths being classified first according to their anatomical structure rather than plant taxonomy (cf. Pearsall and Dinan 1992). While this anatomical classification provides some information on general vegetation, a phytolith classification scheme is needed that is firmly linked to plant taxonomy. The second factor is multiplicity, or the production of many phytolith forms—both known and unknown—by any single plant (Rovner 1971). These factors make describing and classifying phytoliths tedious and create many blind spots in the knowledge of phytolith production (Pinilla, Juan-Tresserras, and Machado 1997). It is not uncommon for an analysis of fossil assemblages to include very distinctive phytolith forms that have not yet been catalogued in the phytolith literature.

Despite these complications, there is an abundance of literature on phytolith classification for some plant families. This is especially true for the Poaceae, the grasses (Smithson 1958; Metcalfe 1960; Twiss, Suess, and Smith 1969; Ellis 1979; Brown 1984; Lanning and Eleuterius 1989; Mulholland and Rapp 1992; Piperno and Pearsall 1993). Such abundance can, however, be a curse as well as a blessing. Terms used for naming and describing grass phytolith morphotypes are not yet standardized. Even the definition of such common, well-recognized morphotypes as cross short-cell type may vary. This lack of consistency, while easily overcome by careful documentation when such terms are used, does create a significant obstacle for researchers attempting to apply phytolith analysis for the first time.

The grass phytolith investigations also provide an example of the taxonomic limits of phytolith classification. Grasses produce a variety of anatomical groups including short-cell, long-cell, tricome (prickle-hair cell), and bulliform phytoliths (figure 13.1). The surveys listed above have consistently concluded that some short-cell phytolith forms are diagnostic, or at least characteristic, of grass subfamilies or tribes. Conical and keeled forms (also called rondels; Mulholland and Rapp 1992), while occurring across almost all grasses, dominate within the Pooideae subfamily. Saddle forms occur only rarely outside of the Eragrostoideae and are characteristic of the Chlorideae tribe. Both Panicoideae and Arundinoideae subfamilies produce bilobate (or dumbell) forms, although separate characteristic variants are diagnostic of each of these forms. If, however, classification of grass phytolith forms is done solely on the abaxial or addaxial outline, then many similar "confusors" (Brown 1984) may be incorrectly classified as Panicoid bilobates (Bartolome, Klukkert, and Barry 1986). However, when three-dimensional shape is included, most

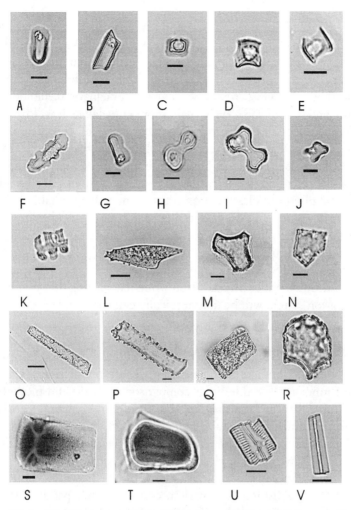

Figure 13.1. Photomicrographs of phytolith types from a 7,080-year-old fossil assemblage, from Little Salt Creek in eastern Nebraska. Grass short-cell types (A–J) conform with Fredlund and Tiesaen (1994): (A) conical, (B) side view of same conical phytolith, (C) pyramidal, (D) side view of keeled form, (E) saddle, (F) sinuate, (G) stipa-type, (H) bilobate, (I) panicoid bilobate, (J) cross. Short-cell phytoliths are shown in abaxial (top) view except for B and D. Other forms: (K) tracheal form, taxa unknown; (I) tricome or prickle form, Poaceae; (M) keystone-type bulliform cell, Poaceae; (N) dicot leaf epidermal polygon, cf. *Celtis*; (O) smooth elongate form, taxa unknown; (P) serrated elongate, Poaceae; (Q) large cubical form, taxa unknown; (R) fan-shaped bulliform, Poaceae; (S) large cubical form, taxa unknown; (T) large tricome or prickle, taxa unknown; (U) broken diatom; and (V) broken sponge spicual. Note occluded organic matter within S and T and severe dissolution pitting on O, Q, and R. Black bars are approximately 10 microns.

of these pseudo-bilobates can be readily distinguished and reclassified. In my studies of the Great Plains grasslands, I refer to these pseudo-bilobates as stipa-type in recognition of the grass genera that most commonly produces them. Distinguishing all true Panicoid-bilobates from those produced by other grass tribes does remain problematic (Ollendorf, Mulholland, and Rapp 1988). As we gain more knowledge, it will be possible to improve the taxonomic integrity of grass short-cell classification.

The above discussion of grass phytolith classification is introduced here not because it is unique, but because it is representative of the complexities of phytolith classification in general. It should not be misconstrued that phytolith classification is taxonomically unreliable, only that it has its limitations. Fossil grass pollen, for example, is identifiable only to the family; phytolith identification is much more taxonomically sensitive and useful in evaluating vegetation change within grasslands. Researchers need to construct functional, reproducible keys to diagnostic forms of the area under investigation while recognizing that no phytolith classification system will be taxonomically perfect.

Establishing Comparative Collections

Even the most complete literature on phytolith production and classification cannot replace the direct comparison of fossils and modern phytolith forms. Researchers may be able to obtain comparative slides of modern phytoliths from established researchers, but extraction of additional modern samples will likely become necessary. Ideally, modern comparative phytolith samples should be linked to herbarium vouchers so that the taxonomy of samples can be verified (Brown 1984). This can be done by establishing a herbarium collection that parallels the phytolith collection by sampling existing herbaria sheets. To use existing herbaria sheets, researchers need to work with curators, who (if they allow it at all) will limit the researcher to taking only a small portion of the plant specimen (for example, a single leaf), which can then be used to extract phytoliths.

The better solution is to establish a parallel herbarium because that allows the researcher to use the entire aboveground portion of a plant. The use of the entire plant is desirable when studying grasses, sedges, and forbs because the entire plant provides information on the relative and absolute production of all phytoliths that would naturally cycle into the fossil record. To reduce the amount of plant materials analyzed, entire plants can be shredded and representative subsamples of the homogenized material processed. Establishing and maintaining parallel herbarium collections is expensive and is, therefore, not always done. Whatever approach is taken, documenting the source of the plant materials, the taxonomy, and who confirmed the identification is critical to establish a comparative phytolith collection.

Extraction and Laboratory Analysis

Various methods are used to extract phytoliths from modern plant materials. These methods are generically grouped into "wet-ashing" and "dry-ashing" techniques. Wet ashing, or wet oxidation, is the chemical oxidation of the nonsiliceous portions of plant material. A wide range of reagents, from Schulze solution (a solution of nitric acid and potassium or sodium chloride) to household bleach (sodium hypochlorite), have been used for this purpose (see Pearsall 1989). Dry ashing is the oxidation of the plant materials in a muffle furnace, typically at temperatures between 400 and 500°C, followed by acid or other washes to remove colloidal byproducts (Pearsall 1989). The white, ash-like residue resulting from either of these procedures typically consists of silt-sized (2- to 50-micron-diameter), pure biogenic opal. These samples represent ideal preservation and often include sheets of articulated phytoliths and delicately silicified tissues that are uncommon in soil assemblages. The phytolith residue is stable and is best dried and placed into a small storage vial.

There is also a fairly standard set of procedures used to extract phytoliths from soil and sediment samples. The basics of the method are well established (reviewed in Piperno 1988 and Pearsall 1989), but improvements and special applications continue to emerge (Fredlund 1986; Powers and Gilbertson 1987; Hart 1988; Lentfer and Boyd 1998; Madella, Powers-Jones, and Jones 1998; Zhao and Pearsall 1998). Typical extraction has three major steps: (1) disaggregation of the sample and removal of clays, (2) oxidation of organic carbon, and (3) specific gravity fractionation of biogenic opal from silicate minerals. The overriding concern during the extraction procedure is for complete and unbiased recovery. Concern for producing a clean and easily analyzed residue is secondary.

Standard laboratory procedures are used to disaggregate and remove clays. Although there are many variations, all are based on differential settling rates for sands, silts, and clays. First, the soil samples are allowed to soak in detergent (e.g., sodium heximetaphosphate). This causes clay-sized particles to lose their cohesion and the sample to fully disaggregate. Clays are then mechanically removed by decanting the supernatant once the silts and sands have settled. Clay removal is critical because clays can cause incomplete phytolith recovery and will obscure phytoliths in the final residue. If the samples include large amounts of sand, it may be removed through a similar process in which the silts are decanted and retained after the sands have been allowed to fall out of suspension. In arid soils or sediments, where concentrated carbonates may bind soil particles, it is necessary to use an acid (e.g., 10% hydrochloric), preferably before the use of the detergent.

The occurrence of large amounts of organic matter in samples may also cause problems in recovery and microscopic analysis. If necessary, organic carbon can be removed with an oxidizing reagent such as hydrogen peroxide. Alternatively, heating the samples in a furnace at controlled temperatures has also been used (Lentfer and Boyd 1998). Some researchers have used the heating approach to remove organic matter after specific gravity fractionation rather than before.

Specific gravity fractionation, also called heavy-liquid flotation, utilizes the low-specific-gravity (less than 2.3 g/cc) biogenic opal. Typically, a 2.30 to 2.35 specific-gravity solution of zinc bromide, or the environmentally safer sodium polytungstate, is used to separate the biogenic opal from other heavier mineral matter. Multiple floatation procedures are required to ensure complete recovery. Some researchers, especially those working in forested environments, have chosen to separate fine silts (5 to 20 microns) from coarse silts (20 to 50 microns), which includes many of the forest phytolith forms, by sieving prior to flotation (e.g., Carbone 1977; Piperno 1988; Runge 1995). This procedure has several advantages. First, it provides a means for comparing total recovery of the two size fractions. This in itself yields valuable information. Second, size separation facilitates identification. The procedure also has drawbacks, however. First, it significantly increases the processing time for extraction. Second, it doubles the number of fractions that must be microscopically analyzed. Third, size separation will inevitably increase some analytical error, thus making results more difficult to replicate. In some situations size fractionation may be justified, but it is not an approach that should be universally adopted.

Materials isolated through heavy-liquid flotation process should then be washed with distilled water, transferred to storage vials, and dried. Phytolith extractions typically include other biogenic silica produced by diatoms, freshwater sponges, and Chrysostomita as well as non-opalin mineral contaminates (figure 13.1). Because of the overlap in specific gravity, volcanic ash is the most commonly encountered type of mineral impurity. In many settings, such as in the Great Plains, significant amounts of volcanic ash may be present. These ash shards are not typically in their primary deposition but in redepositions by wind of other processes from older Cenozoic sediments (Fredlund, Johnson, and Dort 1985). If the mass of the original soil was recorded, the weight of the recovered fraction can be used to calculate relative mass. Standard point-count methods used in optical mineralogy can be used to correct these mass estimates for volcanic ash and other impurities.

The standard biological light microscope is the tool of choice for phytolith analysis, although it is often supplemented by scanning electron microscope (SEM) imaging. Mounting dried phytolith residues for analysis with the microscopes is relatively simple. Various media have been used. Some researchers prefer a fixed mount (Paramount of Canada Balsam) so that individual phytoliths do not migrate and can be easily relocated. Others prefer a liquid mount that allows phytoliths to be rotated by applying pressure on the coverslip. Rotation facilitates the three-dimensional observation and description of phytolith forms. Glycerin is often used as a temporary liquid mounting medium because it has both an acceptable viscosity and a contrasting refractive index. If the coverslip is sealed with paraffin and slides are properly stored, glycerin-mounted reference slides will last for decades. Observations of phytoliths are typically done under moderate magnification (400x to 630x). Higher magnifications (1000x) may be required when observing fine details of surface textures of unusually small specimens.

Taphonomy and Analysis of Modern Samples

Taphonomy is the study of events that intervene between the death of an organism and its incorporation into the fossil record (Shipman 1981). These transformations may include differential phytolith dispersal and destruction. Investigation of these transformations is necessary for accurately inferring vegetation from the phytolith record. Early phytolith studies tended to ignore these taphonomic transformations and implicitly assumed that plant materials were produced, decayed, and joined the fossil record, without alteration, at the spot where the plant grew. In the 1980s, many studies acknowledged these taphonomic processes but continued to use the simple decay-in-place model pro forma (e.g., Lewis 1981).

To investigate effects of taphonomic processes, the researcher must analyze modern samples from situations analogous to the source of the fossil record. This approach, sometimes referred to as methodological uniformitarianism, is a basic principle of all paleoecology (Birks and Birks 1980). Results of modern studies inform the practitioner of potential distortions of the fossil assemblages due to production as well as taphonomy. This approach provides the only means to distinguish random variability inherent in the analysis from meaningful evidence of environmental change. Modern analog studies will become even more critical as phytolith methods move toward statistical methods of inferring past vegetation and climate (Fredlund and Tieszen 1997b).

Applications of the uniformitarian approach show significant differences when forests are compared with grasslands. The evidence from closed forests, although limited in breadth, tend to validate the decay-in-place model. Dolores Piperno's (1988) research in the tropics of Panama is a good example. Working across existing plant community boundaries, Piperno sampled soil and vegetation along transects to demonstrate and quantify the local nature of the phytolith signal. From her data, she was able to infer local change in vegetation through time based on the results of the modern gradient analysis.

In grasslands, however, the validity of the decay-in-place model remains questionable. For example, in a study of modern grassland soil assemblages, which I undertook as a means of inferring vegetation from phytolith assemblages buried in upland soils, I found that differences in local grass phytolith production were often detectable but far less distinctive than a decay-in-place model would predict (Fredlund and Tieszen 1994). I hypothesize that this tendency toward regional homogenization of grassland phytolith assemblages is the product of fire, herbivory, and geomorphic agents, especially wind. Theoretically, these processes can transport an average of 40 or 50 percent of the biomass production in naturally functioning grassland ecosystems. The extra-local deposition resulting from such transportation tends to mute the signature of the local vegetation. Additional modern investigations are needed to understand and quantify phytolith transportation in grasslands. Analysis of vegetation clip plots, dust traps, litter traps, and soils from common localities should provide a means for partitioning potential sources.

Modern analog investigations also shed light on the taphonomic processes of decay and breakage of phytoliths that may occur between production and incorporation into the fossil record. My work with Tieszen in the Great Plains (Fredlund and Tieszen 1994) illustrates the potential problem. Strong evidence suggests that many of the phytolith forms characteristic of the Panicoid grass subfamily (including big bluestem, little bluestem, switchgrass, and Indiangrass) are broken or destroyed between production and incorporation into the soil. Without modern soil analyses, the relative frequencies of these diagnostic phytoliths were assumed to correlate directly with grass productivity. Indeed, low occurrences of Panicoid morphotypes in the fossil assemblages and modern grass distribution have been interpreted by some as evidence for a late Holocene migration of tallgrass prairie species in North America (Brown and Gersmehl 1985). However, analysis of surface samples from numerous tallgrass prairies clearly shows that even relatively low frequencies (15 to 20 percent of grass short-cell forms) in fossil assemblages should be interpreted as tallgrass prairies. Such low frequencies of other diagnostic grass forms, including "saddle" shapes produced by the xeric-adapted Chloridoid shortgrass (including gramma and buffalo grasses), would be far less significant. Inferring shortgrass dominance from a fossil assemblage would require extremely high relative frequencies (ca. 60 percent to 70 percent of short-cell forms).

Variations resulting from both production and taphonomy greatly complicate the task of reconstructing vegetation from the fossil phytolith record. The nature and strength of these processes vary considerably among vegetation types and depositional settings. Yet, even with the limited investigations currently done, it is still possible to generalize. The decay-in-place model is most likely valid for soil investigations of closed forests. In contract, extra-local homogenization of phytolith assemblages is likely to be stronger in open grasslands and other vegetative systems maintained by frequent fires, herbivory, or both. Documentation of phytoliths in smoke and charcoal residue from forest fires is a first step in documenting regional or extra-local homogenization (Komarek, Komarek, and Carlysle 1973). Additional studies of modern phytolith deposition will better quantify the nature of the taphonomic alterations.

Depositional Context of Fossil Records

Fossil phytoliths have been recovered from a variety of depositional setting, including surface soils, buried soils, alluvial fans, alluvial terraces, loess deposits, lakes, bogs, and deep ocean sediments. Research criteria for choosing a locality for study may include fossil preservation, geographical location, chronological resolution, and geographical resolution of the fossil assemblage. Each depositional environment has its own set of advantages and limitations relating to these criteria. Preservation, normally the first concern in fossil analysis, is less critical in phytolith analysis, as these silicate bodies are less susceptible to the chemical corrosion than many fossil types. (Situations with poor phytolith preservation and methods for evaluating preservation are addressed in the section "Preservation.") Choosing a depositional situation with appropriate chronological and geographic resolution is, nevertheless, of great concern.

A common strategy in paleoecological research is to analyze localities that have continuous deposition. Wetlands, especially enclosed drainage lakes, are especially appropriate for this reason, and phytolith studies are increasingly employed in such settings (e.g., Kealhofer and Penny 1998). Lake depositional environments are attractive for several reasons. First, small to medium lakes without through-flowing streams provide a finite source of sediments, including phytoliths. They also limit recycling or redeposit of older fossils that may occur in alluvial sediments. Second, enclosed lake basins often hold the factors of deposition and preservation constant over long periods of time. Rates of sedimentation in enclosed wetlands typically vary less and are less likely to have unconformates than are terrestrial deposits. Third, lacustrine sediments typically lack destructive post-depositional processes that can fragment or dissolve phytoliths. Finally, continuous sedimentation and low rates of sediment mixing may yield high-resolution (decades to centuries) chronological sampling, that would be useful to restoration ecologists.

Phytolith analysis of terrestrial deposits including those in soils, eolian, and alluvial sediments are, however, often the ideal or only sources of fossil evidence for many questions in vegetation reconstruction. There are three general advantages of terrestrial deposits. First, phytoliths may be well preserved in terrestrial deposits while other fossils, including pollen, are not. For example, in arid and semi-arid environments, where lakes are absent, phytolith research may yet become a surrogate to pollen analysis. In such regions, phytoliths may be recovered from landscape positions where sediments have aggregated. Second, terrestrial settings may be more ubiquitous and more directly related to an ecosystem targeted for restoration. Finally, phytoliths provide an invaluable additional line of evidence for the geomorphologist interested in landscape development and patterning that has resulted from changes in climate, soils, geomorphology, and vegetation (Fredlund 1997; Fredlund and Tieszen 1997a).

The disadvantage of terrestrial deposits is that they tend to be more complex than lake or wetland sediments. Just as pollen researchers have had to become limnologists, many phytolith researchers have become more well versed in process geomorphology and soil science. Terrestrial deposits, especially fluvial sediments, typically occur episodically, resulting in highly variable rates of sedimentation and potential erosional unconformitites. When the geomorphic surface becomes stable, soil-forming processes (pedogenesis) take over and introduce differences in phytolith deposition and alterations to the fossil phytolith (Birkeland 1999). Terrestrial fossil records must, therefore, by interpreted with a clear understanding of what geomorphic agents deposited the sediments and what processes, especially pedogenesis, may have altered the record after deposition.

An example from the upper Highland Creek valley of Wind Cave National Park in western South Dakota illustrates my point about depositions in terrestrial environments. Episodic deposition and erosion of alluvial sediments in the upper Highland Creek valley has been ongoing for more than fourteen thousand years at this site (Fredlund and Tieszen 1997a). During the last forty-five hundred years, the geomorphic balance has tilted toward net sedimentary aggradations on the valley floor, with two prolonged periods of surface stability resulting in significant soil development. The earlier of these soils (soil horizon AB2) is now buried beyond the reach of most pedogenic processes. Radiocarbon dating of organic matter from this buried soil provides a minimal (most recent) age for this soil development at 3,870 ± 50 years B.P. Radiocarbon dating of charcoal from the alluvial strata immediately overlying this layer put termination of soil development at 3,620 ± 90 years B.P. The younger surface soil has undergone much greater development than the older buried soil. Although it is difficult to ascertain precisely, the evidence suggests that aggradation of the upper sediments happened fairly rapidly and that the surface soil began developing sometime between one thousand and two thousand years ago. Prior to alteration by soil formation, the sediments were very much like those that now lie between the two soils (soil horizon C1), and that retain laminar structures characteristic of depositional processes.

These sediments have undergone at least one thousand years of pedogenesis under virgin grassland. Analysis of organic matter, calcium carbonate, and particle size illustrates the profound pedogenic alterations of the original alluvial sediments (figure 13.1). Differences in texture that help distinguish the A-horizon from the upper B-horizon (Btj) are the products of downward migration of silts and clays during soil development. Likewise, the bulge of calcium carbonate that extends into the lower B-horizon (Bk) is the result of periodic soil wetting and movement carbonates in solution. Large columnar structures created by these pedogenic processes extend throughout the B-horizon, obliterating all traces of the original depositional structure (soil horizon designations consist with Birkeland 1999).

The phytolith record from this profile is the product of both geomorphic deposition and soil-forming processes (figure 13.2). Our initial observations of the phytolith record for this soil profile include estimates of the percent of mass (% of Wt. Extracted) and the relative purity of the extraction (% Phytoliths) for each sample. The highest rates of recovery occur in the A-horizon of the surface soil, the AB-horizon of the buried soil, and the unaltered alluvial sediments lying immediately above the buried soil. Relatively poor recovery occurs in the B-horizons of both the surface and the buried soils. The cause of this stratigraphic pattern of recovery brings us to the topic of preservation.

Preservation

Preservation is a measure of the condition of the phytoliths found in the fossil assemblage. Several researchers, including myself (Fredlund 1997), have developed scales for describing preservation. For my analysis of grassland phytoliths, I developed a six-point scale (0 to 5) to describe

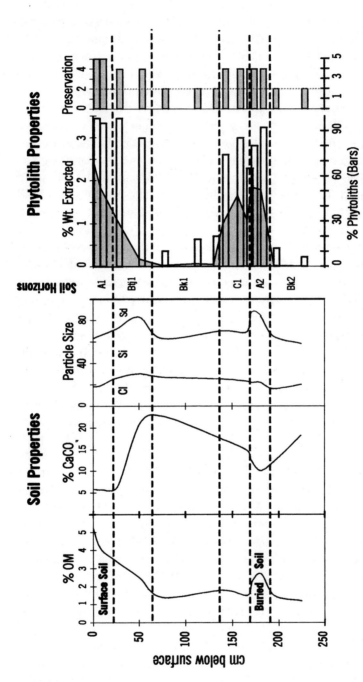

Figure 13.2. Variability of pytolith recovery and preservation related to deposition and soil formation. Note that B-horizon formation has lead to dissolution of phytoliths. Buried soil is radiocarbon-dated at 3870 ± 50 years before present. Sample soil profile from Wind Cave National Park in western South Dakota (Fredlund 1997; Fredlund and Tieszen 1997a).

preservation, where 0 is total absence and 5 is perfect preservation (Fredlund and Tieszen 1997a). A score of 2 on this scale means that the phytolith preservation is judged to be highly altered by dissolution and breakage and, therefore, lacks the integrity required in vegetation reconstruction (figures 13.2 and 13.3). Similar semi-objective scales have been developed for forests and other vegetative communities (Alexandre et al. 1999).

Although phytoliths are resistant to many forms of chemical corrosion, they are subject to dissolution in some soil-forming environments (Wilding, Smeck, and Drees 1977). Although the solution chemistry is complex, high soil pH (greater than 8) is often found to promote rapid silica dissolution. Zones of poor preservation at Highland Creek, Wind Cave National Park, South Dakota, correspond with high-pH, carobonate-rich Bk-horizons and are in keeping with this pattern (figure 13.2). Within the C1-horizon, below the reach of the current soil-forming environment, abundant and well-preserved phytoliths persist. Their persistence in this zone demonstrates that their poor preservation resulted from subsequent soil formation rather than damage incurred before or during deposition. The low content but relatively good preservation also brings into question the relative age of the phytoliths recovered from the Btj1-horizon. Because phytoliths are as susceptible to translocation as any silt, these assemblages may be relatively recently redeposited phytoliths originating in the A1-horizon rather than assemblages that are chronologically older than A-horizon assemblages. This can now be tested through radiometric dating of organic matter occluded within phytoliths (Mulholland and Prior 1993).

Strategies for Vegetation Reconstruction

Approaches to inferring vegetation from fossil phytoliths vary, although the strategies employed have become increasingly sophisticated and quantitative. Statistical approaches to vegetation reconstruction range from basic inferential statistical techniques to multivariate regression and ordination. Today, the application of statistics to phytolith analysis parallels that of Quaternary palynology (Grimm 1988).

The most basic strategy compares differences in phytolith production by forests and by grasslands. Two examples of this approach in conservation management illustrate its limitations. In the first example, researchers used phytolith mass to confirm the stability of forb- and grass-dominated patches in southeastern Ohio, know locally as "buffalo beats" (Kalisz and Boettcher 1990). The authors used bulk phytolith content from soil transects extending across a local prairie-forest border. The significant differences in phytolith mass from the buffalo beats to the forest

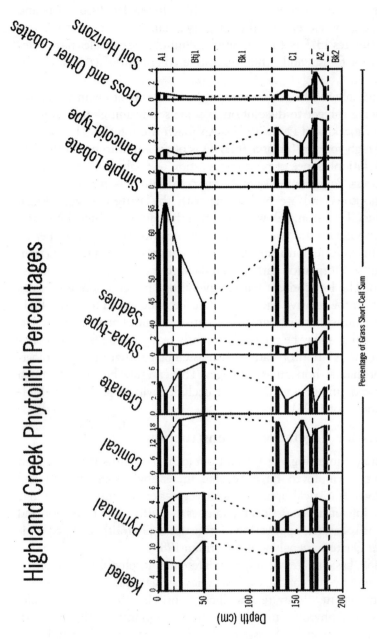

Figure 13.3. Grass short-cell phytolith percentage from Wind Cave National Park soil profile shown in figure 13.2. Percentages for B-horizon samples with poor preservation are excluded from the analysis. Changes in relative frequencies of short-cell percentages are used to infer changes in grassland composition through time.

supported the widely held view that these patches are a relatively stable phenomenon controlled by local soil conditions. In a second example, Fisher and collaborators (1987) used soil phytolith masses to test the instability of the mosaic of pine parkland and grasslands at Devils Tower National Monument in eastern Wyoming. Not finding significant differences along soil transects, they concluded that most pine woodlands are not fixed, but are recent invasions resulting from fire suppression.

In the first example, it is difficult to find alternative explanations because of the positive difference in soil phytolith content across the ecosystem boundary. By contrast, the authors in the second example are arguing from negative findings, and while their conclusions are likely valid, the phytolith evidence remains ambiguous. The lack of significant differences in phytolith content in the study at Devils Tower could also be explained by extra-local sources of phytolith deposition, but because the researchers assumed they were working with a decay-in-place situation, we will not know until further, more sophisticated, research is done.

The most common approaches to vegetation reconstruction using phytoliths are based on percentages of phytolith morphotypes. These attempts to infer vegetation from phytolith percentage data are logical extrapolations from the taxonomic literature (Carbone 1977; Lewis 1981). However, inferring vegetation change from fossil assemblages without modern sample analysis makes a critical assumption. Such inferences assume that observed differences among samples have vegetative significance—meaning that researchers assume they can distinguish analytical variability from a vegetation change. This is very difficult to accomplish without the use of modern sample analysis and means that, at best, such inferences must remain at the relative level. For example, in my early research (Fredlund, Johnson, and Dort 1985), I could speculate that a rise in percentage of Panicoid-type phytoliths represented a relative change in the abundance of tallgrass prairie species, but I could not tell the magnitude of the vegetation change. The lack of analogous modern samples continues to limit phytolith applications to paleoecology.

Once modern analog assemblages are analyzed, more advanced inferences are possible. The basic, and most widely applied use of modern samples is nonstatistical. An analysis of surface and buried soil samples at Capitol Reef National Park in Utah demonstrates the improved level of analysis provided by surface soil assemblages (Fisher, Newell Bourne, and Fisher 1995). In this study, Fisher and his collaborators used phytolith analysis to provide critical evidence for pre-European vegetation at various landscape positions throughout the park. They combined data from modern comparative collections and radiocarbon-dated soil samples to build a convincing reconstruction of pre-Columbian plant communities.

I believe this study is an example of a successful, nonstatistical application of phytolith analysis for determining reference conditions.

My own modern surface-sample studies across the Great Plains, from Texas into Canada (Fredlund and Tieszen 1994), were designed to incorporate the entire range of grassland vegetation change that might have occurred in any locality during the last ten thousand years. As a result, this modern Great Plains data set forms the basis for a pseudo-quantitative comparison and vegetation reconstruction of the fossil record extending back into the late Pleistocene (Fredlund and Tieszen 1997a). I have found the best approach for vegetation reconstruction of the Quaternary fossil record includes broader-scale studies supplemented by exploration of local vegetation and landscape variability for each project. Even a modest analysis of local vegetation can do a great deal to validate inferences based on the phytolith record. For example, Linda Scott Cummins (1996) analyzed six surface samples representative of local vegetation communities near the Mill Iron archaeological site in southeastern Montana to document the range of variability in local phytolith assemblages. However, this local analysis does not capture the range of variability realized in the twelve-thousand-year record of vegetation change documented in the archaeological record.

The grass short-cell phytolith record from the Highland Creek profile discussed earlier helps illustrate this broad-scale local vegetation–type approach (figure 13.3). Based on the analysis of surface soil samples from across the Great Plains, it is possible to infer tallgrass (Panicoid)–dominated grassland from the A2 soil horizon. The shift in phytolith composition toward a dominance of saddle forms in the C1 soil horizon is consistent with changes in vegetation that occurred during the 1930s dust bowl (Fredlund and Tieszen 1994) and would result in a geomorphically unstable landscape. Phytolith assemblages from the Bk1-horizon are not interpretable due to severe problems in preservation. Phytolith assemblages in the Btj1-horizon are presented but are considered problematic because of the low concentrations (figures 13.2 and 13.3). Phytoliths from the surface and near surface represent mixed-grass vegetation of the landscape today resulting from historical cattle and horse grazing of the site before its incorporation into the Wind Cave National Park. Tallgrass (Panicoid) grasses are far less important today than they were three thousand years ago during the formation of the A2 soil horizon. Note that even with modern analog samples, the study is limited to relative statements about vegetation change (e.g., more or less tallgrass).

Marie Kurmann's (1985) investigation in eastern Kansas is one of the few phytolith vegetation reconstruction studies that have employed inferential statistics. Kurmann used analysis of variance (ANOVA) to compare fossil assemblages derived from buried soils with modern assemblages associated with typical local vegetation communities in eastern Kansas. By testing the null-hypothesis that fossil samples were the same as modern assemblages, she was able to place fossil assemblages into broad vegetation community types (i.e., mixed grasslands compared to tallgrass prairie). Although innovative, this study has problems. It fails to consider potential differential preservation as an alternative explanation for some of the observed differences. Also, in order to apply the analysis of variance, Kurmann compared raw phytolith counts rather than relative frequencies. The use of raw counts and ANOVA statistics requires many assumptions that restrict the use of this methodology.

An alternative statistical approach to inferring absolute composition for grassland reconstruction is multivariate regression. Because of the multiplicity of phytolith forms produced by any single species of grass and the persistent fuzziness in classification, this technique is especially appropriate. Although not published, the protocol for applying this approach is the same as that for climatic reconstruction (Fredlund and Tieszen 1997b). First, regression functions are developed using modern percentage data from localities with known vegetation. It is then possible to apply the regression functions to fossil composition to predict the absolute composition in terms of net productivity for many of the dominant grass subfamilies or tribes. In applying such models to problems in restoration ecology, it is critical to remember that they are based on average conditions for the past several hundred years and, therefore, may not match current conditions.

Other multivariate statistical approaches fall into two categories: multivariate ordination techniques and discriminant analysis. In these approaches, phytolith assemblages are matched with vegetation community types as a whole. I know of no published applications of discriminant analysis in phytolith research, but there is reason to think it would be effective. Discriminate functions are constructed on modern multivariate data sets where vegetation communities have previously been calcified. Once constructed, these discriminate functions are used to classify unknown fossil assemblages into the vegetation community types as defined in the modern data.

Multivariate ordination techniques come in too many variations to review in this paper (see Grimm 1988 for a basic introduction to the pollen applications). In general, multivariate ordination techniques are statistical approaches to data reduction. When applied to phytolith analysis, they take a data set of many phytolith types and reduce it to two or three variables that encapsulate the most important aspects of variability. The analyst interprets what these new variables represent. In my application of principal component analysis to modern grassland assemblages (Fredlund and Tieszen 1994), the resulting new variables represented the regional climatic variables that govern regional vegetation composition—temperature and precipitation. Once these new variables are constructed, it is possible to take unknown (fossil) assemblages and plot them along newly constructed variable axes. Vegetation of the fossil assemblage is then inferred by comparing its plotted location to known modern assemblages. Alix Powers-Jones and Joanne Padmore (1993) used another multivariate ordination technique—correspondence analysis—for a similar problem in which they were able to infer the origin of archaeological samples from a range of possible domesticated animals by using samples of modern animal dung.

Conclusion and Future Research Directions

In this chapter I have attempted to introduce all of the major considerations that any practitioner of the art should consider. One of the most basic is classification. At the 1998 International Meeting of Phytolith Research, held in Aix-en-Provence, France, inconsistency in phytolith classification and descriptive vocabulary was cited as the single most important problem facing phytolith researchers. International committees have been appointed to establish a standard lexicon.

A second cluster of problems includes phytolith production, dispersal, and deposition. I have stressed the role of modern sample analysis in validating vegetation reconstruction and in advancing phytolith analysis toward a more quantitative method.

Yet another critical part of vegetation reconstruction is developing a better understanding of the depositional context of fossil assemblages. This is especially critical in using terrestrial samples for vegetation reconstruction. While each depositional situation is unique, some general statements may guide research in historical vegetation reconstruction. The chronological resolution of most terrestrial deposits (typically on the order of several centuries) is adequate for detecting and documenting long-term (millennial) trends in vegetation and climate change (e.g., Fredlund and Treszen 1997a). Significant variation in composition can, of course, be easily hidden within samples of this resolution. If historical reconstruction demands more precise chronological control, then enclosed lakes or other wetlands would likely be a better source of information. In arid and semi-arid environments, rapidly accumulated alluvial fans and terraces may preserve higher-resolution fossil records. Alluvial terraces deposited by larger streams or rivers may not be appropriate, however, as these deposits are potentially a mix of redeposited materials from the upstream drainage basin.

Although the list of caveats in the application of phytoliths for the purpose of ecosystem restoration is long, it should not intimidate the novice researcher. Admittedly, some first-time archaeologist researchers have become discouraged when considering these potential problems (Starna and Kane 1983), yet the problems faced in phytolith analysis are no less daunting than those encountered when applying palynology to paleoecology. The difference between the two techniques is one of maturity. The potential for applying pollen in vegetation reconstruction was recognized and developed much earlier than phytolith analysis. I hope that the reader will view this developmental lag as an opportunity to contribute rather than as a roadblock to the use of phytoliths in restoring historic ecosystems.

References

Alexandre, A., J.-D. Meunier, A. Mariotti, and F. Soubies. 1999. Late Holocene phytolith and carbon-isotope record from a latosol at Salitre, south-central Brazil. *Quaternary Research* 51:187–194.

Baker, G. 1959a. Fossil opal phytoliths and phytolith nomenclature. *Australian Journal of Science* 21:305–306.

———. 1959b. Opal phytoliths in some Victorian soils and "red rain" residues. *Australian Journal of Botany* 7:64–87.

Ball, T.B., J.S. Gardner, and J.B. Brotherson. 1996. Identifying phytoliths produced by the inflorescence bracts of three species of wheat (*Triticum monococcum* L., *T. dicoccon* Schrank, and *T. aesticum* L.) using computer-assisted image and statistical analyses. *Journal of Archaeological Science* 23:619–632.

Bartoli, F., and L.P. Wilding. 1980. Dissolution of biogenic opal as a function of its physical and chemical properties. *Journal of the Soil Science Society of America* 44:873–878.

Bartolome, J.W., S.E. Klukkert and W.J. Barry. 1986. Opal phytoliths as evidence for displacement of native Californian grassland. *Madrono* 33(3):217–222.

Beavers, A.H., and I. Stephen. 1958. Some features of the distribution of plant opal in Illinois soils. *Soil Science* 86(1):1–5.

Birkeland, P. 1999. *Soils and geomorphology*, 3rd edition. New York: Oxford University Press.

Birks, H.J.B., and H.H. Birks. 1980. *Quaternary paleoecology*. London: Edward Arnold.

Bozarth, S.R. 1987. Diagnostic opal phytoliths from rinds of selected Cucurbita species. *American Antiquity* 52:607–615.

———. 1992. Classification of opal phytoliths formed in selected dicotyledons native to the Great Plains. Pages 193–214 in *Phytolith systematics: Emerging issues*, ed. G. Rapp Jr. and S.C. Mulholland. *Advances in Archaeological and Museum Science* 1. New York: Plenum Press.

Brown, D.A. 1984. Prospects and limits of a phytolith key for grasses in the central United States. *Journal of Archaeological Sciences* 11:345–368.

Brown, D.A., and P.J. Gersmehl. 1985. Migration models for grasses in the American Midcontinent. *Annals of the Association of American Geographers* 75:383–394.

Carbone, V. 1977. Phytoliths as paleoecological indicators. *Annals of the New York Academy of Science* 288:194–205.

Carlquist, S. 1988. *Comparative wood anatomy*. New York: Springer-Verlag.

Cummings, L.S. 1996. Paleoenvironmental interpretations for the Mill Iron site: Stratigraphic pollen and phytolith analysis. Pages 177–194 in *The Mill Iron site*, ed. G.C. Frison. Albuquerque: University of New Mexico Press.

Darwin, C. 1846. An account of the fine dust which often falls on vessels in the Atlantic Ocean. *Quarterly Journal of the Geological Society of London* 2:26–30.

Ehrenberg, C.G. 1846. Über die vulkanischen Phytolitharien der Insel Ascension. *Monatsberichte der Königlich Preussischen Akademie der Wissenschaften zu Berlin*. 191–202.

Ellis, R.P. 1979. A procedure for standardizing comparative leaf anatomy in the Poaceae. II. The epidermis as seen in surface view. *Bothalia* 12:641–671.

Fisher, R.F., C. Newell Bourne, and W.F. Fisher. 1995. Opal phytoliths as an indicator of the floristics of prehistoric grasslands. *Geoderma* 68(4):243–255.

Fisher, R.F., M.J. Jenkins, and W.F. Fisher. 1987. Fire and prairie-forest mosaic of Devils Tower National Monument. *American Midland Naturalist* 117:250–257.

Fredlund, G.G. 1986. Problems in the simultaneous extraction of pollen and phytoliths from clastic sediments. Pages 102–111 in *Plant opal phytolith analysis in archaeology and paleoecology*, ed. I. Rovner. Proceedings of the 1984 Phytolith Research Workshop, Occasional Papers No. 1 of the Phytolitharien. Raleigh: North Carolina State University.

———. 1997. Late Quaternary geomorphic history of Lower Highland Creek, Wind Cave National Park, South Dakota. *Physical Geography* 17:446–464.

Fredlund, G.G, W.C. Johnson, and W. Dort Jr. 1985. A preliminary analysis of opal phytoliths from the Eustis Ash Pit, Frontier County, Nebraska. *Institute for Tertiary-Quaternary Studies, Inst. TER-QUA Studies Symposium Series* 1:147–162.

Fredlund, G.G., and L. L. Tieszen. 1994. Modern phytolith assemblages from the North American Great Plains. *Journal of Biogeography* 21:321–335.

———. 1997a. Calibrating grass phytolith assemblages in climatic terms: Application to late Pleistocene assemblages from Kansas and Nebraska. 1 *Paleogeography, Paleoclimatology, Paleoecology* 136:199–211.

———. 1997b. Phytolith and carbon evidence for Late Quaternary vegetation and climate change in the southern Black Hills, South Dakota. *Quaternary Research* 47:206–217.

Fujiwara, H. 1993. Research into the history of rice cultivation using plant opal analysis. Pages 147–159 in *Current research in phytolith analysis: Applications in archaeology and paleoecology*, eds. D.M. Pearsall and D.R. Piperno. Museum Applied Science Center for Archaeology (MASCA) Research Papers in Science and Archaeology 10. Philadelphia: University of Pennsylvania.

Geis, J.W. 1973. Biogenic silica in selected species of deciduous angiosperms. *Soil Science* 116:113–130.

Grimm, E.C. 1988. Data analysis and display. Pages 43–76 in *Vegetation history*, eds. B. Hyntley and T. Webb III. Dordecht: Kluwer Academic Publishers.

Grob, A. 1897. Beiträge zur Anatomie der Epidermis der Gramineenblatter. *Bibliotheca Botanica* (Stuttgart) 7, Bd. 36:1–122.

Hart, D.M. 1988. The plant opal content in the vegetation and sediment of a swamp at Oxford Falls, New South Wales, Australia. *Australian Journal of Botany* 36:159–170.

Jones, R.L., and A.H. Beavers. 1963. Some mineralogical and chemical properties of plant opal. *Soil Science* 96:375–379.

Kalisz, P.J., and S.E. Boettcher. 1990. Phytolith analysis of soils at Buffalo Beats, a small forest opening in southeastern Ohio. *Bulletin of the Torrey Botanical Club* 11:445–449.

Kanno, I., and S. Arimura. 1958. Plant opal in Japanese soils. *Soil Plant Food* 4:62–67.

Kaplan, L., M.B. Smith, and L.A. Snaddon. 1992. Cereal grain phytoliths of Southwest Asia and Europe. Pages 149–174 in *Phytolith systematics, emerging issues*, eds. G. Rapp Jr. and S.C. Mulholland. Advances in Archaeological and Museum Science 1. New York: Plenum Press

Kealhofer, L., and D. Penny. 1998. A combined pollen and phytolith record for fourteen thousand years of vegetation change in northeastern Thailand. *Review of Palaeobotany and Palynology* 103:83–93.

Klein, R.L., and J.W. Geis. 1978. Biogenic silica in the Pinacae. *Soil Science* 126(3):145–155.

Komarek, E.V., B.B. Komarek, and T.C. Carlysle. 1973. *The ecology of smoke particulates and charcoal residues from forest and grassland fires: A preliminary atlas*. Miscellaneous Publication No. 3. Tallahassee, Fla. Tall Timbers Research Station.

Kurmann, M.H. 1985. An opal phytolith and palynomorph study of extant and fossil soils in Kansas (USA). *Palaeogeography, Palaeoclimatology, Palaeoecology* 49:217–235.

Lanning, F.C., and L.N. Eleuterius. 1985. Silica and ash in tissues of some plants growing in the coastal area of Mississippi, U.S.A. *Annals of Botany* 56:157–172.

———. 1989. Silica deposition in some C 3 and C 4 species of grasses, sedges and composites in the USA. *Annals of Botany* 63:395–410.

Lentfer, C.J., and W.E. Boyd. 1998. A comparison of three methods for the extraction of phytoliths from sediments. *Journal of Archaeological Science* 25:1159–1183.

Lewis, R.O. 1981. Use of opal phytoliths in paleo-environmental reconstruction. *Journal of Ethnobiology* 1:175–181.

Madella, M., A.H. Powers-Jones, M. K. Jones. 1998. A simple method of extraction of opal phytoliths from sediments using a non-toxic heavy liquid. *Journal of Archaeological Science* 25:801–803.

Metcalfe, C.R. 1960. *Anatomy of Monocotyledons.* I. Gramineae. Oxford, England: Clarendon Press.

Mulholland, S.C., C. Prior. 1993. AMS Radiocarbon dating of phytoliths. Pages 21–24 in *Current research in phytolith analysis: Applications in archaeology and palaeoecology,* eds. D.M. Pearsall and D.R. Piperno. Museum Applied Science Center for Archaeology (MASCA) Research Papers in Science and Archaeology 10. Philadelphia: University of Pennsylvania.

Mulholland, S.C., and G. Rapp Jr. 1992. A morphological classification grass silica-bodies. Pages 65–89 in *Phytolith systematics, emerging issues,* eds. G. Rapp Jr. and S.C. Mulholland. Advances in Archaeological and Museum Science 1. New York: Plenum Press.

Ollendorf, A.L., S.C. Mulholland, and G. Rapp Jr. 1988. Phytolith analysis as a means of plant identification: *Arundo donax* and *Phragmites communis. Annals of Botany* 61:209–214.

Palmer, P.G. 1976. Grass cuticles: A new paleoecological tool for East African lake sediments. *Canadian Journal of Botany* 54(15):1725–1734.

Parry, D.W., and F. Smithson. 1964. Types of opaline silica depositions in the leaves of British grasses. *Annals of Botany* 28:169–185.

———. 1966. Opaline silica in the inflorescences of some British grasses and cereals. *Annals of Botany* 30:524–538.

Pearsall, D.M. 1978. Phytolith analysis of archaeological soils: Evidence for maize cultivation in formative Ecuador. *Science* 199:177–178.

———. 1989. *Paleoethnobotany: A handbook of procedures.* San Diego: Academic Press.

———. 1998. Phytoliths in the Flora of Ecuador: the University of Missouri Online Phytolith Database www.missouri.edu/~phtyo/. With contributions by A. Biddle, K. Chandler-Ezell, S. Collins, S. Stewart, C. Vientimilla, Dr. Zhijun Zhao, and Neil A. Duncan, page designer and editor.

Pearsall, D.M., and E.H. Dinan. 1992. Developing a phytolith classification system. Pages 37–64 in *Phytolith systematics, emerging issues,* eds. G. Rapp Jr. and S.C. Mulholland. Advances in Archaeological and Museum Science 1. New York: Plenum Press.

Pinilla, A., J. Juan-Tresserras, and M.J. Machado, eds. 1997. *Estado actual de los estudios de fitolitos en suelos y plantas / The state-of-the-art of phytoliths in soils and plants.* First European meeting on phytolith research, September 23rd–26th, 1996, Centro de Ciencieas Medioambientales del Consejo Superior de Investigaciones Cientificas, CSIC, Monografias, 4, Madrid.

Piperno, D.R. 1984. A comparison and differentiation of phytoliths from maize (*Zea mays* L.) and wild grasses: Use of morphological criteria. *American Antiquity* 49:361–383.

———. 1988. *Phytolith analysis: An archaeological and geological perspective.* San Diego: Academic Press.

Piperno, D.R., and D.M. Pearsall. 1993. Phytoliths in the reproductive structures of maize and teosinte: Implications for the study of maize evolution. *Journal of Archaeological Science* 20:337–362.

––––––. 1998a. *The origins of agriculture in the lowland Neotropics.* San Diego: Academic Press.

––––––. 1998b. The silica bodies of tropical American grasses: Morphology, taxonomy, and implications for grass systematics and fossil phytolith identification. *Smithsonian Contributions to Botany* 85.

Powers, A.H. 1992. Great expectations: A short historical review of European phytolith systematics. Pages 47–57 in *Phytolith systematics, emerging issues,* ed. G. Rapp Jr. and S.C. Mulholland. Advances in Archaeological and Museum Science 1. New York: Plenum Press.

Powers, A.H., and D.D. Gilbertson. 1987. A simple preparation technique for the study of opal phytoliths from archaeological and Quaternary sediments. *Journal of Archaeological Science* 14:529–535.

Powers-Jones, A.H., and J. Padmore. 1993. The use of quantitative methods and statistical analyses in the study of opal phytoliths. Pages 21–24 in *Current research in phytolith analysis: Applications in archaeology and paleoecology,* ed. D.M. Pearsall and D.R. Piperno. Museum Applied Science Center for Archaeology (MASCA) Research Papers in Science and Archaeology 10. Philadelphia: University of Pennsylvania.

Rovner, I. 1971. Potential of opal phytoliths for use in paleoecological reconstruction. *Quaternary Research* 1:343–359.

––––––. 1999. Phytolith analysis. *Science* 283:488–489.

Runge, F. 1995. Potential of opal phytoliths for use in paleoecological reconstruction in the humid tropics of Africa. *Zeitschrift für Geomorphologie,* N.F., Supplement-Bd. 99:53–63.

Runge, J., and F. Runge. 1995. Later quaternary palaeoenvironmental conditions in eastern Zaire (Kivu) deduced from remote sensing, morpho-pedological and sedimentological studies (phytoliths, pollen, C-14). Pages 109–122 in *2d Symposium on African Palynology,* eds. A. Le Thomas and E. Roche (Tervuren, March 6–10, 1995), International Center for Training and Exchanges in the Geoscience (CIFEG), Occasional Publication 1995/31. Orléans, France: Frankreich.

Sangster, A.G., and M.J. Hodson. 1992. Silica deposition in subterranean organs. Pages 239–251 in *Phytolith systematics, emerging issues,* eds. G. Rapp Jr. and S.C. Mulholland. Advances in Archaeological and Museum Science 1. New York: Plenum Press.

Shipman, P. 1981. *Life history of a fossil: An introduction to taphonomy and paleoecology.* Cambridge: Harvard University Press.

Smithson, F. 1956. Silica particles in some British soils. *Journal of Soil Science* 7:122–129.

––––––. 1958. Grass opal in British soils. *Journal of Soil Science* 9:148–154.

Starma, W.A., and D.A. Kane Jr. 1983. Phytoliths, archaeology and caveats: A case study from New York. *Man in the Northeast* 26:21–31.

Thomasson, J.R. 1986. Fossil grasses: 1820–1986 and beyond. Pages 159–167 in *Grass systematics and evolution*, eds. T.R. Soderstrom, K.W. Hilu, C.S. Campbell, and M.E. Barkworth. Washington, D.C.: Smithsonian Institution Press.

Twiss, P.C., E. Suess, and R.M. Smith. 1969. Morphology classification of grass phytoliths. *Proceedings of the Soil Science Society of America* 33:109–115.

Watson, L. 1987. Automated taxonomic descriptions of grass genera. Pages 343–351 in *Grass systematics and evolution*, eds. T.R. Soderstrom, K.W. Hilu, C.S. Campbell, and M.E. Barkworth. Washington, D.C.: Smithsonian Institution Press.

Wilding, L.P. 1967. Radiocarbon dating of biogenetic opal. *Science* 156:66–67.

Wilding, L.P., and L.R. Drees. 1968. Biogenic opal in soils as an index of the vegetation history in the prairie peninsula. In *The Quaternary of Illinois*, ed. R.E. Bergstrom. Special Publication 14. Urbana: University of Illinois, College of Agriculture.

Wilding, L.P., N.E. Smeck, and L.R. Drees. 1977. Silica in soils: Quartz, cristobalite, tridymite, and opal. Pages 471–552 in *Minerals in soil environments*, ed. J.B. Dixon and E.B. Weed. Madison, Wisc.: Soil Science Society of America.

Zhao, Z., and D.M. Pearsall. 1998. Experiments for improving phytolith extraction from soils. *Journal of Archaeological Science* 25:587–598.

III

Synthesis
Case Studies Using Reference Conditions

THE CASE STUDIES we chose span the continent from east to west and from north to south. Moreover, they typify the experimental approach being taken in many historical ecology projects.

Peter Dunwiddie's restoration work on Nantucket Island has received much attention; it has been featured in *National Geographic Research*, the *Journal of Forest History*, and *Restoration & Management Notes*. Dunwiddie describes how he used pollen studies (see chapter 9), written historical accounts (see chapter 6), and repeat photography (see chapter 5) to better understand the changes that had taken place to the island's sandplain grasslands, coastal heathlands, and scrub oak barrens. He also describes how land managers, who have limited information about how vegetation groups have assembled themselves over time, are faced with the dilemma of conserving assemblages, such as sandplain grasslands, while at the same time attempting to restore other competing assemblages to their historic condition.

In his report from the Indiana Dunes National Lakeshore, Ken Cole demonstrates how merits of a "multiscale environmental history [allow] for the merging of data from a broad spectrum of disciplines, and across scales of time and space." His study stretches from the late twentieth century, which he and his colleagues studied using permanent vegetation plots and comparative photography (both ground-based and aerial), to the mid-twentieth century, which he studied using aerial photos and fire-scar analysis (see chapter 8); to the catastrophic fires and logging of the nineteenth century, which he studied using GLO surveys (see chapter 6) and documents (see chapter 3); to pre-European settlement conditions, which he describes with the aid of pollen analysis (see chapter 9). What emerges is a study that integrates a variety of data across time and space, using each technique to its best advantage and producing corroborative evidence for vegetative change.

Our third case study takes the reader to the Grand Canyon region, where historical ecology and restoration ecology have come together under the guidance of Wallace Covington and his colleagues at Northern Arizona University. One of Covington's colleagues, Thomas Alcoze, and his student Matthew Hurteau describe how they developed the Archaeoenvironmental Reconstruction Technique to identify the understory species composition of three historic plant assemblages—ponderosa pine, pinyon-juniper, and sagebrush grassland—that occur in the region. They used ecological studies, historic documents, paired photographs, ethnobotanical data from archaeological site reconstructions (see chapter 2), and data from palynological and packrat midden studies (see chapter 10) to develop their species list. This study represents the first successful attempt at discerning the understory species of this region and was done using cross-referential data that were multidimensional in time and space.

In the final case study, Robin Grossinger of the San Francisco Estuary Institute (SFEI) demonstrates how efforts to discover a watershed can be part of a community-based restoration project. Using both volunteers and experts, SFEI's Historical Ecology Project brought together an amazing amount of human expertise in order to gather and interpret their data. Like the authors of the other case studies, Grossinger points to the use of multiple lines of evidence as key to overcoming biases or shortcomings in the data. His chapter also has considerable appeal because he discusses how to map historic landscapes using the data gathered from the community. And, as his talk at the Society for Ecological Restoration annual conference in 1999 in San Francisco demonstrated, these maps serve as powerful visual products not only for the restorationist but also for the general public. Grossinger summarizes the sentiments of many when he writes, "The historical landscape has an undeniable appeal that leads people into the intertwined stories of people and the land."

14

Using Historical Data in Ecological Restoration: A Case Study from Nantucket

Peter W. Dunwiddie

Modern landscapes in the eastern United States have been heavily shaped by human influences (Cronon 1983; Stilgoe 1982; Whitney 1994). More than three centuries of activity by settlers of European descent brought about the clearing of forests, the conversion of vast areas for cropland and pastures, and the birth of towns and villages. Subsequent generations witnessed the disappearance of many of the towns and the regrowth of many of the forests after unproductive farms were abandoned. Later still, burgeoning populations spurred the sprawl of cities and suburbs, summer homes and golf courses. In many areas, these influences were superimposed on a landscape that already had been significantly shaped for millennia by fire and agricultural activities carried on by Native Americans.

Today's landscape is a direct product of these past influences. What we see is the result of centuries of transformation during which soils were tilled, fertilized, and impoverished; fires were set and suppressed; native plants were harvested, planted, logged, and grazed; and new plant species were introduced by accident or design. A similar winnowing and sifting has occurred among the fauna.

One of the greatest tasks faced in restoring landscapes is determining appropriate ecological goals. Identifying the composition, structure, extent, and distribution of vegetation types that existed on a site at the time of settlement by Europeans—a frequently sought-after restoration target—can be extremely difficult due to the magnitude of changes during the last three hundred to five hundred years. This chapter explores some of the approaches used on Nantucket Island to piece together a picture of its historic vegetation and identify the forces that were key in maintaining it, thereby providing a framework on which restoration goals could be developed.

Composition and Significance of Nantucket Vegetation

A primary focus of conservation on Nantucket has been on the remarkable grasslands and shrublands that stand in such contrast to the native forests that occur throughout much of New England. Several related native plant communities occur on the island's gently rolling moraines and outwash plains. Sandplain grasslands have many similarities to midwestern dry prairies, including the dominant grass species—little bluestem (*Schizachyrium scoparium*). Coastal heathlands have a smaller component of forbs and grasses than the sandplain grasslands and a greater abundance of low shrubs with leathery leaves and often evergreen foliage from the Ericaceae and other families. Scrub oak barrens represent a third prominent community on the island. They are dominated by thickets of scrub oak (*Quercus ilicifolia*). These communities intermingle extensively, and collectively constitute a large portion of the native vegetation on the thirty-two-thousand-acre island.

Nantucket has long been recognized for its unique flora, and it continues to draw attention for its high concentration of rare species. A diverse assortment of plants, insects, and birds that are listed as endangered, threatened, or of special concern by the Massachusetts Natural Heritage and Endangered Species Program occurs on the island. These species, together with the three communities in which many of them occur, which also are regarded as rare in New England, are the focus of extensive management and restoration efforts by several conservation organizations.

The open, largely treeless landscape that comprises these communities was more common in the past than it is today along the eastern seaboard, particularly from Long Island to Cape Cod. But recent human activities, especially the development of subdivisions and summer homes, have eliminated vast tracts. For example, the Hempstead Plains on Long Island, a grassland that once covered more than sixty thousand acres, has been reduced to only a few tens of acres as a result of extensive real estate development, particularly following World War II. Similarly, only scattered remnants exist in most areas of Cape Cod and Martha's Vineyard. The several thousand acres of heathland and grassland on Nantucket are the largest vestiges of these communities that survive on a large scale.

In addition to direct threats from development, the heathlands and grasslands are rapidly being invaded by taller woody species, most notably pitch pine (*Pinus rigida*) and scrub oak. Left unchecked, this encroachment will convert many areas to shrub thickets and pine forests, which will be accompanied by a significant loss of rare species and overall diversity. However, this succession raises an intriguing ecological question. The plant communities being invaded appear to be well developed associations of native species. Why, then, are they now disappearing so rapidly beneath a wave of other plants, many of which also are native?

This chapter presents the results of several different lines of investigation that begin to answer this question. These studies were designed to clarify Nantucket's vegetational history and examine the causes of the changes that have taken place since the last Ice Age. As a result of ecological restoration efforts and long-term successional studies at various sites, additional questions emerged that further helped to focus the paleoecological and historical investigations. Have the heathlands and grasslands existed on Nantucket for millennia, or are they anthropogenic communities that resulted largely from post-European activity? What factors helped to maintain these communities in the past? To what extent was the island forested in the past? Was pitch pine, a common species invading many of the heathlands and scrub oak barrens, native to Nantucket? The answers to these questions are critical to the conservation organizations attempting to preserve rare coastal vegetation types throughout the northeastern United States. First, answers are essential in formulating ecological models to help explain the dynamics and relationships among sandplain communities. These models, in turn, provide a rational basis for identifying ecologically sound restoration goals. And finally, an accurate historical perspective is key in developing effective management and restoration strategies.

Sources of Information on Historical Vegetation

Other chapters in this book have described many of the tools available to reconstruct vegetation histories at a site. Each offers a perspective on past vegetation with a different degree of spatial, temporal, and taxonomic resolution. Several of these techniques were used to study past changes in Nantucket's vegetation, including palynology, written historical accounts, and analyses of paired photographs.

Pollen Studies

Studies of plant fossils provide a long-term perspective on past vegetation composition. On Nantucket, I examined fossil pollen preserved in sediments collected from two sphagnum bogs—Taupawshas and Donut Pond Bog—and from the bottom of a shallow pond—No Bottom Pond. Records from the latter two sites are discussed in this chapter.

A continuous record of past vegetation cannot be precisely reconstructed from fossil pollen assemblages due to a variety of factors that alter percentages of pollen in sediments from a direct correspondence with the relative abundance of species in the nearby terrestrial flora. Owen Davis describes many of these factors in chapter 9. Significant differences exist among taxa in terms of pollen productivity, dispersal, and preservation. In addition, aquatic and local bog plants are often greatly overrepresented. These factors apply to all sites, including those on Nantucket. Other problems are unique to particular sites. In Taupawshas Bog, for example, harvesting of peat during the late 1700s removed most of the sediment deposited during the last thirty-five hundred years, creating a hiatus in the record. However, fossil pollen from all three sites describe a similar picture of past changes, although only the diagram from No Bottom Pond is reproduced here.

No Bottom Pond occupies a kettlehole in the Nantucket moraine and is located about 1 km west of Nantucket town. The site is about 6 m (20 ft) above sea level and is encircled by a dense mat of narrowleaf cattails (*Typha angustifolia*). The surrounding vegetation has been highly altered by recent settlement but includes a mixture of shrubs, grasslands, and scattered trees. We took a 5.5-m-long sediment core from near the center of the pond using a piston corer (Wright, Mann, and Glaser 1983). Six samples were taken for radiocarbon dating. Samples for pollen analysis were taken at 10-cm intervals and processed using standard techniques (Faegri and Iversen 1975). Pollen, spores, and charcoal fragments were identified and counted from microscope slide preparations mounted in silicone oil and examined at x400 and x1,000 magnification. At least three hundred grains were counted at each 10-cm interval. Percentages of each taxon were calculated based on the sum of all terrestrial pollen types. Additional details are provided in Dunwiddie (1990).

Similar methods were used at Donut Pond Bog, a site about 5 km east of No Bottom Pond. However, only a single, 145-cm-long core was collected at that site. This core was sampled at closer intervals than No Bottom Pond and provides somewhat greater resolution than the No Bottom Pond core on changes over the last five hundred years.

To be able to recognize fossil pollen assemblages that might have been derived from grassland and heathland vegetation, I collected surface sediment samples from fifteen ponds and bogs on Nantucket. These sites included a range of vegetation types that currently exist on the island. Pollen was extracted and counted in the same manner as with the longer cores.

Written Historical Accounts

I have not come across any eyewitness accounts that depict the native vegetation on Nantucket at the time the island was first settled by colonists, known locally as proprietors, in 1659. Macy (1835) is perhaps the most widely cited early historian of the island, but it is difficult to assess the accuracy of his vegetation portrayals, as he often fails to identify the sources of his information. Such accounts, removed by a century or more from the period they are describing, must always be viewed with caution. Firsthand descriptions of the island's vegetation are remarkably few, even in more recent times. The best that I have encountered are De Crevecoeur's *Letters from an American Farmer* (1782), in which the author provides several graphic descriptions of Nantucket at the time of his visit, and Thoreau's (1906) journal notes from when he came to the island in 1854. These accounts of conditions on the island during the eighteenth and nineteenth centuries, portions of which are cited later in this chapter, lend a vividness and detail absent from the reconstructions of the vegetation based only on palynological evidence.

Repeat Photography

For the last 120 years or so, photographs provide yet another source of information on the rate and extent of vegetation change. A wealth of material is available from numerous photo archives, books, and private collections. The Nantucket Historical Association and the Nantucket Atheneum were particularly helpful, but obtaining sources of old photographs is only the beginning. Only a small fraction of the thousands of available photos are potentially useful in evaluating historic vegetation. A first cut in the selection process was to choose scenes that depict largely natural vegetation. This subset was further reduced by excluding photos that contained no clues as to their location. A set of high-quality prints was then made of the remaining photos.

The next step is to identify the position from which the original photograph was taken. This presents an intriguing challenge, in which one must often rely on subtle clues of roads and fences, pond margins and boulders, to identify sites precisely. One assumption proved especially helpful in relocating many of the oldest photo sites. I postulated that nineteenth-century camera equipment was so unwieldy that few photographers would have ventured far from existing roads. By working with maps showing road locations one hundred years ago, the number of likely sites was quickly reduced. Using this approach, most sites were eventually located, and very few were found to be inaccessible.

Efforts were made to determine the conditions of light, season, and time of day of the original photo to minimize differences that might affect interpretations of vegetational composition and structure. A new photograph was then taken that matched the location, camera angle, field of view, and conditions of the original as closely as possible. Detailed notes were taken of the current vegetation composition. Finally, comparisons were made with the original photograph—often under a dissecting microscope—to identify and describe differences in the vegetation.

Representation of Modern Vegetation in Surface Pollen Assemblages

Pollen in surface samples collected from ponds and bogs on Nantucket provide examples for how different vegetation types appear in pollen assemblages (figure 14.1). In the island's grasslands and heathlands, grass pollen is the most abundant type, averaging 17 percent of the total. Pollen from composites (including Tubuliflorae) and other nonarboreal types are prevalent. Sedge pollen (Cyperaceae) is also well represented in some samples and is probably derived from Pennsylvania sedge (*Carex pensylvanica*), a common graminoid in both sandplain grasslands and coastal heathlands.

The abundance of pine pollen is deceptive. The genus is an abundant pollen producer and is frequently overrepresented in pollen diagrams in relation to its abundance in nearby vegetation. Pitch pine forests have been planted and become naturalized in some parts of Nantucket, and a portion of the pine pollen probably is derived from those trees. Regionally dispersed pollen from the mainland, where pine forests are more common, is a significant additional component. In only one of the Nantucket samples (Site 13, pine-oak heath) does pine pollen approach the levels found in samples on Cape Cod (Winkler 1982), where this taxon averages 31 percent of the pollen total, three times the mean on Nantucket.

Oak pollen is common in all the samples but is most abundant where scrub oaks are prominent in the vegetation. Unfortunately, this pollen type cannot be identified to species. The scrub oak–dominated areas on Nantucket yield pollen assemblages with oak percentages of 20 to 35 percent. These percentages are comparable to those found in black and white oak forests on Cape Cod (Winkler 1982) and in both oak forests and scrub oak barrens on Martha's Vineyard (Stevens 1996).

Birch (*Betula*) pollen, like pitch pine, also tends to be overrepresented compared to nearby vegetation. This species is nearly absent on Nantucket, and its consistent appearance of 5–10 percent in most spectra suggests that it is primarily derived from the mainland. Stevens (1996) made similar observations on Martha's Vineyard with pollen of this genus.

The surface samples from Nantucket suggest that much of the pollen is derived from local, on-island sources. However, as has been documented on a nearby coastal island (Jackson and Dunwiddie 1992), significant transport of pollen also occurs from the nearby mainland, and caution

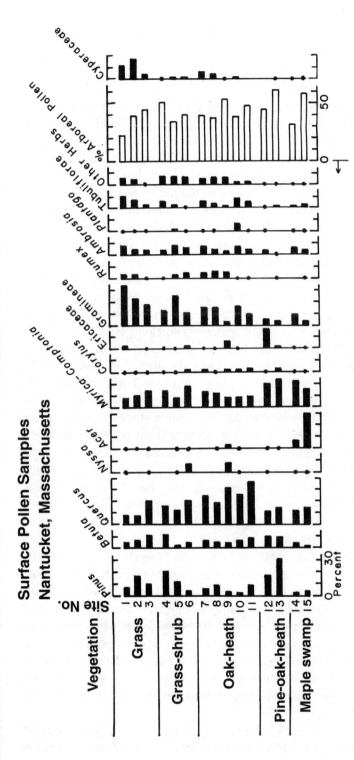

Figure 14.1. Pollen percentages from surface-sediment samples on Nantucket Island. Dominant vegetation surrounding each site is indicated in the left-hand column (from Dunwiddie 1990).

must be exercised in interpreting the island's past vegetation from the fossil pollen assemblages.

Prehistoric Vegetation on Nantucket

Pollen in sediments from No Bottom Pond provide the only uninterrupted record of Holocene vegetation changes from Nantucket Island. Radiocarbon dates provide stratigraphic time control, along with pollen indicators of European settlement about 300 years B.P. The percentage diagram depicting this sequence (figure 14.2) was divided into five informal zones that delineate key changes in the pollen record.

Zone NB-1: 13,790 to 13,000 years B.P. The moraine and outwash plains of Nantucket were deposited by the Pleistocene ice sheets before 14,000 years B.P. The oldest sediments from which pollen could be extracted depict the vegetation that grew in the early postglacial environment. Significant percentages of sage (*Artemisia*) and other composites (Tubuliflorae), grass (Gramineae), sedge (Cyperaceae), heath (Ericaceae), and other nonarboreal pollen types probably reflect a tundralike vegetation. Highly inorganic sediments and low pollen accumulation rates (Dunwiddie 1990) at this time are characteristic of an open, treeless landscape. The presence of several arboreal pollen types in these lowest sediments, including pine, spruce (*Picea*), birch, and oak, probably represent long-distance dispersal from forested habitats to the south and west.

Zone NB-2: 13,000 to 9,300 years B.P. Pine and spruce reach maxima during this period, averaging 45–60 percent of the total. Pollen reflecting either jack (*P. banksiana*) or red pine (*P. resinosa*) dominated early, with white pine (*P. strobus*) becoming prominent later in this zone. Alder (*Alnus*) also attain their highest values at this time. The end of this zone is marked by declines in jack pine and spruce pollen as birch, oak, and grass begin to rise. These data suggest that a boreal forest existed on Nantucket during this period.

Zone NB-3: 9,300 to 5,500 years B.P. Pitch and white pines are the dominant pines in this zone, with white pine disappearing at the end. Birch reaches its greatest Holocene percentages, followed by a large increase in oak pollen. As the postglacial climate warmed, forests dominated by pine and, later, oak replaced the boreal forest vegetation. Heath and sedge pollen can come from local bog or wetland plants as well as from upland vegetation. However, their appearance together with grasses and composites, both common elements in grasslands and heathlands today, suggests that these vegetation types became established during this period as well.

Zone NB-4: 5,500 to 300 years B.P. The beginning of this zone approximately coincides with Nantucket becoming an island as Nantucket Sound

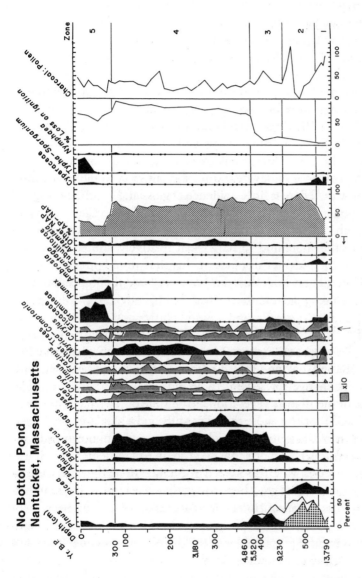

Figure 14.2. Pollen percentages from No Bottom Pond, Nantucket. Proportions of different pine (*Pinus*) pollen types are indicated (stippled = jack or red pine; white = white pine; black = pitch pine). For taxa with low pollen percentages, dots indicate <1 percent, and gray shading depicts changes exaggerated by a factor of ten to enhance detail. Cyperaceae and *Typha-Sparganium* are not included in the arboreal-nonarboreal pollen sum (from Dunwiddie 1990).

was flooded by rising sea level (Oldale 1985). Low pine pollen percentages throughout this zone suggest that pines may have largely disappeared from the island and are represented by long-distance dispersal of pollen from the mainland. Oaks are the dominant taxon throughout this period, with beech, tupelo, maple, hickory, and other hardwoods also present. Sediments are highly organic, reflecting a more extensively vegetated, productive landscape. Oak forests were probably extensive, with a mixture of hardwoods in protected areas.

The island probably continued to shrink rapidly throughout the Holocene. Erosion rates average 3–4 m/yr along the south shore today (Gutman et al. 1979). No Bottom Pond, which presently lies about 5 km from the south shore, probably was several times that distance from the ocean early in this period. Scrub oak thickets may have been prevalent in exposed sites with poor soils, where wind and salt spray would have inhibited forest growth. There is little evidence of grassland-heathland vegetation in the pollen assemblages from this period. These vegetation types may have been present but are likely to have occurred in exposed locations close to the shore and to have been relatively limited in extent. Together with their greater distance at this time from both No Bottom Pond and Donut Pond Bog, this may have obscured their appearance in the fossil pollen records from these sites.

Effects of European Settlement on Vegetation

Zone NB-5: 300 years B.P. to present. At the time the proprietors arrived on Nantucket in 1659, oak and mixed hardwood forests had persisted with little apparent change for several thousand years. Firsthand historical descriptions of the island's vegetation at the time of settlement are lacking. Macy (1835), writing more than a century and a half later, provides a detailed picture of the island, although his sources are unknown and cannot be corroborated. He reports that "At the time of settlement. . . . it was covered with wood, which protected the crops from the raw easterly winds. . . . The wood, that grew here, was of the same kind as that found on the adjacent parts of the continent. A great proportion of it was oak, of an uncommonly hard and firm texture. It was used for the frames of houses and other mechanical purposes: some buildings, now standing, framed of this wood, appear to be as sound as ever."

The first colonial settlements occurred not far from No Bottom Pond on the northern part of the island. The rapid removal of woody vegetation across the island following settlement is marked by an abrupt decline in all the locally derived arboreal taxa in the fossil pollen records from both coring sites. Pollen types thought to be derived primarily from more distant sources on the mainland, such as pine and birch, are virtually unchanged across the settlement stratigraphic horizon. At Donut Pond Bog (figure 14.3), although pine pollen occurs at somewhat higher percentages, much of it represents the white pine (*Pinus strobus*) type, a species that is intolerant of salt spray and is relatively rare on Nantucket today. This lends further support to the contention that the pine pollen was regionally rather than locally derived. Early agricultural fields are a likely source of the increasing percentages of grass, sheep sorrel (*Rumex*), and ragweed (*Ambrosia*) pollen that accompanied the declines in oak and other trees. Increased runoff and erosion from plowed fields contributed to a concurrent increase in inorganic sediments. Fossil charcoal also declined following the settlement horizon, a pattern reported on both Cape Cod (Backman 1984) and Martha's Vineyard (Stevens 1996), suggesting a decline in the frequency or intensity of fire.

Evidence from other sites in southeast New England tends to corroborate this interpretation of changes related to colonial settlement on Nantucket, where a pollen assemblage dominated by oak prior to 1659 is rapidly replaced by a mixture of grass, sheep sorrel, and ragweed. On Martha's Vineyard, Ogden (1959) used various historical sources to suggest that forests at the time of colonial settlement were not substantially different from the mixed oak and hardwood forests found on that island today. Stevens (1996) lent support to Ogden's interpretation in her study of fossil pollen assemblages from twelve sites on Martha's Vineyard. She also found that many presettlement assemblages were dominated by oak pollen, with a major shift toward grasses and forbs after settlement. On Block Island, off the coast of Rhode Island, a pollen assemblage from Fresh Pond was consistently dominated by 50 percent oak pollen for about eight thousand years (Dunwiddie 1990). Here, too, settlement is represented by a significant, albeit somewhat more gradual, decline in oak pollen, accompanied by a simultaneous increase in grass, sheep sorrel, and ragweed as the forests were cleared for pastures.

Arboreal pollen reached its lowest percentage in over twelve thousand years on Nantucket soon after colonial settlement, attesting to the treeless character of the vegetation. Within decades of the proprietors' arrival, firewood was being imported from the mainland (Worth 1904). As the American Revolution disrupted shipping and commerce, Nantucketers became increasingly desperate for fuel. "Peat was found to be excellent firing. All the swamps to the westward of town were laid out for the purpose of digging peat. Some dug up the shrub oaks with their roots, which answered a very good purpose; some, in the winter season, cut brush in the swamps, which burned well, but did not make a durable fire" (Macy 1835). Others made the 25-km round-trip trek across the frozen Nantucket Harbor in winter to cut wood from a small remnant stand of

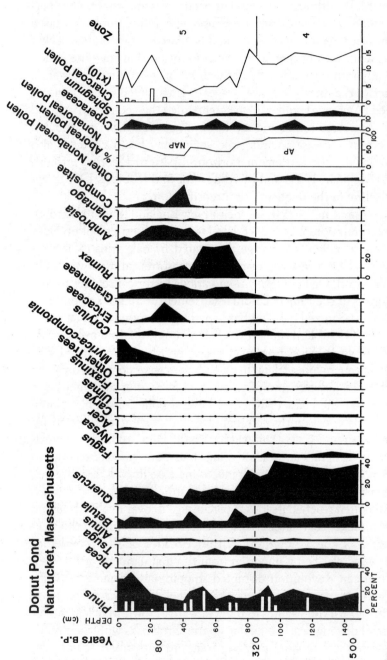

Figure 14.3. Pollen percentages from Donut Pond Bog, Nantucket. Dates were estimated by stratigraphic and pollen indicators. White bars within *Pinus* curve depict the proportion of white pine-type pollen at those intervals; pitch pine-type constitutes the remainder of total pine pollen. Cyperaceae and *Sphagnum* are not included in the arboreal-nonarboreal pollen sum (from Dunwiddie 1989).

oaks at the far northeastern end of the island. Macy, perhaps this time writing from firsthand oral accounts, elaborated on the privations of these woodcutters, remarking that they suffered "weather frequently so boisterous, as to make it hardly safe to expose the human body to its severity."

Cutting of wood for fuel was only one of the reasons for the lack of trees. By 1780, upwards of sixteen thousand sheep were reported on the island (Macy 1835). The impact of such large numbers of animals on the island's vegetation would have been tremendous. De Crevecoeur (1782) noted the "many red cedar bushes and beach grass . . . on the [barrier beach] peninsula of Coitou" but further observed that "the rest of the . . . island is open and serves as a common pasture for sheep." As early as 1672, in an effort to increase forage for grazing, the town fathers voted "that each owner of a share should sow two bushels of hayseed on an acre of land . . . " But few pasture grasses could thrive in the acidic, droughty, and nutrient-poor Nantucket soils. Instead, native grasses and forbs, once found primarily in the sandplain grasslands and heathlands close to the shore, probably spread widely across the newly cleared, sandy plains.

Nantucket since 1850

The stark landscape described by De Crevecoeur in the eighteenth century continued to be remarked upon by visitors to Nantucket seventy years later. Henry David Thoreau (1906) reported a similar scene in 1854: "There is not a tree to be seen, except such as are set out about houses . . . This island must look exactly like a prairie, except that the view in clear weather is bounded by the sea . . . The nearest approach to woods that I saw was the swamps, where the blueberries, maples, etc., are higher than one's head."

Sheep grazing declined at the middle of the nineteenth century for a variety of economic and social reasons. As pressure from the livestock disappeared from the island, the vegetation began to recover. Several changes in the pollen record around this time may reflect some of these changes in land use. Percentages of sheep sorrel declined, as plantain (*Plantago*), ragweed, and other composites (Tubuliflorae) increased. Various woody taxa, such as bayberry (*Myrica*), began to increase, although oaks and most other arboreal pollen never returned to their presettlement abundance.

Increases in pitch pine–type pollen reflect the introduction of this species to the island in the mid-1800s. Josiah Sturgis is reported to have planted pitch pine seeds beginning in 1847—an example followed by others over the next decade. This species has spread widely across the island from these and other early plantings. Thus its story on the island is unusual in that it appears to be both native and introduced. It was prominent in the fossil record prior to about 5,500 years ago but apparently disappeared for unknown reasons. Then 150 years ago, it was reintroduced in a deliberate effort to establish trees on the open, windswept plains.

The earliest photographs of the landscape date from the 1870s and 1880s and graphically illustrate the treeless character of the vegetation. Even by 1900, almost fifty years following the removal of most of the sheep, most photographs show little reestablishment of trees or shrubs. However, over the last century, woody vegetation has returned at an accelerating rate. The photographs reproduced here (figures 14.4 and 14.5, 14.6 and 14.7) depict trends typical of those found in many of the nearly one hundred pairs of photos from Nantucket that I examined. Scrub oak and pitch pine have shown the greatest increase in cover, especially in the eastern part of the island. Elsewhere, other species, such as bayberry, arrowwood (*Viburnum* spp.), black huckleberry (*Gaylussacia baccata*), and blueberry (*Vaccinium* spp.), have become dominant. Several

Figure 14.4. Nantucket, ca. 1890. Only one tree—most likely planted—is visible in this view of the open plains that characterized Nantucket following colonial settlement. It grows in the distance where the driveway from the farm meets the road climbing up the hill. Although sheep grazing had largely ceased on the island by this time, dairy farms were still common. Cows have heavily grazed the fenced pastures on both sides of the road, and several can be seen along the roadside as well. The white patch along the farm driveway in the middle distance is bare sand, probably kept open by the trampling of livestock. The vegetation appears to be closely cropped grasses and other herbs; the only shrubs visible are on the bank at the extreme right edge of the photo. (Henry S. Wyer, Nantucket Historical Association)

introduced species, including Japanese black pine (*Pinus thunbergiana*) and honeysuckle (*Lonicera* spp.) are frequent in some areas as well.

Causes of Vegetation Changes

Long-term changes in climate have had a major influence on the composition of Nantucket's vegetation. The tundra that occupied the landscape following retreat of the Pleistocene ice sheets gave way as climates warmed to boreal communities and later to more temperate assemblages of plants. It is likely that the increasing warmth of early-Holocene climates favored heathland and grassland species, but other factors were probably critical as well, including fire, salt spray, and human influences.

Charcoal is present throughout the fossil record from Nantucket cores, attesting to the occurrence of fire on the landscape. But it is difficult to

Figure 14.5. Nantucket, 1986. A heavy growth of native shrubs and low trees (arrowwood, black cherry, red cedar, bayberry, and others) has screened the original camera position on the roadside bank. The camera in this view was elevated 3 m with a stepladder to approximate the original camera elevation and permit a view of the farmhouse, which appears unchanged since 1890. Scrub oaks and other shrubs have taken over virtually the entire uplands. The only extensive herbaceous vegetation today is found in the salt marsh (middle left) and cattail marsh (hidden by shrubs between the road and the farmhouse). Telephone poles have replaced the rail fences and now trace the edge of the road, which has been relocated to remove the bend. Its old course in the foreground is now a driveway. In the decade since this photo was taken, several large houses were built and now dominate the skyline.

Figure 14.6. Nantucket, 1906. The abandoned sheep commons in eastern Nantucket are visible in this scene looking northeast across the morainal land-scape. Donut Pond Bog is just out of view to the left, about 200 m north. The foreground is dominated by bearberry and little bluestem. Low shrubs occur around the pond, but only about a dozen individual shrubs (probably scrub oak) are visible in the distance. The light color of the hills is produced by grass. Several darker gray patches of clonal shrubs, probably huckleberry or bayberry, are visible (J. H. Wilson, *The Glacial History of Nantucket and Cape Cod*, New York: Macmillan, 1906).

refine the fire history further based on the fossil evidence currently available. Additional study is needed to shed more light on the distribution, intensity, and frequency of fire across the historical landscape and to determine what vegetation types may have been most extensively influenced by such fires. However, some inferences relevant to questions regarding the importance of fire in maintaining native plant communities on Nantucket may be drawn from other evidence. Since lightning is a rare ignition source for wildfires in coastal New England, humans are the only other likely cause of frequent fire. Patterson and Sassaman (1988) suggest that Native Americans played a major role in influencing the frequency and severity of fire in native plant communities. Stevens (1996) has also suggested that burning by Native Americans might account for the presence on Martha's Vineyard of several heathland and grassland-like pollen assemblages that she reported from sites on the outwash plain prior to colonial settlement.

Figure 14.7. Nantucket, 1986. Little bluestem grass persists in part of the foreground, but bayberry, arrowwood, and scrub oak have overtaken much of the area between the camera and the pond. The pond margin is largely unchanged. The hills in the distance are now almost entirely covered by scrub oak, with bayberry and huckleberry occupying most of the space between the taller shrubs. A stand of pitch pine is visible near the right edge, with scattered individuals elsewhere. This landscape has been protected from real estate development by the Nantucket Conservation Foundation. The only obvious sign of human activity is a road that runs north just beyond the pond.

Significant Native American populations are known to have existed on Nantucket prior to European settlement, but the extent to which burning was commonly practiced on the island can only be surmised. No presettlement pollen records have been studied from the southern outwash plain, where grasslands are particularly well developed today. If fires associated with agricultural and other activities were particularly prevalent in the outwash plain, as has been suggested by Stevens (1996), many potential sites that might have recorded such evidence disappeared long ago due to shoreline erosion. The fossil pollen sites studied on Nantucket are all on the terminal moraine, and thus are not optimally located to detect historic grasslands and heathlands that are more likely to have been present farther south along the coast on the outwash plain. Similarly, evidence of frequent fires in the form of abundant charcoal would not be expected as frequently as in more fire-prone locations on the outwash plain. Despite these limitations, it is not unreasonable to assume from the charcoal in the cores that Native Americans set at least occasional fires, and that those fires potentially influenced the structure and composition of the island's vegetation for thousands of years. Once set, such fires are likely to have been extensive, burning unchecked across the island, with little but wetlands and coastal plain ponds to halt their progress. Both the No Bottom Pond and the Donut Pond bog cores depict a decline in charcoal since 300 years B.P. that may reflect a cessation of burning by Native Americans. This closely matches the historical record, where it has been reported that within five years of the time of the proprietors' arrival, the settlers had prohibited Native Americans from burning grazing lands (Tiffney and Eveleigh 1985).

Most of the native terrestrial vegetation on the island is well adapted to fire. In grasslands and heathlands, fires inhibit the growth of tall shrubs and trees that compete with grasses, forbs, and low shrubs. Many oak-dominated communities are also fire adapted, and most species in the scrub oak barrens that cover large portions of the eastern part of the island resprout vigorously following burning (Dunwiddie 1998). However, frequent fires in oak barrens can result in a much more open oak canopy (Finton 1998), allowing the persistence of many herbaceous species that are likely to be missing from oak barrens in which fire is absent.

Another factor that has affected the distribution of vegetation communities on Nantucket is wind, in particular, salt spray. Trees and taller woody plants that are more exposed to the wind are especially affected, exhibiting stunting, deformation, and visible browning of the foliage after storms. Such effects are most pronounced close to the shore, where salt spray is greatest. As a result, grasslands and heathlands, which are more resistant to salt spray effects, are likely to have been most common close to the coastline through much of the Holocene. Trees would have been particularly slow to recolonize such exposed habitats on the outwash plain if fires, agricultural clearing, or extensive firewood cutting created vegetation of low stature.

Various lines of evidence indicate that a diversity of human activities has directly or indirectly impacted Nantucket's vegetation over time. As has already been suggested, burning by Native Americans may have continued for thousands of years and may have helped to shape the composition and structure of communities that were best adapted to frequent fire. Agricultural clearings would also have kept forests at bay in an environment where tree growth was inhibited by salt-laden winds. More recently, settlers of European descent brought about much more extensive changes as they rapidly cleared large acreages of shrubs and trees to create cropland. They also introduced a wealth of species to the island such that today nearly 40 percent of the flora is non-native (Sorrie and Dunwiddie 1996). Grazing by introduced sheep, cows, and horses cropped pastures that mostly comprised native grasses and forbs, and which later saw the return of woody plants as the livestock industry declined.

Implications for Conservation, Management, and Restoration

There is no paleoecological evidence to suggest that grasslands and heathlands were extensive on Nantucket prior to colonial settlement. Their occurrence in many areas today appears to be the product of several centuries of clearing and grazing. Similarly, their disappearance from many of these areas reflects the absence of the grazing livestock, fires, and woodcutting that created and maintained them historically. Yet these communities contain a diversity of native plants and animals, many of which do not occur in other habitats. Of equal note is the relative absence of non-native species in these communities (Dunwiddie, Zaremba, and Harper 1996). The grasslands in particular contain many taxa that thrive only in open, prairie-like landscapes, which are extremely uncommon today in coastal New England. Thus, it seems improbable that these communities are entirely anthropogenic, assembled over the last several centuries from species that grew in oak-dominated forests and barrens that occurred on the island at the time of settlement.

Conservation organizations on Nantucket have worked extensively to maintain and restore sandplain grasslands, heathlands, and scrub oak barrens. These efforts are motivated by the obvious, rapid losses of individual species and entire communities—particularly the grasslands and heathlands—due to the encroachment of taller woody vegetation. These protection efforts continue despite uncertainties about the successional relationships among these communities, about their composition, extent, and distribution prior to extensive modification by European settlers, and about the precise role and importance of different key ecological processes.

As new information on land-use histories or successional processes comes to light, decisions regarding conservation goals and restoration methods can become more difficult. Should diverse heathlands and grasslands that include rare species be maintained in areas where they can be shown to be of relatively recent human origin, or should they be maintained only where they would have occurred "naturally"? What should be managed for when a rare sandplain grassland is being converted by succession to a rare heathland, or a heathland is being invaded by scrub oaks and turning into a rare scrub oak barren?

The decisions that have been made regarding the ecological goals for Nantucket conservation reflect several realities and priorities. While they are partly based on our admittedly limited understanding of how these communities are assembled, they also reflect other, less well-articulated concerns. Some decisions of what to restore, and where, have been made based on expediency—what can be restored most simply? Management units designated for prescribed burning may reflect the presence of features that can be used as firebreaks (or the absence of expensive homes in close proximity), as much as any ecological rationale for burning one site rather than another. This has often resulted in a tendency to maintain communities in locations where they occur now, or are thought to have occurred in the recent past, with little concern for answering difficult questions regarding their likely historical distribution. Another bias has been toward managing for assemblages with a high diversity of native plant species and an abundance of rare species. Thus communities that are shifting toward a dominance of scrub oak—a condition that also tends to be relatively low in herbaceous species richness, although not necessarily in the more difficult to monitor invertebrate species richness—frequently have been managed in ways to slow or reverse this succession and maintain the grassland taxa.

These other considerations have resulted in a particular emphasis on the maintenance of sandplain grassland assemblages. Typically, these are relatively easy to burn, are the most diverse floristically, and often contain conspicuous and attractive faunal elements such as short-eared owls, northern harriers, and regal fritillary butterflies. One is tempted to suspect a certain affinity here as well for open, flower-filled grasslands and charismatic fauna, in contrast to impenetrable shrub thickets with largely invisible, but nonetheless rare, invertebrates with unpronounceable names.

Current ecological management activities in these communities on Nantucket have explored a diversity of methods both to restore the structure and composition of communities, and to maintain them once they have been restored. It is important not to overlook the distinction between these two management activities. The primary conservation goal on Nantucket has been to maintain rare communities by reestablishing processes that historically helped to sustain them. This has included extensive experimentation with prescribed burning to replicate Native American burning, and more limited studies using sheep grazing.

Restoration, on the other hand, has employed additional means, such as herbiciding and brush cutting, to bring communities back to a condition thought to be closer to their original condition.

Future Research

Various studies in oak, pine, and heath vegetation types in the northeastern United States have stressed the importance of land-use history as a primary factor in determining current vegetation community composition (Motzkin et al. 1996; Motzkin, Patterson, and Foster 1999; Finton 1998; Foster and Motzkin 1999; Copenheaver, White, and Patterson 2000). The current distribution of communities on Nantucket is almost certainly no exception to this pattern. In 1996, some colleagues and I proposed successional models among several of these community types, but additional work is needed to determine the validity of the hypothesized successional sequences (Dunwiddie, Zaremba, and Harper 1996). In particular, studies are needed that provide details on past uses of individual parcels of land. Several approaches appear particularly promising.

Historical information can be especially helpful. Paired photographs, such as used in this study, provide a graphic, but relatively superficial and short-term, perspective. Foster and Motzkin (1999) demonstrated the potential for a much more comprehensive approach at a site on Martha's Vineyard, where they used historical accounts, survey records, property deeds, and maps, together with paleoecological data, to provide site-specific information documenting several centuries of use.

Soils can also yield remarkably detailed information on land use. Krauss (1997) explored the use of opal phytoliths preserved in soils (see chapter 13) as a means for reconstructing past vegetation at sites on Martha's Vineyard. Although he related abundance of different phytolith types to vegetation only over the past couple of centuries, such studies may provide valuable evidence when used in conjunction with other site-specific data.

Motzkin, Patterson, and Foster (1999) have been particularly effective in utilizing soils data (see chapter 12) to reconstruct detailed site histories. They obtained information on past agricultural activity derived from observations of presence or absence and depth of plowed soil horizons and combined it with many other types of physical and cultural evidence of past land use. Comparing this information to current vegetation composition at sites helped to explain the many complex aspects of the relationship between vegetation and past land use. Their results have interesting implications for communities on Nantucket. Many of the species they found to be characteristic of unplowed sites in the Connecticut Valley in central Massachusetts (Motzkin, Patterson, and Foster 1999) are also more prevalent in heathlands than in grasslands in southeastern Massachusetts (Dunwiddie, Zaremba, and Harper 1996). Further study of the agricultural histories where these two community types occur today may reveal a similar dichotomy of past plowing versus grazing.

It should be clear that much additional work is needed to better articulate and refine ecological restoration objectives on Nantucket. Other goals should be examined that consider alternative historical scenarios regarding the distribution and extent of grassland and heathland species and a clearer understanding of ecological processes. For example, could many grassland species have existed within an oak-dominated matrix that was maintained in a more open-canopy condition by Native American burning (Finton 1998)? Do prescribed burns in the spring and fall adequately replicate fires set by Native Americans, or were the most ecologically important effects produced by fires that may be more difficult to prescribe, such as growing-season burns during periods of extreme drought? Deciding upon restoration goals becomes even more difficult when several rare communities potentially can exist on a site.

Future management of Nantucket's rare biotic communities needs to be an adaptive process. Considerable caution must be exercised in building restoration models and goals based on the composition, structure, and patterns of rarity in modern communities and landscapes that have undergone centuries of extensive modification. Goals must be set based on the best available historical evidence, and on an understanding of ecological processes that shaped past communities. This in turn necessitates that goals must be frequently and, perhaps, extensively revised as new historical evidence is uncovered, and as our understanding of ecological processes is refined based on well-monitored management and restoration activities. To accomplish this will require innovative studies of the island's ecological history, as well as an extensive commitment to carefully monitor the effects of ongoing ecological management and restoration efforts.

Acknowledgments

Portions of this chapter utilize material previously published in *National Geographic Research* and the *Journal of Forest History*. Both journals have granted permission to use this material.

References

Backman, A.E. 1984. *1000-year record of fire-vegetation interactions in the northeastern United States: A comparison between coastal and inland regions.* M.S. thesis, University of Massachusetts Amherst.

Copenheaver, C.A., A.S. White, and W.A. Patterson III. 2000. Vegetation development in a southern Maine pitch pine-scrub oak barren. *Journal of the Torrey Botanical Society* 127:19–32.

Cronon, W. 1983. *Changes in the land: Indians, colonists, and the ecology of New England*. New York: Hill and Wang.

De Crevecoeur, J.H. St. J. 1782. *Letters from an American farmer*. London: Thomas Davies.

Dunwiddie, P.W. 1989. Forest and heath: The shaping of the vegetation on Nantucket Island. *Journal of Forest History* 33(3):126–133.

———. 1990. Postglacial vegetation history of coastal islands in southeastern New England. *National Geographic Research* 6:178–195.

———. 1992. *Changing landscapes: A pictorial field guide to a century of change on Nantucket*. Nantucket, Mass.: Nantucket Conservation Foundation, Nantucket Historical Association, and Massachusetts Audubon Society.

Dunwiddie, P.W. 1998. Ecological management of sandplain grasslands and coastal heathlands in southeastern Massachusetts. Pages 83–93 in *Fire in ecosystem management: Shifting the paradigm from suppression to prescription*, ed. T.L. Pruden and L.A. Brennan. Tall Timbers Fire Ecology Conference Proceedings, No. 20. Tallahassee, Fla.: Tall Timbers Research Station.

Dunwiddie, P.W., W.A. Patterson III, J.L. Rudnicky, and R.E. Zaremba. 1997. Vegetation management in coastal grasslands on Nantucket Island, Massachusetts: Effects of burning and mowing from 1982 to 1993. Pages 85–98 in *Grasslands of northeastern North America: Ecology and conservation of native and agricultural landscapes*, ed. P.D. Vickery and P.W. Dunwiddie. Lincoln, Mass.: Massachusetts Audubon Society.

Dunwiddie, P.W., R.E. Zaremba, and K.A. Harper. 1996. Classification of coastal heathlands and sandplain grasslands in Massachusetts. *Rhodora* 98:117–145.

Faegri, K., and J. Iversen. 1975. *Textbook of pollen analysis*. Copenhagen: Munksgaard.

Finton, A. 1998. *Succession and plant community development in pitch pine-scrub oak barrens of the glaciated northeast United States*. M.S. thesis, University of Massachusetts Amherst.

Foster, D.R. and G. Motzkin. 1999. Historical influences on the landscape of Martha's Vineyard: Perspectives on the management of the Manuel F. Correllus State Forest. Harvard Forest Paper 23. Petersham, Mass.: Harvard University.

Gutman, A.L., M.J. Goetz, F.D. Brown, J.F. Lentowski, and W.N. Tiffney, Jr. 1979. Nantucket shoreline survey. MIT Sea Grant College Report, MITSG 79-7.

Jackson, S.T., and P.W. Dunwiddie, 1992. Pollen dispersal and representation on an offshore island. *New Phytologist* 122:187–202.

Krauss, D.A. 1997. *The use of phytolith analysis in paleoenvironmental reconstruction and environmental management on Martha's Vineyard, Massachusetts*. Ph.D. dissertation, University of Massachusetts, Boston.

Macy, O. 1835. *The history of Nantucket*. Boston: Hilliard, Gray, and Co.; reprinted New York: Research Reprints, 1970.

Motzkin, G., D. Foster, A. Allen, J. Harrod, and R. Boone. 1996. Controlling site to evaluate history: Vegetation patterns of a New England sand plain. *Ecological Monographs* 66:345–365.

Motzkin, G., W.A. Peterson III, and D.R. Foster. 1999. A historical perspective on pitch pine-scrub oak communities in the Connecticut Valley of Massachusetts. *Ecosystems* 2:255–273.

Ogden III, J.G. 1959. Forest history of Martha's Vineyard, Massachusetts 1. Modern and pre-colonial forests. *American Midland Naturalist* 66:417–430.

Oldale, R.N. 1985. *Geologic map of Nantucket and nearby islands*. Miscellaneous Investigation Series, Map I-1580. Reston, Va.: Department of the Interior, U.S. Geological Survey.

Patterson, III, W.A. and K.E. Sassaman. 1988. Indian fires in the prehistory of New England. Pages 107–135 in *Holocene human ecology in northeastern North America*, ed. G.P. Nicholas. New York: Plenum.

Sorrie, B.A., and P.W. Dunwiddie. 1996. *The vascular and non-vascular flora of Nantucket, Tuckernuck, and Muskeget Islands*. Nantucket, Mass.: Massachusetts Audubon Society, Nantucket Maria Mitchell Association, and The Nature Conservancy.

Stevens, A. 1996. *The paleoecology of coastal sandplain grasslands of Martha's Vineyard, Massachusetts*. Ph.D. dissertation, University of Massachusetts, Amherst.

Stilgoe, J.R. 1982. *Common landscape of America, 1580 to 1845*. New Haven, Conn.: Yale University Press.

Thoreau, H.D. 1906. *Journal 7*. New York: Houghton Mifflin. (Cited by M.A. Rice, *Trees and shrubs of Nantucket*. Ann Arbor, Mich.: Edwards Brothers, 1964.)

Tiffney Jr., W.N., and D.E. Eveleigh. 1985. Nantucket's endangered maritime heaths. In *Coastal Zone '85*, vol. 1, ed. O.T. Magoon, H. Converse, D. Miner, D. Clark, and L. T. Tobin. New York: American Society of Civil Engineers.

Tzedakis, P.C. 1987. *Holocene vegetation changes in Cape Cod, Massachusetts*. M.S. thesis, Brown University, Providence, R.I.

Whitney, G.G. 1994. *From coastal wilderness to fruited plain: A history of environmental change in temperate North America from 1500 to the present*. New York: Cambridge University Press.

Winkler, M.G. 1982. Late-glacial and postglacial vegetation history of Cape Cod and the paleolimnology of Duck Pond, South Wellfleet, Massachusetts. M.S. thesis, University of Wisconsin, Madison.

Worth, H.B. 1904. Nantucket lands and landowners. *Nantucket Historical Association Bulletin* 2:183.

Wright Jr., H.E., D.H. Mann, and P. H. Glaser. 1983. Piston corers for peat and lake sediments. *Ecology* 65:657–659.

15

A Multiple-Scale History of Past and Ongoing Vegetation Change within the Indiana Dunes

Kenneth L. Cole

When reconstructing environmental histories, researchers usually focus on a specific temporal and spatial scale, usually dictated by their particular method. For example, a study using General Land Office (GLO) survey data to compare mid-nineteenth-century and modern forest composition examines forest changes over a temporal scale of about 150 years at a relatively large spatial scale. While contributing valuable information about changes occurring since the settlement period, this comparison of two time periods yields little information on shorter- or longer-term processes of change or at finer spatial scales. Because of the range of space and time scales studied, and the focus on different environmental parameters, results produced by two different retrospective methods can even be contradictory. However, specialists in either method rarely even recognize the disparity in their results because they often belong to different scientific groups (e.g., system ecologists or historians).

In contrast, a multiple-scale environmental history allows for the merging of data from a broad spectrum of disciplines, and across scales of time and space. This approach provides a means to better understand the current trajectories and variabilities of environmental change. While expensive and intellectually taxing for the investigator, a successful multiscale history allows for a more detailed understanding of the often complex trends of change, and for the development of more sophisticated conservation and restoration strategies.

The interaction of variables acting on different timescales confounds a simple understanding of ecosystem history. When discussing why different plant communities may occur adjacent to each other, Henry Cowles wrote, "In order to understand any formation it is necessary to know its history. . . .The study of the cumulative influence of past environments, the lagging of effects behind their causes, is still in its infancy" (1899a, 216). Thus, history can be a series of unrelated events acting on different temporal and spatial scales (Delcourt, Delcourt, and Webb 1982). Complex histories usually resist encapsulation into simple themes, ecological laws, or hypotheses and almost never follow mathematical functions.

My colleagues and I undertook the following case study using an amalgam of historical vegetation techniques, with temporal scales ranging from annual to millennial. The results were used to reconstruct past and recent changes in forests, prairies, and wetlands of the Indiana Dunes, and to guide ongoing conservation activities within Indiana Dunes National Lakeshore.

The Study Area

The Indiana Dunes National Lakeshore is at the southern tip of Lake Michigan, forty miles southeast of Chicago. Most of the areas reported in this chapter are on dunes that were formed during the mid-Holocene high stand of Lake Michigan around four thousand years ago (Nipissing Level) (Larsen 1985). These areas are located in the Dune Acres, Inland Marsh, Miller Woods, and Beverly Shores sections of the lakeshore.

The flora of the Indiana Dunes is exceptionally diverse. The national lakeshore contains 1,445 plant species in an area of less than six thousand hectares, third among all national park units in total species numbers despite its small area (Pavlovic and Bowles 1996). Variable water levels, slope aspects, and fire frequencies generate a mosaic of fen, swamp, wet prairie, mesic prairie, dry sand prairie, oak savanna, oak forest, and mesophytic forest (Bowles et al. 1990). The area is near the tip of the prairie peninsula (Transeau 1935), where the North American tallgrass prairie intergrades with the eastern deciduous forest. Many northerly species, such as common juniper (*Juniperus communis*) and jack pine (*Pinus banksiana*), are near their southern limits in these cool, lakeshore habitats, while some southerly species, such as shellbark hickory (*Carya laciniosa*) and honeylocust (*Gleditsia triacanthos*), are near their northern limits (Little 1971). The intermixing of all of these species suggests that the area is near the junction of multiple gradients in precipitation (east-west) and temperature (north-south), which are further complicated by gradients in lake effect, water table elevation, substrate type, and disturbance. Because changes along different gradients do not necessarily occur at the same time or proceed at the same rate, the vegetational history is very complex. Conservation strategies designed to assist one native plant association can be detrimental to others.

Causes of Vegetation Change in the Indiana Dunes

The Indiana Dunes have been the site of pioneering studies of plant succession since Henry Cowles's classic descriptions of the successive plant societies (Cowles 1899b, 1901). Jerry Olson later strengthened Cowles's observations with more detailed physical, chemical, and geomorphological data (Olson 1958). Both Cowles and Olson conducted their studies by comparing plant associations on dunes of different ages. They described a long-term primary successional sequence starting with bare sand being invaded by the pioneer species marram grass (*Ammophila breviligulata*) and cottonwood (*Populus deltoides*). This pioneer community eventually shifted to jack pine and eastern white pine (*Pinus strobus*), which was in turn invaded by black oak (*Quercus velutina*), white oak (*Q. alba*), and prairie species. The inferred successional sequence is very similar to that proposed for Lake Superior (Maun 1993) and for European coastal dunes (Warming 1909), although the mechanisms driving the sequence are still a topic for debate (Poulson 1999; McIntosh 1999).

Anthropogenic disturbances, such as logging, drainage of marshes, increased fire ignition, fire suppression, air pollution, and invasions of exotic species have also been implicated as major causes of vegetational changes within the dunes (Jackson, Futyma, and Wilcox 1988; Bowles et al. 1990; Cole et al. 1990; Wilhelm 1990; Cole and Taylor 1995; Cole 1995; Pavlovic and Bowles 1996). Although late Holocene climate changes have been minor within the Indiana Dunes compared to those within other parts of the Great Lakes region (Davis et al. 2000; Bartlein, Webb, and Fleri 1984), they still may have been significant. Without a more complete historical record, it is impossible to separate the effects of natural successional processes, anthropogenic disturbances, and climatic change.

Olson (1958) identified plant nutrients such as nitrogen and organic matter as the primary limiting factor in dune succession. Thus, as organic matter and nutrients build up in the bare sand over thousands of years, the plant assemblages change. Recently, however, this natural process of soil development has been radically altered. The Indiana Dunes area currently receives among the highest rates of deposition in North America for nitrate, ammonium, sulfate, and calcium (National Atmospheric Deposition Program 1999). This "artificial fertilization" might result in fewer changes in rich soils, but on the newly formed bare dunes, it probably accelerates the natural successional processes. The increased atmospheric content of carbon dioxide probably also has a large, as yet undetermined, effect on successional processes. Because of these unprecedented atmospheric inputs into the natural systems, and the multiple anthropogenic disturbances, the currently developing plant assemblages of the Indiana Dunes may be unlike any that previously existed. Moreover, the current rapid rates of vegetation change do not seem to have any precedent (Cole 1995).

National Park Service Management of the Dunes

In 1916, Stephen T. Mather, then director of the newly created United States National Park Service (NPS), proposed the creation of a national park encompassing the Indiana Dunes. After decades of efforts, the area was finally protected as Indiana Dunes National Lakeshore in 1966.

The initial NPS surveys of the Indiana Dunes highlighted several areas in immediate need of focus for conservation. More than seven hundred private residences were included within the boundaries of the national lakeshore, and as those residences were removed, restoration plans were required to guide revegetation efforts and removal of the exotic species. In addition, many of the wetlands, which had been drained by ditches, were being taken over by exotic species. Restoration of the original hydrologic conditions was seen as a way to avert those changes. Finally, prairie areas were quickly turning into shrublands and forest because residents in adjacent developments had demanded control of the periodic wildfires.

Acknowledging these problems, park managers sought better data on the current trends of vegetation change and increased understanding of the variables driving the changes. Many initial efforts were focused on simply documenting current existing conditions, especially of wetland and prairie vegetation. After only a few years of sampling, it became evident that these systems were changing rapidly. Obtaining a greater scope of the history of the changes, and the variables likely to have initiated them, was one way to better understand them. As a result, historical and paleoecological studies were started, focusing on the wetland and prairie areas.

In particular, the managers wanted more detailed information on the effects of fire. They needed information on fire history of the dunes in order to guide the fire management plans. In 1984, NPS began an aggressive program of research burn studies to increase understanding of the effects of specific fire prescriptions. Several areas, including Howes Prairie and Inland Marsh, are now burned with fires of varying frequency and seasonality as part of that program.

Because of the multiple variables responsible for change in the system, no single historical or paleoecological technique was capable of reconstructing past and recent changes at all relevant scales of time and space. The research program was fortunate that several very different methods could be successfully employed within the area. Permanent monitoring plots had been established, and abundant vegetational surveys had been completed. Aerial photos had frequently been taken along the Lake Michigan shoreline by the USGS and in nearby agricultural areas by the Farm Service Agency (USDA, formerly ASCS). Detailed surveys of forest cover had been taken in 1834 by the GLO. The many wetlands preserved layered sedimentary records of fossil pollen and charcoal from the past.

Although each of the different methods has a unique scope in time and space, and produced different types of information, they do overlap in many instances. This allows for comparison among the techniques, which increases confidence in the results. Each method, and its result, will now be discussed in order, proceeding from the most recent time to further back into the past.

Late Twentieth Century: Fire Suppression and Rapid Vegetation Change

Vegetation changes of the late twentieth century can be documented using permanent vegetation plots and comparative photography. These data are detailed enough to allow quantification of trends and rates of change. Records often have sufficient detail to study annual variability in climate and species populations. The short-term consequences of various management techniques can also be seen in some records.

Permanent vegetation plots have been used throughout the Indiana Dunes to document this recent vegetation change. Although many were set up earlier, the most thoroughly resampled plots were studied by National Park Service personnel between about 1978 and 1995. Some plot clusters have been resampled as many as eight times over a sixteen-year period through an ongoing program now run by the USGS Lake Michigan Ecological Field Station. Most plots are located within areas that are now subjected to various prescribed burning schedules.

Permanent photo stations have been established at many of the staked plot locations. Each photo station yields photos taken from a tripod set at a constant height above a metal stake along established compass bearings (usually four—north, south, east, and west). While the detailed plot measurements are more quantitative, the comparative photographs provide a more graphic and convincing documentation of vegetation change.

These marked photo locations are essential in this quickly changing land-scape because of the absence of rocks or other permanent landmarks. The pace of vegetation change is so great that comparisons with older pho-tographs with only generalized locations are usually met with skepticism. The permanent photo stations are supplemented by a series of stereo aer-ial photos that have been taken at scales as detailed as 1 inch = 200 feet. This scale is fine enough that the loss of an individual shrub is evident.

The photo stations and aerial photographs show that forest succession at Indiana Dunes is proceeding quickly in areas with fire protection (fig-ure 15.1). Although black oak and white oak dominate the canopy and are still increasing in size, the next generation of mesophytic, fire-sensi-tive trees could be very different. The proportion of shade-tolerant–fire-intolerant species, such as black cherry (*Prunus serotina*) and witch hazel (*Hamamelis virginiana*), is increasing rapidly (figure 15.2). If these rates of change for individual species can be extrapolated into the future, com-munity structure will be very different in twenty to thirty years. These dramatic increases in shade-tolerant, woody species were not recorded in the recently burned portions of the study area (Cole, Benjamin, and Klick 1990).

Study plots subjected to prescribed fires of several frequencies demon-strated a thinning of the forest canopy and understory, and a resultant increase in the light levels required for prairie species (figure 15.3). Canopy black oaks were killed only by the most intense fire conditions—in the vortex of converging flame fronts in areas with several years of accumulated fuel. However, even comparatively light fires were sufficient to top-kill small oak saplings invading the prairie. These oak grubs remained to resprout the next year, but periodic fires keep them from shading the prairie.

Rapid changes in wet prairie vegetation are also recorded in both burned and unburned plots (figure 15.4). Woody species increased in abundance during dry years, such as 1987 and 1988, when a drought cen-tered around the Great Lakes states (Tilman and El Haddi 1992). Repeated fire was ineffective in salvaging the drying grassland during this drought. But the changes were most severe in unburned areas, and a return to wetter conditions in 1991 restored the wet prairies of the recently burned areas.

These results from the late-twentieth-century vegetation plots and photographs demonstrate the essential role of periodic fire in the mainte-nance of prairie and savanna. However, rapid change characterized plots both within and outside of the burn areas. These rapid changes raise the question of how long such changes have been occurring. Are these rapid

Figure 15.1. Early forest succession on an oak savanna in the absence of fire. Between 1986 and 1995 this oak forest developed from a thicket of saplings between taller canopy trees into a more open forest with little understory and nearly 100 percent canopy cover. The site probably last burned in 1965, as indicated by the ages of the multiple-stemmed oaks that resprouted following that fire.

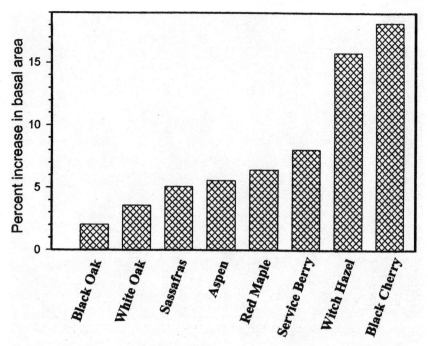

Figure 15.2. Bar graph of mean percent annual increase in basal area for the eight major tree species between 1985 and 1995 in a forest similar to that shown in figure 15.1. Fire-sensitive species are increasing at the fastest rates (adapted from Cole and Taylor 1995).

shifts a natural trend, natural variability, or something with no historical precedent?

Mid-Twentieth Century: Expansion of Oak Forest

Vegetation changes of the mid-twentieth century can be documented using early aerial photography, forest stand structure, and fire-scar analysis. Stereo aerial photographs (see chapter 5) of the Dunes are available, and they document changes since 1929. Although the early photographs are not very detailed, by 1959 the quality is high enough to locate single trees when the photos are viewed as stereo pairs. These aerial photographs form a valuable archive of past vegetation and other periodic events, such as fires and high-water events.

Robert Taylor and I compared aerial photographs from 1959 through 1987 and found an expansion of oak forest canopy into mesic prairie and savanna. Within the photographs shown in figure 15.5, the mesic prairie and savanna declined by 57 percent between 1959 and 1987 (Cole and

Figure 15.3. Thinning of an oak forest into an oak savanna. The 1984 photo shows the forest edge where a dense oak forest (formerly a savanna) abutted an open prairie. After five fires between 1986 and 1995, the forest canopy is now thinned and relictual prairie species between the trees are expanding.

Figure 15.4. Woody invasion of a wet prairie during a drought. In 1984 this area supported primarily wet and mesic prairie grasses. A severe drought in 1987 and 1988 lowered the water table levels. By 1995 populations of gray dogwood (*Cornus racemosa*), gooseberry (*Ribes* spp.), and prairie willow (*Salix humilis*), had expanded to dominate the area. Trembling aspen (*Populus tremuloides*) (foreground) had been top-killed by a 1983 high-water event but resprouted. Similar, but less intensive, invasions even occurred in frequently burned areas nearby, demonstrating that radical changes in the water table can have a stronger effect on vegetation change than fire.

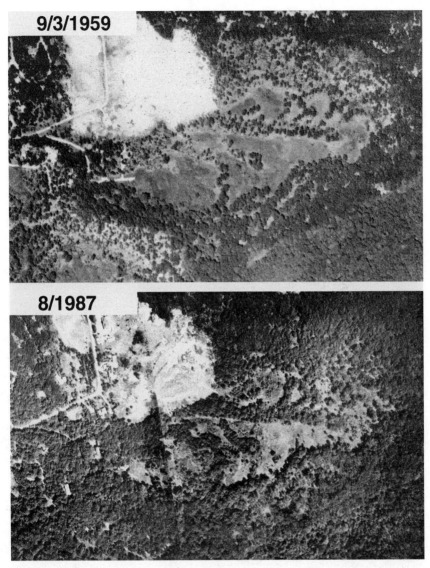

Figure 15.5. Comparison of aerial photographs from 1959 and 1987 showing the invasion of tree canopy into a prairie. Light gray areas are wet and mesic prairie. The white area (upper left of both photographs) is a dune blowout extending southward from the lake.

Taylor 1995). When combined with the analysis of fire effects at permanent plots, these results suggest that fewer fires occurred in the area between 1959 and 1987. This forest invasion occurred mostly in those areas higher than three feet above the typical spring high-water table. Additional data are needed to determine if this is a recent trend of the last three decades, a postsettlement trend of the last 150 years, or an even longer-term trend.

Twentieth-Century Fire Histories

The age structure of the forest trees was determined using increment cores of trees throughout the dunes (see chapter 8). Robert Taylor (1990) reconstructed the fire history using both fire-scar analysis of tree sections and the age structure of multiple-stemmed trees. The dominant trees surrounding the prairie—black oak, white oak, and sassafras (*Sassafras albidum*)—usually resprout with several stems following fire. Consequently, the age structure of multiple-stemmed trees preserves information on fire history in the form of cohorts of multiple-stemmed trees resulting from previous fires. These age structure data are most powerful when combined with fire dates obtained from fire scars on cut slabs of windthrown trees. The combination of methods—multiple-stemmed stand ages and imbedded fire-scar ages—increased the resolution of each (Taylor 1990).

Fire histories from throughout Indiana Dunes demonstrate the large range of fire frequencies and their resulting vegetational effects. Fire-return intervals during the twentieth century range from about two to fifty years. In general, the western dunes burn much more frequently. They are upwind from the higher humidity caused by the lake effect and are transected by numerous railroad lines. Malfunctioning brakes on the railcars create sparks that supply a constant source of ignition.

Isolated oak forests in the western dunes that are transected by railroad lines, such as in Miller Woods, have burned as frequently as they are capable of sustaining a fire, about every one to three years. Occasional dry periods in early spring before leaf-out (usually in April) cause this to be the most fire-prone period. These fires have created a very open savanna with scattered, fire-scarred oaks. The easterly portions of the dunes show evidence of one or no twentieth-century fires. These areas now support a very mesic oak forest with a total canopy cover.

The central dunes, which are the primary focus of this article, are intermediate in fire frequency. For the period between 1900 and 1972, Taylor (1990) calculated that the Howes Prairie and Inland Marsh areas had fire-return intervals of 4.6 and 5.1 years, respectively, based on a liberal interpretation of the data, and 6.9 and 6.0 years, respectively, based on a more conservative analysis (figure 15.6).

Unfortunately, the tendency for fire-scarred black oaks toward heart-rot within about one hundred years of age limited our tree-ring fire chronology to the twentieth century. Most ecologists presumed that the earliest twentieth-century fire frequencies were typical of presettlement

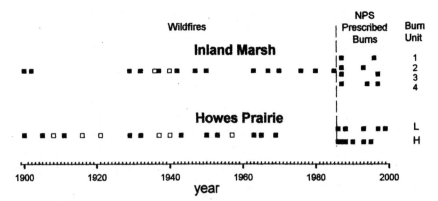

Figure 15.6. Fire histories of two areas on Nipissing-aged dunes (11 km apart). Open boxes indicate less certain date; closed boxes indicate more certain date (modified from Taylor 1990). Pre-1980 wildfires typically burnt entire areas, while recent NPS prescribed research burns covered only a portion of each area (prescribed burn schedule from Noel Pavlovic, written communication).

conditions. This seemed logical because the fire suppression efforts since about 1970 seemed the most likely cause for the resulting woody invasion of the prairies. Because of the lack of older trees, earlier records from other sources were considered.

Nineteenth Century: Catastrophic Fires and Logging of the Pine Forest

Historical changes that took place after the time of European settlement but before more detailed twentieth-century records are documented in historical writing (see chapter 3) and even in oral histories of long-lived residents (see chapter 4). Probably the most valuable documents of the historical era are the GLO surveys (Bourdo 1956; see chapter 6).

The study area was surveyed by the GLO survey in A.D. 1834. Records of forty-nine tree pairs from middle Holocene (Nipissing age) dunes near Lake Michigan were present in the GLO database. I compared these records with data from sixty 100-m² vegetation plots on similar-aged dunes to estimate the 1985 tree density. The comparison of the estimated 1834 tree density for the general area and the calculated 1985 tree density suggests that drastic changes occurred in both total density and species composition during the intervening 151 years (figure 15.7; Cole

TREE DENSITY: 1834 vs. 1985

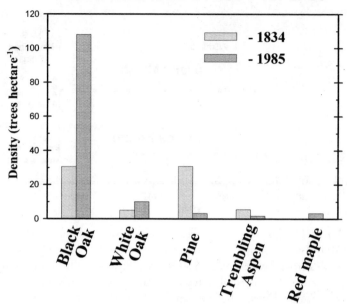

Figure 15.7. A comparison of tree density for trees exceeding five inches in diameter calculated from the A.D. 1834 General Land Office survey data and the A.D. 1985 vegetation sampling for selected taxa (modified from Cole and Taylor 1995).

and Taylor 1995). The total tree density increased from 168 to 329 trees/acre, with black oak responsible for most of the increase. Other species also increased—primarily white oak and red maple (*Acer rubrum*). The density of pine decreased from 77 to 7 trees/acre. Because almost all of the trees used in the GLO survey exceeded ten inches in diameter, most of the pines recorded were probably eastern white pine, rather than the smaller jack pine. Many jack pines are recorded along the shoreline in early photographs, and much reduced stands are still located along undisturbed portions of the shoreline. "Ghost forests" of older dead trees exposed in dune blowouts are almost exclusively white pine.

Written histories of the Indiana Dunes region mention the early logging efforts within the dunes (Moore 1977; Cook and Jackson 1978). However, this logging period, which came earlier than the massive logging efforts that occurred in northern Wisconsin or upper Michigan, was more localized to smaller pine stands. As a result, there is a far less recognized history. But within the local historical records the effects of the logging era were significant. For example, this item appeared in a 1949 newspaper from Valparaiso, Indiana:

Visiting Porter County Dunes are Mr. and Mrs. Freeman E. Morgan Jr. of Takoma Park, Md. Lansing Morgan, a lumberman, purchased eight miles of dune land from the U.S. in 1850 for 30 cents an acre for the stands of white pine. The area purchased encompasses the present Dunes State Park and Beverly Shores. Morgan shipped lumber from his yard to Chicago. ("Looking Back," *Vidette-Messenger,* 1949)

Only a few white pines remain today in the protected Dunes State Park, and almost none survive within Beverly Shores. Logging is probably not the only reason that this once codominant species has been decimated. Growth of seedlings into saplings around the few persisting trees is very rare. Apical meristems of seedlings are quickly eaten during winter by an abundant population of white-tailed deer (*Odocoileus virginianus*). The region also has one of the highest ambient ozone levels in North America, further reducing the vigor of white pine. The final injury preventing the recovery of the white pine stands could be plant succession, but longer-term records are needed to investigate that possibility.

Presettlement and Paleoecological Changes

Sediment cores have provided paleoecological records of fossil pollen (see chapter 9) and charcoal from several marshes and ponds within the dunes (Futyma 1985; Jackson, Futyma, and Wilcox 1988; Cole et al. 1990; Cole and Taylor 1995). The cores were aged using radiocarbon dating, ^{210}Pb dating, and historical changes in pollen spectra.

The results from three sediment cores are shown in figure 15.8. The depth of the horizon at which regional settlement by Anglo-Europeans occurred can be determined by the increase in ragweed (*Ambrosia* spp.) pollen resulting from the proliferation of these weedy species in newly cleared fields between A.D. 1840 and 1855 (Cole et al. 1990). Other indicators of industrialized settlement at this horizon are (1) the reduction of remaining pine stands by logging, (2) the increase in industrial fly ash particles, and (3) the increase in mulberry (probably *Morus alba*), an introduced European species (figure 15.8a).

The two cores from mid-Holocene aged dunes (figures 15.8a and b) both demonstrate a shift from pine-dominated forests to oak and grass several thousand years ago. Thus, these paleoecological studies support the long-term successional replacement of pine forests by oak forests, as was predicted by the dune chronosequence studies of Cowles (1899) and Olson (1958). This threshold between pine and oak is likely a one-way barrier. Now that oaks and fire-spreading prairie species dominate the dunes, it is unlikely that any restoration of the pine forests could succeed without the removal of some soil and plant species in the replanting area.

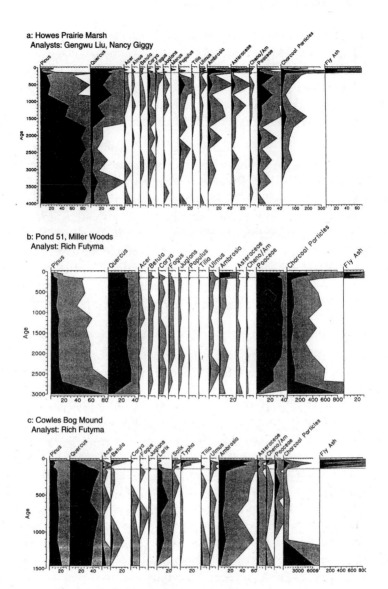

Figure 15.8. Fossil pollen and charcoal taken from three sediment cores within the Indiana Dunes. (a) A 4,000-year core from a mesic prairie surrounded by an oak savanna (modified from Cole and Taylor 1995). (b) A 3,000-year core of an interdunal pond from a savanna area with frequent fires (modified from Jackson, Futyma, and Wilcox 1988; Futyma 1985). (c) A 1,500-year core from a cedar mound surrounded by Cowles Bog (now a cattail marsh and red maple swamp) (modified from Cole et al. 1990). Pollen taxa are quantified in percent of the total terrestrial pollen for each level with the patterned area showing a 5x exaggeration. Dashed line near top shows settlement horizon at about A.D. 1850.

These fire-adapted oaks and prairie species constitute a "guild of arsonists" (Poulson 1999) that facilitate and can survive fires (although above-ground growth is trimmed back). Deer would also have to be excluded from the area until the pine saplings exceeded their browsing height.

Time-Based Restoration Perspectives

Restoration goals are shaped by our understanding of the past and how we interpret "natural" ecosystems. In this case study, the most definitive data on change comes from the last fifty years. During this period, fire suppression and the resulting sudden explosion in woody plant species dominate the record of vegetation change. These changes are proceeding rapidly enough (figure 15.4) to scare even the most conservative land manager.

As a result of previous observations and studies, the National Park Service has been conducting a broad program of fire research and management burns. Fire effects also continue to be monitored and studied through an ongoing USGS research program testing the consequences of varying fire frequency and seasonality. Considering the pace of ongoing changes and their likely links to fire suppression, this program is essential life support for many rare prairie species.

A longer-term perspective on settlement impacts and their effects on "natural" ecosystems during the last two hundred years supports many aspects of the recent perspective. The recent rapid increase in oaks is obvious in both the GLO data (figure 15.7) and the pollen data (figure 15.8). These results further support the need for continued fire management, but they also suggest that other causes, in addition to fire exclusion, are contributing factors in these rapid changes.

The disappearance of white pine from the dunes is obvious in both the GLO and the pollen records. Historical written records further document the removal of pine stands by logging. It is obvious that these pine forests have declined drastically, yet no restoration efforts are even being considered. Nineteenth-century data from fossil pollen, GLO, and written records may be too remote to dictate costly and manipulative management actions. Also, the natural successional pathway away from pine and toward oak and mesophytic assemblages may have crossed a threshold that can be reversed only through the most heroic (and expensive) of management actions. Finally, because the removal of pine seems to be a fait accompli, rather than an immediate crisis, there is far less incentive for action.

Unfortunately, from a genetic perspective, the preservation of these few remaining white pines could be viewed as an imminent crisis. These few trees represent the last vestige of a population that was near the southernmost limit of the species in the Great Lakes states (Little 1971).

They could possibly contain genetic characteristics that would be useful in the warming future. Other species that may have formerly been associated with this pine forest are also very limited. For example, the population of bunchberry (*Cornus canadensis*), a typical associate in white pine forests around the Great Lakes, consists of only forty-one individuals in two small groups within the Indiana Dunes (Wilhelm 1990).

The unrealized prospect of white pine restoration raises basic questions about management goals. It is clear that large white pine stands were present prior to settlement and were eliminated by the actions of an industrialized society. However, the replacement of pine stands with oak forest also seems to be a "natural" successional process, albeit one that has been greatly accelerated through anthropogenic disturbances. If the management goal is to return the landscape to its presettlement character, then restoration of these pine forests needs to be part of the restoration. However, if the goal is merely to retain natural successional processes (regardless of their rate), then we may have already achieved it.

Another prominent feature of the nineteenth-century fossil records is the evidence for the catastrophic fires that occurred in the early phases of settlement and into the late nineteenth century. Except for two samples at the bottom of figures 15.8b and c, all sediment cores taken thus far within the dunes reach their highest charcoal levels during this late-nineteenth-century period. Historic records also document tremendous fires and drainage of wetlands during this period. Furthermore, the first of many railroad lines around the south end of the dunes was completed in 1852 (Moore 1977; Cook and Jackson 1978). Live sparks from steam locomotives were dropped into the newly drained wetlands, and catastrophic fires engulfed the landscape, setting the stage for the eventual dominance of the more fire-tolerant oaks on the uplands once the fires ceased.

The trapping of beaver also increased the development of woody forests in what had been wet prairies and marshes. The ditching of wetlands and the elimination of blockages in natural drainages were also essential parts of the region's residential and industrial development. Sedge meadows, such as Cowles Bog, were also farmed for "hay" produced by the sedges. These meadows are now being invaded by cattails (*Typha latifolia*) (figure 15.8c) as well as common reed (*Phragmites australis*) (Wilcox, Apfelbaun, and Hiebert 1984).

The high water tables that were typical of these dunes cannot be restored without significant flooding of adjacent residential areas. Indiana Dunes National Lakeshore has recently consolidated a small watershed within the dunes (Derby Ditch) and has restored its drainage to a presettlement condition. Future monitoring of this watershed will demonstrate the feasibility of restoration of these wetlands.

Recent Rates of Vegetation Change

The integration of data across several historical scales allows a more complete understanding of vegetation dynamics by setting short-term trends into a larger perspective. The changes in canopy cover and tree density during the last 150 years contrast dramatically with the slow changes recorded in the pollen diagrams over the last four thousand years (figure 15.9; Cole 1995; see Jacobson and Grimm 1986 for methods). Thus, the integration across these timescales dramatizes the extreme magnitude of recent and (by extrapolation) ongoing rates of change.

The extreme rate of change now occurring within the Indiana Dunes has usually been attributed to fire exclusion, and there is little doubt that that is one cause. But other major changes such as logging, the intensive burning of the late nineteenth century, and the invasion of exotic species have increased the rates of change. In addition, the area has a high depositional rate for nitrate and sulfate ions, which is likely helping to accelerate the other changes. Artificial fertilization may be the primary

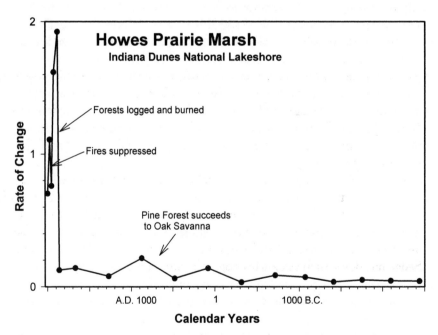

Figure 15.9. Rates of vegetation change in an oak savanna during different time periods as reconstructed by multivariate analyses of changes for plant taxa in the record based on fossil pollen from tree species. Values on the rate-of-change axis are derived from distance between samples in the four primary dimensions of a Decorana ordination divided by the years between samples (modified from Cole 1995; see Jacobson and Grimm 1986 for methods).

factor accelerating succession trends leading to the recent rapid terrestrial changes shown in figures 15.2, 15.4, 15.8, and 15.9. The increase in cattails seen in Cowles Bog (figure 15.8c) is very similar to changes occurring in wetlands receiving nutrient-rich agricultural runoff.

These data should serve as a caution against extrapolating permanent plot data from this century to earlier time periods and "natural" processes of change. The initial surveys from earlier in this century are not representative of presettlement conditions, and the recent rates of change observed are not representative of presettlement rates of change. Successional patterns observed on postsettlement dune chronosequences have been greatly altered from any "natural" presettlement patterns (Jackson, Futyma, and Wilcox 1988), casting suspicion on some previous successional studies (Shelford 1911).

Summary.

This case study demonstrates the integration of several types of data on vegetation change ranging in scale from annual to millennial. Although different changes characterize different time periods, these past changes coalesce into the present pace and direction of change. For example, although the suppression of fire during the last fifty years is now leading to rapid increases in closed-canopy forest, the foundation for this increase may have been laid during the late-nineteenth-century period of intense fires, which, along with logging and drainage, disrupted the natural plant assemblages and replaced them with the more fire-tolerant oak forest. Thus, variables of change, such as fire and water, can transform landscapes in complex directions depending on the timing and severity of the changes.

The integration of these historical studies also illustrates some different variables operating upon dramatically different timescales. Long-term variables, such as soil development, integrate with medium-term variables, such as plant migration and competition. Short-term variables, including individual fire events and annual water levels, can also have dramatic effects. Climate, meanwhile, can drive a system at all scales, but may or may not be the predominant variable.

Acknowledgments

Noel Pavlovic of the USGS Lake Michigan Field Station assisted with many aspects of this research and provided information on the ongoing fire management programs and building the GLO database. Fossil pollen identification and counting was completed by Richard Futyma, Geng-wu Liu, and Nancy Giggy. Numerous other personnel worked on aspects of the project over a fifteen-year period, including Robert Taylor, Kenneth

Klick, Pam Benjamin, Wanda Manek, Mark Englebright, and Sandy Whistler. This chapter was critically reviewed by Noel Pavlovic and Thomas Poulson. This research was funded by the National Park Service, the National Biological Service, and the U.S. Geological Survey.

References

Bartlein, P.J., T. Webb, and E. Fleri. 1984. Holocene climatic change in the northern Midwest: Pollen derived estimates. *Quaternary Research* 22:361–374.

Bourdo, E. 1956. A review of the General Land Office survey and of its use in quantitative studies of former forests. *Ecology* 37:754–768.

Bowles, M.L., M.M. DeMauro, N. Pavlovic, and R.D. Hiebert. 1990. Effects of anthropogenic disturbances on endangered and threatened plants at the Indiana Dunes National Lakeshore. *Natural Areas Journal* 13:164–176.

Cole, K.L. 1995. Vegetation change in national parks. Pages 224–227 in *Our living resources 1994: A report to the nation on the distribution, abundance, and health of U.S. plants, animals, and ecosystems*, ed. E.T. LaRow, G.S. Farris, C.E. Pucket, and P.B. Doran. Washington, D.C.: National Biological Service.

Cole, K.L., P. Benjamin, and K. Klick. 1990. The effects of prescribed burning on oak woods and prairies in the Indiana Dunes. *Restoration and Management Notes* 8:37–38.

Cole, K.L., D.E. Engstrom, R. Futyma, and R. Stottlemyer. 1990. Atmospheric deposition of metals in northern Indiana measured using a peat core from Cowles Bog. *Environmental Science and Technology* 24:543–549.

Cole, K.L., and R.P. Taylor. 1995. Past and current trends of change in a dune prairie/oak savanna reconstructed through a multiple-scale history. *Journal of Vegetation Science* 6:399–410.

Cook, S.G., and R.S. Jackson. 1978. *The Bailly Area of Porter County, Indiana*. Report to the Indiana Dunes National Lakeshore. Porter, Ind.

Cowles, H.C. 1899a. Review of "Pflanzengeographie auf physiologischer Grundlage," by A.F.W. Schimper. *Botanical Gazette* 27:214–216.

———. 1899b. The ecological relations of the vegetation on the sand dunes of Lake Michigan. *Botanical Gazette* 27:95–117, 167–202, 281–308, 361–391.

———. 1901. The phytosociological ecology of Chicago and vicinity: A study of origin, development, and classification of plant societies. *Botanical Gazette* 31:73–108.

Davis, M.B., C. Douglas, R. Calcote, K. Cole, M. Winkler, and R. Flakne. 2000. Holocene climate in the western Great Lakes National Parks and Lakeshores: Implications for future climate change. *Conservation Biology* 14:968–983.

Delcourt, H.R., P.A. Delcourt, and T. Webb. 1982. Dynamic plant ecology: The spectrum of vegetational change in space and time. *Quaternary Science Reviews* 1:153–175.

Futyma, R.P. 1985. Paleobotanical studies at Indiana Dunes National Lakeshore. Unpublished report to Indiana Dunes National Lakeshore. Porter, Ind.

Jackson, S.T., R.P. Futyma, and D.A. Wilcox. 1988. A paleoecological test of a classical hydrosere in the Lake Michigan Dunes. *Ecology* 69:92–936.

Jacobson, G.L., and E.C. Grimm. 1986 A numerical analysis of Holocene forest and prairie vegetation in central Minnesota. *Ecology* 67:958–966.

Larsen, C. 1985. Stratigraphic study of beach features on the southwestern shore of Lake Michigan—New evidence of Holocene lake level fluctuations. *Environmental Geology Notes* No. 112. Champaign: Illinois Geological Survey.

Little, E.L. 1971. *Atlas of United States Trees*, Volume 1: Conifers and important hardwoods. Miscellaneous Publication No. 1146. Washington, D.C.: USDA Forest Service

Looking Back. 1949. *Vidette-Messenger*. Valparaiso, Ind.

Maun, M.A. 1993. Dry coastal ecosystems along the Great Lakes. Pages 299–316 in *Dry coastal ecosystems*, part 2B, ed. E. van der Maarel. Amsterdam: Elsevier.

McIntosh, R.P. 1999. The succession of sucessions: A lexical chronology. *Bulletin of the Ecological Society of America* 80:256–264.

Moore, P.A. 1977. *The Calumet region: Indiana's last frontier.* Indianapolis: Indiana Historical Bureau.

National Atmospheric Deposition Program (NRSP-3)/National Trends Network. 1999. Isopleth maps of national precipitation chemistry available for 1994 through 1998 at nadp.sws.uiuc.edu/isopleths/.

Olson, J.S. 1958. Rates of succession and soil changes on southern Lake Michigan sand dunes. *Botanical Gazette* 119:125–170.

Pavlovic, N.B., and M.L. Bowles. 1996. Rare plant monitoring at Indiana Dunes National Lakeshore. Pages 253–280 in *Science and ecosystem management in the national parks*, eds. W.L. Halvorson and G.E. Davis. Tucson: University of Arizona Press.

Poulson, T.L. 1999. Autogenic, allogenic, and individualistic mechanisms of dune succession at Miller, Indiana. *Natural Areas Journal* 19:172–176.

Shelford, V.E. 1911. Ecological succession. II. Pond fishes. *Biological Bulletin* 14:9–14.

Taylor, R.S. 1990. Reconstruction of twentieth century fire histories in black oak savannas of the Indiana Dunes National Lakeshore. Master's thesis, University of Wisconsin, Madison.

Tilman, D., and A. El Haddi. 1992. Drought and biodiversity in grasslands. *Oecologia* 89:257–264.

Transeau, E.N. 1935. The prairie peninsula. *Ecology* 16:424–437.

Warming, E. 1909. *Oecology of plants*. Oxford, England: Clarendon Press.

Wilcox, D., S.I. Apfelbaum, and R.D. Hiebert. 1984. Cattail invasion of sedge meadows following hydrologic disturbance in the Cowles Bog Wetland Complex, Indiana Dunes. *Wetlands* 4:115–128.

Wilhelm, G.S. 1990. *Report on the Special Vegetation of the Indiana Dunes National Lakeshore*. Indiana Dunes National Lakeshore Research Report 90–02. Porter, Ind. National Park Service.

16

Implementing the Archaeo-environmental Reconstruction Technique:

Rediscovering the Historic Ground Layer of Three Plant Communities in the Greater Grand Canyon Region

Thom Alcoze and Matt Hurteau

Determining reference conditions is a central theme in authentic ecological restoration (Higgs 1997; White and Walker 1997). This means that restorationists must determine the ecological conditions that were present on a site prior to the disruption of the historic ecological conditions and identify the possible causes of the degradation. Obtaining reliable information about reference conditions requires the restorationist to examine both spatial and temporal aspects of the ecosystem being studied. A thorough study of the natural range of variability characteristic of an ecosystem and the variability of that ecosystem over time provides a general framework and working definition for determining reference conditions (Aplet and Keeton 1999). However, the specific limits of these variability parameters range from verifiable details based on scientific research to generalizations derived from direct observations and interpretation.

To solve the problems inherent in this kind of work, we developed a data collection and analysis process—called the Archaeo-environmental Reconstruction Technique (ART)—to help us reconstruct the reference conditions of our project site in the Greater Grand Canyon region (GGCR). These multiple databases extend the information made possible through methods now used to reconstruct historic reference conditions and provide additional ways to triangulate evidence, thus making the resulting data more complex and detailed.

In this chapter we will discuss the events in our research that led to the design of ART, and the analysis of the data collected by this method. First, we will present data gleaned from traditional methods to reconstruct reference conditions for three ecosystems in the GGCR. Then we will present a rationale for using additional methods to examine these ecosystems. We will identify the methods that ART comprises and present the data we collected using this methodology. Finally, we will discuss the conclusions of this study, present the species lists we developed using ART, and discuss the implications of those conclusions for further research.

The original intent of our research was to identify the historic species composition of three plant communities—ponderosa pine, pinyon-juniper, and sagebrush grassland—that occurred in the GGCR between A.D. 800 and the time of European settlement, approximately 1870. In particular, we were interested in determining the species composition of the understory of these communities. Such a study had heretofore not been done, although research by Wallace Covington and his colleagues (1997) suggested that the understory of these plant communities had high levels of diversity. One reason for the lack of knowledge about understory species is that, unlike overstory species that live for centuries and leave obvious and identifiable evidence of their presence on the historic landscape, understory species rarely leave a record of their historic occurrence. This is especially true when ecosystem processes such as decomposition, fire, and erosion decrease the likelihood that evidence will be preserved.

Data Gleaned from Traditional Methods

We know that ecological conditions in present-day ponderosa pine, pinyon-juniper, and sagebrush grasslands have changed dramatically since European settlement. Numerous references by explorers and early travelers provide a qualitative description of the historic sagebrush grasslands of the GGCR (Stoffle and Evans 1978; Lavender 1984). Early descriptions and records of the GGCR consistently include comments about the extent and high quality of grasslands, noting the diverse composition of grasses, forbs, and shrubs. Accounts of fires similar to those reported in nearby savanna-like ponderosa pine and pinyon-juniper plant communities are also included in these early records. Today these grasslands, if they exist at all, are overrun with sagebrush and other shrubs and are encroached upon by pinyon pine (*Pinus edulis*) and juniper trees (*Juniperus osteosperma*). For example, Gumerman (1988) points out that overgrazing in the Hopi Buttes District has allowed snakeweed (*Gutierrezia sarothrae*) and other unpalatable species to take over what were once diverse grasslands. During the last century, present-day ponderosa pine and pinyon-juniper communities have become characterized by increased tree densities, diminished diversity, lower densities of understory species, high fuel loads, and greater susceptibility to disease and catastrophic fire. The species composition for overstory components of these historic ecosystems is determined from analysis of snags, logs, and stumps. Understory species composition for these ecosystems could not be determined with certainty. Analysis of paired photographs (see chapter 5) reveals dramatic changes in ground-layer vegetation from historic times to the present. When contrasted with photographs as recent as the 1940s, contemporary photographs reveal major changes in the density of the ground-layer plants and the encroachment of overstory species in historic grasslands.

A Rationale for Using Additional Methods

We recognized that there is substantial information about the Native Americans of the desert Southwest, who are described as opportunistic in their harvest and use of regional vegetation types (Hawks 1998). In short, Native Americans in this region are known to have harvested any plants of nutritional or utilitarian value, making extensive use of the diversity available to them in the environment. Lavender (1997) notes that the people of the Southern Paiute nation, in particular, are also known for their sophisticated use of frequent low-intensity fires. Furthermore, ethnobotanical data compiled in part through archaeological site reconstruction on Native American lands identify species composition and land management cultural practices of various indigenous peoples of the GGCR (Whiting 1939; Wyman and Harris 1951; Bright 1992; Elmore 1944). The reports of plant and animal remains associated with these site reconstructions, in addition to data from pollen analysis and analysis of packrat middens provide other data sources for the study of the historic environmental conditions of the GGCR.

To summarize, we recognized a need to (1) gather data about historic reference conditions from a wider variety of sources than is currently being used to inform restoration projects; (2) extend data collection to ethnobotanic, archaeological, and cultural databases; and (3) depend on these diverse databases to provide triangulation for thematic and specific evidence of historic reference conditions. We devised a systematic technique to examine research from primary and secondary archaeological sites, ethnobotanical records, and historical documents, a technique we now term the ART.

Once we had resolved these issues, we established a baseline or reference list for the historic species composition of ponderosa pine, pinyon-juniper, and sagebrush-grassland ecosystems in the GGCR. We obtained data on plant community composition from three primary archaeological sites. The archaeological studies provided evidence in the form of pollen (see chapter 9), macro- and microfossils (see chapter 13), and human coprolites, or fossilized human fecal matter (Williams-Dean and Bryant

1975) to identify plant species present in the region in the past. At seven secondary sites, we obtained additional information on the historic understory species composition of the GGCR from packrat middens (see chapter 10) and animal scat analysis. These methods helped identify plant species that were present prior to European settlement but were not used by Native Americans.

Ethnobotanical records for the Navajo, Kayenta Navajo, Hopi, and Southern Paiute nations and other historical documents containing species inventories of the region provided additional historical species composition data. We collected this information from the Museum of Northern Arizona and from library holdings at Northern Arizona University (NAU) in Flagstaff. The records from archaeological excavations were especially valuable because they involved ethnobotanists who were working to reconstruct the cultural practices of the indigenous peoples (see chapter 2). Their work identified plant remains associated with specific sites.

From this evidence we were able to discern that indigenous people harvested an extensive array of natural resources from the region and practiced landscape-scale management that maintained a high diversity of plants and animals in the region. They used plant species for a variety of purposes, including food, medicine, rituals, and construction materials.

After compiling an initial list representing the historic understory species composition for the GGCR from the archaeological data and ethnobotanical records, we compared this list with contemporary reference materials that identify native plant species currently present in Arizona and Utah. The purpose of this comparison was to refine the reconstructed species list to reflect current taxonomic changes. Botanists from NAU and the Bureau of Land Management assisted the project by making revisions to the list, including name changes and identification of exotic species.

Conclusions

The ART used in this study yielded an initial species list that represents a composite of all ecosystems of the GGCR—a total of 446 species representing 279 genera. We then refined this list to categorize the three major plant communities of the GGCR. This effort resulted in four categorical divisions. The species were divided into categories representing ponderosa pine, pinyon-juniper, sagebrush grasslands, and species occurring in two or more of the identified ecosystems.

The historic ponderosa pine forest contained 17 species specific to ponderosa pine ecosystems of the GGCR (see table 16.1). Contained in this list were 53 species that occurred in ponderosa pine and at least one of the other plant communities. Of the 70 species that occurred in the

Table 16.1. Species occurring in the ponderosa pine ecosystem

Species	Common Name	Ecosystem
Abies concolor	white fir	PP
Acer glabrum	Rocky Mountain maple	PP, Riparian
Asplenium trichomanes	maidenhair spleenwort	PP
Bromus ciliatus	fringed brome	PP
Chrysothamnus vaseyi		PP
Cryptantha spp.		PP
Gentiana barbellata		PP, Alpine
Lathyrus arizonicus	Arizona peavine	PP, Alpine
Lazula parviflora	small flower woodrush	PP/streams
Lupinus lyallii	lyall lupine	PP, Alpine
Orogenia linearifolia	Indian potato	PP
Pedicularis parryi		PP
Pinus ponderosa	ponderosa pine	PP
Populus tremuloides	quaking aspen	PP
Prunus emarginata		
var. *emarginata*	bitter cherry	PP
Verbascum thapsus	mullein	PP
Zygadenus elegans		PP

historic ponderosa pine ecosystem, 5 were overstory species and 65 were understory species.

The historic pinyon-juniper woodlands contained 21 species specific to that ecosystem (see table 16.2). There were 111 species that occurred in the pinyon-juniper woodlands and at least one of the other plant communities. Of the 132 species that occurred in the historic pinyon-juniper ecosystem, 10 were overstory species and 122 were understory species.

The list for historic sagebrush grasslands contained 51 species specific to that ecosystem in the GGCR (see table 16.3), and 102 species that occurred in the sagebrush grasslands and at least one of the other plant communities (see table 16.4).

These lists demonstrate that the diversity in these historic plant communities was greatest among understory species. For example, the overstory species characteristic of the historic ponderosa pine ecosystem of the GGCR represented 7.1 percent of the total species composition, while the understory species represented 92.9 percent of the total species composition. Similarly, the overstory species characteristic of the historic pinyon-juniper ecosystem of the GGCR represented 7.5 percent of the total species composition, while understory species represented 92.5 percent of the total species composition.

The ART also revealed 30 plant species that do not occur in the modern vegetation reference lists for Arizona and Utah. At the present time,

Table 16.2. Species occurring in the pinyon-juniper ecosystem

Species	Common Name	Ecosystem
Agave utahensis	Utah agave	PJ
Agave utahensis var. *kaibabensis*	Utah century plant	PJ
Cryptantha fulvocanescens	tawny catseye	PJ
Juniperus californica utahensis	Utah juniper	PJ
Juniperus communis	common juniper	PJ
Juniperus deppeana	alligator juniper	PJ
Juniperus monosperma	oneseed juniper	PJ
Juniperus occidentalis	Sierra juniper	PJ
Juniperus osteosperma	Utah juniper	PJ
Juniperus pachyploea		PJ
Juniperus virginiana	eastern redcedar	PJ
Lycurus phleoides	wolftail	PJ
Phoradendron juniperinum	juniper American-mistletoe	PJ
Physalis fendleri		PJ
Psilostrophe sparsiflora	paperflower	PJ
Tragia stylaris		PJ
Yucca angustifolia		PJ
Yucca angustissima	narrow leaf yucca	PJ
Yucca baccata	datil yucca	PJ
Yucca elata	soaptree yucca	PJ
Yucca glauca	small soapweed	PJ

further analysis is necessary to establish with certainty whether these species are, in fact, absent from the contemporary landscape or represent potentially threatened or sensitive species. The comparison between the list produced using the ART method and modern floral lists also led us to conclude that with few exceptions, the reconstructed historic species composition represents a relatively complete list of the actual plant assemblages of the GGCR.

Implications

We believe that the integrative use of archaeological data with ethnobotanical and historic documents to determine the species composition of historic ecosystems is an example of successfully establishing reference conditions. Prior to implementation of the ART, the goals for restoration projects in the GGCR were based on inferences about ecosystem structure and function obtained from historic photographic evidence, documents from explorers and settlers, and limited scientific research. However, reconstructions of ecological conditions that rely solely on data sets from these and related traditional sources are typically limited to broad generalizations about ecosystem structure. The ART provides multiple, intersecting lines of evidence that can be cross-referenced to assess the accuracy and consistency of data and thus provide more reliable conclu-

Table 16.3. Species occurring in the sagebrush-grassland ecosystem

Species	Common Name	Ecosystem
Agrotis palustris	bent grass	Grass
Amelanchier pallida		Grass
Amelanchier prunifolia	redbud serviceberry	Grass
Amelanchier utahensis	serviceberry	Grass, Riparian
Aristida glauca		Grass
Aristida longiseta		Grass
Aristida pupurea	three-awn	Grass
Aster spinosus	devilweed aster	Grass
Astragalus kentrophyta	vetch	Grass
Astragalus mortoni	Morton loco (milkvetch)	Grass, Riparian
Astragalus sesquiflorus	milk vetch	Grass
Bouteloua hirsuta	hairy grama	Grass
Calamovilfa gigantea	big sandreed	Grass
Calochortus aureus	golden sego lily mariposa	Grass
Calochortus nuttallii	sego lily	Grass
Cercis occidentalis	California redbud	Grass, Riparian
Chrysothamnus greenei	greene rabbitbrush	Grass
Cirsium lanceolatum	bull thistle	Grass
Cirsium ochrocentrum	yellow spring thistle	Grass
Cirsium pulchellum		Grass
Encelia farinosa	brittle bush, incienso	Grass
Enneapogon desvauxii	spike pappusgrass	Grass
Ericameria laricifolia	turpentine bush	Grass
Fraxinus cuspidata	fragrant ash	Grass
Gaillardia pinnatifida	blanket flower	Grass
Larrea spp.		Grass
Lithospermum incisum	narrow leaf gromwell	Grass
Lycium andersonii	Anderson wolfberry	Grass
Machaeranthera pinnatifida	lacy tansymustard	Grass
Monarda fistulosa	wildbergamot beebalm	Grass
Monarda menthaefolia	mintleaf beebalm	Grass
Monarda pectinata	pony beebalm	Grass
Monarda puncata	spotted beebalm	Grass
Muhlenbergia pungens	sandhill muhly	Grass
Nama hispida		Grass
Parosela terminalis		Grass
Parryella filifolia	parryella	Grass
Pectis angustifolia		Grass
Pericome caudata	taper leaf, yerba del chivato	Grass
Plantago purshii	wooly Indian wheat	Grass
Poliomintha incana	wild rosemary mint, wild basil	Grass
Prosopis chilensis	common mesquite	Grass
Ricinus communis	common castorbean	Grass
Sonchus asper	prickly sowthistle	Grass
Sporobolus flexuosus	mesa dropseed	Grass
Sporobolus giganteus	giant dropseed	Grass
Thelesperma megapotamicum	Hopi tea greenthread	Grass
Tribulus terrestris	puncture vine	Grass
Tridens pulchellus		Grass
Verbena bracteata	prostrate vervain	Grass
Xanthium strumarium var. *canadense*	Canada cockleburr	Grass

Table 16.4. Species occurring in two or more ecosystems

Species	Common Name	Ecosystem
Amelanchier alnifolia	Saskatoon serviceberry	PJ, Grass
Artemisia filifolia	sand sagebrush	Grass, PJ
Artemisia frigida	fringed sagebrush	Grass, PJ, PP
Artemisia tridentata	big sagebrush	PJ, PP
Artemisia trifida		Grass, PJ
Asclepias hallii	Hall's milkweed	Grass, PJ, PP
Asclepias verticillata	whorled milkweed	Grass, PJ, PP
Asclepiodora decumbens	spider antelopehorn	PJ, PP
Aster abatus		Grass, PJ
Aster canescens	hoary aster	Grass, PJ
Bouteloua curtipendula	sideoats grama	Grass, PJ
Bouteloua gracilis	blue grama	Grass, PJ, PP
Brickellia grandiflora petiolaris	tasselflower brickellia	Grass, PJ, PP
Castilleja angustifolia	northwestern painted cup	Grass, PJ
Ceanothus fendleri	Fendler ceanothus	PP, Grass
Cercocarpus montanus	true mountain mahogany	Grass, PJ, PP
Chaetopappa ericoides	babywhite aster	Grass, PJ
Chamaebatiaria millifolium	fernbush	Grass, PJ, PP
Chrysopsis hispidum		Grass, PJ
Chrysopsis villosa	hairy goldaster	Grass, PJ
Chrysothamnus nauseosus albicaulis	rubber rabbitbrush	Grass, PJ, PP
Chrysothamnus nauseosus graveolens	greenplume rabbitbrush	Grass, PJ, PP
Cirsium neomexicanum		Grass, PJ
Cordylanthus ramosus	bushy birdbeak	Grass, PJ
Cordylanthus wrightii	Wright birdbeak	Grass, PJ, PP
Cryptantha confertifolia	golden cryptantha	Grass, PJ
Cystopteris fragilis	brittle bladderfern	PJ, PP
Datura meteloides	sacred datura	Grass, PJ
Ephedra nevadensis	Nevada Mormon tea	Grass, PJ
Ephedra torreyana	Torrey Mormon tea	Grass, PJ
Ephedra viridus	green ephedra	Grass, PJ, PP
Ericameria nauseosa var. *latisquamea*	heath goldenrod	Grass, PJ
Erigeron canadensis	horseweed fleabane	Grass, PJ
Erigeron divergens	spreading fleabane	Grass, PJ, PP
Eriodictyon spp.		Grass, PJ
Eupatorium occidentale	western eupatorium	Grass, PJ
Euphorbia robusta	Rocky Mountain spurge	Grass, PJ, PP
Fallugia paradoxa	Apache plume	Grass, PJ
Fendlera rupicola	cliff fendlerbush	Grass, PJ
Festuca ovina var. *brevifolia*		Grass, PJ, PP
Frasera speciosa	showy frasera	Grass, PJ
Gentiana heterosepala		Grass, PP (wet)
Geranium caespitosum	purple cranesbill	Grass, PJ, PP
Gilia aggregata attenuata	skyrocket gilia	Grass, PJ
Gilia longiflora		Grass, PJ
Haplopappus armeriodes	thrift mock goldenweed	Grass, PJ
Hedeoma drummondii	Drummond false pennyroyal	Grass, PJ
Helenium hoopesii	orange sneezeweed	Grass, PJ, PP

Table 16.4. (*continued*)

Species	Common Name	Ecosystem
Helianthus annus	common sunflower	Grass, PJ, PP
Helianthus nuttallii		Grass, PJ
Hordeum jubatum	foxtail barley	Grass, PJ
Hymenopappus filifolius		Grass, PJ, PP
Hymenopappus filifolius var. *lugens*	Idaho hymenopappus	Grass, PJ, PP
Hymenopappus lugens		Grass, PJ, PP
Hymenoxys acaulis	bitterweed	Grass, PJ, PP
Hymenoxys richardsoni	pingue, rubberweed	PJ, PP
Hymenoxys richardsonii var. *floribunda*	Colorado rubberweed	PJ, PP
Juniperus scopulorum	Rocky Mountain juniper	PJ, PP
Laphamia congesta		Grass, PJ
Leptotaenia dissecta multifida	carrotleaf leptotaenia	Grass, PJ, PP
Ligusticum porteri	osha, bear root	Riparian,PJ, PP
Linum australe		Grass, PJ
Lithophragma tenella	slender woodland star	Grass, PJ, PP
Lithospermum multiflorum	manyflower gromwell	Grass, PP
Lupinus brevicaulis	shortstem lupine	Grass, PJ
Lupinus kingii	broadleaf lupine	PJ, PP
Lycium pallidum	rabbit thorn	Grass, PJ (wash)
Medicago sativa	alfalfa	Grass, PJ, PP
Mentha arvensis var. *glabrata*	field mint	Grass, PJ, PP
Nicotiana attenuata	coyote tobacco	Grass, PJ
Nicotiana glauca	tree tobacco	Grass, PJ
Nicotiana spp.	tobacco	Grass, PJ
Nicotiana tabacum	common tobacco	Grass, PJ
Oenothera caespitosa var. *marginata*	tufted evening primrose	Grass, PJ,PP
Oenothera spp.	evening primrose, sundrops	Grass, PJ, PP
Oenothera tanacetifolia	tansyleaf evening primrose	Grass, PJ
Orobanche fasciculata	broom rape	Grass, PJ
Oryzopsis hymenoides	Indian ricegrass	Grass, PJ
Oxytropis lambertii	Lambert crazyweed	Grass, PJ, PP
Oxytropis lambertii var. *sericea*	silky crazyweed	Grass, PJ, PP
Penstemon ambiguus	gilia penstemon	Grass, PJ
Penstemon barbatus var. *torreyi*	Torrey penstemon	PJ, PP
Penstemon laricifolius	larchleaf penstemon	Grass, PJ
Penstemon linarioides	beard tongue	Grass, PJ, PP
Penstemon spp.	penstemon	Grass, PJ, PP
Perezia wrightii	brownfoot	Grass, PJ
Petalostemon candidus	white prairieclover	Grass, PJ
Petradoria pumila	rock goldenrod	Grass, PJ
Phaseolus vulgaris	kidney bean	Grass, PJ
Phoradendron spp.	American mistletoe	PJ, PP
Pinus edulis	pinyon pine	PJ, PP
Prunus fasiculata	desert almond	Grass, PJ
Psoralea tenuiflora	scurvey pea	Grass, PJ
Rhus aromatica trilobata	skunk bush	Grass, PJ
Rhus trilobata	skunkbush sumac	Grass, PJ
Ribes aureum	golden currant	Grass, PJ, PP

Table 16.4 (*continued*)

Species	Common Name	Ecosystem
Ribes inebrians	squaw currant	Grass, PJ, PP
Robinia neomexicana	New Mexico locust	PJ, PP
Salvia dorrii ssp. *dorrii* var. *incana*	desert sage	Grass, PJ, PP
Salvia reflexa	lanceleaf sage	Grass, PJ
Senecio longilobus	thread-leaf groundsel	Grass, PJ
Solanum elaeagnufolium	silverleaf nightshade	Grass, PJ, PP
Sporobolus contractus	spike dropseed	Grass, PJ
Stephanomeria exigua	small wirelettuce	Grass, PJ
Stephanomeria pauciflora	desert straw	Grass, PJ
Stipa arida	Mormon needlegrass	Grass, PJ
Stipa comata	needlegrass	Grass, PJ, PP
Stipa speciosa	desert needlegrass	Grass, PJ
Thelesperma subnudum	Navajo tea	Grass, PJ
Townsendia exscapa	stemless townsendia	Grass, PJ, PP
Townsendia incana	hoary townsendia	Grass, PJ
Townsendia strigosa		Grass, PJ
Verbesina encelioides	golden crownbeard	Grass, PJ
Zigadenus paniculatus	sand corn	Grass, PJ, PP

sions. Using the ART approach to reconstruct historic environmental conditions provided new insights about the diversity of species that occurred historically in the GGCR prior to European contact.

Still, while we have reconstructed the historic species composition for ponderosa pine, pinyon-juniper, and sagebrush-grassland ecosystems in the GGCR, we recognize that our current application is limited. For example, while the results of our study provide an accurate description of the vegetation assemblages characteristic of the GGCR within the limitations of archaeological, ethnobotanical, and historic records, we recognize that they do not provide a means to develop data about species abundance and/or distribution. Nonetheless, we consider the ART to be the critical beginning point to reconstructing this kind of data and suggest that additional analyses of data from the same records that inform ART may be possible to reconstruct abundance and distribution data. The sources of data incorporated into the ART method also provide reliable information concerning the presence or absence of regional vegetation assemblages associated with human use and occupancy in the Greater Grand Canyon Region.

We are currently using the results of the ART to establish the reference conditions associated with the Kaibab Paiute reservation in the Greater Grand Canyon Region. Field surveys are under way to determine contemporary species composition and abundance. Future research will examine and compare modern and historic species composition to further our understanding of the changes in the historic structure, function, and interrelationships in those ecosystems.

References

Altschul, J.H., and H.C. Fairley. 1989. *Man, Models and Management*. Contract No. 53-8371-6-0054, USDA Forest Service, USDI Bureau of Land Management.

Aplet, G.H., and W.S. Keeton. 1999. Application of historical range of variability concepts to biological conservation. Pages 71–86 in *Practical approaches to the conservation of biological diversity*, ed. R.K. Baydack, H. Campa III, and J.B. Haufler. Washington, D.C.: Island Press.

Arizona Ethnobotanical Research Association. 1988. *Official Journal of the Arizona Ethnobotanical Research Association*, Summer Solstice:4–21.

Arizona State Land Department. 1974. Natural Vegetation of State, Private and BLM lands in Arizona. *Arizona Landmarks*, volume 4. Arizona State Land Department.

Bright, W. 1992. *The collected works of Edward Sapir*. New York: Mouton de Gruyter.

Covington, W.W., and M.M. Moore. 1994. Southwestern ponderosa forest structure. *Journal of Forestry* 92(1):39–47

Covington, W.W., P.Z. Fulé, M.M. Moore, S.C. Hart, T.E. Kolb, J.N. Mast, S.S. Sackett, and M.R. Wagner. 1997. Restoring ecosystem health in ponderosa pine forests of the Southwest. *Journal of Forestry* 95(4):23–29.

Cronquist, A., A.H. Holmgren, N.H. Holmgren, and J.L. Reveal. 1986. *Intermountain flora*, volume 1. New York: Hafner Publishing.

Endangered and threatened species of Arizona and New Mexico. 1987. Albuquerque, N.M.: U.S. Fish and Wildlife.

Elmore, F.H. 1944. *Ethnobotany of the Navajo*. Albuquerque: University of New Mexico Press.

Euler, R.C. 1984. *The Archaeology, Geology, and Paleobiology of Stanton's Cave*. Flagstaff, Ariz.: Grand Canyon Natural History Association.

Gumerman, G. 1988. *The Archaeology of the Hopi Buttes District, Arizona*. Research paper no. 49. Carbondale: Southern Illinois University.

Hawks, D. 1998. Personal communication. Bureau of Land Management, St. George. Utah.

Higgs, E.S. 1997. What is good ecological restoration? *Conservation Biology* 11(2):33–348.

Kearney, T.H., and R.H. Peebles. 1951. *Arizona flora*. Berkley: University of California Press.

Lavender, D.S. 1984. *Pipe Spring and the Arizona strip*. Springdale, Utah: Zion Natural History Association.

———. 1997. *The history of Arizona's Pipe Spring National Monument*. Salt Lake City, Utah: Paragon Press.

Lehr, J.H. 1978. *A catalogue of the flora of Arizona*. Phoenix, Ariz.: Desert Botanical Garden.

———. 1980. *A catalogue of the flora of Arizona*, supplement 1. Phoenix: Desert Botanical Garden.

―――. 1982. *A catalogue of the flora of Arizona*, supplement 2. Phoenix: Desert Botanical Garden.

Lindsay Jr., A.J. 1968. *Survey and excavations north and east of Navajo Mountain, Utah, 1959–1962.* Flagstaff: Northern Arizona Society of Science and Art.

Lipe, W.D. March, 1960. *1958 Excavations, Glen Canyon Area.* Salt Lake City: University of Utah.

McDougall, W.B. *Seed plants of northern Arizona.* Flagstaff: Museum of Northern Arizona.

Merriam, C.H. 1890. *North American Fauna.* U.S. Department of Agriculture.

Northern Arizona Society of Science and Art. 1951. *Plants of northern Arizona.* Flagstaff: Northern Arizona Society of Science and Art.

Olsen, S.J., and R.P. Wheeler. 1978. *Bones from Awatovi.* Papers of the Peabody Museum of Archaeology and Ethnology. Cambridge, Mass.

Paiute Forestry. 1994–95. *Evergreen*, special issue, Winter.

Phillips, B.G., A.M. Phillips III, and M.A. Schmidt-Bernzott. 1987. *Annotated checklist of vascular plants of Grand Canyon National Park.* Monograph 7. Grand Canyon, Ariz.: Grand Canyon Natural History Association.

Powell, S. 1971–76. *Excavations on Black Mesa.* Carbondale: Southern Illinois University.

Quirt-Booth, T. 1997. Analysis of leporid remains from prehistoric Sinagua sites, northern Arizona. *Journal of Archaeological Science* 24:945–960.

Stoffle, R.W., and M.J. Evans. 1978. *Kaibab Paiute history: The early years.* Fredonia, Ariz.: Kaibab Paiute Tribe.

Thomas, D. 1989. *Archaeology.* Fort Worth, Tex.: Holt, Rinehart and Winston.

Westfall, D. 1987. *The pinenut site: Virgin Anasazi archaeology on the Kanab Plateau of northeastern Arizona.* Cultural Resource Series No. 4. Phoenix, Ariz.: Bureau of Land Management.

White, P.S., and J.L. Walker. 1997. Approximating nature's variation: Selecting and using reference information in restoration ecology. *Restoration Ecology* 5(4):338–349.

Whiting, A.F. 1939. *Ethnobotany of the Hopi.* Flagstaff: Museum of Northern Arizona.

Williams-Dean, G., and V.M. Bryant Jr. 1975. Pollen Analysis of Human Coprolites from Antelope House. *Kiva* 41:97–111.

Wyman, L.C., and S.K. Harris. 1951. *The ethnobotany of the Kayenta Navaho.* Albuquerque: University of New Mexico Press.

17

Documenting Local Landscape Change
The San Francisco Bay Area Historical Ecology Project

Robin Grossinger

While one can often find richly detailed histories of significant people and social institutions within a region, equally rigorous ecological histories remain relatively rare. A few impressive early maps and accounts may be widely recognized, but a much larger body of historical materials generally remains unassembled (Sauer 1941) and unavailable to people who restore and manage the landscape.

In the San Francisco Bay Area, we have found that diverse historical documents can be integrated into a meaningful set of data through the use of a broad-based, multidisciplinary historical ecology approach (Crumley 1994). Moreover, this way of exploring a historical landscape can provide an open-minded, less confrontational context for information sharing among agency and academic scientists, environmental organizations, and interested citizens. In this way, a range of often neglected community resources—dusty local archives, encyclopedic town historians, longtime residents, experienced local scientists—can contribute to building a picture of the past that is both reliable and trusted. When developed in the form of accessible maps and associated information, this picture can serve as "common ground" for landscape-level thinking and planning, including the development of complementary lines of further research. This regional effort has given birth to a growing number of related, collaborative historical ecology projects, all of which are compiled in the Bay Area EcoAtlas, a GIS (geographic information system) of past and present ecology that supports local and regional environmental planning (figure 17.1; www.sfei.org).

Project Setting

The San Francisco Bay, one of the largest and most extensively modified estuaries in the world (Conomos 1979; Nichols et al. 1986), has experienced a particularly steep trajectory of change. At the time of European

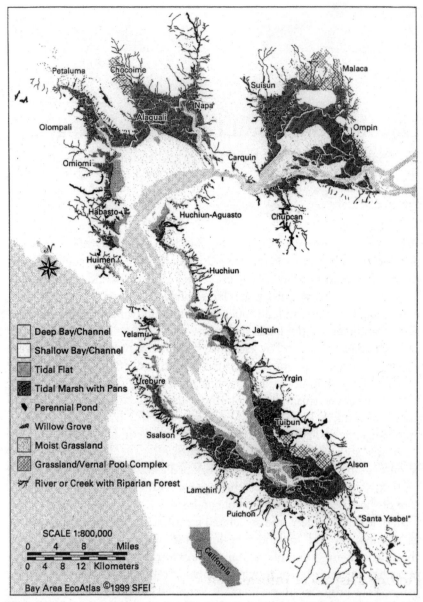

Figure 17.1. Historical extent of San Francisco Bay and related wetland and riverine habitats downstream of the inland delta (ca. 1770–1820), from the Bay Area EcoAtlas. Tribal regions based on Milliken (1995).

contact in 1769, about two dozen tribes, with an estimated population of at least fifteen thousand to twenty thousand people, inhabited the margins of the bay (figure 17.1). By 1820, tribal culture had largely disintegrated (Milliken 1995), and rapid modification of the landscape followed. For example, about 80 percent of the bay's tidal marshlands, which occupied 190,000 acres in 1850, had been eliminated by 1950 (Atwater et al. 1979; Goals Project 1999). Such extensive changes have resulted in a residual landscape composed largely of relatively new, human-constructed habitats—salt-evaporation ponds, flood control channels, "amenity lagoons" in bayside housing developments—interspersed with relatively small patches of habitats that are similar to historical conditions. We find remnants of thousand-year-old marshes adjoining newly formed ones, new riparian forests following new lengths of creeks through diked tidelands, ancient remnants of coastal prairie bordered by eucalyptus stands. This mosaic of both young and old habitats *still* supports dozens of threatened or endangered species, in addition to migratory shorebirds and monarch butterflies, and a few salmon and steelhead runs. So, despite the dramatic changes, there was reason for local scientists and environmental advocates to think that this region could continue to support, and possibly enhance, elements of these native ecosystems. But what ecological resources should be restored? And where, and how? What should a healthy, cohesive landscape look like?

As efforts to establish science-based ecological goals for the region's wetlands began to develop in the mid-1990s, senior managers of the state and federal resource agencies (including Region IX of the Environmental Protection Agency, the San Francisco Bay Regional Water Quality Control Board, the California State Resources Agency, and others) realized that the answers to these questions would require a deeper understanding of historical conditions and environmental change (Goals Project 1999). In 1994, the Bay Area Historical Ecology Project was established to gather, compile, and integrate the historical data needed to develop such an understanding. Housed at the San Francisco Estuary Institute (SFEI)— a regional center for environmental monitoring and data dissemination— the project started small and grew rapidly, especially through the efforts of several dozen volunteers recruited from nearby colleges and universities, and through mentoring by local experts.

Finding Historical Information

We knew that it would take a concerted effort to gather the large volume and wide range of information required for a coherent historical picture— one that would transcend the inherent limitations of individual sources. To recover and organize the resources, we organized a team of enthusiastic volunteer researchers to identify archives, collect materials, and build a database. The level of volunteer support seems to have been due to several factors—the recognition of the professional value of applied internships, the opportunity to contribute directly to local decision making, and the inherent intrigue of exploring the historical landscape.

During a two-year period, project members queried hundreds of local residents and institutions. We were able to identify and collect more than one thousand historical sources, including eighteenth- and ninteenth-century maps, sketches, paintings, photographs, engineering reports, town histories, explorers' journals, mission texts, hunting magazines, naturalists' collections and notebooks, ethnographic records, interviews with living elders, and myriad other indications of historical conditions. Since useful information tends to be widely distributed, researchers with local contacts were often more successful. Major academic libraries and agency archives provided a large part of the information, but researchers also found invaluable data in local historical societies, small museums, and personal collections.

Much of this information had been overlooked in the past, simply because historical data tend to be poorly organized for the purpose at hand, and because they are often of uncertain quality. Yet much of this material is detailed and reliable. For example, narrowly distributed local histories often reflect decades of personal research, and early maps and art with obvious spatial distortions (e.g., several sources shown in figure 17.2) can still provide reliable descriptive information that may not be available in any other form.

Interpretation of Historical Data

In the early design of the project, we realized that its success would depend on a careful accounting of the potential errors inherent in the interpretation of historical documents. In comparison to most environmental data, which are collected according to standardized methodologies, one has no control over the methods that were used to create historical data. Indeed, every document provides a different, incomplete, but potentially important, view of the land. To overcome these challenges, we used several approaches. First, we worked hard to understand the contextual information surrounding the document, including the techniques used to make it, its maker's goals and objectives, and the social context within which it was made.

Second, we worked closely with a range of experts, both recognized professionals and less well-known, but very knowledgeable, "amateur" historians, to help interpret the data. New findings were interpreted in an open and collegiate way, with teams of ecologists and geomorphologists reviewing and using information as it was compiled. We found that interpreting early documents also requires expertise from a number of fields distinct from the environmental sciences. For this reason, we developed an informal group of advisors and reviewers representing decades of

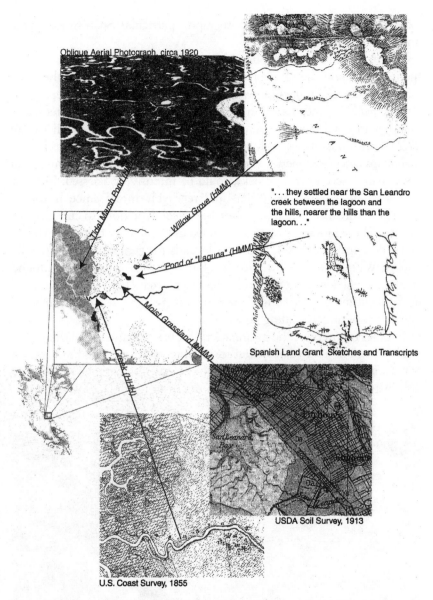

Oblique Aerial Photograph, circa 1920

"... they settled near the San Leandro creek between the lagoon and the hills, nearer the hills than the lagoon..."

Willow Grove (HMM)

Tidal Marsh Pond (HH)

Pond or "Laguna" (HMM)

Moist Grassland (HMM)

Creek (HHH)

Spanish Land Grant Sketches and Transcripts

USDA Soil Survey, 1913

U.S. Coast Survey, 1855

Figure 17.2. Integration of multiple sources to form a composite picture. Sources and certainty levels (presence, size, location; H = high, M = medium, L = low) are shown for several features. See table 17.1 for explanation of certainty codes.

experience with early maps, photographs, particular Spanish explorers, and local history.

Third, we aimed for duplication, acquiring as many different documents describing the same area as possible. Multiple views of the same place provide the single best way to visualize how a document represents a real place. We find that each document provides a highly limited view, but that in combination documents become much more useful (figure 17.2). Fortuitous sites were found where multiple sources, such as historical maps and later aerial photography (figure 17.3) or Spanish and American descriptions of creeks, could be intensively assessed. In a few places where habitats have persisted relatively intact since historical times, we were also able to compare historical depictions to current conditions. These kinds of situations enabled us to calibrate historical vocabulary, descriptive phrases, and map legends for general use around the region. While this level of effort is obviously time intensive, we found that as knowledge about a document and a place increases, the amount of useful, legitimate information one can identify increases greatly, making new levels of understanding possible.

In order to interpret the information properly, we also found that it was vital to work at a range of spatial scales. Intensive, very local integration of multiple sources, using one-of-a-kind local photographs or detailed oral histories, was critical to discover the fortuitous places where docu-

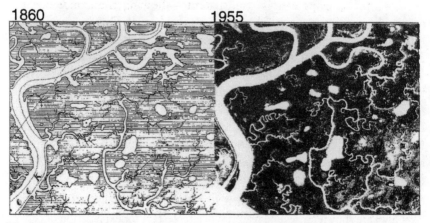

Figure 17.3. Comparison of U.S. Coast Survey Topographic Sheet T817 to 1955 aerial photograph at Petaluma Marsh, Sonoma County. The comparison shows that the map well represents marsh channels and pans to the resolution visible in the photograph. Much of the apparent differences can be attributed to natural processes operating during the period bracketed by the two images.

ments could be compared (Grossinger 1995) and where the most useful, highly detailed reconstructions could be developed. At the same time, many documents, such as federal maps and explorers' journals, cover large areas and become understood only through a regional assessment (e.g., variability among U.S. Coast Survey surveyors; Grossinger and Collins, in press). Historical research projects are often more limited in either detail or scope, but we have found that combining local and regional sources is essential to building a picture that has both consistency and detail.

The relationship between historical findings and current field research has also been important to the project. As might be expected, we found that close communication between historical researchers and other scientists observing remnant habitats and geomorphic features, or analyzing historical conditions through field studies (e.g., pollen, tree-ring, or isotopic analyses) helps develop a cohesive picture that continues to grow as new information is obtained. However, since the past is often quite different from the present, it can be useful to have some amount of naivete about what one is supposed to find, so as not to be overly influenced by what may turn out to be erroneous notions about the past.

Mapping Historical Landscapes

Making maps can be a particularly valuable tool for historical ecology (Sauer 1941), as a way to both integrate diverse information and visualize findings. With rigorous documentation, supported by modern GIS and database tools, maps can be transparent—allowing their audience to access the information on which the map is based. This is particularly important since maps of historical conditions inevitably reflect a range of certainty. Without maps, historical synopses can easily remain unspecific, lacking the spatial details needed to inform on-the-ground efforts. The process of mapmaking forces historical ecology research to be grounded in local geography, showing where and how wide the creek flowed, which hillside was logged in the 1870s, and where the best trout pools were. Maps help to understand relationships between physical processes and habitats, habitats and species, and habitats of different kinds. We are developing different kinds of historical maps to depict the native landscape at the time of European contact (ca. 1770–1820); and subsequent eras (e.g., "Spanish," "Agricultural," "Early Industrial"); the historical distributions of native plants and animals; and the land-use history of individual watersheds.

Some of the challenges involved in making a historical map include (1) the rectification of historical data to modern coordinates; (2) the integration of materials of differing spatial accuracy and contrasting information; and (3) the representation of varying levels of reliability or confidence. We have used several methods to bring information from historical records into modern map projections. We digitized some relatively accurate historical maps that used historical datums and/or projections and then registered them to modern coordinates, using locally developed coordinate shifts (Dedrick 1985) or persistent cultural or physical features that could be found on both historical and modern maps. For most sources, however, it was more practical to compile historical data onto a modern base map, which was then digitized. The compilation of cartographic, pictographic, and textual data onto one base map (USGS 7.5-minute quadrangles) as a single, "best-guess" integrated picture helped to reduce the large volume of data to a manageable compilation of consistent detail. An artist trained in landscape design played a valuable role in translating features visible in oblique photographs, coarse sketches, and narrative descriptions to the base map (Brewster and Grossinger 1998). The resulting map is a composite picture reflecting a range of sources and associated levels of certainty. To record the variations in confidence associated with different parts of the map, we developed a system to (1) document the suite of sources contributing to each mapped feature, and (2) assign and record certainty levels. We assessed each landscape feature (e.g., a creek, a pond, a segment of marsh shoreline) with regard to three types of certainty: presence, size, and location. According to the range of data quality observed during the early part of integration (table 17.1), we developed qualitative or quantitative standards for high, medium, and

Table 17.1. Certainty Level Standards for the EcoAtlas Historical View

	PRESENCE	SIZE	LOCATION
HIGH "Definite"	Reliable, direct data support presence of feature.	Reliable, direct data support mapped size (estimated max. error +/− 10%)	Reliable, direct data support mapped location (est. max. error 500 ft.)
MEDIUM "Probable"	Direct, or strong indirect, data support presence of feature, but with some qualifications.	Direct, or strong indirect, data support size, but with some qualifications. (+/− 50%)	Direct, or strong indirect, data support location, but with some qualifications. (+/− 2000 feet)
LOW "Possible"	Feature supported by only limited/contradictory data. More data needed.	Size supported by only limited/contradictory data. More data needed. (potential error defined by case)	Location supported by only limited/contradictory data. More data needed. (+/− 1 mile)

low certainty for each category. The use of such standards greatly facili-
tated the efficient management of data of widely varying quality. Certainty levels allow the full complement of information to be used
effectively while preventing poorer-quality data from "contaminating"
well-supported parts of the map.

Different methods of cartographic representation can be used to show
this variability. For example, conservation zoning policies in Marin
County required a map of the historical extent of tidal waters along the
bay. Since previous renditions of the historical margin had been challenged for inaccuracy, county planners recognized that the best depiction
would be not only as accurate as possible but also clearly documented
with regard to potential error. The resulting GIS coverage is a series of
223 line segments with attributes indicating each segment's potential
cumulative error in feet, based on errors inherent in the historical source,
its transformation to modern coordinates, the digitization process, and
other factors (Collins et al. 1998). In this way the historical tidal margin
can be shown as a line of varying width, corresponding to variations in
the range of its potential horizontal location (figure 17.4). In other situations, we are finding that a hand-drawn or watercolor map, by project
researcher and artist Elise Brewster, can most effectively represent subtle
gradients and patterns in historical vegetation, and the uncertainty in
those boundaries.

Project Findings

Prior to the creation of the EcoAtlas, a number of important reconstructions of the historical landscape had been carried out in the bay area.
These landmark pictures generally either covered only a small part of the
region (Cooper 1926; Brown 1994) or were intentionally produced at a
relatively coarse scale (Clarke 1952; Nichols and Wright 1971; Mayfield
1978; Atwater et al. 1979). These efforts recognized that there was loss of
habitat, with some specifics, but they did not provide the level of detail
required to inform local or regional restoration and management plans.
Building on the foundation of these earlier efforts, the more intensive historical ecology research has revealed many new choices and opportunities.

Regional Landscape Ecology

The EcoAtlas catalogues a range wetland and related habitats as small as
0.03 acres over about fifteen hundred square miles, allowing spatial characteristics of the past and present landscapes to be quantified and compared. Such data about changes in landscape pattern are often needed to
understand the current use of fragmented modern landscapes (Foin et al.
1997; Ribe et al. 1998).

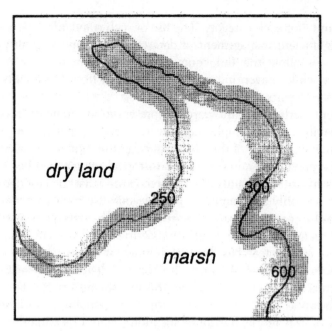

Figure 17.4. Representation of cartographic uncertainity in the horizontal position of the historical boundary between tidal marsh and dry land in a part of Marin County, California. The marshland boundary for the county is composed of 223 line segments, with estimated error ranging from 250 feet to 1,200 feet.

Using the newly developed GIS coverages of the EcoAtlas, we expected to document large decreases in a range of habitat types between the mid-1800s and 1998. However, many of the specific findings about these changes were unexpected. We found, for example, that while the loss of tidal marshland we calculated (−79 percent) is similar to that reported by previous researchers (Meiorin et al. 1991), some parts of the marshland, such as the natural pans or ponds of high tidal marsh (−97 percent), have experienced much more precipitous declines. During the same period, other components, such as low- to mid-elevation tidal marsh (+300 percent), have actually increased greatly. Thus, there has been not only a major loss in overall marsh habitat, but also a large, and less well-recognized, shift in the character of the remaining habitat. In fact, we determined that about half of the existing tidal marshland has actually formed since historical times, often with substantially different ecological functions than ancient marshes. These data suggest that many of the marshes familiar to researchers and managers are not representative of historical conditions, and the data emphasize the need to focus on restoring particular elements of the tidal marsh ecosystem that are currently underrepresented.

Large changes in the patch size of local habitat were also observed. For example, the number of tidal marshes greater than one thousand acres in size has decreased from about fifty to two. Recognizing that projects in recent years have generally been smaller than a couple of hundred acres, recent multi-agency plans based on these data call for the restoration of substantially larger, contiguous habitats (Goals Project 1999).

One of the most interesting results of developing a detailed map of multiple habitat types was that we began to recognize habitat "complexes"—repeating associations of neighboring habitat types—and how they varied regionally. In the Central Bay, for example, associations of large tidal flats, narrow salt marshes, beaches, and small willow groves were characteristic. In the South Bay, there were broader tidal marshes with substantial brackish areas near creeks, larger willow groves, and no beaches. Vernal pools were most common in Suisun, while tidal flats covered tens of thousands of acres in each subregion except Suisun, where lower salinities allowed their colonization by intertidal vegetation (Atwater and Hedel 1976). In fact, the distribution of habitats varied dramatically around the bay, producing a distinct mosaic in each subregion (figure 17.5). These observed patterns could enable restoration projects to emphasize relationships and transitions between habitats of different types, rather than independent marsh, creek, or grassland projects. In concert with the "Modern View" of the EcoAtlas, which displays present-day conservation opportunities and constraints, the "Historical View" helps determine which habitats, and in what proportion, should be restored in different parts of the region so as to reincorporate historical ecological patterns and to benefit from persistent natural processes.

Ecosystem Details

The regional habitat map is further illustrated by finer-grained information about the structure or composition of major habitat types. One important question for the anticipated restoration of thousands of acres of tidal marshland involved the characteristics of tidal channels and pans, which provide most of the functional habitat for fisheries and waterfowl within a marsh. Managers needed to know whether channels and pans,

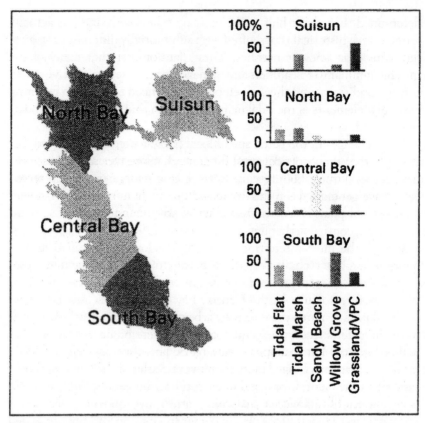

Figure 17.5. Historical distribution of selected habitat types by subregion. Regional acreage totals: tidal flat 50,469; tidal marsh 189,931; sandy beach 205; willow grove 2,547; grassland/vernal pool complex 24,070.

which are not well represented in present-day marshes, were common historically and, if so, under what conditions. We developed a detailed analysis of historical tidal marsh systems, finding that both components were, in fact, ubiquitous in tidal marshes around the bay, but that they varied dramatically in density (amount per unit area of marshland), corresponding to distance from freshwater sources (Grossinger 1995). Salt marshes had numerous small tidal pans and dense, sinuous channel networks, while fresh and brackish systems had fewer and larger pans, and shorter, less sinuous networks (Grossinger 1995).

Most significant to restoration success, observing the relationships between the historical patterns of habitat distribution and physical factors such as topography, climate, and salinity has helped researchers to understand the natural controls on habitat formation and maintenance, and to identify suitable sites for restoration. Since the dominant factors of topography, geology, and rainfall are relatively unchanged since historical times (Goodridge 1990; Goals Project 1999), the past patterns of the habitats they supported can be used as a template for habitat restoration—to restore habitats consistent with more natural controls. These findings enable projects to have more detailed and site-specific objectives, taking into account local environmental differences. Moreover, these kinds of analyses can provide quite specific engineering templates to restoration projects within the bay—for example, aiding the design of tidal channels at Arrowhead Marsh (Oakland) and Pier 98 (San Francisco).

Forgotten Habitats

The historical research also revealed an array of habitat types that were significant components of the pre-European landscape but had been largely overlooked in restoration planning to date. These habitats had been mostly eliminated prior to the careers of local ecologists and environmentalists and thus, without historical research, might have remained underrecognized. For example, sandy barrier beaches adjacent to tidal marshes and lagoons fringed more than twenty miles of the bay shoreline, primarily in the Central Bay, and likely supported several species, such as California sea-blite (*Suaeda californica*) and snowy plover (*Charadrius alexandrinus nivosus*), that are now endangered (Baye 1998). On the adjacent plains, we found that, contrary to expectation, many creeks did not maintain channels to the bay, but instead fanned out into seasonal wetlands, especially dense, stand-alone willow groves as large as 350 acres that dotted the flatlands near the bay's edge. These features were widely documented in the Spanish era, by the term *sausal* (e.g., *sausalito*—little willow grove), and likely provided important habitat for songbirds and amphibians, but have been almost completely (−99 percent) eliminated. Similarly, research using early herbarium records and local flora has uncovered detailed descriptions of plant communities—for example, at the much impacted tidal marsh–upland ecotone—that have changed so greatly as to be difficult to imagine from our present vantage point (Baye 1999).

However, by using the map of historical habitats, we have been able to identify impressive historical remnants, as well as newly formed, functional habitats. In this way the potentially discouraging documentation of these losses actually helps us recognize existing values and opportunities. Moreover, many of these smaller, but significant, elements of the historical landscape, which probably contributed greatly to the regional diversity of species, are now being considered for restoration in the future.

Species Support Functions

With both populations of native species and their original habitats so reduced in the contemporary landscape, it is not always obvious what original array of habitats supported species of concern. Determining what habitats supported a species historically can help define what characteristics constitute "good habitat." For example, the research question "Where were the ducks before duck clubs?" led to the discovery that natural ponds in tidal marshland supported the vast flocks of waterfowl. This finding led us back to the much-storied hunting history of Suisun Marsh (Arnold 1996). Other research has documented the historical location of currently rare tidal marsh plants (Baye 1998), and determined which streams had steelhead and salmon runs, and how recently (Leidy and Sisco, in press).

Local Land-Use History

Once a baseline picture of earliest-documented conditions has been developed, the challenge becomes to explain how subsequent land use has shaped the historical landscape into that which we find today. The cumulative and interrelated effects of local history not only are usually the source of current problems but also can have ongoing effects extending far into the future, strongly shaping a local site's potential for restoration (Aronsen and LeFloc'h 1996; White and Walker 1997). Building upon the regional GIS, the San Francisco Estuary Institute and local partners have initiated several collaborative watershed-based historical ecology projects. These more detailed, local investigations are currently being tested on Wildcat Creek (Contra Costa and Alameda Counties), Permanente Creek (Santa Clara County), and Napa River (Napa County). Even within the relatively small region of the bay area, we are finding that the land-use histories of different watersheds are distinct and significant. Finding out when and where the first railroad bridge was built, the dams constructed, grazing started, the hills logged, and other key events helps interpret current conditions that affect erosion, fishery support, flooding, and other management concerns (SFEI 1998).

Historical Perspective

Not unsurprisingly, as the diversity and grandeur of the landscape have been reduced and simplified, so too have our images of what they used to be. Rapid change and the destruction of indigenous culture have effected a collective lack of social memory of earlier conditions (Nichols et al. 1986). In the face of such large, yet poorly documented, losses, studying historical ecology is an important educational endeavor because it helps us recognize the effects of previous social priorities (Sauer 1975). Despite our general lack of historical perspective, many people from a range of backgrounds are interested in the study of historical ecology, and many have useful information to contribute. In a place so obviously altered as the San Francisco Bay Area, it seems that almost everyone has asked, "What did this place used to look like?" and has attempted to visualize the historic landscape through a neighbor's reminiscence or an old photo on the wall at the local bank.

The Future

Since establishment of the project, its maps, databases, and archives have been intensively used for regional ecological planning (Goals Project 1999) and have become trusted sources of information for local agencies, citizen groups, newspapers, and academic institutions (Watts 1994; Sowers 1995; 1997; Barnum 1996; Foin et al. 1997; Tobin 1999). The project has also generated strong community interest and participation. Several groups have begun to apply our how-to guide (draft version available at www.sfei.org) to develop more detailed pictures of how their local landscape has changed. Indeed, what we have learned is that once an historical ecology project is started, it takes on a life of its own. The historical landscape has an undeniable appeal that leads people into the intertwined stories of people and the land. Many of us involved in these projects have found that despite lifelong environmental interests and decades of experience in the region, it is historical ecology research that has most aided our ability to recognize existing native habitats and natural processes within the urbanized setting (Grossinger 1999). At the same time, we have found that exploring the past seems inevitably to invite consideration of the future. It may well be that you can only look ahead as far as you can look back. As citizens, resource managers, and policy makers become more comfortable with well-validated, locally grown pictures of landscape history, a shared understanding of present conditions and potential future scenarios becomes more possible, and a common vision of the future can emerge.

Acknowledgments

This project would not have been possible, or much fun, without my colleagues Elise Brewster, Josh Collins, Zoltan Der, Christina Wong, and the team of student researchers. I would like to thank Josh for envisioning the project and mentoring our growth as scientists through its development. Paul Smith, Cristina Grosso, and Josh provided valuable comments on this manuscript; Christina Wong produced figures 17.1 and 17.5. We cannot thank enough the many people who have generously contributed time, information, and inspiration to the project.

References

Arnold, A. 1996. *Suisun Marsh history—hunting and saving a wetland*. Marina, Calif.: Monterey Marina Publishing.

Aronson, J., and E. Le Floc'h. 1996. Vital landscape attributes: Missing tools for restoration ecology. *Restoration Ecology* 4(4): 377–387.

Atwater, B.F., S.G. Conard, J.N. Dowden, C.W. Hedel, R.L. MacDonald, and W. Savage. 1979. History, landforms, and vegetation of the estuary's tidal marshes. Pages 347–384 in *San Francisco Bay: The urbanized estuary*, ed. T.J. Conomos. San Francisco: American Association for the Advancement of Science, Pacific Division.

Atwater, B.F., and C.W. Hedel. 1976. *Distribution of seed plants with respect to tide levels and water salinity in the natural tidal marshes of the northern San Francisco Bay Estuary, California*. USGS Open File Report 76–389. Menlo Park, Calif.: U.S. Geological Survey.

Barnum, A. 1996. Bay Area EcoAtlas—A view of habitats past. *San Francisco Chronicle*, October 25, p. A10.

Baye, P. 1998. *Significant historic changes in the distribution and abundance of native vascular plant species occurring in tidal marshes of the San Francisco Bay Estuary*. Draft report prepared for the San Francisco Bay Area Wetlands Ecosystem Goals Project.

Brewster, E., and R. Grossinger. 1998. *Mapping the San Francisco Estuary: The EcoAtlas as a tool for restoration*. Fellows Lecture at the American Academy in Rome, March 11.

Brown, A.K. 1994. The European contact of 1772 and some later documentation. In *The Ohlone past and present: Native Americans of the San Francisco Bay region*, comp. and ed. L.J. Bean. Menlo Park, Calif.: Ballena Press.

Clarke, W.C. 1952. *The vegetation cover of the San Francisco Bay region in the early Spanish period*. Master's thesis, University of California, Berkeley.

Collins, J., Z. Der, R. Grossinger, and C. Wong. 1998. *Cartographic analysis of historical and modern bayland boundaries for Marin County, California*. Report to the Marin County Community Development Agency.

Conomos, T.J. 1979. Introduction. In *San Francisco Bay: The urbanized estuary*, ed. T.J. Conomos. San Francisco: American Association for the Advancement of Science, Pacific Division.

Cooper, W.S. 1926. Vegetational development upon alluvial fans in the vicinity of Palo Alto, California. *Ecology* 7: 1–30.

Cronon, W. 1988. *Changes in the land: Indians, colonists, and the ecology of New England*. New York: Hill and Wang.

Crumley, C.L. 1994. *Historical ecology: Culture, knowledge and changing landscapes*. Santa Fe, N.M.: School of American Research Press.

Dedrick, K.G. 1985. *Modern and historic mapping of tidal marshlands of San Francisco Bay, California*. Unpublished manuscript.

Foin, T.C., E.J. Garcia, R.E. Gill, S.D. Culberson, and J.N. Collins. 1997. Recovery strategies for the California clapper rail (*Rallus longirostris obsoletus*) in the heavily urbanized San Francisco estuarine ecosystem. *Landscape and Urban Planning* 38: 229–243.

Goals Project 1999. *Baylands ecosystem habitat goals: A report of habitat recommendations prepared by the San Francisco Bay Area Wetlands Ecosystem Goals Project.* U.S. Environmental Protection Agency, San Francisco, and San Francisco Bay Regional Water Quality Control Board, Oakland, Calif. Available at www.sfei.org.

Goodridge, J. 1990. *One hundred years of rainfall trends in California.* December 8. Chico, Calif.: self-published.

Grossinger, R. 1995. *Historical evidence of freshwater effects on the plan form of tidal marshlands in the Golden Gate Estuary.* Master's thesis, University of California, Santa Cruz.

———. 1999. Seeing time: A historical approach to restoration. *Ecological Restoration/North America* 17(4): 251–252.

Grossinger, R., and J.N. Collins. In press. *Accuracy and detail of the first coast survey of San Francisco Bay, 1850–1860.*

Leidy, R.A., and Sisco, J. In press. *Historical distribution and current status of steelhead* (Oncorhynchus mykiss irideus), *coho salmon* (O. kisutch), *and chinook salmon* (O. twaschyscha) *in streams of the San Francisco Estuary, California.*

Mayfield, D.W. 1978. *Ecology of the pre-Spanish San Francisco Bay area.* Master's thesis, San Francisco State University.

Meiorin, E.C., M.N. Josselyn, R. Crawford, J. Calloway, K. Miller, T. Richardson, and R.A. Leidy. 1991. *Status and trends report on wetlands and related habitats in the San Francisco Estuary.* Prepared by the Association of Bay Area Governments for the San Francisco Estuary Project. San Francisco: U.S. Environmental Protection Agency.

Milliken, R. 1995. *A time of little choice: The disintegration of tribal culture in the San Francisco Bay area, 1769–1810.* Menlo Park, Calif.: Ballena Press.

Nichols, D.R., and N.A. Wright. 1971. *Preliminary map of historic margins of marshland,* San Francisco Bay, California. USGS Open File Report, Basic Data Contribution 9. San Francisco.

Nichols, F.M., J.E. Cloern, S.N. Luoma, and D.H. Peterson. 1986. The modification of an estuary. *Science* 231: 567–573.

Ribe, R., R. Morganti, D. Hulse, and R. Shull. 1998. A management driven investigation of landscape patterns of northern spotted owl nesting territories in the high Cascades of Oregon. *Landscape Ecology* 13: 1–13.

Sauer, C. [1941]. 1967. Foreword to historical geography. In *Land and life: A selection from the writings of Carl Sauer,* ed. J. Leighly. Berkeley: University of California Press.

———. 1967. *Land and life: A selection from the writings of Carl Sauer,* ed. J. Leighly. Berkeley: University of California Press.

———. 1975. *Man in nature: America before the days of the white man, a first book in geography.* Berkeley, Calif.: Turtle Island Foundation.

SFEI (San Francisco Estuary Institute). 1998. Bay Area Watersheds Science Approach, Version 3.0-The Role of Watershed Science to Support Environmental Planning and Resource Protection. Available at www.sfei.org.

————. 1999. Conceptual models of freshwater influences on tidal marsh form and function, with an historical perspective. Prepared for the City of San Jose, California. March 31.

Sowers, J.M. 1995. Creek and watershed map of Oakland and Berkeley. Oakland: Oakland Museum of California.

————. 1997. Creek and watershed map of San Leandro and Hayward. Oakland: Oakland Museum of California.

Tobin, M. 1999. The natural order of things. Napa Valley Register (Napa, Calif.), May 16, p. 1D.

Watts, N.F. 1994. Etchings outline East Bay wetlands. Daily Review (Hayward, Calif.) April 11, p. A-1.

White, P.S., and J.L. Walker. 1997. Approximating nature's variation: Selecting and using reference information in restoration ecology. Restoration Ecology 5(4): 338–349.

About the Contributors

Thom Alcoze is an associate professor in the School of Forestry at Northern Arizona University in Flagstaff.

M. Kat Anderson is an ethnoecologist for the Natural Resources Conservation Service, National Plant Data Center, working out of the Department of Environmental Horticulture at the University of California–Davis. She is the co-editor of *Before the Wilderness: Environmental Management by Native Californians.*

Kenneth L. Cole is a research ecologist with the U.S. Geological Survey and adjunct professor at Northern Arizona University in Flagstaff. He has conducted research on past vegetation change using numerous paleoecological and other retrospective techniques in the southwestern and Great Lakes states.

Owen K. Davis is a professor of palynology in the Geosciences Department at the University of Arizona in Tucson. He is president of the International Federation of Palynological Societies.

Joseph DeCant is an environmental science major in the Department of Environmental Sciences at Allegheny College in Meadville, Pennsylvania. He has considerable experience and interest in Geographic Information Systems.

Peter W. Dunwiddie is a stewardship ecologist with The Nature Conservancy of Washington in Seattle.

Michael Edmonds is the library director at the State Historical Society of Wisconsin in Madison. He is currently working on a book about American birds and people before Audubon.

Dave Egan is an editor of *Ecological Restoration* and other publications at the University of Wisconsin–Madison Arboretum.

James E. Fogerty is head of the Acquisitions and Curatorial Department at the Minnesota Historical Society in Saint Paul.

Glen G. Fredlund is an associate professor in the Department of Geography at the University of Wisconsin–Milwaukee.

Sana Gardescu is a research associate in the Department of Ecology and Evolutionary Biology at Cornell University in Ithaca, New York.

Robin Grossinger is an assistant environmental scientist at the San Francisco Estuary Institute in Redmond, California. He also serves as the director for the institute's Historical Ecology Project.

Evelyn A. Howell is a professor in the Department of Landscape Architecture and the Institute for Environmental Studies at the University of Wisconsin–Madison. She has been teaching about restoration ecology since 1975.

Matt Hurteau is a student in the Department of Forestry at Northern Arizona University in Flagstaff.

Kurt F. Kipfmueller is a graduate student at the Laboratory of Tree-Ring Research, University of Arizona in Tucson. His interests include dendroecology and dendroclimatology in the northern Rocky Mountains, natural disturbance, and landscape ecology.

P. L. Marks is a professor in the Department of Ecology and Evolutionary Biology at Cornell University in Ithaca, New York.

Michael L. Morrison is an adjunct professor in the Department of Biological Sciences at California State University in Sacramento. He is the lead author of *Wildlife-Habitat Relationships: Concepts and Applications*.

Michael J. O'Brien is a professor in the Department of Anthropology at the University of Missouri–Columbia. He is the editor of *Evolutionary Archaeology: Theory and Application*.

Tina Reithmaier is the program coordinator for the Hermon Dunlap Smith Center for the History of Cartography at the Newberry Library in Chicago. She is also a visiting assistant professor at Concordia University, where she teaches public history.

David Rhode is an associate research professor at the Division of Earth and Ecosystems Sciences, Desert Research Institute in Reno, Nevada.

Thomas W. Swetnam is an associate professor of dendrochronology at the University of Arizona in Tucson, and director of the university's Laboratory of Tree-Ring Research.

Stanley W. Trimble is a professor of geography at the University of California in Los Angeles. He is one of the joint editors of *Catena*, an international journal devoted to the study of soils and geoecology.

Gordon G. Whitney is a lecturer in the School of Forestry and Environmental Studies at Yale University. A historical ecologist, he has studied the changing landscape of the northeastern and midwestern United States. He is the author of *From Coastal Wilderness to Fruited Plain: A History of Environmental Change in Temperate North America from 1500 to the Present*.

Index